BART EHRMAN
and the
QUEST OF THE HISTORICAL JESUS OF NAZARETH

CONTRIBUTORS

RICHARD CARRIER, Ph.D., historian, philosopher, and author of *Proving History: Bayes's Theorem and the Quest for the Historical Jesus*. Dr. Carrier specializes in the religious and intellectual history of Greece and Rome and the modern philosophy of naturalism and Atheism. His next book *On the Historicity of Jesus Christ* will soon be published. To learn more about him and his work see www.richardcarrier.info.

EARL DOHERTY began his research into the question of Jesus' existence in the early 1980s, and in 1996 was the first to create a Web-site presenting the argument for what is now known as Jesus Mythicism. Both the Web-site and his first published book in 1999, *The Jesus Puzzle*, were influential in bringing Mythicism to wide public exposure and popularity. His 2009 opus, *Jesus: Neither God Nor Man*, is perhaps the most comprehensive case yet published for the non-existence of Jesus of Nazareth.

DAVID FITZGERALD is, among other things, a writer and historian on the speaker's bureau of both the Secular Student Alliance and Center for Inquiry; Director of the world's first Atheist Film Festival; an audience favorite at Skepticon; and author of *Nailed: Ten Christian Myths That Show Jesus Never Existed At All* (voted one of the top 5 Atheist/Agnostic books of 2010); and the forthcoming *The Complete Heretic's Guide to Western Religion* (*Book One: The Mormons*) and *Jesus: Mything in Action*.

D. M. MURDOCK a.k.a. Acharya S is an alumna of Franklin & Marshall College and the American School of Classical Studies at Athens, Greece, where she studied under world-renowned classicists and archaeologists. Murdock researches in English, Greek, Latin, Hebrew, French, Spanish, Italian, German, Portuguese and other languages. She is the author of several books, including *The Christ Conspiracy, Suns of God, Who Was Jesus?* and *Christ in Egypt*. Articles by Murdock have been published on several Web-sites and E-zines, as well as in magazines, books, and journals.

RENÉ SALM is An independent researcher, who has investigated the field of religion for almost four decades, producing books on both Buddhism and Christianity. He has had a successful career in the mental health field as well as in music. His controversial book *The Myth of Nazareth: The Invented Town of Jesus* (2008) is an archeological exposé that shows that the town of Nazareth came into existence after the time that 'Jesus' should have been living there. Salm continues to investigate possible historical and religious links between Christianity and Buddhism and maintains several Web-sites, including www.mythicistpapers.com (*Mythicist Papers*) and www.nazarethmyth.info.

ROBERT M. PRICE, Ph.D. in Systematic Theology, Ph.D. in New Testament, is the author of many books including *Deconstructing Jesus, The Widow Traditions in Luke-Acts,* and *The Amazing Colossal Apostle*. He is the host of two podcasts, *The Bible Geek* and *The Human Bible*. Price serves as contributing editor for *The American Rationalist* and *The Humanist*. He is a native Mississippian, lived long in New Jersey, and now happily dwells in remote Selma, North Carolina, with his beloved wife Carol and daughters Victoria and Veronica.

FRANK R. ZINDLER is a linguist, geologist, neurophysiologist, and the editor of American Atheist Press. A former professor of biology and geology, he translated and published an English version of early German Christ-Myth theorist Arthur Drews' *The Legend of Saint Peter*. His *The Jesus the Jews Never Knew*—an exhaustive study of all Jewish literature surviving from antiquity—showed that the ancient Jews had never heard of 'Jesus of Nazareth.' Indeed, they had never heard of Nazareth! Bart Ehrman's *Did Jesus Exist?* has criticized several chapters of the first volume of Zindler's four-volume *Through Atheist Eyes: Scenes From a World That Won't Reason*.

BART EHRMAN

and the

QUEST OF THE HISTORICAL JESUS OF NAZARETH

An Evaluation of Ehrman's Did Jesus Exist?

Edited by

Frank R. Zindler & Robert M. Price

2013
AMERICAN ATHEIST PRESS
Cranford, New Jersey

ISBN-13: 978-1-57884-019-9
ISBN-10: 1-57884-019-8

225 Cristiani Street
Cranford, NJ 07016-0158

FAX: 908-276-7402
www.atheists.org

Printed in the United States of America.

Bart Ehrman and the Quest of the Historical Jesus of Nazareth: An Evaluation of Ehrman's *Did Jesus Exist?*

Library of Congress Cataloging-in-Publication Data

Bart Ehrman and the quest of the historical Jesus of Nazareth : an evaluation of Ehrman's Did Jesus exist? / edited by Frank R. Zindler & Robert M. Price.
pages cm
ISBN 978-1-57884-019-9 (alk. paper)
1. Ehrman, Bart D. Did Jesus exist? 2. Jesus Christ--Historicity. I. Zindler, Frank R. II. Price, Robert M., 1954-
BT303.2.B33 2013
232.9'08--dc23

2013000900

THIS BOOK IS DEDICATED

to that

Child of the Enlightenment and Founding Father

Thomas Paine

who wrote in *The Age of Reason, Part Three*:

Repeated forgeries and falsifications create a well-founded suspicion that all the cases spoken of concerning the person called Jesus Christ are *made* cases, on purpose to lug in, and that very clumsily, some broken sentences from the Old Testament, and apply them as prophecies of those cases; and that so far from his being the son of God, he did not exist even as a man — that he is merely an imaginary or allegorical character, as Apollo, Hercules, Jupiter and all the deities of antiquity were. There is no history written at the time Jesus Christ is said to have lived that speaks of the existence of such a person, even as a man.

Contents

ENVOI

FOREWORD

The struggle here engaged is not just another scholarly quarrel. It is a contest between scholars who see the world through the lens of science and those who cannot yet cut themselves free from the anchors of religious and traditional authority. Until the publication in 2012 of Bart D. Ehrman's *Did Jesus Exist? The Historical Argument for Jesus of Nazareth*, scholars who have denied the historicity of Jesus of Nazareth have for the most part been answered only by religious apologists, not genuine historians or biblical scholars. Only occasionally during the twentieth century did secular scholars take critical notice of the growing Mythicist literature and present arguments against even the most uncertain and vulnerable parts of it. For the most part, the strategy of traditional scholars seems to have been, "If we ignore them, sooner or later they'll give up and go away."

That strategy worked very well, and notice of the so-called Mythicist position was taken neither in Academe nor in pulpit. Until the advent of the Internet, Mythicist evidence and arguments against the Historical Jesus were largely excluded from the ordinary channels of scholarly communication.

Everything changed, however, when the Mythicist position was formally engaged by Professor Bart D. Ehrman, the James A. Gray Distinguished Professor of Religious Studies at the University of North Carolina, Chapel Hill. Ehrman arguably is one of the most famous and professionally respected New Testament scholars in America. In his *Did Jesus Exist?*, specific Mythicists are named and their works are cited and criticized. This is a milestone in the history of Historical-Jesus studies and it lends hope that before too long a genuine Science of Christian Origins will be able to supplant Historical-Jesus Studies in the world of secular scholarship.

The present book provides an opportunity for Mythicists to reply to Professor Ehrman's criticisms in *Did Jesus Exist?* The views expressed in any particular essay do not imply endorsement by any other Mythicist writer, nor by this editor, nor by American Atheist Press. Indeed, it is likely that readers will perceive conflicting images of 'Jesus of Nazareth' in the following pages. Such is the nature of our time—an exciting period in which an old scholarly paradigm is giving way to one that is new and not yet fully formed.

—Frank R. Zindler,
Editor, American Atheist Press

PREFACE

By Frank R. Zindler

Bart Ehrman's *Did Jesus Exist? The Historical Argument for Jesus of Nazareth* may very well prove to be the last book written by an undisputedly first-rank scholar of the New Testament attempting to prove the existence of a Jesus specifically of Nazareth. To be sure, there will be some attempts to show that a shadowy Jesus of *somewhere* once existed. But because there really is no likelihood that credible historical evidence will ever be discovered, such efforts will soon be seen to be fruitless. Most assuredly, however, fundamentalist apologists will never give up the struggle to prove the historical reality of Jesus of Nazareth: they have a vested interest in his historical reality. But scientifically oriented scholars, I expect, will likely soon understand that we are now in the midst of a paradigm shift in religious studies that is as earth-shaking and revolutionary as the adoption of plate tectonics in geology in the 1960s. Indeed, many younger scholars have already abandoned the 'Historical Jesus,' and more than a few senior scholars are assuming an agnostic, wait-and-see stance as the struggle to save the life of an admittedly dead Jesus of Nazareth plays itself out on the Internet and other venues of scholarly and popular discussion.

As I shall explain, for many years now, Mythicists — scholars who are not convinced by the evidence offered to establish the historical reality of Jesus of Nazareth — have hoped for the appearance of a book by a secular, main-line scholar who would make a credibly complete argument for the historicist case. Although many attempts were made during the last half of the twentieth century to produce detailed biographies of a turn-of-the-era Sage from Galilee, and though a number of books contained scattered materials that might be used to construct arguments intended to demonstrate his historical reality, no serious scholar ever attempted to produce a comprehensive treatise marshaling all the best evidence and arguments in order to prove for once and for all that a man styled Jesus of Nazareth once walked the earth obedient to the same laws of physics and physiology that rule the lives of mortals such as we.

Mythicists have hoped for a book such as Ehrman's for a number of reasons. First of all, although Mythicists of the nineteenth and early twentieth centuries had reasonably little difficulty in having their work published, their counterparts of the last half of the twentieth and twenty-first centuries have had to resort to small and obscure publishing houses or simply give up altogether and rely on Internet publication to disseminate their findings. It has been difficult for Mythicists to find a public voice to bring their discoveries to an enlightened reading public. A book such as Ehrman's, it was hoped, would finally bring public notice to at least *some* of the Mythicists' reasons for denying the historicity of Jesus of Nazareth.

Secondly, during most of the twentieth century historicist scholars have scrupulously avoided engaging Mythicists in dialogue or debate. As a result, even the existence of Mythicists has been obscured from public view. Mythicist arguments — when through accident or otherwise, Mythicist claims have been propelled into momentary public view — have been dismissed with claims such as "These ideas long ago were found to be without merit," or "Albert Schweitzer disproved such fanciful claims over a hundred years ago." To have a book appear that takes them seriously would have the effect of rescuing them from the oblivion suffered by Mythicist scholars going back to Charles Dupuis in the 1790s.

Thirdly, it has been hoped that an authoritative and comprehensive statement of the historicist case would allow for a more focused argument. Throughout the twentieth century, Mythicists have had to engage in a sort of shadow boxing. They have never been able to engage historicists in comprehensive, hard-hitting debate regarding *all* the evidences on either side. Only occasional Mythicist arguments have been disputed in particular skirmishes, while their overall case has been ignored. At the same time, it has been very difficult for Mythicists to discover just exactly what the arguments of secular historicist scholars are. Almost all of them claim that the historicity of Jesus of Nazareth is so well established that it requires no further proof. N.T. Wright, for example, in his 1996 *Jesus and the Victory of God* [Fortress] made the incredible claim that:

> I have taken it for granted that Jesus of Nazareth existed. Some writers feel a need to justify this assumption at length against people who try from time to time to deny it. It would be easier, frankly, to believe that Tiberius Caesar, Jesus' contemporary, was a figment of the imagination than to believe that there never was such a person as Jesus.

Fourthly, Mythicists have wished for a book such as Ehrman's for the simple reason that they have been confident that it would be impossible to discover really new evidence for Jesus of Nazareth and that such a book would only be able to collect the various arguments used by apologists and dress them up in more modern, secular garb. Such a book would be extremely easy to refute. By successfully refuting the best arguments of the best historicist scholars, it has been hoped, the Ghost of Galilee might finally be laid to rest — at least in the still-haunted halls of secular Academe.

It is hard, then, to describe the depth of disappointment that Mythicist scholars have experienced after reading Ehrman's long-awaited book. It has been difficult for many to believe that *Did Jesus Exist? The Historical Argument for Jesus of Nazareth* could have been written by the *New York Times* best-seller author who also wrote the masterful *The Orthodox Corruption of Scripture* and the prestigious Loeb Classical Library's new edition of *The Apostolic Fathers.*

Some have hypothesized that the research was done by graduate students and that Ehrman simply reworked the material to stamp it with his characteristically easy style. Ehrman, however, emphatically denies this and avers that he personally studied all the Mythicist sources. Considering the fact that he is a man who gave up Christianity for *ethical* and *moral* reasons (especially the problem of theodicy), categorically we cannot question the honesty of his claim. But alas, if the inadequacy of the book cannot be blamed on graduate students, the responsibility for the failures of scholarship embodied therein — failures that will be detailed in the following pages — must rest with Professor Ehrman.

As noted above, the appearance of *Did Jesus Exist?* left Mythicists in a state of stunned perplexity. It was as though they were reading an apologetic screed written by a religious true believer. If one ignore as non-evidence the fanciful argument of long-lost Aramaic documents underlying the Gospels, one sees that Ehrman has not produced any *new* evidence to support the hypothesis that Jesus of Nazareth was an historical figure. Indeed, it appears that his survey of historicist arguments has been almost as incomplete as his survey of Mythicist evidence. Worse yet — as will be shown by the authors of this volume — Ehrman has committed numerous fallacies of informal logic, has not dealt with the vast majority of the most important Mythicist authors and arguments of the last two hundred years, and seems to have abandoned the methods of serious secular scholars in order to perform for the benefit of his literate *New York Times* best-seller audience. It has even been suggested by some that Ehrman is pandering to a religious audience as well. It is likely that such claims are both scurrilous and unfair. Readers will have to decide that for themselves after carefully reading the following pages.

INTRODUCTION

Surprised by Myth

Robert M. Price

Overkill

This collection of essays addresses Bart Ehrman's book *Did Jesus Exist?* It seeks to serve two purposes. First, most of our authors' works were discussed in it and we feel obliged to respond, to clear the air of misconceptions and even misrepresentations. Though Professor Ehrman is a true scholar, we fear his treatment of our work was, let's say, casual (a euphemism, I'll admit it, for 'slipshod'). Here we seek to set the record straight, not so much in order to vindicate our views as to make it possible for the reader better to evaluate them. Thus these essays are not polemical in nature, but rather counter-polemical, if there's a difference. Maybe it just boils down to who started the fight.

Second, we want to take the occasion to provide something of a symposium on the controversial Christ Myth Theory, which most of us espouse in one form or another. It is important to understand that Mythicism (what I would prefer be called "New Testament Minimalism" in continuity with the revolutionary Old Testament work of Thomas L. Thompson, Philip L. Davies, Mark Zvi Brettler, Niels Peter Lemche and others) is really a family of theories which can be gathered together only once you get to the punch line of each. For the theorists start from various places, seeking to answer various questions, and happen to wind up at more or less the same destination (to the surprise of many of them!). I do not believe any of our contributors began by grinding an ax, determined to destroy belief in the historical Jesus, not that such a chip on the authorial shoulder would absolve anyone of the duty to evaluate the arguments presented. We do not dismiss any Christian apologists' arguments simply because they are plainly offered by believers who want to establish belief. That would be the worst kind of *ad hominem* attack: even if true, so what? They might be right anyway, and only critical analysis can decide that.

So motive hardly matters, but I say that it is my impression that the scholars whose essays you will read here have been spurred on by simple scholarly curiosity. And, again, they have pursued very different paths. Several do not accept the conclusions of others. To those outside it may appear that we belong to some "Christ Myth School," but from the inside, let me assure you, it looks quite different. To us, it is the differences that stand out, while for others our differences may seem almost insignificant. To some extent that is the result of impatience, an itch to get to the bottom line. But such an attitude reveals an unwillingness to evaluate arguments: "That's all I need to know, thank you!" But it isn't. Actually, lumping one's ideological opponents together is an ancient propaganda tactic. As R. Joseph Hoffmann [*Marcion: On the Restitution of Christianity*,[1] "Marcion at Rome: The Genealogy of Error"] demonstrated, early church apologists ('official' historians of the movement like Irenaeus and Eusebius) liked to pretend that all the 'heretics' (thought criminals) were linked together genealogically, each the disciple of the other, or to use the metaphor I prefer, a group of neighborhood laundrymen who stayed in business only by doing each other's wash, This intentional over-simplification was a way of marginalizing thinkers like Marcion, Simon, Menander, Valentinus, and Basilides. The polemical goal was to make it look like they were some little Eccentrics Club, thus concealing the fact that they were really figureheads of whole different types and families of early Christianity over which official Constantinian Christianity eventually won out. These notorious names ought to be seen as islands representing

1 R. Joseph Hoffmann, *Marcion: On the Restitution of Christianity: An Essay on the Development of Radical Paulinist Theology in the Second Century*. AAR Academy Series 46 [Chico: Scholars Press, 1984: 39–44].

the still-visible remnants of a vast sunken continent. Apologists want to keep it submerged. Same with us.

Overview

On the other hand, the outsider perspective is valid in some helpful respects, too, for what seems to insiders an insultingly over-simple stereotype can function also as a valid Ideal Type. This is a heuristic device which delineates a kind of text-book abstraction distilling common features shared by disparate real-world phenomena despite their manifold differences. The point is not to say, "Yessir, all religions (or dying-and-rising god myths or ancient Mystery Cults, or Christians or Buddhists or Republicans) are just like this!" Of course none of them is. This is why you can collect statements from all the major world faiths to the effect that, "Oh, your definition of religion is fine, only ours is not a religion." But Ideal Types are most definitely *not* definitions! Instead, they are like measuring sticks; by holding the Ideal Type of 'a religion' (for example) alongside any one of the actual on-the-ground religions, its unique distinctives leap into focus. We begin to understand each religion better by asking how it came to differ and why. The point is not to reduce them to a lowest common denominator but more fully to appreciate their fascinating diversity. And Christ Mythicism, or New Testament Minimalism, is very diverse.

Whenever historians of theology try to group major thinkers into movements (categories), some living representatives are sure to protest their inclusion: "Hey! Don't tar *me* with that brush!" I was very interested in the Death of God movement of the 1960s. Paul van Buren (*The Secular Meaning of the Gospel*) protested his inclusion alongside Thomas J.J. Altizer (*The Gospel of Christian Atheism*) and William Hamilton (*The New Essence of Christianity*). So did Gabriel Vahanian (*The Death of God*), who once told me, "What Altizer thinks is the solution, I think is the problem!" Yet these very different theologians *did* belong together, or at least under the same microscope, even if, to borrow Paul Tillich's metaphor, some were positioned along the outside and others along the inside of the same circle's rim. And so with me and my fellow inmates in these pages.

Robert M. Price

That little trip down theological memory lane reminds me of another 1960s phenomenon: collections of essays and reviews in the wake of recently popular books. Harvey Cox's *The Secular City*, Bishop Robinson's *Honest to God*, Joseph Fletcher's *Situation Ethics* all called forth a gathering of echoes: *The Secular City Debate, The Honest to God Debate, The Situation Ethics Debate*. I loved these books, mainly because they helped me understand the works under consideration. It was not always easy to be sure one understood what the new thinkers were saying, and it was so helpful to see that, say, Bultmann had spotted the same problem I thought I had noticed in Robinson. Okay, then, maybe I was on the right track. I have a whole shelf of books like this. And of course my point is that I like to think of the present book as something of a late member of this genre. As you perused Professor Ehrman's send-up of our work, did you think you spotted the ad hominem fallacy? The appeal to consensus fallacy? If so, rest assured you were not alone. Did you find yourself thinking, "Hold on a second — I read Earl Doherty, and I didn't think he meant *that!*" Me neither. So let's compare notes.

Overture

My own contribution, "Bart Ehrman: Paradigm Policeman," seeks to locate Professor Ehrman's anti-Mythicist polemic in the hidden sociological-professional framework that governs how mainstream academics see (and don't see) these issues, a perspective helpful for accounting for their public pronouncements when we cannot see how facts or cogent reasoning can have led to them. Then I take the opportunity to defend myself and my published opinions from Professor Ehrman's contemptuous misrepresentations of them.

Richard Carrier's "How not to Defend Historicity" deals with such an array of pseudo-scholarly errors in Ehrman's anti-Mythicist broadside that it is downright startling to read his caution to the reader that he has restricted his treatment to the iceberg tip of Ehrman's most shockingly egregious gaffes. One almost dreads to learn what floats beneath the water line (though, rest assured, the subsequent essays will dredge up yet more). It is not quite as if Carrier systematically engages Ehrman's case either against Jesus Mythicism or on behalf of a historical Jesus. Indeed, his point is that Ehrman makes it impossible to go that far, because his book lingers on the level of sophomoric superficiality. Many of Professor Ehrman's widely read books are popularizations of the party-line consensus of mainstream biblical scholarship, a useful service to be sure, but in *Did Jesus Exist?* the Professor seems to reveal that, when it comes to the needful expertise in adjacent fields, he himself relies on popularized treatments, often outdated at that. This Richard Carrier lays bare with scrupulous and merciless scrutiny. And it is important for him to do so; sometimes being too polite in a critique tends to lend respectability, hence credibility, to an opposing view that deserves neither. If a doctor fears to issue an accurately terrifying diagnosis for fear of traumatizing the patient, no one will apply the serious treatment that is needed.

Acharya S. (pen name of D.M. Murdock) is one of the prime targets for Professor Ehrman's haughty derision. Her chief sin in Ehrman's eyes would appear to be her lack of diplomas on the wall, notwithstanding Acharya's extensive researches, including on-site investigations of archaeological materials, and her extensive documentation of her theories. She dares to plumb neglected and forgotten works by old writers, separating the wheat from the chaff where these old authors lacked the (more recent) knowledge that would have enabled them to tell the difference. Like a scribe who produces from her treasury goods old and new [Matt. 13:52], she has a knack for displaying intriguing data neglected by 'mainstream' scholars who simply do not know what to make of them. Such items of evidence are rejected or ignored by scholars who have long since assembled the jigsaw in a particular way and find that these oddly shaped bits cannot be conveniently inserted. Acharya dissents: she sees the need to start over and to redo the puzzle. One such puzzle piece is the bizarre artifact inscribed with the caption "Savior of the World," a bust of a rooster-headed man whose beak is replaced with an erect penis! Was this thing an improbable caricature of Jesus Christ? An artist's conception of the fabled Antichrist? An idol of the penis god Priapus? Any way you cut it, the ancient world was full of oddities that imply a stranger, more complex picture than many would like to think. Well, Bart Ehrman not only knows not what to make of the dickhead deity (we could forgive him for that); he just wishes it away, declaring it a figment of Acharya's fevered imagination. Such libel only reveals a total disinclination to do a fraction of the research manifest on any single page of Acharya's works. In fact, one inevitably thinks of Erich von Daniken's *Chariots of the Gods?*[2] In it he declares, "Without actually consulting Exodus, I seem to remember that the Ark was often surrounded by flashing sparks." Here Acharya obligingly does what she shouldn't have to do, providing (again!) the documentation for her account of "The Phallic Savior of the World in the Vatican Museum." Are Acharya's hypotheses and speculations debatable? That is no surprise when one ventures, and one suspects that is what Ehrman, safely ensconced in the cocoon of mainstream scholarship, really cannot brook.

Oversights

Refusing to do the necessary fact-checking (a crime for which Richard Carrier has damningly indicted Ehrman) is one thing. How much worse to have had masses of the relevant research literally placed under one's nose only to dismiss it summarily, seemingly without even reading it, and later to pretend no such evidence exists. Such is the disgusting spectacle on display in my co-editor's "Cognitive Dissonance: The Zindler-Ehrman Corresondence." Zindler, a polymath, supplied Dr. Ehrman with truckloads of evidence regarding Docetism, Mithraism, the anachronism of Nazareth in the gospels, and more, in short, all the matters on which Ehrman would later, in print, claim Zindler had supplied no documentation. Mister Short Term Memory.

You know what cognitive dissonance is: as Leon Festinger[3] explained it, cognitive dissonance is the condition of urgent discomfort arising in the mind when one is presented with conflicting data or with truths that collide with cherished beliefs. One cannot long tolerate the blaring klaxons, so one rushes to harmonize the contradictions or

---

2 Erich von Daniken, *Chariots of the Gods? Unsolved Mysteries of the Past.* Trans. Michael Heron [NY: Bantam Books, 1971: 40–41].

3 Leon Festinger, *A Theory of Cognitive Dissonance* [Stanford: Stanford University Press, 1957].

even to repress the offending data. Tillich had already said it: "In this respect fundamentalism has demonic aspects. It splits the conscience of its thoughtful adherents and forces them to suppress aspects of the truth of which they are dimly aware." Bart Ehrman may not be a fundamentalist anymore, but sometimes the old behavior patterns kick in. As seen to great disadvantage in these letters (actually e-mails), the prestigious author of *Did Jesus Exist?* portrays himself as requiring no further education, thank you. Nothing he does not already know can possibly be true. Why waste his valuable time with information that would upset his best-selling apple cart? Sorry to say so. Sorry he says so.

Bart Ehrman just cannot bring himself to take Earl Doherty seriously. Why? Alas, the poor fellow lacks credentials. Never mind that his vast erudition is manifest in both depth and breadth. Who is being sophomoric: he who dares to write without 'proper' credentials? Or he who takes his stand on his sheepskin? Did Earl Doherty publish his own book? So did Hume. The real question is: did Professor Ehrman bother to read it? If he did read the whole thing, it is quite surprising that he treats it as he does in *Did Jesus Exist?* At any rate, Doherty's essay, "Did the Earliest Christians Regard Jesus as God?" raises a fascinating issue as it addresses Dr. Ehrman's dogmatic pronouncement that the earliest Christians were adoptionists who believed Jesus was a righteous man given divine honors in heaven after his death. In other words, Ehrman is saying Mythicists have it exactly wrong when they contend that Jesus was first considered a god existing on the heavenly plane, and only subsequently reconceived as an incarnate demigod walking the earth. What this debate boils down to, I think, is a replay among scholars (even Atheist ones, as both Doherty and Ehrman are) of the Christological controversies among early Christian bishops. Both Doherty's and Ehrman's models of early Christian belief in Jesus are in effect rival Christologies. Ehrman himself is, in effect, an adoptionist, while Doherty is advocating Jesus as God 'incarnated' in an eventual Christian reduction of the original myth. To put it another way, Doherty can be understood as paralleling William Wrede's Messianic Secret theory[4], whereby the evangelist Mark sought to harmonize

4 Willliam Wrede, *The Messianic Secret in Mark's Gospel*. Trans. J.C.G. Greig. Library of Theological Translations [Altrincham: James Clarke, 1971].

the competing beliefs of two adoptionist factions. One believed that Jesus had become God's messiah at his resurrection, while the other believed that Jesus had been the functioning messiah from his Jordan baptism onward. Mark's contrived solution was to posit that, while the messiahship did commence with the baptism, Jesus managed to keep it a secret "till the son of man should have risen from the dead" [Mark 9:9]. Subsequent gospel writers discarded the secrecy motif, rewriting the stories so that Jesus proclaimed both his messianic office and his divine dignity. In the same way, Mythicists argue that the evangelists began with the second-stage belief that Jesus had come to earth in the form of man [Phil. 2:7], keeping his true divine nature a secret [1 Cor. 2:8], allowing occasional glimpses of it (*e.g.*, the mountaintop Transfiguration), but immediately hushing it up [Mark 9:9; 3:11–12]. And the post-Markan evangelists felt less and less inclined to keep the originally suppressed divinity hidden. The essential deity of Christ began to reassert itself not in the life of Jesus but in the evolution of gospel writing. The same sort of progression occurred in the case of Hercules, originally a sun god, subsequently historicized as an earth-bound demigod, full of super-powers, and eventually returning to full godhood, ascending to Olympus at his death.

Doherty's next essay, "'Mythicist Inventions': Creating the Mythical Christ from the Pagan Mystery Cults," calls the bluff of apologetics-influenced scholarship by Jonathan Z. Smith and others, of which Ehrman's assertions are wholly derivative, the kind of thing H.P. Lovecraft called "second-hand erudition."[5] Ehrman, echoing Smith (not to mention evangelicals like Ehrman's mentor Bruce M. Metzger and Edwin M. Yamauchi) pursues what Doherty rightly brands a scorched earth policy of denying not only that Christians could have borrowed Mystery Religion mythemes like that of the resurrected god, but even that such myths existed in the first place! Where such syncretism did exist, why, it must have been the archaic pagan cults cribbing from Christianity, like the *Saturday Night Live* skit where, worried about ratings, Johnny Carson starts remodeling his late-night talk show after Arsenio Hall's. And all this at an early time when Christianity could not possibly have been perceived as a threatening rival to be imitated or coopted.

5 H.P. Lovecraft, *Selected Letters*. Vol. 4 [Sauk City: Arkham House, 1976: 162].

Introduction

Overchoice

David Fitzgerald's "Will the Real Jesus Please Stand up?" does, among many others, two vital things. His main point, as I see it, is to highlight what ought to be obvious but obviously is not. When Bart Ehrman and others denounce Christ-Mythicism, they do so in the name of a supposedly monolithic scholarly consensus on the historical Jesus. But this ostensible unanimity vanishes like the mirage it is once we realize that each of the "historical Jesus" reconstructions is as different from its rivals as any one of them is from Mythicism! A huge menagerie of Jesus theories can be entertained — but not this one. They never let poor Rudolph join in any reindeer games.

This fact that a single "historical Jesus" construct does not exist can be seen as something like a modern form of Docetism. In documents featuring this doctrine (*e.g., Acts of John*), Jesus is seen by different individuals in different forms in the same moment, a tip-off to the fact that, having no single form, he really has no form at all. Shouldn't our intrepid questers for the historical Jesus draw the same inference? What genuine historical figure can give rise to such an array of portrayals?

The second outstanding value of "Will the Real Jesus Please Stand up?" is the role of our foil Bart Ehrman in the essay. Unlike everyone else here, Fitzgerald makes no attempt to call out Ehrman and to dare him to face the music. No, Professor Ehrman appears here in quite a different capacity, a richly quotable source of arguments against gospel historicity. How on earth, ask many readers of both *Misquoting Jesus* and *Did Jesus Exist?* can the same man have written both? If the sources for Jesus are so pathetically unreliable as Ehrman everywhere contends, on what possible basis can Ehrman use them to establish the existence of a historical Christ? He is trying to sit on a limb he has long since sawed off.

My co-editor's "Is Bart Ehrman Qualified to Write about Christian Origins?" is what I would have to call an exercise in Socratic humility. On the surface Zindler is responding to Ehrman's insulting sneers to the effect that Zindler just lacks the necessary expertise which Ehrman himself of course implicitly possesses in spades. Picture Zindler quoting 2 Corinthians 11:18, 21b. "Since many boast of worldly things,

I, too, will boast... But whatever anyone dares to boast of — I am speaking as a fool — I also dare to boast of that." But the underlying point is that, as Van A. Harvey[6] has pointed out, history is "a field-encompassing field." Indeed it is so vast that no one can possibly master it all. This is the reason for collegiality among scholars, all of whom are necessarily specialists and welcome correction and supplementary knowledge from others. At least that is true of most of us. Zindler would never say so, but it is obvious he is a polymath and a Renaissance man. And Ehrman? I think of Alan Quartermain's comment in the movie *The League of Extraordinary Gentlemen*: "I'm waiting to be impressed."

Frank Zindler's "Bart Ehrman and the Art of Rhetorical Fallacy" makes inescapably clear just how little Jesus scholars have any right to take for granted, as well as, ironically, how very much they *do* take for granted. (You can guess which particular New Testament scholar Zindler makes his focus, but the critique applies to many, many more.) In the process, Zindler is obliged to click on the "reveal codes" key to make visible the underlying logical fallacies upon whose currents Ehrman's surface argumentation floats. There is a significant amount of duplicity involved, but one must judge Professor Ehrman self-deceived — you know, like a religious apologist. Ehrman's most blatant errors are easy to catch (except, of course, that *he* has not caught them). He commits again and again the fallacious appeal to majority opinion and the *ad hominem* fallacy, dismissing someone's views because of some perceived personal failure, such as one's damning lack of a doctorate or a prestigious teaching post. On a more fundamental level, Zindler notes, Professor Ehrman commits the logical sin of assuming the consequent: if he pokes enough holes in the various Christ Myth arguments, he thinks he has established the historical Jesus. Not so fast.

Instances of plain old carelessness abound, too. Ehrman tells us that Josephus mentions Jesus *of Nazareth* when in fact Josephus never once names that town, and it matters. Again, Ehrman lumps Mythicists

---

6 Van A. Harvey, *the Historian and the Believer: An Essay in the Morality of Historical Knowledge and Christian Belief* [NY: Macmillan, 1969: 54].

together, as if they were all fast food franchise owners, dutifully using the same recipes handed down by the home office. The views of William Benjamin Smith he ascribes to J.M. Robertson. What's the difference? They're both worthless Mythicist cranks, aren't they?

Zindler shows how heavily Ehrman leans on the weak reed of the appeal to a greater mystery to explain a lesser one, banking, *e.g.*, on the hypothetical gospel sources Q, M, L, *etc.* to close the gap between the gospels and the historical Jesus. Indeed, any appeal to oral tradition about Jesus is hopelessly circular, taking for granted a historical Jesus at the beginning of the process. It is the same when apologists tell us that the few decades between Jesus and the gospels are not long enough to allow for embellishment of the facts. But isn't the starting date one of the issues under debate? If Jesus never existed, the bottom drops out, doesn't it? There is so much, too much, more in the same vein. But I'm afraid we have Ehrman, not Zindler to blame for that.

Professor Ehrman seems to have grown too accustomed to the role he plays in his popular books, as a guide who can authoritatively declaim what he takes for granted, serving it up to an audience who will simply swallow it. Frank Zindler's role, by contrast, is that of a food taster. Or better, that of Chef Gordon Ramsey on *Kitchen Nightmares*.

In "Bart Ehrman's Most Important Critical Method" Frank Zindler takes appreciative note of an axiom Professor Ehrman employs in his field of expertise, New Testament textual criticism (the 'lower criticism' as it used to be called). When considering two possible manuscript readings, the parsimonious explanation is to be preferred, the one that offers the most natural, least contrived accounting for all the evidence. If the longer reading at Luke 22:19b–20, the words of institution of the eucharist mentioning both bread and cup, were the original text, where could the short version, lacking most of the standard formula, have come from? Who would have abbreviated the sacred words? On the other hand, if Luke had written the shorter version, it is easy to imagine some scribe comparing it with the fuller versions of Mark and Matthew and deciding a previous copyist must have fallen asleep at the switch and skipped some text and that it fell to him to "restore" what "must" have been accidentally omitted. Zindler merely wonders why Ehrman does not think to apply the same cogent reasoning to many other questions. For instance, if the Christian eucharist evolved directly from the Jewish Passover seder, as most want to believe, how can one possibly account for the element of ritual blood-drinking, even only symbolically? Can we even begin to imagine Jews adopting such imagery? It would have been like using child-molestation imagery, given the taboos of Leviticus. On the other hand, suppose the ritual came from a religion like those of Osiris or Dionysus, where such imagery is naturally at home. Shouldn't we prefer that explanation? But one is little inclined to favor, or even to think of such an explanation if one despises the heretical notion of early Christian dependence upon the Mystery Religions.

James Barr[7] once observed that scholarly evangelicals often choose to enter fields like textual criticism and archaeology. This enables them to become New Testament scholars with Ph.D. degrees while evading all engagement with the dangerous, faith-threatening questions of biblical historicity, authorship, *etc*. Their acquaintance with these latter is then liable to be second-hand. They may even fall back on the apologetics they learned from InterVarsity Christian Fellowship or William Lane Craig. I can only say that it appears to me this is roughly what happened in Professor Ehrman's case. How interesting that it was not critical scholarship that led him into unbelief, but rather the troubling question of theodicy, the problem of evil. I suspect this is why he seems to cling to the facile and far-fetched rationalizations of evangelical apologetics. He had never gotten to the point of seeing through them before something else made him jump ship. (What explains Jonathan Z. Smith's apologetical posture I cannot begin to guess.)

Overdraft

Zindler strikes again in a brief note on "Bart's Subtitle." In it Ehrman refers to "Jesus of Nazareth," a tag that already begs the question of the historical character of the Christian savior. In fact, the case for

7 James Barr, *Fundamentalism* [Philadelphia: Westminster Press, 1978: 128–129].

the historical Nazareth is even more tenuous than that for its most famous resident. But it is yet another datum Ehrman takes for granted simply because nearly everybody else does. Strikingly, he quips that, even if crank skeptics were able to debunk Jesus' Nazareth origins, it would not undermine a historical Jesus; he would be simply be Jesus from someplace else. What Ehrman fails to see is that Jesus is *already* "Jesus from someplace else," that is, Jesus from wherever theologians need him to be from, and from no one place more than another as long as he belongs *someplace.* Nazareth is another Utopia: both a good place and at the same time *no place.*

Can anything good come out of Nazareth if there was no Nazareth to come out of? René Salm raises that *koan*-like question in his "Archaeology, Bart Ehrman, the New Skepticism, and the Nazareth of 'Jesus.'" He easily shows how Ehrman, while denouncing Salm as being no archaeologist, is in precisely the same position, able to do no more than Salm does: to scrutinize the assertions of archaeologists and popular news (mis)reporters, something Salm does in remarkable depth but Ehrman does not. Ehrman, as Salm shows, is all too eager to take the word of those whose reading of the evidence comports with tradition. Ehrman's defensive reaction to Salm's demonstration that no datable evidence suggests, much less establishes, the existence of Nazareth during the ostensible time of Jesus exactly parallels the umbrage taken by the *Biblical Archaeology Review* alliance of conservative Christians and Jews at the work of Old Testament Minimalists. As there is no archaeological evidence for the Exodus, the conquest of Canaan, or the monarchy of David and Solomon (did God send angels down to vacuum up all the evidence?), so there is no sign of Nazareth. How dismaying for biblical traditionalists to find themselves in the same sinking boat with Mormon apologists who have never been able to scrape up a speck of the once-mighty Nephite and Lamanite civilizations. "Lord, save, we perish!"

Frank Zindler, in his "Mark's 'Jesus from Nazareth of the Galilee'" addresses Dr. Ehrman's sneering dismissal of his claim that the sole occurrence of the place name "Nazareth" in Mark, namely in chapter 1, verse 9, is an interpolation. Needless to say, Zindler thinks (as I and others do) that all the Markan references to "Jesus the Nazarene/

Nazorean" refer to a sect label, not to a town (though later writers, who lived in a time when there was once again a populated Nazareth, did take the epithet to denote Jesus' home town). Ehrman, who dedicated a whole book to the demonstration of extensive scribal 'corrections' of the New Testament text, laughs off Zindler's suggestion as a case of what some call "surgical exegesis:" a verse contradicts your pet theory? Just claim it is not original to the text! But Bart knew better, as he admits somewhere in an endnote (like a newspaper printing a retraction on page 50 of a false report it had the previous day trumpeted on page one). In materials he had earlier sent to Ehrman, Zindler had made an impressive case for Mark 1:9, as well as the whole prologue to which it belongs, constituting an interpolation. He repeats that case in this response essay, then adds an extensive Bayesian analysis of Ehrman's counter claim that a grammatical anomaly in Mark 1:9, relevant to Zindler's theory, was a simple scribal goof. I will admit that I can make as little sense of Bayesian probability calculus as I can of *Star Trek*'s warp drive mechanics — or, for that matter, of setting the clock on my VCR! But suffice it to say that for all of Professor Ehrman's flaunting his Ph.D. like a peacock's tail, Frank Zindler's essay proves once again that New Testament scholarship is too important to be left to the professional academics.

"Was There a Historical 'Jesus of Nazareth'?" by D.M. Murdock (Acharya S.) returns to the holy ghost town of Nazareth. She summarizes the basic work of Frank Zindler and René Salm but goes on to explain how and why the phantom town was conjured from Jesus' sectarian epithet. As she notes, it is far from rare in the history of Jesus scholarship to suggest that "Jesus of Nazareth" aims to paper over the sectarian origins of a historical Jesus who was a Nazirite or a Nazorean. But what if there were no Jesus in the first place? Murdock, like Zindler, acknowledges that, once turned into an earthly figure, Jesus seemed to require some definite place to live. Not to have had one might suggest that the son of man had no place to lay his head because he never touched the ground at all. After Superman comes to earth, when he seeks a semblance of an earthly identity (Clark Kent), he has to hail from somewhere in particular, since all earthlings do. Thus he dwells first in Smallville, then in Metropolis. So Jesus must hail from someplace, too.

But why Nazareth? Why not Hooterville or Gotham City? Here is Murdock's distinctive contribution: 'Nazareth' is a manufactured fulfillment of supposed scriptural prophecies of a messianic Branch (*netzer*) of David's family tree, or of a new Nazirite like Samson who should save Israel from her enemies. Interestingly, her suggestion here strikingly parallels that of Richard Carrier with regard to Arimathea, which will pass for a genuine place name but is very likely a pun for 'best (*ari-*) disciple (*mathetes*) town.'

Finally, we should linger on Murdoch's telling reference to Euhemerism, the theory of the pre-Socratic thinker Euhemerus to the effect that mythology's deities were legendary magnifications of actual historical figures. The historical Hercules, for instance, must have been a mighty warrior, the historical Asclepius a renowned physician. One supposes the real Apollo had operated a tanning parlor. At any rate, is it not clear that 'historical critics' like Ehrman and his SBL brethren are modern day Euhemerists? And one must suspect it is only vestigial theological habits of mind that prevent Ehrman and company from seeing that there is little more likelihood of there having been a historical Jesus than there is of there having been a historical Hercules.

Earl Doherty shows again, in his chapter, " 'Key Data' and the Crucified Messiah," how a self-educated prodigy may have a keener view of the data and a wider horizon for theorizing than someone, a product of the academy, who is, to use Rabbi Yohannon ben Zakkai's description of a pupil, "a plastered cistern that loseth not a drop." Doherty shows with seemingly effortless ease how Ehrman is so absolutely controlled by the assumptions of conventional scholarship that he remains oblivious of glaring contradictions both in his positions and in his defenses of them. He just cannot get the gospels out of his head as he reads the epistles and so reads the former into the latter. He believes that the earliest records depict Jesus as a peasant prophet and teacher, never a dying and rising savior. What records might those be? A collection of SBL seminar papers?

Frank Zindler ("Bart Ehrman and the Crucified Messiah") forms a tag team with Earl Doherty in addressing Bart Ehrman's argument on how no one would have invented a crucified messiah, so there must have been one. If Doherty exposes the shaky foundations upon which Ehrman has built, Zindler goes deeper still. To switch metaphors, we may say that Zindler goes back *before* Square One: never mind the viability of a crucified Christ, what if the earliest "Christians" spoke and wrote, as Suetonius, Marcion, and Tacitus did, not of *Christos* but of *Chrestos* (a common name meaning 'the good')? No messiah at all then. The New Testament texts may even have read this way at first, which would certainly make sense of the fact that, as Werner Kramer[8] demonstrated decades ago, there is but a single place in the whole Pauline Corpus where 'Christ' even *might* make sense as a reference to Jesus as the Jewish messiah [Romans 9:5], everywhere functioning as an alternate personal name, even as most people use it today. Again, how precious little we have any right to take for granted!

Overload

"Bart Ehrman and the Body of Jesus of Nazareth" by Herr Zindler discusses a problem that Bart Ehrman does not seem to know he has, namely, if we start with a historical individual who lived in the first third of the first century of the Common Era, how easy is it to imagine that within another thirty years there grew up a widespread and long-lived belief that this individual had never existed in the flesh but was only what we might call a hologram without weight or substance? This was the 'heresy' of Docetism (from the Greek *dokeo*, 'to seem'). But to call it a heresy implies it was a secondary development, a subsequent mutation from a prior proto-orthodox belief in a real fleshly man (divine incarnation, mere mortal, or demigod as you please). As an Atheist, Dr. Ehrman obviously does not condemn any religious belief as false doctrine (or rather, he condemns them all), however severe he is in branding as thought crimes scholarly theories he does not like. But he does retain the classic Catholic view of church history despite his avowal (in his *Lost Christianities*) of the Bauer thesis (Walter Bauer, *Orthodoxy and Heresy in*

8 Werner Kramer, *Christ, Lord, Son of God*. Trans. Brian Hardy. Studies in Biblical Theology no. 50 [Naperville: Alec R. Allenson, 1966: 42–44].

Earliest Christianity)[9]. Bauer mounted a powerful argument that what eventually triumphed as Catholic Orthodoxy was a secondary development in many areas of the Roman Empire, where the first known churches were Marcionite, Gnostic, *etc*. The later research of James M. Robinson and Helmut Koester (*Trajectories through Early Christianity*)[10] and Burton L. Mack (*A Myth of Innocence: Mark and Christian Origins*)[11] has followed Bauer's hint to demonstrate how the various 'heresies' had equally deep roots in the New Testament canon as later Orthodoxy did—or claimed. But the notion of 'proto-orthodoxy' being coeval with the Ebionite, Gnostic, and Encratite 'Lost Chrsitianities' represents a sneaky compromise with Bauer, as if to admit that, all right, our Christianity's evolutionary prototype may *not* have been the only game in town, thus not after all the earliest, but it was at least as old as the others — and proved the fittest survivor (with a little help from Constantine). But I should say that our Christianity was already a secondary amalgam of elements chosen from earlier types. Pre-existence Christology came from Gnosticism, the sacramental system from the Mystery Religions, *etc*. This is the iceberg of which Frank Zindler explores the docetic tip.

Overhaul

Earl Doherty is up to bat again in "The Epistle to the Hebrews and Jesus outside the Gospels," where he does exactly what scientific theorists do when they inaugurate a new paradigm[12]: he focuses on a bit of hitherto anomalous data, something the conventional framework just could not figure out how to make good sense of, and starts over, making that odd bit of data the center of a new model, whereupon

9 Walter Bauer, *Orthodoxy and Heresy in Earliest Christianity*. Ed. Robert Kraft and Kendrick Grobel. Trans. Philadelphia Seminar on Christian Origins [Philadelphia: Fortress Press, 1971].

10 James M. Robinson and Helmut Koester, *Trajectories through Early Christianity* [Philadelphia: Fortress Press, 1971].

11 Burton L. Mack, *A Myth of Innocence: Mark and Christian Origins* [Philadelphia: Fortress Press, 1988].

12 Thomas S. Kuhn, *The Structure of Scientific Revolutions* [Chicago: University Press, 1962].

the rest of the data fall into place around it in a new and comprehensive pattern. In this way Copernicus revolutionized astronomy by focusing on the mystery of the retrograde motion of the planets, and he discovered that that motion made new sense if only one cast aside the ancient assumption of geocentricity. If one posited heliocentricity, implying that we see the motions of the other planets from a moving platform, the apparent doubling back of the planets turned out to be an optical illusion. Earl Doherty has ventured that if we resolve no longer to read into Hebrews the gospel story of an earthly Jesus, the weird business about Jesus offering his sacrifice in heaven, not on earth, goes from being the nail in the tire to being the hub of the wheel. All the business of Jesus assuming a body [Heb. 10:5] "in the days of his flesh" [Heb. 5:7] is at once seen to mean the same thing it does in *The Ascension of Isaiah*: the descent of the Savior through the cosmic spheres, not to this solid earth, but into one of the lower heavens where the Archons, Principalities and Powers hover, and where they killed him [1 Cor. 2:8; Col. 2:13–15], precisely as the Gnostic Primal Man of Light was ambushed in space above the physical creation at the dawn of time.

Likewise, it suddenly begins to make sense that Hebrews gives no details of any earthly life of a human Jesus, why the words placed upon his lips are all *scripture quotes* — since the whole thing was the product, not of historical memory, but of esoteric scriptural exegesis (decoding).

Over and out

In "Bart Ehrman and the Cheshire Cat of Nazareth," Frank Zindler supplies a review of the numerous factors that make it unlikely that any historical Jesus ever existed. Many have done this, though few so extensively yet concisely. But Zindler is making a point seldom made even by Mythicists. He notes how historical and literary critics have dismantled and discarded so much of the gospel Jesus figure(s) that all that remains is a fading phantom countenance like that of the fictional feline. And this forces the question of what keeps 'critics' like Bart Ehrman believing in the existence of Jesus. Why do his vacuous and circular arguments look good to him? Isn't it the simple and stubborn will to believe? The same thing that motivates evangelical apologists? Reading *Did Jesus Exist?* one begins to suspect that nothing could shake Bart Ehrman's faith, and faith is what we must call it. And then, as Zindler explains, we are talking about a 'belief' that is in principle impossible to falsify, and thus without content. If you can't think of any possible state of affairs that would mean your belief is wrong after all, that means you can't even draw the lines to define it. You're not really believing anything, just spouting slogans. Even so, if all the evidence falls away, what do you even *mean* by 'Jesus'?

The indefatigable Doherty ("Ehrman's Concluding Case against Mythicism") helps wind our book down with his rejoinder to Professor Ehrman's own parting pot shot. Forgive me for being more blunt, less restrained, than the even-tempered Doherty, who is both older and wiser than me. Professor Ehrman, apparently tired of the scholarly pretense he has assumed throughout his condescending screed, finishes by taking off the gloves and smacking Mythicists with one massive *ad hominem* slur. Jesus Mythicism, he avers, is nothing but a cynical weapon aimed by Humanist-Atheist malcontents at the walls of religion. "Hey! Not only is there no God, but your precious Jesus didn't even exist! Nyah nyah nyah *nyah* nyah!" Even if this libel were not a libel, even if Mythicists were such bitter neurotics, that would not reflect in any degree on the validity or invalidity of their arguments. How can an ostensibly serious scholar resort to such tactics?

And the rank hypocrisy of it! As if Ehrman himself did not patently delight, in his many books, in sticking his finger in the eye of the fundamentalists to whose ranks he once belonged. Do not his contemptuous barbs (quoted by Doherty), aimed at a Humanist group who invited him as their convention speaker, betray a smug desire to show himself superior to both those who like him and those who don't? Is not the gist of it "I wouldn't join any group that would have someone like me as a member"?

Frank Zindler ("Bart Ehrman and the Emperor's New Clothes") rounds out this volume with a familiar parable, the application of which will hardly surprise you. Nor, by this time, will you be surprised that it fits so very well.

Robert M. Price

December 22, 2012

PART I. Ehrman's Arguments Engaged

CHAPTER ONE

Bart Ehrman: Paradigm Policeman

Robert M. Price

Copernican Revelations

In his controversial book, *Did Jesus Exist? The Historical Argument for Jesus of Nazareth,*[1] Professor Bart Ehrman appears addicted to the fallacious 'appeal to consensus.' He seemingly never tires of treating New Testament scholarship as a game of *Family Feud*. What hypotheses are to be taken seriously? "Survey says!" If the majority of scholars think A, then A must be the truth. But if one is feeling up to evaluating actual arguments, one will not refer to nose-count epistemology at all. One will not think to take refuge amid the herd. True, Bart no longer defends fundamentalism, but he is an apologist for a new orthodoxy, "mainstream scholarship," the Society of Biblical Literature (SBL) magisterium. I call this the "Stuck in the Middle with You" school of biblical scholarship, where nothing out of the comfortable bell curve of theories can be taken seriously. Berger and Luckmann well describe what Bart is up to: he is a "legitimator," a public relations man for a professional guild.

> The outsiders have to be *kept* out... If... the subuniverse [of meaning] requires various special privileges and recognitions from the larger society, there is the problem of keeping out the outsiders and at

1 Bart D. Ehrman, *Did Jesus Exist? The Historical Argument for Jesus of Nazareth* [New York: HarperOne, 2012].

> the same time having them acknowledge the legitimacy of this procedure. This is done through various techniques of intimidation, rational and irrational propaganda..., mystification and, generally, the manipulation of prestige symbols.[2]

This is, of course, why we see Bart Ehrman (and other members of the academic elite, like Maurice Casey and R. Joseph Hoffmann) trying to undermine the claims of 'eccentric' Mythicists by throwing around talk of who has or doesn't have official credentials and illustrious teaching posts. I know this sounds like sour grapes from me. I don't perceive it that way (though who knows his own heart?). But even if it is, that only reinforces Berger and Luckmann's point and the application of it to the case at hand, doesn't it?

But there is a more serious misunderstanding implied in Bart's ceaseless appeals to "what most scholars think." And here I am thinking of Thomas S. Kuhn's great book, *The Structure of Scientific Revolutions*.[3] Kuhn demonstrates how science advances at least as much by the formulation of new interpretive paradigms as by the accumulation of new data and discoveries. Copernicus had no new data when he rejected earth-centered Ptolemaic cosmology for sun-centered cosmology. He just found a simpler, more natural, economic, and comprehensive way to construe the evidence everyone already possessed. There was the little problem of the retrograde motion of the planets. Usually they seemed to trace a circular course around the earth, but on occasion they seemed to take a step or two backward, shuffle around a bit, then continue on their circular course. Why?

Ptolemaic astronomers posited that the planets were, so to speak, poised atop a fantastic array of meshing gears and wheels which kept them going but with a kind of 'leap-year' jog every once and a while. It was still regular and in principle predictable once you had worked out the schematics. But what a mess! Copernicus realized it would all be much simpler if, say, the earth and the planets revolved

2 Peter L. Berger and Thomas Luckmann, *The Social Construction of Reality: A Treatise in the Sociology of Knowledge* [Garden City: Doubleday Anchor Books, 1967: 87].

3 Thomas S. Kuhn, *The Structure of Scientific Revolutions* [Chicago: University of Chicago Press, 1962].

around the sun. That way, the retrograde motion would be the result of our watching the motion of the other heavenly bodies from a *moving platform*. Bingo!

Martin Luther condemned Copernicus as a madman, but he was like Nietzsche's madman in *The Gay Science*: he was right, but he came too soon. It would take a good while till his public could catch up with him. The same thing happened, for instance, with Alfred Wegener, who first proposed the theory of Continental Drift. He, too, was dismissed as an eccentric, though everyone now knows he was right all along.

Why do new theorists often face such opposition from the scientific establishment? It is facile to vilify the 'mossbacks' who just have too much invested in the way the game is currently played and are not willing to change the rules. Are they just dealing with cognitive dissonance by fending off a new theory that would mean they had been wrong? These things may actually be true, though to pass such a judgment one would really have to be a mind-reader. But it makes no difference. The new theorist *must* run the gauntlet, because his theory must be able to prove itself. For the scientific establishment to jump on the bandwagon at once would be to jump the gun. Theorists will (or should) be only too happy to submit their theories to exhaustive scrutiny (as Paul is depicted doing in Galatians 2:1–2). Isn't that the essence of scientific method? You don't want anyone to take anything by faith. You try to debunk your *own* theory, because that is the only possible way to see if it's got what it takes. If it does, we can expect that the new paradigm will eventually receive recognition, just as Copernicus's and Wegener's did. Here we see the proper and valuable role of scholarly consensus.

Moreover, this means that finding oneself in a tiny minority advocating a theory does not mean one is a weirdo and a crank. You might be, and there are plenty of them, but no one will be able to say so for sure until the elders of the scholarly establishment (the 'paradigm police') get busy scrutinizing the theory. This is what Bart discourages with his Steve Harvey-like appeals to majority opinion. Frank Zindler, Earl Doherty, René Salm, myself, and the other Mythicists he seeks to refute might be Immanuel Velikovsky, sure, but we also might be Alfred Wegener. It's too early for Bart to tell. The fact that we form a tiny minority doesn't by itself mean a damn thing.

Bible College Reunion

I don't want to be unfair. Bart does after all spar with many Mythicist arguments, but it seems clear to me he is simply not ready to think outside the box of his SBL peers. Again and again, as I read the book, I realized that he and I occupy different universes of biblical criticism. He believes the 'lucky seven' Pauline Epistles to be authentic and holds to what I regard as unrealistically early (apologetics-derived) dates for the gospels. He thinks the canned speeches in Acts preserve facts about Jesus even though careful vocabulary and conceptual studies by Earl Richard[4] and others have shown them all to be the creations of the Acts author. By contrast, I am a student of the classic Higher Critics (*e.g.*, F.C. Baur, D.F. Strauss, Wilhelm Wrede, Rudolf Bultmann, Walter Schmithals) and the more extreme Dutch Radical Critics (especially Willem Christiaan van Manen and L. Gordon Rylands).

Like many neo-conservative New Testament scholars today, Bart is on the one hand *un*-willing to entertain the possibility of textual interpolations in the early decades from which no manuscript evidence survives at all;[5] while on the other, he *is* willing to trim away

4 Earl Richard, *Acts 6:1–8:4: The Author's Method of Composition*. Society of Biblical Literature Dissertation Series 41 [Missoula: Scholars Press, 1978].

5 He alleges that Christ-Myth Theorists engage in the *ad hoc* strategy of what some call "surgical exegesis" or what Walter Kaufmann called "gerrymandering the Bible" [*The Faith of a Heretic*. Garden City: Doubleday Anchor Books, 1963: 109], writing off New Testament texts inconvenient for one's hypothesis as later interpolations. I would refer him to William O. Walker, Jr., *Interpolations in the Pauline Letters*. Journal for the Study of the New Testament Supplement Series 13 [London: Sheffield Academic Press, 2001: 18–19] and the material cited there in footnote 54, for 1 Cor. 11:23–26 as an interpolation. Walker is no Christ-Myth kook. Nor was the late Winsome Munro who offers (as Walker does) definite criteria for spotting interpolations from the early period in her *Authority in Paul and Peter: The Identification of a Pastoral Stratum in the Pauline Corpus and 1 Peter*. Society for New Testament Studies Monograph Series 45 [New York: Cambridge University Press, 1983].

What is darn near comical is that it is the author of *The Orthodox Corruption of Scripture: The Effect of Early Christological Controversies on the Text of the New Testament* [New York: Oxford University Press, 1993] who is so zealous for the

the more blatant marks of Christian interpolation from the *Testimonium Flavianum* (what Josephus supposedly says about Jesus) as scribal embellishments because it would allow him to take what's left as a genuine testimony to Jesus. Not that he thinks it would prove much in either case — or does he? Depends on what page you are reading.

Similarly, he *accepts* the claim of Papias, second-century bishop of Hierapolis, that he had met people who claimed to be acquaintances of Jesus' disciples, even though he himself *rejects* everything Papias claimed to have learned from them about the authorship of the gospels. Nor does he mention Papias' cartoonish account of the grotesque swelling of Judas Iscariot to parade-float dimensions, something that surely ruins the good bishop's claim to any credibility. Do I remember correctly that Bart wrote a book[6] on fraud and forgery in the New Testament?

The methodological error here — trying to make bad evidence into good — is a cousin to the error bemoaned by D.F. Strauss[7] so long ago. Protestant Rationalists supposed that, though the major point of a miracle story, the supernatural event, might be rejected, other, tangential features might nonetheless be genuine historical data. Strauss rejected this, pointing out that the ancillary details were there only for the sake of the story's main point and that it was arbitrary to maintain the former while rejecting the latter. But that is essentially Bart's strategy in the case of the speeches in Acts, the Josephus text, and the Papias

---

inviolability of today's 'received text.' In that great book Ehrman demonstrates the frequent tampering with the New Testament texts by ancient Christian apologists who sought thereby to safeguard the scriptures against the use of them by heretics. Surely the further back we go, the more likely it is that more such scribal funny business occurred, in the early period before the texts had donned the halo of inspired scripture. When Ehrman ought to be agnostic *vis-à-vis* possible interpolations, he instead embraces fideism: let's just assume, even insist, that no such tampering occurred. If we don't, it will be much harder to dogmatize based on uncertain evidence. That is, after all, the duty of *a paradigm policeman.*

6 Bart D. Ehrman, *Forged: Writing in the Name of God — Why the Bible's Authors Are Not Who We Think They Are* [New York: Harper Collins, 2011].

7 David Friedrich Strauss, *The Life of Jesus Critically Examined.* Trans. George Eliot (Mary Ann Evans). Lives of Jesus Series [Philadelphia: Fortress Press, 1972: 55].

traditions. He has no business picking up the scraps. He has to throw the bathwater out once he has ejected the baby. But he won't.

In *Did Jesus Exist?* Bart makes repeated fallacious appeals to authority and majority opinion, nor is he loathe to loathe. That is, he aims *ad hominem* attacks like Cupid's arrows. Personally, I do not appreciate it when he invites the reader to write me off as a bitter ex-fundamentalist, implying my work is a mere rationalization of my apostasy. He mistakenly thinks I used to be an evangelical preacher. I did spend a dozen years as a born-again Christian, but I became disillusioned with it precisely because, against my every hope and desire, I found I could no longer accept the apologetical arguments for gospel accuracy and biblical authority. What irritation my writings sometimes display expresses my righteous indignation at the bogus argumentation of the conservative writers. I suspect that Bart has occasionally felt the same way. But at the end of the book he writes all of us Mythicists off as merely pursuing an anti-religious agenda. Is he a mind reader? Does it not occur to him that our embrace of radical criticism might have *led to* our disillusionment with faith rather than being an after-the-fact rationalization of it? Bart sounds like 'Creation-Science' fundamentalists who accuse scientists of espousing evolution merely as a way to escape repenting and believing in God. Is he still thinking in the patterns they taught him at Moody Bible Institute?

When I first discarded evangelicalism (years before I became a church pastor) I held views almost identical to those Bart espouses today: Jesus was an apocalyptic prophet much as Albert Schweitzer described him. And these views were for me no more a function of my rejection of faith than they are for Bart. Again like him, back then I viewed the arguments of G.A. Wells (at the time a Mythicist) with astonishment and skepticism. But as the years went by and I studied more and more perspectives neglected by most scholars I knew, I found myself going in a more radical direction, not because I found the notions particularly attractive, but because I could no longer accept the arguments of moderate critics. And I have paid the price for it professionally, not that I am complaining. Indeed, "the lines are fallen unto me in pleasant places."

Bart Ehrman: Paradigm Policeman

Police Brutality

Let me turn to a few places where I believe Bart gets me wrong or offers ineffective arguments against my views. Most often he just professes to find my arguments implausible or unpersuasive. There is nothing I can do about that. I have to rely upon my readers to make that call for themselves. I trust they will not merely take his word for it. But there are a few points, I say, where I really must raise an objection.

First, he says I misunderstand the criteria of dissimilarity and embarrassment[8] because I am wielding them in the wrong task, like using a hammer to saw wood. These criteria are designed to establish which gospel materials are authentic, but (he thinks) I am using them perversely to demonstrate *inauthenticity*. He says I do not get it, that the proper use of the criteria is to sift through the texts to find those that can jump the hurdles. We should accept, he says, any gospel bit that does not appear so similar to early Christian belief or to current Jewish material that it might have been borrowed from one or the other. Anything that does not match up with early Church or Jewish material must really be from Jesus, something distinctive, a point where Jesus differed from Judaism. Or something he said that went over like a lead balloon, not picked up by Christians.

What about the embarrassment criterion — what John Dominic Crossan calls "damage control"? The idea here is that certain features in the gospel material that gave later Christians theological headaches (Jesus receiving John's baptism of repentance, Jesus denying he is good and therefore that he is God, his cry of dereliction from the cross, his admission of ignorance concerning the time of the end, *etc.*) must be historical, since Christians would never have made them up. (Thus embarrassment is a special case of dissimilarity: if some loose end is conspicuous by the chagrin it caused later Christians, it is dissimilar to their Christian beliefs and thus, ostensibly, could not have been derived from them.) The purpose of the criteria is indeed to help us winnow out the chaff and preserve the wheat. I know that.

8 You can't beat the discussion of these criteria by Norman Perrin in his *Rediscovering the Teaching of Jesus* [New York: Harper & Row, 1976: 39–47].

Robert M. Price

Can Bart possibly miss my point that *none of the material passes the test*? I think I am the first (though who cares?) to note that the basic axiom of form criticism throws a deep shadow over the usefulness of dissimilarity and embarrassment, and here's why. Form critics argue that nothing would have been preserved in the process of oral transmission that was not useful for some purpose (catechetical, homiletic, ritual legitimization, polemical, *etc.*) of the early Christians. Nothing seems to have been preserved for the sake of abstract curiosity. Well, if that is so, then *everything* in the gospel tradition reflects early Christian interests or we would not be reading it now! And that means we cannot be sure *anything* was not fabricated to serve those interests. It's not that we *know* the stuff *was* fabricated; it's just that we can't say it *wasn't* — and that's the point of these criteria, isn't it? To show what wasn't fabricated? And nothing passes the test.

Bart, like all mainstream critics, is less critical than he thinks. In his book *Lost Christianities*[9] (which essentially recycles Walter Bauer's ground-breaking thesis in *Orthodoxy and Heresy in Earliest Christianity*),[10] Bart sets forth the amazing diversity of early Christian religion. Yet his naïve use of the criterion of embarrassment in *Did Jesus Exist?* assumes that all early Christians believed, thought, and practiced the same things. But they didn't. What was embarrassing to one writer or one generation or one sect needn't have been embarrassing to another. It is obvious, for instance, that Mark had no problem with a humble Jesus who could apply to John for a baptism of repentance or who could tell the Rich Young Ruler not to call him good. Mark had no problem with Jesus being surprised at the lack of faith among his townsfolk, or with his inability to heal them. Matthew, however, did, so he changed all this. But that doesn't make the earlier version historical fact.

Bart seems to realize this when he recognizes the presence in Acts, Romans, *etc.*, of vestiges of adoptionist Christology, the belief that Jesus was a mortal man subsequently adopted as God's son, perhaps at

9 Bart D. Ehrman, *Lost Christianities: The Battles for Scripture and the Faiths We Never Knew* [New York: Oxford University Press, 2003].

10 Walter Bauer, *Orthodoxy and Heresy in Earliest Christianity*, translated from 2nd German edition [Mifflintown, PA: Sigler Press, 1996].

his baptism, perhaps at the resurrection. This hardly means Jesus must actually have *been* adopted as God's son somewhere along the line just because the notion undermines the later pre-existence Christology. It just means that an earlier *belief* was embarrassing to later believers. Likewise, just because Matthew wished Mark hadn't depicted Jesus as being baptized in the Jordan confessing his sins doesn't mean that it actually happened.

And this brings me to Bart's lambasting my suggestion that the story of Jesus' baptism might have been rewritten from that of the Persian prophet Zoroaster. Ehrman's service revolver fires two cheap shots at this target. But he is firing blanks. First, he complains that I can't get my story straight, since elsewhere I claim all the gospel narratives were worked up from Old Testament originals. But I clearly stated that there were other sources, too. Besides this, Bart admits that many gospel stories do seem to parallel various Old Testament tales, but he laughs the fact off, pleading that the stories may still preserve a core of historical material even though the tellers of these tales may have added scriptural form and color to them.

What, pray tell, is *left*? Is Bart saying Jesus really *did* multiply food for the crowds and this led the teller of the story to make it look like the similar story where Elisha does the same thing? That won't work: the only thing the two stories have in common is the central 'fact' of the feeding miracle. And isn't it obvious that the 'peripheral detail' consists rather in the change from Elisha as the miracle worker to Jesus? In any case, if a gospel story and an Old Testament story look that similar, isn't the simplest explanation that the Jesus version has been rewritten from the Elijah, Elisha, or Moses version? Bart is not shaving with Occam's Razor. He is positing superfluous, redundant explanations.

Secondly, he, like apologists, likes to seal off the sphere of biblical culture from the adjacent religious world. I can understand that bias on the part of conservatives who want to see Christianity flowing directly out of the Old Testament, without other tributaries, for theological reasons. But Bart allegedly no longer cares to defend such interests. Then why does he ignore the massive influence of Zoroastrianism on Pharisaic Judaism? Many scholars (except perhaps

Bart's professors at Wheaton College) believe Jews derived from Zoroastrianism the belief in an end-time resurrection, the apocalyptic periodization of history, the notion of a virgin-born future savior, the idea of an evil anti-God, and an elaborate angelology. The rabbis thought that Zoroaster was the same man as Baruch the scribe of Jeremiah! That means they were trying to legitimatize the Jewish assimilation of Zoroastrian themes during and after the Exile. T.W. Manson[11] suggested that the traditionalist Sadducees ('Syndics,' 'Councilmen') resisted these borrowings and labeled those who accepted them as *Pharisees* (*i.e.*, 'Parsees,' 'Persians,' 'Zoroastrians'). (Later the Pharisees redefined the term to make it a badge of honor: *Perushim* now denoting 'Separatists,' 'Puritans.' Am I such a nut for suggesting possible Zoroastrian influence on the baptism story?

What I have just mentioned is an example of *synchronic* comparison: tracing possible influence from one phenomenon to another close to it in time and space. Bart gives me hell for my invocation of the fact that Hong Xiuquan, the nineteenth-century Taiping messiah in China, called himself "the younger brother of Jesus" as a possible parallel to the use of "brother of the Lord" for James the Just (Galatians 1:19). Across so many centuries? Far-fetched, right? How can Bart not recognize a *diachronic* comparison (a comparison of analogous phenomena across time)? As I say quite clearly, the Taiping messiah obviously could not have been claiming to be the blood brother of Jesus unless he was Mel Brooks's character the 2,000 Year Old Man. No, he used the title to mean he was the earthly manifestation of another hypostasis of the Godhead, just as Jesus had been. Such a title need not at all imply its holder was the brother of a historical Jesus, either in the first century or the 19th. I don't see what's so funny about that.

Speaking of James the Just, Bart paints me as claiming that James was an eponymous (namesake) ancestor of a tribe, like the Old Testament tribal patriarchs whom the ancients posited, as Hermann Gunkel[12] argued, to cement alliances between hitherto-independent

11 T.W. Manson, *The Servant Messiah: A Study of the Public Ministry of Jesus* [Cambridge: Cambridge University Press, 1953: 18–19].

12 Hermann Gunkel, *Genesis*. Trans. Mark E. Biddle. Mercer Library of Biblical

tribes. With a sure grasp of the self-evident, Bart protests that Christians were not an ethnic group! Nor am I so stupid. I believe I made it pretty clear that the case of the Israelite, Edomite, and Ishmaelite patriarchs is a *historical analogy* for the hypothetical grafting together of James, a sect figurehead in his own right, and Jesus as brothers in order to facilitate the combining of the two sects. I would be much surprised if Bart did not believe that Luke's connecting of Jesus and John the Baptist as cousins is not exactly the same sort of thing.

Murder Mystery

I cringe when Constable Ehrman calls for back-up, appealing to Jonathan Z. Smith's attempts to dismantle the dying and rising god mytheme. He also summons Tryggve Mettinger,[13] who actually demonstrates the existence of pre-Christian myths of dead-and-resurrected deities but remains oblivious of the implications of his own arguments for the resurrection of Jesus. I have dealt with these authors in detail elsewhere,[14] in fact, in books Bart says he has read, including *Deconstructing Jesus*[15] and *The Christ-Myth Theory and Its Problems*.[16] He could at least have done me the courtesy of replying

Studies [Macon: Mercer University Press, 1997: *xviii–xix*].

13 Tryggve N.D. Mettinger, *The Riddle of Resurrection: "Dying and Rising Gods" in the Ancient Near East*. Coniectanea Biblica Old Testament Series 50 [Stockholm: Almqvist & Wiksell International, 2001].

14 Smith seems to think all the relevant myths must exactly match, and he dismisses them because they don't, whereas the point is *to formulate an ideal type* of the dying and rising god myth by distilling the common *fabula* shared by the various myths and then using the result as a yardstick with which to measure and explain each individual myth's distinctions. He claims there is no solid evidence of pre-Christian resurrected saviors, whereas in fact there is plenty, from the Ras Shamra texts featuring Baal, to the Pyramid texts featuring Osiris, to shards depicting the risen Attis. Ehrman denies Osiris was said to have risen in a physical body, but Plutarch, whom he selectively quotes, makes it clear he did. Did pagans pinch the mytheme from Christians? That's absurd: had they known pagans copied the Jesus story, would early apologists have claimed Satan had counterfeited Jesus' resurrection *in advance* by inspiring the *earlier* myths of Adonis, Dionysus, Attis, and the rest?

15 Robert M. Price, *Deconstructing Jesus* [Amherst: Prometheus Books, 2000: 88–92].

16 Robert M. Price, *The Christ-Myth Theory and Its Problems* [Cranford, NJ: American

to my arguments. If he thinks they are stupid, too, he might have done his readers the favor of explaining why.

It is interesting that Stanley Fish blurbs the book, thanking Bart for swatting Mythicism like an annoying fly. Bart's book is a prime example of what Fish himself explains in his great book *Is There a Text in this Class?* There Fish shows how an argument over texts can be meaningful only between those who belong to the same "interpretive community," sharing the same assumptions and methods.[17] Catholics cannot really argue from scripture against Protestants, and *vice-versa*, because one feels free to allegorize the text and the other doesn't. A Structuralist and a Deconstructive critic talk past one another. It would be like two teams in a stadium, one playing baseball, the other football. Each community embraces its own *paradigm*, its own frame of reference which includes its own criteria for the plausibility of readings and arguments. A reading seems "natural" or "the plain sense" if it is the accustomed reading.[18] If you have always read it one way, no new reading can sound plausible to you. Unless of course, you make what Don Cupitt[19] calls "the leap of reason" and try to see it the other guy's way. And then you may find it makes new sense to you.

I remember when I first heard there were scholars[20] who argued that the Sodom and Gomorrah story had nothing to do with homosexuality. My first reaction was to scoff. But then the sheer outlandishness of it made me curious. How on earth could intelligent people think this? I read and pondered their argument — and found myself convinced. At first I thought Deconstruction was the merest nonsense. But then I realized, "Listen, Price, there must be something to this, some game these people are playing, a method to the seeming madness. Let

Atheist Press, 2011: 44–46].

17 Stanley Fish, *Is There a Text in this Class? The Authority of Interpretive Communities* [Cambridge: Harvard University Press, 1980: *e.g.*, pp. 171–172].

18 *Ibid.*: 276.

19 Don Cupitt, *The Leap of Reason*. Studies in Philosophy and Religion 4 [London: Sheldon Press, 1976].

20 Derrick Sherwin Bailey, *Homosexuality and the Western Christian Tradition* [London: Longmans, Green and Co., 1955: Chapter I, "Sodom and Gomorrah," 1–28].

me find out what it is." And I did, and I found it illuminating. And, need I say, I started out the same way with the Christ Myth Theory — outlandish! But the more I looked into it, the more astonished I was at the sense, *better sense* it began to seem, that it made of the evidence.

Again, I am no mind reader, but Bart Ehrman gives every indication of being someone who has not taken the requisite leap of reason beyond the boundaries (and the blinders) of his interpretive community. Certain ideas appear to him outrageous because he has never heard them, or never heard them taken seriously by those whom he deems to be serious scholars — serious precisely because they do not take seriously nutty notions like Mythicism.

Is it too much to hope that Bart Ehrman will one day soon be promoted from a mere paradigm policeman to a genuine detective?

CHAPTER TWO

How Not to Defend Historicity

Richard Carrier, Ph.D.

As a scholar investigating the Jesus-myth theory, even as one who has come to be convinced it is in some sense correct, I have maintained my public criticism of poorly thought-out defenses of the Jesus-myth theory. I do not agree with many of the claims and arguments even of the other contributors to this volume. But I do not give a free pass to defenders of historicity, either. When their arguments are as illogical or ill informed as even the worst defenders of the Jesus myth, I must say so, and have.

I am not alone in this. When I researched my book *Proving History: Bayes's Theorem and the Quest for the Historical Jesus,*[1] I discovered that every mainstream expert who had published a study on the methods employed to defend the historicity of Jesus (by defending specific claims about him) had found those methods to be logically indefensible, across the board, as well as widely abused by essentially everyone in the field. The modern 'consensus' that Jesus existed has simply not been founded on any logically valid or properly employed methodology. I realized I could not examine any theory or move forward at all without a new method, one that actually has demonstrable logical validity. So, I had to solve that problem first.

The result was *Proving History*, wherein I demonstrate extensively the failure of the methods currently being employed to study

1 Richard C. Carrier, *Proving History: Bayes's Theorem and the Quest for the Historical Jesus* [Amherst, NY: Prometheus Books, 2012].

Jesus (consisting of the use of several 'criteria of historicity'), and the unanimous expert agreement on their failure, and then develop a methodology to replace it — a method that is logically defensible and would only have to be applied to soundly established facts to get a more credible result. When I finally applied that method, I found historicity to be far less probable than the consensus imagines. I make a detailed case for that conclusion in my next book on this subject, *On the Historicity of Jesus Christ* (forthcoming).[2]

While I was still completing that second book, Bart Ehrman came out with his case to the contrary, *Did Jesus Exist?*.[3] I had loved all his previous work, and still to this day cite most of it as the very best treatments of the mainstream view of the New Testament available, especially *Jesus Interrupted* and *Forged*. So I was expecting *Did Jesus Exist?* to be the very best — and the clearest — defense of the historicity of Jesus to date, competently and carefully responding to the arguments of the best proponents of the Jesus-myth theory, most especially Earl Doherty, Robert M. Price, and (to a lesser but still important extent) Thomas L. Thompson of the University of Copenhagen.

I was thoroughly disappointed. In fact, I was so shocked at how poorly researched and illogical his arguments were in this book that *appalled* is a better word. Accordingly, I composed a detailed critique not only of his book, but his even more inept claims in an article promoting it in *The Huffington Post*.[4] He then attempted a response to my criticisms

2 In the meantime a *very* brief précis of the case I shall make can be viewed online: Richard Carrier, "So...if Jesus Didn't Exist, Where Did He Come from Then?" Madison Freethought Festival (28 April 2012) at www.youtube.com/watch?v=XORm2QtR-os. You can also view a PDF of the accompanying slideshow (lacking the animations) at www.richardcarrier.info/Historicity_of_Jesus.pdf.

3 Maurice Casey is also due to publish his own defense of historicity, as *Jesus: Evidence and Argument or Mythicist Myths?*, but that has not yet come into print. That leaves Ehrman's book as, at present, the only book-length defense of historicity by a qualified expert in over fifty years.

4 Bart Ehrman, "Did Jesus Exist?" *The Huffington Post* [20 March 2012] at www.huffingtonpost.com/bart-d-ehrman/did-jesus-exist_b_1349544.html. He made several irresponsibly inaccurate, fallacious, or misleading statements in that article that will greatly misinform any lay reader, which I documented in my critique (see following note), but I will not revisit those errors in the present chapter. Here I will focus solely on his book.

— ignoring almost all of them and making newly inept arguments against a select remainder. Some of them, in my opinion, call into question his professional honesty.[5] He would appear to be the very worst defender of the historicity of Jesus. He has become more of a liability to that cause, as his inept and illogical approach to the debate only serves to make the defense of historicity look ridiculous. His example should be a warning to all who would attempt a better argument.

The Overall Problem

The main problem with *Did Jesus Exist?* was the sheer number of errors, fallacies, and misleading statements that fill it. It is important to emphasize this: a handful of errors or fallacies would not condemn any book, as every book has a few (even the best scholars make mistakes and get a few things wrong), and a good book can more than compensate for that by being consistently useful, informative, and on-point in every other respect. But Ehrman's book was so full of gaffes it is simply unsalvageable. It resembles in this respect some of the worst Jesus-myth literature, which I can't recommend to people either, as it will misinform them far more than inform them. Scholars can also correct their errors — if they are inclined to. Ehrman, so far, does not seem at all inclined to.

I could not list all the errors, fallacies, and misleading statements I marked up in my copy of his book. There were hundreds of them, averaging at least one a page. This shocked me, because all his previous works were not like this. Their errors are few, and well drowned out by their consistent utility and overall accuracy in conveying the mainstream consensus on the issues they address. But *Did Jesus Exist?* was a travesty.

In my critical review I chose a representative selection of the worst mistakes, in order to illustrate the problem. Some mistook

5 For my latest recap of this exchange see: Richard Carrier, "Ehrman on Historicity Recap," *Richard Carrier Blogs* [24 July 2012] at freethoughtblogs.com/carrier/archives/1794, which contains a table of links to all of my more detailed articles on this matter, as well as a complete summary of what I argued, and what (if anything) Ehrman said in reply.

that as a complete list, and suggested those weren't enough errors to condemn the book. Although they certainly were (not all of them, but many of them are damning and render the book useless at its one stated purpose), they are *not* a complete list, but just the tip of the iceberg. And that is the bigger problem. The errors I chose to document and discuss are examples of consistent trends throughout the book, of careless thinking, careless writing, and often careless research. This means there are probably many more errors than I saw, because for much of the book I was trusting him to tell me correctly what he found from careful research; but the rest of the book illustrates that I can't trust him to correctly convey information about this subject or to have done careful research.

I think I have an idea what happened, if reports are true that Ehrman has said he takes only two or three weeks to write a book: with the exception of *Orthodox Corruption of Scripture* (and a few related works), which summarizes many years of his own dedicated research (and thus is an excellent piece of scholarship, not aimed at laymen), all his books have been just summaries of 'what he knows' from being a trained New Testament scholar (plus occasionally a small foray into specific independent research, as when he investigated the nature of forgery in the ancient world for *Forged*, which could have been completed in a couple of long days at a library). He is thus relying on field-established background knowledge. This is fine when that's what you are reporting on (as he usually does). But when you are going outside your field, you do need to do a bit more, and you do risk being wrong a bit more often. This is why it's a good idea to field ideas in other venues before committing them to print: it gives you an opportunity to be corrected by other experts first.

I had said it was his "incompetence in classics (*e.g.* knowledge of ancient culture and literature) and ancient history (*e.g.* understanding the methodology of the field and the background facts of the period) that trips him up several times," and that now makes sense. He *is* fully competent to make up for not being a classicist or specialist in ancient history, by getting up to speed on what he needed — which for this task might have taken a year or more — but he chose not to.

Instead, from the armchair as it were, I think he just relied on 'what he knows' — which was all just what he was told or has read in New Testament studies. But that isn't enough. Disaster resulted. Following are only some of the examples I selected to illustrate this.

1. Failing to Engage the Arguments

Ehrman treats Mythicist arguments *only selectively*, never comprehensively. I never once saw him actually engage directly with any single Mythicist's case for a theory of Christian origins — as in, describing the theory correctly, listing the evidence its proponent offers for each element, and then evaluating that evidence and the logical connection between it and the conclusion. You won't find this done once, anywhere in this book, for any author. Ehrman just cherry picks isolated claims and argues against them, often with minimal reference to the facts its proponent has claimed support it. This makes his book useless as a critique. Readers are not given a fair review of what the opposition is saying, and will have to just go and read what they actually say to evaluate it, bypassing Ehrman altogether.[6]

I also took Ehrman to task for hardly treating at all the worst (yet most popular) Mythicist arguments. But I said I could live with that, since addressing the best was at least more important. Yet in Ehrman's response to me, he never addresses that main concern (his failure to properly engage with any of the best Mythicist theories), and only makes his excuses for dealing so little with the worst of them. For that he asserts a principle in his own defense, that "a few indications of general incompetence is good enough" reason to dismiss an entire book as unworthy of further attention. Ironically, that is precisely the principle I applied to *his* book. I found more than a few indications of general incompetence (including failures to fact-check, sloppy and

6 The best works to start with are Earl Doherty, *The Jesus Puzzle* [Canadian Humanist 1999] and *Jesus: Neither God Nor Man* [Age of Reason 2009] and Robert Price, *The Christ-Myth Theory and Its Problems* [American Atheist Press 2011] and *The Incredible Shrinking Son of Man* [Prometheus 2003]. My own work *On the Historicity of Jesus Christ* will adapt and reinforce the best features of these.

careless writing and analysis, illogical arguments, self-contradictory assertions, all by the scores). Yet he dismisses *my* criticism as an unwarranted personal attack. This has led me to wonder: does he regard *his* exact same treatment of *others* as an inappropriate personal attack that *they* didn't deserve? Or as simply a demonstration that the books he examined are incompetently researched and incompetently written, a perfectly valid thing to demonstrate and conclude, and exactly what I did — but that he in his response attacks me for doing?

This is not how to argue for historicity. You have to be able to take the same kind of criticism you dole out. You have to make an effort to research and write your case carefully and responsibly. *You have to actually engage with the theories you intend to rebut.* And when errors and fallacies in your work are identified and demonstrated, you have to acknowledge and correct them, or otherwise prove (not just assert, but demonstrate) that they weren't mistaken or fallacious. Ehrman did none of these things, and still has not.

2. Lying to Cover Up Your Mistakes: The Case of the Priapus Bronze

In response to D.M. Murdock's claim that there is a statue of a penis-nosed cockerel (which she appears to imply is a "symbol of St. Peter") in the Vatican museum, Ehrman says "there is no penis-nosed statue of Peter the cock in the Vatican or anywhere else except in books like this, which love to make things up" [24]. Ehrman evidently did no research on this and did not check this claim at all. Murdock quickly exposed this by providing numerous scholarly references, including actual photographs of the object.[7] Most important of these is an article by Lorrayne Baird published in *Studies in Iconography*, a serious work of modern peer reviewed scholarship.[8]

7 D.M. Murdock, "The Phallic Savior of the World Hidden in the Vatican," *Freethought Nation* [22 March 2012] at www.freethoughtnation.com/contributing-writers/63-acharya-s/669-the-phallic-savior-of-the-world-hidden-in-the-vatican.html.

8 Lorrayne Baird, "Priapus Gallinaceus: The Role of the Cock in Fertility and Eroticism in Classical Antiquity and the Middle Ages," *Studies in Iconography* 7–8 [1981–82: 81–112].

The statue does not have the name "Peter" on it (and Murdock never claimed it did; that it could represent him is only an interpretation), but it apparently exists (or did exist) exactly as she describes.

At the very least I would expect Ehrman to have called the Vatican museum about this, or to have checked the literature on it, before arrogantly declaring no such object existed and implying Murdock made it up. I do not assume Murdock's interpretation of the object is correct (there is no clear evidence it has anything to do with Christianity, much less Peter). But its existence appears to be beyond dispute. She did not make that up. Ehrman's statement to the contrary at worst exposes his carelessness and failure to do proper research; at best, it exposes him as a wholly misleading and unreliable writer — producing a book that will only misinform the public by never saying what he means, thus negating any value it could have had.

A correct statement would have been "the statue she refers to does exist, or once did, but it's not a statue of Peter but of the pagan god Priapus, of which we have many examples; the notion that this one represents Peter comes only from the imagination of theorists like her." But that is not what he said, or anything like it. Notice the difference between what a *responsible* sentence of rebuttal looks like, and what it says, and how it better informs the public, with what Ehrman wrote, which only misinforms, and thus makes things worse than they were to begin with. This is not how to argue for historicity.

In response to his being caught in this mistake, Ehrman insisted that's not what he meant, and that he knew the statue existed all along, and that he was only saying in the book that it wasn't a statue of Peter.[9] Let's look at what he actually wrote in the book. You be the judge:

> [Acharya says] "'Peter' is not only 'the rock' but also 'the cock', or penis, as the word is used as slang to this day." Here Acharya shows (her own?) hand drawing of a man with a rooster head but with a large erect penis instead of a nose, with this description: "bronze

9 In Bart Ehrman, "Acharya S, Richard Carrier, and a Cocky Peter (Or: "A Cock and Bull Story")," *Christianity in Antiquity (CIA): The Bart Ehrman Blog* [22 April 2012), at ehrmanblog.org/acharya-s-richard-carrier-and-a-cocky-peter-or-a-cock-and-bull-story.

> sculpture hidden in the Vatican treasure of the Cock, symbol of St. Peter" (295). There is no penis-nosed statue of Peter the cock in the Vatican or anywhere else except in books like this, which love to make things up.[10]

That's the sum total of what he says about this. It is quite evident to me that when he wrote this, he doubted the drawing came from any source, and believed (and here implies to the reader) that she just made it up. There is no such statue. That is what he is saying. Certainly, the one thing this paragraph *doesn't* say is that the statue she references does exist, is (or at one time was) at the Vatican, and looks essentially just as her drawing depicts it. It also does not say that she is merely wrong to interpret this statue as being of Peter. And it fails to inform the public that statues like this do come from antiquity, and represent the god Priapus. To the contrary, all it says is that there is no such statue, she made this up — which is false. This betrays Ehrman's failure to even check.

But he now claims he did check. Sort of — he says he saw her citations and assumed there were priapic statues; he did not actually say he checked her sources or (as a genuinely concerned scholar might) contacted the Vatican. Some commentators on his blog then tried claiming the statue was never at the Vatican. But their misinformation and mishandling of the sources is thoroughly exposed in an extensive comment by an observer at Murdock's website.[11] The object may have been moved (as I implied was possible in my original review), but Ehrman said it didn't exist anywhere, so its location is moot. And I should add, this is precisely the kind of source analysis that Ehrman should already have worked through and been able to discuss informedly. Yet in comments there he said the original commentator's findings were "very interesting" and "very hard to get around," indicating he didn't in fact do any of this research himself and was never familiar with the source materials on the statue. This is *not* how scholars should behave. If you are going to challenge

10 Ehrman, *Did Jesus Exist?* 24.

11 Comment of 24 April 2012 (2:22pm) by moderator GodAlmighty at freethoughtnation.com/forums/viewtopic.php?p=25634#p25634.

someone's claim, you check their sources, familiarize yourself with the facts of the case, and communicate your findings to the public.

Now, of course, Ehrman claims he never said the statue didn't exist. He only said a statue of *Peter* didn't exist. He thus parses his words hyper-literally to argue that he said the exact opposite of what he said. You see, when he said the statue didn't exist, that it was made up, he meant *a statue of Peter*, and since the statue that Murdock references and presents a drawing of isn't a statue "of Peter," the statue doesn't exist. This is an amusing case of faux metaphysical deepness being used as an excuse to read a sentence as saying a statue simultaneously does and doesn't exist, depending on what one calls it. Even if that is really what he was doing when he wrote the book, this is just a variant of a textbook masked-man fallacy ("That statue exists. She says it is a statue of Peter. No statues of Peter exist. Therefore that statue doesn't exist.").

It's bad enough that, even if this is true and he really meant to say the opposite of what he appears to say, he obviously wrote it so badly he not only sucks as a writer but can't even tell that he sucks as a writer (indeed only after repeated goading in comments did he confess that "maybe I should have phrased it differently"). But trying to use the "I suck as a writer" defense against the much worse crime of careless scholarship requires him to claim the masked man fallacy isn't a fallacy but a perfectly reasonable way to argue. This convicts him of not understanding how logic works. That is a zero net gain for him. Scholars who routinely argue illogically — and don't even know they are arguing illogically — are not reliable scholars.

Before I get to the punchline, *I really must emphasize this point.* Even granting his excuse, the fact that the wording is completely misleading and will misinform the public still confirms my point in citing this example: *we can't trust a book written like this.* If he so badly botched this sentence that he meant the opposite of what he said, then how many other sentences in this book are as badly written and mean the opposite of what they say? Indeed, the fact that he had to be repeatedly goaded before even admitting that this sentence does that means he is not even capable of detecting when a sentence he has written says the opposite of what he meant. That entails we should trust his book *even less*, since whatever filter is supposed to prevent him making these kinds of mistakes is clearly not working in his brain.

As commentator Kim Rottman said:

> The issue is what the average reader of Ehrman's book is going to think he means. Ehrman's statement may be strictly true but I sincerely doubt that a lay person reading that sentence is going to take it to mean something like "there is such a statue but it's not a statue of Peter." They're going to think he means there is no such statue. Period. They're probably also never going to see Ehrman's rebuttal of Carrier's review and thus never know he corrected himself. ... Then he acts like this is representative of all the examples Carrier gave; as if the rest can also be explained away as poor wording and that none of them were anything that's relevant to his overall argument. This response wasn't successful at all. If anything, he's dug himself in deeper.[12]

Indeed. But I fear it may be worse than that. That's because I don't actually believe him when he says he didn't mean to say the statue didn't exist. I suspect that is a *post-hoc* rationalization that he cooked up in an attempt to save face, after his careless and irresponsible scholarship on this matter was exposed. I suspect this not only because his excuse is implausible on its face (read his original paragraph again, and ask yourself how likely it is that someone who wanted to say "the statue she depicts does exist, but it's not a statue of Peter" would say instead what he did), and not only because he still doesn't claim to have researched her sources or contacted the Vatican (in other words, to do what he should have done), but also *because he said in a podcast* (before my review and before Murdock herself exposed him on this) *that the statue did not in any sense exist.*

That's right. On the *Homebrewed Christianity* show, Ehrman says Murdock talks about Peter the cock and shows a drawing of a statue with a penis for a nose and claims this is in the Vatican museum, at

12 Comment of 22 April 2012 (8:11pm) by Kim Rottman at www.patheos.com/blogs/camelswithhammers/2012/04/ehrman-evades-carriers-criticisms/#comment-8150.

which Ehrman declares, with laughter, "It's just made up! There is no such s[tatue]... It's just completely made up." In context it is certainly clear he is saying there is no such statue of any kind, that her drawing is not of any actual object.[13] I must leave it to you to decide what's going on here. From both his own wording in the book and this podcast, it certainly seems that Ehrman had no idea the statue actually existed, until Murdock and I caught him on it. Notably, I had emailed him about this weeks before my review, asking what his response to Murdock was, because I was concerned it didn't look good. I had not yet read his book, so I didn't know this would be such a travesty. Ehrman never answered me (even though he has in the past). Only after my review did he come out with the explanation that he meant to say the statue existed but wasn't connected to Peter. And on that point I suspect he is lying.

I can give more leeway to a podcast interview, where we often forget to say things or say things incorrectly, and we don't get to re-read and revise to improve accuracy and clarity (though this excuse doesn't hold for a book). But here this does not look like an accidental omission or a slip of the tongue. He really does appear to think (at the time of that podcast) that the statue was completely made up. And that certainly appears to be what he says. Did he really also "mean to say" in that podcast that the statue wasn't "completely" made up, that in fact it existed, but that Murdock was only wrong about what it symbolized? In other words, did he once again say, as if by accident, exactly the opposite of what he meant? You tell me.

The clincher is the fact that he gives no argument at all in his book for why Murdock is wrong to conclude this is a statue of Peter. His only argument is that the statue doesn't exist. This only makes sense as a rebuttal if indeed he meant the statue *wholly* did not exist.

---

13 "Bart Ehrman on Jesus' Existence, Apocalypticism & Holy Week," *Homebrewed Christianity* [3 April 2012], timestamp 20:30-21:10, at homebrewedchristianity.com/2012/04/03/bart-ehrman-on-jesus-existence-apocalypticism-holy-week. Note that I put the word "statue" in partial brackets because he speaks so quickly he didn't complete the word but started saying what is obviously the word "statue"; he doesn't pause to correct himself, though, he just quickly segues to the next phrase in animated conversation.

Otherwise, *why is she wrong to conclude it symbolizes Peter*? Ehrman doesn't say. I consider this good evidence that he is now lying about what he really thought and meant when writing the book. Surely, in an argument that she was wrong, he would give a reason why she is wrong. And he gave only one: the statue she drew doesn't exist. But it does — as even he now admits.

Establishing oneself as someone who prefers dishonesty to admitting mistakes is not the way to argue for historicity. Neither is so thoroughly failing at the job of informing the public on the actual facts.

3. Lying to Cover Up Your Mistakes: The Case of the Pliny Correspondence

Ehrman again exposes how careless his research for this book was by horribly bungling his treatment of a key source. He discusses the one letter of Pliny the Younger that mentions Christ, but in a way that demonstrates he never actually read that letter, and misread the scholarship on it, and as a result so badly misreports the facts concerning it that this section of his book will certainly have to be completely rewritten if ever there is a second edition.

The error itself is not crucial to his overall thesis, but it reveals the shockingly careless way he approached researching and writing this book as a whole. In fact, Ehrman almost made me fall out of my chair when I saw this. He made two astonishing errors here that are indicative of his incompetence with ancient source materials — the very same incompetence he accuses Mythicists like D.M. Murdock of. First, he doesn't correctly cite or describe his source (yet in this particular case that should have been impossible); and second, he fails to know the difference between a fact and a hypothesis.

Ehrman says that Pliny discusses Christians in his correspondence with emperor Trajan in "letter number 10," and that "in his letter 10 to the emperor Pliny discusses" the problem of the imperial decree against firefighting societies in that province, "and in that context he mentions another group that was illegally gathering," the Christians.[14] This is all incorrect, and demonstrates that Ehrman

14 Ehrman, *Did Jesus Exist?* 51–52.

never actually read Pliny's letter, and doesn't even know how to cite it correctly, and has no idea that the connection between Pliny's prosecution of Christians and the decree against illegal assembly affecting the firefighters in Bithynia is a modern scholarly inference and not actually anything Pliny says in his letters.

In fact, Pliny never once discusses the decree against fire brigades in his letter about Christians, nor connects the two cases in any way. Moreover, neither subject is discussed in "letter number 10." Ehrman evidently didn't know that all of Pliny's correspondence to Trajan is collected in *book* 10 of Pliny's letters. His letter on the fire brigades in that book is letter 33; and his letter on Christians is letter 96 (and therefore nowhere near each other in time or topic).[15] But Ehrman has still gotten the context wrong. The law against illegal assembly was not a special law in that province, but had long been a law throughout the whole empire — and it was not targeted at fire brigades. Existing law required all social clubs to be licensed by the government, and many clubs were so licensed. This included religious and scientific associations, burial clubs, guilds, and, of course, fire brigades. What was unique about Pliny's province was that the state had been denying these licenses even to fire brigades, and Pliny asked Trajan to lift that injunction. (In letter 10.34, Trajan denies Pliny's request, citing recent unrest there.)

The connection between the Bithynian fire brigades and Christianity is not that there was any special injunction against Christians (Trajan, in letter 10.97, explicitly says there wasn't), but that in letter 96 Christianity appears to be treated by Pliny like any unlicensed club, and both letters (96 and 97) make it clear there was no specific law or decree against Christians. Therefore, modern scholars conclude, the same law is probably what was being applied in both cases (prosecuting Christians and banning firefighting associations). And that's kind of what Ehrman confusingly says — except that he is evidently unaware that *this is a modern conclusion* and is not actually stated in the source.

15 On their possible connection (which I do believe scholars have correctly inferred), see my discussion in Richard Carrier, *Not the Impossible Faith: Why Christianity Didn't Need a Miracle to Succeed* [Lulu 2009: 418–22].

Richard Carrier

Ehrman's treatment of the sources and scholarship on this issue betray the kind of hackneyed mistakes and lack of understanding that he repeatedly criticizes the 'bad' Mythicists of — particularly his inability even to cite the letters properly and his strange assumption that both subjects are discussed in the same letter. These are mistakes I would only expect from an undergraduate. But if even Historicists like Ehrman can't do their research properly and get their facts right, and can't even be bothered to read their own source materials or understand their context, why are we to trust the consensus of Historicists any more than Mythicists? And more particularly, how many other sources has Ehrman completely failed to read, cite, or understand properly? This is not how to argue for historicity.

But it gets worse. After I called him out on this, Ehrman refused to admit his mistake. He claims it was just a typo. I do not believe he's telling the truth. Because the wording in the book does not look even remotely like he knew that two different letters were being discussed, or that their connection was a scholarly inference and not something directly revealed in the context of "the letter" he twice references. I'll quote the relevant section in full (skipping only incidental material, and adding my emphasis in bold):

> ...Pliny is best known for a series of letters that he wrote later in life to the Roman emperor, Trajan, seeking advice for governing his province. **In particular**, letter number 10 from the year 112 CE is important, as it is the one place in which Pliny appears to mention the existence of Jesus. **The letter** is not about Jesus himself; it is dealing with a political problem. In Pliny's province a law had been passed making it illegal for people to gather together in social groups ... The law applied to every social group, including fire brigades ... and so villages were burning.
>
> **In his letter 10** to the emperor Pliny discusses the fire problem, **and in that context** he mentions another group that was illegally gathering together. As it turns out, it was the local community of Christians.

Surely this cannot by any stretch of the imagination be a mere typo. To the contrary, it looks like Ehrman simply didn't consult the actual sources and is wholly unfamiliar with their content and relationship.

He doesn't even know how to cite them properly. This would be impossible for anyone actually looking at the source itself, where the designation by book and letter would be clear — as well as the separation between the subjects of Christianity and the fire brigades. So once again, it appears that Ehrman lied about his mistake, in an effort to avoid admitting his carelessness. Perhaps he did this because such an admission would impugn the whole book, since it would evince a general slackness and unreliability in the way he researched and wrote it. But that is definitely *not* the way to argue for historicity. His dishonesty and inability to admit real mistakes call into question everything he argues. His excuses are destroying his reputation. What else has he misrepresented? What else has he fudged, screwed up, or lied about? Can we ever trust him on this subject?

4. Not Checking or Knowing Essential Facts: The Case of "No Ancient Documents"

Ehrman falsely claims that from antiquity "we simply don't have birth notices, trial records, death certificates — or other kinds of records that one has today" and is adamant not only that we have none, but that such records were never even kept, because he asks "if Romans were careful record keepers, it is passing strange that we have no records."[16] In fact, we have lots of those things. I mean *lots*. (So in answer to Ehrman's question, "Where are they?," probably some are in his own university's library.) But more importantly, Christians *could have* quoted or preserved such documents relating to Jesus or his disciples, as such documents certainly would have existed then. *Thus a historian must explain why they did not.*

A correct treatment of this issue would be to give reasons why Christians didn't quote or preserve any of these records; *not* to claim that no such records existed or could have survived. That is simply false. What he said, therefore, suggests he didn't even check whether his claim was true, and he had no significant experience with ancient documents other than New Testament manuscripts, two marks against him that cast

16 Ehrman, *Did Jesus Exist?* 29.

a shadow over the whole book. And since such documents did exist, and therefore what he actually needs to do is explain why Christians didn't preserve them, the fact that he attempts no such explanation means he doesn't even understand the issues in the historicity debate. If this is how clueless and careless he is, again, what else is as wrong in this book?

At the very least, what he says in the book badly misinforms the public, and that not on a trivial matter, but on a crucial issue in the debate between Historicists and Mythicists. Although his conclusion is correct (I agree we should perhaps not expect to have any such records for Jesus or early Christianity), his premise is false. In fact, I cannot believe he said it. How can he not know that we have thousands of these kinds of records? Yes, predominantly from the sands of Egypt, but even in some cases beyond. I have literally held some of these documents in my very hands. More importantly, we also have such documents quoted or cited in books whose texts have survived. For instance, Suetonius references birth records for Caligula, and in fact his discussion of the sources on this subject is an example I have used of precisely the kind of historical research that is conspicuously lacking in any Christian literature before the third century.[17]

From Ehrman's list, "birth notices" would mean census receipts declaring a newborn, tax receipts establishing birth year (as capitation taxes often began when a child reached a certain age), or records establishing citizenship (Roman or local, there being more than one kind), and we have many examples of all three; as for "trial records" we have all kinds (including rulings and witness affidavits); we have "death certificates," too (we know there were even coroner's reports from doctors in cases of suspicious death); and quite a lot else (such as tax receipts establishing family property, home town, and family connections; business accounts; personal letters; financial matters for charities and religious organizations). As one papyrologist put it:

> A wealth of papyrus documents from the Graeco-Roman era have come to light on the daily lives of ancient people in Egypt, including their love letters and marriage contracts, tax and bank accounts, commodity lists, birth records, divorce cases, temple offerings, and

17 Carrier, *Not the Impossible Faith* 182–87.

most other conceivable types of memoranda, whether personal, financial, or religious."[18]

That Ehrman would not know this is remarkable and suggests he has very little experience in ancient history as a field and virtually none in papyrology (beyond its application to biblical manuscripts). Worse, he didn't even think to *check* whether we had any of these kinds of documents, before confidently declaring we didn't. And spouting unchecked generalizations about antiquity from the armchair is precisely *not* how to argue for historicity.

Ehrman demonstrates how little we can trust his knowledge or research when he says such silly things like, "If Romans kept such records, where are they? We certainly don't have any."[19] He really seems to think, — or is misleading any lay reader to think — that (a) we don't have any such records (when in fact we have many) and that (b) our not having them means Romans never kept them, when in fact it only means those records have been lost, because no one troubled to preserve them. Which leads us to ask why no one in Jesus' family, or among his disciples or subsequent churches, ever troubled to preserve any of these records, or any records whatever, whether legal documents, receipts, contracts, or letters, of Jesus' surviving family or any of the earliest missionaries and congregations.

We can certainly adduce plausible answers for why we don't have any of these documents for Christianity, answers that do not entail 'Jesus did not exist.' That is what a competent author would have done here: admit that we have lots of these kinds of records and know they must have existed for Jesus and the earliest Christian apostles and communities, but due to factors and conditions relating to where Christianity began and how it developed, it would be unreasonable to assume any of these records would be preserved to us.[20] But we also have to accept the consequences of such an answer.

18 J.R. Alexander, "Graeco-Roman Papyrus Documents from Egypt," *Athena Review* 2.2 [1999] at www.athenapub.com/egypap1.htm.

19 Ehrman, *Did Jesus Exist?* 44.

20 See my discussion of the corresponding logic of evidence in regard to the trial records under Pontius Pilate in Carrier, *Proving History* 220–24.

Richard Carrier

For example, we cannot claim the Christians were simultaneously very keen to preserve information about Jesus and his family *and* completely disinterested in preserving any information about Jesus and his family. An example is the letter of Claudius Lysias in Acts (in effect an official court record), which if based on a real letter has been doctored to remove all the expected data it would contain (such as the year it was written and Paul's full Roman name). Moreover, if it was based on a real letter, why don't we still have it? It makes no sense to say Christians had no interest in preserving such records. Furthermore, if a Christian preserved this letter long enough for the author of Acts to have read it, *why didn't they preserve any other letters or government documents pertaining to the early church, just like this one?*

I personally believe we can answer these questions (and thus I agree with Ehrman that this argument from silence is too weak to make a case out of it), but not with his silly nonsense. A *good* book on historicity would have given us educationally informative, plausible, and thoughtfully considered answers and information about ancient documents and the total Christian failure to retain or use them. Instead Ehrman gives us hackneyed nonsense and disinformation.

The relevance of this is that if he failed so badly in this case, how many other statements and claims of his are misinforming us about the evidence and the ancient world? And if he didn't do even the most rudimentary fact checking ("Let's see, *do* we have any Roman documents?") and didn't know so basic a background fact as this about the field of ancient history (that we have tons of these documents, as any ancient historian cannot fail to know, due to having worked with them many times even in graduate school), then how can we assume *any* of his work in this book is competently researched or informed?

This was one of the few criticisms of mine that Ehrman made any attempt to reply to. And his reply only dug his hole deeper, illustrating further his probable ignorance, dishonesty, and illogicality.[21] His reply nonsensically contradicts itself, at one point saying he misspoke and

21 Bart Ehrman, "Fuller Reply to Richard Carrier," *Christianity in Antiquity (CIA): The Bart Ehrman Blog* [25 April 2012], at ehrmanblog.org/fuller-reply-to-richard-carrier.

meant only that we shouldn't expect such records to survive (precisely what I said he should have said in the book, but didn't), and at another point saying that he does indeed deny "any indication that there ever were Roman records of anything" in Palestine. But which is it? Did he mean such records existed, but none survived from early Christianity, even though many survived from other people and groups? Or did he mean no such records were ever created in Palestine, even though they were created abundantly and routinely in Egypt? Such self-contradictory attempts at saving face aside, both of his arguments only further reflect his ignorance regarding the materials in question, thus demonstrating that he didn't even check these facts before pronouncing on them, not in his book, nor even (most embarrassingly) in his subsequent response to accusations of not checking the facts — the one place where surely he should finally go and check the facts and show that he had.

Of his two contradictory responses, the first is probably another lie. Read my quotations from his book above again: is there any plausible way he can be read as saying such documents existed but simply didn't survive? Not really. It looks like he really didn't know any existed. He says we don't have any such documents; he even calls out his opponents for failing to present examples of them to prove they existed, smugly noting that "Freke and Gandy, of course, do not cite a single example of anyone else's death warrant from the first century," an accusation that only makes sense if Ehrman thought there were no extant death warrants (by which I assume he means official records of death sentences).[22] This demonstrates

22 Ehrman, *Did Jesus Exist?*, 29. If instead Ehrman means arrest warrants, we have a 3rd century arrest warrant for a Christian, for example (*P. Oxy.* 3035, described at en.wikipedia.org/wiki/Papyrus_Oxyrhynchus_3035), demonstrating these kinds of records existed — in fact such arrest warrants for all crimes were commonplace: see Christopher Fuhrmann, *Policing the Roman Empire: Soldiers, Administration, and Public Order* [Oxford University Press 2012: 79–81]. If instead Ehrman means merely death certificates, we know those existed, too, even indeed coroner's pronouncements of cause of death (*e.g. P. Oxy.* 3926; *cf.* Darrel Amundsen, "The Forensic Role of Physicians in Ptolemaic and Roman Egypt," *Bulletin of the History of Medicine* 52.3 [Fall 1978: 336–53] and "The Forensic Role of Physicians in Roman Law," *Bulletin of the History of Medicine* 53.1 [Spring 1979: 39–56]). For more mundane death certificates (necessary for purposes of tax and contract law), see discussion in Rafael

that he really believed none existed — when in fact they do. We have numerous documents declaring sentences at trial.[23] In fact, such records were extensively kept, in collections of court decisions used to establish legal precedents, just as we do today.[24] When I called Ehrman out on this, he tried to save face by again claiming to have misspoken. But what argument did he give for why such records didn't survive for early Christianity, while many survived from other people and groups? None. His only argument is that such records didn't exist at all, so we should not expect to have them now. It seems clear that he thought that was true, and was thereby a sufficient rebuttal. Otherwise he makes no mention of any reason why Christians would not have preserved any of the records we know there would have been.

So his first response is probably dishonest, or at least betrays his ineptitude as a writer, saying exactly the opposite of what he meant (suspiciously, again), and thereby badly misinforming the public on the relevant facts of antiquity and completely botching the opportunity to make a valid argument against Freke and Gandy by explaining why, though such records certainly existed, none were preserved by the Christians themselves. And yet even in his dubious revision of what he meant, Ehrman still gets the facts wrong. He now concedes that (at least in Egypt) such records existed and were kept (something he definitely did not tell his readers in the book), but "most of these are not in fact records of Roman officials, but made by indigenous Egyptian writers/scribes." This is twice fallacious (even setting aside his strange assumption that "indigenous Egyptians" could not

---

Taubenschlag, *The Law of Greco-Roman Egypt in the Light of the Papyri, 332 B.C.–640 A.D.* Volume 1[New York: Herald Square Press, 1944: 64–65].

23 For example, see the brief selection discussed in Barry Baldwin, "Crime and Criminals in Graeco-Roman Egypt," *Aegyptus* 43.3/4 [December 1963: 256–63].

24 W. W. Buckland, *A Text-Book of Roman Law from Augustus to Justinian* [Cambridge University Press 1921: 19]. The fact is evident throughout surviving treatises on Roman law, from the *Institutes* of Gaius to the *Digest* of Justinian, which frequently draw on these legal records: see, for example, Bruce Frier, *A Casebook on the Roman Law of Delict* [Scholars Press 1989] and J.J. Aubert, "A Double Standard in Roman Criminal Law? The Death Penalty and Social Structure in Late Republican and Early Imperial Rome," in *Speculum Iuris: Roman Law as a Reflection of Social and Economic Life in Antiquity*, edited by Jean-Jacques Aubert and Boudewijn Sirks [University of Michigan Press 2002: 94–133].

be Roman officials or in their employ): first, *most* is not *all* (so his point is moot — formally, we call this a *non sequitur*); secondly, what he doesn't tell you is that even the private records are frequently the personal copies of government records (for example, the tax receipts I have translated were a private citizen's copy of the very same receipts that entered the government archives).[25] Thus, the fact that we have only the copies, albeit made under official circumstances, often at the same time as the originals, is again moot to the point as to whether the government kept such records. Indeed, that private citizens sought and kept copies of state records proves my point that Christians could have done this too — had they wanted to — which requires explaining why they didn't. And, of course, besides that, we have a lot of the government's own records, too, both directly (in recovered papyri) and indirectly (in their quotation or use in later legal texts and histories) — which Christian historians could later have consulted and quoted if such documents survived long enough in archives they had access to.

Ehrman then says he meant that Romans kept no such records in Palestine (thus trying to have it both ways). He doesn't actually provide any evidence to back this claim, of course, and it's obviously absurd, the kind of implausible armchair assertion we should sooner expect from a Christian apologist. Obviously Romans kept the same records in every province that they kept in any. And we know for a fact that they did so in Palestine, because we have several caches of them.[26] So he again didn't check the facts, but made a completely false armchair assertion, as if he knew what the facts were. And when I called him out on *this*, he made no further reply. If this is how Bart Ehrman conducts his research when defending historicity, we have no reason to trust that research. It is evidently built on armchair assumptions and assertions, not on much of an effort to ascertain what the facts really are. That is not the way to defend historicity.

25 See Richard Carrier, "An Ancient Roman Tax Receipt (*P. Columbia* 408)" (1999) at http://richardcarrier.info/papyrus.

26 See the examples published in *P. Euphrates*, *P. Hever* and *P. Yadin*. On which see Hannah Cotton, Walter Cockle and Fergus Millar, "The Papyrology of the Roman Near East: A Survey," *Journal of Roman Studies* 95 [1995: 214–35].

Richard Carrier

There might not have been a record of Jesus' birth at the time of his birth (that would depend on where he was really born and whether, instead, any state or local Jewish administration kept such records; Josephus implies having records of his own ancestry), but if Jesus or his family ever paid Roman taxes, there would be records of that, and if his family was ever the subject of any Roman census at any time while Jesus was alive, there would be a record of that, and along with it a record of his birth, age, and family relations (Tertullian claimed such records existed, although he is unlikely to have really checked). And certainly, there would have been a record of Jesus' trial, of Pilate's ruling, of the execution, and any recorded witness affidavits. There would also be ancillary records, *e.g.*, other trial records or official correspondence (akin to the letter of Claudius Lysias) discussing Christians and their tussles with the Jews or attempts to get them prosecuted in Roman courts, which would certainly have to mention the historical Jesus and information about him. And besides official records, there were also private. Congregations and apostles, from the very beginning, would have accumulated dossiers of correspondence and contracts.

All we can say is what I myself said in my original critique: we have no reason to expect such records to have been preserved by Christian churches or early Christian scholars — although that requires admitting that no early Christians ever had any interest in preserving or using them. This is not a conclusion welcome to defenders of historicity, but it is a conclusion they must accept nonetheless.

5. Not Knowing or Checking Essential Facts: The Case of Resurrection

Ehrman falsely claims that Osiris "return[ing] to life on earth by being raised from the dead" is a modern fabrication because "no ancient source says any such thing about Osiris (or about the other gods)." And note the hyperbole: no *such* thing about *any* gods.[27] This is multiply false. Many dying-and-rising gods predate Christianity, and we often know this from *pre*-Christian sources. Many effected

27 Ehrman, *Did Jesus Exist?* 26.

their deaths and resurrections in different ways (the differences being moot to the point that they nevertheless died and rose back to life), and some even "returned to life on earth by being raised from the dead" in essentially the same way Jesus did (who, after all, did not stay on earth any more than they did). Whether the one kind of resurrection or the other, these gods include Osiris, Dionysus, Romulus, Hercules, Asclepius, Zalmoxis, Inanna, and Adonis-Tammuz.

In responding to this, Ehrman acted like a Christian apologist, inventing hyper-specific definitions of 'dying' and 'rising' in order to claim that since no god meets his *hyper-specific definition* of those terms, therefore there were no dying-and-rising gods at all. I then demonstrated that there were indeed dying and rising gods even by *his own hyper-specific definition*, and the gods who don't meet his hyper-specific definition are still *sufficiently similar* to the original beliefs of how Jesus died and rose to sustain Mythicist arguments for cultural diffusion and syncretism. To which Ehrman has made no reply. Yet this is crucial to understanding the Mythicist argument and representing it correctly, and thus actually responding to it, rather than a straw man of it.

For his attempted denial of the facts Ehrman relies solely on a single scholar, Jonathan Z. Smith, failing to check whether anything Smith says is even correct. If Ehrman had acted like a proper scholar and actually gone to the sources, and read more widely in the scholarship (instead of incompetently reading just one polemical author), he would have discovered that almost everything Smith claims about this is false. In fact, Plutarch attests that Osiris was believed to have died and been returned to life — literally: he uses the words *anabiôsis* and *paliggenesis*, 'back to life' and 'recreated,' which are very specific, and the very same words used by Christians for the resurrection. Plutarch also attests that in his public myths Osiris did indeed return to earth in his resurrected body.[28]

28 Plutarch, *On Isis and Osiris* 35.364f, 65.377b, and 19.358b (*see also* Plutarch, *On the E at Delphi* 9.389a). See my discussion of the vocabulary in Richard Carrier, "The Spiritual Body of Christ and the Legend of the Empty Tomb," *The Empty Tomb: Jesus Beyond the Grave*, edited by Robert Price and Jeffery Lowder [Prometheus 2005: 105–232; *see also* 154–55].

Although Plutarch also says that in the *private* teachings Osiris' death and resurrection took place in outer space (below the orbit of the moon), after which he ascended back to the heights of heaven in his new body (not "the underworld," as Ehrman incorrectly claims),[29] that is irrelevant to the Mythicist's case (or rather, it supports it, by analogy, since this is exactly what Mythicists like Earl Doherty say was the case for Jesus: public accounts putting the events on earth, but private 'truer' accounts placing it all in various levels of outer space).[30] In fact the earliest Christians *also* believed Jesus was resurrected into outer space: he, like Osiris, ascended into the heavens in his resurrection body, appearing to those below in visions, not in person; the same was true of many other dying-and-rising gods, like Hercules.[31] The notion of a risen Jesus walking around on earth was a late invention (first found in the Gospels of Matthew and Luke).

That these kinds of beliefs about Osiris' death and resurrection long predate Plutarch is established in mainstream scholarship on the cult.[32] But we hardly need point that out, because there is already zero chance that the entirety of Isis-Osiris cult had completely transformed its doctrines in imitation of Christianity already by 100 CE. (I shouldn't have to explain why that is preposterous.) Ehrman's claim that Plutarch is making all this up because he is a Platonist is likewise nonsense. Plutarch's essay is written to a ranking priestess of the cult, and Plutarch repeatedly says she already knows the things he is conveying and will not find any of it surprising. So this was not idiosyncratic, but common doctrine. Moreover, to suggest that Plutarch "invented" the death and resurrection of Osiris from Platonism is to assume a most remarkable coincidence. The Christians start up with

---

29 Ehrman, *Did Jesus Exist?* 228.

30 See my critical review of Earl Doherty's book *The Jesus Puzzle* in Richard Carrier, "Did Jesus Exist? Earl Doherty and the Argument to Ahistoricity," *The Secular Web* [2002] at www.infidels.org/library/modern/richard_carrier/jesuspuzzle.html.

31 See my thorough survey of the evidence in Carrier, "Spiritual Body."

32 S.G.F. Brandon, *The Saviour God: Comparative Studies in the Concept of Salvation* [Greenwood 1963: 17–36; and John Griffiths, *The Origins of Osiris and His Cult*, 2nd ed. [Brill 1980].

the idea of a resurrected Son of God and then, out of the blue, a Platonist invents another one, completely independently?

Plenty of pre-Christian evidence already establishes that belief in the resurrection of Osiris long preceded that of Jesus anyway. So Ehrman's armchair attempt to explain away the facts only betrays his failure to check what the facts were. For example, consider these descriptions of the resurrection of Osiris in the Pyramid Texts:

> "I have come to thee...that I may revivify thee, that I may assemble for thee thy bones, that I may collect for thee thy flesh, that I may assemble for thee thy dismembered limbs, for I am as Horus his avenger, I have smitten for thee him who smote thee...raise thyself up, king, Osiris; thou livest!" (1684a–1685a and 1700 = Utterance 606; *cf.* also 670)
>
> "Raise thyself up; shake off thy dust; remove the dirt which is on thy face; loose thy bandages" (1363a–b = Utterance 553)
>
> "Osiris, collect thy bones; arrange thy limbs; shake off thy dust; untie thy bandages; the tomb is open for thee; the double doors of the coffin are undone for thee; the double doors of heaven are open for thee...thy soul is in thy body...raise thyself up!" (207b–209a and 2010b–2011a = Utterance 676).[33]

So, regarding the death and resurrection of Osiris, clearly Ehrman states what is in fact false.

This is most alarming because much of his case against Mythicism rests on this false assertion. But worse, Ehrman foolishly generalizes to *all possible gods*, repeatedly insisting there are *no* dying-and-rising gods in the Hellenistic period. This proves he did no research on this subject whatever. I shouldn't have to adduce passages such as that from Plutarch, "[about] Dionysus, Zagreus, Nyctelius, and Isodaetes, they narrate deaths and vanishings, followed by returns to life and resurrections."[34] That looks pretty cut and dried to me. But we needn't rely on Plutarch, because for Romulus and Zalmoxis

33 Translations from Samuel Mercer, *The Pyramid Texts* [Longmans, Green & Co. 1952].

34 Plutarch, *On the E at Delphi* 9.388f–389a.

we *undeniably* have pre-Christian evidence that they actually die (on earth) and are actually raised from the dead (on earth) and physically visit their disciples (on earth). Likewise for Inanna: a clear-cut, death-and-resurrection tale for her exists on clay tablets inscribed a thousand years before Christianity (in which she dies and rises in hell, but departs from and returns to the world above all the same).[35]

I was especially alarmed to see that Ehrman never once mentions Romulus or Zalmoxis or Inanna — thus demonstrating he did no research on this. He must not have even read my book *Not the Impossible Faith*, even though he claims to have done so and even cites it. But he can't have actually read it, because I document the evidence, sources, and scholarship on these gods there, yet his book shows no awareness of these gods or any of the evidence I present for their resurrection cults. He ignores as well the evidence I present for many other dying-and-rising gods and heroes. (Do not mistake me for supporting false claims in this category, however; Mithras was almost certainly *not* a dying-and-rising god, and Attis only barely was.)

If Ehrman had done anything like a responsible literature review on this, he would have found the latest peer reviewed scholarship establishing, for example, that vanishing bodies as elements of resurrection tales were a ubiquitous component of pagan mythmaking, for example.[36] And thus a dying-and-rising hero theme was incredibly ubiquitous, even if highly flexible in the different ways this theme could be constructed. The only literature Ehrman does address is Tryggve Mettinger's work on *pre*-Hellenistic dying-and-rising gods.[37] Ehrman dismisses it as questionable

35 *See* Carrier, *Not the Impossible Faith* 17–20 and 85–128.

36 Richard C. Miller, "Mark's Empty Tomb and Other Translation Fables in Classical Antiquity," *Journal of Biblical Literature* 129.4 [2010: 759–76].

37 Tryggve Mettinger in *The Riddle of Resurrection: "Dying and Rising Gods" in the Ancient Near East* [Almqvist & Wiksell International 2001] and "The Dying and Rising God: The Peregrinations of a Mytheme," in W.H. van Soldt, ed., *Ethnicity in Ancient Mesopotamia* [Nederlands Instituut voor het Nabije Oosten 2005: 198–210]. See also M.S. Smith, *The Ugaritic Baal Cycle*, vol. 1 [Brill 1994] and M.S. Smith and W. Pitard, *The Ugaritic Baal Cycle*, vol. 2 [Brill 2009]; and Tikva Frymer-Kensky, "The Tribulations of Marduk: The So-Called 'Marduk Ordeal Text'," *Journal of the American Oriental*

(without giving any good reason for that assessment), but ultimately admits Mettinger might have a case for there being such gods. So Ehrman argues instead, implausibly, that they can't have influenced Christianity (even though all the neighbors of Judea worshipped such gods for centuries right up to the dawn of Christianity — they would have been well-known in Tyre, for example — and Ezekiel 8:14 confirms their presence even in Jerusalem itself). But Ehrman doesn't address any of the evidence for these same (much less other) gods in the *Hellenistic* period, the period actually relevant to Christianity, which proves he did no checking, and isn't even aware of such evidence, nor even thought it was important for him to be. Yet such evidence is abundant.

Ehrman ignores all this evidence and cherry picks his own evidence instead, offering examples of Egyptian beliefs that the corpse of Osiris still lay in its tomb, for example. But those Egyptians (not representing all Egyptians) will have believed Osiris rose from the dead by assuming a new body, and ascending to heaven therein, leaving the old one in its grave. And the first Christians probably believed the very same thing of Jesus, the empty tomb story evolving more than a generation later. There continued to be Christians advocating that same view (of a 'new body' resurrection) for centuries.[38] The particular *kind* of resurrection effected is precisely the kind of distinction that isn't relevant. Osiris is a dead god who still "lives again," escaping the slumber of death, to live forever, as the king of heaven, visiting and revealing himself to the living. Like all the gods that do this, they do it in their divine resurrection bodies, which have replaced their flesh-and blood corpses. This is explicitly stated in the sources for many gods, such as Hercules.[39] Many Jews

---

Society 103, no. 1 [January–March 1983: 131–41], in light of the further analysis and evidence in Mettinger.

38 I discuss the evidence in Carrier, "Spiritual Body," which can be read with its accompanying FAQ at www.richardcarrier.info/SpiritualFAQ.html (which also cites the leading scholars in agreement).

39 For example: Lucian, *Hermotimus* 7; similarly for Romulus: Plutarch, *Romulus* 28.6. See Carrier, "Spiritual Body" 137.

likewise believed the same thing about their own resurrection.[40] And Paul, our earliest Christian writer, appears to say exactly that about earliest Christian belief, declaring that the body that dies is *not* the body that rises (1 Corinthians 15:35–49), that in fact we have entirely new bodies waiting for us in heaven, while our current ones will be left to rot (2 Corinthians 5).

This notion of resurrection for gods and demigods is *not* spirit-survival like the "Witch of Endor," as Ehrman suggests, precisely because these are *gods*, and gods have divine bodies. That's what makes them *gods* (and not just impotent spirits). The Jewish view of resurrection was essentially the same view, only extended to humans, who would all become like gods — a view that actually came from the Zoroastrians, and thus is not uniquely Jewish.[41] It was still called 'resurrection,' and it still involved a literal death, followed (often a few days later) by a literal restoration to life, even if in a newly-minted divine body.

Insofar as even the first Christians — or certainly later ones — believed Jesus rose from the dead in the same body that died, that would be an element of *syncretism* with the Jewish belief in corpse reanimation (held by many but not all Jews), or even an adaptation of other pagan views of gods that experience the same kind of resurrection — most clearly, Zalmoxis and Inanna — and probably Inanna's consort Tammuz, *i.e.*, Adonis. As her consort in the same myth, his celebrated resurrection is not likely to have substantially differed from hers; we just don't have the portion of the text that describes it. (We only have external references to it being part of the same cult's mythology.) Even if the later Christian idea did not come from these pagan 'same-body' resurrection myths, a pagan body-exchange resurrection (returning to earth after their deaths in an immortal glorious resurrection body, as Romulus does, for example) combined with a Jewish resurrection of the flesh *still* gets you the version of dying-and-rising god that we meet with, for example, in the Gospel of John. But that's still just a variant of the same mytheme: a god who dies and is then celebrated as having risen again, in a

40 Documented in Carrier, "Spiritual Body" 109–13, 136–37.

41 See Carrier, *Not the Impossible Faith* 90–99.

more glorious body than he once had. That's why Osiris is said to have returned to life and been 'restored to life' and 'recreated' — the exact terms for resurrection, as even Ehrman admits Plutarch freely uses to describe it. So is it likewise for other gods, from Inanna and Zalmoxis to Hercules and Romulus, and many others besides.

Again, Ehrman exposes himself as completely uninformed on all of these facts, almost willfully incompetent (trusting a single biased scholar and not checking any of the evidence or reading any of the other literature to verify what that scholar says), consistently misinforming his readers on the facts, and thus hiding from them almost everything that actually adds strength to the Mythicist thesis. That he does this on a point so central and crucial to his entire argument is alone enough to discredit his entire book. This is not how to argue for historicity. The fact that dying-and-rising god-cults surrounded Palestine, and were in fact very fashionable at the time, simply has to be accounted for.

This does not entail concluding that Jesus was a fictional person. Rather, even if he was historical, the attribution to him of the properties of pagan deities had to come from somewhere, and cultural diffusion is the obvious source. Ehrman appears to be denying even that, which puts him at the far extreme of even mainstream scholarship. He is implausibly implying that it's just a coincidence that in the midst of a fashion for dying-and-rising salvation gods with sin-cleansing baptisms, the Jews just happened to come up with the same exact idea without any influence at all from this going on all around them. Such a coincidence is simply far too improbable to credit. There were no gods like this in ancient China, but they were all over the Mediterranean. So, if the Jews suddenly decided they had one, too, it is almost certainly a product of cultural diffusion. Why deny this obvious fact?

6. Not Knowing or Checking Essential Facts: The Case of 'Baptism'

Ehrman says "we don't have a single description in any source of any kind of baptism in the mystery religions."[42] That is outright false, and one of the most appallingly incompetent statements in this book.

42 Ehrman, *Did Jesus Exist?* 28.

Apuleius gives us a first person account of baptism in Isis cult, which he describes as a symbolic death and resurrection for the recipient, exactly as Paul describes Christian baptism in the New Testament (*e.g.*, Romans 6:4), a fact that surely undermines Ehrman's entire argument and makes the Mythicist case look significantly stronger.[43] So this is certainly important for him to know (and yet he would know it, if he actually had read my work — which as we've seen, he apparently did not), and it is crucial for the reader to know.

Evidence of baptism in Osiris cult (and that it granted eternal life) exists in pre-Christian papyri, and several other sources.[44] We also know that something like baptism into eternal life was a feature of the cult of Bacchus-Dionysus, and we know this not only because Plato mentions it (discussing Orphic libations "for the remission of sins" that secure one a better place in the afterlife), but also from actual pre-Christian inscriptions (that's right, words actually carved in stone).[45] Both sources (Plato and the inscriptions) also confirm the Bacchic belief that one could be baptized on behalf of someone *who had already died* and thus gain them a better position in the afterlife. It cannot be a coincidence that exactly the same thing, baptism for the dead, is attested as a Christian rite by Paul (1 Corinthians 15:29). We have hints of baptismal rituals in other cults. Tertullian, for example, mentions several pagan rituals of baptism for the remission of sins, clearly understanding it to be a common practice everywhere known.[46] Certainly, in many of these cases the baptism was part of a larger ritual (perhaps involving prayer or incense), but Christian baptisms were not free of their own ritual accoutrements, so those hardly matter to the point.

This also undermines Ehrman's claim that there is no evidence that the death of Osiris (or any other god) "brought atonement for

---

43 See Carrier, *Not the Impossible Faith* 376.

44 See Brook Pearson, *Corresponding Sense: Paul, Dialectic, and Gadamer* [Brill 2001: 206–18, 312–29].

45 Plato, *Republic* 364e–365a; inscriptions are discussed in Hans Conzelmann, *1 Corinthians* [Fortress 1975: 275–76, n. 116].

46 Tertullian, *On Baptism* 5; and *On the Prescription against Heretics* 40.

sin."[47] We know Egyptian afterlife-belief made the physical weight of sin a factor in deciding one's placement in the afterlife (one's soul was weighed against a feather by Ma'at, and too many sins made it weigh more, thus signaling your doom), and that baptism into the death and resurrection of Osiris washes away those sins (as we just saw) and thus lightens the soul to obtain the best place in heaven. It is hard to imagine how this does not entail that the death and resurrection of Osiris somehow procured salvation through remission of sins. Clearly, as we saw even from as early as Plato, a similar belief had developed in Bacchic and other cults.

We could perhaps get nit-picky as to what might be the exact theology of the process, but whatever the differences, the similarity remains: the death and resurrection of Osiris was clearly believed to make it possible for those ritually sharing in that death and resurrection through baptism to have their sins remitted. That belief predates Christianity, and Ehrman is simply wrong to say otherwise. The evidence for this is clear, indisputable, and mainstream — which means his book is useless if you want to know the facts of this matter. Or *any* matter, apparently. This is not how to argue for historicity. It ought to be rule number one: *get the facts right*.

7. Hiding Relevant Facts

Several times Ehrman conceals facts from his readers that are damaging to his case, or that he should certainly address to explain why we are supposed to dismiss them. For example, he falsely claims that "the life, death, and resurrection of Jesus were recent events" (of the 30s CE) is "the view of all of our sources that deal with the matter at all."[48] In fact, some of the sources that "deal with the matter" (such as Epiphanius and the Talmud) date the life, death, and resurrection of Jesus to the 70s BCE, and this would be known to anyone who read up on the basic literature on the historicity debate (as any competent scholar writing a book on the subject would have done).[49] We know there were

47 Ehrman, *Did Jesus Exist?* 26.

48 Ehrman, *Did Jesus Exist?* 247–51.

49 In fact one of the "sources" Ehrman must mean is the Talmud, as he includes it in

actual Christians teaching that Jesus had died in the 70s BCE, and that the Jews who composed the Babylonian Talmud knew of no other version of Christianity than that. This is hard to explain if Jesus was widely known to have lived and died under Pontius Pilate in the 30s CE. But instead of mentioning this or discussing these sources or why we should ignore them, Ehrman gives the impression that Mythicist G.A. Wells was just making up the whole idea.

When I called him on this, Ehrman responded that he didn't mean "all" when he said "all," and that he had his reasons for keeping quiet — reasons he failed to mention in the book. On both points this amounts to confessing that he completely misled and misinformed the readers of his book, by omitting any mention of the fact that Wells' hypothesis was based on actual sources, sources which require a response, an explanation of why Ehrman is rejecting them or Well's inferences from them. I believe it is dishonest to spend several pages rebutting a scholar's arguments (as Ehrman does), and never once mention that that scholar's conclusions are based on sources, or addressing those sources.

Only *after* he was caught doing this did Ehrman offer up a rationale, once again deploying an argument that should have been in the book to begin with: that he discounts those sources on this point because they are late. Although that is in itself a fallacy, since late sources can preserve early tradition and, therefore, you still have to make an argument for why this is not occurring in this case. Indeed, that this was the belief of what appears to be (a) a pre-Pauline sect of Christianity (the Nazoreans still being Torah observant and having a name similar to what Christians were sometimes called in Paul's time, if we are to trust Acts 24:5) and (b) the only sect of Christianity apparently known to the Babylonian Jews, argues against this being some recent novelty. Even the *late* existence of such a tradition is hard to explain on Ehrman's theory of Jesus' historicity (how could such a tradition have arisen?), and thus requires explanation; it can't

his own discussion of "sources" (*ibid.* 66–68), yet the Talmud only knows of a Jesus who lived and died in the 70s BCE. The other source is Epiphanius, *Panarion* 29.3, where a Christian sect is discussed who taught the same. Notably that sect was a Torah-observant sect, still using the movement's original name, located in the Middle East.

just be ignored. Ehrman would prefer to ignore it. Possibly he would even prefer you not to know of it.

Another example of concealing facts is Ehrman's claim that no "trained classicists or scholars of ancient Rome" have ever questioned the authenticity of the reference to Christ in Tacitus.[50] His intended point is clearly that only Mythicists have proposed this, and that it is therefore solely motivated by their need to defend the Jesus myth theory. But in fact several experts throughout history, who were not Mythicists, *have* challenged the reference's authenticity.[51] In fact, one of them (Rougé, the most recent) has made a very impressive argument to that effect, which to my knowledge has never been rebutted.[52] At the very least, it requires rebutting before dismissing. And at the very, very least, one ought to mention that it exists.

It is clear that Ehrman didn't even bother to check. He just assumed that because he'd never heard of any scholars publishing papers to that effect, that there were none. The thought of doing research to find out first does not seem to have occurred to him (if it had, he would have found what I did, and would then be morally obligated to mention it). Once again, if he didn't bother to check this, *what else didn't he bother to check*? It's a serious question. Because given the many examples of this, it really looks like this book was

50 Ehrman, *Did Jesus Exist?* 55.

51 The most important of which are C. Saumagne, "Tacite et saint Paul," *Revue Historique* 232 [1964: 67–110] and Jean Rougé, "L'incendie de Rome en 64 et l'incendie de Nicomédia en 303," *Mélanges d'histoire ancienne offerts à William Seston* [E. de Boccard 1974: 433–41]. For these and other examples see Herbert Benario, "Recent Work on Tacitus (1964–1968)," *The Classical World* 63.8 [April 1970: 253–66; *see* 264–65] and "Recent Work on Tacitus (1974–1983)," *The Classical World* 80.2 [Nov.–Dec. 1986: 73–147; *see* 139]. The matter is also discussed in the leading reference work on the evidence for Jesus: Robert Van Voorst, *Jesus Outside the New Testament* [William B. Eerdmans 2000: 43–44].

52 In fact, despite my long-standing certainty that this reference cannot have been interpolated, upon further investigation I have found Rougé's argument rather convincing, and will be publishing a paper updating his case: Richard Carrier, "The Prospect of a Christian Interpolation in Tacitus, *Annals* 15.44" (in progress). Note, however, that the Jesus myth theory in no way requires this passage to be inauthentic. It has no historical value even if genuine, because it would simply be repeating what early second century Christians were by then saying.

a lazy armchair spinoff, and not a serious work of scholarship. And this also matters here specifically, because part of Ehrman's argument is that Mythicists are defying all established scholarship in suggesting this passage in Tacitus has undergone interpolation, so the fact that there is previous established scholarship (even as-yet unrebutted scholarship) supporting them on this undermines Ehrman's argument and makes him look irresponsible.

Ehrman also argued that he "meant" that no "current" Tacitus scholar doubts the passage, even though that qualification is not in the book, and he still gives no reason to believe it's true (the latest articles against its authenticity have no known rebuttal, so we really don't know if or how many experts share their opinion). But more importantly, it's not a valid excuse, since by concealing the fact that several Tacitus experts have doubted its authenticity, the entire argument he makes is undermined. If qualified experts with no agenda to defend any Jesus myth theory *independently* found reasons to be suspicious of this passage, that is very important evidence in favor of what Mythicists are saying about it. To suppress that evidence is unconscionable; to not know of it is incompetent. This is not how to argue for historicity.

8. Contradicting Yourself: A Sign of Apologetics, Not Scholarship

Ehrman often contradicts himself, failing to follow his own stated principles whenever it suits him. For example, Ehrman attacks Robert Price for using the 'criterion of dissimilarity' negatively, insisting that's a "misuse" of the criterion, and then *defends* using it negatively himself, a blatant self-contradiction.[53] It's also fallacious reasoning. Price was using it 'negatively' (in Ehrman's sense) to show that the case for historicity from the Gospels is weak because for every story about Jesus, the Christians had a motive to invent it. This *is* a logically valid way to argue. Price is rebutting the contrary claim (that some of these stories *must* be true because they didn't have a motive to invent them) and thereby removing a premise that ups the

53 Compare Ehrman, *Did Jesus Exist?* pages 187 and 293.

probability of historicity, which necessarily *lowers* the probability of historicity (by exactly as much as that premise being true would have raised it). Ehrman outright denies this, which betrays a fundamental ignorance of how logic works.[54] Perhaps what Ehrman meant to say was that this argument cannot *alone* prove Jesus didn't exist, but Price never says it does.

Another example of Ehrman's self-contradictory assertions is one of the two main pillars of his case for historicity: his claim that "there were no Jews prior to Christianity who thought Isaiah 53 (or any other 'suffering' passages) referred to the future messiah," therefore only a real crucifixion of a historical Jesus could have inspired it.[55] He does nothing to defend this statement, even though he was well aware of the fact that I had adduced abundant evidence against it, showing that in fact there probably *were* some early Jews who expected a dying messiah to immediately presage the end of the world.[56] He has also carefully worded his statement to conceal the fact (which he must know is indisputable) that *later* Jews did indeed see Isaiah 53 as referring to a future dying messiah (the Talmud explicitly says so).[57] But all that doesn't even matter. Because he couldn't possibly claim to know what *all* Jews thought anyway, among all the *dozens* of divergent sects we know existed at the time Christianity began.[58] And ironically, *Ehrman later makes that very point himself*, insisting that blanket assertions about what "no one thought" cannot be allowed, because we don't know what everyone thought.[59] Thus he contradicts himself by using a rule later in his

---

54 Ehrman, *Did Jesus Exist?* 187.

55 Ehrman, *Did Jesus Exist?* 166.

56 I have surveyed the evidence and arguments in Richard Carrier, "The Dying Messiah Redux," *Richard Carrier Blogs* [14 June 2012] at www.freethoughtblogs.com/carrier/archives/1440. Its content will soon be updated and published as "Did Any Pre-Christian Jews Expect a Dying-and-Rising Messiah?"

57 See *b.Sanhedrin* 98b and *b.Sukkah* 52a–b.

58 On the great number of Jewish sects and our ignorance of their specific beliefs see Carrier, "Spiritual Body" 107–13; on the whole problem of our pervasive ignorance on questions like this: Carrier, *Proving History* 129–34.

59 Ehrman, *Did Jesus Exist?* 193.

own defense that, if applied to himself, would destroy one of the central pillars of his own thesis.[60] That an author would so decisively undermine his own central argument, and not even notice it, is embarrassing.

Ehrman's failure of logic in this case is even worse, since it doesn't merely consist of a factually questionable assertion, a textbook fallacy of arguing from ignorance (and one that does not entail the conclusion he wants even if the assertion were true — since imagining a murdered messiah was demonstrably possible for later Jews, he cannot mean to argue Christians wouldn't have invented it, when later Talmudic Jews clearly had no problem inventing one for themselves), but he leverages it into yet *another* self-contradiction. Ehrman says "the messiah was to be a figure of grandeur and power who overthrew the enemy." Certainly, that was the most common view; but again, it is a fallacy of hasty generalization to assume that that was the *only* view, especially since we don't know what most of the dozens of Jewish sects there were believed about this. But then from this fallacious hasty generalization, Ehrman concludes "anyone who wanted to make up a messiah would make him like that."

Now, I have to ask, can you see why that conclusion *can't* be correct? Why, in fact, what he is suggesting, what he predicts would happen if Mythicism were true, is *impossible*? Answer: the only kind of messiah figure you could invent would be one who *wasn't* like that. Otherwise, everyone would notice that no divine being had militarily liberated Israel and resurrected all the world's dead. This means the probability of that evidence ("anyone who wanted to make up a messiah would make him like that") on the hypothesis "someone made up a messiah" is exactly zero. This means that, to the contrary, if "someone made up a messiah," we can be absolutely certain he would look essentially more like Jesus Christ: a being no one noticed, who didn't do anything publicly observable, yet still

60 Ehrman, *Did Jesus Exist?* 142–44, 156–70. The second of Ehrman's two pillars is the evidence for Jesus having a brother [144–56], which is really the only evidence for historicity there is. It deserves reasonable debate. But alas, Ehrman doesn't provide one, his treatment succumbing to the kinds of errors I document here in other cases. I will treat the subject better in my forthcoming book.

accomplished the messianic task — although only spiritually. That would be precisely the one way against which no one could produce any evidence. In other words, a messiah whose accomplishments one could only 'feel in one's heart'; or see by revelation, as the Corinthian creed declares in 1 Cor. 15:3–8; or discover in scripture, as that same creed again declares — as well as Romans 16:25–26.

These kinds of logical blunders are typical of Christian apologetics, which leap to any argument they can think of in the moment, without stopping to think if they are defensible or even make sense. The result is often a system of self-contradictory assertions, just like Ehrman has produced in his ill-conceived attempt to defend historicity. And yet he is not a Christian apologist. He is just someone who, on this issue, has decided to behave like one. That is definitely not how to defend historicity.

9. Using an Illogical Methodology

Even with sound methods, to start with dozens of false facts (as Ehrman does, as I just demonstrated with a sample of them) will produce false or logically unsound conclusions. That would be enough to discredit the book. One needn't even question his methods. We know he made so many factual errors, we can't trust any of his factual claims. And in light of that even a perfect method couldn't have rescued this book. But the failure of his methods remains important precisely to the extent that other historians in this field might be fooled into trusting them and continuing to use them — and lay readers might similarly be duped into trusting and using them themselves.

I will not address here the one aspect of his methodology that the scholarly literature has already soundly refuted: the 'method of criteria.' My book *Proving History* already does that, in meticulous detail, summarizing all the scholarship and evidence. Yet Ehrman cluelessly relies on that method, showing no awareness of the fact that all peer reviewed studies of it have denounced it as illogical (once again proving he didn't check). Instead, I will here address Ehrman's particularly strange method of inventing sources and witnesses. Ehrman illogically moves from the mere possibility of hypothetical sources to the conclusion of having proved historicity. How does he do that?

Ehrman argues that because Mark, Matthew, Luke, John, Thomas (yes, *Thomas*) and various other documents all have material the others don't, that therefore we "have" dozens of "earlier" sources, which he sometimes calls by their traditionally assigned letters like M, L, and Q. Ehrman is, of course, inexplicably dismissive of Mark Goodacre's refutation of the Q hypothesis, claiming no one is convinced by it, yet cites not a single rebuttal; I myself find Goodacre's case persuasive, well enough at least to leave us in complete doubt of the matter.[61] And the case is even worse for the other hypothetical sources like M. Whether M or L or Q or anything else, we don't in fact have those sources, we aren't even sure they exist, and even if we were, we have no way of knowing what they really said. To illustrate why that matters, take a look at the second redactions of the Epistles of Ignatius and ask yourself how you would know what the *first* redactions of those epistles said if you didn't in fact have them (then go and look at those first editions and see if you guessed successfully!). Just try that, and you'll see why Ehrman's entire procedure is methodologically ridiculous.

According to Ehrman's method, the material added and changed in the second redaction of the Ignatians had a 'source' and therefore we can rely on it. But that's absurd. The material added to the second redactions of the Ignatian epistles is made up. It did not 'have a source' (except in that it repeats common dogmas of later centuries). The same is true of most if not all the material unique to any given

61 See Mark Goodacre, *The Case against Q: Studies in Markan Priority and Synoptic Problem* [Trinity Press International 2002], with Mark Goodacre, *The Synoptic Problem: A Way Through the Maze* [Sheffield Academic Press 2001], and his supplementary website http://www.markgoodacre.org/Q, as well as Mark Goodacre and Nicholas Perrin, ed., *Questioning Q: A Multidimensional Critique* [InterVarsity Press 2004]. Dennis MacDonald has produced the only viable challenge I know, in *Two Shipwrecked Gospels: The Logoi of Jesus and Papias's Exposition of Logia about the Lord* [Society of Biblical Literature 2012]. MacDonald's argument actually confirms Luke's use and redaction of Matthew, but argues that there was a previous lost gospel, written in Greek, employed by all three Synoptic Gospels, which lacked nativity, betrayal, passion, and empty tomb narratives, and was a rhetorical rewrite of Deuteronomy, casting Jesus in the role of Moses.

Gospel. The miracle at Cana is something John just made up. He did not 'have a source for it.' And even if he did, that source made it up. Obviously. That's why no one had ever heard of it before, or anything even remotely like it before, and why it involved a patently impossible event (the transmutation of matter; or if you have a rationalist bent, a deceptive magician's trick that would make no sense in context and could not have any plausible motive). There is no argument for historicity here. The story is false. And false stories cannot support the existence of real people. And yet Ehrman repeatedly cites false stories, even stories he himself confesses to be false (indeed, even false stories in forged documents!) as evidence for the existence of Jesus, which is the most unbelievably illogical thing I can imagine a historian doing.

Ehrman's examples of finding hypothetical Aramaic sources exemplify this fallacy. He cites Jesus' cry on the cross, for example, which Mark gives in Aramaic and translates, as evidence Mark was using an Aramaic source.[62] Well, yes. His source is the Bible. If he was not translating the Hebrew into Aramaic himself, then he was using a targum.[63] Everyone knows this. Scholar after scholar has pointed out that the entire crucifixion scene is created out of material extracted from the Psalms, this specific cry on the cross in particular, which is a quotation from Psalm 22.[64] Ehrman doesn't mention this (misleading his readers again, by concealing rather crucial information that undermines his point). But notice what happens when we take it into account: Mark dressed up a scene by borrowing and translating a line from the Bible, and Ehrman wants us to believe this is evidence for the historicity of Jesus. Really. Think about that for a moment. Then kick his book across the room to vent your outrage.

Mark does the same thing (puts a sentence in Jesus' mouth in Aramaic, then translates into Greek) in the story of the raising of

62 Ehrman, *Did Jesus Exist?* 88.

63 Which could also explain the biblical citations in the Gospels to verses that we can't find in our Bible, like Matthew's Nazarene prophecy (in Matthew 2:23); because the Aramaic targumim often altered the text, and we don't have most of the targumim that were then in use.

64 See my discussion of the evidence and the scholarship in Carrier, *Proving History* 131–33.

Jairus' daughter, which Ehrman again cites as evidence that Mark was using Aramaic sources.[65] Apart from the fact that we should sooner suspect Mark drew this line from the same targum that he used for embellishing the crucifixion (and we just don't have that targum to confirm), the bigger problem is that *everyone knows the Jairus story is fabricated*. It didn't happen. It's a literary creation, a reworking of an Old Testament story (a targum of which may have contained, for all we know, the very line quoted by Jesus), with obvious puns, and a symbolic and allegorical purpose.[66] It's possible it was invented in Aramaic, but why would that matter? How does a story being fabricated in Aramaic prove the characters in that story existed? *Jairus* (whose name means 'he will awaken' or 'be enlightened'), in a story about resurrection and enlightenment) is most likely a fictional character. So why couldn't Jesus (whose name means 'savior,' lit. 'God saves') be just as fictional? But even the notion that the story originated in Aramaic cannot be proved. If Mark is an Aramaic speaker, then he may simply be translating his own Aramaic thoughts and ideas into Greek. And even if he is using an Aramaic source (and that source is not simply a targum), *then that source made this up*. And made-up stories cannot be used as evidence for the existence of the characters in them. Yet that is what Ehrman does with them.

Consider how his 'method' would work if we applied it to the nativity stories (which Ehrman himself concludes are fiction). According to Ehrman's methodology we have six independent sources for the miraculous birth of Jesus: Matthew, Luke, the Protevangelion of James, Ignatius (*Ephesians* 19), Justin Martyr, and Q (because some elements of the nativities in Luke and Matthew are shared in common). And there are probably others. We know these are all made up. Not a stitch of them is true. But Ehrman's method would compel us to assert that we have undeniable proof of the miraculous birth of Jesus. For example, every one of these 'independent' sources attests that a miraculous star or light from

65 Ehrman, *Did Jesus Exist?*, p. 87.

66 See Randel Helms, *Gospel Fictions* [Prometheus 1988: 65–67].

heaven attended his birth. Six independent sources! What better evidence could you want?

These are all different stories, too, written in different words, so (by Ehrman's logic) they "cannot" have been influenced by each other — except where they are nearly identical, then (by Ehrman's logic) they corroborate each other. This is actually the way Ehrman argues for the historicity of Jesus. That his very same method produces absurd conclusions ("a miraculous star or heavenly light attended the birth of Jesus"), demonstrates its logical invalidity. He is simply not allowing for the obvious fact that all the new material in these stories is made up (even if they used now lost sources, the material is still made up, it was just made up in those sources), and that people can use a source by completely rewriting it in their own words and changing any detail they please (which is why nearly every specialist I have read on the Gospel of John disagrees with Ehrman's claim that John did not use Luke as a source; I think Ehrman is not nearly honest enough with his readers about this).[67]

Even with his assumption (never really defended, yet continually employed) that 'hypothesized underlying Aramaic source' = 'source written in Judea in the 30s CE,' Ehrman descends into the illogical, in this case a textbook fallacy of affirming the consequent. Aramaic was not only spoken in first century Judea; it was spoken in parts of Syria and Egypt and Asia Minor and to an extent across the whole diaspora, and continually for centuries. So 'Aramaic source' = 'Judean source written in the 30s CE' is a ridiculous inference. And yet Ehrman repeatedly relies on it, arguing that some lost sources behind the Gospels were in Aramaic (already a double conjecture: that there were sources; and that they were in Aramaic), so therefore they originated in Judea in the 30s CE. Why? Because Aramaic was spoken in Judea in the 30s CE. Ehrman gives no other reason. That's illogical.

This is what he is doing:

67 See bibliography in Richard Carrier, "Why the Resurrection is Unbelievable," *The Christian Delusion*, edited by John Loftus [Prometheus 2010: 312, n. 11].

If **p**, then **q**.	If a source was written in Judea in the 30s CE, then it was probably written in Aramaic.	If a dog ate your homework, then you have no homework to turn in.
q.	The Gospels used sources written in Aramaic	You have no homework to turn in.
Therefore, **p**.	Therefore, those sources were probably written in Judea in the 30s CE.	Therefore, a dog ate your homework.

You can prove anything with logic like this. And the fact that it's illogical isn't even the only thing wrong with this argument. He can't really establish **q** with any certainty, either (*did* the Gospels use sources written in Aramaic? That's been argued but never conclusively proven). Nor can he establish the required inference that 'Aramaic source' entails 'not made up.'

Someday I might compose an article applying Ehrman's method to prove a flying saucer crashed at Roswell and alien bodies were recovered from it. Because I have a dozen independent sources (which by Ehrman's method I can convert into *several* dozen sources, by inventing a 'Q' for material two sources share but change up, and an 'M' for material unique to one source but not in the others, and so on), which contain stories that show signs of deriving from the original language of the time and place the event happened (1940s American English), all written within fifty years of the event (thus an even better source situation than we have for the historicity of Jesus!). So obviously those stories had 'sources' that date from the time and place of the crash! If I limited myself only to material written by 'believers' (and people quoting them or relying on them alone as a source), then by Ehrman's method I would have to believe a flying saucer crashed at Roswell and alien bodies were recovered from it — which is silly.[68]

68 Philip J. Klass, *The Real Roswell Crashed Saucer Coverup* [Prometheus, 1997] and Karl T. Pflock, *Roswell: Inconvenient Facts and the Will to Believe* [Prometheus, 2001].

How Not to Defend Historicity

Not only is fabrication a better explanation of the proliferation of traditions (for Jesus just as for Roswell), the whole notion of using hypothetical sources as 'evidence' suffers from another fatal problem. The fact that we don't have that source also means we don't know exactly *what it said*, and that makes it even more useless for determining historicity. For example, if someone used a book like Revelation as a source for some sayings of Jesus and put those sayings in the middle of Jesus' Galilean ministry, if we didn't have Revelation we would not know that it actually claimed those sayings came from *a vision of Jesus in heaven* and not an actual historical Jesus. Likewise, if we did not have the *Epistle of Eugnostos*, we would not know that the source used for the sayings of Jesus in the *Sophia of Jesus Christ* actually originally identified those sayings as coming from Eugnostos and not Jesus. A Christian just copied them over, adapted them as needed, and changed who said them. Thus, not having the actual source makes it impossible for us to know whether that source would have supported historicity or not. The mere existence of such sources is therefore useless — even when we can confirm there were such sources, which we cannot honestly do with the kind of certainty Ehrman claims anyway. This should not have to be said, because already many leading mainstream scholars do not believe such certainty is warranted.

Needless to say, having surveyed even just a few problems, it's clear Ehrman has no logically credible method. Is this really the only way to defend historicity? Illogical inferences are bad enough, and must be avoided altogether. Historians need to seriously question and verify whether their arguments are logically valid, and not just assume they are thinking or arguing logically.[69] But omitting mention of the kinds of facts I just enumerated is also irresponsible, because most readers won't know these things. Yet concealing this information from them makes Ehrman's case seem stronger than it really is. His readers should rightly feel betrayed by this.

69 Still the best and most comprehensive warning on this point is David Hackett Fischer, *Historians' Fallacies: Toward a Logic of Historical Thought* [Harper & Row 1970]. Answering his concluding call, I demonstrate the universal logic of all historical methods in Carrier, *Proving History*. But an invaluable resource is Bo Bennett's *Logically Fallacious* [eBookIt 2012], a handy collection, and easy lay explanation, of three hundred fallacies.

Richard Carrier

10. Not Knowing How Things Worked Back Then

It also seems that Ehrman did not do any discernible research into ancient literary or educational methods. For example, Ehrman appears to be blithely unaware of the routinely fabricatory nature of ancient biography, as documented throughout the literature on the subject, which demonstrates that things an author said or wrote (even fictionally) were often converted into stories about them, and these legends then spread and were collected by biographers and became the ancient pagan equivalent of 'Gospels' for such luminaries as Euripides, Homer, or Empedocles.[70]

The significance of this is that it demonstrates Ehrman's *naïveté* when it comes to interpreting ancient literature, source materials, and tradition formation. He is evidently not a competent classicist. And yet understanding how the Gospels likely came together requires being at least a somewhat competent classicist: you have to study and understand how ancient literature operated, especially comparable literature like this. For example, one needs to know that schools of the time specifically taught students to redact and alter stories in their own words — contrary to Ehrman's assumption, for example, that John cannot be a redaction of Luke because it does not follow Luke verbatim.[71]

---

70 See Mary Lefkowitz, *The Lives of the Greek Poets* [Johns Hopkins University 1981] and "Biographical Mythology," in Ueli Dill, ed., *Antike Mythen* [de Gruyter 2009: 516–31]; Janet Fairweather, "Fiction in the Biographies of Ancient Writers," *Ancient Society* 5 [1974: 231–75] and "Traditional Narrative, Inference, and Truth in the Lives of the Greek Poets," *Papers of the Liverpool Latin Seminar* 4 [1983: 315–69]; Barbara Graziosi, *Inventing Homer* [Cambridge University 2002]; and Ava Chitwood, *Death by Philosophy: The Biographical Tradition in the Life and Death of the Archaic Philosophers Empedocles, Heraclitus, and Democritus* [University of Michigan 2004].

71 See the studies of Raffaella Cribiore, *Gymnastics of the Mind: Greek Education in Hellenistic and Roman Egypt* [Princeton University Press 2001]; David Gowler, "The Chreia," *The Historical Jesus in Context*, edited by Amy-Jill Levine, Dale Allison, and John Dominic Crossan [Princeton University Press 2006: 132–48]; and Thomas Brodie, *The Birthing of the New Testament: The Intertextual Development of the New Testament Writings* [Sheffield Phoenix Press, 2004: 2–81]. Also of value is the recent contribution of John Dominic Crossan, *The Power of Parable: How Fiction by Jesus Became Fiction about Jesus* [HarperOne 2012].

How Not to Defend Historicity

If things a person said, *or was merely thought to have said*, were routinely transformed into stories about them (for example, Euripides occasionally made remarks about women in his plays that were transformed into a story about his troubled marriage — a completely fabricated story, that nevertheless became a standard element of his biography), doesn't this change substantially how we view the possible tradition history behind the stories in the 'biographies' of Jesus? Especially considering how many times we have caught these authors fabricating, as even Ehrman admits several times in this book. Biographies were also written of non-existent people, like Romulus, Numa, Coriolanus, Hercules, and Aesop. And we know for a fact Jesus said all kinds of things to the earliest Christians *in revelations, not in person*. And Ehrman concedes this is true. So, we don't have any need of a historical Jesus to get sayings of Jesus out of which to construct a life of Jesus any more than we need a historical Daniel to get the narratives and speeches and sayings in the Book of Daniel; or a historical Moses to get the narratives and speeches and sayings in Deuteronomy or Exodus.

The book of Revelation itself is an example of how easily Christians believed this. That gives us an example of where the idea of an apocalyptic Jesus could come from. In this he even delivers pithy sayings and dictates whole letters from heaven! Yet no one would argue that this is therefore evidence of a historical Jesus. At best, it was made up; at worst, it was hallucinated. Paul in his own letters frequently talks about revelation as a source of Jesus' teachings. Again, Ehrman even agrees that some of the teachings of Jesus were probably "learned" that way. But if some, why not all? After all, Paul never once mentions any other source — other than scripture [Romans 16:15–26]. Even Hebrews 10:5-7 records a saying of Christ that is in fact simply Psalms 40:6–7, so evidently Christians were also 'learning the teachings of Jesus' by reading them as hidden messages in scripture. In Galatians 1, Paul explicitly denies not only that he received *any* human tradition, but that such traditions would even have any worth to him or his fellow Christians. That chapter shows human oral tradition was in fact despised. Visions were the only reliable source his congregations trusted.

When we combine that fact, with what we know of the literary practices of the time, in the way stories and biographies were fabricated from sayings by (or merely attributed to) famous people (which often included nonexistent people), the Mythicist case does not look as improbable as Ehrman portrays it. I find this to be yet another example (among the great many I have already cataloged here, which again are just the tip of the iceberg) of how Ehrman didn't do his job as a scholar, and doesn't inform his readers. In fact, he substantially *misinforms* them and comes to silly conclusions based on exactly the kind of naïve ignorance of the relevant scholarship that he accuses Mythicists of.

The Changing Tide

Failures of facts and logic, careless neglect of research, ignorance of essential background knowledge, and inattention to the arguments and evidence offered by his opponents, all typify *Did Jesus Exist? The Historical Argument for Jesus of Nazareth*. Is this the best case for historicity? If so, historicity no longer appears defensible. Pull at any of its threads and it unravels. Why hasn't anyone noticed this before? Dogmatic and institutional inertia, I suspect. But this has also led to a good dose of subtle intimidation, sending the message that no respectable scholar would argue this, which communicates the conclusion that any scholars who do will lose their respect and prestige, perhaps even face professional persecution, losing jobs or privileges or simply just status in the eyes of their peers. But freedom permits resistance, and that resistance is growing.

Ehrman often asks who with advanced degrees or professorships in any relevant field is convinced Jesus might not have existed. The answer is a growing number. Arthur Droge, professor of early Christianity at UCSD, and Kurt Noll, associate professor of religion at Brandon University, have both gone on record as historicity agnostics, a position already shared by the renowned Thomas Thompson, professor of theology at the University of Copenhagen (now emeritus).[72] Those who are increasingly convinced the

72 A.J. Droge, "Jesus and Ned Lud[d]: What's in a Name?" *CAESAR: A Journal for the*

evidence even weighs against historicity include myself (with a Ph.D. in ancient history from Columbia University) and Robert Price (who has two Ph.D.'s from Drew University, in theology and New Testament studies), and now the renowned Thomas Brodie, Director of the Dominican Biblical Centre (affiliated with the University of Limerick, Ireland) has joined us.[73] I think the wind is starting to blow in the direction of historicity agnosticism at the very least.[74]

I predict Ehrman will eventually find that he chose the losing side of the argument. Once you strip away all the illogical, uninformed arguments for historicity, none of any great merit remain; whereas when you do the same for Mythicism, several arguments of significant merit still do remain. So I believe the balance in the end favors the non-existence of Jesus. Or at the very least, uncertainty as to his existence. But to challenge that conclusion, we need something far better researched, written, and argued than the book that Bart Ehrman has given us.

Critical Study of Religion and Human Values 3.1 [2009: 23–25]; Kurt Noll, "Investigating Earliest Christianity without Jesus," *"Is this not the Carpenter?" The Question of the Historicity of the Figure of Jesus*, edited by Thomas Thompson and Thomas Verenna [Equinox 2012: 233–66]; Thomas Thompson, *The Messiah Myth: The Near Eastern Roots of Jesus and David* [Basic 2005] and "Introduction," *"Is this not the Carpenter?"* 1–26.

73 Thomas Brodie, *Beyond the Quest for the Historical Jesus* [Sheffield-Phoenix 201]; Robert Price, *The Christ-Myth Theory and Its Problems* [American Atheist Press 2011].

74 Just read the apt chiding Philip Davies, professor of biblical studies for the University of Sheffield (now emeritus), gives Ehrman and others who attempt the intimidation of scholars entertaining the Jesus myth theory, in "Did Jesus Exist?" *The Bible and Interpretation* [August 2012] at www.bibleinterp.com/opeds/dav368029.shtml. Davies is convinced of historicity but admits there are reasonable doubts, and says "a recognition that [Jesus'] existence is not *entirely* certain would nudge Jesus scholarship towards academic respectability." This is a significant development against Ehrman.

CHAPTER THREE

The Phallic 'Savior of the World' Hidden in the Vatican

Acharya S/D.M. Murdock

In the first edition of my book *The Christ Conspiracy: The Greatest Story Ever Sold* [1999], I included a chapter entitled "The Bible, Sex and Drugs" [275–295], at the end of which I provided a line drawing of a bronze, rooster-headed bust with a phallus for a beak. Under the image, I added the following caption:

Bronze sculpture hidden in the Vatican treasury of the Cock, symbol of St. Peter.
Inscription reads "Savior of the World."

(Note that I do *not* say, here or elsewhere, that the bronze sculpture itself is a symbol of St. Peter, but only the cock or rooster, as in the story of Matthew 26:34, *etc.*, in which Peter denies Christ three times before the cock crows. In several places elsewhere in my book I provide the citation for the cock/rooster being a symbol of St. Peter. I apologize for the ambiguity, but I was not in error here, despite the constant attempts to make me appear as such.)

After providing the image, I then cited it as coming from "Walker, *WDSSO*," a reference to Barbara G. Walker's *The Woman's Dictionary of Symbols and Sacred Objects*, included in my bibliography at the end of the book. Previous to this image [168], I had discussed this theme of the 'peter' or cock, with the esoteric and 'vulgar' meaning:

> "Peter" is not only "the rock" but also "the cock" or penis, as the word is used as slang to this day. As Walker says, "The cock was also a symbol of Saint Peter, whose name also meant a phallus or male principle (*pater*) and a phallic pillar (*petra*). Therefore, the cock's image was often placed atop church towers."

The 'Savior of the World' image appears in Walker's book on page 397, where she remarks:

> It is no coincidence that "cock" is slang for "penis." The cock was a phallic totem in Roman and medieval sculptures showing cocks somehow transformed into, or supporting, human penises. Roman carvings of disembodied phalli often gave them the legs or wings of cocks. Hidden in the treasury of the Vatican is a bronze image of a cock with the head of a penis on the torso of a man, the pedestal inscribed "The Savior of the World."

(There follows her quote cited in the paragraph above.)

Fabricated image or 'celebrated bronze'?

Over the years since *The Christ Conspiracy* was published, this image has been the periodic focus of interest. Of late, in his book *Did Jesus Exist?,* Bart Ehrman has raised up this image in my book and appears to be accusing me of fabricating it. Quoting me first, he comments:

> " 'Peter' is not only 'the rock' but also 'the cock,' or penis, as the word is use as slang to this day." Here Acharya shows (her own?) hand drawing of a man with a rooster head but with a large erect penis instead of a nose, with this description: "Bronze sculpture hidden in the Vatican treasure [*sic*] of the Cock, symbol of St. Peter" (295). [There is no penis-nosed statue of Peter the cock in the Vatican or anywhere else except in books like this, which love to make things up.]

(The "treasure" typo is Ehrman's, while the '*sic*' is mine. The other comments in brackets and parentheses are Ehrman's.)

In insinuating that I drew the image myself, Ehrman is indicating he did not notice the citation under it in my book, clearly referring to Barbara Walker's work. He is further implying that I simply make things up, and he is asserting with absolute certainty that no such bronze has existed in the Vatican, essentially stating that I fabricated the entire story. Contrary to these unseemly accusations, the facts are that I did not draw the image, the source of which was cited, and that, according to several writers, the image certainly *is* "hidden" in the Vatican, as I stated.

In *The Woman's Dictionary* (397), Walker cites the image as "Knight, pl. 2," which, in her bibliography, refers to: Knight, Richard Payne. *A Discourse on the Worship of Priapus*. New York: University Books, 1974. Consulting an earlier edition of Knight's book [1865], we find a discussion of the object in question:

> ...the celebrated bronze in the Vatican has the male organs of generation placed upon the head of a cock, the emblem of the sun, supported by the neck and shoulders of a man. In this composition they represented the generative power of the Ερως [Eros], the Osiris, Mithras, or Bacchus, whose centre is the sun. By the inscription on the pedestal, the attribute thus personified, is styled *The Saviour of the World* ..., a title always venerable under whatever image it be presented.

Here Knight references the image as "Plate II. Fig. 3." Turning to the back of the book, around page 263, we find the image (right), which is hand-drawn because of its age, printed when photography was still not entirely feasible for publishers.

On page 35, Knight mentions the "celebrated bronze" again:

> ...Oftentimes, however, these mixed figures had a peculiar and proper meaning, like that of the Vatican Bronze...

Another source, Gordon Williams in *A Dictionary of Sexual Language and Imagery* [258], comments about this artifact:

> The relationship of cock and phallus is ancient. A bronze bust in the Vatican Museum, bearing the Greek inscription "Redeemer of the World" (Fuchs, *Geschichte der Erotischen Kunst* [Berlin 1908] fig. 103), is given a cock's head, the nose or beak being an erect penis.

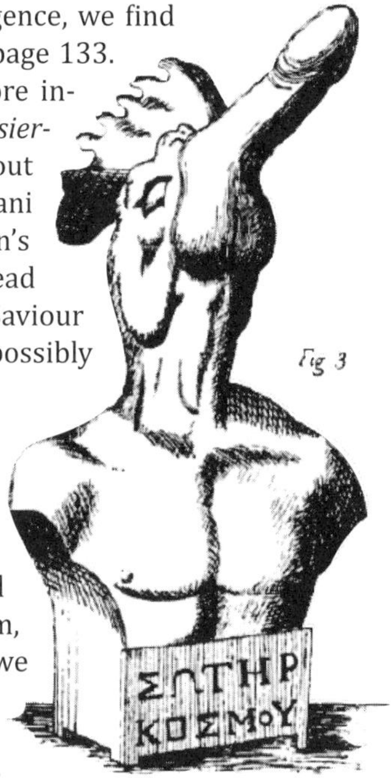

Doing our scholarly due diligence, we find the pertinent figure in Fuchs on page 133. Hot on the trail, we discover more information in Peter Lang's *Privatisierung der Triebe?* [1994:203] about the "small bust known as the Albani bronze, still housed in the Vatican's secret collection..." There, we read further: "Its plinth is inscribed 'Saviour of the World' in Greek, and it is possibly of Gnostic import."

In another mention of the "notorious Albani bronze said to be held in the Vatican Museum," we learn that such Rome phallic representations are called *priapi gallinacei*. [Jones, Malcolm, *The Secret Middle Ages*, 75] As we can see, this bronze image is "celebrated" and "notorious," which means many scholars have written about it, also stating that it is "housed" and "held" in the Vatican Museum.

Romanum Museum, 1692

Continuing the hunt, a discussion of this artifact can be found in a book entitled *Public Characters of 1803–1804* [127], which comments about the "Savior of the World" inscription, written in Greek as ΣΩΤΗΡ ΚΟΣΜΟΥ, a phrase used also to describe Jesus Christ:

> That inscription is found upon an ancient Phallus, of a date of much more remote antiquity than the birth of Christ. The account of this antiquity may be seen at large in "De la Chaussee's Museum Romanum," printed at Rome, in folio, in 1692... The late reverend and learned Dr. Middleton, in that valuable work entitled "Germana quaedam antiquitatis eruditae monumenta, etc." has not scrupled to give the following short account of it...

Tracing the image to De la Chaussee's *Romanum Museum*, we discover a description on page 125 of volume 1:

Diſſertatio de Mutini ſimulac. 125

Priapus in numerum Deorum à Græcis translatus Mutinus dictus 1
eſt, teſte Lactantio lib. 1. ſed in baſe cujusdam imaguncula caput habentis gallinaceum cum pudendo vice roſtri appoſito nobilior inſcriptus eſt titulus, nempe ΣΩΤΗΡ ΚΟΣΜΟΥ. CONSERVATOR MVNDI. Gallum Soli ſacram avem diximus, Sol autem generatricis facultatis præſes habetur: pudendum gallinaceo capiti appoſitum eſt, quòd homo unà cum Sole ad generationem perficiendam concurrat, juxta illud Ariſtotelis lib. 2. Phyſ. cap. 3. *Homo hominem generat, & Sol.* Et ſic uterque genus humanum ex ſe mortale continuâ generatione, vt loquitur idem Philoſophus lib. 2. de gener. & corrupt. cap. 2. perpetuum, & immortale reddit, MVNDIque CONSERVATOREM ſe præbet.

The author follows this discussion with another about the ancient author Macrobius and his work concerning the various gods of the Roman Empire and their solar nature.

The *priapus gallinaceus*

A description of the statue in Latin is also provided by Rev. Dr. Conyers Middleton (*The Miscellaneous Works of the Late Reverend and Learned Conyers Middleton,* 4:51):

> Quod quidem illustrari quodammodo videtur a Symbolica quadam apud Causæum Priapi effigie, cui Galli Gallinacei caput crista ornatum, rostri vero loco, Fascinum ingens datur: cujusque in basi litteris Græcis inscriptum legitur ΣΩΤΗΡ ΚΟΣΜΟΥ. *Servator orbis.* Quae omnia vir doctus ita interpretatur: "Gallum scilicet, avem soli sacram esse; solemque generatricis facultatis præsidem; pudendumque ideo virile Gallinaceo capiti adjunctum denotare, quod a conjunctis solis Priapique viribus, animalium genus omne procreatum et conservatum sit, secundum physicum quoddam Aristotelis axioma, *Homo hominem general et Sol.*"

Here Middleton describes the "priapus effigy" as a rooster with a head crest and the inscription "Savior of the World" or *Servator orbis* in the Latin. A "learned man" interprets the image as a cock, a bird sacred to the sun, a symbol of fertility and generative power. We can see where the term *priapus gallinaceus* comes from, as it refers to the erect member of the god Priapus and the Latin word for 'rooster' or 'cock.' Therefore, we are discussing an entire *genre* of artifacts, evidently dating to before the common era and into it (Gnostic?); other such examples can be cited.

In *The Image of Priapus* [67], Giancarlo Carlobelli writes:

> The "Soter cosmou" portrayed as the central figure appears to be an example of what the classical scholars refer to as "Priapus gallinaceus"; it may be a herm. The illustration had already appeared in De la Chausse...

Continuing our search, we find in Otto Augustus Wall's *Sex and Sex Worship (Phallic Worship): A Scientific Treatise on Sex* [437] a photograph of what appears to be the original bronze statue (or at least its twin). Concerning this artifact, Wall [438] states that "this representation of a bronze figure of Priapus...was found in an ancient Greek temple..."

Phallic 'Savior of the World'

Hidden in the Vatican

In the journal *Studies in Iconography* [7–8:94],[1] published by Northern Kentucky University, after discussing this "Savior of the World" artifact, Lorrayne Y. Baird comments:

> The most remarkable of all the examples of the Priapus gallinaceus grotesque, however, is an antique Roman bronze of the Albani collection. The bronze is a bust with the neck, shoulders and breast of a human male figure, upon which is grafted the crested head of a cock with an erect phallus replacing nose and chin. At the base of the bust appears the inscription ΣΩΤΗΡ ΚΟΣΜΟΥ [Soter Kosmou] ("Savior of the World"). This object was published under papal and royal authority, exhibited for a time in the seventeenth and eighteenth centuries, and is now said to be held inaccessible in the secret collections of the Vatican. During the life of this bronze, officials disagreed upon the probity of the exhibit. One offended cardinal requested that the object be removed from public view; whereupon, Pope Benedict XIV is reported to have answered "that he had no authority over such a personage, being himself but his vicar."

Fig. 257- The god Priapus as a cock, from a Greek temple

Needless to say, what I wrote in *The Christ Conspiracy* concerning this phallic artifact was accurate, per this professional academic's

1 Baird, Lorrayne Y. "Priapus Gallinaceus: The Role of the Cock in Fertility and Eroticism in Classical Antiquity and the Middle Ages." *Studies in Iconography*, 7–8 (1981–82): 81–111.

scholarship. In addition to the fact that Dr. Baird's contentions confirm my research is the astonishing implication of Pope Benedict XIV's words here, which seem to be claiming that he is but a mere vicar to this "personage" of Priapus or, at the least, Yahweh/Jesus as the ithyphallic god/Priapus. The pope here is likewise acknowledging that the sexual connotation of God as Creator is a sacred attribute that he has no right to contravene; hence, these artifacts are sequestered apparently with great reverence.

Baird (95) also relates that, over the centuries, scholars who have studied the Albani bronze have opined that "the Vatican Saviour-as-Phallic-cock was a scandalous satire on early Christians." We are therefore justified in bringing up this artifact and wondering why it would serve as "satire on early Christians," if not for the reasons stated here.

Note also that Baird is not hesitant in stating outright that the University of Naples museum has a *secret collection*, asserted so matter-of-factly that one understands *many* museums possess such secret collections, including the Vatican. The reality is that secret and hidden collections in museums are quite common; as such institutions do not and cannot display everything they possess, obviously. In my travels to some 200 archaeological sites in Greece, I encountered many of these back rooms in museums, since I was traveling with groups of students and scholars who were given access to them. I even worked in one of these storerooms while an archaeology student at Corinth, Greece. Anyone who does not know about these rooms in museums not available to the public has apparently not been to museums in the capacity of a scholar.

The bottom line is that I obviously did not fabricate the image of this artifact, which has been known in scholarly circles for over 300 years. Nor was my contention erroneous that the figure is secreted in the Vatican, according to several authors. Nevertheless, Ehrman continues his imputation by concluding about my book:

> In short, if there is any conspiracy here, it is not on the part of the ancient Christians who made up Jesus but on the part of modern authors who make up stories about the ancient Christians and what they believed about Jesus.

Phallic 'Savior of the World'

As we can see, everything in my book concerning this discussion is cited and accurately represents the original commentary, as found in several publications dating from the 17th century until the present era, reflecting a tradition from antiquity. It is unfortunate when other scholars engage in libelous accusation and gross misrepresentation, of which there are a number of other instances in Ehrman's book *vis-à-vis* my work.

CHAPTER FOUR

Cognitive Dissonance: The Ehrman-Zindler Correspondence

Frank R. Zindler

What did he know of the evidence against a Historical Jesus and when did he know it? Even though generally interested readers of Bart D. Ehrman's *Did Jesus Exist? The Historical Argument for Jesus of Nazareth* (*DJE?*)[1] would not have realized it, for them to *really* understand the nature and significance of the book they were reading they needed to know what Professor Ehrman *could* and *should* have discussed and evaluated but apparently chose not to face up to. Although many readers might well have perceived the inadequacy of Ehrman's 'evidence' supposedly supporting the historical reality of 'Jesus of Nazareth,' they would have had no way to know about the many questions that Ehrman knew needed to be answered but are not even acknowledged, let alone adequately answered in *DJE?*.

Specifically, readers would not know that I and other scholars had sent him books to critique—books that marshal evidence of many kinds to show not only that Jesus of Nazareth never existed, but that the city now called Nazareth was not inhabited at the turn of the era! Although Ehrman mentions some of these books in his recent attempt to refute Mythicist scholarship, readers have no way of knowing that

1 Bart D. Ehrman, *Did Jesus Exist? The Historical Argument for Jesus of Nazareth* [New York: HarperOne, 2012]. Hereafter, *DJE?*

almost all the most important arguments and evidence in those books go unacknowledged and unrefuted in *Did Jesus Exist?* Readers could not know that Ehrman deals with only a tiny fraction of the literature arguing against a historical Jesus of Nazareth.

Generally interested readers, however, are not the only ones who need to know what Ehrman knew and when he knew it. Even the authors of the books just mentioned could not really know, for example, if Ehrman actually *chose* not to deal with their various arguments or simply never got around to reading those parts of their books. Ordinarily, there would be no way to know if Ehrman was deliberately avoiding their arguments and evidence or simply was unaware of them. Ehrman himself states that he does not usually bother to read criticism of his work,[2] and it could be that he also avoids reading material that might *a priori* be expected to call into question his traditional understanding of how Christianity began.

With regard to my own work, however, I have a lot of information concerning Ehrman's awareness and avoidance of my evidence and arguments, even though I too cannot know what he read—if anything—of my book *The Jesus the Jews Never Knew,*[3] or how much he read of my *Through Atheist Eyes: Scenes From a World That Won't Reason, Volume*

2 "I sometimes get asked," Ehrman breezily explains, "usually by supporters, why I do not make a practice of responding to scholars and bloggers who criticize my work and attack me personally. It's a good question, and I have several answers. For one thing, there are only so many hours in the day. If I responded to all the crazy things people say, I would have no time for my other work, let alone my life. Anyone should be able to see whether a point of view is plausible or absurd, whether a historical claim has merit or is pure fantasy driven by an idealogical or theological desire for a certain set of answers to be right" [*DJE?* 142].

We see several defense mechanisms here at play. First of all, by labeling even scholars and bloggers who criticize him as "crazy," he relieves himself of responsibility to recheck his assumptions and facts. Secondly, readers can only use their intelligence to evaluate his "point of view" or "historical claim" if they already have enough background information to be able to appraise the evidence he uses to support his claims. Will even the above-average reader be able to tell that Ehrman is wrong when he claims that Josephus wrote about "Jesus *of Nazareth*"? Once again, relying upon presumed readers' intelligence and knowledge absolves him from the responsibility of perpetually reexamining and reevaluating his facts and assumptions.

3 *The Jesus the Jews Never Knew: Sepher Toldoth Yeshu and the Quest of the Historical Jesus in Jewish Sources* [Cranford, NJ: American Atheist Press, 2003].

One: Religions & Scriptures.[4] The information that I possess and will present and discuss in this chapter is contained not in the books and papers I gave him, but in a voluminous and extensive e-mail correspondence that we exchanged going back to at least August of 2009.

Although it is lengthy, the correspondence record that follows can be read quickly—perhaps too quickly to grasp its significance. Generally interested readers will probably find the exchange interesting—perhaps even fascinating. Disinterested scholars, however, who seek to understand Ehrman's motivations and methods when writing *DJE?* might possibly form a darker opinion of the significance of both that book and its author.

The Correspondence

On August 11, 2009, I wrote to congratulate Bart Ehrman on becoming an Agnostic/Atheist and for his then newly published *God's Problem*:

> Dear Prof. Ehrman,
>
> Although you certainly will not remember me, we spoke briefly on at least two occasions at SBL [*Society of Biblical Literature*] meetings during the 90s. I have followed your career with increasing admiration since that period. I don't remember exactly why, but I do remember after listening to your papers on those occasions I fully expected that your own research would eventually turn you into an Atheist. (Since an Agnostic is without god-belief, an Agnostic is a-theos: an Atheist.) I did not, however, expect that you would lose your faith for much the same reason that I did: theodicy. I just read your book "God's Problem" and am very moved and pleased to detect so kindred a spirit.
>
> Over the years I have read just about all of your books, but I have not been able to follow your journal writings. ...[5] I sent

4 Cranford, NJ: American Atheist Press, 2011.

5 For legal and/or personal reasons involving third parties or institutions, slight redaction of several of the following messages has been necessary.

for all your courses [*The Teaching Company's Great Courses on DVDs*] and have recently finished viewing all of them. ... I must say that your courses seem to me to be about the best that mainline scholarship could produce.

It appears to me, however, that you may well have evolved past the views expressed in your courses. My guess is that you are now poised to re-examine all the "givens" in your field and rebuild your theories ab initio. However the truth may be, I have taken the liberty of attaching to the end of this e-mail the text of a talk I gave to Joseph Hofmann's THE JESUS PROJECT last December at Amherst. I hope you will be able to find the time and motivation to read it.

For Reason,

Frank

Ehrman replied on the following day:[6]

Frank,

Thanks for your note. I'm glad you've enjoyed the books. ...

And thanks for your lecture. I'm afraid I'm too crushed with a writing deadline to be able to give it written evaluation, but I very much appreciate your sending it along.

For what it's worth, I don't think that agnostics are atheists, although I do lean more toward the atheist side of agnosticism ("strong" agnostic, I like to think of myself. :-)). All best,

-- Bart Ehrman

It wasn't until November 8, 2009, leading up to the meeting of

6 I thank Professor Ehrman for graciously having granted me permission to reprint here his messages, provided only that I "acknowledge that they were emails, not written intended for publication."

the Society of Biblical Literature that I was able to continue our correspondence:

Dear Bart,

... I hope you were able to finish your publishing project on time and I hope that you won't become indentured to another project before I have a chance to pick your brain. I suspect, however, that you are a multi-tasker and only told me of one of several simultaneous projects! ;-)

Ann and I will be attending the SBL meeting in New Orleans and I am hoping against hope that you will be willing (and schedule-wise able) to be our guest for dinner on one evening of the convention. I see that you are speaking Sunday morning, and I don't know if you will be staying for the whole show or not. I have a bunch of books and papers I would like to give to you. I could have sent them to you by mail, but I am hoping I will be able to explain the purpose and utility of each item face-to-face. Naturally, I hope to be able to "pick your brain" on the historicity of Jesus issue.

It is always very uncomfortable to find myself in disagreement with scholars as prominent as you. Although I have been a mythicist since the mid-1980s, I try as best I can to keep up with the best thinking on the question, as well as continue my own research. The problem is, I have been a mythicist for so long that it is impossible for me now to put myself into the heads of scholars who still think Jesus was a real man once upon a time. That is why I am hoping you will indulge me by sharing your core reasoning on the historicity issue.

Perhaps because I have been a mythicist for so long now, it is difficult for me to understand why everyone else has not given up the historicity "game." Specifically, I hope to learn what remains for me to prove or disprove in order to to get others to agree with me. I need to know what has to be shown in order for other scholars to agree that Jesus of Nazareth was not an historical figure. ...

Please let me know if we'll be able to get together.

For Reason,

Frank

Although we weren't able to have dinner together, I did have a chance to give him a copy of my *The Jesus the Jews Never Knew* (an exhaustive examination of all Jewish literature prior to the Babylonian Talmud showing that the ancient Jews never heard of 'Jesus of Nazareth' or Nazareth either one!),[7] all the relevant articles that later would be gathered together in volume one of *Through Atheist Eyes,* and some papers I had presented to The Jesus Seminar back in the 1990s.

It was not until October of 2010 that I found occasion to renew my correspondence with Ehrman. A friend of mine received and forwarded to me an e-mail concerning Ehrman and me that was rather startling:

Sent: Thursday, October 14, 2010 4:01 PM

Subject: Dr. Bart Ehrman Comments about Zindlerites on Radio Show

---

7 Ehrman devotes pages 66–68 to discussion of "Rabbinic Sources" relating to a historical Jesus. His endnote 24 on page 351 explains that "Here I am simply summarizing my discussion in *Jesus: Apocalyptic Prophet of the New Millennium*... For fuller discussion, see the classic studies of R. Travers Herford, *Christianity in Talmud and Midrash* (New York: Ktav, 1903), and Morris Goldstein, *Jesus in the Jewish Tradition* (New York: Macmillan, 1950)."

Because Ehrman probably had not read my book, he did not realize that a large part of it was devoted to an exhaustive critique *of the entirety* of Herford's book! It was absolutely necessary for Ehrman to provide an explanation of how it could have been possible for the founders of the rabbinic tradition—working in Tiberias and other places in the Galilee—not to have known anything at all about the religious activist who had been stirring up trouble there just a few decades before them. He needed to explain why 'Nazareth' itself is unknown in the Mishnah and two Talmuds. If he *had* read my book, why did he not deal with my arguments?

[Name redacted], I listened to a radio interview with Dr. Ehrman yesterday. He was specifically asked what he thought about American Atheists and their backing of the idea that Jesus never existed and that Nazareth never existed in the first century AD. His response was "that's completely crazy!... they [are] not doing very well with their history lessons. What are they thinking? (laughs)." As to the claim made by the Zindlerites that Nazareth never existed, Ehrman said "he's making something up."[8] (i.e., a fabrication).

He continued: "It's very hard to prove that Jesus did not exist. I think it is historically virtually certain that Jesus existed. I mean, there's just hummungous [evidence] ... "

This was very startling and quite unexpected. I forwarded the e-mail to Ehrman on October 14, 2010, with the following comment and request:

Sent: Thursday, October 14, 2010 9:06 PM

Subject: FW: Dr. Bart Ehrman Comments about Zindlerites on Radio Show

Dear Bart,

A friend sent me the following account of a radio show you apparently did recently. Is this in fact an accurate account of what

8 It is interesting to note that Ehrman says the same thing in *DJE?* page 212. Criticizing my *hypothesis* that astrologers (the Magi) as the vernal equinox was moving into Pisces "left their cult centers in Phrygia and Cilicia... to go to Palestine to see if they could locate not just the King of the Jews but the new Time Lord," he opines that "Zindler says this in all sincerity, and so far as I can tell, he really believes it. What evidence does he give for his claim that the Mithraists moved their religion [*sic*!] to Palestine to help them find the king of the Jews? None at all. And so we might ask: what evidence could he have cited, had he wanted to do so? It's the same answer. There is no evidence. This is made up." Why did Ehrman think I was suggesting that the Magi would have moved their religious headquarters, when it was clear that an information-gathering expedition would have been meant? Ehrman offers no evidence to support his claim that I could not possibly have had evidence to support my hypothesis or the implied claim that I did not want to cite evidence for my hypothesis. Why did he not ask me about this as he later was to do concerning other Mithraic issues?

you said concerning my research? If so, does it involve a critique of my books and articles that I gave you in New Orleans? Does it involve an evaluation of Rene Salm's book showing that the Franciscan "evidence" for habitation at Nazareth at the turn of the era is pure fancy? Does it reflect a critical rejection of my article in the Journal of Higher Criticism showing that Capernaum was a purely literary invention?

As you know, in science the onus probandi rests with those who assert the existence of a think [*sic*] or process. I would appreciate an explanation. I was disappointed that you did not have time to read my "Prolegomenon to a science of Christian origins" that I sent you almost two years ago when you were trying to get several books through the press. I would ask you now again to be so kind as to read it.

For Reason,

Frank Zindler

American Atheist Press

Seven minutes later, I received the following reply:

Sent: Thursday, October 14, 2010 9:13 PM

To: Zindler, Frank R.

Subject: RE: Dr. Bart Ehrman Comments about Zindlerites on Radio Show

Frank,

Yes, this is my position. And the position of every historian of the NT and early Christianity who teaches in a university or college or divinity school or seminary that I know (I know many hundreds, as you might imagine) in North America, Europe, or Asia, whether atheist, agnostic, main line Christian, or whatever. History is not a science, but there are some things that are beyond reasonable doubt, and I think this is one of them. Sorry you find it offensive!

BTW, I have not done any radio programs for about a year.

-- Bart

Bart D. Ehrman
James A. Gray Professor
Department of Religious Studies
University of North Carolina at Chapel Hill

I was dismayed to see that he didn't even bother to say if he had read the articles and books I had given him or any of the evidence concerning Nazareth and Capernaum! He did not deny that he had accused me of "making something up." Alarmed, lest our dialogue be abruptly terminated before he might answer any of my questions at all, I answered Ehrman later that day:

Bart,

I don't really find it offensive, I find it hard to understand how someone who knows so much about Christian origins would simply appeal to authority and ad populum argumentation without fairly evaluating the evidence against the majority opinion.

In the instant case, the evidence of Nazareth would seem to completely settle the issue. As you know, Nazareth is unknown to the OT, to the Talmud, to Josephus,[9] and everyone else prior

9 It is interesting that that Ehrman repeats this information in his criticism of René Salm on page 193: "Like so many mythicists before him, Salm emphasizes what scholars have long known: Nazareth is never mentioned in the Hebrew Bible, in the writings of Josephus [even though on page 58 he falsely asserts that Jesus of Nazareth *is* mentioned in Josephus!] or in the Talmud. It first shows up in the Gospels." By hohummification of Salms' argument — "what scholars have long known" — Ehrman neatly obscures the fact that scholars have never been able to provide a believable explanation for what they "have long known"!

to Matthew's gospel. It is unknown to "Paul," and is unknown to Mark. (The only mention of Nazareth in Mark is the interpolation 1:9; in that verse, "Jesus" is inarticulate unlike all other occurrences in Mark except for vocatives, etc.)[10] In my articles "Where Jesus never walked" and "How Jesus got a life" I explain the origin of the name. If you have thrown those articles away but would be willing to read them, I would be happy to send them to you again.

---

10 In *DJE?*, on page 191, Ehrman criticizes my argument that the sole mention of 'Nazareth' in Mark's gospel [Mark 1:9] is an interpolation. "Frank Zindler, for example, in a cleverly titled essay, "Where Jesus Never Walked," tries to deconstruct on a fairly simple level the geographical places associated with Jesus, especially Nazareth. He claims that Mark's Gospel never states that Jesus came from Nazareth. This flies in the face, of course of Mark 1:9, which indicates that this is precisely where Jesus came from ("Jesus came from Nazareth in Galilee"), but Zindler maintains that that verse was not originally part of Mark; it was inserted by a later scribe. Here again we see history being done according to convenience. If a text says precisely what you think it could not have said, then all you need to do is claim that originally it must have said something else.[9]"

Had Ehrman forgotten the evidence I cited back on October 14, 2010? Not at all! In footnote 9 [page 356] he completely reverses his charge and lightly comments, "I do not mean to say that Zindler does not cite evidence for his view. [*Although in his main text that is exactly the implication.*] He claims that the name Jesus in Mark 1:9 does not have the definite article, unlike the other eighty places it occurs in Mark, and therefore the verse does not appear to be written in Markan style. In response, I should say that (a) there are two other places in Mark where the name Jesus does not have the article; ..."

This gives one the impression that Ehrman has researched the Greek text better than I did. But in my letter of October 14, I clearly say 'Jesus' is inarticulate unlike all other occurrences in Mark *except for vocatives, etc.* Actually, there are more than two other occasions of 'anarthrous' Jesus, as I discuss in my chapter "Mark's 'Jesus from Nazareth of the Galilee'." In all of those other cases, however, 'Jesus' could not carry the definite article for grammatical reasons. While the changing principles of using the Greek definite article are quite complicated, it is interesting that Mark's use of "*the* Jesus" where the other gospels have simply "Jesus" gives the overall impression that in Mark *Jesus* is still a title—'the Savior'—but has become a personal name in the other, later gospels.

According to Richard Carrier [*Proving History: Bayes's Theorem and the Quest for the Historical Jesus*, 2012: 142*ff*], "Eric Laupot makes a plausible case that the term was originally derived from Isaiah 11:1 as the name of the Christian movement (as followers of a prophesied Davidic messiah), which was retroactively made into Jesus' hometown (either allusively or in error). J.S. Kennard makes just as plausible a case that it was a cultic title derived from the nazirites ("the separated" or "the consecrated") described in Numbers 6 (and the Mishnah tractate Nazir)." It is regrettable that Ehrman is not likely to read Carrier's book, which seeks to bring mathematical rigor to the writing of history.

COGNITIVE DISSONANCE

The history of mythicist research is an honorable one, going back at least to Charles DuPuis in the 1790s. A very long list of eminent scholars has espoused the mythicist position but the scholars have never been refuted, only ignored and buried under claims of refutation.

I asked you several years ago why you thought Jesus was historical, what was the most important evidence in your opinion. To my disappointment, you did not answer me then but it seemed understandable at the time. But now I would really like to know why you think Jesus was a real man. Surely, you must have some reason better than the ad populum excuse.

I got my master's degree in geology at a time when none of my professors accepted my arguments for "continental drift." Yet they were all wrong and I proved to be correct. It is time that history became a science, as I argued in my "Prolegomenon to a science of Christian origins." It was never clear if you read that paper two years ago or not. In any case, I would like to know what you think is wrong with it--apart from the fact that most historians wouldn't like it.

I know it is hard to go against something that is so totally embedded in one's intellectual memory and sense of "common sense." I too was horrified when Madalyn O'Hair announced she was going to write a book showing the non-historicity of Jesus of Nazareth. I immediately set out to find the evidence for Jesus so privately I could deflect her to prevent a public scandal.[11] To my

---

11 I freely confess that this was the 'efficient cause' of my immediate investigation into Mythicist claims. However, I am quite sure I would have done that even if the claim had come from someone less famous than Madalyn Murray O'Hair. I have always tried to understand why people believe crazy things—things that occasionally turn out not to be crazy at all. In decades of debating creationists, again and again I have been alerted to important problems in science that otherwise would have escaped my notice. Although the creationists in every case so far have misunderstood — or misrepresented — the evidence surrounding any given problem, it has always been well worth my while to get to the bottom of it—not only for the joy of being able publicly to explain a particular creationist's error, but for the satisfaction of gaining deeper understanding of some point of science of which I hitherto had been ignorant. This

greater horror, however, I came up with exactly nothing; no evidence whatsoever survives from antiquity to indicate let alone demand the historicity of Jesus. There is no reason to suppose Christianity began in any way different from Judaism, Hinduism, or the other mysteries to which it seems so closely related. Christianity did not begin at all in the way that say Mormonism began. It did not grow as a tree from a basal trunk. Rather, like most "great religions" Christianity grew as a braid woven from various fibers coming from various depths and directions in antiquity that twisted together, frayed out at different times, were joined by new threads, etc. At no time could one point out and say "Here is where Christianity is beginning."[12]

You are a world-renowned authority on the early Christian "heresies," including Docetism.[13] If Jesus was a real person as late as 33 CE, isn't it odd that people as early as the time of the Pauline and Johannine epistles could be arguing that he had not had a real body? Indeed, the refutations of docetism one finds in the NT and church fathers (I very much admire your edition of Ignatius) all seem to imply that the Docetists "got there first," and the NT and early Christian orthodoxies are trying to prove their own "heretical" views that Jesus had a body, in contradiction to earlier teachings of the Christian mysteries. If Jesus had been a real man, how could Christianity have begun as a mystery

would not seem to be a habit shared with Ehrman.

12 Arguably, this is the most important argument not dealt with in *DJE?* Historicists seem never even to consider the possibility that Christianity had no discrete beginning in either space or time. It could not possibly have developed the way the 'heathen' religions did! Detailed comparison of the braid-vs-tree models of Christian origins was urgently needed in *DJE?* In that book, Ehrman does not even hint that his most fundamental assumption concerning Christian origins had been challenged by me two years before publication of *DJE?* Was the braid model of Christian origins cognitively too dissonant for him to remember over so long a time? Was it perhaps too dissonant even to gain his full, conscious attention when he read my e-mail?

13 It is a shock to discover that despite this challenge, the word 'Docetism' or its derivatives is not to be found in *DJE?* All the more is it shocking to see an authority on the earliest Christian heresiologists evading an argument so closely pertaining to his research specialty.

cult? I suppose that is not impossible, but it certainly seems hard to imagine a scenario by which a real man created mysteries about himself.

I know you consider me to be a crank, but that doesn't really hurt my feelings. As a scientist, I have never had to worry about how I was being evaluated personally, only how my evidence was being evaluated. Although I was invited two years ago to speak on the mythicist position in Germany, at the University of Muenster, I have no claim to fame apart from that which should be accorded any honest seeker of truth. Your heroic "coming out" as an agnostic shows that you too are more concerned with truth than with reputation.

I hope very much that we can carry on a dialogue concerning the historical Jesus. I hope we can discuss evidence rather than customary opinions. Of course, one always wishes to know why customs are the way they are, but that too involves discovery and examination of evidence.

Please let me know if you are willing to read any of my stuff.

For Reason,

Frank

Later that same evening, I received the following reply:

From: Ehrman, Bart D

Sent: Thursday, October 14, 2010 10:26 PM

To: Zindler, Frank R.

Subject: RE: Dr. Bart Ehrman Zindler reply

Frank,

I am absolutely not depending on authority! There are compelling grounds for thinking Jesus existed. I assume you know the arguments, or at least I hope you do. (These arguments[14] are compelling to virtually every one who looks at them, and for good reason. You really should take that seriously.)

At the same time, I assume you would not trust geologists who in fact have no training in geology (or creationists who were fundamentalist Bible "scholars" rather than scientists). So let me ask you, since I don't remember (and you are presuming too much if you presume that I haven't looked at your work): what are your qualifications to talk about first century Palestine and the writings of the early Christians? Or do qualifications, in your opinion, not matter?

-- Bart

Bart D. Ehrman

James A. Gray Professor

Department of Religious Studies

University of North Carolina at Chapel Hill

The following day I answered his *ad hominem* message:

---

14 During more than two years of dialogue, Ehrman never explained what "these arguments" were, and it was not until I read *DJE?* that I discovered that almost entirely he was relying on the arguments used by fundamentalist apologists, not real scholars, to support his historicity claims. Why didn't he reveal his arguments to me? Did he understand at some subconscious level that an argument based on something silly such as the 'criterion of embarrassment' could easily be demolished, leaving him with nothing but his much-used appeal to authority? It is almost comical now to reread this e-mail denying that he is depending upon authority, claiming that there are evidentiary grounds for his position, yet giving not even a hint as to what they are. Moreover, I had already devoted hundreds of pages to criticism of the traditional arguments, and Ehrman had repeatedly been made aware of them.

I did not realize at the time the implication of his snide "I assume you know the arguments, or at least I hope you do." All the arguments were dealt with in the books and articles I had given to him, so it is clear that he never read them. Nevertheless, he assures me that "you are presuming too much if you presume that I haven't looked at your work"!

COGNITIVE DISSONANCE

Subject: RE: Dr. Bart Ehrman Zindler reply2
Date: October 15, 2010 10:04:31 AM EDT

Bart,

I will answer your ad hominem questions, but still wonder why you do not state what the "compelling grounds for thinking Jesus existed" are. I do NOT know the arguments, because there simply aren't any good ones. I am quite certain now that I have researched this more deeply than you have.[15] Your unwillingness to present any evidence at all is again very disappointing, given that it repeats the evasion of a year ago or so.

Now to the ad hominem: geology was merely a side excursion in my career. My doctoral studies were in Neurobiology although I never went on to a career in that field. Rather, after being driven from my post as Chairman of the Division of Science, Nursing, & Technology at SUNY-Johnstown because of my public Atheism, I have for nearly 30 years worked as a linguist and editor ... [*for*] a learned society chartered by Congress. I analyze ... research published in all the languages of Europe except for Hungarian, Estonian, Celtic, and Basque. My major assignments, though, are in the Slavic languages--hence my ability to feature Slavonic Josephus so much in my book THE JESUS THE JEWS NEVER KNEW: SEPHER TOLDOTH YESHU AND THE QUEST OF THE HISTORICAL JESUS IN JEWISH SOURCES.

(I gave you a copy of the book in New Orleans. If you were to read it, you would see that I have probably produced the most thorough and extensive investigation of the Testimonium Flavianum ever done.)[16]

---

15 Despite my bragging at this point, it still came as a shock when *DJE?* was published and I could see not only that *I* had researched things more deeply than Ehrman but that *all* of the "amateurs" whom he criticized were more deeply studied in Historicist arguments than he.

16 Despite my hyperbole here, if Ehrman had in fact read my arguments against the *Testimonium Flavianum* (a passage in all extant copies of Josephus' *Antiquities of the Jews* mentioning Jesus) in my chapter "Faking Flavius," he could not have written his

Frank R. Zindler

Because I am able to read all the major European languages in areas even outside of science, I have been able to cover historical Jesus studies in considerable breadth. I also am competent in Latin, Greek, and Hebrew. I get by in Aramaic, Syriac, and Coptic, and have dabbled in Sanskrit and other ancient languages. It must be noted that in almost all the languages with which I work on a daily basis I am entirely an autodidact. In several cases I took college courses in a language after I had already learned it, but for the majority of languages in which I work I am self-taught.

It is more than a bit dismaying that you judge me to be unqualified to write about 1st-century Palestine when you have not--indeed, it now appears, WILL not--read any of the voluminous materials I have given to you.[17]

I ask you once again: what do you think is significant evidence for the historical Jesus? How do you account for Docetism at so early a date?

I also ask you once again to read something--anything--that I gave to you. Or, if you have thrown it all in the rubbish, please ask me to resend something. Do not prejudge me. If I have made

---

criticism of Earl Doherty [pages 59–66 of *DJE?*] the way he did. He would have had to explain why notice of the passage (as well as the death of James the Just or John the Baptist) is missing in the table of contents of a pre-fifth-century Greek manuscript of Josephus but a fifth- or sixth-century Latin version of the table of contents adds "Concerning John the Baptist." Moreover, he would have had to account for the presence of the *Testimonium* in the Slavonic version of *The Jewish Wars*! Oh, yes—he would also have had to explain why Photius [*c.* 810–*c.* 893], Patriarch of Constantinople did not report in his *Bibliotheca* any version of the passage in his review of *Antiquities of the Jews*, even though he would have been highly motivated to exploit the passage had it been in his copy of Josephus.

17 In retrospect, it appears that Ehrman would not read my books and papers simply because I am not a doctoral graduate of a seminary or similar program. Can there any good thing come out of Nazareth? Of course not! Clearly, this hyperparochial attitude has protected him from coming in contact with disturbing stimuli that might "awaken him from his dogmatic slumber," but it made the embarrassment of *DJE?* inevitable.

mistakes in my writings, I genuinely want to know it. I have no axe to grind. At the age of 71 I am past the posturings of pride. I would like to know that I have glimpsed truth before I cash my chips in.

Still in friendship,

Frank

Not receiving an answer to my question about Docetism,[18] I wrote to Ehrman again several days later:

Attached file: Did Jesus Have a Body?

October 19, 2010

Dear Bart,

I just have learned you will be speaking at the Humanist Conference next April 7-10 in Boston.[19] Of course, I too will be there. I hope we can discuss historiography at some time during the meeting.

I have just reread your first reply to me where you allude to all the authorities who believe in an historical Jesus. It now occurs to me that this has even less significance than ordinary ad populum arguments. The reason is that virtually all of the "authorities" who have pronounced upon the historicity of Jesus are handicapped and compromised by their employment by church-related institutions. Certainly, even an Atheist in the

18 Docetism was an ancient form of Christianity that held that Jesus or Christ only *appeared* (Greek *dokein*, 'seem,' 'appear') to have a body of flesh and to suffer on the cross. The Docetists were the 'antichrists' of 2 John 1:7—"For many deceivers are entered into the world, who confess not that Jesus Christ is come in the flesh. This is a deceiver and an antichrist."

19 This was the conference Ehrman mentions on pages 332–334 of *DJE?* At the last minute, I had to cancel my plans to attend the meeting and so missed an opportunity to discuss historicity issues *publicly* with him.

employ of a religious university or seminary would not dare to express mythicist theories. Almost all authorities were themselves educated at sectarian schools and were never exposed to the abundant mythicist literature that has appeared since the 1790s.[20] Virtually all secular historians are not themselves authorities on Jesus of Nazareth, taking the word of religious authorities simply because they have never had any reason to do otherwise. They never had reason to do otherwise because of the effective suppression of mythicist writings.

Thus it is that only outsiders with respect to the sectarian university-seminary world are able even to explore the mythicist aspects of Jesus. You yourself are a rare exception to this, teaching as you are at a public university. You are one of the few scholars who would be free to "come out" with the news that Jesus of Nazareth never lived as a man of flesh and blood.

It also occurs to me that your questioning of my qualifications is beside the point. Why should one need special qualifications to ask a question? Why should one need special qualifications to announce what he thinks is a discovery? If he is unqualified in any genuine way, it is a small thing for a genuine expert to point out the errors of reasoning or failures of fact. While it is true that I would not expect someone with your professional background to be able seriously to challenge my understanding, say, of brain physiology, I would be intrigued rather than offended by such an inquest. I would patiently try to explain what specifically was incorrect about your claim--unless, of course, it turned out that you were correct. In that case, I would change my own mind and adopt your new information into my Weltanschauung. It sounds corny, I know, but I genuinely wish to discover truth. I

20 It surely is significant that Ehrman makes no effort to counter my claims here at any point in *DJE?* but rather repeatedly chides Mythicists for not being properly educated and repeatedly citing the conclusions of the "authorities" here discussed! Because he makes no attempt to deal with this argument, the appeals to authority and *ad hominem* attacks of that book are more glaringly apparent than would be the case if he had tried fairly to deal with my argument here.

don't want to go through what remains of my life assuming errors to be truth.

I think you will have to agree that there isn't a single fact that BY ITSELF requires Jesus of Nazareth to have been an historical figure. By contrast, the Res Gestae inscriptions of Augustus and Tiberius instantly confer reality upon those figures. The many coins of other rulers likewise BY THEMSELVES, even if only a single coin, confer reality. There is nothing concerning Jesus of Nazareth that can confer reality upon him in this way.

It is this very fact of the absence of proof-facts that puts the historical existence of Jesus of Nazareth into a disputable position. It puts him into the same boat as Socrates, Buddha, Lao Tzu, Zoroaster, and now, apparently, even Mohammed. (When I was asked to speak at the University of Muenster on Christian Origins, Stephen Kalisch, the head of the School of Religious Studies, turned out to be a Muslim who disputes the historicity of Mohammed! Since then, a considerable literature has accumulated arguing for the non-historicity of Mohammed.)

You indicate that you have in fact read some of my material. I am glad to learn that. However, I am puzzled even more as to why you haven't pointed out even a single error of fact or reasoning in whatever you have read. I certainly don't think that everything I have written is perfect. I would truly like to know what errors I have made.

I have taken the liberty to attach a draft of a chapter of an up-coming book. The chapter is called "Did Jesus Have a Body?"[21] It follows up my previous comments about Docetism. Since you are one of the few authorities in this field, I would appreciate your critique of this light-hearted essay.

21 This was an early version of the chapter in the present book, "Bart Ehrman and the Body of Jesus of Nazareth." Surely, had Ehrman read "this light-hearted essay," he would have had to say *something* about how the Docetists could have claimed that Jesus didn't have a real body—merely several decades after his supposed death!

For Reason,

Frank

Several days later, Ehrman sent me the following reply. After reading it, I ask readers to reread the letter above and form their own opinion as to whether or not Ehrman's answer was either adequate or fair.

From: Ehrman, Bart D
Sent: Friday, October 22, 2010 7:47 PM
To: Zindler, Frank R.
Subject: RE: Dr. Bart Ehrman Zindler reply3

Frank,

Thanks for your follow-up. There are lots and lots of scholars of early Christianity who teach in secular settings. None of them is a mythicist. That should probably tell you something. Though I know it doesn't. :-)

I certainly don't challenge your right to ask hard questions. I challenge your authority to answer them confidently without serious training in the field. You would like an example where you obviously go wrong. OK. Your claim that Christianity started as a mystery religion. I'm afraid you don't seem to know much about mystery religions.[22] But why should you? It's a very complex field.[23]

22 It is amusing to note that in his scholarly works Ehrman has often had to deal with references to Christian mysteries, but has never been conscious of their significance. On page 267 of *The Orthodox Corruption of Scripture* [New York: Oxford University Press, 1993], for example, he discusses the Greek text of Colossians 2:2: "But it is difficult to know how to construe the syntax of the phrase; does it mean the "mystery of the Christ of God"? Or the "mystery of God, namely Christ"? Or "the mystery of the God Christ" (*i.e.* of God, who is Christ)? ... Some fourteen variations are attested, virtually all of them eliminating the possibility of understanding the verse as equating Christ with God ...[the Father] himself. Thus we have manuscripts that speak of "the mystery of God," or "the mystery of Christ," or "the mystery of God which (neuter, referring to mystery) is Christ," or "the mystery of God the Father of Christ," *etc.*" Do we not get a whiff of something mysterious here? A mystery cult, perhaps?

23 Considering all the books and essays I had given him displaying my technical

All best wishes.

-- Bart Ehrman

Bart D. Ehrman

James A. Gray Professor

Department of Religious Studies

University of North Carolina at Chapel Hill

For personal reasons, I could not reply to this provocative and insulting non-answer until several weeks later. Still thinking that I could engage him at a scholarly level, I wrote the following:

Subject: FWD: Dr. Bart Ehrman Zindler reply4
November 8, 2010 8:37:51 PM EST

Bart,

I meant to reply long before now ... In any case, I now have a moment to reply. Hopefully, we may be able to discuss some of these things in Atlanta in a few weeks.

It is true that the mystery religions are a complex subject, but certainly it is not as difficult as molecular genetics or neurophysiology. My library bulges at the seams with treatises both very old and very new on the mysteries, including their relationship to early Christianity. While my research is just getting off the ground, it almost certainly will establish that Christianity began as an esoteric cult that then spilled out to become an exoteric religion still using the parables and metaphoric scriptures externally associated with the esoteric cult.

competence in biblical studies, this insult was a wake-up call to me, warning me that some powerful defense mechanisms had suddenly been activated. By insulting me, he might get *me* to break off the annoying conversation and he would not have to come up with evidence for Jesus of Nazareth. Perhaps more importantly, he wouldn't have to read the materials I had given to him. Quite deliberately, I worked to keep the dialogue going.

Frank R. Zindler

As you may have noted if you read my Prolegomenon (It just has been published by Joe Hoffmann through Prometheus in a proceedings volume for a meeting of the Jesus Project.), I seek to make the study of Christian origins scientific. Step one for the mysteries, I am collecting ALL uses in Greek of the term "mysterion" ("musterion" for those who have forgotten why a "y" was used in Latin transcription) in the NT, apostolic fathers, apocrypha, church fathers up past Irenaeus, the surviving mystery religious texts, including Hermetic stuff in Greek, etc. (I have used your Loeb edition and will send you an errata list when I have time to compile it.) Also, I will do the same for Latin. Hopefully, I'll live long enough to include Coptic and Syriac.

In conjunction with collecting occurrences and usages of mysterion, I am also compiling statistical data from all the above sources on all the sacred names and titles. With this plus some other statistics, I plan to construct a phylogenetic tree showing the relationships of the various Gnostic, Christian, Jewish, and other ancient philosophic and religious texts (Including Plato and the middle Platonists). Forltunately [*sic*], I can use the same software for this as I use to construct phylogenetic trees of arthropods, primates, or whatever. My use of Thesaurus Linguae Graecae is still rather clumsy, but it will make possible an EXHAUSTIVE survey of my subject field. The problem with historiography as practiced heretofore is that it was never possible to be exhaustive in dealing with any topic. Religious historians have been like the blind man with the elephant. In their arguments they have all been correct while simultaneously being wrong. With computers now we can create a bounded playing field.

As is the case with all scientific endeavors, I can't be certain in advance that my thesis will prove correct. I won't know until the study is finished. However, I will be extremely surprised if an hypothesis with so much heuristic and explanatory power should prove to be incorrect.

I do appreciate your response concerning my mystery-religion hypothesis. I really had hoped, however, that you might have indicated at least one bit of evidence strongly indicating the historicity of Jesus of Nazareth. Lacking that, I discovered your earlier book "Jesus Apocalyptic Prophet of the New Millennium." I hoped you would have presented some evidence of historicity therein. Although I haven't finished the book yet, I must tell you I am disappointed.

The greatest problem seems to be that you repeatedly fall into the petitio principii fallacy. Consider, for example:

"My examples, then, have to do with accounts about Jesus that appear to be contradictory in some of their details. Let me stress that my point is not that the basic events that are narrated didn't happen. Since these particular accounts deal with the birth of Jesus and his death, I think we can assume they are historically accurate in the most general terms—Jesus was born and he did die!" (p. 32)

What's wrong with this? You assume that which is in need of proof—proof that does not exist. Why do you suppose that if you take out all contradictions from two conflicting narratives that whatever remains is true or historical? Do you think that the conflicting accounts of Herakles' miraculous birth and atoning death certify the historicity of Herakles? Do you think the Infancy Gospel also can help to establish the historicity of Jesus?[24]

Jesus of Nazareth lived his life backwards. The earliest documents have the least information about his life; the latest documents have the most. That certainly should give one pause for thought.[25]

24 Shouldn't Ehrman have kept this in mind when staking everything on his 'multiple-attestation' arguments, with his fanciful appeals to Mark, Q, M, L, Thomas, etc.? Shouldn't he have explained why he wasn't including the Infancy Gospel of Thomas and other infancy gospels in his arsenal of 'evidence'? He published a whole book about such scriptures!

25 Ehrman isn't the first apologist or scholar to avoid dealing with this embarrassing

Frank R. Zindler

On pp. 35-36 you write:

"Eventually we'll need to see how we as modern historians—that is, those of us who want to know what actually did happen, and when, and by whom—can get behind these theologically molded accounts to uncover the actual events that lie underneath them."

Why do you beg the question that there ARE in fact historical events underlying them? Isn't it more reasonable, since these are "theologically molded accounts," to suppose that these stories are theopolitical aetiological tales concocted to justify the power structures of various religious groups?

I hope I can find time to finish your book before Atlanta and that we may have some time to discuss it together there.

Frank

It turned out not to be possible for me to attend the SBL meeting in Atlanta and, of course, Ehrman never answered my e-mail. It wasn't until the following spring that I had occasion to resume our correspondence.

Subject: Congratulations on FORGED
Date: March 27, 2011 4:45:17 PM EDT

Bart,

I just received my copy of FORGED and am very pleased. This is a job that was greatly needed and you were the perfect person to do it. It is an argument that needed to be done at book length. Back in 1979 I published a pamphlet "Is the Book of Daniel a Forgery?" in which I too called a spade a spade. From then on, at every opportunity I have used the F-word for many of the same

problem. In debates and publications I have been pointing this out repeatedly for thirty years. In my experience, no one *ever* has tried to explain why the earliest authors knew the least about Jesus of Nazareth and the latest knew the most.

works to which you apply the term. In addition, I routinely use the word "plagiarized" to refer to what "Matthew" and "Luke" did to "Mark." Over the years I have heard all the "explanations" that you demolish so masterfully. Truthfully, I was never very good at debunking them effectively. As I just said, this is an argument that needed to be developed at book length.

In any case, Franx thanx for doing this job!

As I think I told you several years ago, I have been following your career for at least twenty years now and have been gratified to see both your religious-philosophical and scholarly paths come closer to the road on which I have traveled now for almost thirty years. I know you take annoyed umbrage at my implied assertion that you are approaching closer and closer to the mythicist views I have held for so long, but I fully expect that before you retire (more likely, die of exhaustion!) from the exciting scholarly and public life that now is yours, you too will adopt the mythicist position.

There are many reasons for my bold assertion, such as:

(1) Now that you are an Atheist, you are free from the most compelling reason to believe in the historicity of Jesus of Nazareth. It is true that the vast majority even of Atheist scholars still think he was real, but to someone who believes that Jesus was a benevolent god, historicity is sine qua non, but that no longer is an option.[26]

(2) Although using different methods and lines of inquiry, your research and that of many other modern scholars is converging on the results of the Religionsgeschichtliche Schule that long ago found no need for an historical Jesus to explain the phenomena of Christianity.

26 Could Ehrman have actually read this comment and then gone on to spill so much ink charging *all* Atheists with the moral crime of pursuing a nefarious "atheist agenda"?

Frank R. Zindler

FORGED shows the theopolitical motives and purposes for which scriptures are created. It shows that ALL scriptures must be viewed with suspicion. Explaining why a particular work was forged and ascribed to "Peter" should give us clues as to why "Peter" himself was invented. Arthur Drews gave a number of reasons in Die Petruslegende and I won't rehearse them here.

Any of your research that involves understanding the origins of the canon shows how arbitrary the process of canonization was and that it served theopolitical agendas quite independent of historical reality. Indeed, the watch-word might appropriately have been History-be-Damned! If the Docetists had triumphed, just think how differently the gospel story would read! There'd be no controversy at all over the Historical Jesus.

(3) Scholarship since Wettstein's Scholia Hellenistica in Novum Testamentum (a work much needed by modern scholars, IMO) inexorably has shown that the gospel stories are not the products of actual historical events but rather are midrashes or peshers that rework previous materials. Robert Price, Richard Carrier, Dennis Ronald MacDonald, and a host of other scholars have now derived virtually the whole of Mark from the LXX, Homer, Euripides, et al. Even I have made much hay out of the fact that the Q-saying ("We have piped unto you and ye have not danced..." Matt 11:17; Luke 7:32) derives from Aesop's story of the Fisherman and the Flute.

Virtually nothing remains of the Jesus story that cannot be shown to be a fabrication built by recycling of earlier fictions.

(3) There are no contemporary extrabiblical notices of Jesus. Certainly Philo and Justus of Tiberias should have noticed—much to Photius' chagrin!

(4) I have shown what Origen suspected: the geography of the NT is mostly fictive and symbolic, not real. Cheyne & Black were the first to question the historicity of first-century Nazareth. After I went through all the excavation reports published

by the Franciscans, I concluded that there was no proof of habitation at the site at the turn of the era. René Salm (whose book The Myth of Nazareth I gave you last year) reinvestigated ALL the artifacts ever reported from the site and proves quite conclusively that the site was not inhabited when the Holy Family should have been living there. (Christmas 2009 reports of discovery of 1st-century buildings and artefacts from the Nazareth Farm Theme Park development have never been corroborated or published and quite certainly are either grotesque archaeological mistakes or frauds perpetrated to maintain the Christian tourist industry at "Nazareth.")

In my report for the Jesus Seminar "Capernaum—A Literary Invention" I showed that the text of Josephus has been badly misunderstood and misrepresented and that so-called Kfar-Nahum is relatable neither to Josephus nor the gospels.

The Israeli archaeologist Aviram Oshri has shown that there is no evidence of 1st-century habitation at Bethlehem in Judea, and Jodi Magness[27] agrees with his assessment.

Similarly, there is no archeological confirmation for Bethany, Bethpage, Aenon, etc. It is also curious that Jesus never has any adventures in Sepphoris or Tiberias. What does this do to verisimilitude?

In summary: the gospel geography largely ignores the real geography of the 1st century and replaces it with a highly symbolic, fictive landscape.

(5) Although I have not yet gotten all the data into my Excel spreadsheet, it is becoming quite clear that evolution went from Christ to Jesus, not from Jesus to Christ. My survey of the Greek and Latin texts of the NT, Apocrypha (not yet including the Coptic stuff), the Apostolic Fathers, and the Greek and Latin Fathers of the first few centuries indicates quite clearly that the

27 Although Ehrman claims in *DJE?* that Jodi Magness disagrees with my Nazareth claims, he gives no hint that I am wrong about her opinion concerning Oshri and Bethlehem. I wonder why. Although I personally gave her a copy of René Salm's *The Myth of Nazareth: The Invented Town of Jesus*, it seems certain that she never read the book.

evolutionary sequence went from Christ to Christ Jesus, to Jesus Christ, to Jesus with the definite article, to Jesus without the article, to Jesus of Nazareth.

Christ at the beginning was a heavenly character and the subject of an astral mystery cult that formed about the same time the Cult of Augustus formed, in response to the movement of the vernal equinox out of Aries into Pisces. As you know, Augustus was the first to use the word euaggelion, and we have much to learn about Christian origins from the study of the Imperial Cults. (Since few biblical scholars have taken on the task of learning about ancient astronomy or astrology, this admittedly will seem quite kooky, and I won't defend the astral idea further in this letter, other than to note that earliest Christian iconography supports it.)

The bottom line: Earliest Christianity was more like Docetism and earliest forms of Gnosticism. "Jesus," originally a title (still retained in many of the Nag Hammadi MSS that speak of "The Savior" instead of "Jesus") that became a personal name (in Greek it became identical to "Joshua") and then reified into a man with a biography. Docetism is older than Orthodoxy.

(6) It is easier and more parsimonious to reconstruct an evolutionary sequence leading from a Docetic mystery cult with Gnostic affinities than from an historical Jesus to Gnosticism. How can you evolve Thomas the twin of the Savior from Jesus of Nazareth? How could you have people asserting that Jesus of Nazareth didn't have a body — merely several decades after his supposed death?

(7) Only around 18% of all the characters of the NT are known to history, and in most cases the historical characters seem to have been portrayed unrealistically in the NT. Many of the remaining characters clearly are supernatural or made up as symbols. Is it not astounding that—with the arguable exceptions of James the Just and John the Baptizer—there is no historical evidence for the major players of the story? Shouldn't we have evidence of the Twelve Apostles/Disciples? Aren't they zodiacal

figures surrounding the center of a solar cult? Aren't Mary and Joseph clearly made-up characters known only to some of the gospel authors? The silence of history regarding twelve trouble-making apostles amplifies the silence concerning the silence regarding Jesus of Nazareth.[28]

Reading FORGED prompts me to make note of a number of particular things that you might find interesting and relevant to what I have said above.

First of all, Consider 1 Peter 5:1: "The elders which are among you I exhort, who am also an elder, and a witness of the sufferings of Christ, and also a partaker of the glory that shall be revealed..."

Is not the use of "Christ" anachronistic?[29] Would not the "real Peter" have spoken of the sufferings of his master Jesus? Wouldn't he have recalled a man rather than a title?

Secondly, the pericope adulterae: are you aware that this story jumps around? It can also be found in John 21 and Luke 21 in some MSS.

Thirdly, concerning the supposedly authentic Pauline letters: Have you ever read L. Gordon Rylands or van Manen and the other Dutch "Radical Critics"? They make a powerful case against the authenticity of ALL Pauline letters. In reading your discussion of Galatians 6:11 ("See with what large letters I am writing to you with my own hand") I am struck by the fact that this exemplifies so well the forger's use of verisimilitude—the technique you identify so masterfully as a forger's ploy. When "Paul" says "I am not lying," doesn't that give cause for suspicion?

28 It is truly surprising that no Historicist known to me even notices this problem, let alone explains it adequately. Yes, I know that this sentence is repetitiously redundant. I have given up all hope of winning a Nobel Prize in literature.

29 By "anachronistic" I meant in terms of the traditional presumption that theological evolution went from 'low' Christology to 'high.' In fact, however, it appears that 'Judaizing,' low Christologies are the end of the evolutionary line.

Frank R. Zindler

On page 193, concerning James the Just, you say that "The best historical records indicate that he died around 62 CE, after heading the Jerusalem church for thirty years." What "best historical records" are you referring to? Are you referring to Eusebius? I hope not. In a header somewhere in his Praeparatio Evangelica he notes that it is sometimes okay to deceive.

On page 155 you discuss The letter of Pilate to Claudius. I confess, I did not previously know of this letter. You say that "It may seem strange for Pilate to be writing to Claudius, in particular, given the fact that it was Tiberius, not Claudius, who was emperor when Pilate condemned Jesus to death..."

Does this not, however, support Irenaeus' contention that Jesus lived to be around 55 years old and lived into the reign of Claudius? Does not his fundamental disagreement on the placement of the "Historical Jesus" in history itself cause suspicion that we are not dealing with an historical character?

On page 167 you say that "... since the majority of Christians were from the lower, working classes, the weekly meetings as a rule took place either before the work day began, before, dawn, or after it was over, after sundown, that is, when it was dark." What actual evidence do you have that the first Christians were lower-class? This recently has been questioned and someone (I forget who, just now) has found that on the contrary, a very large number of earliest Christians were people of importance. This is of importance since it would undermine the argument against mystery-cult origins of Christianity by supporting the humble explanation for the "secret meetings" of early Christians. I wonder if you have actual data to support this claim or are just following the scholarly tradition.

I especially enjoyed your discussion on page 130 of the argument that falsely using the name of one's patron or teacher in the composition of a pseudepigraphon was common practice:

"I should point out that, as happens so often, neither of these commentators actually provides any evidence that this was a common practice in philosophical schools. They state it as a fact. And why do they think it's a fact? For most New Testament scholars it is thought to be a fact because, well, so many New Testament scholars have said so! But ask someone who makes this claim what her ancient source of information is or what ancient philosopher actually states that this was a common practice. More often than not you'll be met with a blank stare."

I could not have stated the argument against the ad populum fallacy better. It applies a fortiori to claims of the historicity of Jesus of Nazareth. Where is the evidence? Ten thousand historians accept the historicity of Jesus. Even Atheist historians say so. It's stupid to go against the evidence of so many authorities.

I ask you to perform a Gedankenexperiment. Imagine you are preparing to debate a mythicist. Since you will be affirming the positive existence of something, the onus probandi rests upon you. The mythicist need only show that your evidence is either not compelling or isn't even evidence.

You begin by listing a hundred or so historians and biblical scholars who affirm the historical existence of Jesus of Nazareth. After that, you... ? What beyond the ad populum "evidence" could you possibly adduce? Surely, after all the debunking you yourself have done, you cannot use the NT as evidence. What else is there?[30] In my book The Jesus the Jews Never Knew I show that the ancient Jews never heard of Jesus of Nazareth or even Nazareth. You have a copy of my book and can read it to see if my claim holds water or not.

30 The fact that this goading never elicited any response should have told me that no new arguments would be forthcoming in *DJE?* It really looks as though he knew that any 'evidence' he might present in an e-mail would easily be deconstructed and demolished. On the other hand, because of his conviction that I was completely unqualified to understand such matters, he may have thought he would be able to floor me with a book full of Josh McDowell apologetics and wanted to surprise me.

Frank R. Zindler

I know that I am an annoyance to you, and I don't relish playing the role of being an annoyance. However, you arguably now are the most famous NT scholar in America and for perhaps the first time in history you are succeeding in obtaining broad popular and scholarly acceptance for "radical" ideas in NT studies. You are perhaps the only scholar whose reputation could survive the advocacy of the mythicist position. More importantly, you would induce a paradigm shift in NT studies. This paradigm shift almost succeeded in the late 18th century and several times before WWII. Now, however, mythicist studies are building to a critical mass. With your contribution it could sustain a chain reaction and achieve liftoff.

I hope you have been able to read this far. Congratulations again on an excellent book.

Frank

It was of course a wan hope that Ehrman might become a Mythicist so quickly. Nevertheless, I kept the communication channel open.

On Jun 22, 2011, at 1:42 PM, "Zindler, Frank R." wrote:

Bart,

Six or eight weeks ago I ordered your Apocryphal Gospels texts book from Amazon and have kept getting notices that the book is not yet available. Do you have an estimate of when it will be out?

Frank

From: Ehrman, Bart D
Sent: Wednesday, June 22, 2011 2:00 PM
To: Zindler, Frank R.
Subject: Re: Publication date?

July 17 , I *think*.

-- Bart

Sent from my iPad. Apologies for typpos.

Bart,

Franx thanx for the quick reply. I am assuming the book includes the Coptic texts also. Is that correct?

Frank

From: Ehrman, Bart D
Sent: Wednesday, June 22, 2011 3:08 PM
To: Zindler, Frank R.
Subject: Re: Publication date?

We decided not to include Nag Hammadi texts, since they are already so easily accessible in a bilingual edition. But with one proviso: anyone using a book like this would be upset if we didn't include at least the Gospel of Thomas and the Gospel of Mary (not NH, of course, though included in NHL for the same reason)); so we included them, along with everything else, including the History of Joseph the Carpenter (and Gospel of Judas, etc.) Don't know if you know my collaborator Zlatko Plese. He's a premier coptologist.

-- B

Sent from my iPad. Apologies for typpos.

RE: Publication date? Coptic
Date: June 23, 2011 9:18:51 AM EDT

Bart,

Although I have encountered Plese's name several times, I do not own any of his works nor have I ever met him. He might have been sitting right beside me at the Coptic sessions at an SBL meeting and I would not have known it. My Coptic is still rudimentary, but I know enough to be able to zero in on items of interest for my research. As soon as I complete Volume V of my THROUGH ATHEIST EYES: Scenes From a World That Won't Reason, I have vowed to develop full working knowledge of at least Sahidic.

(By the way, did you get the four volumes of my collected short works that I sent to you several months ago? I hope they didn't get lost at the University.)

Also of interest: a year or two ago at an SBL meeting, a PhD candidate at Cambridge named Christian Askeland gave a paper titled "Was there a Coptic Translation of John's Gospel without Chapter 21?" Indeed, there was and he passed out photocopies of the last leaf of a codex(?) that ends with chapter 20. Curiously, instead of viewing this as confirmation of the long-understood fact that chapter 21 is a later addition, Askeland concludes

"The most likely explanation for the low quality of the papyrus, the rapid cursive hand, and the frequent rate of errors is that this manuscript was the product of an exercise in scriptural memory."

Indeed.

Hope you are enjoying a vacation. Are you in Greece?

Frank

Several weeks later, René Salm informed me that Ehrman was actually going ahead with a book to refute the Christ-Myth theory. Given the potentially pivotal position of Nazareth archaeology in that theory, and — quite frankly — doubting that he would actually read Salm's technically challenging book, I wrote a summary of the evidence against a settlement at 'Nazareth' at the turn of the era.

COGNITIVE DISSONANCE

Subject: Comments on Nazareth
Date: July 14, 2011 9:26:29 PM EDT

Bart,

I am very pleased to learn that you are going ahead with your book on the historicity of Jesus of Nazareth and are willing to make a serious effort to refute the Christ-Myth Theory. Even before your book is finished, I am certain it will be a valuable contribution to NT scholarship.

Rene Salm has told me that he is in communication with you concerning Nazareth. I am delighted to hear that you have read his book. As you already know, I am very pleased with his book and feel that it makes a powerful argument against the historicity of Nazareth at the turn of the era. It is perhaps of interest to you to learn that both Rene and I were led to question the historicity of Nazareth by reading Cheyne and Smith's ENCYCLOPAEDIA BIBLICA. In my own case, that led me to question the geographic reality of many other gospel sites, including Capernaum. (A popularized version of my Jesus Seminar paper on Capernaum can be found in Volume I of my collected short works in the chapter "Where Jesus Never Walked," if you care to learn the gist of my geographic studies.)

While most of what I wish to comment on here is found in Rene's book, reasoning is often more effective when condensed into lists of arguments and evidences than when scattered throughout a book. Consequently, I would like to itemize some important points relating to the reality of turn-of-the-era Nazareth.

(1) There is no isnad-like chain of attestation to support the Nazareth identity of the present city of Nazareth. There are at least several centuries separating the gospel habitation from the first verifiable and datable attestations of its location at the present site. (With the exception of Jerusalem, Jericho, Tiberias, and one or two other places, this is true also for nearly all the gospel towns and places.)

(2) Origen, although he lived at Caesarea, just 30 miles from Nazareth, did not know where it was located--even though he had made serious efforts to study the biblical sites. "We have visited the places to learn by inquiry of the footsteps of Jesus and of his disciples and of the prophets."

(3) Origen could not decide if the place was called Nazareth or Nazara, and the MSS of Luke show a stunning uncertainty as to the exact spelling of the name. Reuben Swanson's NT Greek MSS: Luke gives the following variants:

Nazara, Nazaret, Nazareth, Nazarat, and Nazared, and I think more variants could be found in MSS of the other gospels and Church Fathers.

If there actually had been a town with a definite name, how could such differences in spelling have arisen? To be sure, the difference between Nazaret and Nazareth (unaspirated vs. aspirated /t/) are minimal to our English ears, but to a speaker of Koine or Aramaic the difference between /t/ and /th/ was phonemic and would not likely have been confused. But how could Nazaret(h) be confused with Nazara? What actual city name could have given rise to both spellings? (I will discuss the origin(s) of the name later on below.)

(4) Eusebius, like Origen, lived at Caesarea and had occasion to concern himself with Nazareth. Interestingly, he almost certainly never visited the site himself, even though he mentions it in his Onomasticon. When one reads the Greek text concerning Nazareth, it sort of makes sense--until one tries to map out Eusebius' directions onto a map of Roman-era Galilee. It cannot be done. As I indicated, Eusebius himself was substituting handwaving for personal experience.

(5) Like many other holy places of the NT, Nazareth seems to have been discovered by Constantine's mother, with the aid of willing-to-please tour guides.

(6) Nazareth is unknown in the OT.

(7) The Talmud, although it mentions 63 Galilean towns, does not know anything of Nazareth.

(8) Josephus, although he waged war within two miles of Nazareth and fortified the town of Japha nearby, does not list Nazareth among the 45 cities and towns of Galilee in his experience.

(9) No geographer or historian before the 4th century mentions Nazareth.

(10) According to Luke 4:16-30, Nazareth was built atop a hill: 4:28 "And all they in the synagogue, when they heard these things, were filled with wrath, 29 And rose up, and thrust him out of the city, and led him unto the brow of the hill whereon their city was built, that they might cast him down headlong." The Franciscans, whom Rene Salm critiques, accordingly built their shrines on the side of the hill at "Nazareth." Unrealistically, the Biblical city had to be located on the top of the hill, not on the fertile floor of the valley below.

(11) Rene has shown that the Franciscan sites on the hill are not datable to the turn of the era. In doing so, he has refuted the Biblical claims at the same time that he has refuted the Franciscans. (Interestingly, no synagogue has ever been found atop the hill as would follow from Luke 4:29. Indeed, no buildings of any kind existed atop the hill until early modern times.)

(12) Although there doubtless was a city somewhere on the valley floor at the times of the tombs evaluated by Rene, it is extremely unlikely the valley floor was inhabited at the turn of the era. If it had been inhabited, abundant mortuary and agricultural remains clearly datable to that period would be found on the hillside. As you (Bart) well know, the task of the historian is to discover what is or was PROBABLE, not just what is or was POSSIBLE. In science, the onus probandi rests upon the one

positing the existence of a process or thing. Without sufficient evidence forthcoming, the scientist cannot accept the reality of the process or thing posited.

(13) Unlike the case of other archaeological sites that date with certainty to the first centuries BCE and CE, virtually no coins datable to that period have ever been found at Nazareth. By contrast, hundreds to thousands of coins are typically recoverable from other sites inhabited at that period.[31]

(14) Rene has shown that the excavation techniques at Nazareth were completely unscientific, lacking all knowledge of stratigraphic techniques--or at least scorning such techniques in favor of what might be called apologetic archaeological methods. When one reads Bagatti's publications, the Tendenz is palpable--even in Italian! Like "creation scientists," the Franciscan "archaeologists" knew what they needed to find before they started to dig. What a surprise! They found it!

(15) After the publication of Rene's book, a Christmas announcement was made of the discovery of "new evidence" dating from the days of Jesus. Rene gives a full explanation of the "evidence" in a supplement to his book. I hope he will supply a copy of that to you, as it completely deflates the claims. The claims are related rather closely to the projects of the Nazareth Farm Project, a multimillion-dollar theme park[32] planned for the Nazareth Hill. Interestingly, to date none of the claims have yet been published in any scientific journal. Even Jodi Magness has taken note of this "evidence," although she agrees with me that Bethlehem of Judea was not inhabited at the turn of the era (as

31 Recently, claims have been trumpeted about alleging that a small number of Hasmonean coins have been discovered somewhere at Nazareth. Unless those coins are confirmed by at least *hundreds* of other, contemporary coins, we must conclude that the reports derive either from archaeological incompetence or from something even more sinister.

32 Despite this warning, Ehrman uncritically cites the 'evidence' from this commercial operation on page 195 of *DJE?*

shown by Aviram Oshri, the Israeli archaeologist.) It is important that you get this supplemental information from Rene.

(16) Nazareth is never mentioned in ANY of the epistles. Paul NEVER talks about "Jesus of Nazareth," and probably wouldn't have had any idea as to who that might have been. It is clear to me, at least, that even the name "Jesus" was the end of the titular evolutionary line. First was "Christ" (although probably spelled chreistos or chrEstos, not christos). Then came "Christ Jesus," then "Jesus Christ." Belatedly came the name of power, the magical name "Jesus" at which every knee would bow. (I'm sure you are well aware of the early magical literature in which "Yaaysooos" is like the shem: a magical word of command and power.) Although "Lord Jesus" is moderately frequent, "Jesus" alone is rare compared to "Christ" alone. Again, the evolution of divine epithets never gets up to "Jesus of Nazareth."

(17) Nazareth is not mentioned in the Apocalypse.

(18) Nazareth is found only in the Gospels and Acts.

(19) Nazareth is found only ONCE in Mark, Mark 1:9. This seems clearly to be an interpolation made at a time when **"Jesus" had become a name instead of a title meaning "Savior."**[33] The name "Jesus" is inarticulate in this verse, as opposed to at least 80 other places in Mark where the name carries the definite article: "the Jesus," as in "the Savior." It is well to ask the question here, "If verse 9 is authentic, why is it that Mark never mentions Nazareth again, even though he reports events that the other gospels site at Nazareth?"

(20) I have already noted that it is almost impossible to account for the variants "Nazara" and "Nazaret(h)" deriving from a single name of a single place. Rather, it seems evident that both names have been formed by back-formation from an adjective

33 Ehrman unfairly ridicules my argument concerning the lack of the definite article before 'Jesus' in Mark 1:9, apparently refusing to mention this important point.

or title in the way "Paris" could be derived from "Parisian" or "Greece" from "Jimmy the Greek." The question is, what might that descriptive word have been? As you know, the Greek epithets given to Jesus in the gospels are "NazOraios," "NazarEnos," and variants thereof. Presumably, these should be derivable from Aramaic or Hebrew terms that would be of relevance to our character. Rene and I differ somewhat in our derivations, and so I speak only for myself at this point.

In my opinion (and also in the opinion of William Benjamin Smith, who also had the nom-de-plume of "Criticus"), the Hebrew antecedent is the word "netser"--meaning "sprout, shoot," or "branch." It is found most prominently in Isaiah 11:1: "And there shall come forth a rod out of the stem of Jesse, and a BRANCH shall grow out of his roots." As you know, this verse was popular at Qumran. You may not know, however, that according to Epiphanius, before Christians were called Christianoi, they were called Iessaioi--Jessaeans. I think this clearly relates the word "netser" to early Christianity.

The relationship between "netser" and both "NazOraios" and "NazarEnos" seems very strong. The sequence N-Ts-R and N-Z-R is very close when one remembers that the Greek zeta was pronounced [dz] at the turn of the era. That would make it the voiced equivalent of tsadi [ts] in Hebrew. I do not know if tsadi was voiced in intervocalic position in ancient Hebrew or not, but almost certainly [ts] would have become [dz] when dragged into Greek. Thus, Jesus of Nazareth would originally have been "Jesus the Branch"--as in "Branch Son-of-David-ian." (Actually, "Branch Son-of-Jesse-an"!)

Before continuing with this very lengthy e-mail message, it is necessary that we stop to see what became of this technical linguistic argument on page 192 of *DJE?*. Ehrman's misunderstanding or misrepresentation of point 20 above would be embarrassing even if it were written by an undergraduate at a mediocre college:

> Zindler maintains that some early Christians understood Jesus to be the "branch" mentioned in Isaiah 11:1, who would come from the line of David as the messiah. The term *branch* in Hebrew (which does not have vowels) [*sic*!!!] is spelled NZR, which is close (kind of close) to *Nazareth*. And so what happened, in Zindler's view, is that later Christians who did not understand what it meant to call Jesus the NZR (branch) thought that the traditions that called him that were saying he was from a (nonexistent) town, Nazareth.
>
> Zindler does not marshal any evidence for this view but simply asserts it. And he does not explain why Christians who did not know what NZR meant simply didn't ask someone. Even more important, he doesn't explain why they made up the name of a nonexistent town (in his view) to locate Jesus or how they went from "Jesus is the NZR" to "Jesus *came from* Nazareth."[34] The view seems completely implausible, especially given the fact, which we have seen, that multiple independent sources locate Jesus in Nazareth. Moreover, there is the additional evidence, which we will see momentarily, that Nazareth did in fact exist as a small Jewish town in the days of Jesus.

Where to begin? Hebrew doesn't have vowels? Even if what was meant was that the *word* for 'branch' would have been written without vowels, could so sloppy a sentence have been written by the same person who edited and translated the Loeb Classical Library edition of the Greek text of the Apostolic Fathers? Why is Ehrman showing me as using *NZR* as a *Hebrew* word, instead of the consonantal skeleton of a *Greek* word representing the Hebrew *N-Ts-R* (*netser*), the word for 'branch'? Why does he not understand that I was deriving the names *Nazara* and *Nazaret(h)* by 'back formation'

34 Although I had no firm opinion at the time I wrote the e-mail above as to *why* N-Ts-R would be turned into the name of a town, in the course of research for the present book I think I have come up with a convincing explanation: Nazareth was invented to provide a home town as well as a physical existence for Jesus in order to counter the claims of Docetic Christians who believed that Jesus had no real, flesh-and-blood body. If a home town name was *not* a made-up name, it is hard to explain the two competing variants of the name found in the New Testament and church fathers—*Nazaret(h)* and *Nazara*. If the town had really existed, how could the first Christians have become confused as to its *real* name?

from the Greek epithets *Nazoraios* or *Nazarenos*, not directly from N-Ts-R—*and not at all from N-Z-R* (although other scholars whom I respect do thus derive the names)? Why doesn't Ehrman criticize my linguistic/phonetic argument? Why doesn't he even mention that I *have* such an argument?

Ehrman quips, "Zindler does not marshal any evidence for this view [!] but simply asserts it. And he does not explain why Christians who did not know what NZR meant simply didn't ask someone." Neither Josh McDowell nor Lee Strobel could have made a sillier comment. Exactly whom would those Christians have asked? When and where and under what circumstances would they have made such inquiry? Would anyone even *think* to ask someone "Where does Jimmy the Greek come from?"

But to return to my e-mail of July 14, 2011:

> (21) It seems clear that "Jesus of Nazareth" was the end of the evolutionary line for this character in the canonical NT. Almost certainly, he started as a heavenly Christ, but probably not a Christos having messianic signification. The Sibylline double acrostic spells the name ChREISTOS, and Irenaeus (Against heresies, B.I, ch. 15) tells us that "the name Christ the Son (Uios Chreistos) comprises twelve letters... Moreover, Chreistus, he [Marcus] says, being a word of eight letters, indicates the first Ogdoad."
>
> It is likely that early MSS of the epistles would have spelled the title Chreistos, not Christos. The latter would have evolved out of the iotacism that overtook the Greek language at this time. "Chreistos" and "ChrEstos" would both have been pronounced "ChrIstos," and once a messianic connection had been made, would have been the spelling thereafter. The Gnostics, however, seem here as elsewhere to have retained many early traditions and usages. Exactly what "Chreistos" would have meant in early Christianity, however, I do not know and am trying to discover. It is maddening that the MS traditions are of little help here, as only rarely are nomina sacra spelled out. One cannot tell from

the written symbols how the words might actually have been spelled.

All for now.

Frank

PS: Beelzebul has just taken possession of me and is making me type the following comment: "If the Docetists had won the theopolitical battles of the first four centuries, no one today would be debating the physical historicity of Jesus."

Readers who have managed to read my detailed and lengthy message and are still awake at this point may wonder if they will be able to make it through Ehrman's critique and rebuttal to my exhausting arguments. I ask them, however, to persevere to the end. As they say in Italian opera, *Coraggio*! You can do it! Here is his reply:

Sent: Friday, July 15, 2011 3:59 AM
Subject: RE: Comments on Nazareth

Frank,

Interesting argument. Thanks for passing it along. All best,

--Bart

To be fair, though, please note the time stamp on the message. Several hours later the same night, he sent the following message:

From: Ehrman, Bart D
Sent: Friday, July 15, 2011 5:38 AM
To: Zindler, Frank R.
Subject: your book

Frank R. Zindler

Frank,

As it turns out, I've started this morning reading through some of your essays in vol. 1 of your multi-volume magnum opus. Question: is your c.v. available anywhere? And could you explain (would you mind?) how supporting Madalyn Murray O'Hair forced you to leave SUNY? Sounds like there's an interesting story in there.

- Bart

Bart D. Ehrman
James A. Gray Professor
Department of Religious Studies
University of North Carolina at Chapel Hill

The next night I sent him the following reply, attaching a chapter from my yet unpublished memoires detailing how I was forced by county politicians in Upstate New York to give up a nearly twenty-year career as a teacher and professor at SUNY because of my Atheism and support of Madalyn Murray O'Hair in a lawsuit to remove "In God We Trust" from American currency. Not giving up hope that he was still genuinely interested in understanding Mythicist evidence and arguments, I recommended for study my article demonstrating that the Twelve Apostles/Disciples were every bit as unknown to history as was their master.

From: Zindler, Frank R.
Sent: Saturday, July 16, 2011 1:06 AM
To: Ehrman, Bart D
Subject: Zindler story

Bart,

I'm pleased to hear you are looking at some of the stuff

in Volume I of my collected short works. (Actually, it doesn't contain any of my papers for the Jesus Seminar and a bunch of other things such as my legal writings.) Among the things you might want to critique is my chapter "The Twelve: Further Fictions From the New Testament." As you know, I notoriously deny the historicity not only of Jesus of Nazareth but also of the Twelve Apostles/Disciples. As I love to say, the silence of history concerning Jesus is amplified by the silence concerning the Twelve Apostles. The whole purpose of the Twelve was to get attention and be noticed, yet history knows no more of them than of their alleged master.

In any case, it is an honor to have a scholar of your caliber read what I have written even if only to continue to disagree.

Concerning my c.v. and the SUNY/O'Hair epic. I am in the throes of writing my memoirs and will take the liberty of copying parts of several chapters into the message below. These are not finished and will doubtless have to be revised as other parts of the book materialize. Even so, there doubtless will be more here than you really want to know. But I would assume you are a speed-reader even in Greek. ;-)

Frank

Six hours later, it appears he had read my story, but not my comments on 'The Twelve.'

From: Ehrman, Bart D [mailto:behrman@email.unc.edu]
Sent: Saturday, July 16, 2011 7:12 AM
To: Zindler, Frank R.
Subject: RE: Zindler story

Thanks. Scary!

- Bart

Frank R. Zindler

Bart D. Ehrman
James A. Gray Professor
Department of Religious Studies
University of North Carolina at Chapel Hill

Because American Atheist Press was about to publish Dr. Robert Price's *The Christ-Myth Theory and Its Problems*, it seemed desirable to send a pre-publication copy of the book to Ehrman.

Subject: RE: Zindler story2
Date: July 18, 2011 11:14:44 AM EDT

Bart,

The printing of Bob Price's THE CHRIST-MYTH THEORY AND ITS PROBLEMS is being delayed. I expect that I will have a pdf of the book to send him for proofing by the end of the week or early next week. At that time I will send it to you also, so you can include it in your critique. Bob sums up a lot of history of the theory and includes quite a bit of original research as well. It is a rather definitive statement.

Frank

PS I'll try to find a c.v. for you.

Frank

From: Ehrman, Bart D
Sent: Monday, July 18, 2011 11:51 AM
To: Zindler, Frank R.
Subject: RE: Zindler story2

OK, thanks. Are you the publisher at American Atheist Press?

■ B

COGNITIVE DISSONANCE

Bart D. Ehrman

Subject: RE: Zindler story3
Date: July 18, 2011 12:36:34 PM EDT

Yes, since the murder of the Murray-O'Hair family in 1995 I have been the managing editor of American Atheist Press.

Frank

Several weeks passed and then I received the first-ever request for evidence concerning Mythicism and Historical-Jesus studies. It was mildly challenging and had the odor of Church-of-Christ apologetics—apologetics that for many years has denied not only that Christianity began as a mystery cult—certainly a justifiable thing to deny—but also that Christianity at no time had ever absorbed mystery-cult elements.

From: Ehrman, Bart D
Subject: evidence question
Date: August 5, 2011 10:01:10 AM EDT

Frank,

I have a question about some of your claims; I'm not disputing them at this point – but I'm wondering what your authority for them is (i.e., how you know that what you say is right?). Just to pick an example, on p. 64 (of vol. 1 of Through Atheist Eyes) you indicate that Mithra was said to have been born of a virgin on Dec. 25. What makes you think so? I.e., who says that in the ancient world? And so on – that Mithra was worshipped on a Sunday; that he was depicted with a halo; that the leader of his cult was called pope and ruled on the Vatican hill; that his followers celebrated his atoning death; and that he was resurrected on a Sunday. What's the evidence for any of these statements/claims?

Many thanks,

■ Bart

Frank R. Zindler

As welcome as the inquiry was, its timing was awkward. I was away from my library and felt an urgency in supplying the requested information. For reasons now forgotten, I was expecting his book to be published in November or December of that year and knew that he would have to complete his book well ahead of that time. I had to tread water, although as everything turned out his book came out much later than expected and none of the information I would eventually supply to him would find a place in *DJE?*

From: Zindler, Frank
Subject: Mithraism
Date: August 9, 2011 12:26:32 AM EDT
To: Ehrman, Bart

Bart,

Sorry to be so late in reply. I'm traveling in Northern Michigan and haven't checked my e-mail in several days. On top of that, for some reason my Blackberry isn't sending out e-mails reliably and so I had to wait to get to a hotel with Wi-Fi so I could use a lap-top.

As you realize, Volume I is composed of articles written for a popular audience, not a scholarly one. While some of the work in them goes back to primary sources, often the press of deadlines forced me to rely on what appeared to be reliable secondary sources such as Cumont and Ulansey. Such was the case with many of my claims concerning Mithras, although I did examine a large amount of iconographic and archaeological evidence at the time and spent some amount of time puzzling over the so-called Greek "Mithras Liturgy." Over the years, however, I have collected many books giving primary sources for much of the Mithraic mysteries, mostly Greek and Latin authors such as Gregory Nazianzen, Plutarch, Porphyry, Tertullian, Julian the Apostate, Fermicus Maternus, Plutarch, Statius, Dio Cassius, and even Justin Martyr. (I can't remember offhand if Irenaeus weighs in on Mithras or not.)

The stuff about haloes, December 25, virgin birth, etc. has been "common knowledge" amount [*sic*] anthropologists, comparative mythologists, religionsgeschichtliche sholars, and others for over a century now, and until recently I had little reason to question these claims. Many of them derive from Mithraic art and iconography and it is only necessary to cite the particular artifacts and summarize the interpretive arguments associated with them. The case of Mithras is made difficult and confusing by his pleiomorphic nature. Like most deities, he was associated and equated with a host of other deities at one time or place or another. Multiple myths attach to his origins: born of a rock, born of a virgin, born in a cave/stable, etc. In any case, little or no textual material used by the Mithraists themselves has survived (it was, after all, a secret mystery cult), and all we have are the descriptions and invectives of the church fathers and some other ancient writers.

I think I will be able to find an ancient source for all of the stuff you have queried when I get back home this coming weekend. If there are any for which I cannot find a source, I'll have to eat some non-Mithraic crow. [The crow was one of the Mithraic icons, probably the constellation Corvus.]

I hope you will be able to comment on my Prolegomenon as a statement of method. I also hope you will read my "The Jesus the Jews Never Knew: Sepher Toldoth Yeshu and the Quest of the Historical Jesus in Jewish Sources"--including the two appendices containing multiply annotated versions of the Toldoth. Many of my commentary notes therein have broad significance beyond the Toldoth.

If you have other questions, please don't hesitate to ask them.

Frank

A day later, I heard from Ehrman again. For once, he was actually taking notice of something I had written and was actually expanding the focus of discussion. I was overjoyed.

Frank R. Zindler

From: "Ehrman, Bart D"
Date: Wed, 10 Aug 2011 17:20:50 +0000
To: Frank Zindler
Subject: RE: Mithraism

Frank,

Thanks. Yes, I know Ulansey's work quite well, and Cumont, who is no longer regarded as a reliable source. Roger Beck is more "the guy" now. Since all the evidence is archaeological / material (no texts at all!) I don't know where Dec. 25 to a virgin, pope, etc, etc. comes from, although I know everyone repeats it. My suspicion is that everyone thinks it's right because everyone says so!

All best,

■ B

Although this note seemed reasonable at the time, after the publication of *DJE?* some things are worth noting. For one thing, Ehrman's reference to authority is not the sort of *citation* of authority found in scientific practice. In science, "authority" is cited not only to avoid having to reinvent the wheel, but also to give credit or blame for information not the reported discovery of the instant author. "Cumont, who is no longer regarded as a reliable source" not only reveals Ehrman's fixation on authority *qua* authority but betrays his ignorance of Cumont's work apart from his popular *The Mysteries of Mithra*. He seems not to understand that Cumont published most of the *primary, factual data* upon which most interpretations of Mithraism depend. While one may argue that Cumont misinterpreted or misunderstood the *significance* of the artifacts he reported, could Beck or anyone else dispute the reality of the "Mithréum de Sarmizegetusa" whose partial floor plan is depicted on page 280 of Vol. II of his *Textes et Monuments Figurés Relatifs aux Mystéres de Mithra* [1896]?

While it is arguable who had the responsibility to supply the evidence requested, the final sentence of this note is of interest: "My suspicion is that everyone thinks it's right because everyone says so!" Why is it his mere *suspicion*? Why doesn't a famous scholar have a firm, knowledge-based opinion? Did he himself make any preliminary investigation that turned up nothing—as I did for a Historical Jesus in my first encounter with Mythicism—and then decide that there was little point in further searching? Or was he confident that the claims of the traditional apologists were correct and simply did what I would have done in such circumstances—put the burden of proof on the person making an outrageous ontological claim?

It certainly appears that Ehrman had no real knowledge of the primary sources concerning Mithraism let alone the voluminous literature investigating possible mystery-religion ties to primitive Christianity. In any case, I eagerly commenced the search to find answers to his questions.

From: Zindler, Frank
Subject: RE: Mithraism again
Date: August 12, 2011 6:10:56 PM EDT

Bart,

To facilitate this conversation it would be greatly appreciated if you would respond to all 3 of my e-mail addresses above. That way, whether I'm at home, at work, or on the road I will be able to respond in a timely manner. I know it's a bother, but I hope you won't mind doing that.

I have had Roger Beck's work for several years now but have never had time to see exactly where he claims to correct Cumont and Ulansey. I know some of his criticisms but will have to check them out this weekend.

Concerning Cumont, however, his great 2-vol. Textes et Monuments, etc., gives a great deal of documentation for most of these claims, if not all. (I'm still checking.) There are actually quite a few comments and descriptions by church fathers and other early authors. However, a lot can be inferred from ancient coins, inscriptions, remains of mythraea, artwork, etc.[35] For example, coins and bas-reliefs depicting Mithra as sol invictus sporting a halo would clearly indicate a winter solstice birth. I'm still tracking down specific artifacts to cite.

You may be amused to learn that Ulansey disagrees strongly with my precession theory. Even though he argues that "later Mithraism" was created in response to the movement of the vernal equinox from Taurus into Aries, he completely rejects my claim that Christianity was the response to precession from Aries into Pisces, despite the fact of the sacrifice of the lamb replacing the sacrifice of the bull and the fishes (plural) being the earliest symbol for Christianity (except possibly for the chi-rho cross of Chronos, or the simple chi-cross that I think symbolizes the intersection of the celestial equator with the ecliptic). He was quite shocked when I proposed this at an SBL meeting some years ago. So, at least there is one thing in Ulansey's thought with which you might agree! ;-)

While the great scholars of the 19th century and early 20th century certainly made a number of mistakes about all kinds of things, for the most part they were really smart cookies and it is always wise to check them out carefully before rejecting their claims. It is possible, of course, that virgin birth etc. has just been repeated endlessly without foundation, I think that is not probable. In fact, I think I have already found an explanation for the virgin birth part, but I need yet more documentation. I hope I'll be able to give you a reasonable report by Sunday night or Monday. I'm having trouble locating books and manuscripts

35 It is really quite shocking to realize that a scholar as famous as Ehrman would not have known of the classical and patristic literature concerning the mysteries. Surely, if he had ever taken a course in epigraphy he would have understood the importance of inscriptions, coins, art, *etc.* not only with regard to Christian origins but for understanding as well the social world of the first Christians. Surely, he would have encountered *some* Mithraism-related information. It is unfortunate that I had to tell him about this. It is much more unfortunate to discover that none of the information I was to send him had any effect on what he wrote in *DJE?*

in my library, which is not cataloged and pretty much fills up 11 or 12 rooms of my house. …

Frank

Ehrman did not acknowledge receipt of this e-mail.

From: Zindler, Frank
Subject: Zindler reporting
Date: August 14, 2011 11:50:36 PM EDT

Bart,

I had hoped this evening to send you a first installment of my answers to your questions but will only be able to make a bare beginning. Just when I planned to start writing, I received an important e-mail from Robert Eisenman and have spent nearly two hours dialoging with him on important matters …. (By the way, he agrees completely with Salm and me that "Nazareth" was not inhabited around the turn of the era.)

I regret that there will be little logic in the sequence with which I deal with your questions. You would really chuckle, if not laugh out loud, if you could have seen me this weekend running upstairs and downstairs from library to library and file cabinet to file cabinet trying to locate books and papers. My whole house is a repository for books and manuscripts and the tons of correspondence associated with AAP publishing as well as with my research. In any case, I have not yet nailed all the questions but have at least some worked out to my own satisfaction and hopefully to yours as well.

My general impression in looking through Roger Beck's books is that although we disagree on some astrological specifics in interpreting the tauroctony, we agree on many essential points. He is not as rejecting of Cumont as general opinion would have it. Curiously, though, he seems not to have paid much attention to numismatics, which brings me to the question concerning halos.

Frank R. Zindler

[At this point I break off conversational discourse and merely present data.]

HALOS

Franz Grenet (2003) "Mithra, dieu iranien: nouvelles données," *Topoi* 11, pp. 35-58, gives illustrations of a number of coins and seals showing Mithra with a halo.

His Figure 1 shows the head of Mithra on a Bactrian coin of Soter Megas (ca. 80-100 CE) in profile with short rays emanating from his hat and an indented halo surrounding not only his head but the entire representation of his head and shoulders.

Grenet's Figure 2 shows a figure of Mithra on a Bactrian coin of Huvishka (ca. 153-91 CE). Mithra is standing and a rayed nimbus surrounds his head. In addition a whole-body indented halo surrounds the whole picture. It is sort of like the whole-body halo painted around the Virgen de Guadalupe.

His Figure 5 shows the Sassanian monumental bas-relief at Taq-e-Bostan commemorating Shapur II's victory over Julian the Apostate. Mithra, with long-spiked radiate halo, stands on the left behind the king who receives a ribboned ring from Ohrmazd (Ahuramazda).

Figure 6 shows a royal seal of the Greco-Bactrian king Plato (ca. 145 BCE). This shows Mithra as Helios driving a quadriga. The head and shoulders of Mithra are surrounded by a simple-line halo from which in turn emanate rays.

Figure 7 is a Sogdian wood relief depicting Mithra as Helios with his quadriga (only two horses showing).

Figure 8 is a drawing of the painting of Mithra that once decorated the soffit of the niche that contained a 38-meter Buddha at Bamian until 1999 when it was destroyed by the Taliban even before the destruction of the buddhas themselves. It too shows a whole-body indented halo around Mithra being born from the top of Mt. Hara, as described in the *Mihr Yasht*.

Last, but not least, Grenet's Figure 9 depicts an Eastern Sasanian seal depicting Mithr and dating to the late 4th or 5th centuries. This shows the head and torso of Mithra emerging from the top of Mt. Hara (a pile of spherical rocks) as *Mithra petrogenus*. The visible part of Mithra is surrounded by a single-line halo from which emanate long solar rays.

Thus, like all solar beings, Mithra was often depicted with halos.

That's all for now. More to follow tomorrow.

Frank

Ehrman did not acknowledge receipt of this e-mail.

From: Zindler, Frank
Subject: Fwd: Zindler reporting2
Date: August 15, 2011 11:50:58 PM EDT

Bart,

In trying to track down sources with which to answer your questions I have stumbled into a number of Iranian Web-sites dealing with things Mithraic. It appears that there is a substantial apologetic industry thriving in Iran that seeks to discredit Christianity as being derived from Mithraism. What a hoot! It doesn't seem to occur to the Web-sters that by discrediting Jesus they are discrediting one of the Qur'an's prophets as well. Of course, the writers may not really be believing Muslims.

There is, as you probably are aware, a major evangelical apologetics industry in America that seeks to prove that Christianity owes nothing to Mithraism and even that Mithraism is later than Christianity and stole its doctrines from Christianity! Twenty or so years ago I debated a Church of Christ apologist on Cincinnati radio who claimed just that. I pointed out that many Christian churches were built on the ruins of Mithraea, indicating that on those sites, at least, Mithraism got there first. I also pointed out that Mithra [Vedic Sanskrit *Mitra*] was mentioned as a major god in the Rig Veda around 1,500 BCE, and that an entire hymn was devoted to him [Book III, Hymn 59].

I cannot remember the name of my opponent, but I asked him something like "what do you call the pointy hat that Roman Catholic bishops and some popes wear?" He answered "A miter." "Why is it called a miter?" I asked. He not being able to answer me, I explained: "The name of the hat in Latin is *mitra*, exactly the same as the Latin name for *Mithra*. Why do you think that is? Do you think the Mithraists named themselves after a Christian hat?"[36]

[Concerning the mutation Skt. *mitra* > OPrs. *mithra* > Gk. *mithras* > Lat *mitra* I would suggest that the Vedic Sanskrit /t/ probably was a dental *t*. In Avestan and other Old and Middle Persian languages, the cognate sound would also have been a dental, but could have been aspirated or even a fricative /θ̣/. At the time this would have been borrowed into Greek and spelled with a theta, it is well to remember that theta at that time was not the dental spirant θ of Modern Greek. Rather, it was simply an aspirated dental *t* /th/ such as the English *t* in *at*. In Latin, *t* and θ were not separate phonemes. A Roman would not have perceived any difference between *mitra* and *mi*θ*ra*. Both would be pronounced *mitra*.]

Time did not allow elaboration, but I mentioned that early Christian writers such as Justin Martyr [*Dialogue with Trypho*, 70], Tertullian [*De corona*, 15], Origen [*Contra Celsum*, 3:33], and Firmicus Maternus [*De errore*, 22:1] as much as admitted the priority of Mithraism and other mystery religions when they fumed that the

36 It was a crushing disappointment that Ehrman didn't mention this fact when he misrepresented and criticized my claims about Mithraism [*DJE?* 212]: "According to Zindler, the cult figure of the Mithraists, the Persian god Mithras, was said to have been born on December 25 to a virgin [my actual words were "born of a virgin on the winter solstice—frequently December 25 in the Julian calendar"]; his cult was headed by a ruler who was known as a pope, located on the Vatican hill; the leaders of the religion wore *miters*..." [emphasis mine]

rituals and doctrines of the mysteries were counterfeits of Christianity laid out by the devil.

Unfortunately, I did not think of Robert Price's argument of many years later [*Night of the Living Savior*, "The ruin of rationalism," p. 186]: "Had the early Christian apologists been aware of pagan poaching of Christian themes, would they not have made as much of it as modern apologists make when they merely surmise it? Would the ancient Christians ever have fielded such a suicidal argument as this? It is fully as ridiculous as the ancient claim of Philo of Alexandria, who liked to allegorize the Torah as teaching Greek philosophy, that Plato had derived his metaphysics from the Pentateuch of Moses."

I also could have used to advantage the argument of Richard Reitzenstein [*Hellenistic Mystery-Religions*, English translation 1978, p. 149 as cited by Price, *op. cit.*, p. 183]: "... in procedures and perspectives in which Christianity is in agreement with several different pagan mystery-religions, the priority is probably to be credited to the latter. A borrowing of cultic *terms* from Christianity by paganism is more difficult to conceive; here the burden of proof always falls on the person who would assert the priority of Christianity... By way of justification I may add only that most of the Christian authors probably knew something of pagan literature, while only very few of the pagan writers would have known anything of Christian literature, and that in general conversion from paganism to Christianity was more common than conversion from Christianity to paganism. Until this is proved to me to be erroneous, I shall hardly be able to abandon these guidelines, and I must wait for proof that Christianity has influenced the pagan mysteries."

THE EUCHARIST

It is clear from the protestations of Christian apologists that the Mithraic Eucharistic rite was very similar to that of Christianity.

Since we know that Mithraism in some form or other goes all the way back to the Bronze Age, we can be sure that this similarity was not due to Mithraism borrowing from Christianity. Consider Justin Martyrs *First Apology* [Chapter 6]:

"For the apostles, in the memoirs composed by them, which are called Gospels, have thus delivered unto us what was enjoined upon them; that Jesus took bread, and when He had given thanks, said, 'this do ye in remembrance of Me; this is My body;' and that, after the same manner, having taken the cup and given thanks, He said, 'This is My blood;' and gave it to them alone. Which the wicked devils have imitated in the mysteries of Mithras, commanding the same thing to be done. For, that bread and a cup of water are placed with certain incantations in the mystic rites of one who is being initiated, you either know or can learn." [*Ante-Nicene Fathers*]

Then there is the wide-ranging denunciation of the Mithraists by Tertullian [*De paraescriptione haereticorum*, 40:3-4, Geden translation]:

"The devil (is the inspirer of the heretics) whose work it is to pervert the truth, who with idolatrous mysteries endeavours to imitate the realities of the divine sacraments. Some he himself sprinkles as though in token of faith and loyalty; he promises forgiveness of sins through baptism; and if my memory does not fail me marks his own soldiers with the sign of Mithra on their foreheads, commemorates an offering of bread, introduces a mock resurrection, and with the sword opens the way to the crown. Moreover has he not forbidden a second marriage to the supreme priest? He maintains also his virgins and his celibates."

VIRGIN BIRTH OF MITHRA This will have to wait for tomorrow.

Good night for now.

Frank

Ehrman did not acknowledge receipt of this e-mail.

From: Zindler, Frank
Subject: Fwd: Zindler reporting3
Date: August 18, 2011 12:46:08 AM EDT
To: Ehrman, Bart

Bart,

Sorry again for the delay. Ann's computer died, ... and I haven't had any time for fun. In any case, the delay has caused my train of thought to become derailed and all my plans to organize my reports have unravelled. Consequently, I shall have to report answers and partial answers as they come off the piles of books and print-outs.

First, a postscript on the priority of Mithraism: Cassius Dio, in Bk 63, Ch. 10 of his *Roman History* tells of the visit of the Armenian king Tiridates to Nero: "I, my lord [Nero], am son of Arsaces, and brother of the kings Volegeses and Pacoras, and thy servant. And I am come to thee as my god, to worship thee as I worship Mithra, and I will be as thou shalt determine. For thou art my destiny and my fate." [Geden translation] So, Nero was being worshiped as Mithra long before we have any epigraphic or historical record of Christian worship.

Before going into virgin births, I want to reprise the quote from Tertullian and make a few further comments.

Tertullian [*De paraescriptione haereticorum*, 40:3-4, Geden translation]:

"The devil (is the inspirer of the heretics) whose work it is to pervert the truth, who with idolatrous mysteries endeavours to imitate the realities of the divine sacraments. Some he himself sprinkles as though in token of faith and loyalty; he promises forgiveness of sins through baptism; and if my memory does not fail me marks his own soldiers with the sign of Mithra on their foreheads, commemorates an offering of bread, introduces a mock resurrection, and with the sword opens the way to the crown. Moreover has he not forbidden a second marriage to the supreme priest? He maintains also his virgins and his celibates."

This shows that Mithraism practiced baptism to wash away (original) sins. As you know, the Romans had the idea of original sin before it came into Christian theology. Tertullian (*De Baptismo*, 5) notes that "For in certain rites also of an Isis or Mithra initiation is by means of baptismal water."

Mithraism practiced chrismation—the mark on the forehead. (My guess is that the mark was either the chi-cross [the figure imitating the angle of intersection of the celestial equator with the ecliptic path of the sun through the zodiac] or the chi-rho cross, the original symbol for Chronos/Kronos according to a papyrus found at Pompei/Herculaneum. Mithra was equated with Kronos as well as Apollo and Sol Invictus as I shall show below.)

While the "mock resurrection" does not explicitly imply the resurrection of Mithra, it is entirely compatible with the idea. Moreover, since Mithra was a sun god (proof to follow shortly), he would have been a dying and rising god like all the other sun gods. We must remember here, that we are not considering biological, terrestrial events. We must put our minds into the skulls of the average ancient educated person who knew more practical astronomy—and astrology—than the average modern person with a BS majoring in astronomy. [I currently am doing computer modeling of the positions of the planets, constellations, and movements of the vernal equinox along the zodiac at the turn of the era to get a better handle on what exactly the Mithraists and first Christians would have seen and pondered over when they looked up to the sky at night.]

For well over a century, mythicist scholars have argued that the "resurrection" of sun gods phenomenologically is simply the rising of the sun above the celestial equator at the time of the vernal equinox. "On earth as it is in heaven." That is why the Christian resurrection is celebrated in spring around March 21. The "death" of a sun god occurs, correspondingly, at the time of the autumnal equinox, when the sun sinks below the celestial equator. Thus, even without the slightly cryptic comment of Tertullian about mock resurrection, we would know that Mithra died and was resurrected by virtue of the simple fact that he was a sun god.

While I'm on the subject of astronomy/astrology, I might as well add a few more points. Just as sun gods must die in autumn and be resurrected in spring, so too they must be born at the winter solstice, when the sun is at its lowest point below the equator. From that low-point, it "grows" as it climbs to the equator. The sun's fire is rekindled around December 25 (the approximate date of the winter solstice in the Julian calendar).

It is curious that when Christianity trumped the growth of the Baptist cult it had JB be born exactly six months before JC. JB's feast day is the summer solstice! Jn 3:30: "He must increase, but I must decrease." When Jesus the sun is rising upwards toward the celestial equator beginning on December 21/25, JB has already arrived at the summer solstice and is beginning his descent toward the equator. "He must increase, but I must decrease." Interestingly, the Synoptics give JC a sun god's "life" of just one year. Because his life-path is a circle (the circle of the ecliptic), JC is simultaneously the Alpha and the Omega—as is the case for every point in the circumference of a circle![37]

I must tell you that it wasn't easy for me to get into an astrological frame of mine, especially after having studied astronomy (and even taken an honors course in astrophysics) at the University of Michigan. However, studying the ancient philosophers and poets I became convinced that they all were thinking in an astrological world of reference. I have just finished a close reread of the *Aeneid* and the *Eclogues* and am seeing astrology all over the place.

37 I fear that all this information pertaining to astronomy and astrology must have generated far too great cognitive dissonance for Ehrman even to understand my arguments let alone treat them fairly in *DJE?*

Frank R. Zindler

MITHRA THE SUN GOD

Since much of the above argumentation requires Mithra to have been a sun god, I shall now make good on my promise above. Consider, first, the *Clementine Homily* VI.10:

"And I must ask you to think of all such stories as embodying some such allegory. Look on **Apollo** as the wandering **Sun** (Peri-Polôn), a **son of Zeus**, who was **also called Mithras**, as completing the period of a year. And these said transformations of the all-pervading Zeus must be regarded as the numerous changes of the seasons, while his numberless wives you must understand to be years, or generations."

So, Mithra is Apollo, the sun god, and acquires all the characteristics of that deity.

Before proceeding to other proofs of the solar equivalence of Mithra, I must again bemoan the problems and tribulations encountered when dealing with ancient religion/mythology. The rules of scientific or mathematical logic simply do not apply. One is three and three are one, and yet each one remains separate and distinct. Mithra is Sol Invictus is Apollo is Helios is Kronos is Saturn is... (and Saturn can be equated with Yahweh!) And yet each god keeps his name. So, if Sol Invictus was born on December 25, Mithra was born on that date also. However, if it could be shown that one of those equivalent gods had been born on some other date, Mithra too could have acquired that other birth date was well! Are you getting dizzy?

Strabo (*Geographica*, XI.14) tells us that "The Persians therefore do not erect statues and altars, but sacrifice on a high place, regarding the heaven as Zeus; and they honor also the **sun**, whom they call **Mithra**, and the moon and Aphrodite and fire and earth and the winds and water." [Geden translation]

Quintus Curtius (*History of Alexander*, Bk 4, Ch. 13) describes the scene before the battle of Arbela: "The king himself with his generals and staff passed around the ranks of the armed men, **praying to the sun and Mithra and the sacred eternal fire** to inspire them with courage worthy of their ancient fame and the monuments of their ancestors."

Cumont cites several scholia on Lucian's *Zeus Rants* and *The Parliament of the Gods*:

"*This Bendis...* Bendis is a Thracian goddess, and Anubis is an Egyptian [god], whom the *theologoi* call 'dog-faced.' **Mithras** is Persian, and Men is Phrygian. This **Mithras is the same as Hephaestus**, but others say [he is the same as] **Helios**."

"*Mithrês* [*Mithras*]... **Mithras is the sun** [**Helios**] among the Persians.

Then there is the Oxyrhyncus papyrus POxy 1802, a glossary of foreign words: "**Mithras**: **Prometheus**, according to others **the sun** among the Pers[ians]."

The *Wikipedia* article on Mithraism notes that "An altar or block from near SS. Pietro e Marcellino on the Esquilline in Rome was inscribed with a bilingual inscription by an Imperial freedman named T. Flavius Hyginus, probably between 80-100 AD. It is dedicated to ***Sol Invictus Mithras***." [The reference here is confusing. This is either CIMRM 593 or CIMRM 362.]

The Web-site of the Vatican Museum carries a photograph of a bas-relief of a tauroctony [no catalog number given] with the dedication to ***SOLI INVICTO DEO***. 'Nuff said.

MITHRAISM AND VATICAN HILL

The Vatican Museum holds at least three tauroctonies, but no provenances are given. Many books from the 19th and early 20th centuries make the claim that there was a Mythraeum on Vatican Hill, and it seems likely that one of these tauroctonies was taken from it. In this regard, I would like to quote two pages of my translation of Arthur Drews' *Die Petruslegende* of 1910 [*The Legend of Saint Peter: A Contribution to the Mythology of Christianity*, by Arthur Drews, translated by Frank R. Zindler, Austin, American Atheist Press, 1997]:

"In Rome there exists a so-called 'chair of Peter,' allegedly connected to the 'first Roman bishop.' In reality, however, its decoration shows it to be derived from the Mithra cult. In particular, it shows the zodiac as well as the labors of the sun god on its front side,[94] and allows absolutely no doubt that the priest who exercised his powers of office from the chair was not the Christian, but rather the Mithraic *Pater Patrum* [Father of Fathers] or the *Pater Patratus*—as the high priest of the Persian rock god chose to be called. Like the present ruler of Roman Catholic Christianity, he too had his See upon the Vatican Hill. Moreover, he enjoyed the protection of Attis, the dying and resurrecting young god of the Phrygian mysteries formerly recognized by the state, who with his mother Cybele, the archetype of the Christian Mary, had long been worshipped upon the Vatican Hill.[95] Attis also bore the name of Papa, i.e., "Father." And "Father" simultaneously is the name assumed by the high priest of this god who, like the "Successor upon the throne of Peter," wore a tiara upon his head and likewise possessed the power "to bind and to loose." [that from page 40; on page 65 Drews returns to the subject of the chair: "There is, of course, the so-called *sella gestatoria*, 'the chair of peter,' which he is supposed to have used when he was the first bishop. It was exhibited publicly for a while in the sixties of the last century, but then prudently it was withdrawn again from the gaze of the profane crowd. That it had no relationship with Peter was only too apparent."

"There upon the Vatican Hill, where the faithful were 'absolved of their sins' by means of a solemn baptism in blood in the sanctuary of Attis and Mithra—upon that spot is where Peter is supposed to have found his end during the Neronian persecution of Christians. It is the place where the dome of St. Peter's was erected over the so-called 'grave of the Apostle.' [See my chapter "Of Bones and

Boners: Saint Peter at the Vatican" in Volume I for more information about this spot.] It is where originally stood the temple not of the Christian, but rather the pagan, 'man of rock.' It is simply Attis under the name Agdistis, as we have said, a stone-god, one born from rock, a *Peter*. [96]

The references given are:

[94] See the illustration in Franz Xaver Kraus' edition of *La Roma Sotterranea Cristian*a, by Giovanni Battista de Rosse, p. 505.

[95] The Phrygian Cybele is the same as the Babylonian Ishtar, the Egyptian Isis, etc. All these Near Eastern goddesses of earthly abundance and fertility serve simultaneously as mothers and virgins (in consequence of the fact that the constellation Virgo rises in the eastern sky at the time of the winter solstice, when the sun god is born. See Alfred Jeremias: *Babylonisches im Neuen Testament,* p. 35, Note 1; p. 47) and are represented as sitting with the heavenly infant upon their laps.

[96] Compare overall: W. Köhler, *Die Schlüssel des Petrus*, Archiv für Religionswissenschaft VII, 1905, pp. 214-243. Also, Robertson, *Christianity and Mythology*, 1900, pp. 378-384; and his *Pagan Christs*, pp. 331*ff*; 355*ff*.

I am still trying to find archeological evidence for a Mithraeum on Vatican Hill. There are Mithraea near by on the Campus Martius, and all over the rest of Rome. If there *weren't* any on the Vatican Hill, that itself would by [*sic*] a mystery in need of explanation! But in any case, I am continuing to search.

Partial support for Drews' claims come, of all things, from the Web-site of the Vatican Museum, which shows an altar dedicated to Cybele and Attis: "The shrine of the Phrygian goddess Cybele, from which numerous inscribed altars come, was situated in an unidentified place **near the Vatican Basilica**."

Well, I still haven't gotten to Virgin births. Oh, well, perhaps tomorrow...

Frank R. Zindler

Frank

Ehrman did not acknowledge receipt of this e-mail.

From: Zindler, Frank
Subject: Re: Zindler reporting4
Date: August 19, 2011 12:05:10 AM EDT

Bart,

I haven't gotten any "hopped-the-pond" automatic responses, so I assume you're receiving these reports. I will tonight, in fact, finally get to the virgin birth of Mithra. I don't have it nailed down to my complete satisfaction, but I'm getting close.

Temporarily I have stopped paging through my fifty-some books relating to Mithraism and the other mysteries and have been searching on-line as faster, albeit sometimes quite frustrating as in the instant case. There is a popular, English-language women's Web-site called www.irandokht.com. On it I found an article by a certain Manouchehr Saadat Noury, PhD, titled "First Iranian goddess of productivity and values," dealing with the ancient Iranian goddess Anahita. After showing a picture of the great Temple of Anahita at Kangavar, the article says that

"By the HELLENISTIC era (330—310 BC), if not before, Anahita's cult came to be closely associated with that of MITHRA.

"The ANAHITA TEMPLES have been built in many Iranian cities like Kangavar, Bishapur (an ancient city in south of present-day Faliyan) and other places during different eras. **An inscription from 200 BC dedicates a SELEUCID temple in western Iran to "Anahita, as the Immaculate Virgin Mother of the Lord Mithra."** The ANAHITA TEMPLE at Kangavar city of Kermanshah (a western province in present-day Iran) is possibly the most important one. It is speculated that the architectural structure of this temple is a combination of the Greek and Persian styles and some researchers suggest that the temple is related to a girl named Anahita, the daughter of din Mehr, who enjoyed a very high status with the ancient Iranians."

This nicely takes care of the virgin-birth question and points out further parallels between Mithra and Christ/Jesus, the title "Lord" and perhaps even an immaculate conception notion anterior to that of the Virgin Mary Theotokos. Unfortunately, the article doesn't even say what language the dedication is written in, although being Seleucid one would suppose it to have been in Greek. It doesn't say exactly where in "western Iran" this temple is, nor, perhaps not surprising for a popular article, does it give a reference to pursue. I have e-mailed IranDokht to see if I can get more information on this. Meanwhile I will continue to search the standard works.

How, then, can Mithra be born of a virgin (Anahita) and yet be born of rock? Again, caution must be exercised: we cannot expect logic. Rather, something akin to stream-of-consciousness may be the metaphor of choice here.`Websters-dictionary-online.org may unknowingly supply an answer. In its article on Anahita, we read:

"As a cosmological entity

"The cosmological qualities of **the world river** are alluded to in Yasht 5 (see in the Avesta, below), but properly developed only in the Bundahishn, a Zoroastrian account of creation finished in the 11th or 12th century CE. [Worrisomely late!] In both texts, **Aredvi Sura Anahita is not only a divinity, but also the source of the world river and the (name of the) world river itself.** The cosmological legend runs as follows:

"All the waters of the world created by Ahura Mazda originate from the source Aredvi Sura Anahita, the life-increasing, herd-increasing, fold-increasing, who makes prosperity for all countries. This source is at **the top of the world mountain Hara Berezaiti, "High Hara,"** around which the sky revolves and that is at the center of Airyanem Vaejah, the first of the lands created by Mazda. ...

"In the Bundahishn, the two halves of the name "Ardwisur Anahid" are occasionally treated independently of one another, that is, with Ardwisur as the representative of waters, and Anahid identified with the planet Venus.[20] In yet other chapters, the text equates the two, as in "Ardwisur who is Anahid, the father and mother of the Waters" (3.17).

"This legend of **the river that descends from Mount Hara** appears to have remained a part of living observance for many generations. **A Greek inscription from Roman times found in Asia Minor reads 'the great goddess Anaïtis of high Hara**.'[21] On Greek coins of the imperial epoch, she is spoken of as 'Anaïtis of the sacred water.[20]"

[20] Boyce 1983, p. 1004 [Boyce, Mary (1983), "Āban," *Encyclopaedia Iranica*, Vol. I, New York: Routledge & Kegan Paul]

[21] Boyce 1975a, p. 74 [Boyce, Mary (1975a), *A History of Zoroastrianism*, Vol. I, Leiden/Köln: Brill]

As I noted in my first report, there are coins depicting Mithra emerging from the top of "High Hara." That being a concrete datum from which to begin, we may imagine the mythic mind to reason forward that since Mithra was born of Mt. Hara, and since Mt. Hara is also the virgin goddess Anahita, Mithra was born of the virgin Anahita. Reasoning backward from Mt. Hara, one might argue that since Mt. Hara is made of rock, Mithra was born from rock(s).

Another way to look at the virgin/rock puzzle is the following: Anahita is the goddess of waters, yes, but also she is a mountain of rock. She seems to be the equivalent of Gaia. You don't have to be a Hesiod to see the similarity between a god being born from an earth-goddess and a god being born of a rock-goddess.

I can't remember what else you wanted me to document. Let me know if there are other points I should address. As I explained, some of my answers are not yet complete, and I am continuing to search as time allows. Nevertheless, I am increasingly confident that all the major claims about Mithraism made by the major mythicists of the last 150 years can be documented. I am increasingly in admiration of their scholarship. Fully documenting some particulars might, however, be difficult and time-consuming. Imagine being challenged to demonstrate conclusively that George Washington crossed the Delaware River on December 25, 1776. To be sure, you would be able to do it, but I don't think it would be very easy.

While I must confess that I have not completely been able to give fully satisfactory answers to your questions, a solid beginning has been made. It is well to pull back and get a more panoramic view of our discussion. In some of my writings I try to demonstrate that there is no good evidence to indicate the historicity of Jesus of Nazareth, the Twelve Apostles, much of Gospel geography, etc. I point out that the *onus probandi* of necessity is on the person who claims the existence of a thing or process. That is the rule of science, and it must be the rule of any credible historiography.

In other writings such as the one presently in dispute I attempt to explain how the Jesus biography could have come into being if there was no Jesus of Nazareth to serve as a condensation nucleus. **Even if it could be shown that every one of my hypotheses were false, it would not add one whit of evidence to support the claims of the historicity of Jesus**. In fact, my theory (I use the term advisedly) is constantly evolving. While there is little in my "How Jesus Got a Life" that I think is wrong, I now would markedly alter the emphasis on certain points and add a lot of extra components to the mix. I am not stuck to any Tar-Baby hypothesis. I am free to admit errors and set out on any new path that leads to better evidence. I am confident that you can do this too.[38]

Please let me know that you have received this stuff.

All the best,
Frank

38 To my profound dismay, Ehrman gave no hint that I ever told him anything like this when he ridiculed and misrepresented this essay in *DJE?*

Frank R. Zindler

Ehrman did not acknowledge receipt of this e-mail.

From: Zindler, Frank
Subject: Fwd: Zindler reporting5
Date: August 19, 2011 10:37:08 PM EDT

Bart,

I guess I need to thank you for your mildly challenging e-mail of several weeks ago concerning page 64 of Volume I of my *Through Atheist Eyes*. I was actually moving away from my emphasis on the importance of Mithraism in the origins of Christianity. After having been "encouraged" to look into the foundations of Mithraic studies, however, I am now beginning to think I did not emphasize the connection enough. To be sure, I have not had time to nail down all my claims as solidly as you probably would like, but it seems increasingly clear to me that all the great scholars going back to Charles Dupuis in the 1790s weren't all that far off the main highway.

As I catch up on Mithraic studies I find myself being diverted from one interesting finding to another and can't hang on to any particular topic to research it to conclusion. It's kind of like it was many years ago when I decided to read *Webster's Collegiate Dictionary* all the way through. My bookmark might have been on page 123 but in reopening the book my eyes might fall on a word on page 145 and I would get interested on page 145 and only with difficulty could I tear loose to go back to page 123.

A case in point: I was flipping through pages of various books (most of these books either have no index at all or indices that are minimally useful) looking for Vatican Hill Mithriaca. I picked up Volume II of *Mithraic studies: Procedings of the First International Congress of Mithraic Studies* (John R. Hinnells, Editor, Manchester Univ. Press, Rowman and Littlefield, 1975).

I opened the book to the last chapter, chapter 30, "Mithras and Christ: some iconographical similarities," by A. Deman Brussels. In examining the tauroctony from the Heddernheim mythraeum, Brussels finds evidence for the birth of Mithras at the winter solstice, sacrifice at the vernal equinox, etc. Brussels then goes on with numerous illustrations of Christian art to show the structural and thematic parallels to Mithraic models—including evidence to support my claim that the 12 Apostles are zodiacal equivalents. I am going to check out his (?) references to works I don't own at the OSU library. (Ohio State has a surprisingly good classics library.)

All the best,

Frank

Surprisingly, Ehrman did not acknowledge receipt of this e-mail.

From: Zindler, Frank
Subject: Fwd: Zindler reporting6
Date: August 21, 2011 12:34:39 AM EDT

Bart,

I think I found one of the references to Mithriaca on the Vatican Hill that I failed to cite when writing my "Of Bones and Boners: Saint Peter at the Vatican." I was heavily involved with the epigraphic and other works of Margherita Guarducci at the time and I just came across a related item in M.J. Vermaseren's *Corpus Inscriptionum et Monumentorum Religionis Mithriacae* (Martinus Nijhoff, 1956, Vol. I, p. 205.)

The entry is #515:

Marble altar, found in S. Peter's square some meters northern of the Apostle's statue in 1949.
Ghetti-Ferrua e.o., *Espl. S. Pietro*, 14f; *Ann. Ep.*, 1953 No. 238.

Diis magnis / M(atri) d(eum) m(agnae) I(daeae / Attidi sancto menotyranno / Alfenius Ceionius Iulianus / Kamenius v(ir) c(larissimus) VII vir epul(onum) / **pater et hieroceryx sacr(orum)**

s(ummi) i(nvicti) / Mitrae hierofanta Haecatae / arch(i)bucolus dei Liberi / aram taurobolio criobolio/que percepto dicabit / die XIIII kal(endis) aug(ustis) d(omino) n(ostro) Gratiano /Aug(usto) III et Equitio cons(ulibu)s.

19th of July 374 A.D.; *cf.* CIL VI 499 = Dessau, No. 4147 from the same provenance and of the same date. The exact situation of **the Phrygianum in the Vatican city** is unknown, but Margherita Guarducci, *Cristo e S. Pietro in un documento preconstantiniano della Necropoli Vaticana*, Roma 1953, 66 holds it to be situated probably "a sinistra dell' odierna gradinata fra l'arco delle Campane e il Camposanto Teutonico."

Alfenius Ceionius Iulianus Kamenius died in Antium in 395 A.D. (**see No. 206**). He occurs in the following inscription, **which certainly belongs to the same sanctuary**. Cf. O. Seeck in RE III col. 1864 No. 31; H. Bloch in HThR XXXVIII, 1945, 211.

Item 206 is found on page 111 of Vol. I and contains a touching poem and a dedicatory inscription:

Inscription from Antium, found at San Donato in 1884.
Eph. Ep. VIII, 648; MMM II No. 147.
Inter avos proavosque tuos sanctumque parentem
Virtutem meritis et honoribus emicuisti,
Ornamentum ingens generis magnique senatus.
Sed raptus propere liquisti, sancte Kameni,
Aeternos fletus obiens iuvenalibus annis.
Te dulcis coniunx lacrimis noctesque diesque
Cum parvis deflet natis, solacia vitae
Amisisse dolens casto viduata cubili;
Quae tamen extremum munus, solacia luctus,
Omnibus obsequiis ornat decoratque sepulcrum.

Alfenio Ceionio Iuliano Kamenio v(iro) c(larissimo) quaestori candidato /

pretori triumfali, VII viro epulonum, **patri sacrorum summi** /

invicti Mitre, hierofante Aecatae, archibucolo dei Liberi, XV viro /

s(acris) f(aciundis), tauroboliato deum Matris, **pontifici maiori**, consulari / Numidiae et vicario Africae qui vixit annos XLII m(enses) VI d(ies) XIII. /

Rec(essit) II nonas septembr(es) d(omino) n(ostro) Archadio et Fl(avio)

Bautone v(iro) c(larissimo) cons(ulibus).

385 A.D.

Kamenius is also stated in two inscriptions from Rome (See our Nos 515; 516), but there he is still *magister et pater sacrorum*, whereas at his death he bears the grade of *pater patrum*.

Sancte: No. 486.

I won't bother copying the text of #516 as it covers much of the same ground as the inscription just quoted.

I really see no need to doubt that the Mithraists were on Vatican Hill. They were on every other hill in Rome, and some very special explanations would be required to account for their absence on just one of the seven. What better place to stash a *Pontifex Maior*?

Will your book be available on more than one electronic platform? Kindle?

Frank

Ehrman did not acknowledge receipt of this e-mail.

Frank R. Zindler

CONCLUDING DISSONANCE

Bart Ehrman is a scholar who thinks and works in the same 'paradigm'—the same common-sense framework—as that in which Scholastic philosophers, theologians, biblical scholars, poets, romantics, and humanistic historians work. I, on the other hand, gave up thinking in that paradigm at the age of fifteen or sixteen. Since then, I have come to think and work in a hard-headed scientific paradigm. That means that I, when faced with a claim that some thing or process exists or occurs (or once existed or occurred), lay the burden of proof on the person making the existential claim. Ehrman, however, would seem to think that any claim is 'innocent until proven guilty'—that it can be taken seriously until conclusive proof *against* it is forthcoming. As a scientist, when *I* make an existential claim I must not only offer compelling evidence to support it, I must work hard to see if anywhere there lurks evidence against my own claim. As a bible scholar, however, Ehrman not only sees evidence supporting his own views in the flimsiest of arguments, he simply *cannot see* the evidence against his own claims even when they are clearly pointed out to him. Not only does he not seek out disconfirming evidence on his own, he seems not to recognize or apprehend disconfirmation when it is right in front of his nose.

Ehrman thinks within a religious paradigm in which *appeal* to authority not only is valid, it is a requirement. "*Sola scriptura*!" "The Bible says…" "Every qualified historian knows…" I, however, *cite* 'authority' for two purposes: (1) to avoid having to reinvent the wheel, and (2) to indicate where credit or blame should be assigned for work not done by me personally. For me, 'Seeing is Believing'—*seeing* must come before belief. For Ehrman, 'Believing is Seeing'—what he *believes* shapes what he sees.

When anyone is suddenly translated from one frame of reference to another—from one paradigm to a different one—the result is usually what is called 'cognitive dissonance.' Cognitive dissonance is a state of confusion in which one can neither reorient the self in the new landscape nor even locate the major landmarks within it.

COGNITIVE DISSONANCE

Cognitive dissonance is the mental condition in which one writes books like *Did Jesus Exist?* after reading the e-mails reprinted in this chapter. It is the mental condition in which one transforms the simple arguments and evidence of my correspondence with Ehrman into the outrageously distorted and misleading representations of them to be found in his book.

Fortunately, cognitive dissonance is an unstable state—it cannot last forever. If Ehrman continuously is forced to deal with arguments and corrections emanating from the world of science, eventually he will be able to attain a new equilibrium. Experiments in sensory psychology have shown that people made to wear glasses with inverting lenses at first cannot even walk without falling down. Eventually, however, their whole world turns 'right-side-up' and a new perceptual normality asserts itself.

No evidence exists that is sufficient to prove the Historicist thesis, and Mythicists with compelling evidence against it will not give up and go away. The dispute between Mythicists and Historicists is like the struggle between a starfish and a clam. The muscles of the starfish are not very strong, but they have extraordinary endurance. The muscles of the clam, however, are very strong, but tire out quickly. The starfish clasps the clam and tries to pull its shells apart in order to inject digestive enzymes between them to digest the clam. The clam clams up more tightly to resist the starfish. Eventually, however, the massive muscles of the clam become enfeebled. The result? Except for the shell, the clam itself becomes transformed into a starfish. Eventually, the cast-off empty shell may come to be seen as having been functionally useless and empty all along.

Not unlike the clam, 'Jesus of Nazareth' will also be transformed. Almost certainly, the scholars of the future will not *call* him 'The Jesus of Oz,' but that surely is how he will be classified.

CHAPTER FIVE

Did the Earliest Christians Regard Jesus as 'God'?

A critique of Pages 231–240 of *Did Jesus Exist?*

Earl Doherty

This chapter examines the earliest Christian understandings of the nature of Jesus.

- ***Did the earliest Christians see Jesus as 'God'?***
  - *'God' vs. 'an emanation of God'*
  - *Concepts of 'the Son' and 'Logos' : Paul and Philo*
  - *Epistolary descriptions of 'the Son'*
- ***The Synoptic Jesus: 'Man' or 'God'?***
  - *Why Mark's divinity for Jesus is subdued*
- ***The figure in the Philippians hymn: human or divine?***
  - *'Nature' vs. 'image' in the Philippians hymn*
  - *Yet another 'likeness' motif*
  - *What is the "name above every name"? 'Jesus' vs. 'Lord'*
  - *Another smoking gun*

* * * * *

Earl Doherty

Was Jesus 'God'?

Bart Ehrman embarks on what is probably the thorniest problem in New Testament research. How was Jesus regarded, not only by his followers, but by the earliest Christians who spread the faith? Ehrman declares:

> ...the earliest Christians did not consider Jesus God.... scholars are unified in thinking that the view that Jesus was God was a later development within Christian circles. [*DJE?* 231]

But what precisely is meant by the phrase 'Jesus was God'? Much of the problem lies in Ehrman's semantic woolliness. Later Church Councils declared Jesus fully a co-equal with God the Father, of the same substance, two 'persons' within the Trinity. I am aware of no scholarship, let alone any Mythicist, who suggests that this was the view of any segment of earliest Christianity.

But to say that Jesus was an *emanation* of God is something else. The difference between Paul's *Son of God* and Philo's *Logos* as 'an emanation of God' is largely a matter of personhood. Philo does not personalize his Logos; he calls it "God's first-born," but it is not a distinct *person*; rather, it is a kind of radiant force which has certain effects on the world. Paul's *Son* has been carried one step further (though a large one), in that he is a full *hypostasis*, a distinct divine personage with an awareness of self and roles of his own — and capable of being worshiped on his own.

An emanation, however, is not God *per se*. That is why Philo can describe him as "begotten of God." He can be styled a part of the God-head, but he is a subordinate part. (I have no desire to sound like a theologian, but to try to explain as I see it the concepts that lie in the minds of Christian writers, past and present. They are attempting to describe what they see as a spiritual reality; I regard it as bearing no relation to any reality at all.) Paul in 1 Corinthians 15:28 speaks of the Son's fate once God's enemies are vanquished, a passage which exercises theologians because it looks incompatible with the Trinity. For here Paul says that the Son "will be subjected" to God, in the apparent sense of being 'subsumed' back into God, who will then become

One again — "so that God will be all in all." There will only be one 'person.'

The 'intermediary Son' concept

There can be little question that the idea of the Son, Paul's 'Christ' and spiritual Messiah, arose from the philosophical thinking of the era, which created for the highest Deity intermediary spiritual forces and subordinate divine entities to fill certain roles and to be revelatory channels between 'God' and humanity. In Judaism, this was the role of personified Wisdom, though her divinity was relatively innocuous and her 'person' perhaps as much poetic as real. (She may have been a later scribal compromise when an earlier goddess consort of Yahweh was abandoned). In Greek thinking, the intermediary force was the Logos, though in varied versions (the Platonic Logos and Stoic Logos were quite different), and with an independence and personification less developed than Paul's.

Thus 'the Son' which we find described throughout the epistles is viewed in the sense of an emanation of God, not God himself. He has a personification of his own, and he fills certain roles.

Consider three passages:

- **1 Corinthians 8:6** – For us there is one God, the Father, from whom all being comes, toward whom we move; and there is one Lord, Jesus Christ, **through whom all things came to be**, and we through him.
- **Colossian 1:15-20** – [God] rescued us from the domain of darkness and brought us away into the kingdom of his dear Son, in whom our release is secured and our sins forgiven. **He is the image [*eikōn*] of the invisible God**; his is the primacy over all created things**. In him everything in heaven and on earth was created** . . . **the whole universe has been created through him and for him**. And he exists before everything, and **all things are held together in him**. . . .

- **Hebrews 1:2-3** – . . . the Son whom he has made heir to the whole universe, and **through whom he created all** orders of existence: the Son who is **the effulgence of God's splendor and the stamp of God's very being, and sustains the universe** by his word of power.

All three passages present the Son as **the agent of creation (as was personified Wisdom in Jewish tradition).** Two mention his **sustaining power by which the universe subsists**. They also see this emanation as *making the ultimate God 'visible'*: he is the "image" of the Father who is known and communicates with the world through this filial intermediary. In Colossians, his redemptive role is mentioned: through him sins are forgiven and humanity has been released from darkness. (About the only thing never mentioned is the alleged fact of this cosmic Son's incarnation to earth and his identity in that life, but perhaps this was considered unimportant.)

Though Ehrman will argue against it, there can hardly be any question that these epistle writers viewed the Son as a heavenly figure, a part of God who existed on the spiritual plane. That this was an interpretation of the man Jesus of Nazareth is a post-Gospel rationalization, not to be found in the epistles themselves. That some modern scholarship can go further, as we shall see, and regard the epistolary picture as not indicating a belief in its Jesus as divine — whether equal or subordinate to God — is a travesty.

No Jesus as God in the Gospels?

We must now ask, who exactly constituted "the earliest Christians" who Ehrman says did not see Jesus as God? Here is where his argument becomes tangled. For rather than considering the situation in the epistles, Ehrman zeros in on the Gospels:

> It is striking that none of our first three Gospels — Matthew, Mark, and Luke — declares that Jesus is God or indicates that Jesus ever called himself God. Jesus's teaching in the earliest Gospel traditions is not about his personal divinity but about the coming kingdom of God and the need to prepare for it. This should give readers

> pause. If the earliest followers of Jesus thought Jesus was God, why don't the earliest Gospels say so? It seems like it would have been a rather important aspect of Christ's identity to point out. [*DJE?* 231]

Perhaps as the epistles ought to have pointed out, the cosmic Son's human incarnation was an important aspect of *his* identity? Be that as it may, Ehrman, as demonstrated earlier in this series, has jockeyed and massaged the evidence — including fabricating some of it — to produce a dubious witness (indeed, many "independent" ones) prior to the epistles, one which supposedly represented an oral tradition phase which later fed into the Gospels. This alleged tradition, he says, reflected the Synoptic presentation of Jesus as anything but cosmic — as apparently nothing other than human.

'Son of God' vs. 'son of God'

As the first plank in his case, Ehrman points out that many individuals in the Old Testament, such as Solomon, were referred to as "son(s) of God," which did not make them God. Rather,

> (Solomon) was instead a human who stood in a close relationship with God, like a child to a parent, and was used by God to mediate his will on earth. . . . When the future messiah was thought of as the son of God, it was not because he would be God incarnate but because he would be a human particularly close to God through whom God worked his purposes. [*DJE?* 232]

The Synoptic Gospels do indeed downplay the divinity of their Jesus, although there are a few pretty strong suggestions that there is more to being Mark's "S/son of God" than Ehrman has allowed. Mark in 13:32 says:

> But about that day or that hour [the arrival of the End] no one knows, not even the angels in heaven, not even the Son; only the Father.

Here, "the Son" implies a singular spiritual aspect of God (thus needing capitalization, which all translations that I know of give it), inhabiting heaven like the angels. It is not even sure that Jesus is intended to be referring to himself here, just as it hardly seems that he himself is supposed to be the messiah whom he prophesies impostors in the future will be claiming to be. Mark seems to prefer that Jesus think of and refer to himself as the Son of Man, but even this tradition has grown out of a previous expression in the Q tradition wherein such a figure is an apocalyptic one, expected from heaven and thus possessing at least some form of divinity.

Mark's divinity of Jesus

But then Mark throws off the covers in 14:61–2 before the High Priest's questioning: "Are you the Messiah, the Son of the Blessed One?" The latter, of course, means God, and Jesus answers: "I am." Not only is this reference to "the Son" hardly to be put into Ehrman's category of a human particularly close to God, the High Priest declares this claim to be blasphemy, for which Jesus needs to be condemned to death. It was hardly blasphemy to announce oneself as the messiah, nor even the apocalyptic Son of Man; and certainly not to call oneself a "son of God" in Ehrman's sense. It could only be blasphemy if Jesus was declaring himself to be a divine part of God.

We might also wonder at God's extreme reaction to the crucifixion, both in prodigies of nature and in his abandonment of his Chosen People by splitting the veil of the Temple, if this was only a man he felt a close relationship with. And the centurion's reaction would have been an ironic understatement if all Mark wanted him to say was: "Truly, this man was one whom the Jewish God felt particularly close to!"

Besides, what was to be the point of Mark's whole story by including the Passion? Jesus as God's prophet is one thing: "Repent, for the kingdom of God is at hand!" Mark's ministry — though short on actual teachings, let alone memorable ones — might fit a "son of God" of the Ehrman variety. But a trial, execution and rising from his tomb? Something foretold in scripture (as Jesus constantly tells his disciples), whose purpose was a "redemption for many" [Mk. 10:45]? It is difficult to think that Mark would have created such a tale simply in terms of an individual whom he thought of as merely one among many who had been "sons of God."

Distinguishing between Gospels and Epistles

What Ehrman and historicism fail to take into account is the division between the Gospels and the epistles, two quite separate phenomena on the first century scene. The Synoptics grew out of the kingdom-preaching movement of which Mark was a part, represented in Q. (The Johannine community later attached itself to their Jesus character and story). Thus Mark and his redactors were creating an allegorical tale based on quite human traditions: the teachings and activities of the Q prophets themselves and an imagined founder figure who had been developed only later as the sect evolved; that founder was given no death and resurrection, let alone a dimension as part of their god.

The Passion in Mark's Gospel was an insertion into that tradition, quite possibly based on a syncretization with some expression of the heavenly Christ cult (though probably not directly from Paul). That amalgamation with Galilee kept the 'S/son of God' aspect given to Mark's Jesus character on a noticeably lower plane than is found in the epistles. Still, Mark could not avoid according his Jesus some measure of divinity, a personal connection to God whose nature is perhaps hard to pin down from the text. Certainly, he was unable to avoid creating anomalies which would bedevil future scholarship.

The situation in Acts

By claiming an oral tradition origin for the Gospels, Ehrman has transferred the later picture created by Mark to a pre-Pauline period and presented it as the earliest view of Jesus. He backs that up by pointing to the speeches in Acts which allegedly portray Jesus of Nazareth according to a pre-Gospel tradition that Jesus was a human being who was only adopted as 'son of God' in the sense of 'a man special to him' — and then only at his resurrection. That Acts maintains the latter point is by no means clear, and it is hardly compatible with Ehrman's own conviction that Acts was written by the same author who wrote Luke.

Besides, such an adoption only upon resurrection would imply that in his preceding life God did *not* treat the man Jesus as anyone special. That is hardly a view that would have been held by any early Christian, let alone Jesus' former followers. Ehrman has failed to demonstrate that Acts could not have been founded entirely in the Gospels themselves. Given an increasingly popular dating for Acts in the second century, nothing in it can be securely allotted to an initial period of the faith, especially prior to the epistles.

The christological hymn of Philippians 2:6–11

At this point, Ehrman's case becomes thoroughly entangled. For he embarks on a consideration of the christological hymn in Philippians 2:6–11. But this is from the epistolary record, and yet he is offering it as an illustration of how he claims early Christians viewed Jesus not too long after his death. He will use this hymn to show that such a view was simply of Jesus as a "son of God" in the 'special man' category. That certainly bucks centuries of scholarly interpretation, though he points out that the hymn in just about every one of its lines is "much debated" — as is its very identity as a poetic liturgical piece, one of several in the epistles which are regarded as pre-Pauline creations. Still,

> But one thing is clear: it does not mean what mythicists typically claim it means. It does not portray Jesus in the guise of a pagan dying and rising god, even if that is what, on a superficial reading, it may appear to be about. [*DJE?* 233]

One wonders how it can be "clear" that it does not portray Jesus as a dying and rising god, while at the same time it "appears" to be just that on "superficial reading." This alerts us that the "superficial" text is going to need some spin doctoring to overcome that plain reading and render its true meaning "clear." Nor do mythicists need to overplay the "*pagan* dying and rising god" claim; Judaism was capable of coming up with its own version which entailed a distinctive character of its own.

Ehrman lays out the entire passage as follows (the first line in parentheses is not regarded as part of the hymn):

> (Have this mind in yourselves which is also in Christ Jesus,)
>
> [6] who although he was in the form [*morphē*] of God [*alt., being in very nature God (as in NIV)*], did not regard being equal with God something to be seized.
>
> [7] But he emptied himself, taking on the form of a slave, and coming [*lit., becoming*] in the likeness of humans.
>
> [8] And being found in the appearance as a human he humbled himself and became obedient unto death, [even the death of the cross].
>
> [9] Therefore also God highly exalted him [literally: hyperexalted him], and gave to him the name that is above every name.
>
> [10] That at the name of Jesus, every knee should bow of things in heaven, and on earth, and under the earth.
>
> [11] And every tongue should confess that Jesus Christ is Lord to the glory of God the Father.

The words in square brackets in verses 6 and 7 are my own, and I have placed brackets around "even the death of the cross" in verse 8 since most scholars, including Ehrman, regard this as a Pauline addition. In Philippians the hymn is presented in prose, but it seems to have had a chiastic structure: the second half being a mirror image of the first half in terms of poetic lines and meter.

Form = nature? Or form = image?

Ehrman first addresses the opening line of the hymn (verse 6), crucial to his contention about the meaning of "son of God." What does "in the form [*morphē*] of God" mean? Does it mean being in the *image* of God in the way that Adam was made, and all humans are said to be? Or does it mean having the *nature* of God, such as in being an emanation of God, a part of him, and sharing in his divine quality? Traditional scholarship has always taken it to mean the latter, that it is a statement of the *pre-existence* of Jesus, existing with God in heaven from before creation (as had Wisdom in prior Jewish thought).

Ehrman acknowledges that this "may be the right way to read the passage," but he offers qualifications, and will shortly opt for a different understanding. He says,

> Christ was in the "form of God," (but) that does not mean that he was God. [*DJE?* 235]

I am going to assume that by "he was God" Ehrman would allow for the meaning of "he was a part of God," in the sense of an emanation, though he never makes this clear, or that it is not to be equated with Council decisions in later centuries.

> Divinity was his "form," just as later in the passage he took on the "form" of a "slave." That does not mean that he was permanently and always a slave; it was simply the outward form he assumed. [*DJE?* 235]

This is certainly woolly. "Divinity was his 'form'" is particularly obscure. How would one, especially a man, "assume" the outward form of divinity? The line clearly implies that this "form" was his from the first, but perhaps Ehrman is taking this as meaning that the human Jesus had the 'form/image' of God in the same way as any other human being, and so to this extent his form (image) was "divine."

But then we run into trouble. "He assumed the 'form/image' of a slave/servant," supposedly referring to when he became — what? Human? But he was supposedly *already* human. And 'form/image' does not mean 'role,' so it is not referring to when he submitted to death, as a slave/servant to God's will. Besides, a subsequent line repeats a similar idea, saying "becoming in the likeness of men." Was he not in that 'likeness' from the beginning, according to Ehrman?

Ehrman reveals his preference that the solution to the opening of the hymn is that Jesus is seen as being in the *image* of God, as was Adam in the creation account in Genesis. The terms 'image' and 'form' are sometimes used synonymously in the Old Testament, and so Christ is styled as having been another Adam at the beginning, no more. And here Ehrman attempts some sleight-of-hand. Borrowing another motif from Genesis, he suggests that Christ, in not seeking equality with God in the hymn, is being contrasted with Adam who *did* want to be "equal with God" and so "grabbed for the fruit of the tree of the knowledge of good and evil."

But Adam was not seeking equality with God in any sense that he would become God or even a part of God. The serpent's temptation hardly went so far. Adam and Eve would simply "become *like* gods, knowing both good and evil." That is not the same as achieving "equality with God" *per se*, but simply enjoying one of his abilities. Nor would the hymnist be making any point about his figure having a motive like Adam's or being in parallel with him, seeking to acquire the knowledge of good and evil. That would be ludicrous.

If all Ehrman means is that Jesus possessed the 'divine form' of God in the same sense as Adam, that from his birth he had borne this image, why would the hymnist bother making such a point? But as the hymn is constructed, this "form from the first" is meant to present a contrast with the 'form' he adopted as a slave. Such as we might say, John was born of the aristocracy but he led his life among the lower class, helping to lift them from their poverty. **This and the hymn itself implies a stark, wide contrast, one that would be lost if all the first line meant was that Jesus from birth as a human being was in the 'image' of God, no different from Adam or any other human being.**

Clearly, the form that was in 'equality with God' is set against the inferior form he did take on, namely that of a slave or servant. He took on a nature similar to humans, one by which he could suffer and die; he shared one of their key essences.

There is no sense here of an *image* of anything, and thus by being set against the *form* he was initially accorded in the first verse, that first form cannot be understood in the sense of image. (In Colossians 1:15–20, as noted above, the word used for 'image' is not *morphē*, but *eikōn*. And the philosophical concept of the Son/Logos as 'image of God' is not the same as that of man being made in the image of God.)

Moreover, how could a man be said to take on the image or likeness of men? Rather, sharing in the nature of God is being contrasted with sharing in the nature of the slave/servant who undergoes death. In neither case is he said to *be* God or to *be* a man.

Keeping equality with God? Or gaining equality with God?

> Moreover, when it says that he "did not regard equality with God something to be seized," it is hotly debated whether that means that he did not want to "retain" what he already had, or to "grab" something that he did not have. [*DJE?* 235]

Ehrman opts for the latter understanding. But how was a human being to "grab" at equality with God? Why would an early Christian hymnist praise the man Jesus for not grabbing at such equality? Why would such an idea even have been conceivable, let alone formulated so soon after the man's death? Even being exalted upon resurrection would hardly extend to having this man think he could grab equal status with God.

But if Christ Jesus is a heavenly emanation of God, he is subordinate to him, and thus not his equal — just as the Logos was not to be equated with God or considered an equal. It would be natural for a hymnist to praise this 'first-begotten' hypostasis of God for not striving to become God's equal, especially in light of him being willing to go in the opposite direction: he *reduced* his status by assuming the form/nature of a slave/servant obedient to God's wishes — obedient even to death.

Ehrman is assuredly right in saying that if Jesus were already God there was no higher to go, so he must not have already been equal to God. But this inequality does not necessarily spell being human, for a spiritual Son and emanation is by definition less than an equal, something Ehrman has not taken into account. The occasional translation does assume a heavenly equality and understands the 'retain' idea, such as the *Translator's New Testament*: "he did not consider that he must cling to equality with God." But this seems more a faith-based assumption dependent on Trinitarian orthodoxy than allowing that such a meaning could be contained in the words themselves. (The NEB offers as an alternative translation: "yet he did not prize his equality with God." If the hymnist did have such a meaning in mind, it may be that for the purposes of his literary creation he did not bother with the niceties of whether an emanation was exactly equal or not.)

Driving the point home that the Son assumed a "likeness"

Three times does the hymnist make much the same statement:

- he took on the form of a slave/servant,
- becoming in the likeness of men,
- found in fashion as a man.

If this passage is indeed a hymn with metrical lines, this repetition of the same idea was designed to fill in needed lines. But then why not use the available space for some specific reference to a life on earth, to his identity in an incarnation, to some of his activities: teaching, miracle-working, prophesying? Why overwork the likeness motif if he became an actual man? Of course, the explanation here is that this descending figure did not become a man or incarnated to earth; he took on a spiritual equivalent — a likeness — to being human in a part of the corruptible heavens in order to undergo his death and rising at the hands of "the rulers of this age."

Jesus' exaltation

The second half of the hymn has sparked even greater debate. As a result of his obedience to God in submitting to death, this figure — who so far in the hymn has not been named — is exalted. But when Ehrman carries over his "man like Adam" interpretation into the exaltation phase of the hymn, he is led into further problematic exegesis. (Ehrman also suggests that this second half presents an "adoptionist" scenario, that here the man Jesus is being adopted as God's son. But there is nothing in the text to suggest that; there is no allusion to Psalm 2:7. The Son is merely given new power and prestige.)

Earl Doherty

Let's repeat verses 9–11 here for easy reference:

[9] Therefore also God highly exalted him [literally: hyperexalted him],
and gave to him the name that is above every name.
[10] That at the name of Jesus, every knee should bow
of things in heaven, and on earth, and under the earth.
[11] And every tongue should confess that Jesus Christ is Lord
to the glory of God the Father.

[Ehrman has pointed out the "hyperexalted," but that works against him. It implies an exaltation greater than the one he enjoyed before. But what 'exaltation' would the human man have possessed prior to this? The word clearly refers to the Son being raised even higher, with greater power, than he previously stood when he simply 'shared in God's nature' (verse 6).]

The interpretation of verses 9-11 has always been critical. *What is the "name above every name"? The plain reading is that it is "Jesus."* The word 'name' in both verses is the same: *onoma*. This descending-ascending figure, who has pointedly not been identified by any name in the hymn before, is now given a name, and at that name, *Jesus*, all in heaven, earth, and Sheol bow their knee to him. With that understanding, the case for Mythicism has been clinched, for it tells us that no 'Jesus' lived on earth with that name before the resurrection.

But scholarship sees one way out: the 'name' given to the figure in verse 9 is not 'Jesus,' it is something else. And with that other name, the exalted entity who was allegedly already named Jesus receives his new homage. And what is that other "name"? There is only one candidate available. It is 'Lord.' But how much sense does this make?

When is a title a name?

First of all, 'Lord' is a title, not a name. It is sometimes claimed that the word *onoma* can encompass a title. But this is in the sense of a *category* designation, such as Ignatius saying that he is persecuted for his "name" in that he is a "Christian." (See Bauer, def. II.) Even the common phrase "in the name of the Lord" is not making 'Lord' itself a name, but refers to the act of calling upon God, referred to by one of his designations, whether Lord or Most High or Father, and so on. It is not identifying those terms as personal *names* but as *titles*. My father's name was not 'father.' That was a category designation and a form of address. If the hymnist wanted to identify the term given to Jesus as *Lord*, a title designation of God, he should have identified it as a title and not a name.

And what happens if the "name" given in verse 9 is not *Jesus* but some other term? It would be like saying, "He was given the name *George*, so that at the name of *Robert* every knee should bow." There is a rather obvious *non-sequitur* in these verses that the hymnist should not have felt comfortable with. Is 'Jesus' a name that could be called "a name above every name"? It could if it encompassed the meaning of 'Savior,' which it does. This would make it a name greater than any other name of a divine or human entity other than God.

Another smoking gun?

But what if the "name" were *Lord*? Is that "a name above every name"? Since it is a title of God himself it certainly would be, presuming we could take *onoma* as encompassing a title. But the hymnist would then be creating a confusing picture, one in fact which is not just a *non-sequitur* but contradictory. In the usual scholarly scenario, Jesus receives obeisance from the entire universe on the basis of being given the "name above every name" in verse 9. In other words, the denizens of the universe are *reacting to that name*, whatever it is.

But if this "name" is *Lord* then verse 10 isn't compatible, for there it is said that "*at the name of Jesus*" every knee shall bow. But it would *not* be the name *Jesus* which prompts the bending of the knee if it is allegedly the title *Lord*. There is a contradiction here which cannot be resolved. (The statement that "Jesus Christ is Lord"[1] in the final

1 *Editor's note*: In the Septuagint Greek translation of the Hebrew scriptures, the title 'Lord' (Gk. *Kyrios*) is the normal substitute for the ineffable name YHWH (Yahweh). At some point in the evolution of Christianity, 'Jesus is Lord' came to mean 'Jesus is Yahweh.' If the so-called "Kenosis Hymn" here under discussion actually is stating the latter equality, the hymn must be a later composition if Ehrman be correct in his claim that the earliest Christians didn't consider Jesus to be a god. In that case,

verse need not reflect back on the previous verses, for it could as easily mean that the Son now given the name Jesus has become Lord, beside the Lord God himself.) We must return to seeing verse 9's "name" as "Jesus," which brings it into harmony with the statement of verse 10 — and brings Mythicism onto the gold medal podium.

In sum, would Ehrman really have us believe that such a scenario, such an exaltation, would be created for his simple "son of God," even if he had consented to crucifixion? What other "son of God" in Jewish history, even a martyr, was ever given God's own exalted title? What other "son of God" had every knee in the cosmos bent to him? And how would the crucifixion of a *man* give God the means to forgive humanity its sins? (Though that is not the stated effect in this hymn.) Even the author of Hebrews realized that this required *divine* blood. And the Gospel Jesus was eventually raised to divinity precisely because it was perceived that only the sacrifice of a god could bestow redemption.

This picture of the heavenly Son is in keeping with the cosmic portrayal of him in the other hymns we looked at earlier, which Ehrman does not address. Could Philippians 2:6–11 be said to offer a dying and rising god? It certainly looks like it. An entity who was divine to begin with, sharing in God's nature, descends and undergoes death, then rises back to heaven in an exalted state. Ehrman's admission was right: on "superficial reading" it certainly looks to be a duck.

Beyond belief

Ehrman goes so far as to admit:

> This final part of the passage is actually a quotation from Isaiah 45:23, which says that it is to God alone that every knee shall bow

---

he would have to suppose the hymn to be a later composition retrojected into a Pauline text, perhaps for the purpose of attributing its creedal intent to the worthy name of Paul. On the other hand, if 'Lord' does *not* have its LXX meaning of 'Yahweh,' and Paul has actually inserted a pre-existing hymn into his letter, we must wonder how long the Christian community that composed the hymn had been in existence at the time Paul's letter was written. How much time would be needed after the death of a man for an initially disorganized group of people to develop the social and ecclesiastical organization needed to compose and sing hymns to him — and creedal hymns at that? — FRZ

> and tongue confess. However you interpret the rest of the passage, this conclusion is stunning. Christ will receive the adoration that is by rights God's alone. That is how highly God exalted him in reward for his act of obedience. [*DJE?* 237]

Well, it's more than stunning. It is beyond credence. Isaiah 45:23 shows the exalted exclusivity Jews allotted to their God. Were the earliest Jewish Christians willing to contravene that paramount monotheism to the extent of elevating a crucified criminal, calling him "the Lord Jesus Christ" with God's name above every name, to a position beside God himself? Even Ehrman admits that the hymn implies that this man, this "son of God," was after his resurrection exalted to a position worthy of *equal worship* with God." *Equal worship*! And on what basis? That they liked his teachings (for which there is no evidence in the epistles)? That they 'came to believe' based on a rumor, a story, an idea, that he had risen after death — and not even in flesh to earth (as Ehrman will have it)? The whole idea is preposterous.

At this point, Ehrman stands on his wager. The Philippians hymn has Jesus *becoming* someone 'worthy to be worshiped,' and he hedges his description of this new recipient of adoration as someone who was exalted "to a position of divine authority and grandeur," seemingly to avoid styling him a god. But despite such hymns being thought of as written prior to Paul, whose conversion Ehrman puts at two or three years after the crucifixion, and despite them having a depth and sophistication which could hardly have developed overnight, their sentiments, Ehrman declares, do not constitute the *earliest* interpretation of Jesus. No, *that* phase, an entirely human man being declared to have been the messiah despite his crucifixion, *preceded* even the pre-Pauline hymns. Which I guess slots it into the first few weeks after Jesus' death, soon to be followed by the next phase in which he was elevated to being a part of God and given the role of creator and sustainer of the universe.

And if you believe *that*, there are probably swamplands in Florida still available for purchase.

CHAPTER SIX

'Mythicist Inventions' Creating the Mythical Christ from the Pagan Mystery Cults

A Critique of Pages 219–230 *Did Jesus Exist?*

Earl Doherty

This chapter examines Ehrman's arguments against mystery-cult origins of Christianity:

- *Jesus as a dying and rising god*
- *Common creations of the religious mind*
- *The demise of James Frazer's* The Golden Bough
- *The case for borrowing lies in syncretism*
- *Jewish and Greek forms of resurrection*
- *Paul on Jesus' resurrection as "firstfruits"*
- *Jonathan Z. Smith's case against dying and rising gods*
- *The resurrection of Adonis: did the mysteries copy Christianity?*
- *Gunter Wagner on discrediting the mysteries*
- *The appeal of the mysteries*
- *The lack of evidence on the mysteries*
- *Historicist methodology and a Jewish camouflage*

* * * * *

Earl Doherty

If there has been one paramount apologetic concern in the long combat against Jesus Mythicism, it has been the need to discredit any thought of Christian dependence on the Hellenistic savior god traditions. This has led historicism to adopt a 'scorched earth' strategy. Not only must any dependence on the mystery cults be refuted on Christianity's own turf, the war has been carried further afield in an attempt to eliminate even the alleged sources. Thus, the armies of Christian independence are dispatched to the enemy's home territory, there to destroy its own precepts.

No longer do the mysteries believe in dying and rising gods; no longer are they based on the cycle of agricultural death and rebirth; no longer do they practice rites which could have resembled and influenced the Christian one; no longer do they even worship such deities. And no longer do ancient Christians contemporary with the mysteries genuinely know anything about them. But the mysteries knew about Christianity, and they liked what they saw so much that they recast their own ancient beliefs in imitation of the Jesus story.

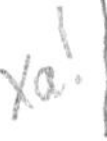

"Did the Earliest Christians Invent Jesus as a Dying-Rising God, Based on Pagan Myths?"

Having asked that question, Ehrman presents the situation this way:

> ONE OF THE MOST widely asserted claims found in the mythicist literature is that Jesus was an invention of the early Christians who had been deeply influenced by the prevalent notion of a dying-rising god, as found throughout the pagan religions of antiquity. The theory behind this claim is that people in many ancient religions worshipped gods who died and rose again: Osiris, Attis, Adonis, Tammuz, Heracles, Melqart, Eshmun, Baal, and so on. Originally, the theory goes, these gods were connected with vegetation and were worshipped in fertility cults. Just as every year the crops die in winter but then come back to life in the spring, so too with the gods who are associated with the crops. They die (when the crops do) and go to the underworld, but then they revive (with the crops) and reappear on earth, raised from the dead. They are worshipped then as dying-rising deities. [*DJE?* 221]

'Mythicist Inventions'

According to Ehrman, the view of almost all Mythicists is that Jesus is an artificial Jewish version of a dying and rising deity of the above type; the significant parallels between the mysteries and the Jesus story prove this claim.

But this is something of a straw man. It envisions that some founder of the movement, or some Jewish study group (a scriptural book review club perhaps?), consciously sat down and 'invented' a new version of an old religion by emulating the latter's features. Occasionally this sort of thing may happen (Ptolemy I deliberately syncretizing two gods into one to create a national-unity religion, or Joseph Smith inventing the whole gold plates business). But more often than not it is 'in the air' concepts and expressions that throw up a new set of ideas and interpretations within a break-away group or a particular cultural or sectarian entity.

Common inventions of the human mind

Almost every sect that looks back to a divine event or interaction with a deity develops a sacred meal as a commemorative thanksgiving or ritual reflection. (What is more fitting, or available, to give to a god than food and drink, or bounty more traditionally associated with a god's own nature?)

If the most fundamental religious impulse is to find a way to believe in a life after death, this is almost inevitably going to take the form of creating a deity who will bestow such a thing; and given our mystical predilections it should not be surprising that a process many would tend to come up with is the principle of the god undergoing the desired goal himself. It would indeed take a god to conquer death, but if we could just find a way to ride through that formidable barrier on his divine coattails. . . .

This is one Mythicist who does not overplay the 'deliberate borrowing' principle to explain the origins of Christianity. And we have to keep in mind that those origins are not to be found in the Gospel story. A proper reading of the epistles—which predate the Gospel traditions, despite Ehrman's efforts to conjure up a reversal—shows that **this was no reaction to a crucified preacher, but a diverse**

interpretation of Jewish scripture inspired by philosophical and religious trends of the day. How much of it was a conscious exercise might be impossible to say. There is much in early Christianity which owes its presence to the Jewish culture it emerged from. But there is also no question that fundamental aspects of the early Christian faith do not have a Jewish character but a Hellenistic one.

So modern historicist scholarship of the last half-century has been forced to adopt a new tack. First, show that the things in pagan religion which allegedly inspired Christianity really didn't exist. Second, show that the earliest Christians did not believe Jesus was a god, so he couldn't have been for them a dying and rising deity.

The Golden Bough goes up in smoke

The first to fall victim to the scorched earth policy is the famous James G. Frazer, whose influential multivolume *The Golden Bough* around the start of the twentieth century set out the picture of a class of dying and rising gods in Near Eastern mythology—Osiris, Tammuz, Attis, Adonis, *etc.*—whose life, death, and resurrection represented the earth's seasonal fertility cycles. Frazer's theories held sway until much later in the twentieth century, when, according to Ehrman, they were clobbered by a "devastating critique" and came to be regarded as discredited.

I am not convinced that this 'discrediting' has enjoyed widespread acceptance outside New Testament circles, and even Ehrman is forced to admit that

> There are, to be sure, scholars here or there [!] who continue to think that there is some evidence of dying and rising gods. But even these scholars, who appear [!] to be in the minority, do not think that the category is of any relevance for understanding the traditions about Jesus. [*DJE?* 223]

That last remark shows that Ehrman is indeed speaking of scholars soldiering in the biblical ranks. One prominent researcher in this area, Tryggve D. Mettinger, has argued for a revival of the Frazer scenario in his *The Riddle of the Resurrection: "Dying and Rising Gods" in the Ancient Near East.* Ehrman challenges Mettinger on two grounds:

- that the actual vocabulary of resurrection (as applied to Jesus, presumably) is rarely found in regard to these gods;
- and that worshiping pagan gods who died and rose lacks any evidence for being present in Palestine in the time of the rise of Christianity.

As for the first objection, I have pointed out previously that the concept of resurrection enjoyed diverse cultural interpretations in the ancient world, and consequently the language used in that context could be expected to be diverse as well. Ehrman also points out that the records of such deities are centuries older than Christianity (I am not sure if that works in his favor), and claims that the language itself can be ambiguous. Since Ehrman does not quote anything to demonstrate that ambiguity, we have to wonder if this is simply his preferred reading of whatever the sources quoted by Mettinger.

No borrowing in sight?

Mettinger does not use his case for reviving the dying and rising gods to explain the Christian faith in Jesus. But his grounds for not doing so are hardly conclusive of anything. I have regularly maintained that we don't need every detail to conform to a source of influence to legitimately postulate a borrowing or derivation. Syncretism is the process of taking certain ideas from one area of thought and combining them with ideas from another area and creating a new synthesis. The Hellenistic gods may ultimately represent cyclical processes in nature, but just because Jesus died only once does not rule out a degree of inspiration from pagan prototypes. (I daresay that devotees of the Attis cult did not view his castration as something that recurred every year—it certainly couldn't recur for the self-castrated Galli! They, too, could be flexible with their sources.) Nor does the uniqueness of the idea that Jesus died as a vicarious atonement for sin rule out syncretism.

As for the claim that there is no evidence anyone in Palestine worshipped a dying and rising god, this would not mean that no one would be *familiar* with the cults. Jerusalem was not exactly the backwater of the empire; the region, from Alexandria to Antioch, enjoyed a heavy Greek presence and influence.

On the other hand, we might say that there is indeed such evidence available. The epistles, when not read with Gospel-colored glasses, present just such a picture in Palestine. Paul sums it up in his gospel of a dying and rising Christ in 1 Corinthians 15:3–4; and in Romans 6:1–6 he encapsulates the principal features of his soteriology: through initiation and ritual the devotee enters into union with the god; he enjoys a rebirth and the benefits of the experiences they share, including resurrection to the kingdom of God. That's all Greek to me.

If we allow ourselves to recognize the debt which Paul owes to pagan concepts, it must mean that the latter were in the Palestinian air at the time.

When is a resurrection not a resurrection?

It is at this point that Ehrman brings up the old canard that none of the dying and rising gods was resurrected the way Jesus was resurrected. I'm tempted to quote Ehrman from earlier in his book: "So what?" What they all had in common was a death, followed by an overcoming of that death and coming back to life. To illustrate Jesus' alleged form of resurrection, Ehrman appeals to Jewish apocalyptic: the expectation of God's imminent kingdom entailed an accompanying resurrection of dead bodies. But the Greeks had no such future mythology, and thus felt no urge to invent for their savior gods a resurrection back to earth in their former flesh. As Martin Nilsson puts it (*The Dionysiac Mysteries of the Hellenistic and Roman Age*: 130):

> The adherents of the Bacchic mysteries did not believe that they would rise up from the dead; they believed that they would lead a life of eternal bliss and joy in the Other World.

By appealing to the Jewish brand of expectation, Ehrman has demonstrated this diversity of cultural views and the reason why there were differences in the idea of resurrection between Christianity's savior god and those of the mysteries. The trouble is, for Ehrman and others, if there is no *exact* prototype, there is no prototype at all.

> If the ambiguous evidence is interpreted in a certain way (Mettinger's), the pagan gods who died did come back to life. But that is not really what the early teachings about Jesus were all about. It was not simply that his corpse was restored to the living. It is that he experienced a resurrection. [*DJE?* 225]

In the context of Jewish apocalyptic expectation, Jesus' 'resurrection' was seen as the prelude to a general resurrection—yet another way (this one relating to context) in which his return to life differed from those of the pagan saviors.

But we know by now that when Ehrman refers to "early teachings about Jesus," he is referring to the Gospel picture of a rising in flesh, a restored body standing on the same earth it had stood on before, with former followers maintaining that they had witnessed him in that restored state. No epistle makes that claim, and even 1 Corinthians 15 can only be so interpreted by reading the Gospels into the passage. To compensate for this, Ehrman has created, through the invocation of his chimerical pre-Markan spirits of oral tradition, a further dimension which contrasts with those of the pagan savior gods, and he assigns it to the very beginnings of Christianity, prior to the epistles.

Pauline "firstfruits"

This, Ehrman contends, is how Paul viewed the importance of Jesus' resurrection, as the "firstfruits" of the general resurrection. But Paul, like the epistles as a whole, does not view Jesus' rising in Ehrman's apocalyptic terms. He has no dimension of a recent Jesus rising in flesh on earth as a prelude to the same sort of resurrection Jews looked for. (If he did, he would never have crafted his argument as he does in 1 Corinthians 15:35–49, failing to introduce an incarnated Jesus with a human body into his pattern, a pattern it would have destroyed.) As shown earlier, all the epistles see Jesus' rising—from wherever it took place—as in spirit only, to God's heaven. Critical scholarship now recognizes this (all but Ehrman, apparently).

By calling Jesus' resurrection the "firstfruits," Paul is not placing his resurrection in the present time, as the first in a general resurrection he believes is just around the corner. That resurrection, occurring at a timeless point in the heavenly world, can serve the same purpose in view of the fact that it has been *revealed* in the present time, through the discovery in scripture of the Son and his acts of salvation. This revelation by God is what has triggered the onset of the End-time and the imminence of the general resurrection, making the revealed resurrection of Jesus the "firstfruits" of the coming harvest.

Jesus' acts—and indeed Jesus himself, the "secret of Christ"—had been kept hidden for long generations, the benefits of his acts stored in a heavenly bank account until, in the time of Paul and other apostles visited by the spirit, God's revelation in scripture had opened that account for withdrawals, with believers being issued the PIN number. This system allows the Son's death and resurrection to have taken place in the heavenly world at any time—or in an essentially timeless setting—which is why the epistle writers are never able to supply a time and place in their countless references to those acts.

Such a revelation by God through scripture is clearly stated in Romans 16:25–27,[1] and implied in 1 Corinthians 15:12–16[2] where Paul declares rhetorically that, if apostles like himself are falsely preaching that Jesus rose, they stand "in contradiction to God," he being the source (in scripture) of the revelation that Jesus rose from death. Moreover, if Christ's resurrection had just happened, Paul would not have described the present time and its progression toward the kingdom's arrival the way he does in Romans 8:22–3[3] and

1 Rom 16:25 Now to him that is of power to stablish you according to my gospel, and the preaching of Jesus Christ, according to the revelation of the mystery, which was kept secret since the world began, 26 But now is made manifest and by the scriptures of the prophets, according to the commandment of the everlasting God, made known to all nations for the obedience of faith: 27 To God only wise, be glory through Jesus Christ for ever, Amen.

2 I Cor 15:12 Now if Christ be preached that he rose from the dead, how say some among you that there is no resurrection of the dead? 13 But if there be no resurrection of the dead, then is Christ not risen: 14 And if Christ be not risen, then is our preaching vain, and your faith is also vain. 15 Yea, and we are found false witnesses of God; because we have testified of God that he raised up Christ: whom he raised not up, if so be that the dead rise not. 16 For if the dead rise not, then is not Christ raised:

3 Rom 8:22 For we know that the whole creation groaneth and travaileth in pain together until now. 23 And not only they, but ourselves also, which have the first-fruits

elsewhere, making not even an allusion to Christ's recent life, let alone allowing it to have played any role in that progression.

It was to take a bit of time for some Christians to come to the conviction that in order to guarantee human resurrection, Christ actually (or "truly," as Ignatius or his forger was to put it) needed to have lived, died, and resurrected on earth and in real human flesh. The first century epistles (and some of the second) still lack that need and conviction.

Jonathan Z. Smith and the denial of dying and rising gods

Ehrman does not enlighten the reader as to what scholarship has offered in the wake of Frazer's alleged discrediting. I've noted in *Jesus: Neither God Nor Man* [128] that some scholars have suggested the mysteries were founded on "male rites of passage" in prehistoric societies. Or that they grew out of "cults of dead kings" such as the Pharaohs in Egypt or the Hittite rulers in Asia Minor. Neither of these options seems adequate to explain a religious tradition that so many placed their hopes in and for so long, and neither has gained much traction, certainly not compared to the Frazer scenario which reigned supreme for decades until its overthrow was deemed in the best interests of historicism.

The commanding generals of this new campaign of revisionism have been principally two: Gunter Wagner, in his 1963 [ET: 1967] *Pauline Baptism and the Pagan Mysteries* (extensively reviewed in my website Supplementary Article No. 13C at: http://www.jesuspuzzle.humanists.net/supp13C.htm); and Jonathan Z. Smith, in a 1977 article for the *Encyclopedia of Religion*, "Dying and Rising Gods," and his more recent 1991 *Drudgery Divine: On the Comparison of Early Christianities and the Religions of Late Antiquity*. (The latter has also been given a detailed review toward the end of article "13B" of the above series.)

---

of the Spirit, even we ourselves groan within ourselves, waiting for the adoption, to wit, the redemption of our body.

Earl Doherty

Ehrman relies heavily on Smith, and quotes this from his 1977 article:

> *"All the deities that have been identified as belonging to the class of dying and rising deities can be subsumed under the two larger classes of disappearing deities or dying deities. In the first case the deities return but have not died; in the second case the gods die but do not return. There is no unambiguous instance in the history of religions of a dying and rising deity."* [*DJE?* 227]

Robert Price takes on Jonathan Z. Smith

There is not sufficient space here to fully debunk Smith's case against dying and rising gods, but let me offer first a few quotes by Robert M. Price from my Web-site book review of his *Deconstructing Jesus*:

> **Smith's first error is his failure, as I see it, to grasp the point of an "ideal type,"** a basic textbook definition/description of some phenomenon under study. . . . Smith, finding that there are significant differences between the so-called dying-and-rising-god myths, abandons any hope of a genuine dying-and-rising-god paradigm. For Smith, the various myths of Osiris, Attis, Adonis, and the others, do not all conform to type exactly; thus they are not sufficiently alike to fit into the same box—so let's throw out the box! Without everything in common, Smith sees nothing in common. . .
>
> Smith's error is the same as that of Raymond Brown, who dismisses the truckload of comparative religion parallels to the miraculous birth of Jesus: This one is not strictly speaking a virgin birth, since the god fathered the child on a married woman. That one involved physical intercourse with the deity, not overshadowing by the Holy Spirit, and so on. But, we have to ask, how close does a parallel have to be to count as a parallel? Does the divine mother have to be named Mary? Does the divine child have to be named Jesus? **Here is the old "difference without a distinction" fallacy.** . . .
>
> **But what does it mean to say someone has descended to the netherworld of the dead?** Enkidu did not deem it quite so casual a

> commute "to Hell and back" as Smith apparently does: "He led me away to the palace of Irkalla, the Queen of Darkness, to the house from which none who enters ever returns, down the road from which there is no coming back." One goes there in the embrace of the Grim Reaper. Similarly, Pausanias: "About the death of Theseus there are many inconsistent legends, for example that he was tied up on the Netherworld until Herakles should bring him back to life." Thus to abide in the netherworld was to be dead, even if not for good. . . .
>
> Osiris, Smith admits, is said even in very ancient records to have been dismembered, reassembled by Isis, and rejuvenated (physically; he fathered Horus on Isis). But Smith seizes on the fact that Osiris reigned henceforth in the realm of the dead. This is not a return to earthly life, hence no resurrection. **But then we might as well deny that Jesus is depicted as dying and rising since he reigns henceforth at the right hand of God in Heaven as the judge of the dead, like Osiris.**

The death and rising of Adonis: copying Jesus?

In one of the myths of Adonis, the god is killed by a boar. Ehrman says:

> It is only in later texts, long after Ovid and after the rise of Christianity, that one finds any suggestion that Adonis came back to life after his death. Smith argues that this later form of the tradition may in fact have been influenced by Christianity and its claim that a human had been raised from the dead. In other words, the Adonis myth did not influence Christian views of Jesus but rather the other way around." [*DJE?* 228]

And so the apologetic specter of the mysteries borrowing from Christianity rears its dreary head yet again. It is hard to know whether Ehrman seriously believes this, or whether he is simply catering to his uninformed readers' ready acceptance of this popular tactic. On the Adonis question, Gunter Wagner floats the same idea. To that, I responded in my Web-site review of his book:

Wagner acknowledges that "*after the beginning of the second half of the 2nd century of the Christian era we hear about the 'resurrection' of Adonis being celebrated in connection with the annual mourning festival*" [198]. . . .

[But he is willing to acknowledge] the idea that "*there is much to support the view that the introduction of a celebration of Adonis' resurrection is to be attributed to the influence of the Osiris cult*" [200]. . . . this would certainly be the prime and preferred candidate for influence on a new Adonis resurrection idea over that of any Christian influence. . . .

But the major anomaly [in Wagner's alternate suggestion that Adonis could have borrowed from Jesus] is the idea that the Adonis cult would be struggling to compete with Christianity. The new Christian religion, throughout the 2nd century, was a despised faith, widely persecuted, and we have no evidence that there were huge numbers of Christians in the empire with whom any of the cults had to 'compete'. . . .

If Adonis, a relatively minor cult throughout the empire, was adopting a resurrection motif from other [Greek] cults, that concept obviously existed in them prior to the mid 2nd century, perhaps at least as early as the 1st century if we can judge by some of the artifacts unearthed at that time and earlier in regard to Attis. Such earlier dates would even more securely rule out Christianity as being the example 'copied' from. It simply wouldn't have exercised that kind of pressure on the pagan cultic organizations. . . .

Celsus has nothing but distaste and condemnation for this young upstart which has borrowed everything from its hallowed predecessors. Could such an outlook in the cults lead to blatantly stealing Christianity's most prominent feature for themselves when they supposedly never possessed it before? [And would Celsus have been likely to be ignorant of such a development in his own culture, one that could hardly be more than a few decades old?]

The evidence for dying and rising gods

We know from primary sources such as Cicero [*De legibus*, II, 14, 36] that membership in the mysteries guaranteed benefits in this life and hopes of a happy afterlife in the next. It would otherwise be hard to understand what their appeal was for the countless men and women who became devotees over the centuries, from the ordinary citizen who could afford the costs, to Roman emperors. (Or why a foundation in male rites of passage or a cult of dead kings, rather than in gods who themselves underwent death and rising, would do anything to generate such benefits and hopes.) Walter Burkert [*Ancient Mystery Cults*: 21] admits that evidence for "the promise of a privileged life beyond the grave for those who have 'seen' the mysteries . . . ranges from the earliest text, the *Hymn to Demeter*, down to the last rhetorical exercises of the Imperial period." And yet Burkert holds on to his doubts:

> "It is tempting to assume that the central idea of all initiations should be death and resurrection, so that extinction and salvation are anticipated in the ritual . . . but the pagan evidence for resurrection symbolism is uncompelling at best."

Heaven forbid that we should give in to temptation. This sort of thing conveys nothing so much as an obsession with avoiding at all costs the 'sin' of connecting the ideas of the pagan cults with the purity of Christian faith. Burkert laments that the evidence is "uncompelling." But is the evidence being downplayed? Is it "uncompelling" because that is the way Christian scholars want to see it? Have they placed the bar so high that it becomes quite *impossible* to see it? Or is it because the gap between the bountiful record left by early Christianity and the meager, *deliberately obscure information* on the pagan cults is so vast? Should not a degree of dispassionate logic be brought to our evaluation of the mysteries, what they promised to their followers and through what spiritual processes those ends were achieved?

Ehrman echoes Smith by stating

> . . . the evidence for such gods is at best sparse, scattered and ambiguous, not abundant, ubiquitous and clear. Such gods were definitely not widely known and widely discussed among religious people of antiquity, as is obvious from the fact that they are not clearly discussed in any of our sources [*DJE?* 230].

Well of course the evidence is not abundant, ubiquitous and clear, or clearly discussed. It was forbidden to be so. Nor do we need a wide discussion of the subject. A few clear references, such as we do have, are sufficient. Anyway, what is Plutarch's *Isis and Osiris,* if not something clearly discussed, even if he avoids a description of the cultic rites? And note that Ehrman slipping in "not widely known" in conjunction with "(not) widely discussed" is an invalid association. The latter does not have to imply the former.

The ancient witness muzzled

Ehrman shares both Wagner's and Smith's **refusal to let the ancient witness speak for itself**. On the one surviving representation of Eleusinian baptism, Wagner declares the portrayal only an "ideal . . . chosen for artistic motives," and cannot be interpreted as signifying "rebirth." Even the evidence provided by Tertullian [*On Baptism*, 5] who says that Eleusinian baptism was meant to produce "regeneration [rebirth] and the remission of the penalties due to their perjuries [a form of 'atonement for sin' by means of a rite]" is a case, says Wagner, of the Church Father "putting a Christian construction upon the pagan festivals he mentions." Elsewhere, he says that "the text from Hippolytus must be set aside." *Clearly, neither the primary nor the secondary evidence from the ancient world is to be accepted as anything but erroneous.* Even Christians who were contemporary with the practice of the mysteries supposedly misunderstood them and were guilty of 'reading into' them the understandings of their own practice.

Even in the fourth century, Firmicus Maternus' famous ridicule of the cult of Osiris for imagining the resurrection of their "god of stone," or his taunt that the devotees are saved because of the god's own resurrection, is not to be taken at face value. Maternus is simply "reflecting his own values," says Wagner, and not accurately reproducing the thought of the Osiris cult. Of course, Wagner allows, if we *were* forced to acknowledge that the cults believed in the resurrection of their gods, *they probably got it from Christianity*!

Smith, too, toes the party line and declares that the view held by Otto Pfleiderer, Rudolf Bultmann, and countless others, that Pauline baptismal thinking was based on pagan precedents, has been proven "wrong" by current opinion in scholarship (as if "opinion" proved anything in New Testament scholarship), although Smith allows a voice like R. C. Tannehill's [*Dying and Rising with Christ: A Study in Pauline Theology:* 32] to be heard: "the question of the relation of this motif [dying and rising with Christ] to the mysteries, then, is not yet settled."

Even ancient Christian writers, says Smith, were guilty of misinterpreting the mysteries they were contemporary with. In addition, he claims that "in the case of Attis, the mythology gave no comfort," leaving us to wonder how it became so popular and survived so long. When he repeats the old red herring that Osiris is not a dying and rising god because he retires to the Underworld after death, we know that the whole modern trend to divorce Christianity from the mysteries is one giant apologetics industry. (Perhaps when the farce is fully exposed, James G. Frazer can be welcomed back into the fold!)

Conclusion

In sum, historicist scholars have carried Christian Gospel-based concepts to the mystery cults and set them against the latter's presentation of 'resurrection' and other features; then they 'expose' them as not properly conforming, which then 'proves' that any resemblance is illusory and that all comparison, along with any suggestion of derivation, is invalid. Quite a methodology!

As I say in my website review of Wagner:

> If one assumes this standard scholarly illusion, Christianity must have possessed an undeniably distinctive asset in a savior who had risen from an earthly tomb, to walk the countryside again in a physical body. And he had done this within living memory, whereas the pagan saviors were a distant mythical echo. What a huge selling point! What a knockout piece of superiority! Yet no epistle writer brings up such a difference [including Paul when he condemns those who take part in the "table of demons" in 1 Corinthians 10].
>
> Furthermore, whether Jesus was claimed to have walked out of his tomb (as in the Gospels), or was resurrected only in spirit (as in

> 1 Peter 3:18), **no one, Christian or pagan, ever says that Christians had a monopoly on the very idea of resurrection**. Certainly Celsus did not. . . . Justin, in defending Christianity against pagan similarities, never declares: "But we have the only god who was resurrected!" This is one reason why we can say with confidence that the pagan mysteries must have had a resurrection concept for their savior deities, even if it wasn't exactly equivalent to that of Christianity—although in the first century and the early second, before the Gospels began to circulate, it might have seemed exactly that.

Thus the entire case presented by Ehrman, Wagner, and Smith, preceded by earlier scholars like H. A. Kennedy and Arthur Darby Nock, is built on smoke and mirrors. Its purpose can only be to conjure up an argument, no matter how shaky or deceptive, to disassociate Christianity's initial mysticism from any connection with the pagan mysteries and root it instead in a safe Jewish soil.

Indeed, scholarship since the mid-twentieth century has in its general study been entirely oriented toward the same end and purpose, to characterize Christianity as essentially if not wholly a child of Israel and bury out of sight the bloody umbilical cord of pre-natal nutrition from pagan influences. This strategy has given scholars the false confidence that they have exploded the problematic mystery cult connection, in much the same way that they assume a false confidence that the idea of Jesus Mythicism has been laid to rest.

CHAPTER SEVEN

Will the Real Jesus Please Stand Up?

Is the 'Jesus of History' any more real than the 'Jesus of Faith'?[1]

David Fitzgerald

Christianity has had a good, long run, but we are long past the point where it's reasonable to be agnostic about the so-called 'Jesus of Faith.' It is ridiculous to pretend that the lack of historical corroboration of the spectacular Gospel events — let alone the New Testament's own fundamental contradictions — aren't a fatal problem for Jesus the divine Son of God.

For example:

- Why does Philo of Alexandria, who was intimately connected to affairs in Jerusalem — his family provided the money to Herod Agrippa to panel the temple gates in silver and gold, and Philo's nephew was briefly married to Agrippa's daughter Berenice (who also appears in Acts 25:13, 23 & 26:30) — have nothing to say about, for example, the multitudes who followed the miracle-worker and bold, radical new teacher Jesus throughout the Galilee and Judea? Why doesn't he mention the long-dead Jewish saints who emerged from

1 From his forthcoming book *Jesus: Mything in Action* [2012].

their freshly opened graves and wandered the streets of Jerusalem, appearing to many?

- If Jesus was really found guilty of blasphemy by the Sanhedrin, why was he not simply stoned to death, as Jewish law required [*Mishnah Sanhedrin 6:4 h & i*]? Why is the original trial account of Jesus so full of other unhistorical details and just plain mistakes that could never have actually happened as portrayed? How can each successive gospel continue to overload the original story with its own additional layers of details that are mutually incompatible with the others?
- Why does Seneca the Younger record all kinds of unusual natural phenomena in the seven books of his *Quaestiones Naturales*, including eclipses and earthquakes, but not mention the Star of Bethlehem, the pair of Judean earthquakes that were strong enough to split stones, or the hours of supernatural darkness that covered "all the land" — an event he would have witnessed firsthand?
- Why can't the Gospels agree on so many fundamental facts about Jesus' life and ministry, such as what his relationship to John the Baptist was — and why John the Baptist's cult was a rival to Christianity until at least the early second century?
- Who were Jesus' disciples, and why is it no Gospels agree on who they were? Why do the disciples disappear so quickly in the New Testament after the Gospels, only to pop up again centuries later when churches start spinning rival legends that they were busy founding Christian communities all along? If any were martyred for their faith, as Christians frequently insist, why don't we have any details of any of the Disciples' deaths in the canonical New Testament?
- When his skeptical Roman opponent Celsus asks the early church father Origen what miracles Jesus performed, why can Origen only respond lamely that Jesus' life was indeed full of striking and miraculous events, "but from what other source can we can furnish an answer than from the Gospel narratives?" [*Contra Celsum*, 2.33]

Will the Real Jesus Please Stand Up?

- Why can't the Gospels agree on so many fundamental facts about Jesus' life and ministry? For instance, was he was born during the reign of Herod the Great, or over a decade later, during the tenure of Quirinius? Or why he was arrested? Or on which day he died? Or whether he appeared alive again for just a single day, or for about a week, or for forty days? Or where and when he appeared alive again, and to whom?
- Why are there so many anachronisms and basic mistakes and misunderstandings about first-century Judean Judaism? Why are the Gospels all written in Greek, not Aramaic? Why do Christians insist that they are eyewitness accounts when none claim to be — or even read as if they were — or if all contain indications that they were written generations later?
- Why is Paul — and every other Christian writer from the first generation of Christianity — so silent on any details of Jesus' life? Why do early writers display so much ignorance of Jesus' teachings and miracles?
- Despite the frequent boasts in the New Testament of Christianity spreading like wildfire, attracting new converts by the thousands with every new miracle or inspired sermon, why did Christianity remain a struggling, obscure cult of feuding house churches on the fringe of Roman society for more than three centuries?
- Why is there not a single historical reference to Jesus in the entire first century — a pair of obviously interpolated snippets in the works of Flavius Josephus notwithstanding?

We could pose similar thorny questions all day and never run out of them. It's embarrassing to have to dignify any of the obvious mythological elements of the Gospels, and yet the better part of 2.1 billion people seem unaware of how ludicrous any of them are. We don't even have to rule out whether or not miracles even *can* occur, or point out that stories, delusions and lies are common while verified miracles are few if any; we merely have to ask: if they *did* happen, *why didn't anyone else notice them?* Christians are perfectly free to put their faith in whichever messiah they please, though it will take more than blind faith and selective hearing to convince the rest of us that their Christ is anything more than a Jesus of their own making. But what about the *real* Jesus?

Apologists love to parrot the old lie that "no serious historians reject the historicity of Christ," but fail to realize (or deliberately neglect to mention) that the 'Historical Jesus' that the majority of historians *do* accept is at best no more than just another first-century wandering preacher and founder of a fringe cult that eventually became Christianity — in other words, a Jesus that completely debunks their own.

For your average Atheist activist, all this should be more than enough to settle the matter. But the truth is, the issue isn't even that cut and dry. What about this 'Historical Jesus' at the core of all this legendary accretion? Can we actually know what the real Jesus of Nazareth really said and did?

Over a decade ago, after reading Ken Smith's hilarious and brilliant *Ken's Guide to the Bible,*[2] I became curious to know the answers to questions like these. (Very) long story (very) short: I began researching the historical evidence for Jesus, a process of pulling a thread that unraveled the whole sweater, as far as I was concerned. The result was my book[3] *Nailed: Ten Christian Myths That Show Jesus Never Existed at All.* And I really mean it; I'm convinced there couldn't even have been an ordinary guy behind our familiar Jesus of Nazareth. No, *really*.

The H Word

Isn't there an Atheist's Jesus? You might think so, from how vehemently some of my fellow heretics defend him. I've long since gotten used to their usual charges: this doesn't matter; this is all old stuff, this was long since discredited by all reputable scholars. Charitable critics call it just minority opinion; the less so call it nothing more than

2 Ken Smith, *Ken's Guide to the Bible* [Blast Books, 1995. ISBN-10: 0-922233-179].

3 David Fitzgerald, *Nailed: Ten Christian Myths That Show Jesus Never Existed at All* [Lulu.com, 2010. ISBN-13: 978-0-557709-915].

historical revisionist nonsense, fringe pseudo-scholarship, junk history, crackpottery, the Atheist equivalent of creationism, *etc*. Robert Price, as usual, answered this crowd best when he asked: "the Jesus Myth theory has been debunked? When did that happen? The truth is, the arguments of the Mythicist camp have never been rebutted — they've been ignored, declared to be mistaken, or simply irrelevant; in short, they've only ever been, in a word, *Harrumphed*."

In fact, ironically enough, comparing Jesus-myth theory with creationism is exactly 100% backwards. Consider: Evolutionary theory first began to be taken up when higher education was completely under the thumb of Christianity. Contrary to popular belief, it did not begin with Darwin. His bombshell was the mass-extinction event, but the cracks had started accumulating in Creationism's official story long before him. Discoveries in biology, zoology, geology and other fields of science all built up a steady pressure on beloved, long-accepted biblical 'facts' of the Flood of Noah, the Garden of Eden, the Firmament, and the like, until the contrary evidence reached such a critical mass that finally — however much it displeased the clergy and their flocks — no intellectually honest academic could deny it. And then the great paradigm shift began.

Not that I'm comparing the Jesus-Myth idea to a concept as earthshaking as Natural Selection, but consider the parallels for a moment. Most historians aren't biblical historians; so when the question of Jesus' historicity comes up, it's only natural that they'll turn to the majority opinion of bible scholars. But who are the majority of biblical scholars? Biblical history has always been an apologetic undertaking in the service of Christianity. Even today it remains perhaps the only field of science still overtly dominated by believers. So to begin with, how many of them do you suppose are open to entertaining the idea that the lord and savior they depend on for their salvation and salaries might never have existed?

So *of course* this is minority opinion — and likely always will be as long as biblical studies continue. As theologian Wilhelm Wrede cautioned in the nineteenth century, facts are sometimes the most radical critics of all. Every single advance in the history of biblical scholarship has begun as heresy. In fact, it's gotten to the point where now, secular biblical historians are the only ones who are actually making progress in the field. The majority is too busy circling the wagons to protect its doctrines and dogma from dangerous new knowledge.

Even among secular biblical scholars, it is difficult to find one who doesn't come out of a religious background. Rabbi Jon D. Levensen, one of today's most prominent Jewish biblical scholars, notes, "It is a rare scholar in the field whose past does not include an intense Christian or Jewish commitment."[4] What's more, religious scholar Timothy Fitzgerald (no relation) points out in *The Ideology of Religious Studies*[5] that theological assumptions are a pervasive difficulty in the field, not merely among practicing believers, but for the formerly religious as well: "even in the work of scholars who are explicitly non-theological, half-disguised theological presuppositions persistently distort the analytical pitch."

But the problem of bias aside, the old paradigm of Jesus studies has long been showing worrisome cracks of its own. Incidentally, in his devastating *The End of Biblical Studies,*[6] Hector Avalos has convincingly demonstrated that cracks are widespread throughout the entire field. First of all, it is a misnomer to even refer to *the* 'Historical Jesus' as if there ever was any such clearly defined thing — nor it is correct to think that there is only one.

Who Do Men Say That I am?

Albert Schweitzer in his *From Reimarus to Wrede: A History of Research on the Life of Jesus* [1906], was already discovering that every scholar claiming to have uncovered the 'real' Jesus seemed to have found a mirror instead; investigators found Jesus to be a placeholder for whatever values *they themselves* held dear. Over a century

4 Jon D. levensen, *The Hebrew Bible: The Old Testament, and Historical Criticism: Jews and Christians in Biblical Studies* [Westminster John Knox Press, 1993: 30].

5 Timothy Fitzgerald, *The Ideology of Religious Studies* [Oxford University Press, 2000: 6–7].

6 Hector Avalos, *The End of biblical Studies* [Amherst, NY: Prometheus, 2007].

later, the situation has not improved — quite the contrary. To say there is still no consensus on who Jesus was is an understatement. A quick survey (Price presents excellent examples in his *Deconstructing Jesus*)[7] shows we have quite an embarrassment of *Jesi*.

Cynic philosopher — The many borrowings from Greek philosophy in Jesus' teachings would make sense if Jesus had actually been a wandering Cynic or a Stoic philosopher, or the Galilean equivalent. Burton L. Mack, John Dominic Crossan, Gerald Downing and others have strongly defended this view, citing plenty of Cynic statements with their equivalents in the Gospels.

Liberal Pharisee — Something like his predecessor, the famous Rabbi Hillel. In *Jesus the Pharisee: A New Look at the Jewishness of Jesus,*[8] historian Harvey Falk argues that virtually all of Jesus' judgments on the *Halakha*, the Jewish law, are paralleled in the Pharisaic thought of that time, as well as later rabbinic thought.

Charismatic Hasid — Similarly, Dead Sea Scroll authority Geza Vermes, an expert on New Testament-era Judaism and author of *Jesus the Jew: a Historian's View of the Gospels,*[9] sees Jesus as one of the popular freewheeling Galilean holy men, unorthodox figures like Hanina Ben-Dosa or Honi the Circle-Drawer. Just like Jesus, they had little respect for the niceties of Jewish law, which of course ticked off the religious establishment.

Conservative Rabbi — On the other hand, Jesus upholds the Torah, insisting "not one jot or stroke of the Law will pass away" [Matt. 5:17–19]. He wears a prayer shawl tasseled with *tzitzit* [Matt. 9:20–22], observes the Sabbath, and worships in synagogues as well as the Temple.

Antinomian Iconoclast — But on the *other* other hand, Jesus then turns around and, point-by-point, dismantles the Torah [Mark 7:15-20,[10] Matt.

7 Robert M. Price, *Deconstructing Jesus* [Amherst, NY, Prometheus, 2000: 12–17].

8 Harvey Falk, *Jesus the Pharisee: A New Look at the Jewishness of Jesus* [Wipf & Stock, 2003].

9 Geza Vermes, *Jesus the Jew: A Historian's View of the Gospels* [Fortress Press, 1981].

10 Mark 7:15 There is nothing from without a man, that entering into him can defile him: but the things which come out of him, those are they that defile the man. ...

5:21–22, 27–28, 31–32,[11] 33–37, 38–42, 43–44,[12] *etc.*] and dismisses the Temple [Matt. 12:6 [13]; Mark 13:1–2; Luke 21:5–6].

Magician/Exorcist/Faith Healer — Morton Smith, discoverer (or more likely, its forger — but that's another story) of the *Secret Gospel of Mark* made the argument that Jesus the Christ was actually *Jesus the Magician* in the book of the same name. Like the pagan miracle workers, Jesus cast out demons and healed the blind, deaf, and mute with mud and spit, using the same spells, incantations and techniques as taught in the many popular Greek magic handbooks of the time [Mark 5:41; 7:33–34].

Violent Zealot Revolutionary — But maybe Jesus was really a political messiah, inciting a revolt against the Romans — like Theudas or "the Egyptian," the unnamed Messianic figure Josephus describes, or the two "robbers" crucified with him (since rebel bandits were commonly referred to as robbers). Why else would it be the *Romans* crucifying him, rather than the Jewish Sanhedrin just stoning him to death for blasphemy? There is evidence one can point to: Luke's Gospel lists a disciple called Simon "the Zealot," and seems to hint that Jesus had other Zealots in his entourage: at the Last Supper, Jesus tells his followers to grab their bags and buy a sword [Luke 22:36]; they tell him they already have two swords on hand [Luke 22:38]; when Jesus is about to be arrested they ask if they should attack [Luke 22:49]. In Mark 14:47, one of the disciples does just that and cuts off the ear of one of the High priest's men (the story grows more details in the other Gospels: Matt. 26:51–52, Luke 22:50–51,

---

11 Matt. 5:31 It hath been said, Whosoever shall put away his wife, let him give her a writing of divorcement: 32 But I say unto you, That whosoever shall put away his wife, saving for the cause of fornication, causeth her to commit adultery: and whosoever shall marry her that is divorced committeth adultery.

12 Matt. 5:43 Ye have heard that it hath been said, Thou shalt love thy neighbor, and hate thine enemy. 44 But I say unto you, Love your enemies, bless them that curse you, do good to those that hate you, and pray for them which despitefully use you, and persecute you...

13 Matt. 12:6 But I say unto you, That in this place is one greater than the temple. 7 But if ye had known what this meaneth, I will have mercy and not sacrifice, ye would not have condemned the guiltless. 8 For the Son of man is Lord even of the sabbath day.

John 18:10). Many capable scholars including Robert Eisler, S. G. F. Brandon, Hugh J. Schonfield, Hyam Maccoby, and Robert Eisenman have thought this is where the real Jesus is to be found, and there are many scholarly variations arguing for the 'Jesus-as-*Che* theory.'

Nonviolent Pacificist Resister — But then again, Jesus isn't called the Prince of Peace for nothing. There's no trace of such political agitation when he instructs his followers "if someone strike you on the right cheek, turn the other also" [Matt. 5:39], or when conscripted by Roman soldier to lug their gear for a mile, to "go with him two" [Matt. 5:41].

Apocalyptic Prophet — This is the Jesus that Albert Schweitzer and many subsequent historians have thought was the real thing: A fearless, fiery Judgment Day preacher announcing that the end was nigh and the Kingdom of God was coming fast. Like Paul (and many other first century Jewish apocalypticists) this Jesus did not expect the world to survive his own lifetime. Bart Ehrman makes a well-reasoned case for such a figure in *Jesus: Apocalyptic Prophet of the New Millennium*

First-Century Proto-Communist — Was Jesus the first Marxist? Milan Machoveč and other leftists have thought so. You have to admit Jesus has nothing good to say about the capitalist pigs of his day [Luke 6:24, 12:15], repeatedly preaching that they cannot serve both god and money [Matt. 6:24, Luke 16:13], that they should sell all they own and distribute the money to the poor [Matt. 19:21, Mark 10:21, Luke 18:22] and most famously, that it is easier to get a camel through the eye of a needle than for the rich to get into heaven [Matt.19:24, Mark 10:25, Luke 18:25] — and don't forget his casting the moneychangers out of the Temple with a scourge. Acts not only depicts the early Christians as sharing everything in common, it even the states the Marxist credo: "From each according to their ability, to each according to their need" [Acts 4: 34–35].

Early Feminist — Or was he the first male Feminist? Some scholars like Elizabeth Schüssler Fiorenza and Kathleen Corley point to his unusual attitudes towards women, some of which seem remarkably progressive for the first century. They say not only that some of his closest followers were women, but he forgave the woman caught in adultery, and challenged social customs concerning women's role in society [John 4:27, Luke 7:37, Matt. 21:31–32].

Earthy Hedonist — Or was he a male chauvinist pig? Onlookers criticize him for being "a glutton and a drunk" who consorts with riffraff like tax collectors and whores [Luke 5:30; 5:33–34; 7:34, 37–39,44–46].

Family Man — but then again, Jesus is a champion of good old family values when he gets even tougher than Moses, ratcheting Old Testament law up a notch and declaring "Whoever divorces his wife and marries another commits adultery against her, and if she divorces her husband and marries another, she commits adultery" [Mark 10:11–12]. He also reminds his followers to honor their father and mother, then sternly warns "whoever speaks evil of father and mother must surely die" [Matt. 15:4].

Home Wrecker — but then when *Jesus* speaks evil of the family, apparently it's okay: "If any man come to me, and hate not his father, and mother, and wife, and children, and brethren, and sisters, yea, and his own life also, he cannot be my disciple" [Luke 14:26]. When Jesus is told his mother and brothers have come to see him, Jesus ignores them and asks, "Who is my mother? Who are my brothers?" [Matt. 12:47–48] "Do not think I have come to bring peace to the earth; I have come not to bring peace, but to bring a sword. For I have come to set a man against his father, and a daughter against her mother, and a daughter-in-law against her mother-in-law" [Matt. 10:34–35].

Savior of the World — But despite all that, Jesus loves everyone; he even preached to Samaritans [John 4:39–41; Luke 17:11–18] and Gentiles [Matt. 4:13–17, 24–25].

Savior of Israel (only) — Well, he loves everyone *except* Samaritans or Gentiles. When a Canaanite woman begs him to heal her daughter he ignores her. After the disciples ask him to make her go away, he first refuses, saying "I am not sent but unto the lost sheep of the house of Israel" [Matt. 15:24]. When Jesus sends out his disciples, he commands them not to preach the good news to Gentile regions or Samaritan cities [Matt. 10:5–6].

Radical Social Reformer — Still others like John Dominic Crossan and Richard Horsley see Jesus as a champion for the Jewish peasants suffering under the yoke of the Roman Empire and its rapacious tax collectors; a Jesus somewhat along the lines of Gandhi and his struggle against the British Empire.

Will the Real Jesus Please stand up?

How plausible are any of these reconstructions? As Price notes in *Deconstructing Jesus* [15], many of the above are quite plausible, make good sense of a number of gospel texts, don't violate accepted historical method, aren't impossibly anachronistic, and are the result of deep and serious scholarship. As far as it goes, all of them have their strengths. None of them are particularly far-fetched. All tend to center on particular constellations of Gospel elements interpreted in certain ways, and reject other data as inauthentic — something all critical historians do, regardless of the subject. All appeal to solid historical analogies for their new take on Jesus. But, as Bart Ehrman points out, one fatal flaw haunts most if not all of them:

> The link between Jesus' message and his death is crucial, and historical studies of Jesus' life can be evaluated to how well they establish that link. This in fact is a common weakness in many portrayals of the historical Jesus: they often sound completely plausible in their reconstruction of what Jesus said and did, but they can't make sense of his death. If, for example, Jesus is to be understood as a Jewish rabbi who simply taught that everyone should love God and be good to one another, why did the Romans crucify him? [*Jesus: Apocalyptic Prophet of the New Millennium*: 208]

Ehrman adds that for most theories, their proposed connections between Jesus' life and his death are at times rather shaky and unconvincing. But to be fair, the problem may go deeper than just poor reconstructions. After all, the original source for all of them, the Gospels, also fail to make a credible link between Jesus' life and death — and disagree with each other on just what led to Jesus' death.

Incidentally, the list above is not the last word on revisionist Jesuses; there are even more reasonably plausible 'Historical Jesuses' to consider before you finally reach all the hopelessly crackpot Jesus theories moldering away at the bottom of the barrel. But this multiplicity of convincing possibilities *is precisely the problem*: the various scholarly reconstructions of Jesus cancel each other out. Each sounds good until you hear the next one. Price makes this very clear:

> What one Jesus reconstruction leaves aside, the next one takes up and makes its cornerstone. Jesus simply wears too many hats in the Gospels — exorcist, healer, king, prophet, sage, rabbi, demigod, and so on. The Jesus Christ of the New Testament is a composite figure...The historical Jesus (if there was one) might well have been a messianic king, or a progressive Pharisee, or a Galilean shaman, or a magus, or a Hellenistic sage. But he cannot very well have been all of them at the same time. [*Deconstructing Jesus*: 15–16]

The Jesus Seminar's John Dominic Crossan has observed this very problem and has frankly complained that the plethora of historical Jesus reconstructions has turned into a circus. In his *The Historical Jesus: The Life of a Mediterranean Jewish Peasant*[14], he puts it bluntly:

> But that stunning diversity is an academic embarrassment. It is impossible to avoid the suspicion that historical Jesus research is a very safe place to do theology and call it history, to do autobiography and call it biography.

The upshot of all this is simply that *all* of the secular reconstructions of the 'Historical Jesus' remain speculative. No one can claim to have cornered the market. And there is a good reason for that — *our problematic primary sources for Jesus.*

What *can* we know? Sources for Jesus

Despite centuries of historical scholarship scrutinizing a figure millennia old, we have not been able to come up with a single verifiable

14 John Dominic Crossan, *The Historical Jesus: The Life of a Mediterranean Jewish Peasant* [New York: Harper San Francisco, 1992: *xxviii*].

fact about Jesus. *Not one.* And how could we? Our only sources are nowhere near trustworthy. What *are* the sources? As I hope I made very clear in *Nailed*, though many people assume there were scores of contemporary historical witnesses who mentioned Jesus (and this assumption is both encouraged and trumpeted by apologists) the truth is that there are exactly — none. Bart Ehrman details the depth of the problem:

> What sorts of things do pagan authors from the time of Jesus have to say about him? Nothing. As odd as it may seem, there is no mention of Jesus at all by any of his pagan contemporaries. There are no birth records, no trial transcripts, no death certificates; there are no expressions of interest, no heated slanders, no passing references — nothing. In fact, if we broaden our field of concern to the years after his death — even if we include the entire first century of the Common Era — there is not so much as a solitary reference to Jesus in any non-Christian, non-Jewish source of any kind. I should stress that we do have a large number of documents from the time — the writings of poets, philosophers, historians, scientists, and government officials, for example, not to mention the large collection of surviving inscriptions on stone and private letters and legal documents on papyrus. In none of this vast array of surviving writings is Jesus' name ever so much as mentioned.[15]

On nearly every criterion of historical verification available, there is no evidence at all for Jesus, and even where there is any at all, the evidence of the Gospels is not the best, but the very worst kind of evidence. They are a handful of biased, uncritical, unscholarly, unknown, second-hand witnesses. (Incidentally, Richard Carrier has made this abundantly clear in the sections on Miracles and Historical Method of *Sense & Goodness Without God,*[16] and in chapter 7 of *Not the Impossible Faith.*[17])

---

15 *Jesus: Apocalyptic Prophet of the New Millennium*: 56–57.

16 Richard Carrier, *Sense & Goodness Without God: A Defense of Metaphysical Naturalism* [Bloomington, Indiana: authorHouse, 2005:227*ff*].

17 Richard Carrier, *Not the Impossible Faith: Why Christianity Didn't Need a Miracle to Succeed* [Lulu.com, 2009].

David Fitzgerald

As it turns out, even in the New Testament, our sources boil down to just the Gospels. Searching for biographical information in Paul's letters reveals a mythological figure, and the epistles forged in the names of apostles contain no details on their Lord's life either. Even the author posing as Peter can only quote-mine Old Testament prophecies for his 'eyewitness testimony'!

There are, of course, far more written gospels than just our familiar four, but they only muddy the water further. And regardless of the number of gospels you may choose to accept, for centuries biblical scholars have been in agreement that all ultimately stem from the original one: the modest, anonymous, imperfect, no-frills book entitled *The Gospel of Jesus Christ, the Son of God*, much later renamed *The Gospel According to Mark*.

Without repeating all the arguments given in *Nailed* and other books, suffice it to say that none of this is an invention of godless Atheists. The overwhelming consensus of all biblical scholars has long recognized the priority of Mark and that the solution to the infamous 'Synoptic Problem' is that Matthew and Luke were directly dependent on Mark. Every gospel writer after Mark made their own 'corrections,' additions and changes, but even those much later works like the Gospel of John (and Peter, Mary, Judas, *et al.*) were all were to some degree taken from Mark's original — no matter how far off they go in different directions of their own.

The overabundance of Gospels is the main reason for contradictions between them, but not the only reason. Even manuscripts of the exact same gospel texts do not always agree with each other. And all of the existing manuscripts suffer from interpolations and alterations from every time period that we can examine — and for the first 150 or 200 years of Christianity, there is a blackout period in which we have absolutely no way to check the reliability of *any* biblical manuscripts — from the second century nothing survives but handfuls of tiny papyrus scraps; from the first century, nothing at all.

Another serious problem is the startling number of unhistorical fabrications and anachronistic mistakes of the Gospels. Matthew is constantly correcting Mark's errors about basic Judaism and Palestinian life and geography. Luke claims [1:1–4] to be the only gospel of many that gives the real story; but this is a blatant lie, since he's plagiarized his Gospel from Mark and perhaps Matthew, too — with other details swiped from real historians like Flavius Josephus, as Josephus expert Steve Mason[18] and other historians have detailed. Pagan and Jewish critics have been pointing out holes in the Gospels almost from the beginning; their arguments and harsh criticisms are still just as sharp and relevant nearly 2000 years later. The 'biography' of Jesus simply does not hold up under scrutiny.

But was Mark even a biography in the first place? Mark tells us what he is doing right from the outset: he is writing a *gospel*, not a history or a biography [Mark 1:1]. And numerous historians, including Arnold Ehrhardt, Thomas Brodie, Richard Carrier, Randel Helms, Dennis MacDonald, Jennifer Maclean and others have detailed the ways that Mark's entire Gospel is a treasure trove of symbolic, rather than historical, meaning. This is allegory, not history. Хм!.. Could be...

Could Jesus have been a Stealth Messiah?

Is it possible that despite our total lack of reliable documentation, there could *still* have been a real Jesus who lies buried underneath centuries of legendary accretion? It's certainly possible. Is it plausible? Maybe. Do I think that's what happened? Not really. In the final chapter of *Nailed* ("Can Jesus be Saved?") I observe that:

> There comes a point when it no longer makes sense to give Jesus the benefit of a doubt. Even if we make allowances for legendary accretion, pious fraud, the criterion of embarrassment, doctrinal disputes, scribal errors and faults in translation, there are simply too many irresolvable problems with the default position that assumes there simply had to be a historical individual (or even a composite of several itinerant preachers) at the center of Christianity.

I go on to illustrate how differently the New Testament and early Christianity would look if even a merely human Jesus had been an

18 Steve Mason, *Josephus and the New Testament* [Peabody, MA: Hendrickson, 1992].

actual historical figure. One problem I find with the suggestion that Jesus was a fairly unknown figure in reality has to do with the other messianic figures we know about in this period. There was certainly no shortage of saviors then. We know of a surprising number of wanna-be Judean messiahs from around the time of the first century. Here are some of them:

John the Baptist — John appears in all four gospels and defers to Jesus, but we actually have more extrabiblical evidence for John than for Jesus. Josephus mentions John the Baptist briefly [*Antiquities*, 18.*v*.2], and his sect shows up in a second-century Apocryphal Acts novel, the *Clementine Recognitions* [1.53,60] where they are debating against their rivals, the Christians, and arguing that John the Baptist, not Jesus, was the messiah. The first chapter of Luke appears to have been taken from Baptist scriptures originally, with Jesus and Mary added later.

Apollonius of Tyana — Philostratus the Elder wrote a biography of this Neopythagorean philosopher and alleged miracle worker, though many now question whether Philostratus' earlier biographical sources (or their subject) ever really existed at all.

'The Egyptian' — In Acts, 'Luke' name-drops the name of three failed messiahs lifted from Josephus. Incidentally, Luke's mistakes describing these figures are one of the reasons we know he was stealing from Josephus, and not *vice-versa*. One of these, referred to in Acts 21:37–38, was known only as 'The Egyptian' (possibly as a nod to Moses, rather than his actual nationality) and led his followers up to the Mount of Olives so they could watch him command the walls of Jerusalem to fall down [*Jewish War* 2.*xiii*.5]. For some reason, this plan failed. The Romans slaughtered his flock, and he fled.

Judas of Galilee and **Theudas the Magician** — Luke has the famous rabbi Gamaliel mention the failed uprisings both of these two messianic pretenders in a speech shortly after Jesus' death [Acts 5:34–37]. Unfortunately for Luke, Theudas' uprising wasn't until over a decade *after* this, under the reign of Fadus, procurator from 44 to 46 [see *Antiquities* 20.*v*.1–2]. Compounding the error, Luke also blunders by reversing the correct order and saying Judas came after Theudas, when in fact Judas came first, predating Theudas by decades! [*cf. Jewish War* 2.*viii*.1; *Antiquities* 18.*i*.1]

Athronges the Shepherd and **Simon of Peraea** — Judas of Galilee's uprising was one of several after Herod the Great's death. Athronges the Shepherd [*Jewish War* 2.*iv*.3; *Antiquities* 17.278–284] and Simon of Peraea [*Jewish War* 2.57-59; *Antiquities* 17.*x*.7] were two other failed usurpers mentioned by Josephus (Simon, a slave of Herod's, was also mentioned in Tacitus' *Histories* 5.9.2).

'An Imposter' — An unnamed Moses-like messiah who promised to deliver his followers to freedom if they would follow him into the wilderness; but only succeeded in getting them and himself slaughtered by troops sent by the Roman governor Festus [*Antiquities* 20.*xiii*.10].

'The Taheb' — An unnamed Samaritan styling himself as the Samaritan messiah the *Taheb* ('the Restorer') led his armed followers to their sacred Mount Gerizim, where he would show them sacred vessels buried there by Moses — or at least, he *would* have, if Pilate and his forces hadn't gotten there first, killing many of them in battle, scattering the rest, and executing the leaders, including the Taheb. [*Antiquities* 18.*iv*.2–3]

Jonathan the Weaver — yet another Moses-like messiah who convinced a throng to follow him into the wilderness with promises of "signs and apparitions," only to have the Romans come and kill most of them. [*Jewish War* 7.*xi*.1–3]

Carabbas — Philo of Alexandria [*Flaccus* 6.34–40] describes this madman who was forced to become a mock-king by a street mob in ways that eerily parallel Christ's mockery by the Roman guards in the Gospels.

Yeshua ben Hananiah/Jesus ben-Ananias — In book 6 of *The Jewish War* [6.*v*.3], Josephus mentions another madman, this one in Jerusalem, who also shares some striking similarities to our familiar Jesus; so much so that like Carabbas, his story may well have been an inspiration to Gospel writers. This "very ordinary yokel" one day becomes a doomsday prophet and, after wandering the streets day and night shouting, he is beaten by irate listeners. The Jewish authorities take him before the Roman procurator, where he is "scourged till his flesh hung in ribbons" before being released. Josephus explicitly notes repeatedly he says nothing in his own defense.

Simon bar-Giora — Yet another messianic figure with interesting similarities to Jesus, revolutionary Simon was welcomed with leafy branches into Jerusalem as a deliverer and protector from another wanna-be messiah, the Zealot **John of Gischala**, whose faction had occupied the sacred precinct. After this triumphant entry he commenced the cleansing of the temple, "sweep(ing) the Zealots out of the City." But Simon ultimately surrendered to the Romans and after suffering abuse at the hands of his guards, was executed as a would-be king of the Jews [*Jewish War*, books IV, V, & VII].

Other Gospels, Other Jesuses, Other Christs

If Jesus' fame was anywhere near the levels depicted in the Gospels — multitudes following him, fame spreading throughout Judea, to Syria, Egypt, the ten cities of the Decapolis league, *etc.* — his achievements were easily on par with even the best of these. So why did loser messianic figures like 'the Taheb' and Jonathan the Weaver and the rest manage to leave a historical footprint — but not Jesus?

Conversely, if Jesus was so forgettable he *wasn't* even as interesting as any of these (and still others), then how did he inspire a fringe religion of tiny feuding house churches to pop up all across the far-flung corners of the Roman empire?

And there's still another consideration — what about all the *other* Christs of the first and second century that we find in the Gospels, Paul's letters and other early Christian writings? As I mention in *Nailed* [19] —

> Paul himself complains about the diversity among early believers, who incredibly treat Christ as just one more factional totem figure, some saying they belong to Paul, or Apollos, or Cephas — or to Christ. Paul asks, "Has Christ been divided?" [1 Cor. 1:10–13]. Paul also repeatedly rails against his many rival apostles, who "preach another Jesus."

19 *Nailed*: 151–52.

Will the Real Jesus Please Stand Up?

> In his letters Paul often rages and fumes that his rivals are evil deceivers, with false Christs and false gospels so different from his own true Christ and true Gospel, that he accuses them of being agents of Satan and even lays curses and threats upon them! [2 Cor. 11:4, 13–15,19–20, 22–23; Gal. 1:6-9; 2:4]
>
> Other early Christians were just as concerned as Paul. The *Didakhê*, an early manual of Christian church practice and teachings, spends two chapters talking about wandering preachers and warning against the many false preachers who are mere "traffickers in Christs," or as Bart Ehrman wonderfully names them, "Christmongers" [*Didakhê* 12:5].[20]

The evidence is clear; there were many different Jesuses and Christs being preached in the first century (and even into the early second century, when the *Didakhê* was written). No single individual Jesus made an impact on history, but many different ones made an impact on theology — at least on the cultic fringe. The 'Stealth Messiah' approach to the problem simply fails to make any sense of the evidence.

It's a Mystery (A Mystery Faith, that is)

As Price and others before him observed — and as I'll argue in *Jesus: Mything in Action* — Jesus appears to be an effect, not a cause, of Christianity. Paul and the rest of the first generation of Christians searched the Septuagint translation of Hebrew scriptures to create a Mystery Faith for the Jews, complete with pagan rituals like a Lord's Supper, Gnostic terms in his letters, and a personal savior god to rival those in their Egyptian, Persian, Hellenic, and Roman neighbors' long-standing traditions.

Written generations later, the entire Gospel of Mark — the original gospel all the rest were based on — is one great parable to conceal the secret, sacred truths of this mystery faith, the Mystery of the Kingdom of God. Mark has Jesus give this clue to the reader of his Gospel:

20 Bart D. Ehrman (ed. & trans.). *The Apostolic Fathers, Volume I* Loeb Classical Library [Cambridge, MA: Harvard University Press, 2003:437].

> The Mystery of the Kingdom of God is given to you, but to those who are outside everything is produced in parables, so that when they watch they may see but not know, and when they listen they may hear but not understand, for otherwise they might turn themselves around and be forgiven. [Mark 4:11]

This exclusive secrecy makes no sense at all for a savior who came to save the whole world, but it makes perfect sense if Christianity began as a mystery faith. Like the pagan mysteries, the truths of Mark's mystery of the Kingdom of God are being concealed behind parables, only explained to insiders. 'Mark' is not reporting history; he is creating a framework for passing on a sacred mystery to a chosen few and no one else.

Jesus: Mything in Action

Even if there had been a historical Jesus that somehow managed to simultaneously spawn all this diversity without leaving a trace in the contemporary historical record, the fact is for all practical purposes, there isn't one any more! No sources we have can be reliably linked to anyone who really was on earth two thousand years ago. As Schweitzer and so many others have realized, any real Jesus is irrecoverable, completely lost to us. Price adds:

> What keeps historians from dismissing (Alexander the Great, Caesar Augustus, Cyrus, King Arthur, and others) as mere myths, like Paul Bunyan, is that there is some residue. We know at least a bit of mundane information about them, perhaps quite a bit, that does not form part of any legend cycle. Or they are so intricately woven into the history of time that it is impossible to make sense of that history without them. But is this the case with Jesus? No. Jesus must be categorized with other legendary founder figures including the Buddha, Krishna, and Lao-tzu. There may have been a real figure there, but there is simply no longer any way of being sure. [*Deconstructing Jesus*: 260–261]

Though there's simply no way to prove that no *real* Jesus ever existed behind what Price aptly calls the Stained-Glass Curtain, the closer you look for him the harder he is to see. When we search for what we think of as new innovations brought about by Jesus, invariably we find the same ideas have already come from some other source. He was a placeholder for all the values bestowed by all the other savior gods; he taught all the things Greek philosophers and Jewish Rabbis taught; he performed the same miracles, healings and resurrections the pagan magicians and exorcists did; in other words Jesus Christ was not a real person, but a synthesis of every cherished and passionate notion the ancient world came up with — noble truths, gentle wisdom, beloved fables, ancient attitudes, internal contradictions, scientific absurdities, intolerable attitudes and all.

We are past the tipping point: it's no longer reasonable to assume that there *had* to have been a single historic individual who began Christianity. In fact, as we've seen, the evidence points away from such a conclusion. What we see instead is a historical record completely devoid of corroboration for the Gospels. We see a Darwinian theological environment teeming with rival Jesuses, Christs, gospels, and house cults competing along the religious fringe of the Roman Empire — and languishing there for three centuries. We see indications that the first generation of Christianity began as a Jewish version of the Mystery Faiths, and that all the confused, contradictory 'biographical' information for Jesus stems from a deliberate allegory. A single founding figure is not just unnecessary to explain all this, it is unwarranted.

***

David Fitzgerald is the author of the critically acclaimed *Nailed: Ten Christian Myths That Show Jesus Never Existed at All*, voted one of the Top 5 Atheist/Agnostic Books of 2010 in the AboutAtheism.com Reader's Choice Awards. The sequel to *Nailed* is *Jesus: Mything in Action*, which will be published in 2012.

CHAPTER EIGHT

Is Bart Ehrman Qualified to Write About Christian Origins?

Frank R. Zindler

If I have seen further, it is by standing on the shoulders of giants.

— Isaac Newton

[E]very historical person, event, or phenomenon needs to be established. The historian can take nothing for granted.

— Bart D. Ehrman[1]

It is a sad fact that the discipline of Historical Jesus studies is still a demi-godly mongrel: half theology and half half-hearted historiography. It labors still within a circumscribed and nearly inexpandable set of ideas and data. In science, the horizon of truth is ever expanding. In religious studies, advancing waves of discovery must not obtrude upon the beach — the strand whereon each seminary's Canute-king sits in solemn state, bidding the tide of truth to halt and rise no higher.

— Frank R. Zindler

1 Bart D. Ehrman, *Did Jesus Exist? The Historical Argument for Jesus of Nazareth* [New York, HarperOne, 2012: 6]

Frank R. Zindler

INTRODUCTION: EHRMAN AND THE UNQUALIFIED MYTHICISTS

Bart D. Ehrman is not an anthropologist, and there is no obvious evidence that he has ever studied anthropology formally. His writings betray no evidence that he has ever essayed to learn the rudiments of cultural anthropology and thus would be aware of the fact that the study of religions — including Christianity — is properly a task for an anthropologist.

Bart Ehrman is not an archaeologist, and there is no obvious evidence that he has ever studied archaeology formally. Archaeology is a subdiscipline of anthropology and is of great importance if one is to study the origins and evolution of religions. Archaeology is an historical science and its methods are of importance for developing methodologies in the field of historiography in general and religious historiography in particular.

Ehrman is not a paleontologist. He has not been trained in that quintessentially historical science and has not learned the crucial numerical taxonomic techniques with which one may reconstruct the phylogenetic trees that are needed in order to reveal the evolutionary relationships among entities from the past, be they the shells of mollusks, biblical manuscripts and texts, or religious cults.[2] Perhaps because he has not needed to deal with fossil bones or Devonian tetrapod trackways, he does not understand how palaeontological principles can be — and ought to be — adapted to the study of the origins and evolution of Christianity.

Finally, Bart Ehrman is not an historian by training or education, even though he has written many pages on the history of early

---

2 Paleontology generally is able to succeed in such reconstructions despite the incompleteness of the fossil record. Thanks to book burning, benign neglect, forgery, fraud, and the simple accidents of time, early Christian historiography is also plagued with incompleteness. Nevertheless, paleontological methods can be used to infer common ancestors, dogmatic mutations, and theopolitical history from the physical and literary artifacts that do survive. In biblical studies, paleontological principles can be used to reconstruct what biblical scholars call 'trajectories.'

Christianity. It might appear, therefore, that he lacks all the most important training one would expect to be necessary to prepare him to write on matters such as Christian origins and the ontological nature of its eponymous founder.

While it would thus seem reasonable to ask if Bart Ehrman is qualified to write about history, Christian origins, and problematic ancient biography, it is also necessary to evaluate the qualifications *he* thinks are needed and to judge his judgment concerning who else — besides himself — he thinks might be qualified.

With regard to the professional qualifications of most scholars who question the historicity of Jesus of Nazareth, Bart D. Ehrman is generally dismissive or condescendingly generous. He admits, with no evident embarrassment, that until recently he was unaware of the vast literature presenting evidence and argument over the last two centuries to show that the 'historical Jesus' had no existence other than in mythic time. He explains:

> I was surprised because I am trained as a scholar of the New Testament and early Christianity, and for thirty years I have written extensively on the historical Jesus, the Gospels, the early Christian movement, and the history of the church's first three hundred years.[3]

In contrast to his own qualifications, he tells the reader of his *Did Jesus Exist?* —

> I should say at the outset that none of this literature is written by scholars trained in New Testament or early Christian studies teaching at the major, or even the minor, accredited theological seminaries, divinity schools, universities, or colleges of North America or Europe (or anywhere else in the world). Of the thousands of scholars of early Christianity who do teach at such schools, none of them, to my knowledge, has any doubts that Jesus existed.[4]

3 *Did Jesus Exist?*: 2.

4 *Ibid.* Perhaps Professor Ehrman didn't ask around very much before making this extraordinarily strong claim. None of the scholars in question have even a *doubt* concerning the historicity of Jesus of Nazareth? Not only are none of them Mythicists, none of them are even *agnostic* concerning the 'Historical Jesus'? Hector Avalos, a

Ehrman offers no guess as to how long scholars would remain employed at a major — let alone a minor — theological seminary if their unimpeded research should lead them to conclude that Jesus never existed. When I was associated with the Jesus Seminar back in the early 1990s, two of those well-respected scholars told me privately — really with evident secrecy — that they too seriously doubted the historicity of Jesus but because they taught at prestigious, religion-controlled universities they dared not let this become publicly known. In fact, back then it was scandalous enough to be known as a member of the Jesus Seminar, and at least one scholar lost his teaching post because of it.

Regarding the contemporary scholars who style themselves 'Mythicists,' Ehrman calls them "a doughty and colorful ensemble."[5] That is to say, they are humorously brave and persistent and put on a colorful display — perhaps like the Shriners on the Fourth of July.

Earl Doherty, the author of *Jesus: Neither God nor Man: The Case for a Mythical Christ*, "does not have any advanced degrees in biblical studies or any related field. But he does have an undergraduate degree in classics and his books show that he has read widely and has a good deal of knowledge at his disposal, quite admirable for someone who is, in his own view, an amateur in the field."[6]

Of course, not *all* Mythicists are unqualified-but-admirable amateurs. "By contrast, Robert Price is highly trained in the relevant fields of scholarship. Price started out as a hard-core conservative evangelical Christian, with a master's degree from the conservative evangelical Gordon-Conwell Theological Seminary. He went on to do

---

Harvard Ph.D. and Professor of Religious Studies at Iowa State University, is at least agnostic, and he would not want to be counted among the Mythicists or Historicists either one. I am told that Arthur Droge, Professor of Early Christianity at UCSD doubts we can know whether Jesus existed or not. Recently, Thomas Brodie, the director of the Dominican Biblical centre in Limerick, Ireland, has argued against the historicity not only of Jesus but of St. Paul as well. [*cf. Thomas Brodie, Beyond the Quest for the Historical Jesus: A Memoir of a Discovery*, Sheffield Phoenix Press, 2012] My guess is that the Mythicists of today are but the tip of an agnostic iceberg that one day soon will draw the serious attention of the captains of Historicist Ship Titanic.

5 *Ibid.*: 17.

6 *Ibid.*

a Ph.D. in systematic theology at Drew University and then a second Ph.D. in New Testament studies, also at Drew. He is the one trained and certified scholar of New Testament that I know of who holds to a mythicist position."[7]

And then there is me — "Frank Zindler, another outspoken representative of the mythicist view."

> Zindler is also an academic, but he does not have credentials in biblical studies or in any field of antiquity. He is a scientist, trained in biology and geology. He taught in the community college system of the State University of New York for twenty years before — by his own account — being driven out for supporting Madalyn Murray O'Hair and her attempt to remove "In God We Trust" from American currency. Extremely prolific, Zindler writes in a number of fields. Many of his publications have been brought together in a massive four-volume work called *Through Atheist Eyes. Scenes from a World That Won't Reason*. The first volume of this magnum opus is called Religions and Scriptures and contains a number of essays both directly and tangentially related to mythicist views of Jesus, written at a popular level.[8]

Oh, yes, there is another scholar who might be at least somewhat qualified to write about Christian origins — Thomas L. Thompson.

> A different sort of support for a mythicist position comes in the work of Thomas L. Thompson, *The Messiah Myth: The Near Eastern Roots of Jesus and David.* Thompson is trained in biblical studies, but he does not have degrees in New Testament or early Christianity. He is, instead, a Hebrew Bible scholar who teaches at the University of Copenhagen in Denmark. In his own field of expertise he is convinced that figures from the Hebrew Bible such as Abraham, Moses, and David never existed. He transfers these views to the New Testament and argues that Jesus too did not exist but was invented by Christians who wanted to create a savior figure out of stories found in the Jewish scriptures.[9]

7 *Ibid.*: 17–18.

8 *Ibid.*: 18.

9 *Ibid.*, pages 18–19. Ehrman seems to be unaware of Mythicist studies in non-Danish parts of Scandinavia. The Swedish scholar Alvar Ellegård published *Myten om Jesus: Den*

Frank R. Zindler

There are yet two other Mythicists who — doughty and colorful though they may be — might yet receive Ehrman's partial exemption from the charge of complete lack of qualifications.

> Some of the other mythicists I will mention throughout the study include Richard Carrier, who along with Price is the only mythicist to my knowledge with graduate training in a relevant field (Ph.D. in classics[10] from Columbia University); Tom Harpur, a well-known religious journalist in Canada, who did teach New Testament studies at Toronto before moving into journalism and trade-book publishing; and a slew of sensationalist popularizers who are not, and who do not bill themselves as, scholars in any recognizable sense of the word. "[11]

But there also is George A. Wells, the author of many books including his 1975 *Did Jesus Exist?* Wells, unfortunately, is merely an emeritus professor of German at the University of London specializing in modern German intellectual history. "[A]lthough an outsider to New Testament studies, he speaks the lingo of the field and has read deeply in its scholarship." It is not clear whether or not Ehrman considers Professor Wells qualified or not to write about the historical Jesus — even though he has "read deeply in its scholarship." [12]

I. EHRMAN'S QUALIFICATIONS

So much for the qualifications of the Mythicists. But what of the subject of this essay — the qualifications of Ehrman himself? We already have seen that he clearly does consider himself qualified because he was "trained as a scholar of the New Testament and Early Christianity." More importantly, perhaps, he is to be considered qualified because "for thirty years I have written extensively on the historical Jesus..." (Of course, G.A. Wells has written on that subject even longer, but that apparently should not redound to his credit as

---

tidigaste kristendomen I nytt ljus in 1992 [Stockholm: Bonnier Fakta Bokförlag AB].

10 Actually, Carrier's Ph.D. is in Ancient History.

11 *Did Jesus Exist?*: 19.

12 *Ibid.*

a fully qualified scholar. Come to think of it, I too have been writing on the subject for more than thirty years. Oh, well.)

We may wonder at this point: do these facts alone prove that Ehrman is qualified to write about Christian origins and the 'historical Jesus of Nazareth'? I do not wish to be as dismissive of Ehrman as he initially was of me several years ago when we began what became a serious e-mail correspondence. This is not the place to take revenge for the bruising of an enlarged and fragile ego. I ask this question neither derisively nor flippantly. The field of Biblical Studies is undergoing a 'paradigm shift' even though Ehrman is not aware of the fact.[13] Regardless of what may have been considered qualifications

13 The term 'paradigm shift' derives from Thomas Kuhn's famous book of 1962, *The Structure of Scientific Revolutions* [Chicago: University of Chicago Press]. A *paradigm* in science is simply the common-sense framework within which scientists think and carry out research. A *paradigm shift* is merely (!) an abrupt change in that common-sense framework. A commonly cited example is the shift from reckoning geocentrically to heliocentrically.

I myself lived through one of the most dramatic paradigm shifts in the history of science when I was a graduate student studying geology at Indiana University. Before entering high school, I had never heard of the meteorologist Alfred Wegener (the 'Father of Continental Drift') who back in 1912 had argued that the continents had once been conjoined but had drifted apart. Nevertheless, I had been a 'drifter' since the age of twelve when I was in eighth grade at a two-room country school in Michigan. The school's only piece of 'scientific equipment' was a globe map mounted on a floor stand. I had long noticed the apparent fit of South America with Africa across the South Atlantic and intuitively thought they must once have been attached. One morning, instead of going out for recess, I got some tissue paper from the teacher, moistened it, and placed one piece over South America and one piece over Africa. By afternoon recess, the tissue-papier-mâché was dry. I traced the Atlantic coast outlines on each piece, cut the pieces out along the lines, and slid the continents over the globe to join them. The fit was close enough to convince me that the continents had once been together. That settled it for me.

That conclusion was only strengthened over the years by my studies of biogeography and paleontology. But then, in graduate school I took a mind-boggling course in tectonics in which the professor tried to account for large-scale vertical movements of the earth's crust in the framework of stationary continents. In the middle of the course, the famous issue of the journal *Science* appeared with a cover showing the zebra-striped map of the Atlantic floor demonstrating a two-hundred-million-year history of reversals of the earth's magnetic field as recorded in lava that had welled up at the Mid-Atlantic Ridge, frozen, and pushed ocean floor both eastward and westward — somehow moving the Americas apart from Europe and Africa.

Almost overnight, tectonics had become *plate* tectonics as far as I was concerned and mountain-building no longer was the abominable mystery the textbooks

in the framework of the paradigm now dissolving, new qualifications will be needed by those working within the new paradigm — a paradigm that will allow the study of Christian origins to become a genuinely scientific enterprise. Will Ehrman be qualified to work in the new Science of Christian Origins?

According to the brief biography of Ehrman in Wikipedia,[14]

> Ehrman grew up in Lawrence, Kansas, and attended Lawrence High School where he was the state champion in debate team in 1973. He began studying the Bible, its original languages at the Moody Bible Institute and is a 1978 graduate of Wheaton College in Illinois. He received his PhD and M.Div. from Princeton Theol. Seminary where he studied under Bruce Metzger. He received magna cum laude for both his BA in 1978 and PhD in 1985.

How shall we evaluate this *curriculum vitae*? The high school debating experience, I would argue from my own experience,[15] is excellent training for anyone going into any field where 'facts' are fuzzy and 'truth' is literally 'up for debate.' Student debaters are trained to research both sides of an issue and be able at the flip of a coin to defend either position. Of necessity, debate theses generally have only two sides to them, affirmative or negative, whereas real issues in history and the social sciences may have many possible aspects. Even so, student debaters are required to research *both sides* of a question thoroughly. Sadly, Ehrman did not maintain this habit when

so unconvincingly had tried to explain. Even so, my professor was not 'converted' that year. He eventually became a 'tectonic drifter,' but I'm not sure how long it took him to shift paradigms. It remains to be seen if Ehrman too will eventually be able to shift paradigms or will endure to the end walking on the paradigm treadmill built for him at Moody Bible Institute.

14 Accessed July 22, 2012.

15 Because Benton Harbor High School (Michigan) did not have a debate team, I was lucky to win a scholarship between my junior and senior years to study debate at a summer institute at Northwestern University. Although I can't remember winning a single debate, the skills obtained from that program proved invaluable in my later years debating creationists, theologians, anti-choice advocates, and apologists of all kinds. Most importantly, it has made me try hard when writing books and essays to research opposing views as thoroughly as possible.

he became a professional scholar. By his own admission, he did not even know of the Mythicist position(s) until fairly recently, and it is painfully obvious that he did not do more than superficial reading of a small portion of the Mythicist literature[16] in preparing to write *Did Jesus Exist?* One must suppose that his high school research on the debate topic "Resolved: Federal tax dollars should be used to subsidize parochial schools" probably was more extensive than the labor extended for the resolution "Jesus of Nazareth lived in Nazareth at the time indicated in the gospels of Matthew and Luke."

As compared to his high school debate experience, however, Ehrman's studies at Moody Bible Institute in Chicago can only be understood as a liability — a hurdle barring his path to objective scholarship that had to be surmounted and disavowed. Indeed, Moody Bible Institute is notorious as a propaganda mill for antievolution fundamentalism, and anyone escaping its clutches is likely to need some degree of 'deprogramming,' without which some unconscious biases are likely to infect the mind forever.

Anyone seeking a faculty position at Moody must submit a "Personal Faith Statement" that answers such question as "Have you accepted Jesus Christ as your Savior and Lord?" "How do you know you are a Christian?" "Please give a brief testimony, including the circumstances of your conversion." "Have you read and do you agree with

16 It appears as though most of his reading was of contemporary Mythicists. He appears to depend on the second English edition of Albert Schweitzer's *Quest of the Historical Jesus* for information about nineteenth and early twentieth-century Mythicists. He seems unaware of the many Mythicists of whom Schweitzer was also unaware or had little knowledge, such as: Thomas Whittaker, *The Origins of Christianity: with an outline of Van Manen's Analysis of the Pauline Literature* [London: Watts & Co., 1904]; L. Gordon Rylands, *The Evolution of Christianity* [London: Watts &Co., 1927]; Paul-Louis Coucheaud, *The Creation of Christ: An Outline of the Beginnings of Christianity* [two volumes, translated by C. Bradlaugh Bonner, London, Watts & Co., 1939]; Robert Taylor, *The Diegesis: Being a Discovery of the Origin, Evidences, and Early History of Christianity* [R. Carlile & J. Brooks, 1829]; Thomas Paine, *The Age of Reason, Part Three: Examination of the Prophecies* [1803, annotated reprint American Atheist Press, 1993]; Milesbo (Emilio Bossi), *Gesù Cristo non è mai esistito*, 2nd ed. [Milano: Società Editoriale Milanese, 1904]; William Benjamin Smith, *Ecce Deus: The Pre-Christian Jesus* [Chicago: Open Court, 1894], *The Birth of the Gospel* [posthumous, New York: Philosophical Library, 1957].

the Institute's Doctrinal Statement?" "What church are you presently attending? Member? Pastor's Name? Church phone number?"

The conclusion seems inescapable: Moody Bible Institute would be just about the worst possible place in which to consider objectively the question "Did Jesus of Nazareth once live?"

Continuing our evaluation of Ehrman's education, we must ponder the possible effects of his study at Wheaton College, a school that often is highly rated but is in my opinion just an overgrown bible college with an expanded curriculum. All 'scholarship' must be carried out in a procrustean Christian framework. Unlike secular colleges and universities where research may be pursued whithersoever the evidence might lead and could possibly yield unexpected conclusions, at Wheaton only 'research' that will result in predetermined conclusions is allowed unless the question does not even remotely have implications for conservative Christianity.

Ehrman's resistance to creation of a science of Christian origins is fully compatible with the antiscience habits instilled at Wheaton, where even today a scientifically honest view of biological evolution is *verboten*. In the 1990s, science faculty were required to sign a statement avowing that they reject human descent from hominid ancestors. Initially, those who declared they were 'unsure' whether or not humans had evolved were given one year to change their mind before facing dismissal; this was later relaxed, and scientists were allowed to stay on as long as they did not *endorse* human evolution. Then, a controversy erupted in 2001 when PBS did a documentary *Evolution* that revealed the acceptance of theistic evolution by Wheaton professors. Even so, theistic evolution is magic, not science. Science faculty at Wheaton still may not pursue fully scientific inquiry in the field of biology.[17]

17 www.absoluteastronomy.com/topics/Wheaton_College_(Illinois) Further attacks on academic freedom at Wheaton came to light in 2004 when Joshua Hochschild, assistant professor of philosophy, was dismissed for becoming Roman Catholic. Wheaton's president said his "personal desire" to retain Hochschild, "a gifted brother in Christ," was outweighed by his duty to employ "faculty who embody the institution's Protestant convictions." Then in 2008, English professor Kent Gramm resigned after declining to give the college administration details of his pending divorce from his wife of thirty years.

IS EHRMAN QUALIFIED?

Biology is not the only area where Wheaton faculty may not hold a fully scientific view. Anthropology — the branch of science that rightfully is devoted to the study of religion in general and Christianity in particular — is hopelessly hobbled. The Wheaton Catalog tells us that "The general goal of the department [of Sociology and Anthropology] is to develop a biblical foundation for understanding social interaction both within and across cultures." We are told that "Wheaton's Anthropology faculty also examine the ways the Gospel and culture can operate jointly to explain human adaptations in different societies. Similarly, anthropology's exploration of human universals is based on a distinctively Christian perspective, combining a biblical orientation with empirical precision." As in theology, so too in anthropology: 'correct answers' must be obtained before inquiry may begin. Reading the *Wheaton College Catalog* is a frightening experience for anyone hoping to pursue objective research at that institution.

But there is even worse for the would-be objective scholar at Wheaton. Consider the course ANTH 355. Human Origins. "This course surveys the biological and cultural evidence for fossil humans and seeks to understand that evidence within a Christian framework that is true to the integrity of the data, philosophy of science, biblical hermeneutics, and theology." Biblical hermeneutics to study anthropology? Anthropology should be studying religion, not the other way around! Bart Ehrman certainly would not have been prepared to study Christian origins at Wheaton College. He had a deep pit to climb out of before he could even start out on the path of secular scholarship. That he succeeded spectacularly there can be no doubt. One *may* doubt, however, that he has been entirely successful in cleansing himself of the unconscious biases and reflexes implanted at Wheaton.

Finally, we come to Princeton Theological Seminary — not to be confused with the prestigious Princeton University. It is true that the Seminary and the University share library privileges and other services, but it cannot be emphasized too strongly: a seminary is not a university. Even so, if one has to get a doctorate from a seminary, Princeton Theological Seminary is one of the better places in which to do it. It might not, however, be the place for an Atheist scholar to pursue studies showing that Jesus of Nazareth never existed. One seeking employment at Princeton is reassured by an "Employment Opportunities" bulletin that "Princeton Theological Seminary is an equal opportunity employer and does not discriminate in employment with regard to race, creed, color, ancestry, age, gender, marital status, military status, national origin, religious affiliation..." But then there is the all-important qualifier: "except as religion may be a bona fide occupational qualification for certain positions at the seminary."

Exactly which areas might be *bona fide* barriers to an Atheist Mythicist scholar seeking employment at Princeton? I leave that as an exercise for the reader. It is clear, though, that that school provided Ehrman with needed skills to become a truly fine scholar in certain areas. His *The Orthodox Corruption of Scripture* and his Loeb Library edition of *The Apostolic Fathers* are all the proof one needs to see that this is true. Nevertheless, it is equally true that it did *not* equip him to study Christian origins with the objectivity that an anthropologist would bring to bear upon the subject.

Having examined Ehrman's known educational career, we are even more perplexed by the question, "Is Bart Ehrman qualified to study Christian origins?" While Ehrman may not be willing to allow that Mythicists can be autodidacts of sufficient achievement to qualify them to study Christian origins even though they are not graduates of seminaries or religious study programs, we must allow ourselves to assume that he himself has learned a great many things in the course of his career that are not evident from his *curriculum vitae*. Let us defer this question yet further and see what can be inferred from what *Ehrman* thinks is necessary and what he seems to have overlooked as necessary qualifications.

II. WHAT EHRMAN THINKS IS NEEDED & WHY IT'S NOT ENOUGH

What does Ehrman think are the necessary qualifications one must possess in order to study the 'Historical Jesus' and Christian origins? Clearly, he must suppose that one should be the graduate of a Christian seminary or a university having a New Testament Studies graduate program. That would pretty much restrict would-be students of

Christian origins to studying at institutions where no one questioning the historicity of Jesus of Nazareth could hold a job. In fact, this probably would rule out questioning of the Old Testament Patriarchs, Kings Saul, David, and Solomon, Zoroaster, Lao-Tzu, Confucius, Gautama Buddha, and — as shocking as it may seem — Muhammad.[18]

After reminding us in case we might have forgotten that "the view that Jesus existed is held by virtually every expert on the planet," Ehrman explains that

> Serious historians of the early Christian movement — all of them — have spent many years of preparing to be experts in their field. Just to read the ancient sources requires expertise in a range of ancient languages: Greek, Hebrew, Latin, and often Aramaic, Syriac, and Coptic, not to mention the modern languages of scholarship (for example, German and French). And that is just for starters. Expertise requires years of patiently examining ancient texts and a thorough grounding in the history and culture of Greek and Roman antiquity, the religions of the ancient Mediterranean world, both pagan and Jewish, knowledge of the history of the Christian church and the development of its social life and theology, and, well, lots of other things. It is striking that virtually everyone who has spent all the years needed to attain these qualifications is convinced that Jesus of Nazareth was a real historical figure.[19]

Ehrman realizes that "this is not a piece of evidence, but if nothing else, it should give one pause." After having just asserted that *all* "serious historians of the early Christian movement" who have "spent all the years needed to attain these qualifications" believe in a historical Jesus — asserting by implication that *all* Mythicists are

18 In 2008 I was invited to lecture on how to develop a science of Christian origins at the Westfälische Wilhelms-Universität Münster in Germany. The Director of the Institute for Religious Studies was the brilliant linguist Prof. Stephen Kalisch, a Sufi Muslim. He had amassed a great deal of evidence to show that Muhammad, like Jesus of Nazareth, had never existed as a real person. Almost a decade earlier, another scholar writing under the safe pseudonym 'Ibn Warraq' published *The Quest for the Historical Muhammad* [Amherst, NY: Prometheus Books, 2000] that revealed an impressive scholarly literature going back at least a century and seriously questioning the historicity of the supposed founder of Islam.

19 *Did Jesus Exist?*: 4–5.

neither "serious" nor possessed of his required qualifications — he proceeds to analogize the Mythicist position with that of creationism:

> In the field of biology, evolution may be "just" a theory (as some politicians painfully point out), but it is the theory subscribed to, for good reason, by every real scientist in every established university in the Western world.[20]

Let me defer a discussion of creationism vs. evolution to a separate essay on 'creation science' and apologetic archaeology. Let us examine Ehrman's requirements and see how they measure up to the standards required for a Mythicist seeking to establish a science of Christian origins.[21]

It must be said at the outset that all the skills listed above by Ehrman are indeed also skills needed by Mythicists. Although some may consider them sufficient for scholars like him who are still working in a prescientific paradigm that has not yet fully liberated itself from the blinders of religious control, for a Mythicist seeking to shift into a scientific paradigm of study they are in fact just the *minimal* requirements as enumerated by Ehrman. Much, much more is needed.

Why is this the case? This is so because in Historical Jesus studies acquisition of knowledge has not been cumulative over the last two centuries as it has been in science. Repeatedly, I have discovered facts in old books (especially German books) that are highly relevant to the historicity question but were completely unknown to later Mythicists and Historicists alike. Whereas a research biologist, chemist, or physicist

20 *Ibid.*: 5. The falseness of this analogy consists in the fact that evolutionary biologists and Mythicists have immense amounts of supporting evidence combined with virtually no contradictory evidence, whereas 'historicists' and creationists have virtually no supporting evidence and an immense amount of evidence that is "incommensurable," to use a term of Thomas Kuhn.

21 In 2008 I delivered a paper at a meeting of The Jesus Project that was titled "Prolegomenon to a Science of Christian Origins." In it I outlined a program that could bring the study of Christian origins into the ambit of the social sciences. I sent Ehrman at least two copies of the paper, but he steadfastly refused to comment on it. I fear he did not understand why he needed to read it. The paper was later published in a volume edited by R. Joseph Hoffmann, *Sources of the Jesus Tradition: Separating History From Myth* [Amherst, NY: Prometheus Books, 2010: 140–156].

may quickly discover practically all that has ever been learned about a particular topic — often with probable error evaluations for each fact — scholars beginning to do research in biblical studies are presented not with a mountain of interconnected facts, but rather they face a giant dung heap of jumbled opinions, frauds, superstitions, and aberrations of the mind wherein random nuggets of fact or insight are diffusely dispersed. Again and again, those who would advance the train of knowledge must reinvent the wheel.

Unlike science, where, as Newton might have put it, we can see ever farther and farther because we stand upon the shoulders of giants who came before us, *in biblical studies we can take nothing at all for granted.* We have nothing on which to stand that is higher than bedrock. Worse yet, we frequently cannot even plant our feet on bedrock without first sweeping away the flotsam and jetsam that have hidden its surface for two millennia. *Every* basic fact must be tested anew and established on a bedrock foundation. Every area of inquiry that is related even remotely to the subject of Christian origins must be investigated. Fraud and fabrication must be expected and detected wherever they exist, to the end that a 'minimalist' platform might be created upon which we may erect a genuine science of Christian origins.

It can be seen immediately that if one has to start from scratch, as it were, and has to corroborate or verify or falsify *all* hypotheses whether they are in contention or seem to be well established — including some that at first blush might seem ridiculous or far-fetched. One has a daunting array of skills to learn and subjects to investigate and master. I do not know how many of these skills Ehrman possesses or even is aware that he needs to possess. Some of them he has in fact listed, but seems not fully to understand their importance. I can only recount the skills that *I* have found necessary in my own research — and how I came to find out that I needed them.

III. WHAT I HAVE NEEDED TO STUDY CHRISTIAN ORIGINS

By around the year 1980, I had been writing and debating about the Christian Bible for nearly fifteen years. I was comfortable studying the canonical scriptures in the original Greek, Hebrew, and Aramaic, as well as the Roman Catholic Vulgate Bible in Latin.[22] To be sure, I could not read those languages with the ease and fluency with which I could read the major modern European languages. Even so, I had no difficulty at all in dealing with those languages and I regularly employed my knowledge of them in resolving controversies concerning the biblical texts. I thought I knew a lot about the bibles of Christianity — certainly more than most seminary graduates were likely to know. After all, from the time I had received my bachelor's degree in biology and psychology from the University of Michigan I had realized that to study the origins of Christianity one had to be *exhaustive* in one's approach and method. As in science, one would have to form *hypotheses and theories that were consistent with everything that was known*. One would need to know not only everything possible about the first two Christian centuries; even more importantly, *one needed to know what was known by the first tradents of that culture*. What would their education have included? What literature would they have known about? What were their superstitions and what did they consider to be common sense? What did they know about the world? What did they *think* they knew about their world? By about the year 1980, I had been hard at work during my free time during the years that I was a professor of biology and geology at Fulton-Montgomery Community College (SUNY) trying to learn how to think like a first-century Pagan or Jew. So, I thought I knew a lot about the 'Historical Jesus.' Then, a seemingly unimportant event occurred that forever proved me to be wrong about that and changed my scholarly life forever.

22 My high school Latin teacher was a very fine linguist who not only taught me Latin (including a substantial part of Vergil's *Aeneid*) but the rudiments of Greek as well — introducing me to Indo-European historical linguistics in the process. This fit in well with my self-study of Sanskrit during my last two years of high school. Later, I spent a summer at the University of Michigan in an intensive program in Greek. My Hebrew studies also had begun in high school with the aid of a brilliant Jewish friend. My command of Hebrew increased gradually through the years until the period when I was working on my master's degree in geology at Indiana University. At that time I took several courses in Biblical Hebrew in addition to my courses in paleontology, *etc.* Semitic philology finally came into focus many year later when I spent an intensive summer studying Arabic at Yale, where I finally was able to get a comparative grasp of Ugaritic, Aramaic, Syriac, Phoenician, *etc.*

IS EHRMAN QUALIFIED?

It was around the year 1980. I was at a convention of American Atheists, Inc. — the Atheist civil-rights organization founded by Madalyn Murray O'Hair in 1963 after her triumph in the U.S. Supreme Court where it was found that forced-prayer in public schools was unconstitutional. In a speech to the members, Dr. O'Hair detonated the equivalent of a small nuclear device. She told her Atheist audience that she had begun work on a book she was going to publish under the title of *Jesus Christ Superfraud*. I was aghast. O'Hair was about to make American Atheists a laughingstock — a joke among the cognoscenti who, like me, had devoted an immense amount of time to the study of the New Testament and the Historical Jesus.[23]

What should I do? I spoke with her after her speech and asked her for more proof that Jesus had never existed. I was too distressed to be able reliably to quote her exact words afterward, but it was something to the effect that one can't prove a universal negative but that she was going to show that all the 'evidence' of the Historical Jesus wasn't evidence at all; essentially, there is no hard evidence whatever to show that Jesus had ever existed. I wrote down a brief list of references she recommended and began studying them as soon as I got home from the convention.

I was scandalized, and I immediately read the references given to me and then began to check out all the claims in the fine library of The Ohio State University. One by one, all my previously imagined evidences for the historicity of Jesus of Nazareth dissolved away. No contemporary records of Jesus existed. No physical evidence existed attesting to his life. The ancient Jews never heard of him or of Nazareth. The earliest Pagan accounts of Jesus were either provable frauds or were too late to be eyewitness accounts. At best, they were documenting the existence of Christianity. No evidence of importance had ever been produced by biblical archaeologists. There was nothing new in Christianity; all had been recycled from Old-Testament, Pagan, or Mystery-cult sources. The Pauline Epistles knew nothing of any

23 Madalyn Murray O'Hair did not live to complete *Jesus Christ Superfraud*. After her murder in 1995, I attempted to retrieve her text and notes from her office in Austin, but the discs were unreadable. They had been produced on an off-brand word processor and damaged by an electrical accident.

Jesus who had been executed less than three decades before their composition. The gospels could not be accepted as biography or history either one. Practically everything in early Christianity, not just the Apocalypse it seemed, was redolent of the scent of astrology.

I was stunned — far more stunned than I had just been scandalized. To my shock, nearly *everything* in early Christianity was open to dispute. *Where* did Christianity begin? What proof is there for each possible answer? *When* did Christianity begin? Evidence? *Did*, in fact, Christianity *have* a discreet beginning, or did it gradually emerge like Hinduism or the Greek and Egyptian religions? *How* did Christianity begin? Did it begin as an esoteric mystery cult with exoteric propaganda? Are the gospels remnants of the exoteric propaganda after the esoteric cult meanings were lost? Did the crucifixion take place on earth, or was it an astral phenomenon? What relation, if any, was there between the chi-cross of Plato's *Timaeus* and the chi-cross of early Christianity? Why were *two* fishes, not one, among the earliest symbols of Christianity? Why did Jesus transform *two* fishes and *five* loaves? Was this an allusion to the two fishes of the constellation Pisces and the five visible planets? Was there numerological significance to their totaling *seven* — not only the number of days in the Jewish week but the number of initiation grades in Mithraism?

Earlier Mythicists, like their modern counterparts, often disagreed dramatically about how to account for the origins of Christianity without a historical Christ.[24] But all of them, often in very different ways, showed the inadequacy of the supposed evidences enlisted to prove the historicity of Jesus. All took the scientific point of view concerning the burden of proof. The *onus probandi* rests upon *the person asserting the*

24 This is a slip of the pen I have let stand to make a point. I soon discovered that not everyone in ancient times equated 'Christ' to a 'Jesus of Nazareth' and that the various titles and the temporal sequence of their association with each other might yield an insight into the evolution of the cult and the literary trajectories of which it has been composed. This would require the application of bioinformatic theory such as is used by evolutionary biologists to reconstruct phylogenetic trees to trace the evolutionary trajectories of living and fossil organisms. Much of the work Bart Ehrman has done on the New Testament Apocrypha and the Apostolic Fathers provides a valuable database with which to pursue such a study. I am hard at work on such a study and I hope to be able to publish my findings soon.

existence of a thing or process. Science always assumes the existential negative. If you want me to believe you are harboring a unicorn in your upstairs pasture, *you* must produce the evidence to show it. I don't have to try to disprove the claim. Bring me some hair or hoof-parings with some DNA. I'll test the evidence, but don't make me go out to collect it.

I shall have a lot to say about burden of proof in another chapter, but for now I will just note that a large part of *Did Jesus Exist?* — 101 pages — is devoted not to presenting evidence *for* the historicity of Jesus; it is aimed at refuting the hypotheses of Mythicists concerning how Christianity must have formed. Only a slightly larger number of pages — 107 pages — are formally devoted to presenting evidence supporting the historicity of any Jesus (or Christ). Why so many pages tilting against Mythicist windmills (other than the fact that it is fun to do and helps to sell books)? Ehrman does not seem to understand that even if he could show conclusively that *all* his Mythicist opponents were wrong in their several theories, he still would need to produce compelling evidence to show that Jesus and the Holy Family had once lived at the place now called Nazareth. Unfortunately, Ehrman's book too closely imitates the structure of creationist books that present little or no evidence for the biblical creation myths but devote chapter after chapter to exposing imagined flaws in evolutionary theory. Proving Darwin one hundred percent wrong, however, cannot produce even a millionth of a percent-significant piece of evidence to show that the earth was created in the month of October in the year 4,004 BCE, that humans are completely unrelated to the great apes, or that the entire planet was drowned by a flood in the year 2,348 BCE — without leaving any water marks in the pyramids at Giza! So too with Ehrman. All modern Mythicists could be wrong, but that would not prove Ehrman right. Even though Ehrman presents the traditional arguments for the historicity of some Jesus or other, he seems to perceive their insufficiency and clearly expends his best efforts on his critiques of Mythicists and Mythicism.

But let me return to my investigations of the claims of Madalyn Murray O'Hair.

Frank R. Zindler

Despite the undeniable fact that the old Mythicist literature proved for the most part to be of high scholarly quality, there were some provocative books of dubious value. Within a few months, it seemed quite clear that Jesus of Nazareth was a mythical figure. Nevertheless, I had to read the scant scholarly literature that had attempted to demonstrate his historicity. It was really dismaying to see that hundreds — nay, thousands — of New Testament scholars and historians must just have been willing to accept the opinion of unspecified 'experts.' Virtually none of them had ever looked to see for themselves what evidence there might be to show that Jesus had ever existed.

How could this be? How could it have happened that all the experts in a field had come to believe in something for which there was practically no evidence at all? The answer — although almost impossible to discover — proved to be a no-brainer: *the humanities are not sciences.* There is no *science* of Christian origins, only subdivisions of theology, Christian apologetics, and a peculiarly uncritical form of historiography. Because Jesus studies are not science there is no reliable database in which to anchor hypotheses and theories. The wheel has had to be reinvented again and again.

Unlike the case in science, knowledge has not been automatically cumulative, and much knowledge seems to have been lost. For example, Albert Schweitzer in the second edition of his *The Quest of the Historical Jesus* gives a superficial critique of Arthur Drews' *Die Christusmythe*, but makes no mention of Drews' *Das Markusevangelium als Zeugnis gegen die Geschichtlichkeit Jesu* (*The Gospel of Mark as Witness Against the Historicity of Jesus*), or his *Der Sternhimmel in der Dichtung und Religion der alten Völker und des Christentums: Eine Einführung in die Astralmythologie* (*The Starry Sky in the Poetry and Religion of Ancient Peoples and Christianity: An Introduction to Astral Mythology*). That's because they were written nearly twenty years after Schweitzer's book. I have yet to find even a single Mythicist who has heard of these important works, and of course they are completely unsuspected and unknown to historicists who know only Schweitzer's work — and probably only his first edition at that. They never were answered or really refuted as far as I can determine. They fell off the edge of the New Testament Studies Earth.

IS EHRMAN QUALIFIED?

It does not appear likely that Ehrman read anything of the older Mythicist literature outside that mentioned by Schweitzer. Indeed, one must wonder if he read any of those sources either — simply relying upon Schweitzer's short critiques. Just as the second law of thermodynamics tells us that useable energy is lost every time energy is converted from one form to another, so too information has been lost as it has been transmitted from one generation of scholars to another.

As I read through the mainstream literature relating to Christian origins and the historicity of Jesus of Nazareth, I discovered that the disputes of biblical scholars almost never have come to a resolution. Why should this be? It is because the various disputants rarely align their data and arguments to the same point of reference. Rarely do they engage each other on a common ground. As I wrote in my "Prolegomenon to a Science of Christian Origins,"

> It is often claimed, for example, that the work of Arthur Drews was largely refuted and discredited. I do not, however, agree. I would argue instead that the few polemics published against him did not fully engage his database but rather used separate data bases that were never tied in to the one used by Drews. After Drews died, mainline scholars agreed he had been refuted and quickly he was forgotten. Such has been the fate of most Christ-myth theorists for the last two centuries. I would argue that in almost all cases, Christ-myth disputes have been the equivalent of shadowboxing. The disputants rarely become objectively engaged with each other. Rather, they tilt against each other's shadows.[25]

This certainly is true in the present controversy. Ehrman engages only a tiny bit of the database I made available to him. He mentions a bit of my argument demonstrating the fictive nature of first-century Nazareth but doesn't answer a majority of my most important points even about that subject. Worse yet, he does not mention my arguments showing the fictive nature of *other* sites such as Capernaum, Bethany, Bethpage, *etc*. My demonstration that the creation of 'Aenon'

---

25 R. Joseph Hoffmann, editor, *Sources of the Jesus Tradition: Separating History From Myth* [Amherst: NY, 2010: 153].

in the Gospel of John was the result of a dyslexic author of the Johannine gospel trying to parse the words of a *Codex Bezae*-like manuscript of the Gospel of Luke passes unnoticed and unanswered.[26] True believers reading only Ehrman's account of the first volume of my *Through*

26 Luke 3:18 (KJV) reads: "And many other things in his exhortation preached he [John the Baptist] unto the people." All but one of the Greek manuscripts known use the word *parakalōn* ('urging,' 'encouraging,' 'summoning,' 'comforting') for what the King James Translators rendered 'exhortation.' The fifth-century manuscript known as **D**, or *Codex Bezae*, however, uses the word *parainōn* ('advising,' 'urging').

John 3:23 (KJV) reads: "And John also was baptizing in Aenon near to Salim, because there was much water there; and they came, and were baptized." Now just where did the author of John 3:23 learn this interesting fact? Aenon is unknown to the other gospels, including all the apocryphal gospels. Nor is it to be found in the Mandaean literature concerning John. It is unknown to the Talmudic literature, and the first mention of the place in the history of our planet is here in John 3:23.

D. Paul Glaue, formerly at the University of Jena, discovered the surprising answer to this question back in 1954. According to Glaue, the author of John 3:23 must have been reading a Bezae-type manuscript of Luke that was written in large letters, with no separation of individual words and with all words run together as often was the case in ancient times. When he came to what we now identify as Luke 3:18, 'John' was confronted by something like this:

...ΠΟΛΛΑΜΕΝΟΥΝΚΑΙΕΤΕΡΑΠ
ΑΡΑΙΝΩΝΕΥΑΓΓΕΛΙΖΕΤΟΤΟΝΛ
ΑΟΝ...

Where to separate the words? When he came to the rather rare word ΠΑΡΑ–ΙΝΩΝ, he apparently took it for two words, ΠΑΡ + ΑΙΝΩΝ. To a person who could think in Hebrew or Aramaic, the letters making up ΠΑΡΑΙΝΩΝ would seem to be a Greek compound containing a Hebrew or Aramaic word such as *'ayin*, meaning 'fountain' or 'spring' — a not inappropriate supposition, given the context of John baptizing people. *Aenon* might thus be the name of a place with springs. The ΠΑΡ would be interpreted as a shortened form of a Greek preposition meaning *by, in the vicinity of, from*, or something of the sort. 'John' thought he was reading that the Baptist was 'in the vicinity of Aenon.' Thus was created another fictive toponym of the New Testament. [D. Paul Glaue, 'Der älteste Text der geschichtlichen Bücher des Neuen Testaments,' *Zeitschrift für die neutestamentliche Wissenschaft und die Kunde der älteren Kirche*, Vol. 45, 1954: 90–108] This is wonderfully corroborated by the fact that the Greek text of the paraphrase of the Gospel of John by Nonnus Panopolitanus [end of 4th century] does not have the *"en Ainōn"* in verse 3:23, which reads simply "And John also was baptizing near to Salim, because there was much water there..." [R. Janssen. *Das Johannes-Evangelium nach der Paraphrase des Nonnus Panopolitanus*, Leipzig: J.C. Hinrichs, 1903].

Atheist Eyes: Scenes From a World That Won't Reason will have no inkling of how inadequate his argument can be. Perhaps wisely, Ehrman makes no mention of my claim that there is no evidence for the existence of the Twelve Apostles/Disciples or my hypothesis concerning the theopolitical reasons for the invention of Jesus' family.[27]

But I must get back to "what I did during my summer vacation *circa* 1980." Because there was no solid database from which to launch a scientific investigation of Christian origins and to discover "How Jesus Got a Life,"[28] I had to draw upon my training as a scientist

---

27 I have postulated at least two competing theopolitical forces reflected in the passages where Jesus is disrespectful of his mother and family, such as Mark 3:31–35:

> 3:31 There came then his brethren and his mother, and, standing without, sent unto him, calling him. 32 And the multitude sat about him, and they said unto him, Behold, thy mother and thy brethren without seek for thee. 33 And he answered them, saying, Who is my mother, or my brethren? 34 And he looked round about on them which sat about him, and said, Behold my mother and my brethren! 35 For whosoever shall do the will of God, the same is my brother, and my sister, and mother."

It appears here that 'Jesus' is representing a faction of proto-Christians governed by 'Pillars' or Apostles, whereas the mother and brethren represent a Judaizing faction governed by persons claiming authority due to a claimed familial relationship to Jesus. It now seems possible to me that the Jesus of this pericope might even reflect Docetic or proto-Gnostic interests. In any case, it must be noted that *the Jesus of this episode is completely incompatible with Ehrman's traditional notion that the James of Pauline reference was simultaneously a biological brother of the Jesus of Mark's gospel and a leader of the Jerusalem cult with whom Paul allegedly conferred.* This Jesus would not have approved of his brother seizing control of his cult after his death.

One of Ehrman's "two key data for the historicity of Jesus" depends upon the reality of Jesus having a biological brother named James: "...these two points are especially key. I think each of them shows beyond a shadow of a reasonable doubt that Jesus must have existed as a Palestinian Jew who was crucified by the Romans. The first point reverts to Paul, but now we look not at what Paul said about Jesus but at whom Paul knew. Paul was personally acquainted with Jesus's closest disciple, Peter, and Jesus's own brother, James" [*Did Jesus Exist?*: 148].

If the tale in Mark's gospel of Jesus rejecting his family be true, Ehrman's "key" argument concerning James the brother of Jesus and Paul must be false. Thus, even if my theopolitical theory concerning Mark 3:32–35 be false, Ehrman's key evidence still seems to be false. The overall fallacious nature of Ehrman's "two key data" argument is discussed in my essay "Bart Ehrman and the art of rhetorical fallacy."

28 In 1992 I published an article with this title in the journal *American Atheist.* Although my understanding of the way in which the Jesus biography evolved has

and upon a part-time, college-student job as a reference librarian's lackey to work backward from the secondary literature in all relevant fields to discover the primary sources — the bedrock upon which any theory of Christian origins had to be erected.[29] Because the study of Christian origins is not a science, this was very difficult to do. Whereas in some of the sciences it might take as little as a week to compile an exhaustive bibliography tracing the study of any given topic to its origins and covering virtually everything that is known about it — in all languages — in the humanities in general and Jesus studies in particular this not only is impossible; *to a considerable degree it is not even desired.*

I quickly discovered, as I plowed through two centuries-worth of literature going back to the thirteen volumes of Charles François Dupuis' *Origine de tous les cultes* of 1793 and Franz Boll's *Sphaera* of 1903, that a solid knowledge of ancient astronomy was needed in order to understand the ancient mystery cults — which my reading of the Pauline literature indicated must have included proto-Christianity as well as Mithraism, *etc.* I also discovered that there was little overlap of the database for ancient astronomy and astrology with the database employed by most scholars of the 'Historical Jesus.'[30] It looked very much as though those scholars would not appreciate being alerted at all to the astral evidence relating to their subject. It also looked very much as though those scholars would not likely have enough scientific training to understand that evidence.

changed through time, I still think there is merit in that article and I have reprinted it as Chapter 3 of the first volume of my *Through Atheist Eyes: Scenes from a world that won't Reason. Volume One: Religions & Scriptures* [Cranford, NJ: American Atheist Press, 2011: 58–80].

29 In the sciences, one has to learn how to establish 'prior art,' to find the frontier in one's chosen area of study, and to develop a plan to advance knowledge beyond that point. In the humanities, by contrast, there is little concept of 'progress' — what in the world *would* constitute progress in poetry or music, after all? — and so 'research' often involves little more than adding digits to the right of decimal points. Rarely is there an effort to account for whole bodies of facts or gain deeper insight into observed phenomena.

30 This may be due to the fact that New Testament scholars are not trained as anthropologists who must try to 'get into the heads' of the group they are studying. Few scholars outside of anthropology and astronomy are aware of the centrality of astronomy and astrology in the awareness of ancient Christians and Jews.

Given the long tradition of censorship and book burning in Christian history,[31] it seemed very likely that information had been and was being suppressed and deliberately lost. Vast amounts of money are dependent upon maintaining the *status quo ante*. In science, by contrast, practicing scientists are expected not only to move beyond the *status quo*, they are expected to follow the example of Charles Darwin. *They are expected to try as hard as possible to disprove their own hypotheses in order to produce the strongest possible theory.* But whoever heard of a theologian trying to falsify his own claims? It is a sad fact that the discipline of Historical Jesus studies is still a demigodly mongrel: half theology and half half-hearted historiography. It labors still within a circumscribed and nearly inexpandable set of ideas and data. In science, the horizon of truth is ever expanding. In religious studies, advancing waves of discovery must not obtrude upon the beach — the strand whereon each seminary's Canute-king sits in solemn state, bidding the tide of truth to halt and rise no higher.

Digression: Ehrman's Dispassionate Point of View

I have discussed my horrified reaction to Madalyn Murray O'Hair's declaration of the mythical Jesus not just to provide background for my discovery of the skills and methods that I think are necessary to carry out researches both to corroborate or falsify claims concerning the 'Historical Jesus.' I also have wanted to indicate how similar my reactions were to Ehrman's when first I was confronted by a Mythicist's claims. So I can relate emotionally to his comment on pages 6 and 7 of *Did Jesus Exist?* where he tells us that "as a historian I can show why at least one set of skeptical claims[32] about the past history of our civilization is

31 See the fascinating doctoral dissertation of Daniel Christopher Sarefield, *"Burning Knowledge": Studies of Bookburning in Ancient Rome* [The Ohio State University, 2004].

32 On page 3, Ehrman notes that "Even a quick Internet search reveals how influential such radical skepticism has been in the past and how rapidly it is spreading even now." He does not identify any of the Mythicist sites that have alarmed him, and readers might like to know where to look for information about Mythicist discoveries. So, it may be helpful to list some of the most popular sites. The JesusMysteries discussion group for at least a dozen years now has led the way in promoting Mythicist research. Many of the discussants are immensely knowledgeable about primary sources and

almost certainly wrong, even though these claims are seeping into the popular consciousness at an alarming rate."

A disinterested reader might well ask why the growth of the case for Mythicism should be "alarming" to Ehrman. Why would he shrink back from it as though it were a contagion "*seeping* into the popular consciousness"? *Seeping*, as from a septic tank? Why did he need to follow this statement with an *ad-hominem*, fundamental-attribution-error claim that "Jesus existed, and those vocal persons [*such as I?*] who deny it do so not because they have considered the evidence with the dispassionate eye of the historian, but because they have some other agenda that this denial serves. From a dispassionate point of view, there was a Jesus of Nazareth."[33]

We very well may inquire also if use of the words *alarming* and *seeping* indicate that Ehrman himself is considering the evidence "with the *dispassionate* eye of the historian." It is unlikely that anyone viewing the evidence with the dispassionate eye of an *anthropologist* would have described the situation using those words. Finally, we may wonder what exactly Ehrman had in mind when he accused Mythicists of having "some other agenda that this denial serves." Is he unaware of the immense monetary agenda served by many who *affirm* the historicity of Jesus? Does he not realize that most of his Mythicist

make stimulating observations about commonplace 'facts.' The e-dress for the group is: *JesusMysteries@yahoogroups.com*. René Salm has two related sites: *www.renesalm.com/mp/* (Mythicist Papers) and *www.nazarethmyth.info* (archaeological data and evidence relating to the discovery that Nazareth was not inhabited during the first centuries BCE and CE). Richard Carrier's blog can be reached through *www.richardcarrier.info* and there is an affiliated site for the Internet Infidels — *www.infidels.org*. Carrier is the author of the important new book *Proving History: Bayes's Theorem and the Quest for the Historical Jesus* and the forthcoming *On the Historicity of Jesus Christ*. Earl Doherty, author of *The Jesus Puzzle*, operates the site at *www.jesuspuzzle.com*, as well as the archival site *http://vridar.info*. Robert M. Price, author of many books including *The Christ Myth Theory and Its Problems* can be followed at *www.robertmprice.mindvendor.com*. Acharya S. (D.M. Murdock), author of the recent *Christ in Egypt* and many other books, operates the site *www.truthbeknown.com*. Dr. Hermann Detering, the eminent German scholar, can be followed both in German and in English at *www.radikalkritik.de/in_eng/htm*. Some of my own work is archived at *www.atheists.org*, the Web-site of American Atheists, Inc.

33 *Did Jesus Exist?*: 6–7.

opponents have come completely unwillingly to their positions and that many have suffered professionally and financially in order to serve their 'agenda' of denial?

However this may be, I need to round out this already long inquiry with a discussion of yet other skills and fields of inquiry I personally have found necessary to study Christian origins. I wish readers to contrast them with what is generally known of Ehrman's qualifications.

IV. WHAT ELSE DO WE NEED TO STUDY CHRISTIAN ORIGINS?

A. Scientific Discipline and Technique

As is the case with any science, in the science of Christian origins it is necessary to have a firm understanding of the philosophy and methods of science — especially of the historical sciences. It is necessary to form hypotheses that are at least potentially testable, *i.e.,* are 'meaningful' in the sense of A.J. Ayer and falsifiable in the sense of Karl Popper.[34] Thus, the statement 'Jesus of Nazareth lived in Nazareth during the first century' is testable and falsifiable, whereas the statement 'The Logos existed before the beginning of time' is neither one. Thus, the discovery by René Salm[35] and me[36] that the town presently called

34 According to A.J. Ayer's *Language, Truth, and Logic,* a statement is 'meaningless' if one could not even imagine a way to test it. A meaningless statement cannot even be false. In the opinion of the philosopher of science Karl Popper's *The Logic of Scientific Discovery,* for a hypothesis or theory to be truly scientific it must at least in principle be "falsifiable" — that is, one should be able to imagine making an observation that would show that the hypothesis was false.

35 For an exhaustive evaluation of *all* the archaeological evidence concerning the Palestinian site now called Nazareth see René Salm's *The Myth of Nazareth: The Invented Town of Jesus* [Cranford, NJ: American Atheist Press, 2008]. Salm shows that the venerated sites owned and operated by the Franciscans could not possibly have been inhabited by observant Jews, due to the presence of tombs that would have made the Holy Family perpetually ritually unclean. Furthermore, the amount of evidence needed to show that those sites were inhabited by anyone at the turn of the era would be several orders of magnitude greater than the scanty and ambiguous material collected by Franciscan archaeologist-apologists. For updates on post-2008 efforts to demonstration first-century habitation at Nazareth, see Salm's Web-site: http://www.nazarethmyth.info/

36 I first reported this startling fact in an article titled "Where Jesus Never Walked,"

Nazareth was not inhabited by anyone during the first centuries BCE and CE is not "irrelevant" — to use Ehrman's word — but rather is crucially important from a scientific perspective. It is sufficient to show that 'Jesus of *Nazareth*' could not have been real, and that Ehrman has to try to prove the existence of a 'Jesus of Somewhere-Else' without resorting to unfalsifiable claims.

In any would-be science of Christian origins it is necessary to assign the burden of proof to anyone who makes an affirmative claim of the existence of any entity or process. *Science always assumes the negative*, requiring sufficient evidence before even provisionally accepting positive propositions. No one needs to prove that Nazareth and Bethlehem of Judea were uninhabited during the Helenistic and Early Roman Period; evidence must be presented by those who claim they were. Before tourists pay out large sums of money to visit 'Joseph's workshop' and 'Mary's kitchen,' tour-guides should be required to show proof of authenticity.

Surprising even myself, I gradually realized that my training as a geologist was of considerable value in the area of biblical criticism, both at the text-critical level and on the higher-critical plane. It helped me to realize that every document of the Christian bibles — not just the canonical New Testament — is actually a stratigraphic palimpsest, not the product of a single authorial deposition. The Gospel of Mark, to give an important example, must be viewed as though it were an erosional landscape — the peaks of which usually represent the latest strata of deposition[37] and the valleys and canyons of which

---

published in the journal *American Atheist* [Winter, 1996–1997] and reprinted it in *Through Atheist Eyes: Scenes From a World That Won't Reason. Volume I: Religions & Scriptures* [Cranford, NJ: American Atheist Press, 2011: 27–56].

37 In geology it is sometimes the case that old strata overlie younger strata as the result of 'overthrusting' — the breaking of the earth's crust downward through the rock strata followed by an upheaval and thrusting of deeper strata over younger and previously higher strata. In the Pauline Epistles, by analogy, we may see this in the form of old material being grafted on top of newer texts, as in the case of putatively earlier creeds being thrust into Paul's discourse. (Of course, given the great amount of fraud and forgery to be expected in the composition and transmission of religious texts, it is quite possible that those creeds are in fact the *latest* deposits in the texts and are actually *later* creeds seeking validation by attachment to the authority of Paul!)

lay bare authorial strata deposited at earlier and earlier times as one sinks deeper and deeper into the scribal topography. The critic of the Gospel of Mark must be prepared to find and recognize remnants of an exoteric form of a secret gospel having some esoteric function in a mystery cult. The critic must expect to find and recognize textual strata of a Docetic tendency, a counter-Docetic tendency, a counter-counter-Docetic tendency, a Judaizing tendency, and strata containing the fallout of the theopolitical wars of those claiming apostolic authority with those claiming Holy-Family hereditary authority, as well as wars between groups as yet unknown or unimagined.

B. Mathematical Skills

Although my formal training in mathematics never went beyond calculus-based statistics and symbolic logic, I have always known that mathematical methods not only are fundamental for the advancement of any science, but are of great utility as well in what might properly be considered the humanities.[38] Whenever possible, I try to imagine the mathematical implications of claims or data sets. Sometimes this can lead to amusing discoveries.

Consider, for example, the tale of the Gadarene Swine as found in the prototypic pig-drowning gospel, Mark. In verses 5:1–13, the best (fourth century) manuscripts — *Codex Sinaiticus* and *Codex Vaticanus* — have the event taking place near *Gerasa*, not Gadara, and the latest have staged the event at *Gergesa*. Now Gerasa was located about 31 miles from the shore of the 'Sea'[39] of Galilee. Those poor

38 A now classic example of this has been Kenneth Neumann's application of statistical analytical methods for the purpose of determining the authorship of the Pauline Epistles. *See*: Kenneth J. Neumann, *The Authenticity of the Pauline Epistles in the Light of Stylostatistical Analysis* [Atlanta, GA: Scholars Press, Atlanta, 1990].

39 The freshwater lake of this story was never called the Sea *of Galilee* before the composition of the Gospel of Mark. It was known as *the Sea* [Heb. *yam*, a word that could be used for any body of water, but usually translated *thalassa* in the Greek Septuagint] *of Kinnereth* [Numbers 34:11; Joshua 13:27] or simply 'Kinneroth' [Joshua 11:2]. By the time Mark's gospel was being written it had become known as 'Lake Tiberias,' after the controversial founding [*ca*. 20 CE] of the City of Tiberias. It may be that the lake was turned into the 'Sea of Galilee' in order to model parts of the gospel after Homer's *Odyssey*. [See Dennis R, MacDonald, *The Homeric Epics and the Gospel of Mark* [New Haven: Yale University Press, 2000: 55–62], although adding *Galilee* to

pigs had to run a course five miles as the Devil flies longer than a marathon in order to find a place to drown! The demonized swine "ran violently down a steep place into the sea, (they were about two thousand;) and were choked in the sea."

Now as realistic as this all may seem, this report has mathematical implications that are astonishingly funny. Let us assume that to be "steep" for the purpose of violent running a slope must be at least 45 degrees. If that be so, then that slope would form the hypotenuse of a right triangle having a base 31 miles long, the sea shore at one end of the hypotenuse, and Gerasa at the other end.

PROBLEM: What is the elevation of Gerasa above the surface of the Sea of Galilee?

SOLUTION: In a 45-degree right triangle, the legs are equal. Therefore, Gerasa would have to be 31 miles above the level of the lake — close to six times higher than Mt. Everest above sea level!

Did anyone in ancient times think about this? Later manuscripts changed the setting to Gadara, about five miles from the seashore, with a computed elevation a bit lower than Mt. Everest. Ultimately, the mass *sui*-cide was discovered to have occurred at a place called Gergesa, and Codex Sinaiticus was 'corrected' to read Gergesa instead of Gerasa. The location of Gergesa — like that of most New Testament towns — is not known, but it has been equated to the remains of Chorsia, located just a few city blocks east of the lake shore. The results of all this geographic revisionism? An immense increase in the verisimilitude of a report of demonic possession.

While mathematics may, from time to time, provide innocent amusement for the scientific student of Christian origins, it is about to become the energy source that will power the shift away from the traditional, theology-bound paradigm for Jesus studies toward a truly scientific paradigm for the study of Christian origins. The harbinger who brings the 'Good News' of mathematics to the world of Jesus Studies is a young scholar criticized by Bart Ehrman, Dr. Richard C. Carrier.

---

the name might well have been due to assonance with the Hebrew term for 'The Great Sea' (Mediterranean) — *ha-yam ha-gaddol.*

IS EHRMAN QUALIFIED?

Early in 2012, Carrier published what I think will become one of the most important books in the field of Jesus studies for the next twenty years at least. Indeed, it may transform the practice of historiography generally. The book is titled *Proving History: Bayes's Theorem and the Quest for the Historical Jesus* [Amherst, NY, Prometheus Books]. A blurb on the dust jacket says much of what needs to be said of this book:

> In this in-depth discussion of New Testament scholarship and the challenges of history as a whole, historian Richard C. Carrier proposes Bayes's Theorem, which deals with probabilities under conditions of uncertainty, as a solution to the problem of establishing reliable historical criteria. He demonstrates that valid historical methods — not only in the study of Christian origins but in any historical study — can be described by, and reduced to, the logic of Bayes's Theorem. Conversely, he argues that any method that cannot be reduced to this theorem is invalid and should be abandoned.

I would add to this merely the point that Bayes's Theorem can be used to weight probabilities and then reweigh them in the light of often seemingly indecisive new evidence. Too often, attempts to apply rigorous mathematical techniques to fields such as historiography that are characterized by the fuzziness of their data become little more than exercises in the 'garbage in — garbage out' process so properly rejected by humanists and scientists alike. Carrier shows how, by using *a fortiori* principles of reasoning, non-numerical evaluations of propositions can be carried out to allow one to select the most probable of competing hypotheses.

Has Ehrman read Carrier's book? I would guess he hasn't. Will he read it? For the sake of protecting the integrity of his spotless scholarly reputation, I think he will. Eventually.

The reason for my optimism in this regard derives from my recent examination of the doctoral dissertation for which he was accorded *magna cum laude* honors by Princeton Theological Seminary. Published in 1986 with the title *Didymus the Blind and the Text of the Gospels* (Atlanta, Scholars press), the dissertation attempts to analyze quotations from the gospels appearing in the commentaries of that fourth century Alexandrian Father in order to focus "on three kinds of issues: (1) Methodological: How can the textual affinities of Didymus's Gospel quotations and allusions best be determined? (2) Textual: What are these affinities? (3) Historical: What does Didymus's Gospel text reveal about the transmission of the NT in Alexandria?"[40]

My optimism derives in particular from his comment that "The scientific study of Didymus's text of the NT — in this case, of the four Gospels — has become possible only within the past several years." I view this casual comment as indicative of the fact that there, at the beginning of his professional career, he consciously valued a *scientific* approach to biblical studies. Moreover, I was delighted to see that a major amount of his study was mathematical — comparing the readings of Didymus's text with each of the major manuscript types and computing percentages of agreement and disagreement in order to infer genetic relationships not only between Didymus and other traditions, but among traditions generally. Unfortunately, his mathematical methods were very elementary: no analysis of variance (ANOVA) was performed, no standard deviations were calculated for manuscripts of each text family, *etc.* It is very likely that there is much more information to be gleaned from his data by someone with the time to carry out the needed mathematical winnowing. It is likely that if Ehrman had used even the most elementary formal statistical techniques such as ANOVA, his advisor Bruce M. Metzger[41]

40 Bart D. Ehrman, *Didymus the Blind and the Text of the Gospels* [Atlanta, GA: Scholars Press, 1986: 2].

41 Neither Metzger nor anyone else seems to have read closely the comment at the bottom of the table of data on page 199: "Obviously Didymus does not stand in as close a relationship to these texts as they stand in relationship to him." Surely, a sentence like that should have been corrected by Ehrman's advisors or rendered less solecistic in appearance.

If Ehrman had received an education in evolutionary biology he would have been better prepared to discover familial and genetic relationships of the various manuscript families of concern to him. Essentially, his concern is one of taxonomy — the classification of texts into hierarchical schemes that reveal genetic relationships. In scientific parlance, a *phylogenetic taxonomy* is needed. He could have gotten off to a flying start on this problem if he had known of the now-classic text *Numerical Taxonomy: The Principles and Practice of Numerical Classification,* by Peter H.A. Sneath and Robert R. Sokal [San Francisco: W. H. Freeman & Co., 1973]. However, even more significant texts have appeared in later years that Ehrman could use to construct a

would have been so dazzled that he would have seen to it that Ehrman would have received *summa*, not just *magna cum laude* honors.

C. Astronomy and Astrology

I have come to realize that no reasonably accurate knowledge of Christian beginnings can be gained without a solid knowledge not only of the science of astronomy, but also of its evil twin astrology. The importance of both disciplines to ancient peoples at the turn of the era is impossible to overestimate. Whereas few modern Christians are even able to *see* the stars and planets due to urban light pollution, and virtually only a handful of modern Americans could tell what month it was by the constellations appearing after sunset in the eastern sky, for the ancients the starry 'firmament' was both calendar and clock. Moreover, it was central to all the religions of the time. A whole book could be written — and probably has been — concerning the astrological significance of the Lord's Prayer phrase "Thy will be done, on earth as it is in heaven." Was not the message of Jesus "The sky-kingdom is at hand"? Wasn't 'the kingdom of heaven' simply a kingdom in the sky in the ancient understanding? Wasn't 'Heaven' simply the sky? Certainly it wasn't the Never-Nowhere Land of modern theology!

Very early in my studies — long before I had become a Mythicist — I had discovered a considerable amount of evidence that a great deal of 'astral religion' had come to form a large part of early Christianity. I simply assumed, however, that such 'pagan elements' had syncretized with the unimpressive early traditions of a yet unsuccessful cult. I didn't realize until much later that those astral elements almost certainly had comprised the mysteries that had spawned the cult in the beginning.

What were the astral elements that needed to be explained? I was shocked to see a color photograph of a mosaic discovered in the

---

phylogenetic tree revealing the genetic relationships among the texts of interest to him. It's never too late for him to start. An old but still useful text is *Cladistics: The Theory and Practice of Parsimony*, by Ian J. Kitching [New York: Oxford University Press, 1998]. Sadly, most of the textbooks that promise "Phylogenetic Trees Made Easy" are completely dedicated to analysis of DNA sequences and can be adapted to textual analyses only with great difficulty.

necropolis beneath the Vatican that depicted Christ as Helios driving his solar chariot. But then it was pointed out to me that Jesus moves among twelve disciples in the course of what seems to be a single year of ministry (according to the Gospel of Mark), just as the sun moves through twelve signs of the zodiac in the course of a year.[42] Jesus is born on the winter solstice, and the feast day of his forerunner John the Baptist is on the summer solstice. Jesus is resurrected at the vernal equinox. Most shocking, for a cult that is supposed to have sprung from Judaism, is the fact that Christ not only is worshipped on the Day of the Sun, he is worshipped at sunrise at Easter and apparently routinely so in ancient times according to Pliny the Younger.[43]

Then too, there was the matter of the 'Kingdom of Heaven.' In ancient ways of thinking, it would have been indistinguishable from what we today would call a 'Kingdom in the Sky.' It would be a real, in some sense physical, kingdom situated above peoples' heads at unknown elevation, but certainly not at the interplanetary distances we take for granted today. After all, the "heavenly host" of the Old Testament was simply a grand army of stars and planets, and they were affixed to the underside of an inverted, solid dome — the *firmament*.

But there was more astral evidence to be discovered. I learned that the oldest symbols of Christianity, the chi-cross and the fish (actually, *two* fish), were very likely symbols for the intersection of the celestial equator with the ecliptic (*à la* Plato's *Timaeus*) and the astrological symbol for Pisces. Gradually an even more startling fact began to emerge: Christianity had developed at the same time that the vernal equinox was moving out of Aries the Ram or Lamb into Pisces

42 The likelihood that the twelve disciples also represent the Twelve Tribes of Israel only increases their astrological significance. It is very probable that the Twelve Tribes are themselves the zodiacal symbols of an Israelite religion that was evolving from a lunar cult into a solar cult and had always had strong astral underpinnings. The Dead Sea Scrolls include solar calendar-related materials and astrological matter such as "Thunder in Gemini."

43 According to a letter written by Pliny the Younger to the Emperor Trajan [Pliny, *Letters* 10.96–97] when he was governor of Pontus/Bithynia [111–113 CE] and had interrogated Christians, "They [the Christians] asserted, however, that the sum and substance of their fault or error had been that they were accustomed to meet on a fixed day before dawn and sing responsively a hymn to Christ as to a god..."

the Two Fishes. Was the Christian 'New Age' actually the precessional great year — the zodiacal Age of Pisces?[44] Was the Christian New Age congruent with the New Age of Augustus — the emperor who was the first to proclaim a 'gospel' (*euaggelion*) and whose nativity had been proclaimed by Vergil in his Fourth Eclogue?

Certainly, not all of these astral and solar features could be accidental. But how do they relate to the astral origins of Christianity? What did the authors of the New Testament know about astrology? What did they know about precession? Did they know about Hipparchus[45] of Rhodes's discovery of the phenomenon?

---

44 Although I was unaware of the fact, about a decade earlier (1977–78), James H. Charlesworth had published a translation and discussion of *The Treatise of Shem*, a new addition to the Pseudepigrapha. In that fascinating paper, he nicely summarized my theory-to-be in a few sentences:

> It is significant that the Treatise of Shem was composed about the time that the vernal equinox (the traditional beginning of the year, the start of Spring) moved from Aries to Pisces, where it has been ever since, although it is about to move into Aquarius. This change, G. de Santillana argued [*Hamlet's Mill: An Essay on Myth and the Frame of Time*], would have evoked strong "astrological emotion" since one age was succeeding another. The Treatise of Shem appears to be an unparalleled record of this monumental shift (the Precession of the Equinoxes). [Page 390 of: Charlesworth, J.H. (1977–1978). "Rylands Syriac Ms. 44 and a New Addition to the Pseudepigrapha: The Treatise of Shem, Discussed and Translated." *Bulletin of the John Rylands University Library of Manchester* 60: 376–403.] I thank Richard Carrier for reminding me of this work.

45 Knowledge of the precession of the equinoxes seems to have been widespread by the turn of the era, especially among the Stoics. Discovered by Hipparchus of Rhodes [*d. ca.* 127 BCE], it seems clear that the phenomenon was known to the Roman poet and Augustan propagandist Vergil [70–19 BCE], who sang of the dawning of a new age in his Fourth Eclogue. As already mentioned, the timing of the New Age of the New Testament seems to be a perfect fit for the passage of the vernal equinox into Pisces. Startling evidence of the sophistication of astronomical knowledge of the first century BCE was discovered in the year 1900 when sponge divers discovered the remains of an ancient shipwreck of the coast of the Aegean island of Antikithera. Ultimately dated to before 76–67 BCE on the basis of the latest coins found by Jacques Cousteau in the 1970s, it was ultimately discovered that the shipwreck had been carrying an ancient astronomical computer, the so-called Antikithera mechanism. The device was originally thought to have been built by Hipparchus himself, because the gearing of the device conforms to the mathematics of his astronomical reforms. Recently, however, it is thought to have been built around 87 BCE or somewhat earlier on the basis of inscriptions on the faces of the mechanism's components. (The device is marked with the Greek signs of the zodiac and tracks the course of the sun through them.) It is thought that the ship was carrying loot from Athens of the Roman general

Frank R. Zindler

It was fortunate that I had had a good education not only in astronomy, cosmology, and astrophysics, but had also read widely in the *history* of astronomy and its anciently popular twin, astrology. I was alarmed when I discovered that David Ulansey had published a book[46] arguing that Hipparchus' discovery that the vernal equinox had moved from Taurus into Aries had catalyzed the creation of Mithraism. Independently and without knowledge of the Mithraic evidence, I had begun to theorize that the New Age of Christianity might have resulted from the observable fact that the equinox was in the process of moving from Aries into Pisces. I feared that Ulansey too must be on the verge of the same discovery and would beat me to publication.[47] Hastily, in order to establish priority, I published my precession theory of Christian origins in the journal *American Atheist* in the form of a popular article entitled "How Jesus Got a Life."[48]

Ultimately, I purchased Voyager® software in order to be able to model and reconstruct the exact appearance of the sky at different times during the first century BCE and the first century CE, showing the positions of the planets, conjunctions, and zodiacal signs. It was necessary to get a feel for what it would have been like for a Mediterranean observer to witness the movement of the vernal equinox into Pisces. Then too, there were so many books and papers on the 'Star of Bethlehem,' an astronomical impossibility that might have had some esoteric meaning.

Sulla in 86 BCE and was on its way to Rome. In any case, sophisticated astronomical knowledge was widespread in the Mediterranean world by the first century of the Common Era. Educated men such as the authors of the Pauline Epistles and Acts of the Apostles would surely have had at least rudimentary knowledge of Hipparchus and his age-turning discovery. (For a popular but scientifically accurate account of this discovery see Jo Marchant's *Decoding the Heavens: A 2,000-Year-Old Computer and the Century-Long Search to Discover Its Secrets* [Cambridge, MA: Da Capo Press, 2009]).

46 David Ulansey, *The Origins of the Mithraic Mysteries: Cosmology and Salvation in the Ancient World* [New York: Oxford University Press, 1989].

47 Some years later, I spoke with Ulansey at a meeting of the Society of Biblical Literature and was astounded to learn than he completely disagreed with me concerning a possible precessional component in Christian beginnings! Precession, it would seem, was not a double-barreled shotgun.

48 *American Atheist*, Vol. 34, No. 6, June, 1992. Reprinted in *Through Atheist Eyes, Volume One: Religions & Scriptures* [Cranford, NJ: American Atheist Press, 2011: 57–80].

Perhaps its meaning could be recovered by astronomical investigations carried out with an understanding of the astrological beliefs of the ancient Mediterranean world. I'm still working on the problem.

D. Historical Disciplines and Techniques Needed

As I have shown elsewhere,[49] before one can create a genuine science of Christian origins it is necessary to have a database of reliable information on which to base hypotheses and test theories. For example, the database required to find all possible clues to the origins and evolving applications of the *nominae sacrae* is essentially an historical one. It must be based on a reliable and exhaustive chronology — with uncertainties clearly noted and attended to in all historical reasoning. It is essential that anachronisms not cloud our thinking. Ehrman, unfortunately, repeatedly and probably unconsciously equates 'Christ' with 'Jesus,' 'Jesus of Nazareth,' 'the Lord,' 'the Son of Man,' 'the Son of God,' 'the Savior,' *etc.* What warrant — scientific or historical — does he have for applying this equation to all phases of the evolution of all ancient forms of Christianity? None at all. What is needed in order to discover how Ehrman's titular equation came about is an exhaustive study of all literature surviving from the ancient Mediterranean world's culture up to at least the fourth century CE.

In the literature (including the epigraphic and numismatic record) containing titles eventually relating to Ehrman's Jesus of Nazareth, it is necessary to discover (1) when and by whom each title can be documented to have been used; (2) to whom it first was applied; (3) when it first was equated to 'Jesus'; (4) how and when different authors combined these titles; and (5) the nature of the theopolitical environment in which the record was created.

With this information in hand, it will be necessary to construct 'trajectories' — phylogenetic trees — to show not only the path leading to the grand-total title equation of Catholic Christianity, but also to reveal all the extinct branches of the Christian evolutionary tree that can be inferred from the ancient literature.

49 Frank R. Zindler, "Prolegomenon to a Science of Christian Origins," in, *Sources of the Jesus Tradition: Separating History From Myth*, edited by R. Joseph Hoffmann [Amherst, NY: Prometheus Books, 2010: 140–156].

Frank R. Zindler

1. The kinds of historical information that are needed

Much of what I shall identify as necessary to form a science of Christian origins includes things that have been done by biblical scholars for centuries. Unfortunately, because what has been done during those centuries was not done scientifically — and more often than not was theologically biased — *everything needs to be done again to see if it can be confirmed.* Every verified datum then must be entered into a database that will — like genuine scientific databases — steadily expand and provide an ever-larger fund of information that can be drawn upon and used as a basis for further discovery. The wheel should never have to be invented again. The Computer Age should make it possible to do *exhaustive* studies of the kind that routinely are done in the sciences.[50]

Some of the most obvious *desiderata* are the following:

(1) *All* literature surviving from the ancient Mediterranean world — including patristic, epigraphic, and numismatic materials — must be an important part of the primary historical material to be studied. This includes all of Greek literature[51] (including poets, dramatists, historians, scientists, theologians, philosophers, the Septuagint, and astrologers); all of Roman Latin literature[52] (Vergil, Horace, Lucretius, Ovid, Cicero, Seneca, Fronto, Statius, *et al.*); Jewish literature

50 The laws and theories of the physical sciences are *exhaustive* in the sense that they are intended to apply to the entire universe. In their formulation, exhaustive inquiry is carried out to see that they comport with everything relevant that is known at the time. Experiments and observations are carried out in order to discover facts that might falsify the reigning theory and cause it to be amended or abandoned. In the historical sciences, of course, this is neither possible nor sought after. However, historical theories and explanations can still be scientific *if they share the exhaustiveness of scientific inquiry.* The exhaustiveness relates not to the entire universe, of course, but rather to the 'universe' of everything that is known about a particular problem. An historical theory must account for everything that is known about the problem. Nothing can be ignored. When new facts are discovered that do not conform to expectations of the current theory, the theory must be amended or abandoned. Thus will progress occur in the historical sciences as has been the custom in the physical sciences.

51 This has already been assembled in the *Thesaurus Linguae Graecae* (TLG).

52 Latin literature is being assembled in the Brepols Library of Latin Texts along lines similar to the TLG.

(including the Dead Sea Scrolls, the Hebrew bible, Old Testament Apocrypha, Elephantine papyri, Talmudic literature, the Targumim and other Aramaic literature[53], *etc.*); Egyptian and Ethiopic literature; the Coptic and Syriac Fathers.

(2) It is imperative that the transmission histories of all texts and manuscripts be determined as completely as possible and those data taken into account. (For example, the fact that the texts of Josephus' works were preserved and transmitted by Christians instead of Jews is of great moment.) In addition, all textual variants known for any given text must be considered and analyzed.[54]

(3) A great number of specific areas of history must be considered, including:

(a) The history of book burning; (b) the history of all religions known to have been known in the Mediterranean world, including especially the history of the mysteries, heresies, especially the congeries of cults known as Docetism and Gnosticism; (c) the history of the classical world; (d) the history of the Jews and other Near Eastern peoples; (e) numismatic history relating to the construction of chronologies and archaeological theories on coins; (f) the history of art (depiction of 'The Good Shepherd,' 'Jesus the Magician,' 'Christ Helios,' *etc.*), architecture (synagogues,[55] house churches, Herod's reconstruction of the Temple of Yahweh[56] in Jerusalem, his construction

---

53 Much is to be expected of the Comprehensive Aramaic Lexicon Project in this regard.

54 In my *The Jesus the Jews Never Knew: Sepher Toldoth Yeshu and the Quest of the Historical Jesus in Jewish Sources* [50–51] I discuss an ancient table of contents in a pre-fifth-century Greek manuscript that lacks mention of the *Testimonium Flavianum* or the deaths of James and John the Baptist, whereas a fifth- or sixth-century Latin version of the table adds "Concerning John the Baptist." On page 63 of that book I show a page of *Codex Vossianus Graec. 72 Olim Petavianus* wherein the *Testimonium Flavianum* has been interpolated into the text of Josephus' *Jewish War* !

55 The Franciscans have attempted to show that there was a first-century synagogue at Kfar Naḥum (supposedly Capernaum) as well as a house church of St. Peter, and so both an understanding of the principles of archaeological excavation and architectural history are needed to evaluate their *outré* claims.

56 According to L. Michael White [*From Jesus to Christianity*, New York: HarperOne, 2005: 30], the temple complex reconstruction begun by Herod the Great [d. 4 BCE] was

of many temples to Roma and Augustus, *etc.*), and decoration; (g) paleographic history; (h) history of philosophy (Pythagoras, Plato, Philo, Seneca, *et al.*); (i) patristic history; (j) historical linguistics, including historical phonology[57]; (k) history of astronomy and astrology; (l) history of dogma; (m) history of liturgies, not just Christian and Jewish liturgies; (n) history of symbols (crosses, monograms, anchors, fishes, dolphins, branches, *etc.*); (o) history of the emperor cults and their influence on various phases of Christian evolution; (p) history of the Christian and Jewish canons, including the Ethiopic and Eastern Orthodox groups; (q) history of Mandaism and Samaritanism; (r) history of worship; (s) text histories of canonical and non-canonical religious texts; (t) compositional history of Jewish texts up to the Babylonian Talmud and beyond; (u) ancient history of mathematics and its devolution into numerology, ciphers, gematria, and compositional structures of sacred texts.; (v) history of the development of religious calendars.

2. Comparative historical studies needed

A science of Christian origins must involve both diachronic and synchronic comparative studies in order to discover how the various threads of tradition came to twine together — how they came to form the temporal braid of cultures that would come to call themselves

not completed until the year 64 CE, just a few years before its destruction 'prophesied' in the 'Little Apocalypse' of Mark 13:2 ("And as he went out of the temple, one of his disciples saith unto him, Master, see what manner of stones and what buildings are here! 2 And Jesus answering said unto him, Seest thou these great buildings? There shall not be left one stone upon another, that shall not be thrown down."). If this had actually happened around the year 33 CE, the curiously anonymous disciple would actually have asked, "Master! Behold these heavy stones! How shall the one be set upon the other?" If Jesus had really been a prophet, he would have answered "They shall use the craft of Rome to build this temple to the top, but it shall avail them naught; for even as the roof be placed upon the pillars, a legion of the Romans shall set upon it: verily I say unto thee, there shall not be left one stone upon another."

57 In my "Bart Ehrman and the Crucified Messiah" I argue that the Greek vowel shift known as *itacism* that took place around the turn of the era turned the name or title *Chreistos* or *Chrēstos* into *Christos* (derivable then from Greek *chriō* — 'anoint') and allowed the identification of the indicated character with the Messiah of Jewish expectation.

Christian. Minimal programs of study should consider the following *desiderata*:

(1) The study of comparative mythology and (2) comparative religions is *sine qua non.* Especially needed is a thorough knowledge of the ancient mystery religions. (3) A knowledge of the techniques of comparative anthropology is needed in order to reconstruct the *Weltanschauung* of the early tradents of Christian culture. (4) A knowledge of comparative literature is needed in order to discover such startling phenomena as a phrase from Aesop's "Fable of the Fisherman and the Flute" issuing from the mouth of Jesus of Nazareth. (5) One must be able to carry out comparative analyses of Hebrew and Greek texts in versions in other languages in order to find clues to the evolutionary pathways traveled by biblical texts.

E. Critical Skills Needed

Not surprisingly, all the traditional types of biblical criticism are needed: (1) Text criticism to determine the best or original readings of each text, and (2) Higher or historical criticism to discover the original and subsequent meanings of a text and to reconstruct the historical *Sitz im Leben* of the author and recipients of the text. Historical criticism includes (a) form criticism, (b) redaction criticism, (c) source criticism, and (d) intertextual analysis. In addition, it may include (e) performance criticism, and (f) what I would call *Tendenz* criticism or theopolitical criticism.

F. Language Tools and Linguistics

Bart Ehrman rightfully asserts that a scholar studying Christian origins must be able to read modern languages such as French and German,[58] and ancient languages such as Greek, Hebrew, Latin, Aramaic,

58 Perhaps not surprisingly, Ehrman does not list Dutch, the language of 'Radical Critics' such as Willem Christiaan van Manen who presented evidence to show that *none* of the so-called Pauline Epistles can be considered to be authentic. Quite surprising, however, is his omission of Italian, the language of vast amounts of Roman Catholic scholarship. When I was investigating papal claims that the actual bones of Saint Peter had been found in the ancient necropolis beneath the high altar of Saint Peter's Basilica, it was necessary to read hundreds of pages of Vatican reports and related materials. My exposé of the fraudulent claims — "Of Bones and Boners: Saint

Syriac, and Coptic. It may be a good idea to explain how I too have found use for these languages, and why, alas, they are not quite sufficient.

1. Greek

The centrality of Greek for Jesus studies can scarcely be exaggerated. Not only were all the documents of the canonical New Testament composed in Greek,[59] virtually the entirety of the apocryphal literature up until Mediaeval times was written in Greek — the most important Nag Hammadi Coptic documents for the most part are derived from Greek *Vorlagen*. Greek was the language of the Septuagint versions of the Hebrew scriptures cited by the New Testament authors. *Indeed, Christianity itself largely appears to have been a Hellenistic confection decked out with Jewish flavoring and frosting.*

Greek was the language of the Apostolic Fathers and the earliest Church Fathers, the earliest heresiarchs, the ancient mystery religions, and Homer — whose Odyssey finds reflections in the Gospel of Mark according to the eminent scholar Dennis R. MacDonald.[60] Greek is the language of 'Aesop' — whose fable "The Fisherman and the Flute"[61] was adapted by an author of the so-called Q-Document to produce the famous line in Matthew and Luke, "I have piped and ye have not danced." Greek is the language of important ancient geographers such as Strabo [*ca.* 63 BCE–*ca* 21 CE] and historians such as Flavius

---

Peter at the Vatican" — has been reprinted in volume one of my book *Through Atheist Eyes: Scenes From a World That Won't Reason.*

59 Matthew Black [*An Aramaic Approach to the Gospels and Acts*, Third Edition 1967, reprinted by Hendrickson, Peabody MA: 1998] attempted in 1946 to demonstrate an Aramaic substrate for the gospel documents based on alleged Aramaisms and syntactic peculiarities of the Greek texts. The purpose, of course, was to establish their relationship to the Targumim and the supposed language of Jesus of Nazareth. I, however, agree with the Roman Catholic scholar Joseph Fitzmyer who finds Black's evidence unconvincing. Aramaisms do indeed exist in the New Testament, but they are entirely to be expected in a Greek koine spoken by bilingual residents of the eastern part of the Roman Empire during the first and second centuries of the Common Era.

60 Dennis R, MacDonald, *The Homeric Epics and the Gospel of Mark*, [New Haven: Yale University Press, 2000: 55–62],

61 For the Greek text of Aesop's fable *"Alieus aulōn,"* see Ben Edwin Perry, *Aesopica* [Urbana: University of Illinois Press, 1952: 326].

Josephus [37–*ca*. 95 CE] whose writings seem to have been in need of 'improvement' by ancient Christians and Baptists alike.[62]

Very early in my study of the non-historical Jesus I was confronted with claims of astral mystery-cult origins of Christianity. This quickly led me to study not only the ancient Greek astronomer Ptolemy, but his even more important predecessor Hipparchus of Rhodes [*ca*. 190–*ca*. 120 BCE] who discovered the precession of the equinoxes[63] and his Cilician or Tarsian predecessor Aratus [*ca*. 315–240 BCE], whose *Phaenomena* verse 5 is quoted by the author of Acts 17:28 ("For in Him we live and move and have our being, as some of your own poets have said, '*We are also his offspring*.'")[64] In fact, that same verse begins with a quotation from the Hymn to Zeus of the Stoic philosopher Cleanthes, the pupil of Zeno the founder of the Stoic School: "For in him we live and move and have our being."[65] The

62 Chapter two of my *The Jesus the Jews Never Knew: Sepher Toldoth Yeshu and the Quest of the Historical Jesus in Jewish Sources* is titled "Faking Flavius" and deals with Christian alterations of both Josephus' *Jewish Antiquities* but also his *Wars of the Jews*. The third chapter, "James the Just, John the Baptist, and Other Perversions of Josephus," gives evidence for textual tampering by both Christians and followers of John the Baptist for the purpose of providing Jesus with an earthly brother (instead of the celestial twin of Gnostic lore?) and documentation of uncertain importance concerning the Baptist.

63 In my essay "How Jesus Got a Life" [*Through Atheist Eyes, Volume One: Religions & Scriptures*: 57–80] I explain that discovering that the vernal equinox ('Easter') had moved from Taurus into Aries and was in the process of entering Pisces may have been the trigger-stimulus for the founding not only of the Mithraic Mysteries with their sacramental Taurobolium but also of the Christian Mysteries with their symbols of two fishes, crucifixion, and chi-cross. Just as Mithras had been the god of the Age of Aries, Christ would have been the god ('chronocrat') of the New Age of Pisces. I did not realize at that time that the 'New Age' cult of the Caesars also was based on the same astronomical phenomenon.

64 I take it as evidence that the author of Acts knew about the precession of the equinoxes the fact that he quotes Aratus, because the most likely source of his knowledge of Aratus probably would have been Hipparchus' commentary on the *Phaenomena*. If he was reading Hipparchus, he would have known about precession — something that was common knowledge to the Stoics of the first century. A necessary but insufficient evidence of the precession-stimulated origin of Christianity is that the first Christians were aware of the phenomenon. If it should be shown that the first Christians did *not* know of Hipparchus' discovery or disavowed it, my hypothesis would be falsified.

65 Practically the same thing is found in the "Hymn to Jupiter" by Cleanthes of Troas:
With Jove we must begin; nor from him rove;

same verse also quotes the *Cretica* attributed to the half-legendary Epimenides (*ca.* 600 BCE):

> "They fashioned a tomb for you, O holy and high one — The Cretans,[66] always liars, evil beasts, idle bellies! But you are not dead; you live and abide forever, *For in you we live and move and have our being*."[67]

A working knowledge of Greek (as well as Latin and Hebrew) is crucial for studying the material remains surviving from antiquity — epitaphs, inscriptions, coins, artworks, *etc.*, and for understanding the context of archaeological discoveries. But perhaps most of all, Greek is needed to read the main philosophers whose ideas dominated earliest Christian thinking.

If one is to pursue an anthropological — that is to say, *scientific* — investigation of Christian origins it is necessary to learn how to think like early Christians. It is necessary to study the philosophers whose *Weltanschauung* (perhaps 'paradigm' might be a more appropriate term here) informed the conscious and unconscious framework in which proto-Christians thought, spoke, and wrote. Pythagoras' notion of metempsychosis can be seen in the gospels where it is reported that Jesus was thought by some to be the reincarnation of Elijah or John

---

> Him always praise, for all is full of Jove!
> He fills all places where mankind resort,
> The wide-spread sea, with every shelt'ring port.
> Jove's presence fills all space, upholds this ball;
> All need his aid; his power sustains us all.
> *For we his offspring are*; and he in love
> Points out to man his labour from above...
> — Adam Clarke (1856)

66 For discussion of Epimenides in relation to the lying Cretans in Titus 1:12 ("One of themselves, even a prophet of their own, said, The Cretans are always liars, evil beasts, slow bellies.") see pages 107–109 of *The Anchor Bible Volume 35 The Letter To Titus*, by Jerome D. Quinn [New York: Doubleday, 1990]. The "prophet" in Titus 1:12 is identified by Clement of Alexandria as Epimenides [*Stromata*, i. 14]. In this passage Clement mentions that "some say" Epimenides should be counted among the seven wisest philosophers.

67 Greek text reconstructed by J. Rendel Harris from a ninth-century Syriac commentary on Acts by Isho'dadh of Merv [*Expositor*, April 1907: 332–37]

the Baptist.[68] But perhaps even most important of all the philosophers that must be read by any student of Christian origins is Plato. The psychophysical universe of Plato's *Timaeus* is probably the theater on whose stage the entire New Testament drama is acted out, and the Platonist/Stoic Philo of Alexandria [20 BCE–50 CE] bequeathed the Logos of John's gospel to some early Christian group.

As if this all were not enough reason to know how to read Greek, there is the need to use Greek as a tool with which to carry out both text-critical and higher critical studies of the New Testament writings and manuscripts. Greek manuscripts must be compared in order to form a theory of the evolution of the New Testament texts and to discover the many interpolations and deletions that have been made for theopolitical purposes.

I might conclude that no important *original* research can be done without a working command of Greek, although important work can be done with secondary sources in modern languages.[69] But unless

---

68 **Mark 6:14** "And king Herod heard of him; (for his name was spread abroad) and he said, That John the Baptist was risen from the dead, and therefore mighty works do shew forth themselves in him. 15 Others said, That it is Elias. And others said, That it is a prophet, or as one of the prophets. 16 But when Herod heard thereof, he said, It is John, whom I beheaded: he is risen from the dead."

Matthew 16:13 "When Jesus came into the coasts of Caesarea Philippi, he asked his disciples, saying, Whom do men say that I the Son of man am? 14 And they said, Some say that thou art John the Baptist: some, Elias; and others, Jeremias, or one of the prophets."

Luke 9:7 "Now Herod the tetrarch heard of all that was done by him: and he was perplexed, because that it was said of some, that John was risen from the dead; 8 And of some, that Elias had appeared; and of others, that one of the old prophets was risen again. 9 And Herod said, John have I beheaded: but who is this, of whom I hear such things? And he desired to see him." (There is no follow-up on Herod & Jesus)

69 An astonishing example of such work was done by Thomas Paine, one of America's Founding Fathers. Paine could only read English and a little French. Nevertheless, his critical analysis of the King James Bible led him not only to reject the supposed divine inspiration of that work but reject the historicity of Jesus as well. In his *The Age of Reason, Part Three: Examination of the Prophecies*, which I edited and copiously annotated for an American Atheist Press edition in 1993, he says that "[R]epeated forgeries and falsifications create a well-founded suspicion that all the cases spoken of concerning the person called Jesus Christ are *made cases*... that so far from his being the Son of God, he did not exist even as a man — that he is merely an imaginary or allegorical character, as Apollo, Hercules, Jupiter and all the deities of

one is extremely lucky in finding sources that are essentially without error or blinding bias, there is the danger that important facts have been overlooked and that errors are being repeated.[70]

2. Latin

Latin is of importance not only because it, along with Syriac, appears to have been the second or third language in which earliest Christians communicated, but also because a fair number of apocryphal gospels and Christian miscellanea were composed in it and important Church Fathers such as Tertullian and Augustine wrote in Latin. It was the *lingua franca* of the European scholarly world up until the end of the eighteenth century and an immense amount of information concerning lost books, manuscripts, artifacts, and other aspects concerning the evolution of Christianity almost surely lies waiting to be rediscovered in Latin manuscripts and books in the libraries of Europe.

Perhaps surprisingly to most readers, Latin is of greatest importance not because it is the language of the Vulgate Bible, but because it is the

---

antiquity were. There is no history written at the time Jesus Christ is said to have lived that speaks of the existence of such a person, even as a man."

In a letter written to Andrew Dean of New York (August 15, 1806) he explained that "The fable of Christ and his twelve apostles, which is a parody on the sun and the twelve signs of the zodiac, copied from the ancient religions of the eastern world, is the least hurtful part [of the bible]. ... Everything told of Christ has reference to the sun. His reported resurrection is at sunrise, and that on the first day of the week; that is, on the day anciently dedicated to the sun, and from thence called Sunday — in Latin *Dies Solis*, the day of the sun; as the next day, Monday, is Moon-day..."

70 The Pauline epistles present a particularly great danger in this regard. They include a substantial amount of technical vocabulary — astrological and Gnostic jargon — that would never be recognized as such in any English New Testament known to me. This includes words such as *archōn* ('ruler,' but also one of the seven world-creating archons comprising the Hebdomad); *aiōn* ('age,' but also a Valentinian rough equivalent to an archon or a time-god like Chronos, a specific Aeon being Stauros — 'Cross' — who functions as a circumvallation and boundary of the Pleroma); *ektrōma* ('miscarriage' or 'abortion,' but also specifically the abortion of Sophia — 'Wisdom'); *sophia* ('wisdom,' but also an aeon and the creative element (*ḥokmah*) of Proverbs 3:19); *stoicheion* ('element,' but also *a sign of the zodiac*); and many other seemingly ordinary words. In his treatise *St. Paul and the Mystery-Religions* [London: Hodder and Stoughton, 1913], H.A.A. Kennedy devoted a lengthy chapter to the topic "St. Paul's Relation to the Terminology of the Mystery-Religions." It should be required reading for anyone desiring to plumb the esoteric depths of the Pauline Epistles.

language of Plautus,[71] Fronto, Horace, Tacitus, Cicero, Statius, Ovid, Apuleius, Seneca, and Vergil. Vergil: author of the famous "Fourth Eclogue" announcing the birth of the miraculous child and the beginning of a new era — the Age of Saturn.[72] Publius Vergilius Maro: composer of the *Aeneid*, the magnificent propaganda gospel of his patron Augustus Caesar.

3. Indo-Iranian Languages

Long before I became a Mythicist I had learned of the immense influence of Indian and Persian thought in the early evolution of Christianity but I supposed that influence had somehow been incorporated by syncretism some while after the time of Jesus. It never occurred to me that those influences even indirectly (say, via Philo or

71 The Roman comic dramatist Titus Maccius Plautus lived from *ca.* 254 BCE to 184 BCE. His hymn to Jupiter in his Punic comedy *Poenulus* [*Poen.* 1187–89] is echoed in Acts 17:28, which reads "For in him we live, and move, and have our being; as certain also of your own poets have said, For we are also his offspring."

Plautus has "O Jupiter, who cherishes and nurtures the race of man; through whom we live and draw the breath of being, in whom is the hope of the life of all men..." (*Iuppiter, qui genus colis alisque hominem, per qui vivimus / Vitalem aevom, quem penes spes vitae sunt hominem / Omnium*...)

If the author of Acts was familiar not only with Greek Stoics but Latin literature as well, it seems highly likely that he would have been aware of the Latin Stoic Seneca. Seneca's possible connection to the Apostle Paul was the source of much ancient Christian speculation, culminating in the forgery of the apocryphal *Correspondence Between Paul and Seneca*. The author certainly knew of Seneca's older brother Lucius Junius Gallio Annaeanus (the Gallio who was the proconsul [51/2–52/3 CE] of the new senatorial province of Achaia of Acts 18:12–17). Even if the pericope in Acts was made up for the purpose of situating Paul's life in the framework of Roman chronology, we know that whoever wrote that part of Acts knew of a Stoic intimately related to Seneca. That being the case, it remains reasonable to suppose Stoic influences upon that author. Drawing the thread even thinner, it remains possible but in no way proven that he knew of Hipparchus' discovery of the precession of the equinoxes. Did he know he was living in the New Age of Pisces? It would have been more than a century after Vergil's Fourth Eclogue and the self-conscious awareness of that fact, and Christianity's New-Age astral origins may very well no longer have been remembered. In any case, it seems clear that 'Luke' derived his information from earlier authors who must have been well aware of that celestial phenomenon.

72 The Romans would have been able to equate Saturn with Yahweh of the Jews, whose sabbath-day was equivalent to 'Saturn's Day.' Saturn occupied the seventh heaven, with only the firmament of the fixed stars being more exalted. This fact almost certainly was of significance to the origins of Jewish and Christian Gnosticism, and there is pressing need for research to elucidate the implications of this theological equation.

Plato or Pythagoras) could have been initial catalysts in the formation of the various cults we might now describe as proto-Christian. Even so, my high school efforts to teach myself Sanskrit proved to be of great value in understanding the position of Christianity in the cultic landscape of the early Christian centuries. Although I never gained full mastery of the language, I learned enough to be able to follow technical arguments concerning comparative religions and comparative mythologies when primary sources were quoted and now I see that to really learn the nature and extent of Indic influence on Christian origins one really should be able to have a good working knowledge of the language. For several centuries it has been suggested that the title 'Christ' is not really derived from the Greek *chriō* and does not mean 'anointed,' but actually, by means of unspecified phonetic mutations, it is related to the Sanskrit name Krishna (*kṛṣṇa*, 'black'). (It is intriguing to note that just as Christ is the second member of the Christian Trinity, Krishna is the second member of the Hindu trinity!)

It is known that Brahman and Buddhist missionaries visited the Mediterranean world in the days of Philo of Alexandria and long before,[73] and it is even claimed that Pythagoras studied in India. The stage certainly would have been set for Indian influence upon nascent Christianity. More than that, however, there is a reasonable possibility that Mithraism and the Magi also were influenced by Indian as well as Persian ideas. In trying to sort out the complex relations between Pythagoras, Plato, Mithraism, Zoroastrianism, Buddhism, Judaism (Pharisaism) and Hinduism, a working knowledge of Sanskrit is needed but is not sufficient. (To unravel Buddhist influences, knowledge of a Prakrit such as Pali is also useful.) Old Persian, Avestan, Pehlevi, and modern Farsi are also needed — particularly in order to read the epigraphic materials reported in Iranian scholarly journals and Web-sites, as well as to understand modern Iranian commentaries

73 Long before being awakened from my historicist slumber by Madalyn O'Hair, I had fallen under the spell of Will Durant's *The Story of Civilization* and had read all but the last-appearing volume of that wonderful monument of Western civilization. In his very first volume [*Our Oriental Heritage*: 449] he told of the Indian King Ashoka [*r.* 273–? BCE] who became a Buddhist and, according to his Rock Edict XIII, sent Buddhist missionaries to the west, including Egypt, Syria, and Greece.

and descriptions relating to those materials — especially the coins and inscriptions. Palestine and Asia Minor were long ruled by Persia, and one must expect a strong Persian influence upon Israelite religions. Whether or not that influence came into Christianity via proto-Judaism, Greek philosophy, or directly via missionaries is a problem for which an answer is urgently needed.

It was clear to me long ago that there were strong similarities between the proto-Christian mysteries hinted at in the Pauline literature (as well as in the gospels and the literature of the Gnostics and other earliest Christians) and the Greco-Roman Mystery religions — especially Mithraism. Although Mithraism as we know it seems to have developed shortly after the discovery of the precession of the equinoxes by Hipparchus [d. *ca.* 120 BCE], Mithra, the eponymous focus of the mysteries, goes back to the ancient Zoroastrian *Avesta*. Clearly, a working knowledge of many Indo-Iranian languages are needed to evaluate the many claims asserting Indian and Persian influences in Christian origins, and they are basic for any serious comparative studies of mythologies and religions.

4. Semitic Languages

Hebrew is a major language of the Dead Sea Scrolls, the Jewish scriptures, the Mishna, ancient inscriptions, and coins. Modern Hebrew is a language in which much important archaeological research is published that never is translated into English. Christianity is alleged to have arisen from Judaism, and so anyone wishing to test that hypothesis perforce must be able to get along in Hebrew. The Jesus biography is largely comprised of 'Old Testament' elements and both the Greek Septuagint and the Hebrew scriptures must be explored thoroughly if one is to determine the extent to which the Jesus 'biography' comprises anything new beyond its inheritance from the Jewish scriptures.

Because the Samaritan religion and its scriptures are closely related genetically to the Hebrew bible and the Israelite religions, it is necessary to be able to work with Samaritan forms of Hebrew, Aramaic, and even Arabic in order to study the evolution of the biblical texts.

Frank R. Zindler

Most intriguingly, according to Arthur Drews' intriguing little book *Die Petruslegende*,[74] there is more than a little evidence to suggest a close genetic relationship between the Christian Saint Peter, the Samaritan Simon Magus of Acts 8:9–24, and the Samaritan version of Hercules, Melkart. That things Samaritan lay at the very taproot of the proto-Christian tree seems clear from the fact that the second-century church father Irenaeus [130–202 CE] identifies Simon Magus as the "master and progenitor of all heresy" — thus asserting a Samaritan origin for most of the forms of Christianity of his day![75]

Other Semitic languages I have found necessary in the course of my investigations of religion in general and Christianity in particular include Assyro-Babylonian or Akkadian, Phoenician, Ugaritic, Aramaic, Syriac, Arabic, and Ethiopic. Assyro-Babylonian cuneiform tablets are of immense importance for understanding not only the evolutionary origins of the major myths of the Old Testament, but also in order to investigate the claim that there was an ancient Babylonian mystery play that closely resembled the passion narrative of the canonical gospels. Phoenician has been useful for comparative linguistic studies relating to purportedly genuine or false inscriptions and artifacts relating to the Old Testament.

Aramaic is needed to read the Targumim and the commentaries on the Mishna known as the Babylonian Talmud and the Talmud of Jerusalem. It also is needed in order to evaluate claims that Jesus not only existed but that his mother tongue was Aramaic and that there are Aramaic echoes in the texts of the gospels and Acts. The closely related Syriac is the language of Ephrem the Syrian, who wrote polemics against Marcion and Mani and a commentary on Tatian's *Diatessaron*. Most importantly, however, it is the language of the extremely important *Codex Sinaiticus Syriacus*, the manuscript

---

74 Arthur Drews, *Die Petruslegende* [Frankfurt am Main: Neuer Frankfurter Verlag, 1910]. In 1997 I published my English translation of this book as *The Legend of Saint Peter* [Austin, TX: American Atheist Press, 1997]. I greatly expanded Drews' text with a foreword and appendix of selected texts referenced by Drews that I presented in full-text English translation to give readers a better understanding of the context of Drews' arguments.

75 Irenaeus, *Adversus Haereses*, I, 27.

in which there is no virgin birth of Jesus in Matthew's genealogy: "... and Jacob begat Joseph, and Joseph begat Jesus..." (It would seem, however, that Ehrman disagrees with my assessment of both the significance and importance of this particular document.)

Quite unexpectedly, Arabic proved to be of great value in my religious studies. I had studied Arabic by 'total immersion' one summer at Yale, intending to find employment in Saudi Arabia. I was offered the post of Editor-in-Chief of the Saudi Geological Survey at Jedda, but before the contract could reach me the job was snapped up by someone who better understood the cryptomonetary mechanisms with which business of all kinds is transacted in that country. When in like manner a post teaching human neuroanatomy at Faisal Medical School in Riyadh slipped from my grasp, I abandoned all Arabian plans for employment.

Despite this dashing of all hope for handsomely rewarding employment, my study of Arabic was not in vain. My Arabic studies proved invaluable for understanding comparative and historical linguistics of the Semitic languages in general, including Ugaritic and the newly discovered Eblaite. Then too, the language was useful in studying the Qur'an not only for its own sake but also for reconstructing the types of Christianity and Judaism that were catalysts in the development of Islam. Then too, when it became necessary to study the Coptic translations of the canonical New Testament, I discovered that many of the important manuscripts had glosses in Arabic that were important in their own right. I regret that in later years my command of Arabic has decayed to the point where I can decode Arabic documents only with great effort.

There is one more Semitic language that I have found to be potentially of immense significance for students of Christian origins: Ethiopic, or Ge'ez. Ethiopia seems to have been the *Ultima Thule* of earliest Christian missionary expansion, and relict forms of Christian scriptures and beliefs have survived there to this very day. Ethiopia lay beyond the reach of the book burners who shaped the canon of the so-called Great Church, and so Ethiopic Christianity and its scriptures seem to be what a biologist would call "living fossils."[76] The canon of the Ethiopic Orthodox Church comprises 81 books, as compared to the 66 that make up the bibles of Protestant Christians. The Ethiopic *Book of Enoch* is of immense value in understanding the astrological aspects of Christian origins. It is with deep dismay that I resign myself to the now-apparent fact that I shall die without ever having made any headway in the study of this critically important language.

5. Slavic Languages

It might be supposed that Slavic languages would not be needed in order to do New Testament studies. However, repeatedly I have found my knowledge of Slavic linguistics to be of utility, not only to read the critical general works of the Communist-era Russian authors so summarily dismissed by Ehrman, but also to read the archaeological literature written in Russian and Serbo-Croatian. Finally, in order to study the interesting Christian interpolations in so-called *Slavonic Josephus*, written in a dialect of Old Russian distinct from Old Church Slavonic (Old Bulgarian), it was necessary to gain at least a rudimentary understanding of that extinct language as well.

6. Other Languages

Bart Ehrman lists Coptic as a useful language for Jesus studies, and I can only emphasize his correctness in this regard. Just recently, he published a valuable book with coauthor Zlatko Pleše, *The Apocryphal Gospels: Texts and Translations*. Pleše contributed the texts and translations for the Coptic materials and Ehrman supplied the Greek and Latin. All of these texts have already proven to be valuable for certain statistical studies I am carrying out. It has been necessary also to obtain the Coptic New Testament in both its Sahidic and Bohairic versions. At the 2009 meeting of the Society of Biblical Literature in

76 In biogeography it is often the case that plants and animals that have survived the least altered from archaic forms are found in regions furthest from their zone of origins or greatest development. Thus, *Amborella*, the most primitive Angiosperm (flowering plant) known is found only on the remote island of New Caledonia. Lemurs, among the most primitive of Primates, have survived only on Madagascar — a long way from North America where the oldest primate fossils are found.

New Orleans, Christian Askeland, then a PhD candidate at the University of Cambridge, showed photographs of a crudely constructed Coptic document[77] containing the ending of the Gospel of John. The manuscript clearly *ended* at the end of chapter twenty! Was this proof of the theory held for over a century by a number of scholars that the twenty-first chapter of John's gospel was a later addition to the text? Was there a Greek *Vorlage* lacking a twenty-first chapter somewhere in the text transmission history underlying this document?

Askeland did not think this was the case. His conclusion was that "The most likely explanation for the low quality of the papyrus, the rapid cursive hand, and the frequent rate of errors is that this manuscript was the product of an exercise in scriptural memory." It seems to me, however, that even if Askeland is correct, the question still presses: Was this an exercise in memorizing just the end of chapter twenty, or an exercise in memorizing the end of John's gospel? Not only is Coptic language skill needed to resolve such issues, papyrological and palaeographic knowledge is also required.

Finally, although of apparently minor importance but needing to be explored more fully, there is archaeological and epigraphic literature written in Romanian and Turkish. Considering the importance of Asia Minor in the earliest history of Christianity, it is highly likely that Turkish-language descriptions and discussions exist pertaining to archaeological sites, artifacts and inscriptions that are of importance for both Old and New Testament studies.

THE SUMMING UP

Having thus summarized the skills and knowledge bases that I personally have discovered to be requisite for studying Christian origins scientifically, I am quite daunted. Some of the requirements I fulfill not at all, and a majority of the skills that I do possess should have been greatly improved and strengthened. I can only take heart in the knowledge — knowledge as certain as any can be in a social science — that I have labored in a new paradigm that will eventually

77 Bodleian manuscript, MS.Copt.e.150(P)

supplant the discipline of Historical Jesus Studies. The new science of Christian origins will be the product of *interdisciplinary* teams of scholars, not just isolated amateurs such as I. Bart Ehrman is clearly correct to claim that I am not fully qualified to write about Christian origins. Lamentably, at the age of seventy-three there isn't a lot more — try as I shall — that I can do to achieve full qualification. Moreover, it seems obvious that progress in the study of Christian origins will result from a sort of multidisciplinary cross-fertilization effected by teams in which members can teach each other to think 'outside the box' of each particular discipline's paradigm. It's too late for me. But Bart D. Ehrman is still young and growing, and the title question of this essay remains: Is Bart Ehrman qualified to write about Christian origins? Is he *fully* qualified? Does he need outside help?

CHAPTER NINE

Bart Ehrman and the Art of Rhetorical Fallacy

Frank R. Zindler

Bart D. Ehrman is a very good writer. His style is always clear, easily understood, and engaging. He is, after all, a *New York Times* best-seller author, and his recent *Did Jesus Exist? The Historical Argument for Jesus of Nazareth*[1] (*DJE?*) seems likely to become another publishing triumph. Felicity of style, however, may often pose potential danger to unwary readers. A style that is *too* engaging, *too* glib, can often carry readers over hidden crevasses in logic and vast evidential voids. It is the task of this chapter to discover if such dangers have been hidden in the arguments that Ehrman uses to persuade his readers that 'Jesus of Nazareth' once roamed the hills of Galilee and shed his blood on Calvary.

Few of the fallacies for which I shall search will be fallacies of formal logic, although arguments drawn out over many pages — even throughout an entire book — sometimes can conceal even a formal fallacy. Rather, I mostly shall be looking for what I like to call *fallacies of rhetoric*. Such fallacies can sometimes be devilish to detect and, as a consequence, are the mainstay of religious apologists of all stripes. Although most of this chapter will be devoted to such 'informal' types of fallacy, I wish to begin with an examination of a formal fallacy that Ehrman has incorporated into the macrostructure of *DJE?*

1 Bart D. Ehrman, *Did Jesus Exist? The Historical Argument for Jesus of Nazareth* [New York, HarperOne, 2012].

Frank R. Zindler

Affirming the Consequent

Although it is not likely to be realized until one has read the entirety of *Did Jesus Exist?* — if even then, if a reader has not activated critical faculties when commencing to read the book — the entire book is the embodiment of a fallacy of formal logic. It is, however, a global fallacy that must be mastered if one is to prosper, say, as a professional apologist or debater supporting 'creation science' in opposition to evolutionary biology. Creationists who commit this fallacy publish books with titles such as *The Evolution Deception, The Evolution Lie*, or *Evolution? The Fossils Say No!* They think that if they can disprove evolution, young-earth creationism has been proven to be true.

The fallacy committed by creationists and Ehrman alike is known as *Affirming the Consequent*. Structurally it takes the form:

> If **p** then **q**.
>
> | **q**. |
>
> Therefore, **p**.

A verbal example might be the following:

> If it's raining, then the streets are not dry.
>
> The streets are not dry.
>
> Therefore, it's raining.

This is, of course, fallacious reasoning. A street might not be dry for many reasons. Street urchins may have opened all the fire hydrants in order to cool off in the summer's heat. A milk truck may have exploded, or little Dutch girls may just have finished scrubbing it. So too it is with the creationists' attempts to prove Genesis by refuting Darwin. Every evolutionist who ever lived might be wrong, but that would no more establish the truth of any one of the four creation myths[2] in the Christian bible than it would prove that the Moon Goddess made

2 The four myths of creation are found in Genesis 1:1–2:4; Genesis 2:5–25; John 1:1–5; and Proverbs 3:19–20.

us or that Old Man Coyote created men and women from the hairs of his right and left arm pits, respectively.

Sad to say, the fallacy of Affirming the Consequent makes up the overarching structure of Ehrman's book. He acts as though he can prove the historicity of Jesus if he can show that all mythicist theories of Christian origins are wrong. Ehrman's implicit reasoning seems to be the following:

> If Jesus of Nazareth existed, then the
> Mythicists are wrong.
>
> The Mythicists are wrong.
>
> Therefore, Jesus existed.

Of the nine chapters of *Did Jesus Exist?,* only four (chapters 2, 3, 4, & 5–107 pages) ostensibly are devoted to providing evidence for the historicity of a Jesus — although not necessarily the Jesus of Nazareth advertized in the book's subtitle. Three chapters (chapters 1, 6, & 7–101 pages) attempt to discredit mythicist claims and theories, and two chapters (chapters 8 & 9–64 pages) fantasize about the 'real' historical Jesus.

If the purpose of the book were really to present "the historical argument for Jesus of Nazareth," why would there be any chapters about Mythicists at all? Given the historical circumstances surrounding Ehrman's decision to write the book, however, it was inevitable that some mention of Mythicists and their theories would have to be made. I, for example, had been having an e-mail discussion with him for about two years, continuously requesting that he share with me whatever evidence he might have to support the historicity of Jesus of Nazareth. As a courtesy, I sent him copies of my *The Jesus the Jews Never Knew*, the four volumes of my *Through Atheist Eyes: Scenes From a World That Won't Reason*, and a few articles and a lecture. He was provided with a copy of René Salms' *The Myth of Nazareth: The Invented Town of Jesus,* and Robert M. Price's *The Christ-Myth Theory and Its Problems*. Astonishingly, during our entire dialogue up until shortly before it broke off, Ehrman never provided any evidence at all to show why Jesus of anywhere at all had ever lived. Finally, after being pestered for two years he wrote something to the effect of "for all the standard reasons. I'm sure you know what they are."

Despite the fact that Ehrman was provided with a great amount of evidence indicating that there *was* no evidence to support the historicity of Jesus of Nazareth, he ignored almost all of it. Then, providing no substantial or even quasi-objective evidence for a Jesus of Nazareth involved in the genesis of Christianity, he devoted much space and energy to refutation of Mythicist attempts to explain how Christianity could have begun without a historical Jesus. Ehrman never provided the evidence requested.

It turns out, however, that I have taken Ehrman's subtitle too seriously, supposing that the purpose of *DJE?* was to demonstrate what needed to be proved, *viz.*, that Jesus of Nazareth once existed. Ehrman sets the record straight on page 173:

> Jesus certainly existed. My goal in this book, however, is not simply to show the evidence for Jesus's existence that has proved compelling to almost every scholar who has ever thought about it, but also to show why those few authors who have thought otherwise are therefore wrong.

Who could have known? Only careful readers who got past the first 172 pages of *DJE?*

Obvious Fallacies

Everyone that I know who has read *DJE?* has been struck by Ehrman's blatant use of the three most fundamental fallacies of informal logic — fallacies that every beginning student of logic or philosophy learns to recognize. These are the *argumentum ad hominem* fallacy, where one attacks the arguer instead of the argument; the appeal to authority (*argumentum ad verecundiam*); and the three-million-Frenchmen-can't-be-wrong fallacy (*argumentum ad populum*). It is really shocking to see a hitherto admired scholar descend to the tactical level of a religious apologist — especially when the scholar in question has become an Atheist. Having little ambition to capture and classify such easy literary prey, I invite my own readers to buy a copy of *DJE?* and see how many of these fallacies they can identify in the first 34 pages.

Fallacy of False Attribution

Actually, there are two distinct fallacies that often are termed 'fallacy of false attribution.' The first, more literal meaning, is simply incorrectly — whether accidentally or deliberately — attributing authorship, information, or a quotation to a particular source. The second version of the fallacy — less likely to be accidental — is the false imputation of motivation to a person or group. Ehrman's *DJE?* provides at least two examples of the first, and a large but uncounted number of examples of the second.

An attribution error of the first type appears on page 58 of *DJE?*, where Ehrman makes a statement that would likely warrant a D-grade if written by one of his undergraduate students:

> In his various writings Josephus mentions a large number of Jews, especially as they were important for the social, political, and historical situation in Palestine. As it turns out, he discusses several persons named Jesus, and he deals briefly also with John the Baptist. And on two occasions, at least in the writings as they have come down to us today, he mentions Jesus *of Nazareth*" [*emphasis added*].

What's wrong with this attribution? In the e-mails and literature that I provided to Ehrman — literature that he claims to have read — I make much noise over the fact that 'Nazareth' was completely unknown to Josephus, who fortified a town less than two miles from present-day Nazareth and he mentions 45 cities and villages in the tiny territory of Galilee. Clearly, if Josephus never, ever mentioned *Nazareth*, he cannot have mentioned Jesus of Nazareth. As I pointed out to Ehrman, if it could be shown that the Land of Oz never existed, the Wizard of Oz would also be a fiction. He knew that I had compared Nazareth to Oz and Jesus to the Wizard. If indeed it had been true that Josephus had in fact authentically mentioned Nazareth, my whole argument against the historicity of Jesus would collapse by virtue of the fact that Jesus *of Nazareth* is probably the only Jesus whose existence can be tested in a scientifically meaningful way.

A perhaps even more revealing error of attribution is to be found on pages 16–17 of *DJE?* Ehrman writes:

> The mythicist view was taken up some decades later in English-speaking circles by J. M. Robertson, sometimes considered the premier British rationalist of the beginning of the twentieth century. His major book appeared in 1900, titled *Christianity and Mythology*. Robertson argued that there were striking similarities between what the Gospels claim about Jesus and what earlier peoples believed about pagan gods of fertility, who, like Jesus, were said to have died and been raised from the dead. These fertility gods, Roberson and many others believed, were based on the cycles of nature: just as the crops die at the beginning of winter but then reappear in the spring, so too do the gods with which they are identified. They die and rise again. Jesus's death and resurrection was based, then, on this primitive belief, transposed into Jewish terms. More specifically, while there once may have been a man named Jesus, he was nothing like the Christ worshipped by Christians, who was a mythical figure based on an ancient cult of Joshua, a dying-rising vegetative god who was ritually sacrificed and eaten. Only later was this divine Joshua transposed by his devotees into a historical figure, the alleged founder of Christianity. [*DJE?* 16–17]

I was quite surprised to see John Mackinnon Robertson being credited with the notion of a pre-Christian Joshua cult and to learn that Joshua, according to Robertson, was "a dying-rising vegetative god who was ritually sacrificed and eaten." It had been almost thirty years since I had read *Christianity and Mythology* [1900] — the only work of Robertson's cited by Ehrman — but I had no memory of such ideas forming any part of that book. Rather, the idea of a pre-Christian Jesus/Joshua was famously the theoretical centerpiece of the mathematician, physicist, linguist, and all-around polymath William Benjamin Smith, whose *Der Vorchristliche Jesus* [*The Pre-Christian Jesus*] of 1906 was critiqued by Albert Schweitzer in the second edition of his *Quest of the Historical Jesus*. In that and subsequent books, Smith had adduced evidence to show that there was a Joshua-cult in the Near

East at the turn of the era. Since the Greek LXX spelling of name 'Joshua' is the same as the Greek New Testament spelling of 'Jesus,' it is easy to perceive a genetic relationship between the putative cult of Joshua and the historical cult(s) of Jesus.

It appeared that Ehrman had not read any of the early Mythicists himself, but had simply relied upon Schweitzer's critiques and had gotten the particular scholars mixed up. (Schweitzer gives considerable space to critiquing W. B. Smith and other scholars curiously not mentioned by Ehrman.) Was that in fact the case? Several hours of scrutinizing *Christianity and Mythology* discovered no mention of a Joshua cult involving a dying-rising vegetative fertility god — concepts seemingly more at home in the thirteen volumes of *The Golden Bough*, by Sir James George Frazer. Did Ehrman find this in some other book of Robertson's? If so, if *DJE?* were to be considered a work of serious scholarship, shouldn't he have referenced the source?

It must be acknowledged that all the components of the paragraph quoted above can indeed be found in the writings of various Mythicists, but I don't know of any single authority whose opinion includes all of them. Rather, it appears that Ehrman has merely jumbled together ideas current in the early twentieth-century community of Mythicist scholars. Anyhow, who might be expected to check his references?

Attribution errors of the second type are, alas, extremely frequent in *DJE?* Indeed, Ehrman ends his book with an entire section titled "The Mythicist Agenda," in which vaguely beneficent as well as sinister motives are imputed to all Mythicists who are Atheists. "I refuse to sacrifice the past in order to promote the worthy cause of my own social and political agendas," he writes. "No one else should either" — as though Mythicists have no scientific or intellectual motives (let alone evidence!), but attack historical Jesus studies purely for sociopolitical purposes.

Imputing to Mythicists a blindness engendered by passion, Ehrman informs us that "From a dispassionate point of view, there was a Jesus of Nazareth" [*DJE?* 7] Referring to my own argument that the mention of Nazareth in Mark 1:9 is an interpolation, and without citing in his main text any of the evidence that I e-mailed to him supporting that claim, he informs his readers that "Zindler maintains that that verse was not originally part of Mark; it was inserted by a later scribe. Here again we see history being done according to convenience. If a text says precisely what you think it could not have said, then all you need to do is claim that originally it must have said something else" [*DJE?* 191]. I am not certain how to identify precisely the motives being imputed to me here, but one thing seems likely: any of his readers who do not already know me personally probably would not want to meet me — or let me get between them and a doorway.

Proof by Proclamation

Another rhetorical fallacy that is hard to pin down when it has been stretched across the space of an entire book is the fallacy I like to call *proof by proclamation*. In my little spoof "Bart Ehrman and the Emperor's New Clothes" at the end of this book, I quip that "Ehrman is seeking evidence for the existence of Jesus of Nazareth. Mythicists are seeking evidence for the existence of Ehrman's evidence." Having tried but failed to find convincing evidence in *DJE?* supporting the historicity of Jesus of Nazareth, I think it is now fair to claim that Ehrman has repeatedly tried to prove his history simply by saying that it's so — proof by proclamation. Here are some examples of Ehrman whistling past the graveyard in which all historical Jesuses have been buried.

> The reality is that whatever else you may think about Jesus, he certainly did exist. [*DJE?* 4]

> From a dispassionate point of view, there was a Jesus of Nazareth. [*DJE?* 7]

> It is striking that virtually everyone who has spent all the years needed to attain these qualifications is convinced that Jesus of Nazareth was a real historical figure. [*DJE?* 5]
>
> For now I want to stress the most foundational point of all: even though some views of Jesus could loosely be labeled myths (in the sense that mythicists use the term: these views are not history but

> imaginative creation), Jesus himself was not a myth. He really existed. [*DJE?* 14]

> Before countering the claims of the mythicists, I will set out the evidence that has persuaded everyone else, amateur and professional scholars alike, that Jesus really did exist. [*DJE?* 34]

> Even though there are innumerably historical problems in the New Testament, they are not of the scope or character to call seriously into doubt the existence of Jesus. He certainly lived... [*DJE?* 37]

> ...and my claim is that once one understands more fully what the Gospels are and where they came from, they provide powerful evidence indeed that there really was a historical Jesus who lived in Roman Palestine and who was crucified under Pontius Pilate. [*DJE?* 70]

> What I think is that Jesus really existed but that the Jesus who really existed was not the person most Christians today believe in... For now I want to continue to mount the case that whatever else you may want to say about Jesus, you can say with a high degree of certainty that he was a historical figure. [*DJE?* 143–44]

Finally, Ehrman ends his little book — a book that actually is amazingly long, considering the fact that not enough real evidence exists in it to fill a pamphlet — with a proclamation that is actually a book-length *non sequitur*:

> Jesus did exist, whether we like it or not. [339]

Just how amazing this final declaration truly is can be understood only when one reads Ehrman's catalog of evidences we do not have with which to demonstrate the quondam existence of the most important man who ever lived:

> To begin with, there is no hard, physical evidence for Jesus (eighteen hundred years before photography was invented), including no archaeological evidence of any kind. [*DJE?* 42]

> We also do not have any writings from Jesus. ... It is also true, as the mythicists have been quick to point out, that no Greek or Roman author from the first century mentions Jesus. [*DJE?* 43]

> Still, to press yet further on the issue of evidence we do not have, I need to stress that we do not have a single reference to Jesus by anyone — pagan, Jew, or Christian — who was a contemporary eyewitness, who recorded things he said and did. But what about the Gospels of the New Testament? Aren't they eyewitness reports? Even though that was once widely believed about two of our Gospels, Matthew and John, it is not the view of the vast majority of critical historians today, and for good reason. [*DJE?* 46]

> In fact, we do not have any eyewitness report of any kind about Jesus, written in his own day. [*DJE?* 49]

In the face of the crippling fact that there is no evidence of any kind — physical, archaeological, or literary — that two thousand years of searching has been able to find to indicate that the Docetists were wrong and Jesus was real, Ehrman thinks he has been able to prove that "Jesus did exist, whether we like it or not." It is interesting that he does not end his book claiming that "Jesus *of Nazareth* did exist." That was, of course, the Jesus specifically promised in the subtitle of *DJE?* Perhaps he secretly realizes that René Salm's archaeological analysis[3] shows conclusively that Nazareth was not inhabited at the turn of the era and Ehrman understands that if there was no Nazareth of Jesus there could not have been a Nazareth of Jesus!

On the other hand, Ehrman is a master debater and may be aware of a forensic trick that when handled well can be quite effective. The trick involves mentioning one's opponent's best points repeatedly, interspersed with irrelevant arguments and confident periodic comments implying that the opponent's points have been refuted.

Concealed Fallacies

A skilled rhetorician is able to practice the art of rhetorical fallacy so subtly that readers are not likely to notice them unless they are

3 René Salm, *The Myth of Nazareth: The Invented Town of Jesus* [Cranford, NJ: American Atheist Press, 2008]. See also his chapter in this book, "Archaeology, Bart Ehrman, and the Nazareth of 'Jesus' "

logicians or have reason *a priori* to be suspicious of the soundness of the book they are reading. Usually, the fallacies thus committed are concealed by being only implied, mixed with several other fallacies, and distributed over a space of text in such a way as to avoid drawing attention to the fallacies by stating them too baldly. Ehrman's skill in the art of rhetorical fallacy can be seen at the very beginning of *Did Jesus Exist?,* in the very first paragraph of his introduction. Let us examine this paragraph and see what all is hidden in it. The paragraph reads:

> For the past several years I have been planning to write a book about how Jesus became God. How is it that a scarcely known, itinerant preacher from the rural backwaters of a remote part of the [Roman] empire, a Jewish prophet who predicted that the end of the world as we know it was soon to come, who angered the powerful religious and civic leaders of Judea and as a result was crucified for sedition against the state — how is it that within a century of his death, people were calling this little-known Jewish peasant God? Saying in fact that he was a divine being who existed before the world began, that he had created the universe, and that he was equal with God Almighty himself? How did Jesus come to be deified, worshipped as the Lord and Creator of all? [*DJE?* 1].

Let us deconstruct this paragraph sentence-by-sentence.

We are told that Ehrman has *"been planning to write a book about how Jesus became God."* This already begs the question (*petitio principii* fallacy) that Jesus existed. Further, it begs the question that religious evolution proceeded from man to 'God,' rather than from a god to a mortal. Moreover, it begs the question that it is *possible* to reconstruct various historical stages by which a man became a god.

Because Ehrman's second sentence constitutes the great bulk of the first paragraph, I shall examine it phrase-by-phrase.

"How is it that a scarcely known, itinerant preacher..." Once again, this begs the question of Jesus's existence and implies that despite his obscurity, we can know that he existed. Further, it implies that the gospel descriptions of his itinerancy — despite the contradictions — are historically accurate, and that a core of historical truth is to be

found in the gospels. It implies that Jesus didn't stay in his hometown (whatever that might have been) but roamed around preaching — even though there is no evidence for this outside the gospels, not even in the Epistles or Revelation. It implies that the gospels are history, not the first-century equivalents of historical novels or religious dramas or passion plays.

"...from the rural backwaters of a remote part of the empire, ..." As it is throughout the book, we see here evidentiary existential claims hidden in virtually every phrase. Jesus existed. He existed in an agrarian environment, not an urban one. Further, it implies that the ancient *Roman* empire was the temporal and spatial setting for the life of Jesus and that Jesus lived out his life far away from Rome. Although no specific timeframe is implied, readers automatically can be expected to think of the first century CE generally and the period from the death of Herod the Great [4 BCE] to the reign of Tiberius specifically.

"... a Jewish prophet who predicted that the end of the world as we know it was soon to come,..." Where to begin? Jesus was Jewish? What evidence is there for this claim outside the New Testament and related writings? This presumes, without evidence that is ever to be presented, that Christianity began in Palestine. It asserts without evidence that Jesus was a prophet as well as a preacher. Whole books have been written claiming that Jesus was neither one! To be sure, at the end of *DJE?* Ehrman argues for an apocalyptic-prophet type of Jesus, but here everything is implied to be accepted without proof. Presumably, the last major part of *DJE?* argues that Jesus was an apocalyptic prophet, but I see no significant proof adduced to support that notion, only assertive imagination at work. We know for a fact that Jesus of Nazareth predicted the end of the world because... (???)

"... who angered the powerful religious and civic leaders of Judea..." Jesus angered *powerful* religious and civic leaders? How does Ehrman know they weren't low-level bureaucrats rather than potentates? How does he know it wasn't a mob he angered by telling them they needed to repent of their sins? How does he know that the story didn't start with a local notary and got inflated in importance to involve Pilate and the High Priest as the tale grew and grew? It is implied

that we know specifically who these leaders were, and that Pilate was one of them. It implies that the gospels are accurate in their depiction of the involvement of *both* religious and secular authorities, and once again it assumes the Gospel accounts are real history, not historical fiction or religious dramaturgy. Where's the proof?

"... *as a result was crucified for sedition against the state*..." Wow! Could anything more be packed into this phrase? Jesus was *crucified* rather than *stoned* as recorded in the *Toldoth Yeshu* — as required by Jewish law! He was crucified on a *cross* rather than a tree, no doubt, and the cross was a crisscross type rather than a bare pole. Moreover, this crucifixion involved *nails* going through his hands and feet, rather than mere tying of the victim to a stake to die in great pain from inanition. The crucifixion took place *on earth*, not at the intersection of the celestial equator and ecliptic. Jesus was guilty of *sedition*, despite the fact that there is no strong indication (let alone evidence!) of this in the gospels or epistles, still less in extrabiblical sources. Whatever happened to blasphemy? How much of the contradictory passion tales are we to swallow along with the 'bare fact' of crucifixion? Is crucifixion the solitary commonality of the passion narratives Ehrman thinks is true? If he discards everything else in the passion accounts as fictive — as every scientifically thinking person must do — on what ground would he retain the crucifixion? Multiple attestation, no doubt.

"... *how is it that within a century of his death*, ..." This implies that (a) we can reliably and precisely date the composition of the epistles and gospels; (b) we can know that their present contents are reliable indicators of their original contents; (c) even though we have virtually no New Testament manuscripts earlier than the third century, we know that those documents are accurate historical records; (d) we can assume that the third-century manuscripts that have been preserved are representative of the entire gospel tradition during the first and second centuries; (e) we can ignore macroevolutionary features of gospel history (*e.g.*, the production of major variant gospels such as those of Marcion, the Docetists, Gnostics, Nazarenes, *et al.*) and theorize with just the data derived from a study of the microevolutionary development of the canonical works; (f) we can know for certain that Jesus once existed; and (g) we can reliably determine *when* (and probably *where*) Jesus died.

"... *people were calling this little-known Jewish peasant God*?" How many people are we to understand were calling the peasant God? The authors of the four canonical gospels? They, plus the authors of the so-called apocryphal gospels? The authors of the various epistles and apocalypses? Or are we to imagine crowds of worshippers whipped up by preachers who read the gospel stories to them?

But perhaps Ehrman wants us to think of ordinary people at a time before the composition of the epistles and gospels — people who supposedly had actually interacted with Jesus. We must remind ourselves that there is absolutely no reason to think that such "people" are anything other than the invention of the New Testament authors, especially the author of Acts of the Apostles. We know even less about the existence of such people than we do about Jesus of Nazareth. If Ehrman tries to use them to explain Jesus, he is committing the *ignotum per ignotius* fallacy — explaining the unknown by the even more unknown.

Ehrman assumes not only that Jesus existed, but that he was a Jewish peasant as well. He knows Jesus was a peasant because...? He was a peasant because he was a royal descendant of King David, perhaps? How came it to be that a royal scion had fallen so far down the social ladder? Okay, all that Royal David stuff is mythical and not to be believed. So, how much else about Jesus can't be believed? How did a peasant become a god? Of course, that's precisely the question to be dealt with in the phrase under scrutiny here. We know that the *god* Orpheus became The Good Shepherd; a musically talented, friendly *shepherd* did not become the god Orpheus. Why should the god Christ Jesus be different from Orpheus?

"*Saying in fact that he was a divine being who existed before the world began,...*" Implicit here once again is the assumption that the evolution of the Jesus myth proceeded from mortal man to immortal god. What evidence does Ehrman plan to present to show this notion is preferable to the converse idea, *viz.*, that an immortal god was understood to have become (in some sense) a mortal man? Will he shave with Occam's razor to decide which mythic evolutionary direction is the easier and more economical to reconstruct? Does he understand what would count as scientifically meaningful evidence? Probably not.

"... *that he had created the universe,...*" What gapless chain of historical events will Ehrman be able to forge (no pun intended) in order to connect a Jewish peasant with the creator of the universe? Will he distinguish the 'universe' as we conceive it from the 'world' or 'worlds' of the early Christians — including Gnostic Christians? What objective evidence will he adduce in support of his historical model? Will he realize he even needs to do that? Probably not.

"...*and that he was equal with God Almighty himself* ?" Exactly which god was the first to be equated with Jesus? The Demiurge? Yahweh? The ineffable supreme god of the highest Gnostic heaven? Inquiring minds will want to know.

"How did Jesus come to be deified, worshipped as the Lord and Creator of all?" Are we talking specifically about Jesus of Nazareth, or a Jesus of not-Nazareth? Will we trace the evolutionary path not only from Ehrman's country bumpkin to the god of Orthodoxy, but also show how that hayseed became the gods of Marcion, the Docetists, the Nazarenes, and the Gnostics as well? It is stunning to see how much there is that Ehrman takes for granted as self-evidently true and not in need of proof. That is the case, of course, because Ehrman is still locked inside the traditional Historical-Jesus paradigm. He knoweth not how much he knoweth not.

Ignotum per Ignotius

One of the most characteristic fallacies of non-scientific, theological reasoning is the fallacy that Mediaeval philosophers termed *ignotum per ignotius* — trying to explain the unknown in terms of the even more unknown. For practical reasons, I expand the definition so that it also includes trying to explain the unknown in terms of *more unknowns* — in common parlance, raising more questions than providing answers. The more narrow definition of *ignotum per ignotius* is more abstract and often difficult to apply precisely. Nevertheless, it might be exemplified in the following way.

Suppose that I am waiting for a train that is late. I don't know why the train is late, and there are many possible reasons for its lateness. Nevertheless, I seize upon the possibility that it is delayed because it hit a car at a railroad crossing and had to stop. Without yet having any evidence to show that that is what has delayed the train, I wonder why the train hit the car. It probably hit the car because the brakes had failed. But why did the brakes fail? Perhaps the driver didn't take it in for its quarterly maintenance. Why didn't she do that? Perhaps... At each successive stage of abstraction from the immediate problem of the late train, the unknown is compounded, not just multiplied.

We already have seen that Ehrman employs this fallacy in the very first paragraph of *DJE?* in his concealed claim "people were calling this little-known Jewish peasant God." Even so, no better example of the commission of this fallacy can be seen than the controversy during the eighteenth-century concerning the nature of lightning. The Christian clergy — explaining the unknown in terms of the more unknown — argued that lightning strikes were chastisements wrought by a wrathful Jehovah. Benjamin Franklin, by contrast, was a scientific thinker of the Enlightenment who held to a completely naturalistic explanation of the phenomenon. Franklin had experimented with electricity both in the laboratory and in the atmosphere. He had postulated, based on his observations of electrical phenomena, that lightning was just an enormous amount of electricity. If that were so, lightning should exhibit the same behavior as electricity — in particular, it should flow through metal rods, wires, and other types of filaments Franklin had observed to be capable of conducting electric charges into Leyden jars or to the ground. Seeking to explain the unknown (lightning) in terms of the known (electricity), he carried out his dangerous kite-flying experiment in 1752 and settled the question for all practical purposes. Armed with this understanding of lightning, Franklin was able to invent the lightning rod and, ironically, become the savior of most of the church steeples of the future world.

After a devastating earthquake at Boston on November 18, 1755, however, the divines of that city compounded their *ignotum-per-ignotius* false reasoning by attributing *the earthquake* to the wrath of an angry Jehovah who was punishing Boston for the circumstance that Boston had more of "Franklin's wicked iron points" than did any other city. The compound complexity of their faulty reasoning is delicious, as we shall see.

We must, however, first consider some particularly important known facts that the divines were hard-pressed to explain. Why was it that trees and church steeples were hit so often? Why were taller trees and higher steeples hit more often than short ones? Why was Jehovah's wrath not usually exercised when the sky was clear? What was it about church steeples that angered Jehovah, when the very churches of which they were a part were intended to please him? Clearly, the likes and dislikes of Jehovah were more inscrutable than the phenomenon of lightning. Indeed, we now can affirm that they *can't* be known because they are scientifically *meaningless* — in the sense that no imaginable test or experiment could be performed to determine them.

To return to the compound fallacy of the Boston divines: attributing the earthquake to Jehovah's anger having been aroused by lightning rods was appealing to a greater unknown than the unknown appealed to in order to explain lightning. That in turn was greater than the scientifically investigable unknown phenomenon of lighting with which we began. Such is the reasoning of the theophrastic mind.

It is hard to get the chill of childhood religion out of one's bones; it is even harder to purge the brain of religious modes of thinking. Despite the fact that it is now 2012, not 1755, and Bart Ehrman is now an Agnostic or Atheist, *Did Jesus Exist?* is as riddled — an amusingly apt term — with the *ignotum per ignotius* fallacy as is any treatise on theology. We may begin our examination of Ehrman's use of this fallacy with a passage from pages 78–79 of *DJE?*:

> What is sometimes underappreciated by mythicists who want to discount the value of the Gospels for establishing the historical existence of Jesus is that our surviving accounts, which began to be

> written some forty years after the traditional date of Jesus's death, were based on earlier written sources that no longer survive. But they obviously did exist at one time, and they just as obviously had to predate the Gospels that we now have. The opening words of the Gospel of Luke bear repeating: "Whereas many have attempted to compile a narrative of the things that have been fulfilled among us, just as the eyewitnesses and ministers of the word delivered them over to us, it seemed good to me also, having followed all these things closely from the beginning, to write for you an orderly account" (1:1–3).

We must remind ourselves that the fundamental question we are trying to answer is, did Jesus of Nazareth once exist? We must try to answer this in the complete absence of physical evidence of any kind, with no contemporary ancient witnesses to his existence or to that of his alleged twelve apostles. In lieu of direct evidence indicating the historicity of Jesus of Nazareth, Ehrman resorts to indirect evidence — the canonical gospels. Thus, at the very beginning of our analysis, we detect the *ignotum-per-ignotius* fallacy, since indirect evidence *a priori* is less knowable than direct evidence.

From the start, we see that Ehrman's argument is erected on shakier ground than that of Boston in 1755. That is because an appeal to the gospels raises more questions than answers. For example:

(1) What is the literary genre of the canonical gospels?

(2) Are they all the same genre? Are any of them like the Book of Mormon? How can we tell?

(3) Were the gospels intended to be read as history?

(4) If so, how reliable are they? How can we determine that?

(5) Are they allegories?

(6) If so, are they allegories having a person as their referent, as does my tale "Bart Ehrman and the Emperor's New Clothes" at the end of this book?

(7) If they refer to a person, was that person a contemporary of the authors? A worthy of the past? How far back in the past?

(8) Are they rather allegories of cosmic history, contemporary history, astrology, or something else?

(9) Are the gospels midrashes or peshers on Septuagint or apocryphal books of scripture?

(10) Are the gospels exercises in historical-future allegory? That is, are they using the common technique of employing perfect-tense narrative to indicate actions that *must* come to pass — *i.e.*, be 'perfected' in the sense of 'carried out'? Is the Jesus of Nazareth of the later gospels or the Jesus of the Gospel of Mark someone expected to appear in the future, but had not actually existed in the authors' past? Is this an example of the ancient magical belief that one can bring about an action by claiming that it has already come to pass?

(11) Are the gospels etiological myths created to justify and authenticate theopolitical power structures such as transfer of authority by apostolic laying on of hands rather than, say, by hereditary transmission through a family claiming descent from the family of Jesus?

(12) Are the canonical gospels *more* or *less* relevant to the problem of Jesus' existence than the so-called apocryphal gospels?

(13) How can we justify ignoring the gospels that clearly picture Jesus as a superhuman, non-historical, mythic being? How can we leave out the witnesses that would answer "no" to the question, "Did a man called Jesus of Nazareth ever live in Palestine?"

(14) Were the canonical gospels created to supplant gospels that were systematically destroyed — gospels that might have painted a very different picture?

(15) Since all the canonical gospels are clearly composites resulting from multiple authors, redactors, and interpolators, how can we know what was the 'original intent' of each document?

(16) What is the significance of the fact that the gospels are mutually contradictory? How can we know if any one of them is 'true'?

(17) Even where all four mutually agree, how can we know they are attesting to a historical fact and not to the existence of an element in a myth? After all, Mark, Q, M, L, and John *all attest to the reality of angels*, and they are strongly corroborated by the Book of Mormon. Would Ehrman accept this as evidence that angels once existed?

The list of unknowns, uncertainties, and questions concerning the gospels could be greatly expanded even further, but the list above suffices to show that when Ehrman appeals to the gospels to explain the unknown Jesus of Nazareth, he has been forced to explain the unknown by means of the even less known. Nevertheless, he assures us that "*our surviving accounts* [the gospels]... *began to be written some forty years after the traditional date of Jesus's death*..."

Once again, we explain the unknown in terms of the more unknown. On top of all the uncertainties about the gospels themselves, we now pile on the uncertainties concerning the date of authorship of the surviving gospels and the questions of when Jesus died, before we have established that he ever lived! Can it be disputed that the unknowns surrounding the alleged death of Jesus of Nazareth must perforce be greater in number and difficulty than the unknowns attending the question of his alleged existence? Is it possible for them to be resolved before it is established that he actually existed?[4] Can begging the question[5] of his existence be a legitimate way to date his death and then in turn date the composition of the gospels?

4 Even if a papyrus record were to be discovered containing the autopsy report on Jesus of Nazareth written and signed by Pontius Pilate's coroner, at best, the life of Jesus would be established *simultaneously* with his death. At worst, well, we may leave such speculation as an exercise for the reader.

5 Employment of the *ignotum per ignotius* fallacy often implies or is actually accompanied by the *petitio principii* fallacy as in this case. It may be that begging the question is needed to avoid having to deal with the rhetorical burden of concealing the ever-greater numbers of questions arising with each step further into the more unknown.

Surely, a hypothetical source that no longer survives is more unknown than an existent document. To be sure, hypothetical sources may sometimes prove to have been real, as in the case of the sayings source Q.[6] But even after their quondam existence has been established — something requiring far more than Ehrman's *maestro dixit!* declaration — we must stare into the broad and deep chasm of our uncertainty as to their original nature and purpose. Did they originally have anything at all to do with the Jesus of Nazareth of Ehrman's subtitle? Or were they, like *The Sophia of Jesus Christ*,[7] non-Christian literature that was swallowed whole and then regurgitated undigested, with remains of the Last Supper soaked into its fibers?

"But they obviously did exist at one time," Ehrman assures us, *"And they just as obviously had to predate the Gospels that we now have."* Obviously? Whatever happened to the Aramaic oral traditions hypothesized to serve the same functions? And what is Ehrman to make of Antoinette Clark Wire's *The Case For Mark Composed In Performance*,[8] that argues that the Gospel of Mark was not composed by a single man from scattered accounts, but was the result of people telling Jesus stories over a period of decades?

---

6 I must admit, however, that I am being forced to reconsider my acceptance of the reality of Q and my theory of its nature by recent publications of Thomas L. Brodie, especially his *The Birthing of the New Testament: The Intertextual Development of the New Testament Writings* [Sheffield, UK: Sheffield Phoenix Press, 2004].

7 The Gnostic library discovered at Nag Hammadi in Egypt provides some examples of how non-Christian materials could have been appropriated for Christian purposes and even displays the smoking gun of revelation-in-the-making-up. James M. Robinson, the editor of the Nag Hammadi materials published in English, tells us that

> The Nag Hammadi library even presents one instance of the Christianizing process taking place almost before one's eyes. The non-Christian philosophic treatise *Eugnostos the Blessed* is cut up somewhat arbitrarily into separate speeches, which are then put on Jesus' tongue, in answer to questions (which sometimes do not quite fit the answers) that the disciples address to him during a resurrection appearance. The result is a separate tractate entitled *The Sophia of Jesus Christ*. Both forms of the text occur side by side in Codex III. [James M. Robinson, *The Nag Hammadi Library*, 3rd rev. ed. (San Francisco: Harper, 1988: 55)]

8 Eugene, OR: Cascade Books, 2011.

All this renders the earlier written sources far more unknown than at first appears and raises the obvious question, "How can we be sure the evangelists didn't just make stuff up?" — as Ehrman likes to assert is the habit of Mythicists. He argues that these written sources are "obvious" because of his translation of the prologue to the Gospel of Luke:

> Whereas many have attempted to compile a narrative of the things that have been fulfilled among us, just as the eyewitnesses and ministers of the word delivered them over to us, it seemed good to me also, having followed all these things closely from the beginning, to write for you an orderly account (1:1–3).

While it is likely that a majority of qualified scholars would agree with Ehrman's rendering, it is nevertheless appropriate to contrast his translation of the first verse of Luke's Gospel with that of the King James Version translators: "Forasmuch as many have taken in hand to set forth in order a *declaration* of those things *which are most surely believed among us*..." When we appeal to the authority of sources behind, say, the Gospel of Luke, exactly what are we appealing to? *A narrative of things that have been fulfilled in the experience of 'Luke' and his sources*, or, *a declaration of things that have been dogmatic 'knowledge' in the Lukan community*?[9]

Regardless of whose translation be considered correct, it cannot be denied that a massive amount of uncertainty has accumulated in Ehrman's argument. But why would he want to appeal to the prologue of Luke anyway? He agrees with me that the birth narratives in Luke and Matthew are fictive, and he knows that Marcion's version of Luke did not contain its first two chapters.[10] (It seems to be

9 The word in dispute here is the Greek passive participle *peplērophorēmenōn*, a form of the verb *plērophoreō*, which Ehrman renders "have been fulfilled" and the KJV translates "are most surely believed." Gerhard Kittel's *Theological Dictionary of the New Testament* [VI:309] explains that in the active voice this verb means "to bring to fulness," and that it can mean "'to satisfy someone completely,' erotically (magic)." In the passive, "plainly so" we are told, it can mean "to be fully convinced of something, to come to full certainty." [Kittel cites in this regard 1 Cl., 42, 3; Ign. Mg., 11, 1; Sm., 1, 1.] The unabridged Liddell & Scott *A Greek-English Lexicon* indicates that in the passive (of persons) this verb means "have full satisfaction, to be fully assured."

10 Thus, Marcion's version of Luke lacked all but one of that Gospel's mentions of

general opinion, moreover, that Marcion's *Evangelion* also lacked the prologue as well.) The Jesuit scholar Joseph Fitzmyer tells us further that Ephraem the Syrian's commentary on Tatian's *Diatessaron* considered Luke 1:5–2:52 to be a later insertion.[11] Fitzmeyer opines that both the birth narrative and the prologue were added some time after composition of the gospel's torso, but supposes all three to have been written by the same hand.

It is well to stop at this point to compare the size of Ehrman's claim about the "value of the Gospels for establishing the historical existence of Jesus" — 139 words — with the length of my incomplete discussion of the unknowns and uncertainties entailed in that claim. Not counting the present paragraph, I expended 1,571 words in that cause and I end my discussion of that claim here simply because I am as weary of it as must be any reader who has been able to stick it out this far.

Two Key *Ignotius* Data: Part I. Whom Paul Knew

With considerable justification, scholars who have been criticized in *DJE?* have accused Ehrman of not engaging their best arguments and evidence but, rather, picking and choosing which arguments he can most easily refute or ridicule, without even acknowledging — let alone engaging — the most important Mythicist research and reasoning. Fortunately, it will be easy for me to avoid having the same claim lodged against me in this book. Ehrman himself has conveniently labeled "Two Key Data for the Historicity of Jesus"[12] — although it is unclear to what degree they may apply to Jesus *of Nazareth* in particular. Nevertheless, despite the uncertainty as to which particular Jesus he intended to prove historical, I engage both "key data" in this book. The second one of the key data, "The Crucified Messiah," I deal with in considerable detail in the chapter "Bart Ehrman and the Crucified

---

Nazareth as well.

11 Joseph A. Fitzmyer, *The Gospel According to Luke I–IX*. The Anchor Bible [Garden City, NY: Doubleday & Co., 1981:311].

12 *DJE?*:142–174.

Messiah," although I will nevertheless revisit it in this chapter in the context of the *ignotum per ignotius* fallacy. The first of the key data, "Paul's Associations," should be considered next, although I need to point out a rhetorical stratagem that went unnoticed until I began to write this paragraph.

Instead of immediately identifying even one of the "two key data" advertised in the title of chapter five, Ehrman begins his chapter [*DJE?* 142] by explaining why he doesn't respond "to all the crazy things people say," and then proceeds to discuss *The Ehrman Project*, a critical Web-site launched by a less-than-worshipful former student. He ends with the opposition-disarming claim, "I believe that better arguments will win out, if people approach the question without a bias in favor of one view or another. Maybe I'm too trusting."

Still not getting to the point of the chapter's title, he laments the likelihood that because of *DJE?* he'll "be getting it from all sides" [*DJE?* 143] — both Mythicists and conservative Christian readers will be annoyed and/or upset by what he has to say. But, he assures us, "Consensus scholarship is like that; it offends people on both ends of the spectrum. But scholarship needs to proceed on the basis of evidence and argument, not on the basis of what one would *like* to think." [*DJE?* 143]

Was it really necessary to delay the revelation of his "Two Key Data" in order to explain that his opponents often say crazy things, that his student's Web-site is not worrisome, although he may be too trusting to assume that people reliably will be able to identify his "better arguments"? Is Ehrman simply poorly organized and has put irrelevant material into the beginning of chapter five, or was there a strategic purpose for placing it here? I leave speculation to my readers.

Late better than never, Ehrman does eventually get around to discussing the first of his two key data at the bottom half of page 144, although readers are left in suspense as to what the second one might be. It is only on page 156 that the second datum is presented: "The Crucified messiah." Ehrman sort of eases into his statement of what his first datum is, and I must quote the entire paragraph:

THE ART OF RHETORICAL FALLACY

> What I think is that Jesus really existed but that the Jesus who really existed was not the person most Christians today believe in. I will get to that latter point toward the end of this book. For now I want to continue to mount the case that whatever else you may want to say about Jesus, you can say with a high degree of certainty that he was a historical figure. In this chapter I will wrap up my discussion of the historical evidence by stressing just two points in particular. These two points are not the whole case for the historical Jesus. A lot of other evidence that we have already considered leads in precisely the same direction. But these two points are especially key. I think each of them shows beyond a shadow of reasonable doubt that Jesus must have existed as a Palestinian Jew who was crucified by the Romans. The first point reverts to Paul, but now we look not at what Paul said about Jesus but at whom Paul knew. Paul was personally acquainted with Jesus's closest disciple, Peter, and Jesus's own brother, James. [*DJE?* 143]

The very last sentence contains the entire argument: *We know that Jesus — a Palestinian Jew who was crucified by the Romans — existed because 'Paul' said he had visited with his brother James and his disciple 'Peter'* [Gal 1:18–19]. Now, how compelling an argument is *that*? Is it more or less believable because Paul solemnly swears, "Before God, I am not lying" [Gal 1:20]?

To prove the existence of a Jesus of [*fill in the blank*] for whom, Ehrman admits, no objective evidence whatsoever exists, he invokes the alleged witness of an equally unknown 'Paul' who — we must suppose — had hallucinations of the Risen Jesus but nonetheless is to be considered a reliable witness. This Paul assures us, not only that he received various messages from 'the Lord,' but also had met someone named Cephas in Jerusalem — as well as a certain James, "the brother of the Lord" [Gal 1:18-20]. The *ignotum-per-ignotius* aspects of this argument are too complex to discuss in an integrated analysis, and so I must simply enumerate the appealing unknowns that lurk within this paragraph.

1. There is no objective evidence that 'Paul' ever lived. There are no genuine relics, no contemporary records. How do we know

that Paul was a historical figure?[13] How can we be sure he is not a literary invention? In the face of this uncertainty, how can we use him in any way as evidence to argue that 'Jesus' was something more than a literary creation? According to the *Panarion* of Epiphanius, in the Ebionite *Ascents of James* it was claimed that Paul's parents were Pagans and that he was a proselyte and was circumcised in order to marry a priest's daughter. When he was not successful, however, he turned against Jewish customs. Will the real Brother of the Lord please stand up? What evidence can Ehrman adduce to show that the conflicting canonical accounts of Paul are any more accurate than that of the Ebionites? If Paul was actually a Pagan, what does that do to the reliability of Acts and the so-called Pauline Epistles?

2. We know that at least some of the New Testament letters attributed to Paul are forgeries or at least falsely attributed to his authorship. How can we be sure that the Dutch Radical Critics at the turn of the twentieth century were not right — *all* of the Pauline epistles are pseudonymous? If Paul didn't write *any* of the letters attributed to him, who exactly *was* Paul? Can that question be answered with-

13 The nineteenth-century scholar Ferdinand Baur not only thought Paul existed, he thought there must have been at least four of him! On the other hand, Epiphanius' discussions on the Carpocratians tell us that their eponymous founder Carpocrates (who, like the Paul of Acts hailed from Asia Minor) worshiped images of Jesus, Paul, Homer, and Pythagoras. Now, the historicity of Homer and Pythagoras has long been questioned. In light of the fact that Paul was being worshiped as a god almost as early as was Jesus, shouldn't we now question the historicity of Paul as well?

The Dominican Thomas L. Brodie recently has done exactly that and has produced what is certain to become a Mythicist classic — *Beyond the Quest for the Historical Jesus: Memoir of a Discovery* [Sheffield: Sheffield University Press, 2012]. In his chapter titled "Paul: The Penny Finally Drops," Brodie reminisces,

> What hit me was that the entire narrative regarding Paul, everything the thirteen epistles say about him or imply — about his life, his work and travels, his character, his sending and receiving of letters, his readers and his relationship to them — all of that was historicized fiction. It was fiction, meaning that the figure of Paul was a work of imagination, but this figure had been historicized — presented in a way that made it look like history, history-like, "fiction made to resemble the uncertainties of life in history" (Alter 1981:27). [145] ... The figure of Paul was built up not only by the epistle writers, but also by Luke. And in a striking addition, Paul's name was connected to further places, monuments and events — a variation on the process by which the Roman Empire used architecture and iconography to communicate its message, a message that included the foundational epic in Virgil's Aeneid. [154]

out recourse to *ignotum-per-ignotius* argumentation? Can testable hypotheses be formulated to investigate the question?

3. Why should we 'believe' the stories told by the author of the so-called authentic Pauline epistles any more than those told by the other authors — for example, the author of Hebrews? Why should we believe any of them?

4. When was Galatians written? Is all of the present text original? Has anything been interpolated? Is Galatians the only document in the New Testament that has *not* been altered over the course of time?[14] What if Galatians was composed much later than the traditional date (*ca.* 58 CE)? Wouldn't that completely vitiate Ehrman's argument? Some Dutch Radical Critics have strongly challenged the traditional dating of this letter.

5. Assuming that Paul existed, how can we be sure that "Paul was personally acquainted with Jesus's closest disciple, Peter"? How can Ehrman know that "Cephas was, of course, Simon Peter" when explicating the I-swear-to-God-I'm-not-lying claim in Galatians 1:18 that "after three years I [Paul] went up to Jerusalem to consult with Cephas"? How can he know they are the same 'rock'? How can we know that neither one of them refers to 'the rock' Mithras?

Is Ehrman aware of the manuscript irregularities concerning the use of the names 'Cephas' and 'Peter' in the first two chapters of Galatians? The name *Cephas* (Aramaic, 'Rock') occurs three times in these chapters: Gal 1:18 ("... I did go up to Jerusalem to get to know Cephas"); Gal 2:9 ("And when James, Cephas, and John, who

---

14 It is curious that Ehrman did not think of his own answer to this question when writing chapter five of *DJE?* and quoting from Galatians. In his *The Orthodox Corruption of Scripture* [New York: Oxford University Press, 1993] he discusses corruptions of Galatians 2:20, 3:16, 3:17, 4:4, 5:11, and 6:17. Of particular interest is his discussion of Galatians 4:4 ["God sent his own son, born of a woman, born under the law..."] and Romans 1:3–4 ["...Jesus Christ our Lord, which was made of the seed of David according to the flesh"] in the context of anti-Docetic corruptions of scripture. "A similar corruption occurs in Romans 1:3–4," he tells us on page 239, "a passage I have already discussed in a different connection. ... As was the case with Galatians 4:4, the change was a matter of the substitution of a word in the versions and of a few simple letters in Greek (from *genomenon* to *gennōmenon*), so that now the text speaks not of Christ "coming from the seed of David" but of his "being born of the seed of David."

seemed to be pillars, perceived the grace…"); and Gal 2:11 ("but when Peter [*Cephas* in best MSS] was come to Antioch, I withstood him to the face…"). The name *Peter* (Greek, 'Rock') appears twice in most manuscripts: Gal 2:7 and 2:8. These two verses are rather odd and have a complicated history in the manuscripts. Before considering the Greek text, it is of interest to contrast the various bewildering attempts to render them in English.

The King James Version: "7 But contrariwise, when they saw that the gospel of the uncircumcision was committed unto me, as *the gospel* of the circumcision *was* unto Peter; 8 (For he that wrought effectually in Peter to the apostleship of the circumcision, the same was mighty in me toward the Gentiles:)"

The New English Bible: "but on the contrary acknowledged that I had been entrusted with the Gospel for Gentiles as surely as Peter had been entrusted with the Gospel for Jews."

The Oxford New International Version: "7 On the contrary, they saw that I had been entrusted with the task of preaching the gospel to the Gentiles, just as Peter had been to the Jews. 8 For God, who was at work in the ministry of Peter as an apostle to the Jews, was also at work in my ministry as an apostle to the Gentiles.

The Anchor Bible translation of J. Louis Martyn: "7. On the contrary, they saw clearly that I had been entrusted by God with the gospel as it is directed to those who are not circumcised, just as Peter had been entrusted with the gospel to those who are circumcised. 8. For he who was at work in Peter, creating an apostolate to those who are circumcised, was also at work in me, sending me to the Gentiles." Martyn comments, "However syntactically disjointed it may be, the long and complex sentence of vv 6–10 is consistently focused on the leaders of the Jerusalem church." He then goes on to discuss the grammatical complexities of the sentence.

The Hermeneia commentary on Galatians [Philadelphia: Fortress Press, 1979], written by the highly respected *Hans Dieter Betz*, does not present a connected translation as such but rather comments on the Greek text. The extent of the *ignotius* invoked by Ehrman in using the Paul of Galatians as evidence of a historical Jesus begins to be visible in Betz's comments on the "long and difficult sentence" of present interest:

> Interesting is also the fact that non-Pauline language is used for the description of the content of the insight. Erich Dinkler emphasized that the notions of the "gospel of the uncircumcision" as well as the "gospel of the circumcision" are not Paul's language and that these concepts contradict his statement in Gal 1:6–7. Surprising is also the name "Peter," instead of the usual "Cephas," in this passage. Karl Holl and Adalbert Merx proposed a solution of the problem of the name by textual emendation, assuming that "Peter" was inserted by later redactors for whom this was the standard name. Ernst Barnikol thought of a later gloss which intended to put Peter and Paul on an equal level. Holl assumed that "Peter" was the name of the missionary, while "Cephas" was the name of the apostle at Jerusalem. Others expressed doubt that the two names refer to the same person. John Chapman argued that Paul formulated Gal 2:7 under the influence of Matt 16:16–19" [96–97; *footnote reference numbers deleted from text*].[15]

As if the translation muddle displayed above were not sufficient to show that Ehrman is trying to explain the unknown in terms of the more unknown, a consideration of the manuscript text history of Gal 1:18 & 2:7–8 promotes his *ignotius* to *ignotissimus*. First of all, *Cephas* in verse 1:18 is found only in the oldest and best manuscripts;[16] all later manuscripts and 'corrections' read 'Peter.' Clearly, this was done to force a Cephas=Peter identity. Secondly, some very important, early manuscripts of verse 2:8 (F, G, ℵ*) *do not contain the second mention of 'Peter'!*

---

15 The pericope of Matt 16:13–20 takes place at Caesarea Philippi, the scene of a grand temple to Augustus and Roma built by Herod the Great. Instead of inveighing against the idolatry of emperor worship, Jesus asks his disciples "Whom do men say that I the Son of Man am?" [Matt 16:13]. Simon Peter replies "Thou art the Christ, the son of the living God." This is followed by a blatant bit of theopolitical invention — the charter for the authority of the Roman Catholic Church: "16:17 Blessed art thou, Simon bar Jona ... 18 And I say also unto thee, That thou art Peter, and upon this rock I will build my church; and the gates of hell shall not prevail against it." Then, 'Peter' is given the magic keys to the gates of the heavens (*tōn ouranōn*) — keys formerly owned by Mithras.

16 B, ℵ*, A, 𝔓[51], 𝔓[46], *etc.*

It is interesting to note that wherever 'Paul' is referring to his own experience, his own interactions, he uses the name 'Cephas.' When, however, he is speaking abstractly, about what God (?) has done for him, he uses the name 'Peter.' It seems to me likely that the 'Peter verses' are later glosses inserted to give a theoretical, theopolitical meaning to the first-person narrative.

The unknowns in this Galatians pericope would seem to make one thing almost certain: the syntactic mess of the Peter passages could not have been original in the text. No one, not even 'Paul,' could have been so poor a writer. Despite all this, not knowing any of the uncertainty surrounding the text of Galatians, Ehrman is certain: "Cephas was, of course, Simon Peter" [*DJE*? 144].

6. It will be remembered that Ehrman claims that we can be sure that Jesus existed because Paul (not Saul?) says he visited "Jesus's own brother, James." Of course there is no evidence for this outside the New Testament. But is there any unambiguous evidence for this *inside* the New Testament?

Young's Analytical Concordance to the Bible lists ten entries under "James the brother of the Lord Jesus," of which only half *by themselves* might imply that Jesus had a brother named James. The other five references might conceivably be relatable to the ones I shall examine here, but clearly to appeal to them would be to appeal to an unknown yet a further degree less known than the problems presented by the 'obvious' verses.

Let us begin with the curious case of the gospels, where at the very beginning of the gospel tradition — the Gospel of Mark[17] — Jesus is thought to be "the brother of James, and Joses, and of Juda, and Simon." Although this 'fact' is copied by 'Matthew'[18] in his requisition

17 Mark 6:3 Is not this the carpenter, the son of Mary, the brother of James, and Joses, and of Juda, and Simon? and are not his sisters here with us? And they were offended at him. 4 But Jesus said unto them, A prophet is not without honour, but in his own country, and among his own kin, and in his own house. 5 And he could there do no mighty work, save that he laid his hands upon a few sick folk, and healed them. 6 And he marveled because of their unbelief.

18 Matt 13:55 Is not this the carpenter's son? is not his mother called Mary? and his brethren, James, and Joses, and Simon, and Judas? 56 And his sisters, are they not all

of most of the Greek text of Mark's gospel, it is hard to explain why it wasn't repeated by 'Luke' — unless he was advancing theopolitical purposes not quite the same as those of Mark and Matthew.[19]

What might have been a theopolitical purpose of Mark? It seems clear — from another of Mark's stories (Mark 3:31–35, repeated with variation in Matthew 12:46–50 and Luke 8:19–21), the story in which Jesus rejects his family and argues that "whosoever shall do the will of God, the same is my brother, and my sister, and mother" — that there's more to this than meets the eye of a speed reader.

First of all, it seems clear that this story is meant as metaphor, not biography. Although both Matthew and Luke copy it, they frame it *in completely different narrative contexts*. If this be biography, it is inexplicable. If it be metaphor with a theopolitical purpose, however, this is literarily unexceptional.

Secondly, it seems to be metaphor with at least two theopolitical purposes. One purpose might have been to undercut the claims to church authority made by persons claiming descent from Jesus' family. It would tie in nicely with another 'hard saying,' Luke 14:26: "If any man come to me, and hate not his father, and mother, and wife, and children, and brethren, and sisters, yea, and his own life also, he cannot be my disciple." Another — perhaps more important — theopolitical purpose might have been to thwart Docetist claims that Jesus only *seemed* to be a man of flesh and blood.[20]

Thirdly, it is highly significant that no specific names are given by Mark in 3:31–35 — not even for 'Mary.'[21] This is typical of fairy

---

with us? Whence then hath this man all these things? 57 And they were offended in him. But Jesus said unto them, A prophet is not without honour, save in his own country, and in his own house. 58 And he did not many mighty works there because of their unbelief.

19 There is also another, more intriguing possibility. If 'Luke' were copying from an early edition of a Docetist-friendly 'proto-Mark,' there may not yet have been mentions of Jesus' family to copy.

20 Perhaps not too surprisingly, the Matthaean passage was also used to prove the exact opposite, *i.e.,* that Jesus *wasn't* human. Epiphanius, in a digression in his *Panarion* chapter on the Ebionites tells us that Cerinthus and Carpocrates used this pericope to argue *against* the humanity of Jesus!

21 Mark 3:31 There came then his brethren and his mother, and, standing without,

tales. That being the case, however, how can we explain the fact that specific names *are* mentioned in the 'carpenter verses'? Could those specific names have found resonance in the theopolitical struggles of the first and second centuries? While that can't be proved, it does indicate, once again, that we are wandering farther and farther into the unknown in order to find 'proof' of the historicity of Jesus of Nazareth. It is interesting to note that although *James* (of course, actually *Jacob*) appears in all surviving manuscripts of Mark 6:3 and Matthew 13:55, at least one of the names in the list is unstable. For the second name in the list, Matthew has *Iōsēf* [B, ℵ^c, *etc.*], *Iōannēs* [ℵ*, D, *etc.*], *Iōsē* [S^c, 118, 157, *etc.*], and *Iōsēs* [Y, K, L, W, Δ, *etc.*]. Mark, from whom Matthew borrowed, has *Iōsētos* [B, D, L, Δ, Θ, *etc.*], *Iōsēf* [ℵ], *Ēōsē* [K], and *Iōsē* [A, C, 𝔐, M, N, U, W, *etc.*]. This raises a question: How much can we trust to a stable element (*James*) in an unstable list? Regardless of what the correct answer may be, being able justifiably to raise the question indicates further movement into the more unknown.

Fourthly, why did Matthew change Mark's "Is this not the carpenter?" to "Is this not *the son* of the carpenter?" Why are later manuscripts of Mark 6:3 changed to agree with Matthew? Questers of the historical Jesus must puzzle this out without resorting to even more unknown 'facts.'

'Brother of the Lord'

7. Let us now turn our attention to the passages in which Ehrman places the most trust: Gal 1:19;[22] 2:9;[23] and 2:12.[24] Here we come to

---

sent unto him, calling him. 32 And the multitude sat about him, and they said unto him, Behold, thy mother and thy brethren without seek for thee. 33 And he answered them, saying, Who is my mother, or my brethren? 34 And he looked round about on them which sat about him, and said, Behold my mother and my brethren! 35 For whosoever shall do the will of God, the same is my brother, and my sister, and mother.

22 Galatians 1:19 But other of the apostles saw I none, save James the Lord's brother. 20 Now the things which I write unto you, behold, before God, I lie not.

23 Galatians 2:9 And when James, Cephas, and John, who seemed to be pillars, perceived the grace that was given unto me, they gave to me and Barnabas the right hands of fellowship; that we should go unto the heathen, and they unto the circumcision.

24 12 For before that certain came from James, he ['Peter'] did eat with the Gentiles:

a question that Ehrman considers a no-brainer: Who — or what — is *a/the brother of the Lord*? If James *were* such a being, would that make him a sibling of Jesus 'according to the flesh'? *Pace*, Bart Ehrman; that cannot be so. Once again, investigation into the meaning of 'Lord' and 'brother' raises more questions concerning James, Paul, and Jesus than can be answered reliably.

As with most Christian believers, Ehrman equates *Lord* with *Jesus of Nazareth* as well as with *Christ*. "Come Lord Jesus, be our guest..." "Christ the Lord is risen today..." Can any equation be more self-evident? The ancient 'Separatists' discussed by Ehrman in his *The Orthodox Corruption of Scripture* would not have thought so. They separated Christ from Jesus — as we must do also if we are to identify the unknowns that disconnect the links in Ehrman's chain of reasoning. In at least some cases, I think, only *Christ* was 'the Lord.' Christ (or, more probably, *Chrēst)* was a heavenly being from the start. But what would that have meant? There is a clue in the fact that the authors of the canonical New Testament relied on the Septuagint Greek translation of the *Tanakh* — the Hebrew Bible — rather than the Hebrew scriptures themselves. This is relevant to our brother-of-the-Lord problem in a very interesting way.

Like many deities of old as well as ordinary mortals, the God of the Jews had a *secret name* — a name of power called the *shem* that, if found out would convey magical powers upon the discoverer. He (or even *she*!) would be able to force that deity to do his bidding. Ancient priests were believed to have formed covenants with particular deities, by virtue of which they claimed to have learned the secret name in exchange for promises to exercise special duties of worship, sacrifice, and praise. Thus, ordinary people could take presents to the priests, in exchange for which the priests would use their magical powers to bend the deity to the will of the supplicant. At least, that was the theory of theurgy.

In the case of the Israelite god, the forging of the first 'covenant' involved a bit of haggling before the god of the burning bush would

---

but when they were come, he withdrew and separated himself, fearing them which were of the circumcision.

trade his name to Moses in exchange for the sacrifices of the Yahwist cult — if the third chapter of Exodus is to be believed. Moses tries to trick the god into revealing his secret name: 13 "And Moses said unto God, Behold, when I come unto the children of Israel, and shall say unto them, The God of your fathers hath sent me unto you; and they shall say to me, What is his name? what shall I say unto them?" Nice try. 14 "And God said unto Moses, I AM THAT I AM (Heb. *'ehyeh 'asher 'ehyeh*): and he said, Thus shalt thou say unto the children of Israel, I AM (*'ehyeh*) hath sent me unto you."

Sometime later, it appears, the secret name — the *shem* — was found to be *Yahweh*. However, the name was never — under pain of death[25] — to be pronounced or written in a manner that would reveal its correct pronunciation. In the Hebrew scriptures this was not a problem, as short vowels[26] were not displayed in writing. The *shem* was simply written as four consonants: Y-H-W-H — the *Tetragrammaton*. Furthermore, it was often written in Palaeohebrew script to further disguise its pronunciation. When the Hebrew scriptures were translated into Greek, however, there was a problem. Greek no longer had a separate letter for /h/ (*h* in initial position was sometimes indicated with an accent-like 'rough breathing'), and the *digamma*, once used to indicate the consonant /w/ had not been used for centuries. It might have been possible to transcribe the *shem* phonetically, but that only could have been done by indicating the vowels as well. That would mean death, however, so the translators of the so-called Septuagint Greek version simply substituted the word *Kyrios* ('Lord') for YHWH.

---

25 Leviticus 24:16. "Whoever utters the name of the LORD [*YHWH*] shall be put to death: all the community shall stone him; alien or native, if he utters the Name [*shem-YHWH*], he shall be put to death." [NEB]

26 On page 192 of *DJE?* Ehrman criticizes my theory that the name 'Nazareth' was derived from the Hebrew word *netser* ('branch'). Creating a straw-man argument and falsely reporting that I claim this comes from a Hebrew "term" *NZR*, he makes the preposterous assertion that "The term *branch* in **Hebrew (which does not have vowels)** is spelled *NZR*..." One wonders if he learned this astonishing fact in his Hebrew studies at Moody Bible Institute or at Wheaton College.

So, what has all this to do with James as 'brother of the Lord'? I think it means one of two things: (1) either James was in some symbolic sense a 'brother' of Yahweh, or (2) Jesus had been equated with Yahweh *right from the beginning*, and the term 'brother' would be equally symbolic. That is to say, 'Brother of the Lord' would equally be a *title*, not a *description*, whether it referred to Yahweh or Jesus. It is likely that if the James in question is to be identified as the 'James the Just' of early Christian tradition, he must have been a leading figure in a religious brotherhood especially devoted to Yahweh. If James the Just had ever uttered the slogan "Jesus is Lord," he would not have meant that his brother Baby Jesus was his master; he would have meant *Jesus was Yahweh*.

8. Having used the Gospels to elucidate problems raised by Ehrman's evidence from the Pauline Epistles, we proceed now to the Book of Acts, which seems to have the closest association with the Pauline Epistles, and might be the most instructive in understanding just what sort of brotherhood might be implied by Ehrman's 'Brother-of-the-Lord.' Let us begin with Acts 21:17.

> 21:17 And when we were come to Jerusalem, the brethren [*hoi adelphoi*] received us gladly. 18 And the day following, Paul went in with us unto James; and all the elders were present.

Who were the brethren? Were they merely fellow believers? Hardly. That they were higher officials likely to hold titles of some sort — including 'Brothers of the Lord' — is seen by the fact that they appear to be considered 'elders' [*presbyteroi*] and the office of Presbyter still survives in various churches to this day. Moreover, common sense indicates that Paul would not be making so much effort just to confer with untitled believers. In fact, in verse 21:16 we read that "There went with us also certain of the disciples [*tōn mathētōn*] of Caesarea, and brought with them one Mnason of Cyprus, an old disciple [*mathētē*] , with whom we should lodge." Who were these disciples? Certainly they were not 'The Twelve.' It is not even clear that in this case the term 'disciple' is even a title. It may simply mean believers who are still undergoing initiation. In any case, disciples are far below the station of brethren.

Another instructive passage to consider is Acts 12:17.

> Acts 12:17 But he [Peter] beckoning unto them with the hand to hold their peace, declared unto them how the Lord had brought him out of the prison. And he said, Go shew these things unto James and to the brethren [*tois adelphois*]. And he departed, and went into another place.

Here James appears to be one of a number of 'brothers,' although it might be argued that James is here being distinguished from individuals called brothers. If that be true, at least this passage reinforces the hypothesis that high officers of the Jerusalem cult formed a brotherhood. On the other hand, it could be argued that what was meant to be said was "unto James and to the other brethren," and that James was the only one named because he was the only one whose name was known.

Finally, there are two passages in Acts where both Peter and James, during the circumcision debate, address a subgroup of their colleagues as brothers:

> Acts 15:7 And when there had been much disputing, Peter rose up [*D* adds "in spirit," 614 & 2412 add "in holy spirit, " and* 𝔓[45] *interpolates part of verse 2 here*] and said unto them, Men and brethren [*Andres, Adelphoi*]
> Acts 15:13 And after they had held their peace, James answered, saying, Men and brethren [*Andres, Adelphoi*], hearken unto me...

Are 'brothers' a group separate from 'men'? Possibly. On the other hand, both Peter and James are speaking to their fellow leaders of the cult, and one might expect a homogeneous, fraternal assemblage being addressed — a brotherhood. It is likely this is not only an assemblage of Brothers of the Lord Jesus, but simultaneously of Brothers of the Lord Yahweh. This can be seen in the fact that in all these episodes involving interactions with the leadership, Jesus is rarely if ever mentioned. Prayers are offered "to the Lord," "the Lord" gets Peter out of jail, *etc.* Is this not 'the Lord' [*ho Kyrios*] of the Septuagint? Is this not more easily understood to be Lord Yahweh? If so, once again it would appear that "James the brother of the Lord" was not the physical brother of a physical Jesus of Nazareth. Rather, he was the spiritual brother of Lord Jesus the avatar of Yahweh.

And so, despite the ample amount of speculation larded into what I have written above concerning 'the brother of the Lord,' the discussion shows once again that Ehrman could not have chosen a worse 'key datum' than the notion that James was a biological brother of some Jesus-or-other of Somewhere-or-other. The deeper one investigates the relevant texts,[27] the more unknown and uncertain the meanings come to appear. *Ignotum per ignotius per ignotius per ignotius.*

Seeming to be Pillars

9. The problems Ehrman is presented with by his key verses in Galatians are not over even yet. In Gal 2:9 we learn that James 'the brother of the Lord' has another title as well — a title he shares with Cephas and John: "And when James, Cephas, and John, who seemed to be *pillars* (*styloi*), perceived the grace..." Now, whatever 'pillar' may mean — I shall add to the speculation about this anon — one thing is clear: it is a title of religious office. Clearly, the story indicates that James held some sort of high office along with Cephas and John. Why couldn't he also hold a *second* office — Brother of the Lord?

While there has long been speculation concerning the meaning of the term *pillar*, there is another aspect of this verse that seems to me to be really bizarre but is never discussed. The three "*seemed to be* (*dokountes*, a plural present participle) pillars." If Paul had actually visited them in Jerusalem, wouldn't he have *known* they were pillars? If 'pillar' was an office in a mystery cult, of course, 'Paul' or his inventor might not have been able to be sure. *If Paul himself was not historical, the unknown author of the Galatians tale would have had to speculate about the situation Paul would have encountered in Jerusalem.*

While we cannot be sure what it meant to say that James and Cephas and John "seemed to be pillars," we can be sure that *actual* pillars were associated with most of the religions of the Mediterranean

27 For the most thorough, comprehensive, and probing analysis of Acts and the related Pauline material of which I am aware, consult Richard I. Pervo's commentary in the Hermeneia series, *Acts: A Commentary* (2009).

world. According to 1 Kings 7:21, in Solomon's temple — apparently modeled after the temple to Hercules at Tyre — there were two great pillars. One of them bore the name *Boaz* ('strength'), the other was named *Yachin* (*i.e.*, 'he erects,' 'he founds,' 'he upholds'). According to Arthur Drews, Hercules bearing pillars was a favorite symbol in antiquity for arduous, oppressive labor. He reminds us also that the Tyrian Hercules Baal-Khon was not only a god of battle, but was also a mediator and savior of the Syro-Phoenician cultural world who maintains the universe upright against the monster Typhon. Drews cites an image of Hercules bearing two crossed pillars — reproduced here as *Fig. 1: Hercules as Crucifer* — and relates this to Christianity:

> There is also a mystical image related to the pillars: the cross of Christ. The god who staggers along, stooped by the weight of the pillars, reappears in the New Testament itself in the image of the savior who collapses under the weight of the cross. The two-armed cross is, however, also in Christianity the symbol of a new life and a divine world order, just as the two pillars in the cult of the Tyrian or Libyan Hercules, or of Shamas or Simon. Small wonder, then, that the three synoptic evangelists add to the cross-bearing savior another cross-bearing character — one who not only is named Simon, but is supposed to come from Cyrene (*i.e.*, Libya), where the myth of the pillar-bearing Hercules[28] most likely was born. According to one ancient description, the shape created by Hercules carrying the pillars was the form of a cross. This provides the source for the legend of the cross-bearing Simon of Cyrene.[29]

28 Clement of Alexandria [*Stromata* I 15:73] tells us that "Herodotus relates that Hercules, having grown a sage and a student of physics, received from the barbarian Atlas, the Phrygian, the columns of the universe; the fable meaning that he received by instruction the knowledge of the heavenly bodies." Chapman's translation of Homer's *Odyssey* on the other hand tells of the pillars' donor: "... Atlas, who of all alive the motion and the fashion doth command With his wise mind, whose forces understand The inmost deeps and gulfs of all the seas, Who (for all his skill of things superior) stays The two steep columns that prop earth and heav'n ..."

29 Arthur Drews. *The Legend of Saint Peter*. Translated from the German, with Foreword and Appendix of Selected Reference Texts by Frank R. Zindler [Austin, TX: American Atheist Press, 1997: 28–29].

THE ART OF RHETORICAL FALLACY

HERCULES AS CRUCIFER

Maffei

Figure 1, copied from Plate CXXVII in Volume I, Part II of *L'Antiquité Expliquée,* by Bernard de Montfaucon (1729). According to de Montfaucon, the figure was engraved upon an ancient gemstone in the possession of a certain *"M. le Cavalier Maffei, gentilhomme du Pape,"* a famous antiquarian of his time.

***

Drews notes that many ancient temples were built with great free-standing pillars beside or before them, and that Lucian of Samosata (*De Dea Syria*) tells us that Syrian temples to Dionysus had two such pillars that actually were giant phalli. Drews opines that the tall steeples of Christian churches are the end-point of pillar evolution.

If Christianity began as an astral mystery cult, pillars might be expected to be important esoteric symbols, perhaps including the axial pole of the universe. It should be remembered that the famous ICHTHYS double acrostic in the Sibylline Oracles ('Jesus Christ, God's Son, Savior') actually contains a sixth word — *stauros*. Although this word almost always is translated 'cross,' its original meaning was 'pole.' Thus, according to one of the earliest of Christian 'scriptures,' James and John and Cephas weren't the only pillars: Jesus was one too!

After this divagation about the term 'pillar,' we must remind ourselves that it has not been for the purpose of proving a hypothesis contrary to Ehrman's historicity hypothesis, but rather to show that there are grounds for considering the "key data" to be ambiguous and uncertain, and thus, to see that Ehrman's reliance on the Galatians pericope involves the addition of further uncertainty to his reasoning. Instead of providing firm answers, it raises yet more questions and is far from producing airtight evidence for any brother of a flesh-and-blood Jesus of Nazareth. Once again, it shows that Ehrman is employing the fallacy of *ignotum per ignotius*.

Disciples and Apostles

10. How do we know there were disciples? How do they correspond (if at all) to the apostles? There are no contemporary accounts of any of them, and the contradictions and inconsistencies in their names in the New Testament documents and manuscripts make it clear that they are theopolitical inventions, perhaps invented to undercut authority of church leaders claiming descent from the family of Jesus. Would the churches have had to manufacture so many fake relics of the apostles if they had ever been real? How can characters as unknown as the disciples — who might also have been apostles — be used to prove the existence of a Jesus who might not have come from Nazareth?

The Unknown Sources of 'Luke'

11. According to Richard I. Pervo's *Acts: A Commentary,*[30] the author(s) of the Gospel of Luke and the Acts of the Apostles definitely

30 Hermeneia. Minneapolis: Fortress Press, 2009: 12.

drew upon certain sources that are still extant, *viz.*, the LXX, the Gospel of Mark, a collection of Paul's letters, and some of the writings of Josephus. [12] It is also likely that he or they drew upon some of the Jewish historians such as Artapanus and Eupolemus, as well as classical source such as Homer and Euripides, and even Virgil's *Aeneid*.

Ehrman places great emphasis on the opening lines of the Gospel of Luke, in which the unknown author acknowledges his awareness of previous accounts "of the things that have been fulfilled [or believed] among us," but assumes that this means that "Luke... knew of 'many' earlier authors who had compiled narratives about the subject matter that he himself is about to narrate, the life of Jesus." [*DJE?* 79]. But are the previous authors writing about Jesus of Nazareth? Or are they writing about how the Christians came to have the dogmas extant at the time of composition? Or, like the hypothetical Q, were they collections of wise sayings that had come to be attributed to Jesus? Or, like Josephus, Homer, and Euripides, were they merely providing historical and literary frameworks for the narratives of Luke-Acts?

Now it is entirely possible that Richard Pervo and the herd of scholars from whom he has drawn his claims about Luke's sources are partly or entirely wrong. But, unless Ehrman has information to prove them wrong and his own presumption of lost sources concerning Jesus specifically is correct, he is resorting once again to explaining the unknown in terms of more unknowns as well as the more unknown. As Ehrman admits, "No one knows how many there actually were" [*DJE?* 83].

Two Key *Ignotius* Data: Part II. The Crucified Messiah

I have devoted an entire chapter of this book — "Bart Ehrman and the Crucified Messiah" — to the second 'key datum' with which Ehrman imagines he can prove the historicity of a Jesus of Somewhereorother. That is the notion that no one would have made up the idea of a crucified messiah and so, perforce, Jesus must have been real. Ehrman clearly supposes this is the joker that can trump all the other cards in the mythtoricity game. In this section I shall briefly consider mostly the *ignotum-per-ignotius* aspects of his argumentation. Ehrman assures us that

> Paul also knew that Jesus was crucified. Before the Christian movement, there were no Jews who thought the messiah was going to suffer. Quite the contrary. The crucified Jesus was not invented, therefore, to provide some kind of mythical fulfillment of Jewish expectation. The single greatest obstacle Christians had when trying to convert Jews was precisely their claim that Jesus had been executed. They would not have made that part up. They had to deal with it and devise a special, previously unheard of theology to account for it. And so what they invented was not a person named Jesus but rather the idea of a suffering messiah. That invention has become so much a part of the standard lingo that Christians today assume it was all part of the original plan of God as mapped out in the Old Testament. But in fact the idea of a suffering messiah cannot be found there. It had to be created. And the reason it had to be created is that Jesus — the one Christians considered to be the messiah — was known by everyone everywhere to have been crucified. He couldn't be killed if he didn't live. [*DJE?* 173]

Uniting the beginning of this paragraph with its ending, we have the premise and conclusion of a would-be syllogism:

> "Paul also knew that Jesus was crucified. ... He couldn't be killed if he didn't live."

Ehrman's argument hidden somewhere in the middle appears to be this:

Paul *said* that Jesus had been crucified.

Therefore, Paul *knew* that Jesus had been crucified.

Therefore, Jesus *was killed* by crucifixion.

Jesus could not have been killed if he had not ever been alive.

Therefore, Jesus once lived.

THE ART OF RHETORICAL FALLACY

The Ascents of Bartholomew

Ehrman's flight into the progressively stratospheric unknown passes through more heavens than a Gnostic soul in its passage through the heavenly gates to the Pleroma:

To reach the first heaven, he tries to prove the existence of Jesus of Nazareth by referring to what is said about him by a character sometimes named Saul and sometimes named Paul in various canonical New Testament letters and the Book of Acts.

To reach the second heaven, he decides the two characters are the same character.

To reach the third heaven, he decides that that character was a single, real person, not one or two literary inventions. Unfortunately, the archon unlocking the third gate for him has no record of any visit from any person matching Ehrman's description of Paul/Saul.

To reach the fourth heaven, Ehrman creates a composite, lowest-common-denominator 'Paul' by selective harmonization of the Book of Acts with the 'Pauline Epistles' of his choice.

To reach the fifth heaven, he decides that the Orthodox understanding of Christian origins is more likely to be correct than the Marcionite, Docetic, or Gnostic view. Actually, he doesn't *decide* this. He doesn't even *think* of the possibility that heretics need to be taken seriously.

To reach the sixth heaven, he decides that the Paul of his inference is more like the Paul of Orthodoxy than the Paul of Marcion, Gnosticism, or Docetism.

To reach the seventh heaven — doubtless a disappointment when it is discovered not to be the highest heaven — he decides that although the Greek text of the Pauline Epistles contains a great number of words that were part of Gnostic jargon, those words should be understood to carry their common, everyday meanings.

To reach the Ogdoad — what should be the eighth and highest spot in the universe, a heaven of heavens — Ehrman decides that wherever Paul speaks of 'Christ' or 'the Lord,' he is talking about 'Jesus of Nazareth, the character whose historicity he had thought would have been established before now.

We watch him as he proceeds up to a hitherto unknown ninth heaven. He achieves that by deciding that everything that Paul tells us is true. After all, Paul himself assures us — "Before God, I am not lying!"

Needing yet to get up to a tenth heaven, Ehrman is denied entry unless he agrees that although Paul suffered hallucinations, he nevertheless was a reliable witness to real-world events.

The gate to the eleventh heaven is unlocked when it is decided that Paul's hallucinations of the Risen Jesus were actually visions that conveyed veridical information to him.

Ehrman is allowed entry to the twelfth heaven only if he can believe simultaneously that (1) Paul was a reliable witness when he said that "no man" gave him his knowledge of Christ crucified, and yet (2) he must actually have gotten his information from St. Peter and from James, the 'Brother of the Lord,' who doubtless was a blood brother of either Jesus of Nazareth or Jesus of not-Nazareth.

Requirements for entry into the thirteenth heaven are multiple: one must avow not only that both James the Brother of the Lord and Peter were real persons, but that they were telling Paul the literal truth about a physical rather than theological Jesus.

Ehrman easily enters the fourteenth heaven upon confession that he had decided long before he began his flight into the unknown that Peter and James must have been eyewitnesses to the physical crucifixion of Jesus of Nazareth.

The fifteenth heaven's gate springs open when Ehrman loudly proclaims that when Paul said that *Christ* was crucified, he was actually reporting the eye-witness accounts of Peter and James concerning *Jesus of Nazareth*, rather than information he received during one of his reported hallucinations.

At last, Ehrman reaches hexadecimal heaven — the furthest place to which a flight of fancy can be carried, the Pythagorean empyrean where only the sixteenth derivative of any fact is to be found. He's run the race. Although hearsay evidence is not admissible in a court of law, he decides that his *inference* from hearsay that a real person named Paul heard it said by two men — whom we infer to have been real — that Jesus of Nazareth had been crucified must be a logically compelling conclusion is true and ... perhaps we should end this sentence here.

Thus satisfied intellectually, and encouraged by each flight of fancy further beyond the world of known facts and hard data, Ehrman has achieved gnosis. He marks the boundary of the cosmic void that yawns before him with a sign. More enlightened than the voyagers of old who marked the edges of their earth with a warning — "Here be dragons" — he erects a billboard to announce his wondrous discovery: "Jesus couldn't have been killed if he didn't live."

Before Jesus Was the Crucified Messiah

We have just taken an amusing look at the *ignotum-per-ignotius* backbone of Ehrman's argument in the paragraph quoted above. More such reasoning is concealed, however, in his understanding of the historical significance of the terms 'Christ,' 'Christian,' and 'messiah,' and I analyze these terms at great length in my chapter "Bart Ehrman and the Crucified Messiah." Here I wish to comment on a false implication of his reasoning in that paragraph.

For everyone to *know* the messiah had been crucified as Ehrman claims, it was necessary that everyone must have identified Jesus of Nazareth with the messiah. Ehrman supposes this fact is concealed in the word *Christ* — meaning 'anointed one,' *i.e.*, a messiah. But if that were true, the first believers in Jesus of Nazareth might reasonably be expected to have been called Christians from the start as Ehrman logically supposes. Alas for his logic, this appears not to be the case. According to Epiphanius, Bishop of Salamis [*Panarion* 29.1.1; 29.4.9], early Christians were called *Jessaeans* and *Nazoreans / Nazareans / Nasareans* before they were called Christians. Moreover, they were called *Galileans* (*Galilaioi*) also at a very early date and for a long time thereafter.

The Phrygian Stoic philosopher Epictetus [*ca.* 50–120 CE], whom many early church fathers viewed as a pagan saint because his teachings resembled the imagined teachings of Jesus so closely, referred to

Christians as 'Galileans' (*Galilaioi*)[31] — the same term of address used by the angels in Acts 1:11. A contemporary and friend of the Emperor Hadrian, Epictetus thus refers to Christians with a term that gives no hint that such people were noted for the messianic beliefs Ehrman supposes are implied by the names *Christos* and *Christianoi*. It is interesting, therefore, to discover a hint even in the New Testament that the first Christians may have been known as Galileans.

This is not obvious, however, in the King James Version's report of two angels saying "...Ye men of Galilee, why stand ye gazing up into heaven?" Every translation I can find, likewise renders the Greek *andres Galilaioi* as 'men of Galilee,' even though that's not what the text says. It says, *Men! Galileans!* not *Men of Galilee!* Both *andres* and *Galilaioi* are vocative plurals; *Galilaioi* is not in the genitive case. It looks as though the author of Acts is unwittingly or otherwise misrepresenting an earlier term as meaning simply 'someone from Galilee,' rather than a member of a sect that somehow was associated with Galilee. (This would parallel his misrepresentation of *Nazōraios* as meaning 'a person coming from Nazareth.' The scene is set at Mount Olivet — "a Sabbath's journey" [about a thousand paces] from Jerusalem — as though to acknowledge that the apostles all came from someplace else. But the craft of the author is revealed when one reflects that quasi-omniscient angelic beings would not have addressed the Christians as *Men! Galileans!* They would simply have called out *Men!* Only a native of Jerusalem (or novelist) would draw attention to their 'foreign' origins.

Now, as a friend of the Emperor Hadrian [76–138 CE], Epictetus would have been a contemporary of the author of Acts and may have obtained his information concerning Christians from some of the same sources and traditions as did 'Luke.'

That the epithet 'Galilean' was early in common use seems certain from its enduring use even after the Council of Nicaea [325 CE]. The Emperor 'Julian the Apostate' [331–363] wrote an entire treatise "Against the Galilaeans" (*Kata Galilaion Logos*) in his effort to return

31 W.A. Oldfather. *Epictetus: The Discourses. Books III–V. Fragments. Encheiridion.* Vol. II, Book IV, Chapter VII:6. The Loeb Classical Library. [Cambridge, MA: Harvard University Press, 1928:362–63].

the Roman Empire to its pre-Christian pagan purity.[32] In Book I of that treatise, in parts that were preserved in hostile Christian attempted refutations, the Emperor refers to "the sect of the Galilaeans" (*tēs Galilaiōn ontas haireseōs*).[33]

The surviving fragments of Julian have much to teach us, even though the best must surely have disappeared into the flames and smoke of Orthodox knowledge pyres. They show that 'of Nazareth' was still not recognized as an epithet of Jesus. Julian refers to 'Jesus the Nazōraean' (*Iēsous ho Nazōraios*), employing the definite article before 'Nazōraean' in apparent understanding that the word is a title, not a toponym or demonym.

Scornful of Jesus and Paul alike, he scoffs, "Jesus the Nazarene, yes, and Paul also, who surpassed all the magicians and charlatans of every place and every time, assert that he is the God of Israel alone and of Judaea, and that the Jews are his chosen people."[34] Interestingly, Julian's assessment of Paul might actually accord with that of Ehrman: "Paul… keeps changing his views about God, as the polypus changes its colours to match the rocks…"[35] He scoffs at the notion that stories such as we find in the Book of Acts could be considered history: "But if you can show me that [the events surrounding] one of these men [Cornelius the Centurion and Sergius the Proconsul] is mentioned by the well-known writers of that time — these events happened in the reign of Tiberius or Claudius — then you may consider that I speak falsely about all matters."[36]

Finally, Julian asserts that 'John' is the only evangelist to call Jesus God. He could do this, Julian claims, because John had heard that the tombs (*mnēmata*) of Peter and Paul were being worshipped and so those apostles must actually have been gods themselves.[37]

32 Wilmer Cave Wright. *The Works of the Emperor Julian,* Vol. III. The Loeb Classical Library. [Cambridge, MA: Harvard University Press, 1961].

33 *Ibid.*, 320–321.

34 *Ibid.*, 340–341.

35 *Ibid.*, 342–343.

36 *Ibid.*, 376–377.

37 *Ibid.*, 412–413.

So, Ehrman is left with the problem of the *ignotius* Paul. Which Paul's Jesus is the one he needs to prove? The Jesus of the several Pauls of the Pauline Epistles? The Jesus of the Paul of canonical Acts? Of *The Acts of Paul*? Of *Paul and Thecla*? The Jesus of the Paul of *The Correspondence between Seneca and Paul*? Of the Paul of *The Apocalypse of Paul*? The Jesus of the god Paul reported by Julian? Or...?

Onus Probandi

Any argument for a historical Jesus of Nazareth must be compatible with and subject to the rules of science. Ehrman's *DJE?*, however, is not compatible with science in one crucial, fundamental aspect. It falls afoul of the scientific rules concerning burden of proof — the so-called *onus probandi*. Ehrman develops a rhetorical fallacy for which there is yet no name — the fallacy of bypassing scientific rules of evidence and claiming that someone who does argue scientifically is somehow misguided. Ehrman criticizes the New Testament scholar Robert M. Price:

> What about the historical existence of Jesus? It has become somewhat common among mythicists to think that the default position on the question of Jesus's existence should be that he did not exist unless someone can demonstrate that he did. This is the position expressed cogently by Robert Price: "The burden of proof would seem to belong with those who believe there was a historical man named Jesus." I myself do not think that is true. On one hand, since every relevant ancient source (as we will see) assumes that there was such a man, and since no scholar who has ever written on it, except the handful of mythicists, has ever had any serious doubts, surely the burden of proof does not fall on those who take the almost universally accepted position. On the other hand, and to be a bit more generous to Price and his fellow mythicists, perhaps the matter should be put more neutrally. As my former colleague, E.P. Sanders, an eminent professor of New Testament studies at nearby Duke University, used to say, "The burden of proof belongs with whoever is making a claim." That is, if Price wants to argue that Jesus did not exist, then he bears the burden of proof for his argument. If I want to argue that he did exist, then I do. Fair enough. [38–39]

"Fair enough"? Not in science, it isn't. In science the burden of proof rests on *the person who asserts the existence of a thing, event, or process*. Science always assumes the negative. If someone claims that phlogiston is the essence of fire, I don't have to try to find evidence against it. All I need to do is demonstrate that the evidence adduced to prove its existence is inadequate or faulty. Those who claim that the animal frequenting their walk-up pasture is a unicorn must bring the DNA samples to me for analysis. I have no responsibility to go up there to collect fecal samples to show it's really a rhinoceros.

Because he is not a scientist, E. P. Sanders can make the facile claim "The burden of proof belongs with whoever is making a claim." Does this mean that everyone who says that 'God is real' or 'Jesus is Lord' must bear the burden of proof and produce the evidence? How wonderful it would be if only it were so! Sanders' claim is, however, at once self-serving and indicative of why progress is so rapid in the sciences and so snail-paced or even moribund in religious studies. "Surely," Ehrman argues, "the burden of proof does not fall on those who take the almost universally accepted position." I suspect that the Boston divines who all universally agreed that lightning was the wrath of Jehovah would have agreed with Ehrman and Sanders. Ultimately, in order for their pointy-topped business buildings to survive, they had to put their faith in science. So too, biblical scholars and historians who wish their work to survive in the world of intellectual respectability will have to adopt scientific methods of inquiry, including acceptance of the fact that the burden of proof rests upon anyone making an existential claim — even if the existential claim happens to involve the *status quo* consensus opinion.

In science, the *status quo* is always a position to which someone has been led by evidence. Consequently, the evidence that has led to that position is always close to hand and can be shown to anyone who questions the *status quo*. An evolutionary geologist, when challenged by a young-earth creationist to prove the *status-quo* view of the antiquity of the earth, can readily point to the millions of microfossil-containing varves (paper-thin layers of rock) in the Green River Shale to show that time past was as real as time present. By contrast, when the creationist asserts that the entire planet was destroyed by a flood in the year 2,348 BCE, he can find neither the source of the water that could have drowned Mt. Everest nor demonstrate how a shell of water five miles thick could "recede continuously" off the surface of a spherical earth. A scientific historian, when challenged by a biblicist such as N. T. Wright to prove the historicity of Tiberius Caesar can point to the evidence of thousands of coins and inscriptions such as the *Res Gestae* of his adoptive father Augustus. Like Ehrman and Sanders, however, Wright does not think it really necessary to prove the existence of Jesus of Nazareth — because he can't.

Unlike the present-day discipline of religious studies, science is a self-correcting, ever-improving and expanding body of knowledge and system of inquiry. That is so because in science, the *status quo* is always open to change whenever a new existential claim is successfully defended that proves the existence of some thing, process, or event that contradicts the *status quo* opinion in some important way. Then the *status quo* must be amended, corrected, or abandoned, and a new and better *status quo* must be adopted. As before, the evidence supporting the new *status quo* must ever be open for examination and evaluation. For this reason, science is self-correcting and ever open to improvement. Scientific progress is real and rapid.

By contrast, in biblical studies, the *status quo* is as stagnant as the Dead Sea. Its volume of actual knowledge hardly ever increases. New 'truths' when they are added tend to become lost amidst the great volume of errors and eventually disappear, never to become the basis for any advance in genuine understanding. New truth rarely can accrete to old truth in the way it can do in science. The stagnation in religious studies is largely due to the fact that upholders of the *status quo* do not — probably dare not — accept the burden of proof and try to assemble whatever evidence there was that led their academic forebears to create the *status quo* that now is being challenged. Ehrman's refusal to accept the burden of proof not only explains why so little of the book makes any serious attempt to find evidence specific for the Jesus of Nazareth promised by his subtitle, it means that *DJE?* cannot be considered a work of scientific significance. It will not become a contribution to the new science of Christian origins.

CHAPTER TEN

Bart Ehrman's Most Important Critical Method

Frank R. Zindler

One of the most important — perhaps *the* most important — methodological procedures that Bart Ehrman employs in his seminal work *The Orthodox Corruption of Scripture: The Effect of Early Christological Controversies on the Text of the New Testament*[1] can be found in his analysis of the problem of reconstructing the original text of Luke 22:19–20, where the most important manuscript readings fall into one of two main categories: long or short. This comprises the Eucharistic pericope that reads as follows (italicized words absent in the short version):

"And taking bread, giving thanks, he broke it and gave it to them, saying, 'This is my body *that is given for you. Do this in my remembrance.' And the cup likewise after supper, saying, 'This cup is the new covenant in my blood that is poured out for you*. But behold, the hand of the one who betrays me is with me on the table'."

After a masterful examination of the "intrinsic probabilities" of vocabulary, style, theology, and structure of the passage in regard to their importance for choosing the long or the short version of this important pericope, he concludes with an examination of "transcriptional

1 New York: Oxford University Press, 1993.

probabilities" for and against the long and short versions. Without drawing attention to the fact that this will be the most conclusive argument of all, he observes matter-of-factly:

> In point of fact, no one has been able to provide a convincing explanation for how the shorter text came into existence if the longer text is original.

Paleontologists and biologists will easily recognize in this statement a quintessentially evolutionary argument akin to the problem of determining which anatomical features of an animal are ancestral and which are derived. (For example, could the wings of birds have evolved from the arms and hands of feathered dinosaurs, or did the anterior appendage of feathered dinosaurs evolve from the wings of birds?)

This method of inquiry, it seems to me, is absolutely fundamental in trying to answer such questions as "Did Christianity evolve out of Judaism?" and other equally crucial questions.

Let us apply Ehrman's method to this problem. It would seem, if the Pauline corpus (and 1 Corinthians 11:23–29)[2] really is as early as commonly supposed, that a Eucharistic meal was a feature of the earliest Christian mysteries. If it is possible to retroject current Roman Catholic understanding of the Eucharist back to the primal mystery cult, we are faced with the problem of explaining how a mock cannibal feast — a theophagy — could possibly have arisen from any form of Judaism known to have existed at that time. (We are reminded

2 1 Corinthians 11:23 For I have received of the Lord that which also I delivered unto you, That the Lord Jesus the same night in which he was betrayed took bread: 24 And when he had given thanks, he brake it, and said, Take, eat: this is my body, which is broken for you: this do in remembrance of me. 25 After the same manner also he took the cup, when he had supped, saying, This cup is the new testament in my blood: this do ye, as oft as ye drink it, in remembrance of me. 26 For as often as ye eat this bread, and drink this cup, ye do shew the Lord's death till he come. 27 Wherefore whosoever shall eat this bread, and drink this cup of the Lord, unworthily, shall be guilty of the body and blood of the Lord. 28 But let a man examine himself, and so let him eat of that bread, and drink of that cup. 29 For he that eateth and drinketh unworthily, eateth and drinketh damnation to himself, not discerning the Lord's body.

of the most important proof-text for the Jehovah's Witnesses, Deuteronomy 12:23: "Only be sure that thou eat not the blood: for the blood is the life; and thou mayest not eat the life with the flesh.") The likelihood that anyone could find a convincing explanation of how this could have occurred seems virtually nil.

On the other hand, if Christianity evolved from a mystery cult of the sort that celebrated a sacred meal (such as Mithraism) and that the meal had already evolved a theophagous significance, the Judaic features of the religion can easily be seen to be later additions that allowed Christianity to distinguish itself from all the other mystery cults of the time.

Similarly, in trying to see how Christianity could have arisen from a single man at a single place at a single time, we find that everyone trying to "connect the dots" between the death of Jesus of Nazareth in Jerusalem at about 33 CE and the earliest archaeological and firmly established textual and historical remains of the Christian cult falls into a morass of conflicting assertions, assumptions, and implausible scenarios.

For example, if Jesus of Nazareth once existed, nearly everyone agrees he would have spoken and taught in Aramaic. How, then, can we connect the dots from outdoor lectures in Aramaic to the oldest known New Testament writings which are written in nonclassical but decent Greek and contain not only quotations from the Septuagint Greek bible instead of the Masoretic Hebrew text, but have Jesus recite a fragment of Aesop's "Fable of the Fisherman and the Flute"?[3] Was Aesop's fable originally written in Aramaic? Did the Aramaic oral tradition claimed by Ehrman somehow turn into a Greek oral tradition and thereafter was committed to writing? Exactly how does an oral tradition change from one language to another? Bilingual bards, perhaps? Were there uneducated but bilingual disciples who commissioned amanuenses with good editorial Greek-language skills? Is it even possible for such a thing to happen?

I think not. I think it is far more plausible to suppose that the first Greek compositions containing 'biographies' of a Jesus of somewhere

3 Matt. 11:17; Luke 7:32 "We have piped unto you, and ye have not danced..."

or other were mythic stories framed and set in an Aramaic-speaking, Palestinian environment. How simple!

Ehrman's method should be applied to the problem of evaluating my claim that Christianity began at no single place and at no single time as does a tree that sprouts from a single seed and then branches out in various ways from a single rootstock. As I wrote in my "Prolegomenon to a Science of Christian Origins,"[4]

> *When*, exactly, did Christianity begin? Did Christianity, in fact, *have* a beginning? Can we visualize the origin and early evolution of Christianity better as a tree, with a single trunk producing many branches, or as a multifilamentous braid, with the oldest threads appearing out of the mists of religious and philosophical antiquity?
>
> Did these strands of tradition then twine together, pick up new threads and incorporate them as time went by? Did other threads then fray, branch, or break off the main braid from time to time? Did Christianity — like Mormonism — have a discrete, clearly defined beginning that we might trace to a single historical figure, or was it rootless like Hinduism or the ancient religions of Egypt and Mesopotamia?

If Christianity did *not* begin with a single man, at a single place, at a single time, however, but rather condensed as a braid of religious traditions around the turn of the era, it is easy to see how a divine concept or character could have been reified — brought to earth as it were from the sky in order to save the souls of an initiated elect.

Relatedly, we must inquire how all the forms of Docetism and so-called Gnosticism could have evolved from an actual Jesus of Nazareth or from anything that we might agree to call proto-Orthodoxy. It is, however, very easy to derive proto-Orthodoxy from the mysteries if it developed as a reifying 'heresy' of a Docetic, proto-Gnostic mystery cult with strong astral elements. Paul's common use of Gnostic technical vocabulary (*e.g., ektroma, Sophia, stoicheia, aion, archon, etc.*) can easily be explained as Gnostic remainders trapped in a text

4 R. Joseph Hoffmann (editor). *Sources of the Jesus Tradition: Separating History from Myth* [Amherst, NY: Prometheus Books, 2010: 145].

that has been forced into the Procrustean bed of historicity. They are terms that were allowed to remain in the text because their Gnostic meanings had been forgotten or misunderstood. But how can we explain the collocated presence of these jargon elements if proto-Orthodoxy evolved before proto-Gnosticism?

Questions of New Testament geography also can be illuminated if not perhaps completely answered using Ehrman's method, and they relate fundamentally to the braid-vs.-tree theories of Christian origins. As applied to the geography of the Gospels, Ehrman's method lends strong support to my thesis that the geography is fictive, not real. The notion that many of the place names are symbolic creations accounts quite simply for the fact that (1) they are not mentioned in any of the epistles or even in Acts; (2) they are unknown to ancient, contemporary geographers, the Old Testament, Josephus, and the two Talmuds; (3) there is no *isnad* (chain of transmission) of any tradition linking those sites securely to the time of Constantine's mother Helena; (4) their precise loctions are disputed even today; archaeology at the alleged sites of Nazareth, Capernaum, and even Bethlehem in Judaea, if not totally disconfirming their identities *vis-à-vis* the gospel stories is wildly more contentious and apologetic than the archaeology of most Near Eastern sites. If Nazareth, for example, had actually been the home of Jesus and the Holy Family, why is there no record of the apostles and others having gone back there? Or to Capernaum? Why did Origen think that the place-names of the gospels had symbolic meanings of great importance, lived only thirty miles from 'Nazareth,' but didn't know where it was located?

One more puzzle to be riddled out with Ehrman's method: A number of early (third-century) Latin Christian inscriptions begin with the superscription "D M" (*Diis Manibus,* 'to the Spirits of the Dead') or "D M S" (*Diis Manibus Sacrum,* 'to the Spirits of the Sacred Dead').[5] If Christianity began as a Jewish splinter sect, how could it so quickly have absorbed the veneration — or even worshipful placation — of

5 An example of "a Christian inscription still with the symbols D M S proper for a Pagan epitaph" is given by Pasquale Testini on page 331 of his *Archeologia Cristiana: Nozioni Generali Dalle Origini Alla Fine Del Sec. VI*, Desclée & C. — Editori Pontifici, Roma (no date; 1958?).

the ancestors? By what specific pathway may we imagine "Go not into the way of the Gentiles" [Matt. 10:5] could have been transformed into a dedication "to the Spirits of the Sacred Dead"?

Another exercise with which to practice Ehrman's method: If the authors of Mark's gospel had had recourse to oral traditions derived from actual events that occurred in the Galilee, would they have made the geographically implausible claim that Jesus and the disciples traveling from Tyre on the Mediterranean to the Sea of Galilee, thirty miles inland, would have gone by way of Sidon [Mark 7:31]? Sidon is twenty miles north of Tyre, so 'Mark' has Jesus walk round-trip forty unnecessary miles to get to where he was going.

In the case of the 'Gadarene Swine,' the King James Version tells us that Jesus went sailing on the Sea of Galilee "and they came over unto the other side of the sea, into the country of the Gadarenes" [Mark 5:1]. Unfortunately, the oldest manuscripts have Jesus disembarking at *Gerasa*, not *Gadara*. Whereas Gadara was about five miles from the shore, Gerasa was over thirty — and in a different country, the Decapolis. (Ultimately, it was written that Jesus actually disembarked at Gergesa, which may actually have been a coastal town.)

So, what is the more parsimonious way to explain such geographical errors? Is it (1) the earliest account of the earthly life of Jesus (supposedly written about forty years after Jesus' death) was derived from informants who themselves had not been eyewitnesses of the events and got mixed up concerning details of the stories recounted? Or (2) the 'errors' were merely fictional devices with which to reify an astral allegory — to bring down to earth a celestial figure and have him engage in symbolic acts on a terrestrial stage? It must be admitted that the better choice between these two alternatives is not exactly obvious and is debatable. Nevertheless, it is a debate that needs to take place if we are to formulate a genuine science of Christian origins.

Ehrman's method may be applied also to the question of how one could possibly get from the Gospel of Mark to the Apocalypse of John — the Book of Revelation. The Apocalypse is a completely otherworldly composition, describing Jesus as a heavenly Lamb

(Aries?). Bruce Malina[6] and other scholars have recognized the astrological nature of the work. Can we — by any believable scenario — imagine the Apocalypse of John evolving from the supposedly historical character starring in the Gospel of Mark? Is it not easier to imagine that the Heavenly Lamb of John has been given an earthly biography by 'Mark' than to think that an earthly 'Lamb of God' not only lost his life and was taken into heaven, but lost his biography as well during the trip?

Is it not easier to derive a Jesus of Nazareth living in a specific place at a specific time from a celestial being who at some unspecified time came to earth at some unspecified place, took human form and then substance — in short, was reified — than to derive the multitudinous Docetic, Gnostic, Separationist, and other early forms of Christianity from a real man who had lived completely unnoticed just a few decades earlier?

At the most fundamental level, Ehrman's method must be applied throughout the New Testament and related writings to decide if we are dealing with history or story. For every pericope, fact, and facet of our texts, we must determine if it is better explained as part of a purposeful story or as the result of an actual historical event. Is it *possible* to connect any given datum to an historical event or person with an *unbroken* thread of imagined process? Only if the answer is 'yes' can we then proceed to weigh its probability against the probability that the datum is part of a story crafted for theopolitical or other purposes. If, as I have argued, 'Christianity' is actually the product resulting from the braiding of several or many cultural, theological, political, and — yes — even historical traditions, we may expect that in at least some of the cases, it *will* be possible to 'connect the imaginary dots' to draw a conclusion favoring historicity of *components* of the traditional, overall story of the evolution of the various forms of Christianity (including all the heterodoxies) from a Jesus of Nazareth. However, I doubt that a comprehensive scenario can be constructed for the entire Orthodox tradition, or even a major part

6 Bruce J. Malina, *On the Genre and Message of Revelations: Star Visions and Sky Journeys* [Peabody, MA: Hendricson, 1995].

of it. It may be argued that the examples presented in this chapter evince a 'confirmation bias' — looking only for evidence supporting my views and not seeing evidence disconfirming it. That is always a worrisome possibility in any field of research, especially in the historical sciences. We must see if Bart Ehrman or anyone else can disconfirm my thesis.

It is very exciting to contemplate the revolution in the study of Christian origins that will be effected by the wide-scale application of Ehrman's method. It is an odd irony of fate that what at first glance appeared to be a methodology useful in justifying belief in a historical Jesus of Nazareth would prove to be *sine qua non* in bringing about his demise.

PART II: The Problem of Nazareth

CHAPTER ELEVEN

Bart's Subtitle

Frank R. Zindler

The subtitle of Bart Ehrman's *Did Jesus Exist?*[1] (*DJE?*) promises *The Historical Argument for Jesus of Nazareth*. This leads prospective readers to expect that the Jesus of concern in the book is to be associated with Nazareth and that it is this identifying tie between Nazareth and Jesus that will be the major investigative concern of the book. One would expect to find evidence supporting the historical existence of not just any-old Jesus. Rather, one anticipates learning the evidence supporting the existence of a Jesus who lived in a place called Nazareth at the turn of the era.

Evangelical and fundamentalist readers might further expect to learn whether or not the Nazareth from which Ehrman's Jesus came was the place described in the gospels — a town big enough to have a synagogue placed "on the brow of the hill" [Luke 4:28–30].

Alas, the Jesus of Nazareth found in the subtitle is almost completely absent from the book. Only eleven times in the 360-page book can we find the expression 'Jesus of Nazareth,' although the word 'Nazareth' occurs 87 times. Three of the eleven appearances of 'Jesus of Nazareth' occur on the title page, the copyright page, and a section heading. He appears two more times in the references at the back of the book, leaving a total of six places in the book where "Jesus of Nazareth" is actually employed by Ehrman himself. This averages

1 Bart D. Ehrman, *Did Jesus Exist? The Historical Argument for Jesus of Nazareth* [New York: HarperOne, 2012].

one occurrence for every sixty pages! This does not promote the impression that Jesus of Nazareth is the actual character whose historical existence Ehrman intends to establish.

But it seems I have miscounted the number of places where Ehrman himself refers to Jesus of Nazareth. One of the six actually turns out to be a quotation from Albert Schweitzer:

> There is nothing more negative than the result of the critical study of the life of Jesus. The Jesus of Nazareth who came forward publicly as the Messiah, who preached the ethic of the Kingdom of God, who founded the Kingdom of heaven upon earth, and died to give his work its final consecration, never had any existence... [*DJE?* 12–13]

It is hard to see how this quotation *supports* Ehrman's thesis, even though it is true that Schweitzer himself believed in the existence of an historical Jesus from *somewhere* or other. (In fact, Ehrman nonchalantly comments on page 191, "If Jesus existed, as the evidence suggests, but Nazareth did not, as this [mythicist] assertion claims, then he merely came from somewhere else."

So there you have it! Ehrman's book proving the historical existence *of Jesus of Nazareth* might actually be proving the existence of Jesus of Hoboken, Jesús of Rancho Cucamonga, or even the Jesus of Timbukthree instead! In the second edition of this book, I would suggest the subtitle be changed to read *The Historical Argument for Jesus of Fill-in-the-Blank*.

Of the remaining five places where Ehrman uses the phrase "Jesus of Nazareth," one of them is a misrepresentation of the writings of the ancient Jewish historian Josephus:

> In his various writings Josephus mentions a large number of Jews, especially as they were important for the social, political, and historical situation in Palestine. As it turns out, he discusses several persons named Jesus, and he deals briefly also with John the Baptist. And on two occasions, at least in the writings as they have come down to us today, he mentions Jesus of Nazareth. [*DJE?* 58]

Contrary to Ehrman's claim, however, Josephus *never* refers to Jesus of *Nazareth*. (Amazingly, Ehrman actually quotes the two disputed Josephan passages in his book where readers can immediately see that Nazareth does *not* occur in the passages quoted!) This is an egregious gaffe, because Josephus, although he refers to forty-five places in Galilee and fortified a town less than two miles from present-day Nazareth, *knew nothing of Nazareth itself*. Naturally, then, he could not be witness to any character styled 'Jesus of Nazareth.' Moreover, Josephus was from a priestly family. How could he have ignored a *polis* that had a synagogue? [Luke 4:16]

What tricks of the mind must have been playing upon the James A. Gray Distinguished Professor of Religious Studies at the University of North Carolina, Chapel Hill when — although he must have been attending closely to scholarly arguments asserting the quoted passages to be Christian interpolations in the text of Josephus — he nevertheless formed the impression that the arguments he was evaluating pertained to Jesus *of Nazareth*?

This leaves four references to Jesus of Nazareth for us to examine amidst 360 pages of expectedly well-written prose. One of the three remainders is a rather anecdotal comment about Ehrman's personal experience at a Humanist conference where many of the participants expressed Mythicist leanings:

> ...many of them were completely taken aback when they learned that I have a different view, that I think that there certainly was a Jesus of Nazareth, who was crucified under Pontius Pilate, and about whom we can say a good deal as a historical figure. [*DJE?* 334]

Formally, this is merely a reference to personal experience. Even so, it makes the concealed unsubstantiated claim that "we can say a good deal [*about Jesus*] as a historical figure." One easily can forget that this hidden claim is a wild exaggeration. We can say a good deal about Jesus of Nazareth? Really? Why, then, does Ehrman say virtually nothing *specifically* pertaining to Jesus of *Nazareth* in his entire book?

Two of the remaining three references to Jesus of Nazareth are simple instances of the fallacies of informal logic known as the appeal to authority and the *ad populum* ('three million Frenchmen can't be wrong') fallacies. The first quotation of this sort is from his argument that Mythicists generally do not have enough specialized education to qualify them to write about a mythical Jesus of Nazareth. They aren't experts.

> It is striking that virtually everyone who has spent all the years needed to attain these qualifications is convinced that Jesus of Nazareth was a real historical figure. [*DJE?* 5]

The second passage embodying these fallacies is found in the section of his book entitled "The Gospels and Their Written Sources."

> Once it is conceded that the Gospels can and should be treated as historical sources, no different from other historical sources infused with their author's biases, it starts to become clear why historians have almost universally agreed that whatever else one might say about him, Jesus of Nazareth lived in first-century Palestine and was crucified by the prefect[2] of Judea. [*DJE?* 74]

Now, simply stating the obvious fact that the vast majority of New Testament specialists are historicists is not evidence for the concealed proposition "Jesus of Nazareth once lived in Roman Palestine and was crucified by Pontius Pilate." That is a statement in

2 Ehrman corrects Tacitus' *Annals* 15:44 concerning Pilate's title. In the disputed passage in the *Annals*, Tacitus gives Pontius Pilate the title of *procurator*. As Ehrman notes on page 56, epigraphic evidence proves that Pilate's title was *prefect*. Curiously, he claims that "Tacitus evidently did know some things about Jesus," even though the possibly-forged passage makes no mention of any *Jesus* from anywhere. Rather, it mentions 'Christians' and a 'Christus' who was put to death by an erroneously titled Pilate.

Despite his own scholarly blunder, Ehrman takes to task Mythicists who claim such Pagan attestations to be interpolations. "...and so when they find any such reference, they claim the reference was not original but was inserted by Christians. But surely the best way to deal with evidence is not simply to dismiss it when it happens to be inconvenient." [*DJE?* 55]

But surely, the two pages detailing strong evidence of forgery in my essay "Did Jesus Exist?" — which Ehrman read in volume one of my *Through Atheist Eyes* — cannot be considered dismissal of evidence by me. Rather, it seems that Ehrman simply dismissed evidence that *he* found inconvenient.

need of proof—proof for which Mythicists seek in vain in the pages of Ehrman's book.

That leaves us with only *one passage* in the entire book where Ehrman uses the name 'Jesus of Nazareth' as an integral part of his argument. This is found in his discussion of methodology to separate the miraculous Jesus from the mundane Jesus.

> The reason this line of reasoning is in error is that we are not asking whether Jesus really did miracles and, if so, why they (and he) are not mentioned by pagan sources. We are asking whether Jesus of Nazareth actually existed. Only after establishing that he did exist can we go on to ask if he did miracles. If we decide that he did, only then can we revisit the question of why no one, in that case, mentions him. [*DJE?* 43–44]

We are left, therefore, with a book that isn't really intended to prove the existence of a god-man who came from a place called Nazareth. Ehrman has hedged his bets and is attempting to prove the existence of *any* Jesus who can be pressed into service to explain a unitary origin of Christianity.

One may fairly ask at this point, "Why should this initiating stimulator have been named *Jesus* either? Wasn't he named *Jesus* because the Aramaic equivalent (*yeshua'*) means 'Savior'? In Septuagint Greek, the word *IESOUS* can also represent the name Joshua. Maybe we should be looking for a Joshua instead of a Savior?

But why, exactly, would Ehrman suppose that Jesus is the first name of his putative character, rather than a title or epithet? He knows that *Christ* is a title, not a name. Why not *Jesus*? Moreover, wasn't 'Jesus' the *ultimate* name bestowed upon Paul's "Christ Jesus" in the so-called Kenosis Hymn [Philippians 2:5–11]?

> Wherefore God also hath highly exalted him [*Christ Jesus*], and given him a name which is above every name: that at the name of *Jesus* every knee should bow, of things in heaven, and things in earth, and things under the earth.

Isn't *Jesus* here a name of magical power given to a being who was referred to as "Christ" before he was titled Jesus? Isn't that why we still find occasional references to *Christ Jesus* instead of Jesus Christ?

Is it not the case that if — as the consensus of historicist scholarly opinion holds — unlike Hinduism and traditional Egyptian, Greek, and Roman religions, Christianity began at a single point in time and was initiated by a single person, couldn't that person have been named Ichabod as well as Savior? Couldn't the name of Savior have been given to him after his death? If we no longer have to think of Christianity having been founded by Jesus of Nazareth, couldn't it have been founded by someone named anything at all?

The unfulfilled promise of Ehrman's subtitle would not be unexpected by anyone who has read his earlier books — none of which has much to say about a character named Jesus of Nazareth. As a glaring example, we may consider his *Jesus: apocalyptic prophet of the new millennium* [New York: Oxford University Press, 1999]. 'Jesus of Nazareth' appears only four times in 274 pages of very small print.

In the Preface, Ehrman tells us "I really don't have a lot to say to scholars who have already spent a good portion of their lives delving into the complex world of first-century Palestine and the place that Jesus of Nazareth occupied within it."

The second sentence in chapter one tells us that the peculiar Christian delusion that the world was about to end "can be traced all the way back to the beginning, to the teachings of Jesus of Nazareth."

'Jesus of Nazareth' puts in an amusing appearance in the first sentence of chapter six, where Ehrman reminds us that "We have spent a good deal of time looking at the historical sources that can inform us about Jesus of Nazareth." "A good deal of time?" "Historical sources?" The only places where Jesus of Nazareth has been mentioned at this point are the two places at the beginning of the book — in sentences having nothing whatsoever to do with historical sources for anything!

Fourth and finally, we learn on page 98 that "Jesus is said to have come from Nazareth in all four Gospels… and is sometimes actually *called* "Jesus of Nazareth" in other ancient sources (*e.g.*, Acts 3:6)." Unfortunately, there are some problems with this claim.

First of all, even the King James Version does not place 'Jesus of Nazareth' in that verse of Acts. It has "In the name of Jesus *Christ* of Nazareth rise up and walk." Since the name there is being used for magical purposes, the distinction between 'Jesus Christ of Nazareth' and mere 'Jesus of Nazareth' almost certainly would have been crucial! Uttering the words 'Jesus of Nazareth' would have healed a man lame since birth about as well as saying *hocus-pocus*.

The second problem is really quite shocking in its implications regarding the quality of Ehrman's scholarship when writing books for popular consumption. It appears that he did not check any Greek version of Acts 3:6. *No Greek manuscript is known in which the city name Nazareth is found in that verse*. Instead, all known manuscripts have an epithet that might be rendered something like *the Nazorean* in English. Such an error or misrepresentation might be expected in an apologetic work by Lee Strobel or Josh McDowell, but it is utterly unexpected in a book written by the author of the excellent Loeb Classical Library edition of the Apostolic Fathers.

In *Did Jesus Exist?* Ehrman claims to have presented evidence for the existence of Jesus of Nazareth. Mythicists in the rebuttals of this volume, however, seek evidence for the existence of Ehrman's evidence.

CHAPTER TWELVE

Archaeology, Bart Ehrman, and the Nazareth of 'Jesus'

René Salm

I. *DJE?*[1] & the New Skepticism

When I first learned that Dr. Ehrman was writing a book combating the Mythicist position, I was elated and knew in advance that this was a 'win' for Mythicists, regardless of what the good doctor might write. After all, his book would finally bring Jesus Mythicism before a general readership. Ehrman's book — slim though it may be in substance — has also opened the door for other efforts attacking Mythicism.[2] This is all laudable from a Mythicist perspective, for Ehrman, Casey, Hoffmann and others are — through their generally vociferous, often emotional, and always poorly argued denunciations — firmly placing Jesus Mythicism on the radar screen of scholarship. It's about time.

A scant few years ago the word 'Mythicist' was unknown to everyone, including biblical scholars. We have now turned a page. Though mainstream scholars may by and large continue to ignore the Mythicist position — that Jesus of Nazareth was an invention —

1 Bart D. Ehrman, *Did Jesus Exist? The Historical Argument for Jesus of Nazareth.* [New York: HarperOne, 2012].

2 One is planned by Maurice Casey, PhD, and another by a consortium of scholars edited by R. J. Hoffmann.

the position now demands address. This is the fundamental significance of Ehrman's book, not what he writes.

After all, *Did Jesus Exist?* has all the earmarks of being lightweight both in content and argument. It is a book to be read with the TV on or while cooking dinner. In fact, I think this was definitely Ehrman's (and/or his editor's) intention. It does not have the scholar and the seminar room in mind, but the "millions of people [who] have acquired their 'knowledge' about early Christianity — about Jesus, Mary Magdalene, the emperor Constantine, the Council of Nicaea — from Dan Brown," author of *The Da Vinci Code* [*DJE?* 4]. The great fear is that skeptical claims "are seeping into the popular consciousness at an alarming rate" [*DJE?* 6–7].

Thus *DJE?* properly locates itself not in academe but in America's increasingly hot culture wars. This explains the immediate and vociferous reactions from both traditional and skeptical sides of the issue. We cannot suppose that those reactions constitute validation that Ehrman's *opus* in any way marks a signal advance in learning. The hundreds of Mythicist rebuttals are something of a celebration — they are celebrating the coming of age of Jesus Mythicism.

But Ehrman is not writing for Jesus Mythicists whom he caricatures from the start as "conspiracy theorists" resisting "a traditional view [which] is thoroughly persuasive" [*DJE?* 5]. Rather, his goal is to inoculate the general reader against the dangerous new heresy of Jesus Mythicism. It is a pre-emptive strike, hopefully carried out before Mythicism has a chance to gain a firm foothold in the culture. Unfortunately for him, Ehrman is too late.

DJE? seeks to influence rather than to inform. Thus it is at heart a book of propaganda. *Propaganda* is the perfect word, for Ehrman skews, ignores, caricatures, and uses all the rhetorical tools of the publicist who cares far more for appearance than for rigorous argument. But rhetoric is not the problem with *DJE?* — every good writer uses it, and Ehrman is a good writer. The main problem with his book is its astonishing lack of rigorous argument. Instead, the reader is time and time again regaled with a cheap appeal to authority. But in our time — when every scintilla of data regarding Jesus of Nazareth is subject to the most careful scrutiny and often to strident disagreement — authority is hardly enough, even if it comes in the form of pronouncements from the James A. Gray Distinguished Professor of Religious Studies at the University of North Carolina at Chapel Hill. And, after 339 breezy pages, we read the ultimate pronouncement in *DJE?*'s final sentence: "Jesus did exist, whether we like it or not." Ironically, like the book which preceded it, the affirmation is surprisingly empty and carries absolutely no weight.

Mohandas Gandhi famously said, "First they ignore you, then they ridicule you, then they fight you, then you win." In the first reactions to *DJE?*, one Mythicist pundit opined that "Ehrman's book presents the paradigm shift from Ignore to Ridicule. As such, it is an important milestone." I doubt this book qualifies as a milestone, or that it is even important. Yet *DJE?* proves that we have progressed beyond the "ignore" stage. Traces of ridicule are readily available, as when Ehrman often invokes majority opinion against Mythicism:

> I agree with Schweitzer and *virtually all scholars* in the field since his day that Jesus existed, that he was ineluctably Jewish, that there is historical information about him in the Gospels, and that we can therefore know some things about what he said and did. [*DJE?* 14, emphasis added.]

For Mythicists there are three great errors in this citation: (1) that Jesus existed; (2) that he was "ineluctably Jewish"; and (3) that there is historical information about him in the Gospels. The first point is the thrust of *DJE?*. Yet Ehrman demonstrates that he is not well read in Mythicist literature — apparently he has merely scanned the most recent crop of books from Acharya S. to G. A. Wells. He indeed grapples with the thesis that 'Christ' was a spiritual entity (Doherty *et al.*), but is woefully unaware of other issues important to Mythicists, such as the critical distinction between 'Jesus' and 'Christ' (Ehrman tiresomely equates these, *e.g.*, page 52); the priority of Greek *Chrestos* (meaning 'good') over *Christos* (meaning 'anointed'); not to mention provocative theories that identify *Chrestos* with the 'prophet,' 'soothsayer' (*chrestes*) of the Delphic mysteries, and 'Jesus' with John the Baptist (Ory, Price) or with the Teacher of Righteousness (Eisenman, others). All of these, for Ehrman, are unknown, unexplored, or *off the table*. They are not within the purview of respectable discussion. But they are important to Jesus Mythicism with the result that, for him, Mythicism is itself largely off the table. From *DJE?* one can say that Ehrman treats a subject that he neither knows nor likes, with the result that he does so neither rigorously nor even seriously.

Though the 'meat' of the Mythicist position may still be off the table, and though Ehrman treats Mythicism with a good dose of haughtiness, I am optimistic that his book marks a somewhat more advanced level than Gandhi's second stage, Ridicule. For if Ehrman were simply ridiculing Mythicism then he wouldn't have bothered to write a whole book about it — which was not a joy, as he states on page 6: "I need to admit that I write this book with some fear and trepidation."

The real reason Ehrman wrote the book has already been noted — it stems from alarm over the recent progress of Jesus Mythicism. Yet, Jesus Mythicism is not new. After all, Albert Schweitzer dedicated a chapter to rationalism, skepticism, and Mythicism in his expanded (German) version of the *Quest* (*Geschichte der Leben-Jesu-Forschung*, 1913). However, the tradition — to which Schweitzer very much belonged — has always been able to marginalize Mythicist voices. If I am not mistaken, for the first time the tradition has blinked. One century after Schweitzer's book the gathering forces of skepticism are demonstrating unparalleled vigor, numbers, and the remarkable and perhaps unprecedented ability to advance their agenda despite a most uneven playing field.

And the playing field — lest any one doubt — is unevenly biased against the Mythicist. While Ehrman is handsomely paid for the books he writes, has no trouble finding a publisher, and is a lauded luminary in the field of New Testament studies, Mythicists are unfunded, may lose their academic positions because of their views, and often must research and write for free and in their spare time. Saying that Mythicists are not professionally engaged academics — as Ehrman does repeatedly in his book — is simply unfair, for a Mythicist may possess all the customary credentials yet still be unable to find work in academe. A case in point is Dr. Robert Price, a scholar who possesses not one but two doctoral degrees in the field of religion. Thus it is not the lack of credentials that ultimately bars Mythicists from the guild — it is their views.

Personally speaking, I long ago perceived this state of affairs and knew that — given my radical views — pursuit of a doctorate in religious studies was essentially a waste of time. I can give two reasons: (1) no job would await me upon completion of my coursework; and (2) for years of university study I would subject myself to cant and to the narrow-minded mores typical of religious institutions. Rather than embark on such a stifling and expensive road, I determined to do the necessary learning on my own, taking occasional classes in language and history at the local university. To the academic who would say that it is not possible to get the equivalent of a PhD in religious studies outside the classroom, I would simply respond that it is not desirable to get such a PhD *inside* the classroom.

The credentialed often hurl the term 'amateur' at the Mythicist. However, I for one am proud of such standing and consider it an indiscretion to mingle truth with a paycheck. *Amateur* is a most laudable qualification for the student of religion. Indeed, there may be no finer endorsement.

At the same time, seething discontent within the field of Biblical Studies (including both Old and New Testaments) is producing a flood of literature decidedly favoring skeptical views. Many academics are straining against the bit which the tradition has long placed in their mouths. The tenor of our age favors this New Skepticism in two important ways. Firstly, recent years have seen Christianity stumble repeatedly, as one ethical compromise after another diminishes its former respect and drives away the faithful. Secondly, the uneducated public has shown itself finally able to cast aside traditional views inculcated over the millennia. Skepticism regarding Jesus is no longer the province of fringe would-be academics. It has infected the population at large, thanks to a steady stream of best-selling books and movies which not long ago would have been considered sacrilegious.

All this demonstrates that the time is ripe for Jesus Mythicism. It is a product of our age. That recognition, too, is causing alarm in the

Christian tradition. The result is that ridicule is no longer an appropriate nor satisfactory response. Now at the beginning of the third Christian millennium, we are entering Gandhi's third stage: Engagement ('fight'). The fact that a leading scholar like Bart Ehrman has written a book called *Did Jesus Exist?* witnesses to the new reality: Mythicism is finally being taken seriously.

Well — up to a point... Ehrman's book is not serious and certainly it is not scholarly. He still has one foot planted in the Ridicule stage, while the other tentatively seeks a foothold in unfamiliar territory that was, until his tome, outside polite discussion. Ehrman's book does not satisfactorily engage with Mythicist issues. An immediate deluge of Mythicist rebuttals on the Internet (some extensive, such as those of Earl Doherty and Richard Carrier) immediately revealed how shallow and wanting are many of his positions.

Now, I have little doubt that Ehrman could have written a more scholarly tome had he wished to address Mythicism in more depth and, it should be said, with more respect. Had he done so, however, he would have lost his vast intended readership which is not other savants, but the largely uneducated public. Mythicists were hoping for a serious treatment validating the serious nature of their proposition. But Ehrman withholds such validation. He seems never to have intended that *DJE?* be part of the scholarly conversation but that it be part of America's cultural conversation.

The upshot is that Ehrman's book could have been written equally poorly by just about any freelance writer. The fact that it was written by a scholar of Ehrman's stature is one more symptom that, as regards 'the historical Jesus,' academe has dropped the ball. Let me spell out the fundamental lesson learned from the last two hundred years of biblical scholarship: in its First Quest, its Second Quest, and now its Third Quest, academe has not been able to seriously grapple with the question of 'the historical Jesus.' Its repeated failure reflects an erroneous goal, and more success will surely attend the emerging quest for 'the *ahistorical* Jesus'

At this time, we still cannot rely primarily upon scholarship for that Fourth Quest. Valuable and significant advances are being made today by the disenfranchised outside the guild. At the same time, the most courageous within academe are trying to break out of the imposed straitjacket of tradition and of religious conservatism. These two camps — radical outsiders and rebellious insiders — are edging towards fragile cooperation. The coming years may not see a breakthrough so much as a realignment of forces behind the lines as it were. In fact, there is evidence that such a realignment is already taking place.

Centuries ago the Church burned heretics. When that was no longer possible it excommunicated them. That was once a serious penalty which amounted to loss of livelihood and social ostracism, but today excommunication carries little weight. With the secular trends of the last centuries the Beast of the Church has thus slowly been de-fanged. The arc of history is clearly bending away from the tradition.

Nonetheless, Jesus Mythicists should not become complacent nor unduly optimistic, for we are speaking of a struggle that is centuries old and that cannot be resolved overnight. It is sobering to read old assessments of the imminent demise of Christianity, such as the following by the much maligned Theosophist and Jesus Mythicist Helena Blavatsky:

> I have no intention of repeating here stale arguments and logical exposés of the whole theological scheme; for all this has been done, over and over again, and in a most excellent way, by the ablest "Infidels" of England and America. But I may briefly repeat a prophecy which is a self-evident result of the present state of men's minds in Christendom. Belief in the Bible *literally*, and in a *carnalized* Christ, will not last a quarter of a century longer. The Churches will have to part with their cherished dogmas, or the 20th century will witness the downfall and ruin of all Christendom... The very name has now become obnoxious, and theological Christianity must die out, *never to resurrect* again in its present form.
>
> — "The Esoteric Character of the Gospels," II, *ca.* 1890.
>
> (Emphasis in the original.)

Today, literal belief in the Bible is still widespread and belief in a "carnalized Christ" is well-nigh universal. We have not witnessed "the downfall and ruin of all Christendom." Yet the cracks in its walls are today more pronounced than ever. I believe those cracks will ultimately prove lethal. But who can predictably time the demise of this global institution now almost two thousand years old? In the near term the pendulum may swing yet again. Secularism may yield to the gathering forces of a reactionary fundamentalism, forces which even today threaten America.

II. What's in a Name?

I mentioned above that Ehrman fails to make a critical distinction in *DJE?* — that between 'Jesus' and 'Christ.' The two names are not interchangeable, as Mythicists, skeptics, and even mainstream liberal scholars have long appreciated. The French Mythicist Georges Ory showed that Paul knew only the *Christ,* while the canonical gospels knew only *Jesus*. The union of the two names was relatively late and entailed the wholesale revision of both the Pauline corpus and of the gospels.[3]

The history of these names is much more complex and revealing than most traditionalists suspect. 'Jesus' alone can produce considerable confusion when going from Semitic to Greek — it has manifestly different forms, histories, and allusions in each linguistic realm. Then we have the English name 'Jesus' which corresponds to the Semitic 'Joshua' (*Yehoshua* = 'Yah saves'). It is important to digest this critical fact which I shall now repeat: *The English name Jesus corresponds to the Semitic Joshua.*

If one asked a Hebrew at the turn of the era, "Who was Yehoshua?" that Hebrew would answer without hesitation: "He was the great prophet who came after Moses and who led the children of Israel into the Promised Land." For the Jews, then, Jehoshua/Jesus was both *the* quintessentially successful conqueror and also the successor to

3 Georges Ory, *Le Christ et Jésus.* [Brussels: Éditions du Cercle d'Éducation Populaire, 1968: 29–38].

Moses. He was very much a messianic figure. The Samaritan *Book of Joshua* (*Sepher Yehoshua,* quite different from the O.T. book of that name)[4] even witnesses to a pre-Christian cult in which Yehoshua/Joshua/Jesus had twelve appointed disciples. Such, I submit, is eminently fertile ground for an investigation into Christian origins. But this line completely escapes Ehrman (and the tradition), for whom a pre-Christian Jesus is definitely *persona non grata*.

Now, if one asked the same question above of a Greek-speaker at the turn of the era, the wording would be: "Who was *Iesous*?" *Iesous* is the Greek form of Yehoshua/Joshua as found, for example, in the Septuagint. So we see that in the Greek language *Iesous* has a pre-Christian history going back at least to *ca*. 250 BCE when the Septuagint began to be translated. Now — to make matters even more interesting — *Iesous* also closely corresponds to the Greek *Iaso, Iason* (Jason), and *iaomai*, "to heal." This aspect of the name Jesus has long been overlooked and is only recently receiving attention (*e.g.*, J. Moles, "Jesus the Healer," *Histos* 5 [2011: 127*ff*]).

Those in the Roman Empire who were not Jews would have had little familiarity with, and also little interest in, the Old Testament heroes such as Joshua/Iesous. Ehrman points out that linguistic proficiency in antiquity was far less than it is today in the developed world, and that only about 10% of ancients could read at all [*DJE?* 47]. If one presented them — say, in Corinth, Ephesus or Antioch — with the Greek name *Iesous* then their most immediate association would be to the name 'Jason' (*Iēsōn* in Ionic) and the verb *iaomai*, 'heal.' The long history of the Semitic name Joshua, and its many associations in the Old Testament, would be entirely lost on those Hellenists — at least on the vast majority who were not Jews.

Figuratively speaking, then, when going from Semitic into Greek, the name *Jesus* passes from the semantic field of a conqueror to that of a healer.

Today we have quite forgotten the above associations and have even ignored a most basic one — that *Yehoshua* yields *both* 'Joshua'

4 See J. Bowman, *Samaritan Documents Relating to their History, Religion and Life.* [Pittsburgh: The Pickwick Press, 1977: 61 *ff*].

and 'Jesus.' In ancient times — indeed, at the birth of Christianity — *Jesus* was separated from *Joshua* as the religion split along linguistic, cultural, and theological lines (*cf.* the friction between Hellenists and Hebrews, Acts 6:1*f*). Accompanying this split, I would suggest, was a linguistic sleight of hand which corresponds with the invention of the new *theios aner* Jesus. In other words the birth of Christianity had a lot to do with the splitting off of Hellenist followers in the first century CE — in fact, that's when the birth of Christianity occurred.

A Jesus Skit

If any professor thinks my above argument is nonsense, or is tempted to brush it off as no more than an irrelevant linguistic distinction of no importance, I challenge him or her to conduct the following somewhat jocular experiment in an upcoming History of Christianity class: whenever the name Jesus comes up, let the professor say instead "Joshua." After all, the two names are precisely equivalent in Greek (*Iesous*). I guarantee it will only be necessary to do this for a few minutes before the class descends into total confusion.

And with that as introduction, I invite readers to enjoy the following brief skit:

Two Co-Ed's are friends and both students in a religion class at a conservative college in the Bible Belt. We shall call them Co-Ed A and Co-Ed B. They like to sit in the back row and occasionally whisper to one another. The professor has announced that there will be a pop quiz at the end of the class.

Professor: When Joshua rises from the dead...

Co-Ed A [*whispers to Co-Ed B sitting next to her*]: Did he say "Joshua"?

Co-Ed B: Yes...

[*Both frantically open their Bibles to the Book of Joshua looking for where he rises from the dead.*]
Professor: ...After three days Joshua rose from the dead, and he appeared to many, many people.

Co-Ed A: [*Still looking frantically in the Book of Joshua.*] I can't find anything. It's all about him conquesting Israel.

Co-Ed B: Oh, I think I know... It's in the New Testament. Remember, at the Transfiguration Jesus goes up the mountain. The prophets from the Old Testament are there. That must be when Joshua rises from the dead.

Co-Ed A: Oh, yeah... [*Both frantically turn to the New Testament and find the story of the Transfiguration in Mark chapter 9.*]

Co-Ed B: Wait a minute. My Bible says Elijah and Moses were there... And Peter. "And they were exceedingly afraid."

Co-Ed A: I see "Jesus" but not "Joshua"!

Co-Ed B: Didn't the prof say there'll be a quiz at the end of this class?

[*Blankly stare at each other.*]

Together: OH MY GOD!!

The *separation* of 'Jesus' and 'Joshua' is only one problem when it comes to the name of 'the prophet from Nazareth.' Scholars routinely confound *Jesus* and *Christ*, as if these two words — in *any* language — were synonymous. Thus, Bart Ehrman can write: "Moreover, Pliny informs the emperor, the Christians 'sing hymns to Christ as to a god'... That is all he says about Jesus" [*DJE?* 52]. Hence, he suggests that the reader take Pliny's letter as evidence for the man Jesus. Of course, Pliny makes no mention of *Jesus* but only of "Christ" and of "Christians." This may appear nitpicking, but it is only after a careful treatment of the primary evidence that the ancient evidence for the man 'Jesus of Nazareth' evaporates.

The Mythicist thesis relies upon such care. Now, Ehrman the consummate historian chastises Mythicists for not being careful (he begins the book by virtually destroying Acharya S and Freke and Gandy on this account) but it is clear that the pot calls the kettle black.

Like the name 'Jesus,' the name 'Christ' is also a complex issue, for we are dealing not only with the Hebrew *Meshiach* and Greek *Chrestos* and *Christos*, but also with Latin *Christus* — as well as with some evident tampering of the texts that has changed "*Chrestianos*" (Tacitus) and "*Chresto*" (Suetonius).[5] It is little appreciated by traditionalists that *Chrestos* in Greek was a common name in antiquity meaning 'good,' 'wholesome,' 'auspicious.' But that is all I will say on these significant matters that impinge on the existence of 'Jesus Christ' and 'Jesus of Nazareth' but which are entirely bypassed by Ehrman.

III. The Nazareth Controversy

Bart Ehrman devotes seven pages to the archaeology of Nazareth and four pages (193–97) to my work. It is a cursory treatment which does not grapple with the seminal issues. For example, he does not make any mention of the Nazareth oil lamps, a central element of my argument. Perhaps Ehrman doesn't do so because the earliest oil lamps from the Nazareth basin incontestably date to CE times [*MON*[6] 170]. In any event, his superficial treatment of the Nazareth issue is characteristic of *Did Jesus Exist?*

At his request, I personally mailed a copy of *The Myth of Nazareth* to Prof. Ehrman in August of 2010. Therefore he possessed a copy almost two years before the publication of *Did Jesus Exist?* Had

5 Erik Zara, ThD, "The Chrestianos Issue in Tacitus Reinvestigated" (2009) http://www.textexcavation.com/documents/zaratacituschrestianos.pdf; "A Minor Compilation of Readings of Suetonius' Nero 16.2," 2011 http://www.textexcavation.com/documents/zarasuetoniuschristiani.pdf (both online).

6 René Salm, *The Myth of Nazareth: The Invented Town of Jesus*. [Cranford, New Jersey, 2008].

he cared to do so, he had ample time to read my book and to study its contents.

Since Ehrman critiques my work, one would expect that he was and is familiar with the issues of Nazareth archaeology and with the main points of my argument. However, given the cursory treatment of Nazareth in *Did Jesus Exist?*, I am not so sure.

My book's argument can be summarized as follows:

A. The material finds reveal the following:

(1) the lack of demonstrable material evidence from *ca.* 700 BCE to *ca.* 100 CE;

(2) the 25 CE+ dating of the earliest oil lamps at Nazareth;

(3) the 50 CE+ dating of all the post-Iron Age tombs at Nazareth, which are of the kokh type;

B. The following points impinge upon the question of pious fraud:

(4) the existence of Middle Roman tombs under the Church of the Annunciation.

(5) The non-rigorous nature of 'Christian archaeology' wherein priests train in seminaries and are unable to conduct a rigorous modern excavation;

(6) The monopoly exercised in Nazareth by the Catholic Church, evident in Church ownership of the so-called "Venerated Sites" where most of the digging has taken place (thus limiting access, evaluation, and publication);

(7) A persistent history of error, internal contradiction, and outright fraud which continues to mar critical findings from Nazareth.

Let me say at the outset that the case for or against Nazareth at the turn of the era rests entirely on part (A) above — that is, on the material finds in points 1–3. We may inveigh all we wish against shoddy digging, lack of access, and fraud, but once seen for what they are, these can and must be put aside so that we can focus on the verifiable material record regarding the turn of the era. That material record is damning as regards the existence of a settlement at Nazareth at 'the time of Jesus.'

In his book Ehrman does not address most of the seven points above. In fact, he does not directly deal with the Nazareth evidence at all but with conclusions that others have made regarding that evidence (Bagatti, Dark, Alexandre, Pfann). However, a primary thrust of my book was to return to the material evidence and to show that those conclusions are generally inconsistent with the evidence. By accepting the conclusions of his colleagues on faith and without further ado, Ehrman entirely bypasses my book's arguments and, in fact, writes as if the book had never been written. After all, *The Myth of Nazareth* shows that the conclusions of biblical archaeologists emphatically *cannot* be taken on faith — for the reasons itemized in points 5–7 above.

Ehrman pulls rank. He focuses on my right to make assessments, "since Salm himself is not an archaeologist" [*DJE?* 194]. What he fails to appreciate, however, is that I have not made any archaeological assessments at all. I have collected, read, and cited the published reports of eminent specialists in many subfields of biblical archaeology. It is *their* verdicts regarding specific Nazareth finds that have decided the case. Moreover, I have not relied upon unpublished and quite unverifiable claims such as Ehrman is willing to do — as with Alexandre's claim of a "house from the time of Jesus," or the claim that coins from Mary's Well date to Hellenistic times.

Ehrman's appeal to authority is, in this case, doubly wrong. Firstly, as just mentioned, he misinterprets my role, which is not that of an "archaeologist," but merely that of a careful compiler. Secondly, by appealing to credentials he ignores (or rejects) my imputation of fraud in Nazareth archaeology (point 7 above). That much is clear. A reasonable person would decide the issue on the basis of the material findings — *not on the basis of authority*. And therein lies the difference between Ehrman and myself.

ARCHAEOLOGY AND THE NAZARETH OF 'JESUS'

The lack of turn-of-the-era evidence

I shall systematically proceed to consider Ehrman's remarks according to the first three points above. Thus, the next several pages will address point number one — whether Ehrman provides any "demonstrable material evidence from *ca.* 700 BCE to *ca.* 100 CE." This is perhaps the most critical aspect of any discussion regarding the archaeology of Nazareth in 'the time of Jesus.'

To begin, Ehrman notes my claim that there was a hiatus in settlement. He writes:

> [Citation #1] Salm's basic argument is that Nazareth did exist in more ancient times and through the Bronze Age. But then there was a hiatus. It ceased to exist and did not exist in Jesus's day. Based on archaeological evidence, especially the tombs found in the area, Salm claims that the town came to be reinhabited sometime between the two Jewish revolts (between 70 CE and 132 CE), as Jews who resettled following the destruction of Jerusalem by the Romans relocated in northern climes [*DJE?* 193–94].

This is a mischaracterization. First of all, "Bronze Age" above should read "Iron Age." The difference is five hundred years. The error indicates remarkable sloppiness and is one clue that Ehrman probably did not, in fact, read my book.

Secondly, I don't claim that "the town came to be reinhabited" but that the *site* came to be reinhabited. It may seem like a minor detail, but the first chapter of my book shows that a settlement indeed existed in the basin in the Bronze and Iron Ages. It was not called "Nazareth" but "Japhia" [*MON* 53–55]. Again, one wonders if Ehrman paid attention to the book.

Thirdly, my argument is not based "especially [on] the tombs found in the area." Here Ehrman omits the two other mainstays of my argument: the lack of demonstrable material evidence from *ca.* 700 BCE to *ca.* 100 CE; and the 25 CE+ dating of the earliest oil lamps at Nazareth. *Ehrman does not mention these two critical points at all.*

René Salm

The "Great Hiatus," as I have called it, lasted 800 years: *ca.* 700 BCE–*ca.* 100 CE. Of course, if that hiatus in the Nazareth settlement existed then the case for a village at the turn of the era is closed. If Ehrman wishes to contest this, his task is simple: he must point to material evidence of human presence at Nazareth before the turn of the era — particularly in the first century BCE, for that would establish the existence of a village when Jesus was supposedly born [*MON* 288].

Of course Ehrman does not do this — even though he claims to do so. Here is what he writes:

> [Citation #2] *Many compelling pieces* of archaeological evidence indicate that in fact Nazareth did exist *in Jesus's day*... [*DJE?* 195, emphasis added]

My response is simple: *Where, then, are those many compelling pieces?* Certainly they are not in the literature of Nazareth published prior to 2008, as examined in Chapter Four of *The Myth of Nazareth* [*MON* 153–210]. There I show that there is no evidence datable to the turn of the era ("Jesus's day"). I treat in turn: pottery, stone vessels, oil lamps, tombs, ossuaries, sarcophagi, inscriptions, graffiti, 'domestic installations,' basins, and coins. All I came up with that could *possibly* date to the turn of the era were two stone vessels. Roland Deines, a specialist who studied these very two Nazareth vessels, writes that such vessels continued to be manufactured into the second century CE. Hence, their presence at Nazareth constitutes no evidence at all of human presence at the turn of the era.

There is much pressure now on the tradition to produce evidence for Nazareth at the turn of the era. Several much-publicized but poorly validated feints have been made in this direction since publication of my book. Ehrman swallows the bait each time — hook, line, and sinker.

Let's continue to look for Ehrman's "many compelling pieces" of evidence. Perhaps he means the following:

> [Citation 3] For one thing, archaeologists have excavated a farm connected with the village, and it dates to the time of Jesus [*DJE?* 195].

Ehrman is referring to the "Nazareth Village Farm Report" (NVFR), a 61-page boondoggle that brings "Christian archaeology" to a new low. That report was published in the 2007 issue of the *Bulletin of the Anglo-Israel Archaeological Society* (*BAIAS*). My eight-page "Response," published in the subsequent issue of *BAIAS*, showed that nothing in the NVF report reflects settlement at the turn of the era.[7] The core issue is the report's characterization of eleven pieces of pottery as "early Roman" (*i.e.*, potentially dating to the time of Jesus) or even "Hellenistic." The archaeologist responsible for the NVF pottery datings is a certain Yehuda Rapuano. I took him to task in my rebuttal, showing that in every case the shards in question could have been produced as much as a century after 'the time of Christ' — this according to the standard dating references that Rapuano *himself* used. My published conclusion as stated in *BAIAS*: "in every case where Rapuano suggests a pre-70 dating, he offers no support" [2008:102]. In other words, he arbitrarily assumed the *earliest possible dating* for these shards. On that arbitrary basis, the entire NVF report claimed settlement contemporary with 'the time of Jesus.' In fact, the artifacts in question fit in very well with my overall thesis that Nazareth was first settled in the years between the two Jewish revolts. As with the two stone vessels mentioned above, they constitute no evidence at all for human presence at the turn of the era.

Incidentally, there were several other problems in the NVF report, *e.g.*, some of the artifacts were given different dates, findspots, and even descriptions from one page to another ('double dating'). In all, it was a very embarrassing report, which is why it had to be completely rewritten after my rebuttal appeared.

At the minimum, the NVF excavation is controversial and constitutes weak evidence indeed (much less the principal evidence) for a village "at the time of Jesus." Yet Ehrman claims that this evidence is "compelling," presumably solely on the basis of Rapuano's authority as an "archaeologist." But I will affirm here that authority is not sufficient, for *authority does not replace evidence.*

7 For the continuation of the tit-for-tat regarding this excavation, please visit my online website devoted to Nazareth archaeology, www.nazarethmyth.info, "Scandal 5."

The Nazareth Village Farm is associated with a multimillion-dollar megaresort called the Nazareth Village. The resort's stated vision is to recreate streets and stone houses "inhabited by actors and storytellers in authentic garb, [who] will illuminate the life and teachings of Jesus. A Parable Walk, museum, study center and restaurant are also planned..."[8] It has been well funded by an international consortium of Christian groups called the Miracle of Nazareth International Foundation. Since the project's inception the consortium has raised over $60 million towards the venture. Contributors in the U.S. have included former President Jimmy Carter, Pat Boone, and Rev. Reggie White, the former Green Bay Packer football star.

Here the intimate connection between academia and commerce is patent, witnessed also by the fact that the Nazareth Village resort is under the auspices of the evangelical University of the Holy Land (UHL) whose Director, not surprisingly, is none other than Stephen Pfann — the principal author of the NVF excavation report.

The "house from the time of Jesus"

To continue our review of "demonstrable material evidence from *ca.* 700 BCE to *ca.* 100 CE" (point #1), Ehrman points to the much-touted 2009 excavation of a "house from the time of Jesus" [*DJE?* 196–97] — excavated by the now-familiar Yardenna Alexandre, an archaeologist working for the Israel Antiquities Authority (IAA).[9] News of this small excavation broke just before Christmas 2009:

> On winter solstice morning a veritable gaggle of international media representatives were assembled on Franciscan property in Nazareth, Israel, for the promised news. They stood outside the Church of the Annunciation, a few yards from the fabled spot where the fourteen-year old Virgin Mary received the assignation

8 *Biblical Archaeology Review* [May–June 1999: 16]. At the time of this writing (August 2012) the Web-site for the Nazareth Village is http://nazarethvillage.com/home.php.

9 I also have addressed this bogus claim elsewhere: "Christianity at the crossroads — Nazareth in the crosshairs." *American Atheist* [July–Aug. 2010: 8–12]. PDF online at: http://www.nazarethmyth.info/naz4article.pdf. *See also*: http://www.nazarethmyth.info/scandalsix.html.

> from the archangel Gabriel that she would be bearing God, or the Son of God, or God with Us ("Emmanuel," Mt 1:23)...
>
> AP, UPI, Reuters, and Agence France Presse were all present (I mean, at last year's press conference, not at the fabled Annunciation for which there were no witnesses). By nightfall the news had circled the globe. HOUSE FROM THE TIME OF JESUS FOUND IN NAZARETH screamed the FOX headline...[10]

The timing smacked of propaganda, not news, but a couple of other aspects of the excavation also aroused my suspicion. First of all, results of this excavation have never been published in any scholarly way. ("Publication" here must be carefully distinguished from the plethora of "news articles" that appeared in the general press.) A possible exception was a short one-paragraph statement from the IAA that was briefly on the Internet. It made no mention of first-century remains, much less of evidence from the turn of the era ("time of Jesus"), but only to "the Roman period" which, of course, lasted into the fourth century CE.

Once again we see Ms. Alexandre evading professional responsibility by not publishing her results so that the rest of the world can verify that what she claims is true. In the Nazareth house excavation she made vaunted claims which immediately circled the world but she failed to produce evidence to substantiate them. We will see this again in the coin imbroglio below.

A second suspicious aspect of this house excavation is that *the site was quickly covered over by a Christian tourist venue so that no further authentication nor verification is possible.* The "Mary of Nazareth International Center" now stands on the site. Hence, we have (1) no verification in the published literature, and (2) not even the possibility of verification due to subsequent construction at the site. No one can ever really know what was at the "Nazareth house."

All this is simply background to Ehrman's glib affirmation that the house Alexandre excavated "dates to the days of Jesus" [*DJE?* 196]. Ehrman writes that he had "personally written to the principal archaeologist, Yardena Alexandre," and she told him all kinds of

10 "Christianity at the crossroads — Nazareth in the crosshairs." *American Atheist* [July–Aug. 2010: 9]

things which he believes *without published evidence.* This is the problem with Nazareth archaeology: scholars are trusting their peers in lieu of relying upon verifiable evidence. In an article for *American Atheist* I wrote — almost a year before the Christmas 'discoveries':

> Archaeologists have been digging at Nazareth for over a hundred years and, as my book attempts to show, all the recovered finds include not a single artefact that can with certainty be dated before 100 CE. In other words, no demonstrable evidence dating either to the time of Jesus or to earlier Hellenistic times has been found...
>
> We should all look with great suspicion on new evidence "coming to light" which conflicts with the evidentiary profile of the last hundred years, new evidence which astonishingly reopens the case for settlement in the time of Christ. Given the revelations documented in my book, and the lengthy history of duplicity associated with Nazareth archaeology, we have every right to insist that any new evidence be rigorously documented as to findspot, circumstances of discovery, and description (preferably accompanied by photo or diagram). Any claim of new, pre-70 CE evidence, should raise an alarum red flag. Such a claim tells us more about the persons making it than about Nazareth.[11]

To show the vacuity of Ehrman's sources, he closes his Nazareth section by discussing an AP story. *Nota bene*: here we witness a premiere New Testament scholar arguing on the basis of information from the Associated Press. Ehrman's parting summation is vacuous: "Jesus really came from there, as attested in multiple sources." Presumably, those sources which he finds so persuasive include AP, Reuters, and Agence France Presse.

Hellenistic coins?

Our search for Ehrman's "many compelling pieces" of evidence continues. He mentions a rather curious story involving coins [*DJE?* 195] that I shall now address. The coins in question already enjoyed

11 "Nazareth, Faith, and the Dark Option," *American Atheist* [Jan. 2009: 12 (online at http://www.nazarethmyth.info/naz3article.html).

a rather sordid history in the Nazareth literature before the appearance of *DJE?*, but Ehrman now adds a new twist.

He writes that 165 coins were found at Nazareth and that some of them dated as early as Hellenistic times. These coins have, in fact, been passed from scholar to scholar in the recent literature with apparently no concern for where the coins were found nor for any precision regarding the dating of individual coins. I will here recap the growth of this brouhaha, which seems to have become a pet claim for those who are now arguing the traditional case for Nazareth's existence at the 'time of Jesus.'

It should first be noted that, prior to 2006, very few coins had been found in the Nazareth basin (a resumé is below in Citation #4). I dispose of the coin evidence in two short paragraphs of *The Myth of Nazareth* [*MON* 196]). The earliest coin from the Nazareth basin *that has been documented* dates to the time of Emperor Constantius II (*r.* 337–351 CE). In 1997–98 Ms. Alexandre excavated near Mary's Well at the northern end of the Nazareth basin. The first notice of this excavation appeared much later in the form of a "pre-publication notice" for the IAA dated "1st May 2006" which — curiously — has to my knowledge not been published. Alexandre shared that signed notice with me via an email attachment during my research for the book. It is a standard half-page report and looks entirely official both in format and wording, similar to those produced for the IAA and routinely published in the Israeli journal *Atiqot* [*See Figure 1, p. 350*].

In her report Ms. Alexandre notes remains from the excavation which date generally "from the Roman, the Crusader, the Mamluk and the Ottoman periods." She signals the presence of "Middle Roman pottery." She notes no material dating earlier than this. As regards coins, Alexandre mentions them three times in a context of the Crusader, Mamluk, and Ottoman periods (11th century CE onwards). She notes "the dredging of many 14-15th century small denomination coins" and "coins from Feodalic France" (9th to 15th centuries CE). In the same paragraph she also signals the presence of "worn coins." The latter were unearthed around the Mamluk vaulted Fountain House together with "considerable quantities of broken jars and other vessels, coloured glass bracelets, [and] wire earrings" which in the previous sentence she dates to the Mamluk period. Nothing in her description suggests that any of the coins or other material goes back to Roman times or to late antiquity. I did not even mention Alexandre's report in my book because it was "pre-publication" and because it contained no verifiable material evidence dating to Early Roman times, that is, to the time of 'Jesus of Nazareth' or to BCE times.

The small, unobtrusive Mary's Well excavation received no further scholarly attention for several years. Then, in Dec. 2007, appeared the NVF "Final Report" in *BAIAS* authored, we recall, by Stephen Pfann, Ross Voss, and Yehudah Rapuano.[12] On page 39 we encounter a section entitled, "Area A: finds made during the construction of the Nazareth Village" where we read:

> [Citation #4] Various finds were made during the construction of the Nazareth Village Project in 2000–2002 and were recorded by Mark Goodman. These conprise [*sic*] a number of unstratified finds including a coin and pottery vessel fragments from Area A (Figs. 19 and 20).[13] This represents the latest Byzantine coin that has been found in the Nazareth area.
>
> From Bagatti's excavations in Nazareth 4 coins were found, all Byzantine (mid-fourth to early fifth century) and 2 coins from the vicinity: one Late Roman (the earliest coin, mid-third century) and one Byzantine (late fifth to early sixth century). These were recorded as follows: Grotto no. 25: 3 unidentifiable Byzantine (one with head of Emperor; two very small, typical of late fourth to early fifth century AD) (Bagatti 1969:I: 46). Grotto No. 29 (embedded in the plaster): one with head of Emperor, apparently Constans (AD 337–350) (Bagatti 1969: I, 210, Fig. 172). In addition there were finds from the village: one coin of Anastasius (AD 491–518) (Bagatti 1969: I, 234). Surface find from

12 The 61 page NVF report begins with the following sections: "The Nazareth Farm site discovery and survey," "The Nazareth Village Farm: initial survey," "GPS mapping survey," followed by a lengthy "Summary of excavated areas," and then "The stone quarries."

13 Fig. 19 follows. It is a coin from the time of Tiberius II (578–82 CE). The authors add a few lines of description of the coin which, incidentally, includes the Chi-Rho staurogram. Fig. 20 is of a Gaza Ware bowl of the Early Bronze III.

> ploughing the land around the village: one coin of Gordian III (AD 238–244) (Bagatti 1969: I, 251). More than 60 other coins from the Islamic to Mamluk Period were unearthed in the 1955 excavations (Bagatii 1969: II, 194–201). *In addition, 165 coins were uncovered by Yardenna Alexandre in the 1997-1998 excavations at Mary's Well, Nazareth. The coins were overwhelmingly Mamluk, but also included a few Hellenistic, Hasmonaean, Early Roman, Byzantine, Umayyad and Crusader coins (Alexandre, forthcoming).*
>
> The unstratified pottery vessels included a complete Gaza Ware bowl (Fig. 20), which was found during the clearance operations which preceded the construction of the Nazareth Village... [NVFR 39–40. Emphasis added.]

I was amazed to read the italicized words above. In her IAA report communicated to me [*See again Figure 1, next page*], Alexandre had mentioned *nothing* about coins from "Hellenistic, Hasmonaean, Early Roman" times. Had such critically important coin evidence been found in her excavation, she surely would have included it in her official report. It is also interesting that *the official report has never been published*, despite the regular dust-off "Alexandre, forthcoming" — we are now almost fifteen years after the original excavation and her report has still not appeared!

My first response to this coin anomaly was an article that appeared in *American Atheist* [Jan. 2009:10–13]. I cite the pertinent paragraphs:

> [Citation #5] Undoubtedly there is great pressure on the tradition now to discover such telling evidence from Nazareth. Continuing pilgrimage depends on it. The incipient Nazareth Village depends on it. Perhaps the entire Jesus-story depends on it. This is the time for stalwart defenders of the tradition to exercise their resourcefulness and acumen in defense of the Christian story and to prevent a wound to the Achilles' heel from festering and becoming fatal. Let's not be too surprised if remarkable new 'finds' at Nazareth conveniently appear in the next few years — finds substantiating a settlement there at the time of Christ. To fit the demands of the tradition that are now in print, the forthcoming material will have to be early and non-funereal.

René Salm

Well, guess what? According to the NVF report, a cache of Hellenistic and Early Roman coins has recently been 'found' at Mary's Well (at the Northern end of the Nazareth basin). Wow. Nothing remotely similar has ever been found in the Nazareth basin. The earliest coin found there dates to about 350 CE. A cache of Hellenistic and Early Roman coins is exactly the sort of evidence which the tradition needs in order to decide the matter in its favor.

ARCHAEOLOGICAL EXCAVATIONS AT MARY'S WELL, NAZARETH

Yardenna Alexandre, Israel Antiquities Authority
1st May 2006

Archaeological excavations were carried out in the Fountain Square and in the adjacent St. Gabriel's Square in 1997-1998 by the Israel Antiquities Authority under the direction of Yardenna Alexandre on the initiative of the Government Tourist Ministry and the Nazareth Municipality in the context of the Nazareth 2000 development programme.

The main excavations were carried out under the modern 1960s concrete Fountain House, which was demolished with the aim of reconstructing the ruined Ottoman stone Fountain House. The archaeological remains exposed dated from the Roman, the Crusader, the Mamluk and the Ottoman periods. From the Roman period part of a covered dressed stone channel was exposed, as well as some wall stubs and Middle Roman pottery. Major construction works carried out in the Crusader period produced finely-dressed stone pools paved with marble slabs, a fine plastered arched reservoir and large and small stone channels, the major of which may have carried water from the spring the the Church of the Annunciation. The evidence indicates that a clear Crusader presence at the site, including a variety of local and imported glazed wares and coins from Feodalic France. In the early Mamluk period the Fountain House continued in use, without destruction and in the fourteenth century the Mamluks built a new vaulted Fountain House, whilst the old Crusader pools served as a 'shop', or small storeroom for a local potter's wares. The activity around the Fountain House is reflected in considerable quantities of broken jars and other vessels, coloured glass bracelets, wire earrings and worn coins. A fifteenth century destruction of the shop seems to have been followed by a period of delapidation. A clean-up including the dredging of many 14-15th century small denomination coins, may date the Franciscan efforts in the early 17th century (known from the written records), but David Roberts drawing from the 1840s indicates that the Fountain House was in a bad state of repair. The vaulted Fountain House was rebuilt in the 1860s and stood until it was replaced in the 1960s.

The limited excavations in the St. Gabriel's Church Square were carried out as some ancient walls were exposed when the infrastructures were being renewed. The excavations revealed a complete underground vaulted reservoir with four well openings in a row, overlain by a stone-paved courtyard. This plastered reservoir or cistern was in use in the 18th-early 19th centuries. Two large stone channels were exposed here, the ancient of which seems to have been part of the Crusader channel that originally transported the water from the source, under and past the St. Gabriel's church and down to the water house. The vaulted reservoir, however, captured these waters and cut off the connection with the Fountain House. The second channel was built after the vaulted reservoir, to bypass this reservoir and again allow the waters to reach the Fountain House. Some fragmentary stone walls and floors were cut by the vaulted reservoir, thus indicating that there was some occupation here in the Hellenistic, Crusader and Mamluk periods.

Figure 1. Yardenna Alexandre's prepublication IAA report.

> My skepticism is increased by the fact that I possess a pre-publication report (dated 2006) from the Israel Antiquities Authority signed by the archaeologist who dug at Mary's Well. In it she mentions no early coins at all. The only datable coins she signals were from the 14th–15th centuries CE. Hmm... What's going on here?
>
> All of a sudden, claims of Jesus-era evidence are being made at Nazareth. Putative turn-of-the-era evidence is popping up all over the place — on the surface at the Nazareth Village Farm (see above), at Mary's Well... Where next?

So far, then, we have an imputation of turn of the era evidence: the NVFR authors (Citation #4) are imputing such evidence to Yardenna Alexandre. Also curious is that Pfann *et al.* had no obvious reason to bring up Alexandre's findings at all: her excavation had nothing to do with the Nazareth Village Farm but was conducted two kilometers to the north. Why, I wondered, were the NVFR authors bringing up an excavation that had taken place a decade earlier and far away, and why were they alleging finds there that were not even in Ms. Alexandre's own IAA report?

The next development is a four page "Reply to Salm" published in the subsequent issue of *BAIAS*. In it, the Nazareth Village Farm proponents (once again) impute early evidence to Alexandre. Now, however, they go one step further and claim to have received a verbatim statement from her attesting to their Early Roman coin claim:

> [Citation 6. Pfann and Rapuano write...] Pace Salm, Dr. Alexandre herself provided the following text to quote in our report: 'In addition, 165 coins were uncovered by Yardenna Alexandre in the 1997–1998 excavations at Mary's Well, Nazareth. The coins were overwhelmingly Mamluk, but also included a few Hellenistic, Hasmonaean, Early Roman, Byzantine, Umayyad and Crusader coins' [*BAIAS* 2008:106].

So, Pfann *et al.* are here alleging that the two critical sentences from their former 61-page report were a verbatim quotation from "Dr. Alexandre herself." A glance above at Citation #4, however, shows that the sentences under examination lack quotation marks and are simply part of *their* prose. If it were indeed a quotation it would be a curious one for several reasons: (1) Dr. Alexandre would be referring to herself in the third person; (2) Pfann and Rapuano would have embedded two of her verbatim sentences into their prose without signaling that to the reader; and (3) they would have done so without any acknowledgment of attribution. Hmm... Presumably, then, in this whole boondoggle regarding the Nazareth coins we are to believe the following sequence of events:

> – Alexandre excavated 165 coins at Mary's Well but *omitted* critical information about Hellenistic and Roman coins in her official IAA report which she shared with me;
>
> – While *withholding* such early coin information from myself (and presumably also from the IAA), Alexandre subsequently selectively shared it with Pfann *et al.* working at the other end of the Nazareth basin;
>
> – Pfann *et al.* included that *unprecedented* early coin information (relating to Alexandre's excavation) in their 2007 report dealing with the NVF;
>
> – After being critiqued by myself, Pfann *et al.* alleged that the two sentences under scrutiny were a *verbatim* quote from Alexandre, despite the fact that the original passage doesn't look like a quotation and despite the fact that in substance their claim conflicts with Alexandre's IAA report which I already had in my possession for two years.

Finally, Ehrman enters the fray, decidedly aligns himself with the tradition, and adds a disturbing new twist. The following passage occurs directly after Ehrman's over-the-top statement of "Many compelling pieces" of Jesus-era evidence being found at Nazareth [*DJE?* 195]. He writes:

> [Citation #7] For one thing, archaeologists have excavated a farm connected with the village, and it dates to the time of Jesus. [Ehrman is speaking of the NVF, and he bases this assertion on Rapuano's eleven pieces of 'evidence' falsely dated to the time of Jesus.] Salm disputes the finding of the archaeologists who did the excavation (remember that he himself is not an archaeologist but bases his views on what the real archaeologists — all of whom disagree with him — say). For one thing when archaeologist Yardena Alexandre indicated that 165 coins were found *in this excavation*, she specified in

> the report that some of them were late, from the fourteenth or fifteenth century. This suits Salm's purposes just fine. But as it turns out, among the coins were some that date to the Hellenistic, Hasmonean, and early Roman period, that is, the days of Jesus. Salm objected that this was not stated in Alexandre's report, but Alexandre has verbally confirmed that in fact it is the case: there were coins in the collection that date to the time prior to the Jewish uprising. [*DJE?* 195. My comments in brackets and emphasis added.]

"In this excavation"? Ehrman doesn't seem to understand that we are speaking of *two different excavations:* one at Mary's Well and one at the NVF. He is apparently now claiming that the alleged Hellenistic, Hasmonean, and early Roman period coins were found at the NVF! I am carefully putting us on notice here because, given past shenanigans at Nazareth, anything and everything is possible. Who knows? Given the prominence of Ehrman's book, pretty soon the tradition may run with this novel and *very false* line that Jesus-era coins have been found at the Nazareth Village Farm (by Alexandre?). I wouldn't put it past an increasingly desperate tradition.

Let us be clear here: when Ehrman writes "Alexandre has verbally confirmed that in fact it is the case" he is reporting hearsay. Without published finds at Mary's Well from the pen of Alexandre (and she has dragged her feet on this) any imputation of Hellenistic to Early Roman coins ascribed to her is just that: an imputation. It is not "evidence."

Regarding these coins, we can conclude the following: (a) In 1997–98 Alexandre excavated a large cache of 14th–15th century CE coins near Mary's Well at the northern end of the Nazareth basin. Her IAA report noted no coins dating prior to the fourteenth century CE. (b) Turn-of-the-era coin finds were later imputed to Alexandre by Pfann, Rapuano, and now by Ehrman — finds which have never been published. (c) Poor scholarship mars the work of all the above academics, in that the NVF report was riddled with errors (as my "Response" in *BAIAS* 2008 shows, requiring the publication of a wholesale "Amendment"). Furthermore, Ehrman conflates two excavations into one. Finally, Alexandre herself has been reported to admit that her original IAA notice omitted critical Jesus-era evidence and was not definitive — yet she has refused to set the record straight via publication.

I leave the reader to decide whether all these irregularities are merely atrocious sloppiness on the part of several scholars or whether they are evidence of collusion and unethical behavior.[14]

Shama's Roman bathhouse

On page 196 of his book Ehrman defers on several issues to Ken Dark and the latter's "thoroughly negative review" of my book [*BAIAS* 2008:140–146]. I have dealt with Prof. Dark's comments elsewhere.[15] There is nothing in his review which impacts the material record from the Nazareth basin at the turn of the era. Unfortunately, the material record seems less interesting to Ehrman than hearsay and the robust veneration of credentials.

The business about "hydrology" that Ehrman mentions [*DJE?* 196] is borrowed from Dark's weak review of my book (which also appeared in *BAIAS* 2008). It is a straw man who, apparently, gives Ehrman the opportunity to engage in invective: "Salm has misunderstood both the hydrology (how the water systems worked) and the topography (the layout) of Nazareth."

I deal with the topographical aspects of the Nazareth argument later in this chapter. As for the hydrology, I may understand it better

14 *Editors Note:* When Hellenistic, Hasmonean, Early Roman, and Byzantine coins were pulled like rabbits from a hat out of Alexandre's cache of 14th–15th-century coins, did anyone consider the implications of finding coins dating to a period 332–63 BCE *in the same cache* with coins nearly two thousand years younger? Does this mean that she had come upon the safety deposit pot of a rare-coin collector? Does this mean that the circulation half-life of Hellenistic coins was almost a millennium in magnitude? If Hellenistic coins had circulated so long, why weren't more than "a few" Byzantine coins found? Was their circulation half-life for some reason much shorter than that of the Hellenistic coins? If those Hellenistic coins should ever be proved to exist, what evidence is there that they had ever been to 'Nazareth' before the fifteenth century? If Alexandre ever gets around to publishing her official report, may we hope that she will provide therein some explanation for this numismatic mystery? As a scientist, Ms. Alexandre may be assumed to be proficient in mathematics; and, since this problem is ideal for application of Bayesian analysis, we would hope that she would include the findings of such an analysis in her publication. — FRZ

15 "Nazareth, Faith, and the Dark Option." *American Atheist* [Jan. 2009: 10–13] (online at http://www.nazarethmyth.info/naz3article.html). See also my response to Dark's review at http:// www.nazarethmyth.info/bibl.html (#10).

than Dark and Ehrman aver, yet it is quite irrelevant. Hydrology has absolutely no bearing on the existence or non-existence of a settlement at the turn of the era. No one has argued that it does — except a certain entrepreneurially gifted owner of a souvenir shop in Nazareth by the name of Elias Shama. His shop is near Mary's Well and is called "Cactus" — at least it was a few years ago (whether or not it still exists I do not know). Shama claims that a Roman bath house exists directly under his shop, a bath house which he dates to the turn of the era. His claim has attracted an enormous number of tourists to his shop, though archaeologists — including Ms. Alexandre herself — have dated those waterworks to at least one millennium after the turn of the era [*MON* 133]. Nevertheless, Mr. Shama's outlandish claims have received much publicity on the Internet and in traditionalist print outlets such as conservative religious journals and tourist releases geared toward Christian pilgrims to the Holy Land.

The oil lamps and tombs at Nazareth

The preceding discussion refers to the first of the seven points with which I began this rebuttal of Ehrman's section on Nazareth archaeology. *Point two* refers to the 25 CE+ dating of the earliest oil lamps at Nazareth. This — together with the 50+ CE dating for all the post-Iron Age tombs at Nazareth (point 3) — forms the backbone of my thesis that the settlement of Nazareth could not have existed at the turn of the era. Ehrman does not once mention the oil lamp evidence, perhaps because it is summarily damning to the tradition's case. After all, what possible rebuttal is there to the scholarly verdict that the earliest oil lamps excavated in the Nazareth basin date no earlier than 25 CE [*MON* 170]? I say "scholarly verdict" because that dating is not mine but is the professional conclusion of oil lamp specialists as noted in my book. This being the case, how then is it possible to envisage a village existing in Hellenistic times and at the turn of the era when every single oil lamp recovered from the basin (scores have been found in over one century of digging) dates to the common era?

Bow-spouted in form (mislabeled "Herodian"), the earliest Nazareth oil lamps were still being produced as late as the Bar Kochba rebellion. They can be no earlier than 25 CE, but that is a charitably early dating for any of them. In all likelihood these lamps were manufactured between the two Jewish revolts — the same time that the settlement of Nazareth came into being (*MON* 207).

Though Ehrman conveniently ignores the oil lamp evidence, he devotes more than a page to the Nazareth tombs. *Point three* in the seven point template above notes that all the post-Iron Age tombs at Nazareth date later than 50 CE. These tombs are of the well-known kokh type (also called loculus tombs) which consist of single-burial shafts radiating from a central chamber [*MON* 158*ff*]. Ehrman does not contest this point. He merely notes that kokh tombs were expensive and speculates, therefore, that in the first century the poor Nazarenes used shallow burials which have not been found. His is a convenient argument from silence, for there is no evidence for such shallow burials at Nazareth.

We can summarize the foregoing Nazareth discussion as follows:

(1) **The lack of demonstrable material evidence from *ca.* 700 BCE to *ca.* 100 CE.** Ehrman rejects this but provides no evidence for settlement before 70 CE. He simply asserts the existence of "many compelling pieces of archaeological evidence" from the time of Jesus. This bold but bald-faced untruth ranks with other egregious misstatements by reputable archaeologists documented in my book.

(2) **The 25 CE+ dating of the earliest oil lamps at Nazareth**. Ehrman does not even mention oil lamps.

(3) **The 50 CE+ dating of all the post-Iron Age tombs at Nazareth.** Ehrman grudgingly accepts this dating of kokh tombs, a dating which has forced the tradition to revise its model of Nazareth's beginnings (see below).

Thus Ehrman's treatment of Nazareth archaeology amounts to very little. Regarding the first major point he provides no evidence to buttress his cause. The second he simply ignores, while the third he accepts. In sum, Ehrman brings nothing at all to the table as regards Nazareth archaeology.

Burden of Proof

The remainder of this chapter addresses the tradition's fall-back position as regards Nazareth, as reflected by Ehrman's book, and by other recent developments. That defensive position is now coalescing four years after publication of *The Myth of Nazareth*. It is a posture which — while overtly in rank denial — grudgingly accepts that the material evidence at Nazareth indeed points to post-Jesus times. So, Ehrman challenges [*DJE?* 194]: "just because later habitation can be established in Nazareth, how does that show that the town was not inhabited earlier?" Note the burden of proof: it is entirely upon the shoulders of the skeptic, while the traditional view is assumed to be correct until *proven* wrong. It is the latter part of this proposition that is most egregious — the tradition, apparently, can say whatever it wishes (no matter how outlandish) without the need for evidence. Furthermore, it will continue to do so *until that is no longer possible.*

Ehrman falls into the double negatives characteristic of a desperate argument: 'Well, even though the evidence is post-Jesus, that *doesn't* prove that Nazareth *didn't* exist in the time of Jesus!' In an American court of law, of course, the accused is innocent until proven guilty "beyond a shadow of a doubt." A similar standard of protection seems to be assumed by the tradition — it is correct (that is, 'innocent') even if the weight of evidence is against it. It is even correct if the substantial totality of evidence is against it. Indeed, it is correct until it is *proven* wrong!

Apparently the tradition assumes a free pass as regards evidence. It is, in effect, saying to Mythicists: "You haven't *proved* that Nazareth wasn't there." This same *modus operandi*, of course, is elsewhere extended to protect pious beliefs regarding the life of Jesus, his miracles, and his resurrection from the grave. In all these cases the tradition challenges nonbelievers to prove a negative. However, this is often impossible (as the tradition is well aware). In one of my articles for the journal *American Atheist* [January, 2009] I explain how it's formally impossible to disprove a myth — especially when common sense is jettisoned:

> After all, neither you nor I can prove that Santa Claus doesn't exist. We can go to the North Pole, can dig up there (under water and ice!) all we want, and can find absolutely no evidence for his gift-packing facility nor for his team of flying reindeer. But to a believer, we can't prove those don't exist. All the believer has to say is, "Well, you didn't look in the right places," "He's hiding," or even "He's invisible." Unfortunately, common myths involving Jesus are every bit as weird [*DJE?* 12].

I discuss such arguments from silence in my book [*MON* 288–91], where I sum up the material evidence from Nazareth in two short columns:

I BCE **Evidence of Nazareth at the Time of Jesus**	**I CE** **Evidence of the birth of Nazareth in the common era**
— none —	After 25 CE: All oil lamps After 50 CE: All post-Iron age tombs After 50 CE: All pottery and other movable evidence

It is clear that we are dealing here with an extremely tilted playing field. The tradition arrogates correctness to its position which, after all, is purely speculative — that is, *without any evidence.* The proof of the pudding is my work. It has shown that the tradition has not actually produced any Nazareth material from the time of Jesus in one hundred years of digging — despite Ehrman's absurd claim of "many compelling pieces of archaeological evidence."

However, archaeology is thankfully now able to prove the negative — simply by digging in the ground. With today's very careful and advanced excavation tools (where sometimes even pollen[16] is counted!)

16 Editor's note: If the NVF theme-park project had any scientific purposes at all, it would have carried out radiometric, dendrochronological, and palynological studies of the soils and archaeological matrices of the NVF area in order to determine the types of crops being grown there (if any) and the agricultural microclimate at the turn of the era. The fact that such studies were not done belies the apologetic nature of the 'archaeology' associated with the venture. — FRZ

what is *not* found can be as significant as what *is* found. As I write in the introduction to *The Myth of Nazareth*:

> This is what gives the Nazareth issue such great potency. Unlike aspects of the gospel story that are quite beyond verification — the miracles of Jesus, his bodily resurrection, his virgin birth, or even his human nature — the existence of Nazareth two thousand years ago can be proved or disproved by digging in the ground. Because the archaeology of a site is empirically demonstrable, "Nazareth" is in a category apart. To this day, it preserves the explosive potential to either prove or disprove the gospel accounts [*MON xii*].

This is just common sense. When one looks for something and doesn't find it, one doesn't say: "Well, I don't see it — but I think it's there." Such a statement would be absurd, yet it is precisely the situation that obtains with a turn-of-the-era Nazareth. People have been looking for over one hundred years and there is not a shred of material evidence for human habitation at the "time of Jesus." My exhaustive review of *all* the evidence shows that only two artifacts — both stone vessels — *could* date to the turn of the era. However, such vessels continued in production as late as the Bar Kokhba revolt (135 CE). Hence their presence in the Nazareth assemblage is as diagnostic of human presence in the second century CE as it is for before 70 CE.

Thus, Ehrman and the tradition have even lost the argument from silence. All that remains to them is rhetoric. Presently, the following illogic obtains: (a) no evidence is forthcoming from Nazareth at the turn of the era; (b) all the evidence is demonstrably later; yet (c) the tradition *insists* these evidentiary results do not invalidate the supposition that Nazareth existed at the time of "Jesus." This is the irrational last stand of a faltering tradition.

As long as skeptics are placed in the position of needing to prove *anything* and *everything* to traditionalists they are playing by the wrong rules and have already lost the fight — for traditionalists can simply refuse to be convinced, even if in doing so they must resort to quaint irrationality ('faith'). Indeed, evidence and reason have never had much influence over the pious Christian. The antidote is simple: common sense.

The burden of proof should reside on the shoulders of the one who takes a position contrary to common sense. In the case of Nazareth, this means that it resides squarely on the shoulders of the tradition which insists on the existence of a village at the turn of the era — but does so without evidence.

Common sense, unfortunately, draws little water for the person of faith. Faith constitutes a curious blind spot in our human psychology, a mental drunkenness in which jettisoning reason is altogether laudable — 'for the glory of God.' Somehow, the abdication of reason for 'God' is validation of one's commitment:

> For the word of the cross is folly to those who are perishing, but to us who are being saved it is the power of God. For it is written, "I will destroy the wisdom of the wise, and the cleverness of the clever I will thwart."
>
> Where is the wise man? Where is the scribe? Where is the debater of this age? Has not God made foolish the wisdom of the world? For since, in the wisdom of God, the world did not know God through wisdom, it pleased God through the folly of what we preach to save those who believe. For Jews demand signs and Greeks seek wisdom, but we preach Christ crucified, a stumbling block to Jews and folly to Gentiles, but to those who are called, both Jews and Greeks, Christ the power of God and the wisdom of God. For the foolishness of God is wiser than men, and the weakness of God is stronger than men. [1 Cor. 1:18–25]

Here is a great divide in biblical studies: to believers faith is sufficient, while to reasoning people it is foolishness. Thus, skeptics and believers speak different languages and are talking past one another. One group provides evidence, while the other stentoriously proclaims the officially sanctioned message carefully crafted long ago:

> We believe in one Lord, Jesus Christ, the only Son of God, eternally begotten of the Father... For us and for our salvation he came down from heaven: by the power of the Holy Spirit he became incarnate

> from the Virgin Mary, and was made man. For our sake he was crucified under Pontius Pilate; he suffered death and was buried. On the third day he rose again in accordance with the Scriptures; he ascended into heaven and is seated at the right hand of the Father. He will come again in glory to judge the living and the dead, and his kingdom will have no end. [Nicene Creed, 325 CE]

As the data of science accumulate in favor of skeptics, they will continue to show that the above has no rational basis and is, indeed, foolishness. Psychiatrists, too, will eventually step in and diagnose the malaise of Christianity for what it is: wishful thinking carried to a delusional extreme. Historians, also, can show that the growth and resilience of Christianity has had as much to do with the aggrandizement of power as with loving one's neighbor. They can show that the quest for global domination is not restricted to the Hitlers and Stalins of the world, but that 'dominionism' is part-and-parcel of organized religion.

The location of the ancient village

Like the post-Jesus dating of the oil lamps and the tombs, the presence of tombs under the Venerated Area at Nazareth is damning for the tradition. After all, there can be little that is more embarrassing than discovering not one but several tombs under the house where the Virgin Mary allegedly grew up. How to explain this to the flood of tourists who are continually visiting the church? "Well," we can imagine the pious tour guide saying, "here is where the Angel Gabriel announced to Mary, 'Blessed art thou amongst women,' and [walking a few feet in *any* direction] here is a tomb, and here is another one, and here another'..." Of course, this interesting scenario does not actually take place, and one will find not the remotest mention of a tomb in any of the literature handed out to tourists. Bagatti scarcely even mentions tombs in his two-volume tome. But the tombs are there, carefully documented in my book and known since the end of the nineteenth century. At least three exist directly under the Church of the Annunciation, and two to four more are close by [*MON* Illus. 5.3 & 5.4].

The inescapable conclusion is that the alleged home of the Virgin Mary lies in a Jewish cemetery. Of course, Jews were proscribed from living near tombs, a source of ritual impurity. The Catholic Church did not take sufficient note of this fact before the Second World War, and several of their amateur archaeologists gleefully described and even diagrammed the tombs in question, hoping one of them might be the tomb of, say, St. Joseph himself. But the presence of tombs in the Venerated Area is fatal to the traditional view of Nazareth. Incorporation of this inconvenient evidence has required a 'return to the drawing board,' as it were. The steep slope, lack of domestic evidence on the hillside, and the presence there of tombs is all exceedingly uncomfortable for the tradition which is now scrambling to concoct a scenario to satisfy all the data, one whereby Jesus' Nazareth somehow existed before the tombs were constructed. The tradition seems now disposed to propose the following curious sequence of events:

A. Mary and her future husband Joseph were neighbors living on the steep slope above Nazareth at the turn of the era;

B. Mary received a visitation from the Archangel Gabriel telling her that she would conceive a child;

C. Mary wed Joseph and gave birth to Jesus;

D. Jesus, Mary, and Joseph lived at Joseph's home (the Church of St. Joseph 100 m north of the Church of the Annunciation);

E. Several generations later Nazareth 'moved' from the hillside to the valley floor;

F. In the second century CE tombs were constructed where Mary and Joseph used to live.

For those who have read my book, this is a return to the "mobile Nazareth" hypothesis of Clemens Kopp, a Catholic priest who, in the mid-20th century attempted to accommodate the gospel version of Nazareth to the incoming scientific evidence. In fact, Kopp had claimed that the settlement moved twice [*MON* 65–60]. What we have above is the only scenario remaining to the tradition, for none other will accommodate both the exigencies of scripture and the material evidence revealed in my work. Recognizing this, Ken Dark — and now Ehrman — insinuate that Nazareth moved and that tombs from a later time do *not* prove there was *no* village earlier. This is the double negative alluded to earlier. Ehrman writes:

> It is hard to understand why tombs in Nazareth that can be dated to the days after Jesus indicate that there was no town there during the days of Jesus. That is to say, just because later habitation can be established in Nazareth, how does that show that the town was not inhabited earlier? [*DJE?* 194]

I have already shown that archaeology can indeed show the absence of settlement. However, Ehrman seizes upon the fact that no one has dug on the valley floor — which is where he supposes the settlement existed *later*. He writes:

> This view [that archaeologists have never excavated the Nazareth valley floor] creates insurmountable problems for [Salm's] thesis. For one thing, there is the simple question of logic. If archaeologists have not dug where Salm thinks the village was located, what is his basis for saying that it did not exist in the days of Jesus? [*DJE?* 195]

I have two problems with this tack. Firstly, Ehrman *specifically asked me this question via e-mail* when he was researching the book. My answer was clear and his feigning ignorance here I find a tad deceitful:

> Bart, July 13, 2011
>
> Thanks for the email. To answer you... I take a scientific approach, looking at the evidence, and drawing conclusions therefrom. There is absolutely nothing in the material evidence to suggest habitation in the Nazareth basin at the turn of the era. I think my book makes that clear. Is there anything to suggest that Nazareth was NOT on the valley floor at the turn of the era? Well, yes — there is no evidence whatsoever on the hillsides of their presence at that time. What has been excavated at Nazareth is more than ample to infer a dating for the people who lived on the valley floor, for they

> of course are the ones who built the tombs and agricultural installations on the hillsides... — Rene

In other words, from the ample evidence (which all dates to CE times) on the hillside, we can with certainty infer a dating for the settlement on the valley floor. It's a no-brainer, for the people who lived on the valley floor are obviously the same ones who worked the agricultural installations and built the tombs on the hillside. Thus, the dating of the ample material on the hillside (numbering hundreds of objects and 20+ tombs) is quite diagnostic and conclusive and requires us to date the settlement to CE times.

But Ehrman is asking us to believe in the previous existence of a village without material evidence for its existence. This may be acceptable for believers, but it will not be for scientists. Secondly, Ehrman quite ignores the elephant in the room: the embarrassing *siting* of the tombs — they are precisely in the Venerated Area itself! He conveniently does not address this issue, but the scenario above with points A to F is the logical outcome of his thinking.

I urge Ehrman and other traditionalists to carefully consider the consequences of their argument and whether this is really the direction in which they wish to go, for it is a non-starter with several unforeseen complications.

First of all, one must propose that Nazareth moved in the century after Jesus. The natural question is: *Why?* No one has proposed a reason.

Secondly, and more importantly, **if the tombs are dated after the time of Jesus** (as both Dark and Ehrman agree) ***then all the artifacts found in them must also be dated after the time of Jesus***. In the case of Nazareth, we are here referring to the lion's share of material evidence, for most of the oil lamps and pottery were found in kokh tombs.

What this means is that the tradition is in a *Catch-22*: **if it dates the tombs later than Jesus, then it must also date the evidence later**. On the other hand, **if it defies science and dates the tombs earlier, then it will be dating tombs *in Mary's house* precisely to the time in which she allegedly lived**.

Ehrman's arguments, however, are not seeking a logical solution. They are essentially *ad hominem* and rhetorical — scoring points based upon authority and playing upon the ignorance of the average layperson in these rather arcane matters. Nevertheless — to those who care — the material evidence must eventually speak, and it can only be a matter of time before Ehrman's arguments fall of their own weight.

Two mutually-intertwined elements now inform the Nazareth discussion: (a) the hillside location of the ancient settlement; and (b) the tombs under the Church of the Annunciation. The tombs are hardly mentioned at all by the tradition — they are simply too embarrassing. As mentioned, they are also lethal to ongoing Christian pilgrimage at the site. Thus, it is understandable that Israeli tourist interests have aligned with Christian evangelical interests to smother any scintilla of truth which threatens the Nazareth revenue stream.

The hillside location of the village and the tombs are intertwined elements because tombs are incompatible with settlement in their immediate vicinity. Not less than two dozen Roman-era tombs have been discovered on the hillside of Nazareth. The work of H. P. Kuhnen shows that those tombs all post-date 50 CE. This creates two complications for the tradition. One is raw dating — if the tombs post-date Jesus, how then can the village predate him? Ehrman parries this threat: "Based on archaeological evidence, especially the tombs found in the area, Salm claims that the town came to be reinhabited sometime between the two Jewish revolts... [The kokh tombs] were not in use in Galilee the middle [*sic*] of the first century and thus do not date to the days of Jesus. And so the town did not exist then" [*DJE?* 194]. Ehrman then asks, 'how does this prove that Nazareth did not exist before the tombs were constructed?' His ultimate recourse is the argument of silence discussed above — somehow the settlement existed even though we have no evidence for it.

The slope of the Nazareth hill is quite steep (averaging a 14% grade in the Venerated Area). Topography mitigates against settlement on the hillside, especially when the relatively flat valley floor beckons. Tombs confirm the location of the village on the valley floor beginning in the second century CE.

Whether or not other villages in Roman Galilee were situated on the sides of steep hills (as Dark asserts) is quite beside the point — there is no evidence at all of such a siting at Nazareth. In addition, no one has found terracing in the Franciscan area of Nazareth which would permit structures. Nor has domestic evidence suggesting houses (such as hearths) been found on the hillside, despite many generations of digging.

The above points A to F constitute the evolving traditionalist scenario, lately implied by Ken Dark and now by Bart Ehrman. It is immediately invalidated by the *documented* evidence itself. According to that evidence (in Bagatti's book and in the primary archaeological reports from Nazareth) *all* the pottery, oil lamps, *etc.* discovered on the hillside date *after* the time of Jesus. How then, are we to suppose that a village first existed on the hillside if it left *absolutely no evidence* there? After all, the hillside Venerated Area is precisely where Bagatti excavated and where generations of Christians have dug. The fact that they unearthed not one shard dating with certainty before 100 CE [*MON* 205] alone disposes of the "early Nazareth located on the hillside" thesis. For — to any reasonable person — it is inconceivable that the Nazarenes lived on the hillside, worked agricultural installations there, yet *did not leave any evidence there of their presence*.

We now come to one final bizarre complication of Ehrman's rhetoric:

> [Salm claims] that, in his opinion, the village that eventually came into existence (in the years after 70 CE) would have been located on the valley floor, less than a kilometer away. He also points out that archaeologists have never dug at that site.
> This view creates insurmountable problems for his thesis. For one thing, there is the simple question of logic. If archaeologists have not dug where Salm thinks the village was located, what is his basis for saying that it did not exist in the days of Jesus? This is a major flaw. . ." [*DJE?* 195]

Ehrman is here confusing the elements of his own thesis. Both he and I *agree* that there was no village on the valley floor in the time of Jesus. He claims that the village was on the hillside (and *then* it moved to the valley floor — see above).

The major difference between Ehrman's position and mine is this: he claims there was a village on the hillside in the time of Jesus, whereas I deny this. So, Ehrman's inveighing against "insurmountable problems" for my thesis is mere rhetoric and quite misplaced, for I never claimed a village on the valley floor *in the time of 'Jesus.'*

Furthermore — and this is the bizarre twist — Ehrman is counting on evidence being found on the valley floor in the future, evidence which dates to the time of Jesus — *all the while arguing that the settlement was actually on the hillside!* Remember — Jesus, Mary, and Joseph lived on the hillside... So it is that the tradition twists itself into increasingly complicated knots in its efforts to avoid the plain truth: there was no Nazareth in the time of 'Jesus.' The village came into existence between the two Jewish revolts and was located on the valley floor. The Nazarenes constructed tombs on the hillside in II CE and thereafter, and they also worked agricultural installations on the hillside. This scenario is not only simpler than the points A to F above, but it is also plain as can be.

Where do we go from here?

As regards Nazareth, the tradition has painted itself into a corner. It insists (per scripture) that the ancient village was on the hillside — yet that happens to be the venue of tombs. So, the tradition speculates that the village moved to the valley floor when the tombs were constructed in the second century CE — but it can't show evidence either for an earlier settlement on the hillside nor for a later one on the valley floor. We now appear to have reached a point in Nazareth archaeology where the tradition is confused and does not know *what* to claim.

Allow me to play the devil's advocate and suggest a possible next step. It is not a good solution but, it seems, the following is the best option that Christianity has in order to perpetuate its curious version of Nazareth archaeology: the tradition should claim that, at the turn of the era, Nazareth existed *both* on the valley floor and on the hillside of the Nebi Sa'in. In the second century CE the Nazarenes then abandoned the hillside where they began to construct tombs.

Unfortunately, it is a very weak solution. There is, after all, no evidence that an ancient village existed *either* on the valley floor *or* on the hillside at the turn of the era. The only evidence we have is from the second century CE and onwards — when the tombs were built. Those tombs powerfully witness to the presence of a settlement on the valley floor in Middle and Late Roman times.

The most desperate option — and one hinted at by Ehrman — is for the tradition to throw in the towel regarding Nazareth and simply to claim 'irrelevance.' Thus he closes his Nazareth discussion with the following words:

> Again I reiterate the main point of my chapter: even if Jesus did not come from Nazareth, so what? The historicity of Jesus does not depend on whether Nazareth existed. In fact, it is not even related to the question. The existence (or rather, nonexistence) of Nazareth is another Mythicist irrelevancy.[*DJE?* 197]

I call his bluff and challenge the tradition at this late stage to jettison its beloved epithet "Jesus of Nazareth," perhaps in favor of 'Jesus of Somewhere Else.' Let the tradition engage in what is tantamount to open heart surgery and call it "irrelevant." I invite the Christian world to change all its Bibles to read "Jesus of Somewhere Else" or perhaps "Jesus of _____" (a blank can be inserted at all the requisite places of the New Testament and in the millions of books about Jesus)! Ehrman blusters as if this is a small thing. I suggest, however, that it amounts to another revolution in Christianity no less epochal than the Reformation itself.

CHAPTER THIRTEEN

Mark's 'Jesus from Nazareth of the Galilee' (*Iēsous apo Nazaret tēs Galilaias*)

Frank R. Zindler

For many years I have argued that the place called Nazareth was unknown to the authors of the Gospel of Mark. It is true that the toponym can be found in verse 9 of the first chapter of that gospel: "And it came to pass in those days, that Jesus came from Nazareth of Galilee, and was baptized of John in Jodan." However, I have argued that that verse — wholly or in part — was an interpolation into the text.[1] Unfortunately, I have been able to publish my evidence for this only partially and in popular works not intended for use by scholars. Now, however, thanks to René Salm's book *The Myth of Nazareth, The Invented Town of Jesus*[2] and the paradigm-shifting publication of Richard Carrier's *Proving History: Bayes's Theorem and the Quest for the Historical Jesus*[3] it has become possible to reargue my case in a more scientific and hopefully convincing way.

In order to evaluate my hypothesis more scientifically, a mathematical investigation of the relevant textual data is desirable. For that purpose, this chapter presents the relevant data I have collected

1 Frank R. Zindler, "Where Jesus Never Walked," in: *Through Atheist Eyes: Scenes From a World That Won't Reason, Vol. I: Religions and Scriptures* [Cranford, NJ: American Atheist Press, 2011: 36–37].

2 Cranford, NJ: American Atheist Press, 2008.

3 Amherst, NY: Prometheus Books, Amherst, 2012.

that are required in order to perform a Bayesian as well as frequentist[4] statistical analysis of the problems presented by Mark 1:9. The need for this is more urgent than ever before, as I have recently come to the opinion that the toponym 'Nazareth' was created out of the need to provide a physical home for a Jesus of flesh and blood, in order to counter Docetist arguments that Jesus only *seemed* to have a body and a physical nature. As part of that larger hypothesis, it is important to know if the author of the oldest Christian gospel knew of Nazareth or whether it was the invention of the birth legends of Matthew and Luke.

In the Greek text of the Gospel of Mark,[5] the name *Jesus* (*Iēsous*) is written with the definite article 72 times — not counting the occurrences in the long and short endings added to the text found in the best witnesses. The name is found only seven times without the article. Of these occurrences, four [1:24; 5:7; 10:47a; 10:47b] have *Jesus* in the vocative case where a definite article could not be used. In two more cases [1:1; 16:6], Jesus is part of a compound name or title (*Jesus Christ*; *Jesus the Nazarene*) where it is not Markan style to use the definite article with the first part of a compound name or title. (Incidentally, Mark 1:1 is the *only* occurrence of the compound name *Jesus Christ* to be found in the entire Gospel.)

That leaves only one case out of seven [Mark 1:9] where the definite article is suspiciously absent. It is the only case out of 73 cases where the definite article would be grammatically or stylistically possible to use with *Jesus* that the article is absent. Does this result from an early interpolation into the text? The article is absent in critical editions of the Greek text of Mark's gospel, and Bart Ehrman[6] argues that it is simply the result of scribal error. He appears to accept

4 The *frequentist* notion of probability considers it to be the long-run expected frequency of occurrence of an event. The *Bayesian* view of probability relates it to the degree of justifiability of belief and provides a measure of the plausibility of an event given incomplete knowledge. Bayesian probabilities can be revised in the face of new knowledge.

5 Kurt Aland, Matthew Black, Carlo M. Martini, Bruce M. Metzger, and Allen Wikgren, *The Greek New Testament*, Third Edition [New York: United Bible Societies, 1975]

6 Bart D. Ehrman, *Did Jesus Exist? The Historical Argument for Jesus of Nazareth* [New York: HarperOne, 2012: 356].

the claim that this is contrary to Markan style but rejects the claim that this is an interpolation. Rather, he argues, this is probably a scribal error.

Criticizing my popular essay "Where Jesus Never Walked," Ehrman comments that "...Zindler maintains that that verse [Mark 1:9] was not originally part of Mark; it was inserted by a later scribe." Sarcastically, he adds "Here again we see history being done according to convenience. If a text says precisely what you think it could not have said, then all you need to do is claim that originally it must have said something else[9]" [191].

Ehrman makes it look as though my critique of Mark 1:9 is purely *ad hoc*, if not downright disgraceful from a scholarly perspective. That certainly is the impression readers are left with if they read only the main text and don't follow up by reading the end-note referenced at the end of the passage quoted above. If one turns to end note 9 on page 356, however, one is startled to read the comment that "I do not mean to say that Zindler does not cite evidence for his view," and Ehrman goes on to criticize my argument that the name 'Jesus' in Mark 1:9 is written without the Greek definite article (*i.e.*, simply *Jesus* instead of *the Jesus*), in violation of the style of 'Mark,' who uses the article wherever it is grammatically or stylistically possible. (Elsewhere I shall examine the possibility that 'Mark' here is remembering the literal meaning of 'Jesus' ('Savior') and is actually using the word as a title as he also appears to do with 'the Peter' and 'the Iscariote.'

Leaving aside for the moment the question of the validity or not of his critique of my grammatical evidence — evidence implied not to exist according to his main text — it is hard to understand how he could have claimed that I was guilty of doing history "according to convenience," and that "all you need to do is claim that originally it must have said something else." This seems both unfair and untrue.

Let us now look at Ehrman's technical criticism of my allegedly *ad hoc* claim that Mark 1:9 appears at least in part to be an interpolation. First, he notes that "(a) there are two other places in Mark where the name Jesus does not have the article," not realizing that there are actually *seven* cases where the article is absent! (He should have known of these other occurrences because in an e-mail of October 14, 2010, I had told him of other inarticulate occurrences of 'Jesus' that had to be excluded for grammatical or stylistic reasons.) I have already shown above that there are good reasons why six of those cases are not relevant or suspect. Then he argues that "(b) if the problem with the entire verse is that the name Jesus does not have the article, then if we posit a scribal change to the text, *the more likely explanation is that a scribe inadvertently left out the article.*" [emphasis added]. We shall evaluate that likelihood presently, but can only wonder how it is that a scholar who has done so much to expose "Orthodox Corruption of Scripture" and forgery in the New Testament would not assign a higher probability to the likelihood of interpolations into the text of the earliest gospel.

The *pièce de resistance* of Ehrman's argument, however, is point (c): "there is not a single stitch of manuscript evidence to support his claim that the verse was interpolated into the Gospel. This latter point is worth stressing since it is the reason that no serious scholar of the textual tradition of Mark thinks that the verse is an interpolation." [356] Apart from the implied *ad hominem* that I am not a "serious scholar," this reveals that Ehrman has never read the writings of William Benjamin Smith — a mathematician, physicist, philologer, poet, and Renaissance polymath whose early works (*e.g., Der Vorchristliche Jesus* of 1906) were critiqued at length by Albert Schweitzer in the Second Edition of his *Quest of the Historical Jesus*. Since Schweitzer does not discuss the problem of Mark 1:9, Ehrman would not know what Smith had had to say about it — unless he took the time to read Smith himself instead of merely relying on Schweitzer's epitome. In his magisterial *Ecce Deus* of 1912, in a section dealing with the origin of the terms 'Nazoraios,' 'Nazara,' and 'Nazareth,' Smith wrote:

> Even in Mark I, 9, we read that "Jesus came from (*apo*) Nazareth of Galilee." This seems like a later addition to the narrative as indicated by the title *'Iēsous*, used here without the article, but elsewhere regularly with it, in this Gospel. Moreover, the text is uncertain; the reading *eis* for *apo* may be older. In Matthew (xxi, 11) we find "the prophet Jesus *ho apo* Nazareth," and the same Greek

phrase also in John I, 45; Acts x, 38. We may now understand this phrase. It seems to be nothing but an attempt to explain *Nazoraios*, precisely as *apo karyōtou* is an attempt to explain *(I)skariot*.[7]

I will have a lot to say about "manuscript evidence" and text preservation and transmission elsewhere. Suffice it to say here that there is no reason to suppose that the same processes of tendentious alteration of texts Ehrman has discovered in surveying extant manuscripts did not take place during the information-blackout centuries prior to them. Like new tomcats killing all the kittens sired by previous top-cats, succeeding winners of the Christian definition wars destroyed the documents that defended the doctrines of vanquished, previously 'orthodox' cults. It took more than a thousand years, for example, before a lucky accident at Nag Hammadi revealed the immensity of our information void regarding Gnostic Christianity.[8]

Let us now return to Ehrman's argument alleging scribal error dropping a definite article rather than interpolation of part or all of verse 1:9 into the text of Mark's gospel. It would seem reasonable that 0tion of the name Jesus should be 1/73, since the name occurs 73 times in the gospel where it is grammatically or stylistically possible to have the definite article, but only in one of those occurrences is it lacking.[9]

It is important to note, however, that this same verse is the only case in the entire Gospel of Mark where the place-name Nazareth occurs. What is the probability that the only inarticulate occurrence of *Jesus* should occur *in the same verse* as does the sole mention of the name *Nazareth*?

There are 666 verses in the Gospel of Mark, so the chance of Nazareth occurring in any particular one of them is 1/666. The

7 William Benjamin Smith. *Ecce Deus: Studies of Primitive Christianity* [London: Watts & Co., 1912: 314–315].

8 For an understanding of how book burning may have contributed to our problem here, see Daniel Christopher Sarefield's doctoral dissertation *Burning Knowledge: Book-burning in Ancient Rome* [The Ohio State University, 2004].

9 Richard Carrier informs me that this actually should be 1/74 (*i.e.*, even more favorable to my hypothesis) in accord with Laplace's Rule of Succession, by which the probability that Mark would write 1:9 as it now is would be (s + 1)/(n + 2), where s = 0 and n = 72, so that the probability that Mark originally had the article here is 1/74.

combined frequentist probability that Jesus without the definite article should be found in the same sentence as the name Nazareth is, therefore, $1/(73 \times 666) = 1/48{,}618 = 0.00002$ — about one in two hundred thousand.[10]

It might be objected that not all sentences are suitable in subject matter to allow for the presence of the word *Nazareth*. Certainly this is true, and it might be more reasonable to *use the number of chapters* in the Gospel of Mark, it being logical to assume that in the space of any chapter of a story about Jesus of Nazareth the occasion should occur at least once to employ the word *Nazareth*. That would bring the combined probability of finding an inarticulate *Jesus* with the name *Nazareth* to $1/(73 \times 16) = 1/1168 = .00086$ — about one chance in 86 thousand. That would increase the probability of finding the only scribal error involving the deletion of the definite article before *Jesus* in the same sentence where we find the only mention of Nazareth in the entire Gospel of Mark by about one order of magnitude, but the probability is still negligibly low.

So even with this relaxation in selecting criteria for determining the most appropriate reference class in which to work we find it extremely unlikely that the absence of the definite article in Mark 1:9 is due to a scribal deletion, and so it is only just to think if there might be a yet better reference class in which to place the word 'Nazareth.' Although Mark 1:9 is in fact the only place in the gospel where the name *Nazareth* actually occurs, it is a curious fact that the translators of the King James Version used that name five times in their translation. In four of those cases they were creating the title 'Jesus of Nazareth' when in fact the Greek text should have been rendered something like 'Jesus the Nazarene' or 'Jesus the Nazorean.' There is much debate concerning the meaning of the Greek words *Nazōrenos*

10 Ideally, calculating such odds would involve calculating the frequency of scribal error generally as well as the frequency of accidentally dropping articles in particular prior to the first manuscript verification of the contents of verse 1:9. Conceivably, Ehrman could refute my calculations by determining those rates and showing that they favor the accidental-deletion hypothesis strongly enough to alter favorably these calculations. It is ironic that Ehrman needs to find a very high error rate here, whereas Christian apologists are forced to agree with me that scribal errors of this sort are of very low frequency!

and *Nazōraios*, but the translators of the Authorized Version clearly thought they meant someone coming from a place called Nazareth. So it might be argued that it is more just to consider the probability of finding *Nazareth* instead of *Nazōraios* in this particular occurrence as 1 out of 5. That would bring the combined probability of finding the name Nazareth in the same sentence as the postulated scribal error to the value $1/(73 \times 5) = 1/365 = 0.00274$ — that is, about three chances in a thousand. The chances that this is *not* a scribal error are thus about 332 to 1. Not particularly close; no cigar.[11]

BAYESIAN ANALYSIS OF MARK 1:9

Before attempting a Bayesian analysis of the verse Mark 1:9 to see if it is the result of interpolation, scribal error, authorial intention, or other cause, it is necessary to assemble the available relevant 'background information' concerning the Gospel of Mark and this particular verse. The following information seems to be most appropriate to collect:

Background I. We know that the Gospel of Mark has been interpolated at least three times: addition of the long ending,[12] the short

11 As already noted, the probability of finding an accidentally dropped article in the same verse as that containing the only mention of Nazareth depends upon the frequency overall of accidentally dropped articles. But how many article droppings in Mark can we expect there would have to be before manuscript evidence could be expected to show them? If, as Richard Carrier argues in his book *Proving History*, we argue *a fortiori* and pick an absurdly high number such as 20, it will be seen that Ehrman's hypothesis is not helped nearly enough to save it.

Let us now consider the odds that one of those 20 deletions just happened to occur here, at the precise spot where Nazareth makes its sole appearance in the entire Gospel of Mark. A generous computation would find that probability to be 20/666 = 0.03. However, there are actually four places in Mark 1:9 where an article could be dropped. That means that the probability of dropping the article specifically in front of the word 'Jesus' would be 0.03/4.00 — in other words, less than one chance in a hundred that this was a scribal accident. If Ehrman argues for an error rate significantly above 20, the entire integrity of the transmission of the text of Mark collapses.

12 The oldest manuscripts of Mark end with verse 8 of chapter 16: "And they went out quickly, and fled from the sepulchre; for they trembled and were amazed: neither said they any thing to any man; for they were afraid." Verses 9–20, constituting the so-called long ending, add the post-resurrection appearances of Jesus and the verse so beloved of snake-handling Pentecostals: "They shall take up serpents; and if they

ending, and a combination of the two. It has also been hypothesized that some degree of interpolation[13] may have occurred in order to harmonize Mark with later gospels, especially Matthew and Luke.

Background II. In order to get some sense of the frequency of purely innocent scribal errors, we should count up the number of text variants of all kinds in Reuben Swanson's reference volume[14] showing major manuscript variations in the Gospel of Mark and try to see how many aren't likely to be deliberate and how many seem to be tendentious.

Background III. We need to decide on the proper reference class in which to place the location of the name 'Nazareth.' As we have seen, it could be the class of all 666 verses in the gospel, the class of all sixteen chapters in the gospel, or the class of five places where the King James translators rendered the Greek word as 'Nazareth.'

Background IV. We need to decide on the proper reference class in which to place the inarticulate occurrence of the name Jesus. It seems to me that this must be the entire class of 73 occurrences of the name *Jesus*, not the class of 7 occurrences without the definite article, where the article is absent for obvious grammatical or stylistic reasons.

---

drink any deadly thing, it shall not hurt them" [16:18].

A shorter ending also was added that reads [NEB] "And they delivered all these instructions briefly to Peter and his companions. Afterwards Jesus himself sent out by them from east to west the sacred and imperishable message of eternal salvation."

13 Ehrman might rightfully argue that throughout this chapter I am assuming too high a rate of interpolation as compared to the relevant rate of scribal errors. This is the most significant point where my hypothesis might be endangered. It is possible that he might be able to reexamine the data from his *The Orthodox Corruption of Scripture* to establish a baseline rate for interpolations and show that the actual rate is too low. However, that would amount to establishing a measurement baseline for determining motivation to alter scriptures — something I find ridiculous on its face.

14 Reuben Swanson (editor), *New Testament Greek Manuscripts: Variant Readings Arranged in Horizontal Rows Against Codex Vaticanus: Mark.* [Sheffield, England: Sheffield Academic Press, 1995].

Mark's 'Jesus from Nazareth of the Galilee'

Background V. We must consider how to deal with the MS variants of the Greek words for *Nazareth* in Mark 1:9 [*Nazaret* (B,W); *Nazarat* (A,P); *Nazareth* (D,1071)] as well as the variants for *Nazarene* in Mark 1:24 [*Nazarēne* (B,ℵ,Δ,C); *Nazarēnai* (D,Θ,28); *Nazarine* (E,H,69); *Nazōrinai* (1424)]. The variants in Mark 10:47 [*Nazarēnos* (B,W); *Nazorēnos* (D*); *Nazōrēos* (D^c); *Nazoraios* (E,700); *Naraios* (K*); *Nazōrinos* (28); *Nazōraios* (ℵ,A,C,Majority, K, *etc.*)] and the variants and grammatical forms found in MSS of Mark 16:6 **[(Missing in ℵ* and D!)**; *Nazarēnon* (B,124); *Nazōraiōn* (L); *Nazarinon* (U,13,1346); *Nazōraion* (Δ); *Nazarēnon* (565); *Nazorinon* (579); *Nazōrēnon* (1071); *Zarinon* (1424)] are also of possible interest when trying to understand the etymology of the toponym. Patristic MSS are also of relevance. Origen, for example, couldn't decide if the place should be called *Nazara* or *Nazaret(h).*

Background VI. We need to look to see if there are stylistic preferences for the forms *Nazorenos/Nazoraios* among the authors of Mark, Matthew, and Luke. Do Matthew and Luke use the same forms as Mark when copying him but differ in other cases? This needs to be checked.

Background VII. We should consider the possibility that Mark has been reharmonized with later gospels, especially Matthew's. 21:11: "And the multitude said, This is Jesus, the prophet of Nazareth of Galilee. (*'Iēsous ho apo Nazareth tēs Galeilaias*)."

Background VIII. We need to examine the possibility that the entire prologue of Mark is not original. To do this we may begin with the curious reincarnation pericope in Mark 8:27*ff*: "And Jesus went out, and his disciples, into the towns of Caesarea Philippi: and by the way he asked his disciples, saying unto them, Whom do men say that I am?: And they answered, John the Baptist: but some say, Elias; and others, One of the prophets." In this context, the Baptist is not a defunct contemporary of Jesus; he is an ancient worthy of the distant past. Jesus clearly could not be the reincarnation of someone only six months older than he (St. John the Baptist's birthday is celebrated at the summer solstice, exactly six months before the winter solstice) and had been alive for years after Jesus was born!

We then proceed to the prologue of Mark's first chapter. We start with what appears to be a superscript: "The beginning of the *gospel* of Jesus Christ." (Some witnesses add "the Son of God.") Instead of then beginning to learn of the gospel *message*, we begin with Isaiah, John the Baptist, and the baptism of Jesus — *Iēsous apo Nazaret tēs Galilaias.* Jesus then spends forty days in the wilderness — presumably a wilderness not located in Galilee — and the next thing we read is verse 14:

> Mark 1:14 *Now after that John was put in prison,* Jesus came into Galilee, preaching the gospel of the kingdom of God.

The gospel message itself finally begins in verse 15:

> Mark 1:15 And saying, The time is fulfilled, and the kingdom of God is at hand: repent ye, and believe the gospel.

What has happened between the Baptist's interaction with Jesus and now? Why was he put in prison ("delivered up")? It is taken for granted that *already, before verse 15, readers know all about the story of John the Baptist!* Things get even stranger, however, when we later learn all about John the Baptist in a flashback in chapter 6. Before analyzing that pericope, however, it may be noted that verse 14b would make a very fine beginning for the original gospel:

> Mark 1:1 The beginning of the gospel of Jesus Christ, the Son of God... 14b Jesus came into Galilee, preaching the gospel of the kingdom of God, and saying, The time is fulfilled, and the kingdom of God is at hand...

It is of interest to note that the translators of *The New English Bible* (NEB) separate the prologue from the rest of the book and graphically begin the Gospel of Mark with verse 1:14. It is the style of the NEB to begin chapters and major sections of books with a number of words written in solid capital letters. Thus, we begin the specially separated section titled "In Galilee: success and opposition" with the intro-scription "AFTER JOHN HAD BEEN ARRESTED" — nicely demarcating words I think have been interpolated and separating them from what I think was the original beginning of the text!

Chapter 6 begins with Jesus returning to his home town, teaching in the synagogue — in a village (*polis*!) big enough to have a synagogue but so obscure that it is unknown to the OT, the two Talmuds, Josephus, and all ancient geographers? — offending the locals and his family, and leading up to the famous "a prophet is not without honour, but in his own country, and among his own kin, and in his own house." He then sends out The Twelve, giving them their hiking instructions.

> 6:12. And they went out, and preached that men should repent. 13. And they cast out many devils, and anointed with oil many that were sick, and healed them.

We then launch into the gory story of Herod's beheading of John the Baptist and the plot outline for Richard Strauss's opera *Salome*:

> 6:14. And king Herod heard of him [*why not 'them'*?]; (for his name [*Jesus, not The Twelve*] was spread abroad;) and he said, That John the Baptist was risen from the dead, and therefore mighty works do shew forth themselves in him. ... 16. But when Herod heard thereof, he said, It is John, whom I beheaded: he is risen from the dead.

The story of John the Baptist continues then as a flash-back through verse 29:

> 6:29. And when his [*John's*] disciples heard of it, they came and took up his corpse, and laid it in a tomb.

The very next verse, then resumes the pericope of the disciples/apostles who had been sent out by Jesus:

> 6:30. And the apostles gathered themselves together unto Jesus, and told him all things, both what they had done, and what they had taught.

By Frank R. Zindler

Are we not in the presence of a glaring interpolation into the text of chapter six? Do we not see seams interrupting a previously seamless text? If we remove the story of John the Baptist, we have a smooth flow of text:

> 6:12. And they went out, and preached that men should repent. 13. And they cast out many devils, and anointed with oil many that were sick, and healed them. 6:30. And the apostles gathered themselves together unto Jesus, and told him all things, both what they had done, and what they had taught.

And so, it is not *a priori* implausible that verse 1:9 is an interpolation. The entire prologue might have been interpolated, leading to the interpolation in chapter 6 to explain the enigmatic "after John was delivered up..."

Background IX. It is interesting to note that the main function of Mark's prologue seems to be to achieve a typically Matthaean purpose: to demonstrate how Jesus and his deeds are the fulfillment of 'Old Testament' prophecies. *It seems to me quite possible that the Markan prologue was created in the process of harmonizing Mark with Matthew* — perhaps shortly after 'Matthew' adapted most of 'Mark's' Greek text to create the narrative skeleton of his own gospel!

Apart from it being a fact that Mark 1:9 is the only place in the oldest gospel where Jesus is styled 'Jesus of Nazareth' instead of 'Jesus the Nazarene' or 'Jesus the Nazorean' or the like, the expression *Jesus of Nazareth* is peculiar in a rather unexpected way. The usual translation of the verse is straightforward:

> "...Jesus came from Nazareth of Galilee..."

The name *Jesus* is connected to the name *Nazareth* by the preposition *apo* — 'from.' This is reasonable and appropriate: Jesus has just come *from* Nazareth in Galilee. The preposition *apo* fits the context.

What is peculiar is that essentially the same expression is found in Matthew, John, and Acts, but in those cases the preposition does not carry the meaning of 'from' in the sense of motion away from a place. Rather, it simply means 'of.' In Matthew 21:11, for example, we read of "...Jesus the prophet of Nazareth of Galilee..." (*ho apo Nazareth tēs Galeilaias*). In John 1:45 we read of "...Jesus of Nazareth, the son of Joseph" (*...Iēsoun...ton apo Nazareth.*)

Interestingly, *'Jesus apo Nazareth' is not found at all in the Gospel of Luke*, but he does appear in Acts 10:37-38, where "...after the baptism which John preached ... God anointed Jesus of Nazareth (*Iēsoun ton apo Nazareth*) with the Holy Ghost."

It seems to be likely that Nazareth was the invention of Matthew and was taken up by the later John and the author of Acts. It could easily have been placed into Mark by someone trying to harmonize Mark with Matthew after the latter had taken Mark's material in an unexpected direction. **It is striking that only in Matthew and Mark do we find the extended expression "Jesus *apo* Nazareth of the Galilee."** At the same time, it is curious that only in Acts is the shorter *Jesus apo Nazareth* directly associated with baptism.

Background X. A preliminary Bayesian analysis of Mark 1:9 is needed, in particular, to gather stylistic statistics of the use of the word *Iēsous* with and without the definite article in Greek texts and manuscripts of the Gospel of Mark according to the Aland-Black *Greek New Testament.*

Before we can test Bart Ehrman's hypothesis that the absence of the definite article with the word *Iēsous* (Jesus) in Mark 1:9 is due to a scribal deletion, it is necessary to examine Markan and scribal usages as witnessed by the most important manuscripts and the critical Greek texts based upon them.

To obtain a general orientation to the nature of the evidence, however, before examining the somewhat bewildering evidence of the MS traditions of relevance it is helpful to begin with the Aland-Black *The Greek New Testament* (Third Edition). A careful examination of that Greek text reveals that the word *Iēsous* occurs 79 times in the Gospel of Mark. In 72 of those cases, *Iēsous* is articulate; it lacks the article in seven cases. Of those seven cases, six are cases where the article would not be grammatically or stylistically possible in Mark

— the name being in the vocative case, for example, or forming the first element of a compound name or title. Mark 1:9 is thus the only instance of the use of the name *Jesus* without the definite article. Wherever it is possible, we read about *the Jesus*, not just *Jesus*.

Bayesian analysis of the hypothesis that the absence of the definite article before *Jēsous* in Mark 1:9 is due to a scribal error

Let us begin by presenting the Bayesian formula for computing the likelihood of any hypothesis:

$$P(h|e.b) = \frac{P(h|b) \times (P(e|h.b)}{[P(h|b) \times P(e|h.b)] + [P(\sim h|b) \times P(e|\sim h.b)]}$$

The elements of this equation are defined as follows:

h = (the hypothesis to be tested) It represents the proposition:

'The word *Iēsous* in Mark 1:9 is not preceded by the Greek definite article because of a scribal error (not because of interpolation of part or all of the verse).'

e = (the evidence to be accounted for by the hypothesis) It represents the data statement:

'The verse contains the only occurrence in Mark of 'Jesus' without the definite article where grammatically and stylistically it could have been used. The verse also contains the only occurrence in Mark of the word 'Nazareth' instead of *Nazarene/Nazorean*. The name 'Jesus' occurs 72 times with the article. It is inarticulate 6 times for grammatical or stylistic reasons. *Nazarene/Nazorean* is used 4 times instead of *Nazareth*.'

b = (background evidence, being the frequentist estimation of the probabilities of the likelihood of this particular occurrence of 'Jesus' being inarticulate in the same verse containing the only occurrence of 'Nazareth' instead of the related words *Nazarene* or *Nazorean*, which occur 4 times in Mark)

P(h|b) = (the probability that our hypothesis would be true given only our background knowledge) = 1/73 = 0.0137.

P(e|h.b) = (the probability that we would have all the evidence we actually do have, given all our background knowledge, if our hypothesis were indeed true) = 1/73 × 1/5 = 0.0027

P(~h|b) = (the probability that our hypothesis would be false given only our background knowledge) = 72/73 = 0.9863

P(e|~h.b) = (the probability that we would have all the evidence we actually have, given our background knowledge, if our hypothesis were instead false) = 4/5 × 72/73 = 0.7890

P(h|e.b) = (the probability that our hypothesis is true, given the evidence and all our background knowledge) =

$$P(h|e.b) = \frac{(1/73) \times (1/73 \times 1/5)}{[(1/73) \times (1/73 \times 1/5)] + [(72/73) \times (4/5 \times 72/73)]}$$

$$P(h|e.b) = \frac{(0.0137) \times (0.0027)}{[(0.0137) \times (0.0027)] + [(0.9863) \times (0.7890)]}$$

$$P(h|e.b) = \frac{(0.00003699)}{(0.00003699) + (0.7781907)}$$

$$P(h|e.b) = 0.000047531$$

To summarize: 0.000047531 is the dismal probability that our hypothesis of scribal error is true, given the evidence and all our background knowledge to this point.

Thus, considering only the evidence of the Greek text of Mark found in the Aland-Black *The Greek New Testament*, it appears that the likelihood that the absence of the article occurring in the same verse as the only use of Nazareth being due to unintentional scribal error is around *five in a hundred thousand.*

It is somewhat startling, after careful examination of a critical edition of the Greek text of the Gospel of Mark to turn to *Young's Analytical Concordance to the Bible* (22nd American Edition)[15] to discover that the King James Version of Mark contains the word 'Jesus' not 73, but 95 times — including its solitary appearance in the form of *Jesus Christ* — a character who appears only once in the entire gospel (and in the title at that!).

Quite obviously, the Byzantine text at the disposal of the King James translators differed from the text of Aland, Black, *et al.* It seems necessary, then, to survey the entire manuscript tradition of Mark to gain a statistically more informative picture of Markan and scribal usage of the definite article with the word '*Iēsous*' and to put Mark 1:9 more sharply in perspective.

The most convenient way to do that is to examine Reuben Swanson's *New Testament Greek Manuscripts: Variant Readings Arranged in Horizontal Rows Against Codex Vaticanus: Mark.* That volume summarizes the texts of 67 of the critically most important New Testament manuscripts that survive to our time. (Swanson has told me privately that the so-called '*apparatus criticus*' to be found at the foot of most pages of the major editions of the Greek text of the New Testament is riddled with errors — as well as being an outrageously unwieldy tool to handle.)

The greater magnitude of the data obtainable from Swanson's book makes it possible to carry out a more informative (Bayesian) statistical analysis with which to evaluate Ehrman's claim of scribal

15 Robert Young, *Young's Analytical Concordance to the Bible*, Twenty-second Edition, revised Wm. B. Stevenson [New York: Funk & Wagnalls Co., 1936].

deletion versus my own allegation of some degree of interpolation in the ninth verse of the first chapter of Mark's gospel.

Background XI. Bayesian analysis employing 'new evidence' from Swanson's collation of the texts of 67 critically most important manuscripts of the Gospel of Mark.

To carry out such an analysis, seven different searches of the 67 manuscript texts were performed to answer the following questions:

(1) How many verses in Mark contain *ho Iēsous* in at least one manuscript? [There are 117 such verses.]

(2) How many verses in Mark contain the word *Iēsous* without an article in at least one manuscript? [There are 11 such verses.]

(3a) How many verses have *Iēsous* without the article where the article would be possible and the article is present in most manuscripts? [There are 5 such verses.]

(3b) How many verses lack the article where it would be possible and the article is lacking in most manuscripts? [There is just 1 such verse, Mk 1:9.]

(4) How many verses contain the article but lack *Iēsous* where *Iēsous* is present in most manuscripts? [There are 24 such verses.]

(5) How many verses lack both *Iēsous* and the article where the two are present in most manuscripts? [There are 21 such verses.]

(6) How many verses have added inarticulate *Iēsous* where it is lacking in most manuscripts? [There are only 2 such verses]

(7) How many verses have added both the article and *Iēsous* where both are lacking in most manuscripts? [There are 34 such verses]

One of the useful aspects of Bayesian analysis is the fact that probabilities calculated with previously available data can be modified and updated to accord with the discovery of new evidence. While the results of all seven of the above tabulated searches are of potential value as 'new evidence,' the findings of Search 3a appear to be most clearly of relevance and, indeed, potentially able to improve the probable likelihood of the hypothesis that the inarticulate Jesus of Mark 1:9 is the result of scribal omission of the article.

Search 3a answered the question, "How many verses have *Iēsous* without the article where the article would be possible and the article is present in most manuscripts?" That is to ask, how many cases can we find in the manuscripts where the absence of the article with *Iēsous* appears to be due to scribal deletion of the article? It turns out that five such instances can be found in Swanson's texts as compared to the 117 cases where *Iēsous* appears with the article.

It would seem that five inarticulate occurrences of *Iēsous* out of a total of 122 (117 + 5) appearances of *Iēsous* is more supportive of Ehrman's hypothesis than was one case out of 73. So, let us see how much this 'new' evidence increases the likelihood that **h** — the scribal deletion hypothesis — is true. We shall use the results of our first Bayesian analysis as the 'prior' probability to substitute into Bayes' formula:

$$P(h|e.b) \quad = \quad \frac{P(h|b) \times (P(e|h.b)}{[P(h|b) \times P(e|h.b)] + [P(\sim h|b) \times P(e|\sim h.b)]}$$

$$P(h|e.b) \quad = \quad \frac{(0.000047531) \times (5/122)}{[(0.0000475) \times (5/122)] + [(0.9999) \times (117/122)]}$$

$$P(h|e.b) \quad = \quad 0.000002031$$

Perhaps surprisingly, adding the new 'favorable' data actually *decreased* the likelihood that Ehrman's hypothesis is true. Moreover, the results of the other searches in Swanson's manuscripts can be expected to further reduce the probability that the inarticulate Jesus of Mark 1:9 is the product of scribal error.

First of all, it appears to be the case that when scribes have omitted part of 'the Jesus' they have omitted the 'Jesus' more often than the 'the'! While we have found five cases where 'the' appears to have been dropped, 24 cases have been found where 'Jesus' has been dropped, leaving the article to serve as a pronoun.

Secondly, scribes have tended to drop *both* 'the' and 'Jesus' more often than the five cases where they dropped just the article. 'The Jesus' is absent in 21 verses where most manuscripts have both 'the' and 'Jesus.'

Thirdly, it seems to be the case that in the transmission of the Greek text of Mark, scribes have had a marked tendency *to add*, not subtract 'the Jesus' from the text: 34 additions as compared to 21 deletions!

HYPOTHESES FOR EHRMAN TO TEST WITH BAYES' THEOREM

Bart Ehrman might easily dismiss the Bayesian analysis above as just so much garbage-in/garbage-out procedure against which I myself have cautioned. He could do that, however, only if he himself does not learn the method well enough to evaluate it fairly. It is quite possible that I myself have made errors in this chapter — my first attempt at applying Bayesian analysis to biblical criticism. It would, however, be very unfair if Ehrman were merely to dismiss my work without learning the method himself well enough to produce better analyses. Convinced still that he is not only a great scholar but an honorable man, I ask him to try the Bayesian technique himself, by evaluating propositions that hold the potential to alter my conclusions markedly or disconfirm them completely. I recommend he cut his Bayesian teeth on the following propositions:

By Frank R. Zindler

1. Mark 1:9 was not interpolated at all.

2. Mark 1:9 was interpolated totally as a deliberate alteration of the text.

3. Mark 1:9 was interpolated partially, merely adding 'Nazareth.'

4. Mark 1:9 originally had no articulate 'Jesus' but had 'Nazareth.'

5. Mark 1:9 originally had no articulate 'Jesus' and no 'Nazareth.'

6. Mark 1:9 originally had articulate 'Jesus' and 'Nazareth.'

7. Mark 1:9 originally had articulate 'Jesus' and no 'Nazareth.'

8. Mark 1:9 originally had no articulate 'Jesus' but had 'Nazarene'/'Nazoraios.'

9. Mark 1:9 originally had articulate 'Jesus' as well as 'Nazarene'/'Nazoraios.'

10. Mark 1:9 'Nazarene' was original but changed to 'Nazareth' by Mark.

11. Mark 1:9 'Nazarene' was original but changed to 'Nazareth' by later editor.

After Bart D. Ehrman completes the analysis of at least three of the propositions above, I ask him to say whether or not he would make the same declaration regarding the present chapter as he did concerning my previous books, *viz.*, "Here again we see history being done according to convenience. If a text says precisely what you think it could not have said, then all you need to do is claim that originally it must have said something else" [*DJE?*: 191]. I would ask further that he render his judgment in his next *New York Times* best-seller.

CHAPTER FOURTEEN

Was There a Historical 'Jesus of Nazareth'?

The use of midrash to create a biographical detail in the gospel story

D.M. Murdock

In the New Testament, Jesus Christ is depicted as having been brought up in a city called 'Nazareth,' a purported biographical detail upon which much speculation has been hung over the centuries as to a 'historical' Jewish messiah figure in the gospel story, buried somewhere underneath layers of pious elaboration.[1] In this regard, countless Jesus biographies have been constructed significantly around this purported place of origin that would indicate a historical personage.[2] Indeed,

1 This position is called 'euhemerism' or, for pronunciation's sake, *evemerism*, after the ancient Greek philosopher Euhēmeros/Euhemerus, who surmised that the gods were ancient kings, queens and heroes whose legends had been deified by the addition of fabulous fairytales and mythical motifs. This process is also called *apotheosis*, which did happen with some prominent figures such as Alexander the Great and the Egyptian physician Imhotep. All pharaohs and many other kings and rulers have been considered to be living 'gods on Earth.' Each case must be weighed on its own merit. Thus, Mythicists demonstrate specifically that the 'Jesus Christ' of the New Testament is a fictional composite of characters, real and mythical, and that such a composite of multiple 'people' is therefore no *one*. In other words, when the mythological and midrashic layers, *etc.*, are removed, there remains no 'historical core' to the onion.

2 As an example of the use of the concept 'Jesus of Nazareth' as the basis for a 'historical Jesus,' in 2012 New Testament scholar Bart Ehrman released his book *Did Jesus Exist?*, which was subtitled *The Historical Argument for Jesus of Nazareth*. As Frank Zindler shows in his rebuttal, "Bart's Subtitle," Ehrman fails to meet the burden of proof for this supposed historical personage from a purported place called Nazareth.

whenever scholars wish to distinguish between the 'historical Jesus' and the 'Christ of faith,' they use the designation *Jesus of Nazareth* to depict the former.

Despite all of this speculation, there exists no hard scientific evidence that the *polis* or 'city' of Nazareth as depicted in the New Testament even existed at the time when Christ was supposedly being raised there. Although there exists a centuries-later 'historic Nazareth' in Israel, archaeological explorations during the past century have failed to demonstrate any such city of the time in the general vicinity. In reality, it appears that Jesus was made to be *of Nazareth* so that he could be called a 'Nazarene' or 'Nazoraean/Nazorean,' a member of an ancient pre-Christian sect, of which the Old Testament hero Samson was said to have been an adherent as well.

The 'City' of Nazareth?

The apparent fact that Nazareth was not a bustling 'city' at the time of Christ's purported existence has been demonstrated through historical records and archaeological evidence. As independent scholars Frank Zindler, René Salm, and others have shown via thorough analysis, there is no mention of a 'Nazareth' or 'Nazara' in the Old Testament or even in Josephus centuries later.[3] The first reference to Nazareth in Jewish literature does not occur until the ninth century AD/CE, "only in two songs of lamentation...as the seat of a priestly division..."[4] It seems that, after the 'city' became the subject of interest because of the gospels, only then do we find the area inhabited to any significant degree, evidently beginning no earlier than the fourth century CE.

As Zindler remarks in "Where Jesus Never Walked":

---

3 Transliterations of other relevant terms in the New Testament include *Nazareth, Nazar*at and *Nazarath*. The variations may be difficult to explain, for writers purported to be familiar with a city by that name, from which their all-important Lord and Savior had emanated, as well as in consideration of the fact that the evangelists are claimed to have been inspired infallibly by the Holy Spirit. The city-name 'Jerusalem' also varies in the New Testament, appearing as *Hierosolyma* (G2414) and *Hierousalēm* (G2419).

4 Luz, 148.

Was there a historical 'Jesus of Nazareth'?

> Nazareth is not mentioned even once in the entire Old Testament, nor do any ancient historians or geographers mention it before the beginning of the fourth century. The Talmud, although it names 63 Galilean towns, knows nothing of Nazareth. Josephus, who wrote extensively about Galilee (a region roughly the size of Rhode Island) and conducted military operations back and forth across the tiny territory in the last half of the first century, mentions Nazareth not even once — although he does mention by name 45 other cities and villages of Galilee. This is even more telling when one discovers that Josephus does mention Japha, a village which is just over a mile from present-day Nazareth! Josephus tells us that he was occupied there for some time. Today, Japha can be considered a suburb of Nazareth, but in Josephus' day, I'll wager, the people of Japha buried their dead in the tombs of the unnamed necropolis that now underlies the modern city called Nazareth.

In the fifth century, Church father Jerome (*Onomasticon*) claimed Nazareth was a *viculus*, a 'little village' or 'hamlet,' an indication that it was founded long after its supposed existence as a 'city.' Considering the interest in the site and that pilgrims eventually flocked there, this small stature seems inexplicable, unless the case is that any such locality eventually named 'Nazareth' (or other variant) in reality was styled *after* an allegorical place based on Old Testament midrash ('interpretation,' 'commentary') and New Testament contentions.

Despite claims to the contrary, it appears that outside of the New Testament there exists no unambiguous evidence for such a place as the *city* called Nazareth that could have hosted a historical Jesus. In view of all the time and effort spent to find what would likely be numerous artifacts demonstrating these contentions of a pre-Christian Nazareth, it remains noteworthy that no such hard proof has been discovered, again, not for want of looking and digging. In ongoing excavations at the site of 'historic Nazareth,' now and again archaeologists claim to have found "Jesus's neighbor's house" or some other such artifact such as coins from "before the Jewish uprising."[5] It has

5 In December 2009, the media announced that "Jesus's neighbor's house" had been found at Nazareth. René Salm analyzed the account and declared it to be false. See my articles "Jesus neighbor's house found?" and "Nazareth scholar: 'No house from Jesus's time found there.'" Concerning this purported find, Salm further remarks: "Typically, no

likewise been asserted that a "necropolis" preceded the city; yet, the earliest tombs in the area so far discovered appear to date to the middle to late first century AD/CE, if that early, decades after Jesus was purported to be living in the midst of this proposed cemetery.

In an article entitled, "Nazareth, Faith and the Dark Option," in response to critics of his book *The Myth of Nazareth: The Invented Town of Jesus*, Salm remarks:

> This important article reviews the problem-ridden history of the site's archaeology, revealing that Jesus-era evidence has often been invented in the past by the tradition, is possibly being invented now, and may continue to be invented at Nazareth in the future.[6]

Salm further states:

> Archaeologists have been digging at Nazareth for over a hundred years and, as my book attempts to show, all the recovered finds include not a single artefact that can with certainty be dated before 100 CE. In other words, no demonstrable evidence dating either to the time of Jesus or to earlier Hellenistic times has been found. This is quite sufficient to decide the issue against the traditional view of Nazareth. The case is closed! No one, of course, is opposed to ongoing research at Nazareth, but that research will inform us about the nature of the Late Roman-Byzantine village, not about a mythical settlement at the turn of the era. That question has already been answered, and answered convincingly.

With such obviously painstaking searches for a century designed to expose a bustling biblical *polis* of tremendous significance to

---

evidence dating to the turn of the era ('time of Jesus') has been forthcoming. In addition, the small excavation site was quickly covered up, so that no subsequent investigation is possible. A recently opened pilgrim center now rises on the site, known as the Mary of Nazareth International Center — with boutique, restaurant and theatre!" In his article "Nazareth: René Salm's preliminary response to Bart Ehrman," Salm also addresses the claim regarding coins raised by Ehrman. Even if coins were found at Nazareth, where is the 'city?'

6 In a number of articles, Salm has addressed the various criticisms of the Nazareth-myth thesis in general and his book in particular, such as in the reviews by Ken Dark and by Stephen J. Pfann and Yehudah Rapuano.

Christendom, one would think there would be a much more conclusive archaeological record. Thus, despite the attempts at painting a thriving metropolis at a place called Nazara/Nazareth in pre-Christian times, no material artifact unambiguously illustrates that claim. Proponents' generalities, sophistry, and evasions aside, Salm reiterates that the fundamental issue remains "that no evidence of human habitation at Nazareth is extant from *ca.* 730 BCE–*ca.* 70 CE."

Moreover, it has been surmised that Nazareth lay on a hill, because Luke 4:29 says Jesus was brought to the city pinnacle in order to throw him off. However, the hill in the vicinity of the 'historic Nazareth' is too steep for dwellings. This verse in Luke is not a 'historical fact' but possibly a midrashic interpretation of an Old Testament 'messianic prophecy.' The scripture 2 Chronicles 25:12 employs the same verb *katakrēmnizō*, meaning 'to throw down a precipice,' as appears in Luke. Using this same Greek term during the first century BCE, historian Diodorus Siculus [*Library*, 16.28.3] discussed a military conquest in which the prisoners were made to hurl themselves off a precipice. In the second century AD/CE, Roman historian Appian [*Mithridatic* 5.34, *Punic* 17:114, and *Syrian Wars* 7.42] also used the word to describe the treatment of vanquished enemies. Obviously, this 'biographical motif' in the New Testament could simply be a literary invention based on a well-known tactic to terrorize one's enemies.

Furthermore, the passage in Luke in which Jesus is said to have been brought up in Nazareth also happens to be one of those biographical details missing from Marcion's *Gospel of the Lord*, which was part of the first 'New Testament,' published in the middle of the second century. Although early Church fathers claimed that Marcion had mutilated Luke's gospel by excising supposedly biographical material such as this part about Jesus having been brought up at Nazareth, the evidence points to the redaction or editing as having occurred in the opposite direction, with the author Luke adding to Marcion's gospel. Hence, we have even more reason to suspect this passage about Jesus being from Nazareth constitutes midrash or *fiction*.

Rather than representing a real 'city,' it appears that Nazareth was included in the gospel story in order to 'fulfill prophecy,' as part of a mass of 'messianic scriptures' used as blueprints to create the New Testament figure of 'Jesus Christ.' This allegorical creation follows a long series of precedents in Judaism, devised through the process of midrash — again, the interpretation or commentary of a biblical passage to illustrate a certain point.

Nazareth as Midrash and Misinterpretation

The midrashic use of an Old Testament messianic scripture to create a New Testament motif is illustrated at Matthew 2:23, in which it is claimed that Jesus was supposed to live in Nazareth in order to "fulfill prophecy":

> And he went and dwelt in a city called Nazareth, that what was spoken by the prophets might be fulfilled, "He shall be called a Nazarene."

The original Greek is:

*kai elthōn katōkēsen eis polin legomenēn **Nazaret** hopōs plērōthē to rhēthen dia tōn prophētōn hoti **Nazōraios** klēthēsetai.*

Here we see the words '*Nazaret*' and '*Nazoraios*,' the latter usually rendered *Nazarene* or *Nazorean* in English.[7] The Greek New Testament word *Nazōraios* is defined by *Strong's Concordance of the Bible* (G3480) as:

> Nazarite = "one separated." 1) an inhabitant of Nazareth; 2) a title given to Jesus in the NT; 3) a name given to Christians by the Jews, Ac. 24:5

Thus, Nazarene/Nazoraios is equated with *Nazarite* or *Nazirite*, as found in the Old Testament, a designation not of a place but of

7 Other spellings, transliterations, and terms related to or confused with *Nazarene/Nazorean* include *Nazrene, Nazarean, Natsarene, Nasaraean, Nasorean, Naassene, etc.* For an extensive discussion of these various terms, see the work of Robert Eisenman, who shows that the New Testament character James the Brother could be deemed an "extreme Nazarite."

a religious cult, to which Samson likewise was said to belong. Concerning Matthew's implication that 'Nazarene' comes from 'Nazareth,' Hebrew scholar Robert Eisenman remarks, "This cannot be the derivation of the term, as even in the Greek, the spelling 'Nazareth'' and 'Nazoraean' differ substantially."[8] Eisenman also comments that "the scriptural reference [in Matthew] clearly aims at evoking *Nazirite*..."[9]

The title *Nazoraios* occurs 15 times in the New Testament, but it is rendered 13 times in the King James Bible (KJV) as "of Nazareth," while only twice in the KJV is Jesus identified as a "Nazarene." An alternate spelling *Nazarēnos* (G3479), defined as "a resident of Nazareth," occurs at Mark 1:24, 14:67, 16:6, and Luke 4:34. In these four verses, this usage would constitute a *demonym* or name/cognomen designating a citizen of a particular place, derived not from the Nazarites of the Old Testament but from the supposed city of Nazara/Nazareth.

At Mark 1:24, Christ is called *Iēsou Nazarēne*, or "Jesus Nazarene." At Mark 14:67, the phrase appears as *tou Nazarēnou Iēsou*, which reads "of the Nazarene Jesus," not "Jesus of Nazareth." Mark 16:6 says:

> *Mē ekthambeisthe Iēsoun Zēteite ton Nazarēnon*

This verse translates literally as:

> Do not be terrified Jesus you seek the Nazarene

In the KJV or Authorized Version of the Bible, this noun *Nazarēnos* in each instance is rendered in English not 'Nazarene' but 'of Nazareth.' The fact is that *Nazarēnos* does not appear in the Greek Old Testament/ Septuagint or other extant pre-Christian literature. Why is there no previous such designation, if Nazareth was already a "city" at the time Jesus was supposedly raised there? It appears that the term *Nazarēnos* was specifically created to describe Jesus, as the word 'Christians' likewise was invented for his followers. Thus, either pre-Christian

8 Eisenman, 1998: 243.

9 Eisenman, 1998: 249.

residents of 'Nazareth' were never called by a comparable name in Greek, or there evidently *were* no other such 'Nazarenes,' as a strict demonym, running about the Levant before Christianity.

It is true that many individuals in antiquity were identified by their place of origin, such as Lucius Cyrenensis and Diodorus Siculus. It is likewise apparently true that there was no such place as the 'city of Nazareth' during the era in question, that there *was* a brotherhood called the Nazarites, and that many people in antiquity *also* were called by religious designations. In the New Testament itself, for example, we read about *Simōn ho zēlōtēs*, or 'Simon the Zealot' (Acts 1:13), so named for his zealotry for the Jewish law.

This scenario of a religious *title*, not a demonym, constitutes the only logical way in which the messiah as 'Nazarene' could represent 'fulfillment of prophecy'" in scripture. The fact remains that this demonym *Nazarēnos* apparently did not exist until it was devised in the New Testament, for the specific purpose of identifying Jesus as having come from a place called Nazareth — for which there is no real evidence of the time — conflating this concept instead with the religious order of the Nazarites/Nazirites.

Concerning titles and demonyms in the Bible, biblical scholar Robert M. Price comments:

> In the same way Micah the Levite would be thought in one period to mean "Micah the oracle," but in another "Micah from the tribe of Levi," Jesus the Nazorean would first be understood as "Jesus the Sectarian" and only later as "Jesus from Nazareth."[10]

Moreover, it has been pointed out that, if the intent was to designate a resident of a city, the proper demonym would be *Nazarethenos, Nazarethanos* or *Nazarethaios*, rather than *Nazoraios, Nazorean* or *Nazarene.*[11] These latter designations would be appropriate for a noun from the Hebrew root words *naziyr* (H5139)*, also transliterated nazir, and nazar* (H5144)*, meaning 'dedicate,' 'consecrate,' or 'separate' in a religious fashion.*

10 Price, 54.

11 Guignebert, 82.

Was there a historical 'Jesus of Nazareth'?

No 'Jesus of Nazareth'

The various New Testament references to "Nazareth, where he had been brought up" [Lk 4:16] are obviously designed to explain the supposed prophecy that the awaited deliverer would be styled '*Nazoraios*,' '*Nazarene*,' or '*Nazarite*.' *Appearing a mere dozen times in the New Testament, t*he word for "Nazareth," which is also written *Nazará* (Strong's G3478), *is defined as:*

> Nazareth = "the guarded one": 1) the ordinary residence and home town of Christ

However, Christ is actually never called "Jesus of Nazareth" in the Greek gospels. He is "Jesus the Nazoraios/Nazarene," "Jesus the one from Nazareth" or "Jesus the prophet from Nazareth of Galilee," this latter as at Matthew 21:11: *Iēsous ho prophētēs ho apo Nazaret tēs Galilaias.*

Mark 1:9 comes next close of the evangelists to writing "Jesus of Nazareth":

> And it came to pass in those days, that Jesus came from Nazareth of Galilee, and was baptized of John in Jordan.

The relevant Greek here is *ēlthen Iēsous apo Nazaret tēs Galilaias*, which could be rendered "came Jesus from Nazareth of Galilee." In this case, however, the phrase is not a moniker or demonym; rather, "*in those days* he came *from* Nazareth to the Jordan" refers to a *journey* at that time.

In Luke's gospel, Jesus is never even associated with Nazareth in the same verse in which the city-name appears; hence, no phrase "Jesus of Nazareth" appears in that book either. We do find, however, at Luke 24:19 a reference to *Iēsou tou Nazōraiou,* or "(of) Jesus the Nazoraios."

In John 1:45 we read "*Iēsoun ton huion tou Iōsēph ton apo Nazaret*." or "Jesus the son of Joseph the one from Nazareth." The grammar makes it clear it is the son who is from Nazareth, not Joseph, but, again, there is no direct "Jesus of Nazareth" designation.

Furthermore, in this passage John specifically states that this "Jesus the son of Joseph the one from Nazareth" had been prophesied by Moses and the prophets, when in reality we find no such specific 'prophecy' in the Bible. What we *do* discover are many 'messianic blueprints' that could be cobbled together and elaborated upon to create such a figure in the New Testament.

Concerning this passage, Eisenman comments:

> At this point, too, John is anxious to mask the true thrust of the "Nazoraean" terminology, which, as we have been discovering, means "Keeper" — either "Keeper of the Law" or "Keeper of the Secrets" — transforming it into Nazareth.[12]

Following this passage in John, at 1:46 we read the famous line "Can anything good come out of Nazareth?" Perhaps not, if it was only a necropolis at the time John's gospel was written, sometime during the *second* century.[13]

When Christ is on the cross in John 19:19, he is designated "Jesus the Nazoraios," not "Jesus of Nazareth," the sign reading: *Iēsous ho Nazōraios ho basileus tōn Ioudaiōn* — "Jesus the Nazoraios, King of the Jews."

Nazoraios or *Nazarene* — as referring to a cult and not an ethnic designation — is also indicated when Paul is deemed the "ringleader of the Nazoraioi" in the book of Acts [24:5], specifically said there to be a *sect*, not a demonym, appropriate since neither the apostle nor any of his followers was said to be from Nazareth. The argument could be made, of course, that by this time followers of 'Jesus of Nazareth' were called 'Nazarenes,' even though they did not come from there. However, again, the term here is not the demonym *Nazarenos*,

---

12 Eisenman, 1998: 841.

13 Although the canonical gospels are frequently dated to the last quarter of the first century, there remains no clear and unambiguous evidence of their emergence in the historical record before the last quarter of the *second* century at which point they suddenly begin to be discussed by a number of Church fathers. For more information, see my books *Suns of God* and *Who Was Jesus?*, as well as Walter Cassels' excellent study *Supernatural Religion*.

but the same word defined by Strong's as 'Nazarite,' the sect/cult in the Old Testament.

Essentially the same word *Naziraioi* was used by Josephus [*Ant.* 4.4.4; 19.6.1], while before 77 AD/CE, Pliny [*Nat. Hist.* 5] discussed the *Nazerini*, whom he dates to the first century BCE.

The closest we get to the phrase "Jesus of Nazareth" in the New Testament is also in Acts [10:38], a book that, according to scientific inspection, does not emerge clearly in the literary/historical record until long after the purported events: To wit, we find no trace of this text until the last quarter of the *second* century.[14] In Acts, Jesus is referred to as *Iēsoun ton apo Nazaret,* or "Jesus the one from Nazareth."

Thus, only once do we find in the New Testament a comparable designation as "Jesus of Nazareth" — in *Acts*, not the gospels — and the rest of the time he is either "a prophet from Nazareth" or "Jesus the Nazarene," *etc*. This fact remains largely unknown because translations consistently render "Jesus the Nazarene" as "Jesus of Nazareth."

In addition, in citing the later word used for 'Christians' by rabbinical Jews, *Nozrim*, Eisenman remarks:

> The term probably cannot derive from the word "Nazareth," although Nazareth could derive from it — that is, there could be a city in Galilee which derived its name from the expression *Nazoraean* in Hebrew, but not the other way around as the Gospels seem to prefer.[15]

The conclusion appears to be that the 'historical' Jesus from a city called 'Nazareth' in reality consists of messianic blueprints designed to make of the awaited savior a Nazarite or consecrated member of an evidently important religious order. In other words, the gospel writers created an allegorical or midrashic 'Nazareth' in which to place their fictional messiah, who was to be consecrated to God as a Nazarite, from the womb and for life.

---

14 See the detailed scholarship of Cassels' *Supernatural Religion*.

15 Eisenman, 1998: 250.

Nazara as 'the Truth'

The concept of 'the Nazoraios' as a religious title, rather than serving as a demonym of a historical individual, is exemplified also in the non-canonical Gospel of Philip:

> The apostles who were before us had these names for him: 'Jesus, the Nazorean, Messiah,' that is, 'Jesus, the Nazorean, the Christ.' The last name is 'Christ,' the first is 'Jesus,' that in the middle is '"the Nazarene.' 'Messiah' has two meanings, both 'the Christ' and 'the measured.' 'Jesus' in Hebrew is 'the redemption.' 'Nazara' is 'the truth.' 'The Nazarene,' then, is 'the truth.' 'Christ' has been measured. 'The Nazarene' and 'Jesus' are they who have been measured.[16]

Here we see that 'the Nazorean/Nazarene' is a *title* comparable to 'the Messiah' and 'the Christ.' It is meant to designate not a *place* called *Nazareth* but that Jesus is *allegorically the truth*.

We receive a further indication of these facts from Church father Epiphanius. As Price remarks:

> Epiphanius, an early Christian cataloguer of "heresies," mentions a pre-Christian sect called "the Nazoreans," their name meaning "the Keepers of the Torah," or possibly of the secrets (see Mark 4:11...). These Nazoreans were the heirs, supposedly, of the neoprimitivist sect of the Rechabites descending from the times of Jeremiah (Jer. 35:1–10). They were rather like Gypsies, itinerant carpenters.[17]

Of this heresy-cataloguer we also read:

> Epiphanius uses the spelling *nasaraioi* (Νασαραίοι), which he attempts to distinguish from the spelling *nazoraios* in parts of the New Testament, as a Jewish-Christian sect. According to the testimony of Epiphanius against the 4th century Nazarenes, he reports them as having pre-Christian origins. He writes: "(6,1) They did not call themselves Nasaraeans either; the Nasaraean sect was before Christ, and did not know Christ. 6,2 But besides, as I indicated, everyone called the Christians Nazoraeans," (*Adversus Haereses*,

16 Barnstone, 91–92.

17 Price, 53.

29.6).[18]

A tortuous effort is made by Epiphanius to differentiate these various groups, but it is clear that the reason for Christ being called a Nazarene is according to a 'prophecy' that could only have revolved around a religious sect, the same order in the Old Testament, which was pre-Christian.[19]

Blueprint Not Prophecy

As is the case with much else in the Bible, the 'prophecy' supposedly fulfilled at Matthew 2:23, in which the messiah was to be called 'Nazoraios,' is not a prophecy at all. The very phrase 'fulfill prophecy' in the New Testament, in fact, is an indication of midrash of a messianic 'blueprint' from the Old Testament.[20] In this regard, no such prophecy is known from the Old Testament. Some have surmised that the so-called prophecy being cited in Matthew 2:23 is from Isaiah 11:1, which discusses the "branch" (Heb. *netser)* from the "roots" of Jesse[21] and is one of the most famous messianic scriptures, as is much of the rest of the book. Indeed, one could analyze the rest of Isaiah as well for numerous blueprints used in the creation of the composite Christ character. If this prophecy involves Isaiah 11:1, then it refers to a *title*, not a place, and no such place is necessary to make of Jesus a Nazarite.

Moreover, it is also possible, if not probable, that the 'Nazarene prophecy' derives from the *past* story of Samson, in which the

18 "Nazarene (title)," en.wikipedia.org/wiki/Nazarene_(title)

19 For a further discussion of Epiphanius and Nazareth, see Eisenman, 1998: 243; 2006: 513; *etc.*

20 See my article "Did Jesus Fulfill Prophecy?" and the chapter by the same name in my book *Who Was Jesus?* for examples of Old Testament 'prophecies' or other scriptures used overtly in the New Testament.

21 In his article "Jesse's 'Lineage Tree' and Its Buddhist 'Branch,'" Michael Lockwood points out the interesting correspondence between this concept and that of Buddhism, including Aśōka/Ashoka's Buddhist medical missionaries. It is possible that these Buddhists noticed this idea in Jewish scripture and assisted in the midrash that eventually led to the creation of the Christian 'branch.' He compares this concept with the 'shoot' of the Bodhi tree under which Buddha had purportedly attained enlightened that Aśōka reputedly sent to Sri Lanka.

awaited one who would "deliver Israel out of the hands of the Philistines ['immigrants']" was to be a Nazarite or Nazirite, one who is consecrated. [Jdg 13:5, 7; Num 6:2, 13, 18, *etc.*] The Greek word for 'Nazarite' at Judges 13:5 is *nazir*, from the Hebrew *naziyr* (H5139), *meaning: 1) consecrated or devoted one, Nazarite: a) consecrated one; b) devotee, Nazarite; c) untrimmed (vine)*

The word translated 'Nazarites' at Lamech 4:7 is *Naziraioi*. *A Handy Concordance of the Septuagint* cites the word *nazeiraios* as an alternate for *nazi* and *nazir*. The term 'Nazarenos' never appears in the Old Testament and, again, was evidently created specifically to deem Jesus *a Nazarene*, as a demonym of a resident from 'the city of Nazareth.' There is no indication before that time of any such city or residents with this moniker.

The Greek word for 'to deliver' at Judges 13:5 is *sōsai*, from the verb *sōzō*, meaning 'to save.' Hence, in this Samson myth we have a Nazarite/Nazarene who will save Israel from its enemies — not unlike the Jesus savior figure of the New Testament. Samson, whose very name (Heb. *Shimshown)* means 'like a sun' (H8123), 'of the sun,' 'man of the sun' or 'the little sun,' possesses a number of solar attributes — such as his 'hair' or rays 'cut' by *Delilah*, the moon goddess[22] — and we can see in this tale a Jewish precedent for elaborating on ancient *myths* to inflate and validate religious claims.

As a related aside for further research, the pre-Christian Nazarites may have become the Natsarenes or Nasoreans, priests of the Mandaeans, who have been associated not only with John the Baptist

22 The name *Delilah* means 'feeble' (H1807), apparently referring to the waning moon, which 'robs' the sun's rays and drains *his* strength as *she* fades away. Delilah is also surmised to be the winter months, again robbing the sun of its rays and strengths. Samson's 'life' as depicted in the Bible in 12 episodes has been dissected as representing a solar year. See, *e.g.*, James Edwin Thorold Rogers's *Bible Folk-lore*, 96*ff.* In the past century, much effort has gone into dismissing this entire body of literature, but the grounds upon which this endeavor has been taken are not as solid as proponents would like. Indeed, after the declaration that "solar mythology is dead," we now have a new crop of superb scholars like Mark S. Smith and J. Glen Taylor to show that there is more to biblical solar mythology than meets the eye. See, *e.g.*, *Yahweh and the Sun: Biblical and Archaeological Evidence for Sun Worship in Ancient Israel*: "Probably the most provocative issue related to the nature of sun worship in ancient Israel...is the specific claim that Yahweh was identified with the sun." (Taylor, 20)

but also, significantly, have evidently served as a *carpenter* sect.[23] In *James the Brother of Jesus* and *The New Testament Code*, Robert Eisenman goes into greater detail as to what it meant to be a Nazarite/Nazirite, providing extensive discussions of various religious sects and the consecrated ascetic status. He also highlights the importance of such pious 'separation' in the Dead Sea scrolls, tracing this lineage to the New Testament and Christian tradition as well.

When these various scriptures and the many more so-called messianic prophecies, such as the "Man of Sorrows" and "Suffering Servant" of Isaiah 53, are factored together, it becomes evident that, in the composition of the New Testament, the Old Testament or *Tanakh* was used to flesh out a *midrashic* or *fictional* messiah figure.

Considering all the time and effort spent to find what would undoubtedly be numerous artifacts demonstrating a pre-Christian Nazareth, it remains noteworthy that no such hard proof has been discovered. Even if there was some sort of a settlement — not a 'city' (*polis*) — we are left with no confirming evidence of a Jesus from there who rose to tremendous prominence during the first third of the first century.

Rather than serving as biography and history, the tale about Nazareth constitutes interpretive midrash. It is designed not to record a biographical detail of a historical Jesus but to explain the purported

23 For more on this subject of Mandaeans, Nazoreans and John the Baptist, *etc.*, see my book *Suns of God: Krishna, Buddha and Christ Unveiled* (531*ff*). There is much reason to surmise that John the Baptist, rather than representing a purely 'historical' figure, constitutes a compilation of characters such as the Babylonian god Oannes the Water-god and the Egyptian god Anubis the Purifier. Again, see *Suns of God*, as well as my book *Christ in Egypt* for more information. We have seen Price's comment above about "itinerant carpenters." In the *Encyclopedia Britannica* ("Mandaeans," 17:557), we read, "As regards secular occupation, the present Mandaeans are goldsmiths, ironworkers, and house and ship carpenters." It is further suggestive that the Gospel of Philip emphasizes the occupation of Jesus' stepfather, Joseph, as a carpenter. (Barnstone, 96) The same can be said of the emphasis on the carpenter in the Gnostic/Mandaean *Book of John the Baptist*, in which we can see the relationship between the allegorical carpenter and divinity: "Let me warn you, my brothers, of the god which the carpenter has joinered together. If the carpenter has joinered together the god, who then has joinered together the carpenter?" (See G.R.S. Mead) The god or hero as carpenter is a recurring theme in mythology. (See, *e.g.*, *Suns of God*, 366*ff*.)

Old Testament prophecy of the awaited messiah as a Nazarite, a member of an obviously important religious order. This detail is evidently intended at once to fulfill this apparent 'messianic scripture' and to anchor the fictional Jesus character in 'history.'

Was there a historical 'Jesus of Nazareth'?

Bibliography

"Nazarene (title)." en.wikipedia.org/wiki/Nazarene_(title)

"Nazareth." en.wikipedia.org/wiki/Nazareth

Acharya S. *Suns of God: Krishna, Buddah and Christ Unveiled*. IL: AUP, 2004.

(See also "Murdock, D.M.")

Barnstone, Willis, ed. *The Other Bible*. HarperSanFrancisco, 1980.

Cassels, Walter Richard. *Supernatural Religion: An Inquiry into the Reality of Divine Revelation.* [London: Watts & Co., 1902].

Dark, Ken. "The Myth of Nazareth: The Invented Town of Jesus." *Bulletin of the Anglo-Israel Archaeological Society, vol. 26* [2008: 140–146].

Ehrman, Bart D. *Did Jesus Exist? The Historical Argument for Jesus of Nazareth.* [New York: HarperOne, 2012].

Eisenman, Robert. *James the Brother of Jesus: The Key to Unlocking the Secrets of Early Christianity and the Dead Sea Scrolls*. Penguin, 1998.

— *The New Testament Code: The Cup of the Lord, the Damascus Covenant, and the Blood of Christ*. [London: Watkins Publishing, 2006].

Guignebert, Charles. *Jesus*. [New Hyde Park, NY: University Books, 1956].

Lockwood, Michael. "Jesse's 'Lineage Tree' and Its Buddhist 'Branch'."

Luz, Ulrich, *et al*. *Matthew 1–7: A Continental Commentary*. [Augsberg, MN: Fortress Press, 1989].

Murdock, D.M. "Jesus neighbor's house found." freethoughtnation.com/contributing-writers/63-acharya-s/224-jesus-neighbors-house-found.html

— *Who Was Jesus? Fingerprints of The Christ*. [Seattle, WA: Stellar House Publishing, 2007].

(*See also* "Acharya S")

Pfann, Stephen, and Yehudah Rapuano. "On the Nazareth Village Farm Report: A Reply to Salm." *Bulletin of the Anglo-Israel Archaeological Society*, vol. 26 [2008: 105–108].

Price, Robert M. *The Incredible Shrinking Son of Man*. [Amherst, NY: Prometheus Books, 2003].

Rudolph, Kurt. *Mandaeism*. [Leiden: E.J. Brill, 1978].

Salm, René. "An Essential Nazareth Bibliography." www.nazarethmyth.info/bibl.html

— "Nazareth, Faith, and the Dark Option — an Update." www.nazarethmyth.info/naz3article.html

— "Nazareth: René Salm's preliminary response to Bart Ehrman." vridar.wordpress.com/2012/05/16/nazareth-rene-salms-preliminary-response-to-bart-ehrman/

— "Nazareth scholar: 'No house from Jesus's time found there'." freethoughtnation.com/contributing-writers/53-archaeology-archaeoastronomy/225-nazareth-scholar-no-house-from-jesuss-time-found-there.html

Salm, René. *The Myth of Nazareth: The Invented Town of Jesus*. ed. Frank Zindler. [American Atheist Press, 2008].

Taylor, J. Glen. *Yahweh and the Sun: Biblical and Archaeological Evidence for Sun Worship in Ancient Israel*. [Sheffield, England: Sheffield Academic Press, 1993].

Zindler, Frank. "Bart's Subtitle." freethoughtnation.com/contributing-writers/76-frank-zindler/685-jesus-of-what-a-response-by-frank-zindler-to-bart-ehrman.html

— "Where Jesus Never Walked." www.atheists.org/content/where-jesus-never-walked

PART III: Crucified Messiahs

CHAPTER FIFTEEN

"Key Data" and the Crucified Messiah
A Critique of Pages 156–74 of *Did Jesus Exist?*

Earl Doherty

This chapter examines the conflict between messianic expectation and result:

- *Assumptions based on the Gospels and Acts*
- *Why did Paul persecute the early church?*
- *Paul's gospel vs. Ehrman's view of early church beliefs*
- *Christ as "curse" for being "hanged on a tree"*
- *Paul switching horses in mid-stream*
- *A new view of Christian origins*
- *The traditional Jewish Messiah*
- *Jesus as lower-class Galilean peasant*
- *Who would make up a crucified Messiah?*

* * * * *

Earl Doherty

A conflict between expectation and history

To introduce his second piece of "Key Data" which confer a "high degree of certainty that (Jesus) was an historical figure" [144], Bart Ehrman offers this:

> These early Christians from day one believed that Jesus was the messiah. But they knew that he had been crucified. [156]

This is a good example of what happens when one's thinking is stuck firmly inside the box. The point Ehrman is making is that the concept of the 'messiah,' the expectation of what he would be and what he would do, conflicted with the fact that Jesus had been crucified. In other words, historical expectations were at odds with (alleged) historical events. But if that is indeed one's starting assumption, and if it is wrong, then it will lead us down all sorts of problematic garden paths and into conclusions which are not only erroneous but unnecessary.

The first part of *this assumption, entirely based on the Gospels and Acts*, is that certain people made judgments about a certain historical man. If that were the case, then an anomaly would certainly have existed between traditional ideas about the messiah and what the life of that man actually entailed. Why, then, the question arises, did those people come to such a judgment when it conflicted so much with standard messianic expectation?

But all we have to do is ask: *what if no judgment was initially made about any historical man?* Everything that follows would then be entirely different, and perhaps more amenable to understanding how Christianity began and showing a conformity to what the majority of the texts themselves are telling us.

Paul's persecution of the church

> For reasons that may not seem self-evident at first, claiming that Jesus was crucified is a powerful argument that Jesus actually lived. [156]

Ehrman's route to supporting this statement is a complicated one. He first calls attention to Paul's persecution of the church in Judea prior to his conversion. He notes that Paul says nothing specific about what the beliefs of that early church were, or on what particular grounds it was subjected to persecution by the authorities, with himself acting as their agent. Nothing daunted, Ehrman steps into that breach. *But because he has made the initial assumption that an historical man was interpreted as the messiah, he embarks on a chain of speculation which not only contains problems, but also looks to be completely off the path of reality.*

To begin with, Paul refers to those persecuted as "the church of *God*" [Gal. 1:13], whereas if this were a movement proceeding out of belief in and reaction to a human man, we might expect it to call itself "the church of *Jesus*." Then to set the scene of his argument, Ehrman slips into the same kind of question-begging as he did in the first part of the chapter dealing with "brother of the Lord." From his inevitable contact with the people he was persecuting, Ehrman surmises that Paul must have learned about Jesus from them. No doubt. But what sort of 'Jesus' was that? Ehrman simply assumes the very issue under debate: that it was the Jesus portrayed in the Gospels, the human man who had been crucified only a few years earlier.

What Paul "learned" about Jesus

And what were they saying about this Jesus?

> These Christians were not calling Jesus a dying-rising God. They were calling him the Jewish messiah. And they understood this messiah to be completely human, a person chosen by God to mediate his will on earth. That is the Jesus Paul first heard of. [157]

I guess Ehrman hasn't read Paul and the other epistles lately, *which constitute the only early record extant*. Perhaps he's forgotten Paul's gospel as laid out in 1 Corinthians 15:3–4: that Christ died, was buried, and rose to life on the third day.[1] Perhaps he's lost sight

1 1 Cor 15:3 For I delivered unto you first of all that which I also received, how that Christ died for our sins according to the scriptures; 4 And that he was buried, and that

of Romans 6:1–6 as well, in which believers were baptized into his death, lay buried with him, and will as a consequence be one with him in a resurrection like his.[2] So far, it's pretty much all dying and rising, something which provided salvation, a very un-Jewish concept especially in regard to the expected messiah. And there are a host of other references throughout Paul and the other epistle writers to Jesus' suffering and death (though never in any recognizable correspondence to the Gospel story), and to his rising.

Would this be "calling (Jesus) the Jewish messiah"? Obviously, there is an anomaly here between what, according to Ehrman, "Paul first heard" about Jesus from the earliest Christians, and what his stated set of beliefs about him are in his surviving letters. How does Ehrman deal with that anomaly?

An "offensive" doctrine

Ehrman has just identified Jewish messianic expectation as something that was at odds with the fact of Jesus' crucifixion. In other words, Jewish expectation did not include a dying and rising for its messiah — salvific or otherwise. According to Ehrman, Paul learned from the Jewish believers he persecuted that the man Jesus was the messiah, although this was something that would not have been blasphemous to Jews, some of whom had the occasional habit of declaring this or that person to be the messiah.

But then why were these people with their non-blasphemous beliefs being persecuted by the authorities? Ehrman suggests that Paul, and presumably those authorities, were "offended" by the idea that a crucified man could be declared the messiah. All of this, of

---

he rose again the third day according to the scriptures.

2 Romans 6:1 What shall we say then? Shall we continue in sin, that grace may abound? 2 God forbid. How shall we, that are dead to sin, live any longer therein? 3 Know ye not, that so many of us as were baptized into Jesus Christ were baptized into his death? 4 Therefore we are buried with him by baptism into death: that like as Christ was raised up from the dead by the glory of the Father, even so we also should walk in newness of life. 5 For if we have been planted together in the likeness of his death, we shall be also in the likeness of his resurrection: 6 Knowing this, that our old man is crucified with him, that the body of sin might be destroyed, that henceforth we should not serve sin.

course, is pure speculation on Ehrman's part. There is nothing, not a hint in the early record, that anyone was declaring *a recently crucified man* as the messiah and that the authorities were offended by this. (It isn't even in Q, the supposed earliest reference to Jesus, which *never* refers to their perceived founder figure as the messiah, or even to his death.)

We might particularly note that such a thing is entirely missing in 1 Corinthians 1:18–24 which says that the "doctrine of the cross," the concept that the Christ had been crucified, was a "stumbling block to Jews and a folly to Greeks."[3] There is nothing said (though it is always, of course, read into the text) about a *human man* who was crucified being the messiah. Now, considering that in this same epistle [8:6] Paul is clearly seen to regard his Christ Jesus as a part of God,[4] this 1 Corinthians passage must entail the idea that this "Christ crucified" which Paul preaches *is a divine figure* — even if it were the case that he had formerly been a human being.

But in that case, **the Jews' "stumbling block" over a crucified messiah would have been vastly overshadowed by their apoplexy at the blasphemy that *Paul and his fellow Christians had identified a human man with God.*** Paul makes no defence of this blasphemy because there is no sign that such an objection has been raised by anyone. And there is certainly no sign, here or anywhere else, that Paul felt any need to explain why his own view of Jesus has been carried so vastly further, and in such a new and blasphemous direction, than the Jewish church he formerly persecuted and to which he was converted.

3 1 Cor 1:18 For the preaching of the cross is to them that perish foolishness; but unto us which are saved it is the power of God. 19 For it is written, I will destroy the wisdom of the wise, and will bring to nothing the understanding of the prudent. 20 Where is the wise? where is the scribe? where is the disputer of this world? hath not God made foolish the wisdom of this world? 21 For after that in the wisdom of God the world by wisdom knew not God, it pleased God by the foolishness of preaching to save them that believe. 22 For the Jews require a sign, and the Greeks seek after wisdom: 23 But we preach Christ crucified, unto the Jews a stumblingblock, and unto the Greeks foolishness; 24 but unto them which are called, both Jews and Greeks, Christ the power of God, and the wisdom of God.

4 1 Cor 8:6 But to us there is but one God, the Father, of whom are all things, and we in him; and one Lord Jesus Christ, by whom are all things, and we by him.

Earl Doherty

Christ as a "curse"

Ehrman points to Galatians 3:13 as an indication of the 'offensiveness' that would have been caused by those Jews adopting a crucified man as the messiah:

> Christ bought us freedom from the curse of the law by becoming for our sake an accursed thing; for scripture says, "Cursed is everyone who is hanged on a tree" [Deut. 21:23].

Ehrman links this ancient view with the Roman method of execution by crucifixion, thinking to cast light on why Paul was offended. But it would have been useful if anywhere in his letters Paul had actually spelled out that he had been offended by hearing that an historical man 'cursed for being hanged on a tree' was thought of as the messiah. It would have been useful had he anywhere even intimated that it was information like this which he had learned from the people he persecuted. Certainly he makes no such connection in Galatians 3:13.[5] Neither does the writer of 1 Peter in 2:22–24 who speaks of Christ hanged on a tree[6] while giving us, by way of 'biography' about that event, simply a paraphrase of verses from Isaiah 53.[7] That was his apparent source of such a biography.

5 Gal 3:13 Christ hath redeemed us from the curse of the law, being made a curse for us: for it is written, Cursed is every one that hangeth on a tree: 14 That the blessing of Abraham might come on the Gentiles through Jesus Christ; that we might receive the promise of the Spirit through faith.

6 1 Peter 2:21 For even hereunto were ye called: because Christ also suffered for us, leaving us an example, that ye should follow his steps: 22 Who did no sin, neither was guile found in his mouth: 23 Who, when he was reviled, reviled not again; when he suffered, he threatened not; but committed himself to him that judgeth righteously: 24 Who his own self bare our sins in his own body on the tree that we, being dead to sins, should live unto righteousness: by whose stripes ye were healed.

7 Isaiah 53:4 Surely he hath borne our grief's, and carried our sorrows: yet we did esteem him stricken, smitten of God, and afflicted. 5 But he was wounded for our transgressions, he was bruised for our iniquities: the chastisement of our peace was upon him; and with his stripes we are healed. 6 ... and the Lord hath laid on him the iniquity of us all. 7 He was oppressed, and he was afflicted, yet he opened not his mouth: he is brought as a lamb to the slaughter, and as a sheep before her shearers is dumb, so he openeth not his mouth.

"Key Data" and the Crucified Messiah

Paul switching Jesuses in mid-stream

Ehrman now has to face that anomaly head-on. He has postulated that before his conversion, Paul found offensive the idea that a crucified man was the messiah, but this was "before changing his mind and becoming a follower of Jesus." And what a change of mind! *Ehrman has embroiled himself in all sorts of contradictions here.* The Jewish followers of Jesus whom he was persecuting were, by Ehrman's measure, traditional Jews innocent of blasphemy who did not regard Jesus as divine, just the messiah. One wonders, then, what this "church of God" who believed a crucified man was the messiah thought this unorthodox messiah had been good for. Had he overthrown the Romans? Had he elevated the Jews to supremacy? Had he inaugurated the Kingdom?

How could any group of Jews possibly have imagined that, quite unlike their traditional expectations and regardless of what scripture had led them to expect, it had really been God's plan to send his messiah to earth on a preliminary visit: to be ignominiously killed, but with the promise of coming again, and *then* he would fulfill the expectations that the messiah was famed for. Nor would those Jews have thought the reason for his death on the first visit was to redeem the world's sins, since Ehrman assures us that, contrary to the atonement doctrine later Christians were to adopt (they read it into passages like Isaiah 53), traditional Jewish outlook contained no such concept.

But wait a minute. What, then, was Paul 'converted' *to*? The belief that a human man who was *not* a part of God had been the messiah? That he was *not* a dying and rising savior, but simply "a person chosen by God to mediate his will on earth"? The former would have been a pagan idea, and Ehrman tells us that this was a group governed entirely by Jewish principles. Another pagan idea would have been the concept of the believers joining themselves with the savior, becoming a 'part' of him and he of them, so presumably Ehrman has ruled this out as well.

Earl Doherty

An impossible contradiction

The problem is, most of Paul's beliefs, as far as we can see, were the *direct opposite* of what he had allegedly learned from the Judean church he converted to. His Christ *did* die and rise. He saved through his death and resurrection. Romans 6:1–6 speaks of joining with the Son, being "baptized into union with Christ Jesus," of being "buried with him," of "becoming one with him in a resurrection like his." Paul's Christ was a part of God; as I've said before, to claim otherwise is to perform extreme violence on the texts (or ignore them altogether), as with 1 Corinthians 8:6, or Colossians 1:15–20.[8]

Is Ehrman saying that Paul was converted to the non-blasphemous variety of faith, and then subsequently did another about-face and betrayed all the principles of the church he had converted to, adopting a blasphemy it would have roundly condemned? Where is the evidence of such a conflict with and divorce from the 'church of God in Judea,' especially if the latter were in any way connected to the Jerusalem pillars as is often suggested? (In fact, Paul declares in 1 Corinthians 15:11 that he and the latter proclaim the same thing.)[9] Where is the record, even an implication, of this *double conversion* by Paul?

Indeed, such a thing has to be ruled out. In Galatians 1:23, Paul declares that

> Christ's congregations in Judea . . . heard it said, "Our former persecutor is preaching the good news of the faith which once he tried to destroy."

8 Col 1:15 Who is the image of the invisible God, the firstborn of every creature: 16 For by him were all things created, that are in heaven, and that are in earth, visible and invisible, whether they be thrones, or dominions, or principalities, or powers: all things were created by him, and for him: 17 And he is before all things, and by him all things consist. 18 And he is the head of the body, the church: who is the beginning, the firstborn from the dead; that in all things he might have the pre-eminence. 19 For it pleased the Father that in him should all fullness dwell; 20 And having made peace through the blood of his cross, by him to reconcile all things unto himself; by him, I say, whether they be things in earth, or things in heaven.

9 1 Cor 15:1 Moreover, brethren, I declare unto you the gospel which I preached unto you, which also ye have received, and wherein ye stand.

"Key Data" and the Crucified Messiah

But Paul's gospel of a dying and rising part of God was, according to Ehrman, precisely *not* the faith of the Judaean church he persecuted. Yet that church, according to Paul, remarked that he now *did* preach their faith. *This is an unresolvable contradiction.* Moreover, would Paul, in the course of his supposed second about-face, switch from a focus that was entirely on a human man to one which focused exclusively on a heavenly deity with no reference to or interest in its human predecessor? That lack of interest has become so profound that he dismisses the human man entirely, portrays the faith movement as impelled by God and the Spirit, makes no room for a recently incarnated Jesus in the course of salvation history, and takes for himself the role of inaugurating the new covenant in parallel with Moses' dispensation of the old.

That's not a 'change of mind.' It's a brain transplant.

And no one called him on any of it!

Revising Christian origins from outside the box

Ehrman cannot see that this convoluted mess he is presenting to his readers is far less likely — indeed it is ludicrous — than the obvious alternative: *that the earliest form of the faith Paul persecuted and then was converted to had nothing to do with a human man* who had been crucified, but with a Son and sacrificial Savior who, as Paul and others regularly say, was discovered in scripture after lying unknown for long ages until God and the Spirit revealed him (as in Romans 16:25–27).[10] Either he lived at some unknown time in the past (the view of G. A. Wells), or he lived, died, and was resurrected entirely in a non-material dimension, in the supernatural heavenly world.

But not a single epistle writer ever offers us a statement that he had lived on earth at an unknown time in the past. They never show

10 Romans 16:25 Now to him that is of power to establish you according to my gospel, and the preaching of Jesus Christ, according to the revelation of the mystery, which was kept secret since the world began, 26 But now is made manifest, and by the scriptures of the prophets, according to the commandment of the everlasting God, made known to all nations for the obedience of faith: 27 To God only wise, be glory through Jesus Christ for ever. Amen.

the slightest inclination to speculate on any details of that unknown life (they certainly could have consulted scripture for such things, as the evangelists were later to do). And the occasional human-sounding language can easily be understood in the context of Platonic philosophy and cosmology — with the occasional passage or document, such as 1 Corinthians 2:8[11] and the Ascension of Isaiah,[12] not to mention Hebrews' picture of a heavenly sacrifice, *actually placing it in a spiritual dimension*. Thus the Wellsian type of theory should be rejected in favor of the heavenly alternative.

The traditional 'Anointed One'

Ehrman now digresses to give us a capsule summary of the history of the Jewish concept of messiah. Originally it simply enjoyed its literal meaning of 'Anointed One,' referring to the practice of anointing a king or high priest, or one enjoying God's special favor. It was the mark of a special representative of God. This, when Israel lost its independence under a succession of foreign overlords, led to the concept that there was a unique 'Messiah' promised by God who at some point in the future would restore the nation to its independent kingship under a descendant of David. One of the Psalms of Solomon most thoroughly encapsulates this complex of expectations,[13] one in

---

11 1 Cor 2:7 But we speak the wisdom of God in a mystery, even the hidden wisdom, which God ordained before the world unto our glory: 8 Which none of the princes of this world knew: for had they known it, they would not have crucified the Lord of glory.

12 The key verses in Ascension of Isaiah are 9:14–15, but a convincing placement of the sacrifice in a spiritual dimension is the product of the analysis of their larger context, including even other chapters.

13 *Editor's note*: Psalm 17, a lengthy work, contains lines such as

> See, Lord, and raise up for them their king,
> the son of David, to rule over your servant Israel
> in the time known to you, O God.
>
> Undergird him with the strength to destroy the unrighteous rulers,
> to **purge** Jerusalem from gentiles
> who trample her to destruction;
> in wisdom and in righteousness to **drive out**
> the sinners from the inheritance; ...

which there was no thought of redeeming the world or its sinners.

Ehrman also gives us alternative concepts about a messiah existing at the same time. One — or rather a duality of concepts — is found in the Dead Sea Scrolls, in their expectation of "two messiahs, one who would be a ruler-king and over him the priestly messiah." Then there was this:

> [The messiah] would be a cosmic figure, a powerful angelic being sent from God to destroy the enemy and set up God's kingdom on earth. This figure was often modeled on the "one like a son of man" in the book of Daniel (for example, 7:13–14). In an apocryphal writing known as 1 Enoch, probably from about the same time, comes this prediction about the future messianic Son of Man:
>
>> [The Son of Man] shall never pass away or perish from before the face of the earth. But those who have led the world astray shall be bound with chains; and their ruinous congregation shall be imprisoned; all their deeds shall vanish from before the face of the earth. Thenceforth nothing that is corruptible shall be found; for that Son of Man has appeared and has seated himself upon the throne of his glory; and all evil shall disappear from before his face (1 Enoch 69). [162]

The Jewish sect represented in 1 Enoch (in the section known as the "Similitudes of Enoch," probably from some time in the first century) has envisioned for itself a spiritual messiah who is a cosmic figure and powerful angelic being residing entirely in heaven and whose arrival they await on the day of judgment; with this Messiah/Son of Man/Elect One the righteous on earth identify themselves, and from him they receive certain future guarantees. (None of 1 Enoch contains the concept of a sacrificial messiah, or a death and rising for him.)

And he will **purge** Jerusalem
(and make it) holy as it was even from the beginning...

[*Old Testament Pseudepigrapha*, ed. J.H. Charlesworth, Vol. 2 Garden City, NY: Doubleday, 1985:667]

Could this have been a model for Jesus' cleansing of the temple? — FRZ

Why not, then, *another* Jewish sect which has envisioned out of scripture a figure they see as God's own Son, in the spirit of the Logos or personified Wisdom; only *this* one also underwent a sacrifice at the hands of evil angels, but came back to life as a guarantee of eternal life for the devotees who have joined themselves with him through faith and ritual? All the concepts of the time were available to create such a perceived 'revelation' of a hitherto hidden truth. Like the "Similitudes of Enoch," this was a transformation of the traditional idea of an earthly messiah into a spiritual and Platonically-based version, one taking on a dimension of divinity.

He, too, would be a judge and establisher of the Kingdom. And when he came into contact with an imagined sage who had preached in Galilee and came to be identified with a different group's expectation of a similar End-time figure they called the Son of Man — though this one, too, had no death and rising dimension — a fusion took place. The heavenly Son fell to earth to join with his composite partner to create, under Mark's hand, a powerful symbol of an entire religious trend: Jesus, ultimately of Nazareth.

The Jewish messiah and the crucified Jesus

In his attempt to accommodate the crucified man Jesus to the concept of the Jewish messiah, Ehrman makes a number of unsupportable declarations. The first is

> In all our early traditions (Jesus) was a lower class peasant from rural Galilee . . . [163]

I hardly need to point out that no such thing is witnessed in the early traditions that are contained in the epistles. Even if Ehrman has postulated (on dubious grounds) oral traditions, including Aramaic ones, which he claims go back to immediately following Jesus' death, he can hardly claim that "all" early traditions make Jesus out to be a peasant from rural Galilee. Even if the epistolary view of Christ were claimed to be a subsequent development, we would hardly see in such a wide range of documents and writers, only a decade or two after his death, an utter absence of any sign of its supposed predecessor.

Then there is this declaration:

> That Jesus died by crucifixion is almost universally attested in our sources, early and late. We have traditions of Jesus's bloody execution in independent Gospel sources (Mark, M, L, John, Gospel of Peter), throughout our various epistles and other writings (Hebrews, 1 Peter, Revelation), and certainly in Paul — everywhere in Paul. The crucifixion of Jesus is the core of Paul's message and is attested abundantly in his writings as one of the — if not the — earliest things that he knew about the man. [163]

Once a question-beggar, always a question-beggar. I've already dealt elsewhere with the claim that all those "Gospel sources" are to be seen as independent. As for all those non-Gospel writers, including Paul, to which we can add many non-canonical documents, crucifixion is indeed the centerpiece. What is *not* part of that centerpiece, however, is its location on earth, or the fact that a recent human man was involved, or that he was crucified by human agencies. Indeed, *some of them specify the agents to be the demon spirits,*[14] and one or two actually give a location in the heavens.[15] It's one thing to beg a question; it's another for that question to be allowed to stand in contradiction to a major part of the evidence.

14 There are two principal references to the demon spirits as crucifiers of Christ. 1 Cor. 2:8 tells us of a mystery "which none of the rulers of this age knew: for had they known it, they would not have crucified the Lord of glory." The phrase "rulers of this age" is a widely accepted reference (including in ancient times) to the demon spirits. The argument is whether they did it directly or, as defenders of an historical Jesus maintain, through earthly authorities. The other is the reference to "the god of that world laying hands upon the Son and hanging him on a tree" in Ascension of Isaiah 9:14, which is a reference to Satan and his minions doing so in the firmament, as the passage can be shown to indicate.

15 A location in the heavens is derivable from Ascension of Isaiah 9:14, and with somewhat less obviousness from Colossians 2:15, which presents a heavenly setting for the cross in which Christ is triumphant over the demons and leads them in a captive procession. A more involved argument for support for a heavenly setting can be derived from the New Testament Epistle to the Hebrews.

Earl Doherty

Who would make up a crucified messiah?

Ehrman now asks the question that many historicists consider something of a slam-dunk. Would any first century Jew make up the idea of a crucified messiah — meaning out of nothing, out of no historical event, as Mythicists claim? But once again, Ehrman is doing his thinking from inside the box. What if the question, asked from outside the box, were:

> What would have led certain Jewish thinkers, influenced by Greek ideas and widespread religious trends, to survey scripture and find that it told of a part of God who had undergone a sacrifice in the supernatural world at the hands of evil angels, some of those thinkers seeing this as a way of overcoming the demons and rescuing present and future souls of the Jewish righteous from Sheol, others broadening their view and seeing it as a way of redeeming the sins of the entire world?

What a different picture of the origins of Christianity Ehrman might have come up with then!

Unfortunately, Ehrman does not ask that question.

CHAPTER SIXTEEN

Bart Ehrman and The Crucified Messiah

Frank R. Zindler

ABSTRACT

Bart Ehrman is mistaken in his argument that the first Christians "from day one" knew that their Messiah, Jesus, had been crucified. It is argued that the term 'Christ' was originally spelled differently and had a different etymology than that usually supposed. It did not derive from a verb meaning 'to anoint.' Thus, the earliest Christians did not worship a Messiah. Epigraphic, manuscript, and literary evidence is presented to show that *Chr?stos* was originally spelled with *ei* and *ē*, not *i*. Then, when the great vowel shift known as iotacism or itacism transformed Ancient Greek into something more like Modern Greek, *ei* and *ē* merged with *i* and 'Christ' was born. In support of the thesis that the first Christians worshiped a celestial Chr?st before they worshiped a terrestrial Jesus, it is noted that crucifixion of Jesus with nails was added late in the tradition, and that lack of nails makes more supportable the idea that the crucifixion of Chr?st was a celestial, not terrestrial, event.

Frank R. Zindler

EHRMAN'S POSITION EXAMINED

Chapter Five of Bart Ehrman's *Did Jesus Exist?* is titled "Two Key Data for the Historicity of Jesus." The first datum concerns the alleged fact that the Apostle Paul "was personally acquainted with Jesus's closest disciple, Peter, and Jesus's own brother, James." The datum that concerns us here, however, is the second one dealing with the problem of "The Crucified Messiah." As Ehrman explains,

> ...I am devoting this chapter to two pieces of evidence that argue with particular cogency that there must have been a historical figure of Jesus. There is a good deal of other evidence that has proved compelling to just about everyone who has ever considered it with a dispassionate eye, wanting simply to know what happened in the past, wherever the evidence leads. But these two points are especially compelling. The first had to do with whom Paul knew... The second has to do, by contrast, with what Paul knew even earlier. And not with just what Paul knew but with what everyone among the early followers of Jesus knew. These early Christians from day one believed that Jesus was the messiah. But they knew that he had been crucified. [*DJE?* 156]

The logically fallacious rhetoric inhering in this passage — especially the informal fallacy known as *ignotum per ignotius* (explaining the unknown in terms of the even more unknown) — I shall deal with elsewhere. Here I must concern myself with the question, "*Did the earliest Christians "from day one" believe that 'Christ' was the equivalent of the Jewish Messiah?*" I note admiringly that Ehrman is an acknowledged and valuable authority on deviant, non-Orthodox early forms of Christianity and their scriptures. This compels me to inquire: Could Marcion or the various Docetists or Gnostics have possibly equated 'Christ' as distinguished from 'Jesus' with the Jewish Messiah? Could their 'Jesus' or 'Savior' be so equated?

It is curious that in the entire Pauline corpus — which Ehrman believes to be the earliest source of information concerning what "early Christians from day one believed" — never once does the Greek word *messias* appear, although it is to be found in what is probably the last completed of the canonical gospels, the Gospel of John. Moreover, the Pauline 'Christ' or 'Christ Jesus' is never identified with the messiah as overtly as in the Gospel of John — the only document in the entire canonical New Testament that does so.

John 1:41 tells us that "The first thing he [Andrew] did was to find his brother Simon. He said to him, 'We have found the Messiah' (which is the Hebrew for 'Christ')." John 4:25 (the only other occurrence of the word *messias* in the entire New Testament) says that "The woman answered, 'I know that messiah' (that is Christ) 'is coming. When he comes he will tell us everything.'" [NEB]

These verses, found only in a presumably late tradition, have to explain to readers that a Messiah is a Christ — 'the so-called Christ' (*ho legomenos Christos*) according to the Greek text. I do not know how Ehrman would explain the need for such an explanation if all early Christians "from day one" knew that 'Christ' meant 'Messiah,' but I shall posit below that the word that has come down to us as *Christos* (spelled with *iota* in Greek and appearing to derive from the Greek verb *chriō* meaning 'smear,' 'anoint') was originally spelled differently and meant something else in the proto-Christian mysteries. Only later did it come to be spelled with *iota* and be identified with the Jewish Messiah. It would appear that the explanations in John's gospel were needed to deal with this newly acquired identity for the focal figure of Christian worship.

We must admit, however, that it is almost universally supposed that the epithet 'Christ' is derived from the Greek term *christos* ('anointed one') and is therefore equal to the Hebrew *māshīaḥ* ('anointed one,' 'messiah'). The reason why this is so is not hard to discover. It is a title given to a savior god who — at some point yet to be determined — became identified with a messiah whose coming was awaited by various Jewish groups at the turn of the era. As Ehrman explains,

> The word messiah is Hebrew and means 'anointed one.' As I pointed out earlier, the Greek translation of the term is *christos* so that Jesus Christ literally means 'Jesus the Messiah.' The origin of the term goes back into the ancient history of Israel, to the time when the nation was ruled by kings, who were said to have been specially

> favored, "anointed," by God. In fact, the king was literally anointed during his inauguration ceremonies, when oil was poured on his head... Other persons thought to be God's special representatives on earth, such as high priests, were sometimes anointed as well... [*DJE?* 159]

But we must return to Ehrman's "data for the historicity of Jesus," in particular the 'fact' that "What Paul appears to have found offensive [*before his conversion*] was that Jesus in particular was being called the messiah. The reason that was offensive is that Paul and everyone else knew that Jesus had been condemned to death by crucifixion. Jesus could scarcely then have been the messiah of God..." [*DJE?* 157–58] Ehrman then presents a number of arguments attempting to prove that no Jewish group expected its Messiah to be executed as a common criminal and that Old Testament proof-texting to demonstrate that the Messiah must suffer is *ad hoc* apologetic to account for the fact that a real Jesus had been crucified. Jesus could not therefore be shown to have been the Messiah unless Old Testament passages could be mined for 'evidence' to show that the Messiah would have to suffer.

> ...there were no Jews prior to Christianity who thought Isaiah 53 (or any of the other 'suffering' passages) referred to the future messiah. We do not have a single Jewish text prior to the time of Jesus that interprets the passage messianically. So why do Christians traditionally interpret it this way? For the same reason they think that the messiah had to suffer. In their view Jesus is the messiah. And Jesus suffered. Therefore the messiah had to suffer. And this must not have come as a surprise to God; it must have all been planned. And so Christians found passages in the Hebrew Bible that talked about someone suffering and said that it referred to the suffering of the future messiah, Jesus. Jews roundly and loudly disagreed with these interpretations. And so the arguments began. [*DJE?* 166]

Ehrman then tries to show that all these attempts to explain away the crucifixion of the Christian Messiah is a compelling proof of the existence of Jesus:

> That no Jew would make up such an idea is made crystal clear by Paul himself in one of his letters. When writing to the Corinthians Paul makes the intriguing and compelling statement that the fact that Christians proclaimed a messiah who had been crucified was the single greatest "stumbling block" for Jews (I Corinthians 1:23) and a completely ridiculous claim to Gentiles (same verse). That is to say, Jews didn't buy it. And why not? Because for Jews this very claim — the heart of the Christians' affirmation of their faith — was absurd, offensive, and potentially blasphemous. [*DJE?* 170]

Then, with no proof whatsoever for these assertions and assumptions being presented for our evaluation, we are presented with a triumphant claim:

> Yet this is what a very small group of Jews, sometime before the year 32, were saying about Jesus. Not that he was God. And not that he was the great king ruling now in Jerusalem. He was the crucified messiah. It is almost impossible to explain this claim — coming at this place, at this time, among this people — if there had not in fact been a Jesus who was crucified. [*DJE?* 170]

I shall deal with the logical and evidentiary problems of this argument elsewhere. For the purpose of this chapter, however, we shall merely indulge in an exercise of 'thinking outside the box' and see where the train of thought pulls us.

What if some Jews *did* expect their Messiah to 'suffer' *à la* Isaiah 53? What if a Messiah had in fact been killed — but that that messiah had *not* been Jesus of Nazareth? Several minutes of searching on the Internet does in fact yield reason to think Ehrman is wrong in his claim that no Jews expected their Messiah to suffer. Israel Knohl[1] has shown that several documents belatedly published from the Dead Sea Scrolls show not only that the Qumran community expected a Messiah would have to suffer *à la* Isaiah 53, one of its leaders — a certain Menahem (the 'Paraclete') — actually seems to have arrogated that prophetic experience to himself! Knohl identifies him as the

1 Israel Knohl, *The Messiah before Jesus: The Suffering Servant of the Dead Sea Scrolls*, S. Mark Taper Foundation Imprint in Jewish Studies, translated by David Maisel [Berkeley: U. Cal. Press, 2002:200].

leader of the Essenes who wrote of himself in Suffering-Servant terms and appears to have been killed in the uprising after the death of Herod the Great in 4 BCE.

But let us hop back onto the train of thought to see where else it might take us. What if it *wasn't* sometime before the year 32? What if it wasn't a very small group of *Jews*? What if the story didn't begin in *Jerusalem*? What if it wasn't originally *a messiah* that had been crucified? What if the crucifixion didn't take place on 'Golgotha' — or anywhere else *on earth*? What if proto-Christians worshiped a 'Christ' before they worshiped a 'Jesus'? Indeed, if they *had* worshiped a Jesus before they worshiped a Christ, wouldn't we be talking about *Jesianity* rather than Christianity? (What are we to make, in this connection of Epiphanius' claim that before believers were called Christians at Antioch they were called Jessaeans,[2] in honor of David's father Jesse? What if most or all of Ehrman's unproved assumptions should prove to be false? This chapter will focus mostly on just one of these questions — the possibility that something other than a messiah had originally been meant by the title 'Christ.' I shall deal with the other questions elsewhere.

THE ANCIENT AND MODERN GREEK LANGUAGES

The hypotheses that something other than a messiah might have been meant by the title 'Christ' or that the character might not have been 'crucified' on earth are greatly illuminated by some seemingly trivial facts about the phonetic evolution of the Modern Greek language. It is not much of an exaggeration to say that Modern Greek differs as much from Classical Greek as Modern Italian differs from its parent language, a form of Latin. Due to various drastic phonetic changes, Modern Greek upon first hearing is virtually unintelligible to scholars even if they might be thoroughly comfortable when dealing with Classical Greek.

Although some odd changes occurred in pronunciation of the

2 J.P. Migne, *Patrologiae Cursus Completus, etc., Series Graeca Prior; Patrologiae Graecae Tomus XLI, S. Epiphanius Constantiensis in Cypro Episcopus, Adversus Haereses*, Paris, 1863, columns 389–390.

ancient consonants, the most significant changes of relevance to this discussion are the pervasive changes in pronunciation of the ancient vowels and diphthongs — some of the latter even becoming consonants! For example, *au* (originally pronounced as in *gown*) came to be pronounced *av* or *af*. The diphthong *eu* (originally pronounced as in *few*) came to be pronounced *ev* or *ef*.

As important as such changes might appear to be, they are of minor significance as compared to the pervasive shift in vocalization known as *iotacism* or *itacism* that completely transformed the pronunciation of the Greek language during the first few centuries of the Common Era. As might be inferred from the fact that the term contains the word *iota* — the Greek vowel originally pronounced *i* or *ī* as in *hit* or *heat* — iotacism describes the convergent transformation of various vowels and diphthongs that ended up with all of them being pronounced like *iota*. Thus, *ēta* (η, *ē*, originally pronounced as in *hay*), *upsilon* (υ, *y*, originally pronounced like French *u* or German *ü*), *oi* (οι, originally pronounced as in *boil*), *ui* (υι, originally pronounced as in French *lui*), and *ei* (ει, originally pronounced as in *gray*) all came to be pronounced *ee* as in *feed*.

How does all this pertain to the crucifixion of Ehrman's Messiah? It could not relate more fundamentally. It would appear that the Messiah of Christian belief was the creation of the impersonal agency of itacism. It seems likely that the *christos* that became the Christ who became the Messiah was originally the title of some other being — a title that was spelled and pronounced differently. What might that name or title have been? Let us consider all the possibilities.

We may hypothesize five words that might have been transformed into *christos* by iotacism: *chrēstos, chrystos, chreistos, chroistos, and chruistos.* A quick check of the great, unabridged *Greek-English Lexicon* of Liddell & Scott[3] turns up no entries for *chreistos*, but it does reveal the verb *chrei-oō* ['have force, prevail'] from which one might imagine deriving the word *chrēstos* and then *christos*. A search for *chroistos* discovers nothing very close, only the verb *chro-īzō*

3 New Edition with a Supplement, compiled by Henry George Liddell and Robert Scott, rev. by Sir Henry Stuart Jones, Oxford, 1968.

['touch, touch the skin of a body, lie with a woman'], and nothing at all resembling *chruistos* is to be found. No *chrystos* as such is to be found either, but one is tantalized to find the verb *chrysoō* ['make golden,' 'gild']. (If one independently could show that 'Christ' was the deity depicted as Helios with the solar chariot in the Vatican necropolis mosaic this etymology might be worth reconsidering.) With the word *chrēstos*, however, we seem to hit the jackpot.

Under the heading *chrēstos* itself we find that the word as an adjective can mean 'useful,' 'good of its kind,' 'serviceable,' 'valiant,' 'true,' 'auspicious' — of victims and omens, 'good' — in a moral sense as opposite of *bad* or *evil*, "of the gods, *propitious, merciful, bestowing health or wealth*," "of a man, *strong, able* in body for sexual intercourse." As the noun *chrēstotēs*, we have 'goodness,' 'honesty,' 'uprightness.' Also as a noun, we have the intriguing word *chrēstōr*, which we are told can mean the same thing as *mantis* — a seer, prophet, or oracle.

But there is more. We have the related noun *chrēstēs* (also written *chreistēs*), which we are told means "one who gives or expounds oracles, prophet, soothsayer." There also are verbs: *chrēsteuomai*, 'be kind or merciful'; *chrēizō*, 'deliver an oracle,' 'foretell'; and *chrēstēriazō*, 'give oracles, prophesy.'

But the greatest surprise is yet to come — one that makes reading unabridged Greek dictionaries worth one's time. Under the heading *chrēsis* we have the seemingly unimportant meaning "*employment, use* made of a thing; in concrete sense, *example* of a word or use." Although it is difficult to perceive any relevance here to our *christos* problem, we are startled all the more to see that this word could be abbreviated with the *chrismon* ☧ — the chi-rho cross of early Christianity — in two third-century papyri from Oxyrhynchus [Anon. Oxy. 1611, 56; An. Ox. 2. 452]!

What can we make of this odd fact? I long have known that the chi-rho cross ☧ was used as a symbol for the time-god Chronos in a copy of Aristotle's *Constitution of the City of Athens* discovered at Herculaneum/Pompeii.[4]

4 Edward Maunde Thompson, *An Introduction to Greek and Latin Palaeography* [Oxford: At the Clarendon Press, 1912: 78, 79, 81]; M. Edmond Saglio, *Dictionnaire*

Bart Ehrman and the Crucified Messiah

Given the relationship between Chronos and the mystery religions, especially Mithraism, and the evidence supporting the notion that Christianity originated as New Age cults observing the passage of the vernal equinox from the zodiacal sign of Aries into Pisces, it has always seemed to me that the *chi-rho* symbol was the severed umbilical cord left over from the birth of Christianity from an astral mystery cult — a cult that was watching and measuring the departure of the Heavenly Lamb and the coming of the Two Fishes. (Unlike the bumper-sticker usage of modern fundamentalist Christians, ancient Christians used *two* fishes or dolphins to symbolize their religion. Could one fish have been Jesus, the other his zodiacal twin Thomas as in ancient Gnostic belief?)

In addition to the link between time-god Chronos and the symbol for the new-age religion that would come to be known as Christianity, there is a tantalizing further possible connection we might hypothesize. Kronos, one of the Titans and father of Zeus, for unclear reasons came to be associated with the Golden Age and, as such, he likely became amalgamated at least partially with Chronos — especially by Latin speakers who would pronounce *Cronus* and *Chronus* the same way. The fact that Kronos (as distinct from Chronos) was associated with the Golden Age awaited by the Roman poet Virgil and his Augustan readers, and the fact that Kronos was associated with the deity Saturn — the equivalent of the Hebrew deity Yahweh — makes this discovery even more exciting.

But *chrēsis*? 'Employment'? 'Use made of a thing'? 'Example of a word or use'? I confess that this confounds all my expectations and theories. In any case, we have a lot of words in the *chrēstēs/chreistēs* family whose meanings seem relatable to the title of a divine character who might have metamorphosed into a Christos — who in turn could be transformed into a Hebrew Messiah. If that is in fact what happened, the first Christians would not have been concerned with

---

des Antiquités Grecques et Romaines d'Après les Textes et les Monuments. Vol. 4 [Paris: Librairie Hachette et Cie, 1918: 1133–34; (on-line edition: Tome 4, Volume 2, pages 329–330, article "Scriptura"]. Perhaps I overstretch a bit here. In that document the symbol ⳩ is used for the word *chronos* generally. Only once, in a poem of Solon, is 'Time' personified in Aristotle's *Athenian Constitution*.

a Jewish Messiah.

MANUSCRIPT EVIDENCE FOR A PRECURSOR OF CHRIST

It is great fun to rummage through dictionaries in search of data with which to form hypotheses to explain phenomena in need of explanation. But hypotheses are worth less than a dime a dozen unless they can be tested and evaluated. Are there any sources of information with which to weigh the words I have pulled out of a dictionary so that we might assess the probability that any of them could have been a pre-Messiah name or title for the proto-Christian savior? Indeed there are: (1) manuscripts (papyri, biblical manuscripts, literary manuscripts, *etc.*) and (2) inscriptions (on coins, tombs, tombstones, stelae, *etc.*). We shall consider both of these in turn, starting with ancient literary witnesses.

The Evidence of Ancient Biblical Manuscripts

Trying to trace the evolutionary history of the word *Christos* in ancient biblical manuscripts presents a special problem: the word almost never is spelled out completely. Rather, it usually is abbreviated to various degrees as a so-called *nomen sacrum*, or it is represented by a sacred symbol such as the *chrismon* or chi-rho cross ☧. And so, various surrogate words must serve as indirect indicators of the early spellings of Christos. (Remember, we wish to know if the word originally derived from the Greek verb *chriō*, meaning 'anoint,' as with a messiah, or whether the word was spelled in such a way as to indicate some other etymology and thus signified something other than a messiah.) Such words as *Christian* and *Antichrist* are the most desirable surrogates, but other words may also be of use as we shall see.

B. Jobjorn Boman has informed me (private e-mail communication) that in *Codex Vaticanus*, 'Christians' is spelled 'Chreistiani," and in *Codex Sinaiticus* it was originally spelled 'Chrestiani," but then corrected. As is usual, 'Christ' is abbreviated as a *nomen sacrum*, but 'Antichrist' is spelled correctly (*Antichristos*) in *Sinaiticus*, but is spelled with *ei* instead of just *i* (*Antichreistos*) in *Vaticanus*.

The Evidence of Ancient Non-Biblical Literature

Taking a phrase from Bart Ehrman, I will close the manuscript discussion of this chapter with "two key data" indicating that the earliest 'Christ' had nothing to do with the Messiah awaited by the Jews. Both of these two key data attest the spelling *Chreistos*, not *Christos* — and do so with far-reaching import and significance. The first of these key data involves numerological theologizing in the writings of the Church Father Irenaeus that show that the Gnostics clearly believed in a Chreistos, not a Christos. The second datum involves the famous FISH (ΙΧΘΥΣ) two-level acrostic found in the *Sibylline Oracles* and in the writings of other ancient authors.

Datum 1: Irenaeus *Against Heresies* I.XV.1–2

In his refutation of a certain Gnostic called Marcus, Irenaeus reproduces and ridicules the numerological system upon which the Gnostic creation myth is based — a numerological system which also was claimed to explain the origin and significance of divine names and titles such as Christ (*Chreistos*, as we shall see), Christ Jesus, Christ the Son, *etc*. The fifteenth chapter of Book I of his *Against Heresies* almost paralyzes the mind of a scientific thinker. Fortunately, for our purposes we may ignore the theosophical import of the text and focus on several simple numerological statements. Even so, we must provide some context for these statements and shall quote a fair amount of Irenaeus's text.[5]

> "Moreover, that name of the Saviour which may be pronounced, *viz*., Jesus [IHCOUC] consists of six letters, but His unutterable name comprises four-and-twenty letters. **The name *Christ the Son* (UIOC XPEICTOC)[6] comprises twelve letters,** but that which

5 The translation is that of Alexander Roberts and James Donaldson, *The Ante-Nicene Fathers: Volume I. The Apostolic Fathers — Justin Martyr — Irenaeus* [Grand Rapids, Michigan: Wm. B. Eerdmans Pub. Co. 1985: 339].

6 Professor Hector Avalos (personal communication) cautions me that the eight-letter spelling XPEICTOC does not actually appear in surviving manuscripts of the

> is unpronounceable in Christ contains thirty letters. And for this reason he declares that He is *Alpha* and *Omega*, that he may indicate the dove, inasmuch as that bird has this number [in its name].
>
> 2. But Jesus, he affirms, has the following unspeakable origin. From the mother of all things, that is, the first Tetrad, there came forth the second Tetrad, after the manner of a daughter; and thus an Ogdoad was formed, from which, again, a Decad proceeded: thus was produced a Decad and an Ogdoad. The Decad, then, being joined with the Ogdoad, and multiplying it ten times, gave rise to the number eighty; and, again, multiplying eighty ten times produced the number eight hundred. Thus, then, the whole number of the letters proceeding from the Ogdoad [multiplied] into the Decad, is eight hundred and eighty-eight. **This is the name of Jesus**; for this name, if you reckon up the numerical value of the letters, amounts to eight hundred and eighty-eight. Thus, then, **you have a clear statement of their opinion as to the origin of the supercelestial Jesus**. ... [*i.e., no terrestrial or virgin birth, etc.*]
>
> Moreover, **Chreistus,** he says, **being a word of eight letters**, indicates the first Ogdoad, and this, when multiplied by ten, gives birth to Jesus (888). And Christ the Son, he says, is also spoken of, that is, the Duodecad. For the name Son (UIOC) contains four letters, and **Christ (Chreistus [XPEICTOC]) eight,** which, being combined, point out the greatness of the Duodecad.

There can be little question here that the 'Christ' of the Gnostic Marcus is actually a 'Chreist' *spelled with eight letters in Greek* and cannot represent an anointed 'Messiah' of Israel who, for lack of a diphthong, is spelled with *seven letters.* Although the forms of Gnosticism of which we have detailed information are, because of their

Greek text of Irenaeus. Rather, the seven-letter spelling XPICTOC is to be seen. He warns me of the danger of extrapolating backward before the evidence of actual manuscripts. Indeed, Migne's *Patrologia Graeca* volume of Irenaeus shows the seven-letter spelling along with the eight-letter description of the word. Avalos directs my attention to Migne's footnote that indicates the possibility that the Greek χ was double-counted because in Latin it is rendered as *ch* (= 2 letters) and so *Christos* = 8 letters. Certainly this is possible, but I think it is unlikely. The same Latin footnote cites Petavius to the effect that just as *Sige* had been spelled *Seige*, so too *Christos* must have been spelled *Chreistos*. Interestingly, the note cites the evidence of the compound acrostic in Constantine's oration at Nicaea, discussed here in the next section.

intricate and obviously evolved features, unlikely to be older than the proto-Orthodoxy we read into the Apostolic Fathers and Ante-Nicene Fathers, it seems almost certain that Gnosticism *as a method rather than a body of doctrines* is considerably older — probably deriving from Pythagorean mysticism and Platonic works such as the *Timaeus*. For the proto-Gnostics who first claimed the Christian identity, therefore, it would seem highly probable that both their Chreist and their Jesus were, if not perhaps originally numerologically derived characters, at least they were theoretically apprehended beings discovered by acts of pure reason. Clearly, they would have held no doctrine that their Chreist had had an earthly origin in Roman Palestine. Still less could they have believed their *Iesous* had been born in "a one-dog town" [*DJE?* 189] called Nazareth or Nazara.

If one should dispute the idea that proto-Orthodoxy was derived from a Docetic type of proto-Gnosticism, but rather that the course of evolution ran in the opposite direction, we should have to apply 'Ehrman's Method' and consider the question: **Is it not easier to derive a Jesus of Nazareth living in a specific place at a specific time from a celestial being who at some *unspecified time* came to earth at some unspecified place, took human form and then substance — in short, was reified — than to derive the multitudinous Docetic, Gnostic, Separationist, and other early forms of Christianity from a real man who had lived completely unnoticed *just a few decades earlier*?**

Just exactly how might a bumpkin from a one-dog town such as Ehrman imagines 'Nazareth' to have been, become transformed into a Tetrad, an Ogdoad, and a Decad in a few decades? Was it before or after the alleged martyrdom of St. Paul that "the Decad, then, being joined with the Ogdoad, and multiplying it ten times, gave rise to the number eighty," *etc.*? Did one of the Disciples suffer from a brain tumor that mixed up his memories of Jesus of Nazareth and blended them with notes he had made while studying Pythagoras?

Datum 2: The Sibylline Compound Acrostic (*Sib. Orac.* VIII: 284–330; Eusebius *Orat. Const.* XVIII)

When the emperor Constantine lectured to the 'saints' gathered together at the Council of Nicaea, he did what Lactantius [*e.g., Divine Institutes*, IV xiii; VII xx, *etc.*] and others had done before him: he quoted from pagan poets and oracles to demonstrate that *Christ* — Jesus is only mentioned once by the long-winded ruler in his own words — and Christian doctrine had been foretold not only by the Hebrew prophets, but by pagan prophets as well. The Erythraean Sibyl, he told the sacred assemblage, had "lived in the sixth generation after the flood" and he declared that she had plainly foretold the advent of *Jesus* — Constantine's only mention of the name apart from his quotation of the Sibyl. She did this, the theologically talented emperor alleged, in an acrostic that read "Jesus Christ, God's Son, Savior, Cross" — "ΙΗΣΟΥΣ ΧΡΙΣΤΟΣ ΘΕΟΥ ΥΙΟΣ ΣΩΤΗΡ ΣΤΑΥΡΟΣ."

The acrostic mentioned by Constantine is a remarkable construction. It is found in Book VIII of the *Sibylline Oracles* as they have come down to us.[7] The acrostic is constructed of hexameter lines of Greek verse, the first line beginning with *I* — the first letter of ΙΗΣΟΥΣ (JESUS) — and then each successive line beginning with the next letter of the name followed by the rest of the words in the acrostic. If in turn, however, we take the first letter of each of the first five words in the acrostic, we obtain *a second-order acrostic* — the Greek word for 'fish,' ΙΧΘΥΣ!

Although we have already noted that Constantine alleged the acrostic contained the word *Christ*, in reality, however, the word was spelled out with *eight* lines of verse, not seven. The word that

7 The Greek text of Constantine's speech and the Sibylline text was published by Fridericus Adolphus Heinichen in his *Eusebii Pamphili Vita Constantine et Panegyricus atque Constantini ad Sanctorum Coetum Oratio. Eusebii Pamphili Scripta Historica*, Vol. II [Lipsiae: Hermann Mendelssohn, 1869: 225–226]. An English translation of Constantine's words by Philip Schaff and Henry Wace is reprinted in *Eusebius: Church History, Life of Constantine the Great, and Oration in Praise of Constantine*, Nicene and Post-Nicene Fathers of the Christian Church, Second Series, Vol. I [Grand Rapids, MI: Wm. B. Eerdmans, 1982: 561–590].

emerged from the oracle was *Chreistos* (ΧΡΕΙΣΤΟΣ), not *Christos*. This accords with the Gnostic spelling we have already seen in Irenaeus' refutation of Marcus, and prompts us to inquire if a Gnostic *Chreistos* — whatever the title might have meant — was the progenitor of the Orthodox *Christos*.

We have just seen that *the first five words* of the Sibylline acrostic yield a second-order reading of ΙΧΘΥΣ ('FISH'). What about the sixth word — ΣΤΑΥΡΟΣ — you might be wondering? That is a good and fascinating question!

Although Eusebius recites the acrostic in its entirety in Chapter XVIII of his *The Oration of Constantine*, the sixth word of the first level of the acrostic disappears from Orthodox Christian tradition. St. Augustine produced a Latin translation of the acrostic in Chapter XXIII of the Eighteenth Book of his *City of God*, but gave no hint that there was a sixth word to the acrostic. Indeed, he appears deliberately to have hidden the fact. "The verses are twenty-seven," he says even though they are thirty-four in the oracular text, "which is the cube of three. ... But if you join the initial letters of the five Greek words (ΙΗΣΟΥΣ ΧΡΙΣΤΟΣ ΘΕΟΥ ΥΙΟΣ ΣΩΤΗΡ) which mean 'Jesus Christ the son of God, the Savior,' they will make the word ΙΧΘΥΣ, that is, fish, in which word Christ is mystically understood, because he was able to live, that is, to exist, without sin in the abyss of this mortality as in the depth of waters."

Before considering reasons why Augustine and everyone after him might have wanted to pretend there had only been five words in the Sibylline acrostic, I wish to point out that that there are twenty-*six*, not twenty-seven letters in the five Greek words quoted by Augustine. That's because he has changed the spelling of *Chreistos* — which is spelled out correctly in the vertical sequence of the Latin verses of his translation — into the *Christos* of subsequent Christian tradition.

So why did Augustine and everyone else sweep the sixth word of the acrostic under the rug of Christian tradition? I think that is because the sixth word was ΣΤΑΥΡΟΣ (*stauros*, 'cross'), and wouldn't fit into the Greek word for 'fish.' But I also think it is because there were Gnostic meanings for the word ΣΤΑΥΡΟΣ, and Gnostic priority in the worship of 'Christ' might be revealed if inquiry be focused on the word. The word ΣΤΑΥΡΟΣ, I think, was a smoking gun with Gnostic fingerprints all over it.

It is a fact that 'cross' in the sense of 'crisscross' was not the primal meaning of the Greek word *stauros*. Its root meaning is 'poll,' 'stake,' 'pale,' or even 'palisade.' In Gnostic theosophy, moreover, Stauros is a heavenly personage. In the apocryphal Gospel of Peter, for example, we read of a cross that came out of a tomb and spoke! Bart Ehrman tells us[8] that "the Gospel narrates an account of Jesus' emergence from his tomb. He is supported by two gigantic angels whose heads reach up to heaven; his own head reaches above the heavens. Behind them emerges the cross. A voice then speaks from heaven, 'Have you preached to those who are sleeping?' The cross replies, 'Yes' (vv. 39–42)."

Even more embarrassing to Orthodox tradition than the presence of the word *stauros* in the acrostic is the fact that it is in direct apposition with all the previous titles of Chreist. That is, not only is Jesus to be equated with Chreist, the Son of God, and the Savior, he is to be identified *with* the 'Cross' not *by* it! That is to say, the 'Stauros' is a heavenly character equivalent to Jesus Chreist, not an instrument of torture on which he died. Just a guess: as the Christ of Gnostic theosophy was seen as an intermediary between the High God in the Pleroma and pneumatics here on earth, is it not possible that in the role of Stauros he was the palisade (*staurōma*) around the Gnostics' Pleroma? Is it likely? I don't know.

CHR?ST IN THE INSCRIPTIONS

In the literature we have found impressive evidence that 'Christ' was not always spelled with an '*i*' and that the word probably would *not* have meant 'anointed' or 'messiah.' As we turn now to epigraphic evidence we shall see that the *ei* spelling for *Chr?stos* is well attested, and that other spellings also once abounded.

8 *Lost Scriptures: Books That Did Not Make It Into the New Testament* [New York: Oxford University Press, 2003: 31].

Bart Ehrman and the Crucified Messiah

I. Inscriptions Reported in German Literature

Many modern academic scholars who study Christian origins, including, it would appear, Bart Ehrman, seem to despise authors and research reported before 1950. While it is true that by modern *scientific* standards, the *methods* employed by nineteenth-century scholars often fall far short of what modern academic scholarship must require, many modern scholars ignore the fact that the *data* reported by earlier scholars may be completely accurate. Regretably, they also seem unaware of the fact that many of the data to be found in older literature can no longer be rediscovered independently due to loss of manuscripts and artifacts in the destruction of libraries and museums during the many wars that have ravaged the European continent.

While I personally used to try to research every important biblical topic back at least to the time at which all European scholarship pertaining to it was written in Latin, this obviously had to become an ideal rather than a routine. Even so, I am frequently astonished by what I have overlooked in old books that have been in my personal library for half a century or more. One such book, of great relevance to this excursus, is the *Handbuch Der Altchristlichen Epigraphik,* by Carl Maria Kaufmann.[9] Although I shall not be able to extract all the information from that book relevant to this chapter, I shall nevertheless cite enough examples to prove — even without further evidence — that the *Christ* of Christian worship was not always spelled with an *i*-vowel.

The *Handbuch* provides a number of illustrations of Greek inscriptions that spell 'Christian' with the diphthong *ei*. (As with manuscripts, 'Christ' is rarely spelled out in inscriptions, being abbreviated as a *nomen sacrum* or represented by a symbol such as a fish, a *chi-rho* cross ☧, or a *tropos* cross ⳨.) On pages 60 and 61, Kaufmann illustrates and describes a funerary inscription from the fourth century that bears the text *XREICTIANOI ΔE PANTEC ENECMEN* ('We,

9 Herdersche Verlagshandlung, Freiburg im Breisgau, 1917.

however, all are Christians.').

Another extremely important inscription — Kaufmann provides most of the examples I have found so far concerning the complete spelling of 'Christ' — is to be found on page 140. It includes the phrase *EN ΘΕΩ KUREIΩ XREISTΩ* ('In God, the Lord Chreist'). It is indicative of the relative unimportance of Jesus — a man who had just recently existed according to majority scholarly opinion — that here as in numerous other early inscriptions and Christian literature, Jesus is not mentioned; only 'Chreist' is the object of devotion.

Kaufmann also presents [151] another instance of *Chreistos* itself, an interesting litany-like fifth-century inscription from Jebel Riha (in Syria?) in which each line of text is followed by the Syroantiochene Christ-Litany response *IHCoXREICTOC* ('Jesus the Chreist'). Although Jesus is mentioned here (although in the abbreviated form IHC=IHS of modern usage), it is hard in this context to suppose that a Jewish Messiah is the intended referent of this litany.

A late third-century inscription from the Melos catacombs [page 159] presents us with yet another view of 'Christ' — naked, with all his vowels showing: *Iēsou Chreiste boēthei tō grapsant panoiki* ('Jesus Chreist, stay by the writer and his house').

Although this chapter is primarily concerned with phonetic and referential evolution of the title 'Christ,' it is worth noting an inscription that Kaufmann records from the Cemetery of St. Hippolytus (third century?) on the Tiburtine Way [page 163]: KITE BIKTOR ΚΑΤΗΧΟΥΜΕΝΟC ΕΙΤΩΝ ΕΙΔΟCΙ • ΠΑΡΘΕΝΟC ΔΟΥΛΟC ΤΟΥ ΚΥΡΙΟΥ ΕΙΗCΟΥ ☧ — ('Here lies Victor the catechumen, 20 years old, a virgin, a slave of the Lord Jesus [Chr?st']). In this inscription, EIHCOUC (Jesus) is spelled not with *I* (*iota*) but with the diphthong *EI*. (It also shows that the Greek letter *beta* had already evolved into *veeta*, and that the Latin consonantal semivowel /*w*/ had become /*v*/.)

Elsewhere I have argued that the site of present-day Nazareth could not have been the place described in the Gospel of Luke and was not inhabited at the turn of the era, so that 'Jesus of Nazareth' was perhaps the latest epithet to be bestowed upon the Christian savior god before the compositional completion of the canonical gospels. (René Salm, in his *The Myth of Nazareth: The Invented Town of Jesus*[10] has convincingly refuted the claims of Nazareth habitation made to the contrary by Franciscan 'archaeologists' and other apologists.) It is interesting, therefore, to discover what Kaufmann claims to be the earliest epigraphic evidence [516 CE] referring to Jesus as a *Nazarene* (*i.e.*, not 'of Nazareth')[11] : *Iēs(ous) ho Nazōreōs, ho ek Marias genneth(e)is, ho u(io)s tou Th(eo)u...* ('Jesus the Nazorean, born of Mary, the son of God'...). Even at so late a date, we have Jesus the *Nazorean*, not Jesus *of Nazareth. If Jesus had in fact come from a place called Nazareth, wouldn't he have been called Jesus of Nazareth from the beginning?*

One last example attesting directly to *Chr?stos* spelled with *ei* is found on page 201. Apparently dating to some time before the Peace of the Church in Asia Minor, a long inscription is presented that contains the phrase *en hageiō e topō heu*[*de*] *Chreistou achranto*[*u*] ('he sleeps in the holy place of Chreist the immaculate').

We take leave of Kaufmann's *Handbuch* with an inscription from the S. Giovanni cemetery in Syracuse that describes the deceased young woman Euskia as *XRHCTEIANH* (*Chrēsteianē*) — Christ-like or Christian. The use of the long vowel *ēta* (H) here attests to the spelling *Chrēstos* which, as we have seen, provides a great number of etymological clues to the meaning of Chr?st before the term was equated to the Jewish Messiah.

II. Inscriptions Reported in Italian Catholic Literature

Although all Roman Catholic publications must be read with great caution and critical attention, handled carefully they can be a gold mine in which to find valuable nuggets of information pertaining to Christian origins. One such publication is the treatise by

10 American Atheist Press, 2008.

11 Page 164.

Pasquale Testini entitled *Archeologia Cristiana: Nozioni Generali Dalle Origini Alla Fine Del Sec. VI* (*Christian Archeology: General Concepts From the Beginning to the end of the Sixth Century*)[12]

Testini presents considerable epigraphic evidence that shows that 'Christ' was not always *Christos*, but at different times and different places was known as *Chreistos* or *Chrēstos*. Understandably, as a Roman Catholic he does not understand the significance of this fact and considers these spelling — as well as the surrogate words *Chreistianos* and *Chrēstianos* — to be "*errori*" [363–64].

One of the *errori* presented by Testini [359] involves an inscription from Refâdeh (IGLS, 428) that comprises both *Chrēstos* and the Sibylline Acrostic-derived title 'FISH' (ΙΧΘΥΣ) — even though the 'X' in the Sibylline Acrostic spells the corresponding word with *ei* and not *ē*: *CHREISTOS*! It reads:

ΙΧΘΥCΙΗ
COΥCΧΡΗCΤ +
+ ΟCΘΕΟΥΥΙ
ΟCCΩΤΗΡ

"*Ichthys*: Jesus Chrēst, of God Son, Savior"

A further witness to the *ēta* spelling of 'Christ' is presented [395] in the form of an inscription from the Tusculan Catacomb. It reads:

ΕΥΨΥΧΕΙ • ΜΟΥCΕΝΑ ΙΡΗΝΗ
Η CΗ ΨΥΧΗ • ΑΘΑΝΑΤΟC
ΠΑΡΑ ΧΡΗCΤω

"Be of good cheer, Musena Irene, your soul is immortal in Chrēst"[13]

Another inscription attesting to 'Christ' spelled with *ēta* is found on page 413. Commencing with a *tropos* cross (⳨) with *alpha* and

12 Desclée & C.–Editori Pontifici, Roma [no date; 1958?].

13 F. Grossi Gondi, *Catacombe tusculane: Roma e l'Oriente* [1914: 298].

omega, it reads: *"O Theos mnēsthēti tou doulou sou Auxanontos tou makariou chrēstianou"* — "O God, remember your slave Auxanontos, a blessed Chrēstian."[14] Testini presents evidence that 'Christ' could be spelled with an *ei* as well as with *ēta.* On page 411 we find an inscription reading *"en Theō Kyreiō Kreistō"* (CIG IV, 9816), *i.e.*, "in God Lord Chreist." Fig. 204 [433] shows an inscription of the Lateran Museum that reads *"Ermaeiske, phōs zēsen theō kyreiō Chreistō"* — "O, Ermaisco, light, live in God Lord Chreist." Perhaps significantly, we may note that these two inscriptions read *Lord* Christ, not *Jesus* Christ.

While the great majority of the inscriptions presented by Testini and other authorities are clearly supportive of the theses advanced in this excursus, there are one or two that are of unclear significance — supporting some of my hypotheses but appearing to contradict others. The most puzzling of these is an inscription shown on page 477. Testini notes, "In qualche caso le affermazioni dommatiche favorirono le composizioni ampollose ed eccitarono la fantasia cabalistica, come l'esempio sequente che può essere considerato come un unicum del gènere per le bizzarrie dell'autore." — "In some cases dogmatic affirmations will foster bombastic compositions and excite cabalistic fantasy such as the following example which may be considered one of a kind due to the weirdness of the author."

The inscription[15] is structured like a litany:

+Athanatos ōn, p(ol)la path<i>ē hypeminen,
Iēsous ho Chreistos.
Genous Daouid ouranios klados,
Iēsous ho Chreistos.
[D]oxazomenos, <m>onogenēs athanatos, en pase tē gē,
⳨ Iēsous ho Chreistos.
Elee<i k>a[tēlthe]n ex ouranōn epi gēs,
Iēsous ho Chreistos.
Zoēs alēthou[s] <ap> eonos didaskalo[s]

14 Syracuse Cemetery of S. Giovanni: Agnellos *Silloge*, I.

15 A Šnân nell'Apamene: IGLS, 1403.

Iēsous ho Chreistos.
Θ IX EC
I M

Eusebios Sympa[nt]os etelesen.

Testini renders this:

"Being immortal, he has suffered many torments: Jesus the Christ.
Of the line of David, Heavenly Branch: Jesus the Christ.
Glorified, only (son), immortal, on all the earth: Jesus the Christ.
[or: Deathless *Monogenes* ('one-of-a-kind,' the Gnostic deity)...]
Out of pity, he descended out of the sky onto the earth: Jesus the Christ.
Master of the true life for eternity [or for the Aions]: Jesus the Christ.
... Jesus Christ ... born of Mary ...(?)
Eusebius has fulfilled al this.[16]

While the inscription gives ample testimony to my thesis that Chr?stos originally was not spelled with *iota* (and thus did not originally equate to a Jewish Messiah), we find our *Chreistos* here identified as the "heavenly branch of the house/clan of David"! Admittedly, this looks like a reference to the Davidic Messiah of the Dead Sea Scrolls[17]

16 "Essendo immortale, ha sofferto numerosi tormenti; Gesù il Cristo.
Della razza di Davide ramo celeste; Gesù il Cristo.
Glorificato, (figlio) unico immortale, su tutta la terra: Gesù il Cristo.
Per pietà è discesso [from the heavens] sulla terra; Gesù il Cristo.
Maestro della vera vita per l'eternità (απ'αιωνος): Gesù il Cristo.
...Gesù Cristo ... nato da Maria ... (?)
Eusebio ha tutto compiuto.

17 Ehrman insists — it's one of his "Two Key Data" proving the historicity of Jesus of Nazareth — that no Jewish group at the turn of the era expected its Messiah to be crucified, or even to 'suffer.' Apparently influenced by Bultmann, he avers that Christian apologetic use of the 'Suffering Servant' of Isaiah 53 *etc.* was *ad hoc* scripture mining to account for the embarrassing 'fact' that Jesus was being called the Messiah but had been executed like a common criminal. Christians never would have made up the idea that their messiah had been executed if they hadn't been forced to do so. Thus, Jesus must have existed and been crucified.

Israel Knohl, however, as we have already noted, has shown that several documents

or to a *Christos* in the anointed sense of Orthodox tradition. However, we must note Testini's comment that this "can be considered as unique due to the oddity of the author" and that such affirmations of faith "will arouse cabbalistic fantasy." We must note that *Iēsous ho Chreistos* is a *heavenly* branch descended from David, not an *earthly* one. Moreover, if Testini's reconstruction of the text is correct, the verb *katēlthein* ('descend') used in line 7 is the same verb as that used in Marcion's proto-Luke used to describe the descent of Jesus from the sky right into a synagogue in Capernaum.

Although it is hazardous to affirm any meanings too strongly when dealing with an inscription as out of the ordinary as this — where even common words may have technical meanings — I am tempted to conclude that the *klados* ('branch') of line 3 refers to the *branch* (Hebrew *netser*) of Isaiah 11:1: "Then a shoot shall grow from the stock of Jesse, and a branch [*netser*] shall spring from his roots." [NEB] Although *klados* is not found in the LXX text of Isaiah 11:1, the word *is* used to translate *netser* elsewhere in the LXX, and branches of one sort or another are frequent decorations on Christian funerary inscriptions. (I have theorized elsewhere that the place name *Nazara/ Nazareth* is derived from the Hebrew word *netser*, and so I find this particularly suggestive.)

One last point of possible relevance to a non-earthly 'House of David': Testini makes little attempt to decipher the Greek letters at the bottom of the inscription ("...Jesus Christ... born of Mary...?") and the attempt is clearly inadequate. The 'I' and the 'M' commonly stand for 'Jesus' and 'Mary.' The Θ almost certainly stands for 'God' (*theos*) leaving the problematic IX and ES. While the IX commonly may stand for *Iēsous Christos,* the meaning of ES is left uncertain. It seems to me likely that the four letters *together* stand for a single word — ΙΧΘΥΕΣ ('fishes') — and refers to the constellation Pisces. (I shall discuss the astrotheological background of Christian origins

belatedly published from the Dead Sea Scrolls show not only that the Qumran community expected a Messiah would have to suffer *à la* Isaiah 53, one of its leaders — a certain Menahem — actually arrogated that prophetic model to himself! [Israel Knohl, *The Messiah before Jesus: The Suffering Servant of the Dead Sea Scrolls,* S. Mark Taper Foundation Imprint in Jewish Studies, translated by David Maisel, U. Cal. Press, Berkeley, 2002:200].

elsewhere.)

Testini presents further inscriptional witnesses to Chreists and Chrēsts, but we shall pass over them and close our survey of his epigraphic evidence with a Montanist inscription found at Chiusi dal Ferrua that may further muddy the etymological holy water font and make us wonder if we are *christening, chreistening, chrēstening* — or *chrestening* our children. Testini tells us [528] that this inscription is not earlier than the second half of the fourth century (*"non anteriori alla secunda metà del IV secolo"*) and that it pertains to a "ΦΡΑΝΚΙ<ΟΣ> ΧΡΕΣΤΙΑ–ΝΟΣ ΠΝΕΥΜΑΤΙΚΟΣ ['Phrankios, a spiritual Chrestian'] (RAC 1955: 97ss)." The use of *epsilon* (a short *e*) is reminiscent of the Latin "Chrestus" of Suetonius, who says that "As the Jews were making constant disturbances at the instigation of Chrestus, he [Claudius] expelled them [the Jews] from Rome."[18] Although there is scholarly debate concerning the 'e' spelling of 'Chresto,' B. Jobjorn Boman has established that the oldest manuscripts are spelled with 'e,' although other variants exist — including *Recresto, Cheresto, Cherestro*, and a *Cristo.*[19]

III. Phrygian Inscriptions

I wish now to turn to a more modern, although more narrowly focused, source of epigraphic information relating to the problem of discovering who 'Christ' was before he was transformed into Christ by the great vowel shift of the first few centuries of the Common Era. This is a little book by Elsa Gibson, *The "Christians For Christians" Inscriptions of Phrygia.*[20] As the title of the book indicates, the great majority of the funerary inscriptions recorded were found in Phrygia, especially in the Upper Tembris Valley. All the inscriptions are dated after 212 CE and appear to have been carved during the

18 *"Iudaeos, impulsore Chresto, assidue tumultuantis Roma expulit." Lives of the Twelve Caesars, Claudius* 25.

19 "Impulsore Chrestro? Suetonius' *Divus Claudius* 25.4 in Sources and Manuscripts," *Liber Annuus* 61 [2011: 355–376].

20 Harvard Theological Review Harvard Theological Studies, Number 32. *The "Christians For Christians" Inscriptions of Phrygia: Greek Texts, Translation and Commentary by Elsa Gibson* [Missoula, Montana: Scholars Press, 1978].

remainder of the third century and early part of the fourth.

As noted above, epigraphically as in the manuscripts "Chr?st" is generally written as a *nomen sacrum* or as a symbol such as a ☧ or ⳨, and so 'Chr?stian(s)' must be employed as a surrogate. As in the epigraphic sources previously examined, a good number of these surrogate readings testify to a *Chreistos*[21] (12, by my count) and *Chrēstos*[22] (I count 19), as well as three attesting to *Christos*.[23]

21 **Inscriptions Attesting to *Chreistos***
CFCIP Inscription 1. Chreistianoi Chreistianois [9]
CFCIP Inscription 2. Chreistianoi Chreistianois [11]
CFCIP Inscription 22. Chreistianoi Chreistiano[is] [56] [248/9 CE]
CFCIP Inscription 32. Chreistianoi [103] [from Akmonia]
CFCIP Inscription 33. Chreistianē [105] [from Akmonia]
CFCIP Inscription 34. Chreistianō [106] [from Akmonia]
CFCIP Inscription 35. Chreistianou [107] [from Akmonia]
CFCIP Inscription 37. Chreistianos [110] [Hierokaisareia, Lydia]
CFCIP Inscription 38. Chreistianōn [111] [from Apameia]
CFCIP Inscription 41. Chreistianos [117] [Eumeneia] [242/3 CE]
CFCIP Inscription 43. Chreistianōn [120] [Karapinar] [prob. 4th C CE]
Unnumbered Montanist inscription. Mountanē Chreistianē [138] [probably 4th C]

22 **Inscriptions Attesting to *Chrēstos***
CFCIP Inscription 3. †rēstianoi †rēstianois [12] [a Roman cross substituting for the chi]
CFCIP Inscription 6. Chrēstianois [17]
CFCIP Inscription 8. †rēstianoi †rē<s>tianois [19] [*ca.* 305 CE]
CFCIP Inscription 9. Chrēssianoi Chrēssianō [22] [*ca.* 305 CE]
CFCIP Inscription 10. Chrēstianē [24] [*ca.* 305 CE]
CFCIP Inscription 11. Chrēstianois [26] [*ca.* 305 CE]
CFCIP Inscription 12. Chrēstianoi Chrēstianō [29] [*ca.* 305 CE]
CFCIP Inscription 13. †rēstianoi †rēstianois [30] [*ca.* 305 CE]
CFCIP Inscription 14. Chrēstianoi Chrēstianois [32]
CFCIP Inscription 19. Chrēstianoi Chrēstianois [50]
CFCIP Inscription 20. Chrēstianoi Chrēst[ian]ō [52]
CFCIP Inscription 21. Chrēstianoi [Chrēst]ianē [54]
CFCIP Inscription 24. Chrēstianoi Chrēstianois [58]
CFCIP Inscription 27. Chrētianoi Chrēstianois [71]
CFCIP Inscription 28. Chrētianoi Chrēstianoi[s] [77]
CFCIP Inscription 29. [Chrēstianoi Ch]rēstianois [81]
CFCIP Inscription 30. Chrēsianoi [100]
CFCIP Inscription 44. Chrēstianou [121] [Apollonia]
CFCIP Inscription 45. Chrēst[iano?] [124] [Amorion]

23 **Inscriptions Attesting to *Christos***
CFCIP Inscription 7. Christia[noi Christi]anois [18]
CFCIP Inscription 18. [Christi]anoi Christianoi[s] [49]

In addition, there are two curious 'hybrid' readings.[24] One combines *ē and ei* in the same word (*chrēsteianoi*) and the other uses *i* in one word and *ē* in the next (*Christianoi Chrēstianois*).

It is worth noting also that several of these inscriptions date to *ca.* 305 CE and employ Roman crosses (✝) to substitute for the initial *chi* in Chr?stianoi. This is considerably earlier than 'common knowledge' would allow.

Elsa Gibson comments on the variant spellings encountered in the upper Tembris Valley [page 17]:

> In the upper Tembris Valley the form with *ēta* predominates; XRIC- or XREIC- is used in only five inscriptions apart from the present one [5], namely, nos. 1, 2, 18, 22, and 33. ...the forms with *ēta* seem to be deliberate; the word "Christian" was **mistakenly** thought to be derived from *chrēstos*. Use of the correct form with *iota* in the same area however sometimes created confusion, as seems to be the case in the present inscription[s] [emphasis mine].

Gibson makes some observations on language evolution that seem to me to be ignored at risk by scholars seeking to understanding the origins of Christ in particular and Christianity in general [96–97]:

> The spelling of the Greek in our inscriptions..., alternance in spelling between ει and ι, the beginning of conflation of οι and υ, αι and η, even ι and η, and the versification by stress of the hexameters are of great interest, for these features show not only how the language was pronounced but also, first, that it was being spoken... The dative begins to disappear from the Greek of Asia Minor as early as the late second or early third century... and by the fourth century the dative and the genitive or accusative are being frequently confused in inscriptions...
>
> The same evolution was taking place all over Asia Minor, as inscriptions show, and these features of pronunciation and syntax foreshadow those of modern Greek, facts which are ignored by those

CFCIP Inscription 23. Christianoi Christianō [58]

24 **Hybrid Readings**
CFCIP Inscription 17. Chrēsteiano[i] [47]
CFCIP Inscription 5. Christianoi Chrēstianois [15]

(even Petrie!) who consider the existence of this non-Classical Greek to be evidence that the spoken language of Phrygia was Phrygian. Many of the elements of modern Greek are here already.

I cannot agree with Ms. Gibson, however, in her claim that the engravers were mistaken in their understanding of the etymology of *Christos/Chrēstos*. It seems obvious to me that in these inscriptions we are witness to the vowel shift *in medias res* and a *new* etymology about to become developed. Although we must suppose it highly probable that in proto-Orthodox communities 'the Christ' had already been equated to the Jewish Messiah, relics of a pre-messianic savior seem here to lie exposed upon the graves of Phrygian believers of the third and early fourth centuries.

IV. ITACISM IN EGYPT

There is a powerful objection that can be raised against my thesis that *christos* was not the original spelling of *chr?stos*. How can we tell that *chrēstos* and *chreistos* aren't just regional misspellings of *christos*? Indeed, Francis Thomas Gignac's *A Grammar of the Greek Papyri of the Roman and Byzantine Periods* provides data that show that itacism did not proceed regularly or uniformly even in the territory of Roman Egypt. There is evidence that *reverse*-itacism also could occur, with ι → ει or η being copiously attested. So how can we tell if *christos* is the itacistic development from *chrēstos* or *chreistos* on the one hand, or whether the latter are the reverse-itacistic developments from *christos*?

Even though the dating of many papyri surveyed by Gignac is imprecise, it is possible to graph his phonetic mutation data in order to get a visual impression of the course of itacism in Egypt. Such a graph shows that the mutation of ει → η starts in 27 BCE and is heavily attested during the first three-fourths of the first century and continues steadily through the second and third centuries. Direct mutation ει → ι starts in the first decade of the first century and increases at the end of the century and then again at the end of the third century. Itacistic change of η → ι is strongly represented by papyri of the first century and then again from the middle of the third to mid-fourth centuries.

The mutation η → ει (*semi*-reverse-itacism?) is seen from about 20 CE to the middle of the second century, and then is seen sporadically into the fourth century. The mutation η → ει is, however, much less frequent at all periods than the change from ει to η.

Genuinely reverse itacism, of ι → ει or ι → η, begins during the first decade of the first century and proceeds steadily into the fourth century. Indeed, the amount of reverse itacism is almost equal to the sum of (ει→η) + (ει→ι) + (η→ι). Nevertheless, although uncertainties in dating of many of the manuscripts does not allow rigorous statistical analysis of the papyrological data, a slight trend is still perceptible that indicates an overall evolutionary sequence of (ει→η) → ι.

We must now ask, how does this analysis impact an evaluation of my thesis regarding the evolutionary origins of the title Christos?

Because of the phenomenon of reverse itacism, the development of itacism generally has to be followed by studying the spellings of words whose meanings are clear and unambiguous in their context, and so can be equated to the standard spellings of words in a Greek dictionary. Such words usually are words of common occurrence or words for which there is only a single 'anchor-word' in the dictionary to which they may be compared. Variant spellings of words can be equated to anchor spellings of words in a dictionary *only if their meanings can be established to be the same as a specific anchor-word in the dictionary*. In the case of a word such as *chr?stos*, however, where the meaning cannot be established *a priori*, and where there are several possible anchor words relatable to them, it is very difficult to determine the 'correct' spelling of the word in the absence of evidence from other lines of inquiry.

At a minimum, the evidence from the papyri certainly does not disconfirm my thesis that the title 'Christ' with a meaning of 'Messiah' is the result of itacistic phenomena transforming an etymologically unrelated title that originally had no messianic, Judaic reference. (Indeed, one may argue that 'Christ' in the Pauline Epistles also has no such meaning.) It is, however, altogether possible that a more detailed and statistically rigorous analysis of Gignac's papyri might be able to support or disconfirm the thesis.

V. FOR WANT OF A NAIL

Although the major focus of this chapter has been on the question of the original spelling of the term *Chr?stos* in order to test the hypothesis that the title was not originally messianic in meaning, I have hinted several times that the 'crucifixion' may not have been a physical occurrence taking place on earth. While I shall deal with this question in more detail elsewhere ("Bart Ehrman and the Body of Jesus of Nazareth"), it may be pointed out here that it is highly likely that the passion narrative account of a physical crucifixion — like the mention of Nazareth and the virgin birth story and the bloody sweat on the brow of Jesus on the Mount of Olives — was composed to counter the Docetists. Certainly, the story of Doubting Thomas has the Docetists in view when Thomas is invited manually to inspect the wounds of the risen Christ or Jesus. If *inspection* of the wounds was invented for polemic purposes, *why not the wounds themselves*?

The Greek word for 'nail' (*hēlos*) is found only in the Gospel according to John, 20:25: "The other disciples therefore said unto him, We have seen the Lord. But he said unto them, Except I shall see in his hands the print of the nails, and put my finger into the print of the nails, and thrust my hand into his side, I will not believe." Amazingly, not even in the Gospel of John is it ever said that Jesus *was nailed* to the 'cross.' Only in post-resurrection retrospect do we learn that nails were used in the crucifixion — a punishment that more often than not did not involve affixing the victim to the stake with nails.

In the oldest of the canonical gospels, Mark, they simply crucify (*staurousin*) Jesus and there is no description of what exactly that entailed. Since there are no post-resurrection appearances of Jesus in the best manuscripts of this gospel, there are of course no hints of wounds at all, still less of nails.

In Matthew 27:35 there is remarkable disinterest in the details of the most important operation ever carried out in the history of the world. It is tossed of with a participle: "After crucifying (*staurōsantes*) him, they divided his clothes among them..." To my amazement, at least, there is no hint in this gospel — even in the post-resurrection material — that Jesus had been physically wounded during the crucifixion process. Even in verse 28:17 — where we read that "When they [*the eleven disciples*] saw him [*the risen Jesus*], they fell prostrate before him, though some were doubtful" — a golden opportunity to display some bloody wounds was lost. No indication that any nails had been part of the story.

In the Gospel of Luke also, we learn nothing at all about how Jesus might have been attached to the pole: "...and when they reached the place called The Skull, they crucified (*estaurōsan*) him there..." [Luke 23:33] We do, however, begin to get a hint that the feet and hands of Jesus might have been injured during his execution. In the fish-eating-Jesus section of chapter 24 — the section clearly invented to confute the Docetists — the risen master orders his doubting disciples to "Look at my hands and feet. It is I myself. Touch me and see; no ghost has flesh and bones as you can see that I have." [Luke 24:39] For good measure, some manuscripts here add "After saying this he showed them his hands and feet." Take *that*, Docetic swine!

Modern readers, of course, interpret this hands-and-feet show-and-tell episode as evidence of nails that had been used to affix Jesus to the 'cross.' But of course, they already know about nails only because they have read about "Doubting Thomas" in the Gospel of John, [John 20:25]! An ancient reader who knew only the text of Luke's passion story, however, would have no reason to think of nails. As the story stands, it is nothing more than a further attempt to demonstrate the physicality of Jesus *even after his resurrection*. Furthermore, what *other* parts of his anatomy might we expect a fully clothed, formerly dead man would display? Judging from old photographs of the long-haired savior, earlobes probably would not have displayable.

So, if nails were not an original feature of the crucifixion story — and no passage in the entire New Testament directly states that Jesus or Christ was nailed to the 'cross' — we begin to suspect that 'crucifixion' is a greater mystery than generally supposed. If nails had been used for certain, the crucifixion of Jesus or the Christ would of necessity have had to take place on earth. Without nails, however, a mystery cult-type celestial event becomes at least possible. Perhaps the 'cross,' being not of this world, was too ethereal to support a body anchored with nails? My hypothesis that the 'crucifixion' occurred at the intersection of the celestial equator and the ecliptic when the vernal equinox had moved into Pisces, however, awaits further evidence.

CONCLUSION

One of Bart D. Ehrman's major arguments for the historicity of at least *some* Jesus or other is that the earliest Christians knew "from day one" that he had been crucified, but yet they identified him with the Messiah of the Jews. Because no Jews expected their messiah to 'suffer' let alone be crucified as a common criminal, Jews couldn't accept the Christian Messiah. So, proto-Christians had to hunt for 'Old Testament' scriptures 'proving' that the messiah would have to suffer. If Jesus had *not* in fact been crucified, Ehrman argues, all this would not have been necessary. It *was* necessary, however, because Jesus *had* been crucified, and so of necessity he must have existed.

Israel Knohl has shown, however, that the Essene leader Menahem *was* a 'Suffering Servant' *à la* Isaiah 53 and was killed in the uprising after Herod's death in 4 BCE. This fact alone is sufficient to nullify Ehrman's argument. Nevertheless, I have presented evidence to support the thesis that the earliest Christians did not identify their 'Christ' with the Israelite Messiah, but considered him to be a celestial figure created by theopoietic methods of a Pythagorean, Platonic, Docetic, and proto-Gnostic nature.

I have presented evidence from ancient inscriptions and manuscripts in order to show that the title *Christos* was originally spelled with *ei* or *ē*, not *i*. I have argued that the etymology of the title leads not to *chriō* ('anoint,' 'smear') and thus to the Greek equivalent of the word for Messiah, but rather it leads to Greek terms associated with goodness, rightness, usefulness, prophesy, divination, and oracles. Exactly what the proto-Christians conceived their Chr?st to be remains to be explored. However, once the great vowel shift called iotacism or itacism transformed Ancient Greek increasingly into Modern Greek, both *Chreistos* and *Chrēstos* would have been transformed into *Christos* and a messianic meaning could be adopted for the title.

Finally, I have argued that the earliest accounts for the crucifixion of Jesus did not indicate that nails were used to fix him to the stake. Nails come into the story explicitly in the late Gospel of John — and even then, it is in retrospection, not description of immediate action. For want of nails, I suggest, the crucifixion need not have occurred on earth. This may force us to inquire what the proto-Christians meant by Greek words usually translated as 'cross' and 'crucify.' Elsewhere I shall argue that this takes us into the realm of astrotheology.

Ultimately, though, it may not matter what the original meaning of 'Chr?st' or 'Chr?stians' may have been. If we are to believe St. Epiphanius [*ca.* 310–402 CE], Bishop of Salamis in Cyprus, the first Christians weren't called that at the beginning anyway! In his *Panarion* ('Medicine Chest,' the antidote to the poison of all heresies), in the chapter about the 'Nazoraeans,' he claims that before Christians received that appellation at Antioch [Acts 11:26] they were called Nazoraeans and Jessaeans, and he opines that the latter name derives from Jesse, the father of David.

Now even if Bart Ehrman has never read Epiphanius, he should know about the Jessaeans: not only are they discussed on the specific pages of my book that he criticizes in *DJE?*, I discussed them also in at least one e-mail that I sent to him. That being the case, one wonders what he could have been been thinking when he wrote the following: "These early Christians from day one believed that Jesus was the messiah. But they knew that he had been crucified" [*DJE?* 156]. Throughout this chapter I have focused attention on the "crucified" part of his claim. In closing, however, we must question the first part of that claim. If 'Christ' means 'anointed' and is a synonym for 'messiah,' and if Christians "from day one" believed that Jesus was the messiah, why didn't they call themselves Christians? If it is true that they originally were called Nazoreans or Jessaeans, doesn't that mean they did not yet think Jesus (or Christ) was the messiah? Doesn't that imply they *didn't* believe Jesus was the messiah from day one? Perhaps it wasn't until day one thousand?

What I have presented in this chapter is a scientific hypothesis to be tested and weighed by further research. It is possible that I am wrong. Nevertheless, even if I am wrong, that would not mean that Ehrman is correct in his claim that "from day one" early Christians "believed that Jesus was the messiah." It is possible that even if *Chr?stos* was originally spelled with iota and did in fact mean 'anointed,' it might not have had anything at all to do with any Jewish *messiah*. It could easily have involved a *celestial anointing* with heavenly oil such as we find in 2 Enoch. In 2 Enoch 22 we read that Enoch was in the tenth heaven and he underwent an anointing of an astounding nature:

> And the LORD said to Michael, "Go, and extract Enoch from [his] earthly clothing. And anoint him with my delightful oil, and put him into the clothes of my glory." And so Michael did, just as the LORD had said to him. He anointed me and he clothed me. And the appearance of that oil is greater than the greatest light, and its ointment is like sweet dew, and its fragrance myrrh; and it is like the rays of the glittering sun. And I looked at myself, and I had become like one of his glorious ones, and there was no observable difference.[25]

We see that Enoch not only had been anointed with oil in a celestial setting, he had become "like one of the glorious [*i.e., glowing*] ones." Had he not *ipso facto* become a heavenly *Christos*? Wasn't that *Christos* more exalted than a mere terrestrial messiah? Might not the 'Christ' of the first Christians also have been a being more exalted than the lowly would-be messiah of Ehrman's argument? We may hope that research carried out in the new paradigm of a science of Christian origins will soon discover convincing answers to this and related questions raised by Ehrman's attempt to defend traditional views.

NOTE ADDED IN PROOF

As this volume was about to go to press, I received a copy of Chrys C. Caragounis' *The Development of Greek and the New Testament*

25 Translated by F.I. Andersen, "2 (Slavonic Apocalypse of) Enoch (Late First Century A.D.)" in: *The Old Testament Pseudepigrapha. Volume I. Apocalyptic Literature and Testaments*, ed. James H. Charlesworth [Garden City, NY: Doubleday & Co., 1983: 138].

[Wissenschaftliche Untersuchungen zum Neuen Testament. Tübingen: Mohr Siebeck, 2004: 493–4]. In his discussion of MS text variants resulting from copyist errors due to "faulty hearing" involving itacism, Caragounis lists "1 Pt 2:3: chrēstos, Christos."

Intrigued, I turned to 1 Pt 2:3 in the KJV and read, "If so be, ye have tasted that the Lord is gracious." That being a bit odd, I consulted the NEB, which informed me that "Surely you have tasted that the Lord is good." Wondering what sort of Greek text could spawn such disparate translations, I consulted the Third Edition of The Greek New Testament, edited by Aland, Black, Martini, Metzger, and Wikgram. Their Greek text read: "*ei* [or *eiper* or *eisper* or *hoper*] *egeusasthe hoti chrēstos ho kyrios*."

Now it just so happens that 1 Pt 2:3 is a quotation from Psalms 34:8: "Taste, then, and see that the LORD is good" [NEB] or "O taste and see that the LORD is good" [KJV]. In the LXX the equivalent verse is 33:8: "Taste and see that the LORD is good," rendering the Greek "*Geusasthe kai idete hoti chrēstos ho Kyrios*." [*The Septuagint with Apocrypha: Greek and English*. Sir Lancelot C.L. Brenton (London: Samuel Bagster & Sons, 1851)]

If we recall the fact that in the LXX *Kyrios* is the equivalent of *YHWH* in the MT, we see that this psalm is equating *chrēstos* with *YHWH*, just as the New Testament equates *Christos* with *Kyrios/ YHWH*.[26]

It seems obvious that the expression *chrēstos ho Kyrios* in 1 Pt 2:3 is formally identical to *Christos ho Kyrios* — 'good is the Lord' and 'Christ is the Lord.' Philosophically, it is an easy step to go from an adjectival reading of 'good' to make it an abstract Platonic noun — 'the good.' It takes no mental effort to go from saying "Yahweh is good" to saying "Yahweh equals the Good" — *Chrēstos ho Kyrios*. With Yahweh thus the embodiment of goodness, *ho chrēstos* would become a title — an epithet of Yahweh.

It is easy to imagine a cult involving *Chrēstos* as a personification of Yahweh, with *Chrēstos ho Kyrios* as a slogan. Then, with the progression

26 Luke 2:11: For unto you is born this day in the city of David a Savior, which is Christ the LORD (*sōtēr hos estin Christos Kyrios*).

of itacism, the slogan in a trice could become *Christos ho Kyrios* — 'the anointed one is Lord.' And so, with the change of a single vowel, the predicate 'the Messiah is the Lord' would emerge from the postulate 'the Good is the Lord.' A messiah whose body could be crucified would have sprung from a word — an ideal substance too ethereal to be touched, let alone to be transfixed by nails.

PART IV: Farewell to Earth

CHAPTER SEVENTEEN

Bart Ehrman and the Body of Jesus of Nazareth

Frank R. Zindler

If the Docetists had won the war, we would not be debating the historicity of Jesus of Nazareth in the twenty-first century. Indeed, we wouldn't even know that this was *the twenty-first century!*

ABSTRACT

The earliest 'heresy' of which we have evidence is Docetism, which denied the corporeality of Jesus. Docetism may very well be ancestral to proto-Orthodoxy, as it is more realistic to derive proto-Orthodoxy from Docetism than *vice-versa,* when a mere thirty years were available for the transformation. Many passages in the Epistles and Gospels show evidence of having been created for anti-Docetic polemic purposes. This includes the genealogies and birth narratives in Matthew and Luke. It is likely that the 'polis' of Nazareth was derived from the epithet *Nazōraios/Nazōrenos* to create a hometown for a deity who had acquired a real body. Nazareth is missing not only in Marcion's *Evangelicon* but in almost the entirety of the apocryphal literature published by Ehrman.

Frank R. Zindler

Like modern Christians and Muslims, Bart Ehrman appears to take it for granted that Jesus of Nazareth once existed as a man — a human being. Although the ostensible purpose of his recent book *Did Jesus Exist? The Historical Argument for Jesus of Nazareth* (*DJE?*)[1] was to prove the historicity of a religious prophet who lived in a place called Nazareth, Ehrman presented no new arguments in the book to prove the historicity of the Nazarene and, I shall argue, presented no positive evidence for his thesis at all. Much of Ehrman's energy is devoted to refutations of the theories of Christian origins that have been advanced by several contemporary Mythicists — as though simply disproving rival theories could somehow substitute for positive evidence in support of an existence claim. Can Ehrman prove that there really is a unicorn in his garden by showing that Ehrorman's claim that it's actually a rhinoceros is silly?

As we learn from Ehrman's repeated use of the three-million-Frenchmen-can't-be-wrong argument, the vast majority of modern scholars also accept the historicity of Jesus of Nazareth on no more evidence than that presented by Ehrman. They take it as axiomatic — even if they are Atheists who do not believe that Jesus the Man was also a god. If asked the question "Did Jesus have a body?" believers and skeptical scholars alike would consider it a no-brainer. Of *course* Jesus had a body! If he once existed as a man, *a fortiori* he had a body. Despite his expertise regarding the ancient 'heresy' called Docetism (more of which anon), Ehrman also seems quite convinced not only that *Jesus* had a body, but *Jesus of Nazareth* in particular once had a body that was fully capable of converting food and air into greenhouse gases and manure.

Whereas even skeptical scholars would consider their affirmative answer to the corporeality question to be a logical necessity, believers could adduce further 'proof' of the physicality of Jesus' corporality from the New Testament of the Christian bible. Was not Jesus born of the Virgin Mary? Mary was a human mother, and women don't give birth to ghosts!

1 New York: HarperOne, 2012. Bart Ehrman recieved a shorter, earlier version of this chapter but seems not to have been able to answer my claims, as no mention whatsoever of my arguments is to be found in *DJE?*

Bart Ehrman and the Body of Jesus of Nazareth

Furthermore, even after Jesus was killed and resurrected, he had a physical body. Did not Doubting Thomas verify the fact when he thrust his hand into the risen Jesus' side [John 20:27–28]? Did not Jesus eat a breakfast of bread and fish with the Disciples when he appeared to them on the shore of the Sea of Galilee [John 21:12–15]?

It is a curious fact that the answer to this simple question — so obvious to *modern* Christians — was not at all obvious to many *ancient* Christians. The earliest 'heresy' that we know of appears to be that of *Docetism*. The Docetists took their name from the fact that they believed that Jesus only *seemed* (Greek *dokein* 'to seem') to have a physical body and only *seemed* to suffer on the cross but was, in fact, a heavenly spirit. (Docetists actually were not a specific type of 'heretic'; a variety of early Christian groups did not believe that Christ and/or Jesus did not have a physical body.) Now of course we can be quite confident that Doubting Thomas never explored the peritoneal cavity of Jesus of Nazareth and that Jesus of Nazareth did not celebrate a 'Last Breakfast' on the shore of the 'Sea' of Galilee. As scientific thinkers, we can be quite sure these stories were made up. But *why* were they made up? Was it to contradict the Docetists? We shall see.

Docetic forms of Christianity appeared so early and were so successful that some of our earliest Christian witnesses — the so-called Apostolic Fathers — were moved to denounce the Gnostics and anyone else who held Docetic beliefs. (Ehrman, it must be noted, is a world-renowned expert on the Apostolic Fathers, being the author and editor of the new Greek text edition and translation of the Apostolic Fathers in the prestigious Loeb Classical Library.)

In or about the year 110 CE, St. Ignatius, Bishop of Antioch, sent a letter to the Christians of Smyrna in present-day Turkey. In that epistle Ignatius told the Smyrneans that "[Jesus] suffered all these things for us; and He suffered them *really*, and not in appearance only, even as also He truly rose again. But not, as some of the unbelievers, who … affirm, that in appearance only, and not in truth, He took a body of the Virgin, and suffered only in appearance, forgetting as they do, Him who said, 'The Word was made flesh' [Jn 1:14]… I know that he was possessed of a body not only in His being born and crucified, but I also know that he was so after His resurrection, and believe that He is so now."[2]

Let us think about this for a moment.

Jesus is supposed to have died somewhere around the year 33 CE. Within 77 years, church leaders were in serious dispute over whether or not he had had a body! Let us translate this to a modern context. Imagine Jimmy Carter and Gerald Ford arguing over the question of whether or not William McKinley had had a body. But the facts of Christian history are even more absurd than is this modern scenario.

It is clear that Docetism was a problem even in the days when letters now attributed to the Apostles Paul, Peter, and John were being written. How do we know this? Consider the following verses:

> **Galatians 4:4–5.** But when the fullness of the time was come, God sent forth his Son, *made of a woman*, made under the law, To redeem them that were under the law... [A.D. 58]
>
> **Romans 1:3.** Concerning his Son Jesus Christ our Lord, which was made of the seed of David according to the flesh... [A.D. 60]
>
> **Romans 8:3.** For what the law could not do, in that it was weak through the flesh, God sending his own Son in the likeness of sinful flesh, and for sin, condemned sin in the flesh... [A.D. 60]
>
> **Colossians 1:21–22.** And you, who once were estranged and hostile in mind, doing evil deeds, he has now reconciled in his body of flesh by his death... [A.D. 64]
>
> **1 Timothy 3:16.** And without controversy great is the mystery of godliness: God was manifest in the flesh, justified in the Spirit, seen of angels, preached unto the Gentiles, believed on in the world, received up into glory. [A.D. 65]
>
> **1 Peter 3:18.** For Christ also hath once suffered for sins, the just for the unjust, that he might bring us to God, being put to death in the flesh, but quickened by the Spirit... [A.D. 60]

2 *Ignat. Smyrn.* Chapters 2–3] [*The Ante-Nicene Fathers, Vol. I. The Apostolic Fathers — Justin Martyr — Irenaeus*, [Grand Rapids, MI: Wm. B. Eerdmans (reprint), 1985: 87].

Bart Ehrman and the Body of Jesus of Nazareth

> **1 Peter 4:1.** Forasmuch then as Christ hath suffered for us in the flesh, arm yourselves likewise with the same mind; for he that hath suffered in the flesh hath ceased from sin... [A.D. 60]

> **1 John 4:1–3.** Beloved, believe not every spirit, but try the spirits whether they are of God: because many false prophets are gone out into the world. Hereby know ye the Spirit of God: Every spirit that confesseth that Jesus Christ *is come in the flesh* is of God: And every spirit that confesseth not that Jesus Christ *is come in the flesh* is not of God: and this is that spirit of antichrist, whereof ye have heard that it should come; and even now already is it in the world. [A.D. 90]

> **2 John 1:7.** For many deceivers are entered into the world, who confess not that Jesus Christ *is come in the flesh*. This is a deceiver and an antichrist. [A.D. 90]

Before going further, I must confess that the dates given with each quoted verse is the date assigned to it by the infamous Archbishop James Ussher [1581–1656] — the same guy who determined the biblical 'fact' that the world was created in the year 4004 B.C. Even so, a very large number of Christian scholars even today would assert that these dates are essentially correct.

It should be noted that in all of the verses I have quoted the writers seem to have gone out of their way to stress that Jesus had a body — something that one might think would be a given. Why would these sacred authors bother to mention such a fact? If I were writing about my childhood and talking about the exciting times I had with my grandfather, wouldn't it seem more than odd if I mentioned even once, "By the way: my grandfather had a body"? What if I told you, "My grandfather had a mother"? Clearly the verses quoted were written to contradict rival Christians who were claiming that Jesus only *seemed* to have a body. Docetists were the antichrists of the first century.

Now let us think about this a bit more. If the Epistle to the Galatians was in fact written in the year 58, and Jesus was crucified in the year 33...

Frank R. Zindler

I can hear Franklin D. Roosevelt arguing with Herbert Hoover: "Did Theodore Roosevelt have a body?" "Did Mittie Roosevelt really bear Teddy?"

The fact that Docetic actors are standing on the Christian stage as early as the raising of the first curtain of our passion play is of considerable explanatory significance. If Jesus of Nazareth never existed as an actual man of flesh and blood, but rather began as a god who had come to earth to help the souls of men and women find their ways back to their heavenly home, there would arise lots of questions concerning what he had actually been like when he was on the earth. Very early on, we might expect to find squabbling theological factions engaging in arguments concerning his terrestrial nature.

Did a god perhaps take possession of the body of some human and then fly back to heaven when that body died? Was a fully human organism 'adopted' by Yahweh, becoming a god in the process? This actually was an early 'Adoptionist' view of Jesus that is reflected in some manuscript readings (including that of the ever-fascinating *Codex Bezae*) of the story of the baptism of Jesus found in Luke 3:22.[3] These have a voice from heaven tell Jesus as he emerges from the water "Thou art my Son; this day I have begotten thee." After the crucifixion, we must suppose, the god abandoned — "My God, my God, why hast thou forsaken me?"[4] — the physical body of Jesus and flew back to heaven.

3 Bart Ehrman gives a thorough account of the scribal and scholarly struggles over the 'original' wording of this verse on pages 62–67 of *The Orthodox Corruption of Scripture*. Concerning the reading "this day I have begotten thee," he writes: "...in the view of many scholars, it makes little sense for Luke's divine voice to declare that Jesus has *become* the Son of God at his baptism when he had already been *born* the Son of God (from a virgin mother) two chapters earlier [*emphasis original*]." Still a cautious scholar, though, he adds: "Unfortunately, as happens so frequently with arguments of this kind, it is difficult to see which way the knife is more likely to cut."

The metaphor seems apt and I would suggest a possibility beyond those Ehrman discusses with regard to this verse. The adoptionist reading "this day have I begotten thee" would not conflict with the virgin-birth account in chapter two *if* — as in Marcion's gospel — *chapter two had not yet been prefixed to the story*. It seems to me that the adoptionist reading of Luke 3:22 is in fact the best reading and that it thus adds to the evidence supporting the thesis that the genealogy and birth narrative are not original in Luke.

4 Mark 15:34b; Matthew 27:46b.

Bart Ehrman and the Body of Jesus of Nazareth

Did a god — as Orthodoxy now holds — impregnate a mortal woman in the way that Zeus had done on a number of occasions? Was Jesus then simultaneously a god and a man of flesh and blood? Was his mortal human mother then literally 'the Mother of God'?

Or were the Docetists and Gnostics correct? When the god came to earth he only *seemed* to be the mortal man Jesus. Throughout his enactment of this divine drama, Jesus never had a mortal body, but continued to the end to be composed of whatever ectoplasmic essence it is that gods are made of. How could Jesus have been mortal if he was a god? How can a god die? Gods are immortal — that's the main difference between gods and humans. If Jesus had had a physical body, *ipso facto* he could not have been a god. Q.E.D.

Scholars who believe without positive evidence that there once was a man called Jesus of Nazareth surely must experience a bit of *Angst* because of this silly situation. This must be made even more anxiety-provoking by the fact that René Salm has shown, in *The Myth of Nazareth: The Invented Town of Jesus*,[5] that 'Nazareth' was not inhabited at the time Jesus should have been living there. No matter. I'm sure that Jesús de Rancho Cucamonga had a body made of flesh and blood.

If the Pauline epistles are indeed as early as most scholars suppose, it is abundantly clear from the passages examined above that Docetism was a very early form of Christianity — perhaps representing the original type of belief shared by the groups we might label as the first Christians. Might reaction to Docetism have left traces in the canonical gospels as well? As we shall see a bit later on, Bart Ehrman in *The Orthodox Corruption of Scripture: The Effect of Early Christological Controversies on the Text of the New Testament* (*OCS*)[6] has demonstrated beyond cavil that this is indeed a fact. But before we look at Ehrman's evidence it may be of interest to see what I have discovered on my own without his help.

Irenaeus of Lyons,[7] in his *Against Heresies* [*ca.* 180 CE: Book III, chapter xi.7], tells us that the Ebionites preferred Matthew's gospel;

5 Cranford, NJ: American Atheist Press, 2008.

6 Oxford University Press, NY, 1993.

7 *The Ante-Nicene Fathers, Vol. I. The Apostolic Fathers — Justin Martyr — Irenaeus*, edited by Alexander Roberts and James Donaldson [Grand Rapids, MI: Wm. B. Eerdmans Pub. Co., 1985].

Marcion preferred his "mutilated" version of Luke; the Valentinians preferred John's gospel; and "Those, again, who separate Jesus from Christ, alleging that Christ remained impassible [*incapable of suffering*], but that it was Jesus who suffered, preferring the Gospel by Mark..." It seems obvious that the unnamed group of separationist heretics who held that *Christ* (*nota bene*, not *Jesus*) could not suffer were Docetists of some sort.

Now an easy question: Why would Docetists at the time of Irenaeus have preferred Mark to, say, Matthew or Luke? An easy answer: Because Mark has no genealogies to prove a human ancestry for 'the Jesus'; no birth legend to indicate that he had been composed of flesh and bones; and no tales of a childhood that might imply that he had been away from heaven for a long time before getting around to proclaiming his 'Good News.'

Further reason and evidence to support the notion that Docetism was the earliest form of Christianity of which we have record come from what will seem to be a rather shocking understanding of the theopolitical motivations that governed the evolutionary development of the Synoptic Gospels.

The earliest of the three Synoptic Gospels, 'Mark,' as we have noted above has no concern for the birth, genealogy, or early life of 'the Jesus' — a character probably understood as 'the Savior,' not a regular guy named Joshua or Jesus. The two gospels that were derived from it — 'Matthew' and 'Luke' — have added genealogies and birth narratives to the Markan story framework.[8] Why is that?

8 According to Bart Ehrman [*The Orthodox Corruption of Scripture*], "Most of the fathers from the early second century (Papias) to the late fourth (Jerome) claimed that it [the Ebionite gospel] comprised a truncated form of Matthew ... written in Hebrew, one that lacked its opening chapters, that is, the narrative of Jesus' miraculous birth." [51] Referring to Adolph von Harnack in explanatory note 42 on page 102, he explains further: "Thus, the adoptionistic Ebionites were commonly accused of using a truncated form of the first Gospel. Moreover, the docetist Marcion, who denied the virgin birth for entirely different reasons, used a version of Luke that was similarly abbreviated (because Christ could not have been a part of the material world, he could not have been born; he therefore descended fully grown from heaven in the fifteenth year of Tiberias Caesar)."

Nota bene: this is *not* during the reign of Augustus or the census of Quirinius and is long after the death of Herod the Great in 4 BCE!

Bart Ehrman and the Body of Jesus of Nazareth

The writings of the Church Fathers provide a clue. Like modern Christians, the Church Fathers did not perceive the genealogies and birth narratives of Matthew and Luke to be additions to the text of Mark. Rather, they supposed Matthew and Luke were independent witnesses who simply were a bit more thorough than Mark. When they encountered non-Orthodox groups whose gospels lacked these elements, they accused them of mutilating the gospel texts — excising these important parts of the Jesus story for evil ends.

Now that we know that Matthew and Luke are expansions of Mark's text, however, we see that it is not likely that various 'heretical' groups were "truncating" Matthew and Luke as Irenaeus and other Church Fathers claimed, but rather they had retained earlier versions of these gospels dating from a time before the birth narratives were invented. Is it not highly likely, therefore, that the birth narratives had been added only after the proto-Orthodox had become engaged in a struggle to extinction with the Docetists and others who believed that a man of flesh and blood could not be or become a god? Is it not, moreover, likely that the earliest gospel, Mark, lacks a birth story for the simple reason that it is nearer to the Docetic roots of the Christian movement? *Is it not easier to derive Orthodox Christianity from Docetism than the other way around?* If the Christian gospel began as an abstraction conveyed in metaphor and symbolism, it would not only be easy to reify everything and make the abstract concrete, it would be practically inevitable. Dullness and ignorance will always be more successful than intelligence and understanding in the course of religious evolution.

Ehrman is absolutely spot-on when he notes [*OCS* 54] "Since the orthodox struggle with adoptionists centered in part on the doctrine of Jesus' virgin birth, we might expect to find a theological battle waged over the first two chapters of Matthew and Luke, the only New Testament passages that affirm the belief."

Indeed.

It might be argued against both Ehrman and me that the genealogies and birth narratives were created simply because of a natural human desire to know more about a man who had become a god.

But where would the needed information have come from? If it were a *reliable* source, why would Matthew and Luke have come up with completely contradictory genealogies and mutually exclusive tales of Jesus's birth and childhood? Why would idle curiosity have driven Matthew and Luke to invent such stories out of thin air?

Well, what if there were a motivation *other than idle curiosity* — a motivation much, much stronger than idle curiosity moving the several authors of those gospels to invent their stories? What if there were theopolitical reasons? What if the political ascendance of someone's church and its authorities were at stake? What if there were a *theopolitical* reason to demonstrate that Jesus had been born a child of flesh and blood? What if one needed to show that Jesus wasn't a phantom as the Docetists claimed as they seemed poised to corner the religion market?

Indeed, *what if the genealogies and birth legends were made up to confute the Docetists*? How might this have been accomplished? It seems likely that once the title *Chreistos* had evolved phonetically into *Christos* [see chapter "Bart Ehrman and the Crucified Messiah"], Christ-Jesus could become Messiah-Jesus and would warrant a genealogy from King David and perhaps from a Joseph as well. Not only would that establish Christos's *bona fides* as a Jewish Messiah, it would prove beyond doubt that he had been a man of flesh and blood — a man whose newly acquired name *Iēsous* just happened to mean *Savior* and implied divinity.

In the case of the Gospel of Matthew, the genealogy almost certainly was added first to the Markan narrative, before the birth legends were added to the tale. Like any good Jewish genealogy, it traced the lineage of Jesus — now equated with Chreistos/Christ — paternally from King David to Joseph. While a long series of 'begats' connecting Jesus to King David would be all that was really needed to trump the claims of the Docetists, there was the problem that now the god Chreistos-Jesus was *too* human, too mundane.

What to do? A miraculous birth was needed: *miraculous*, to retain the signs of divinity; *physical birth* from a woman, to keep the Docetists out of the religion markets in the better neighborhoods. A *virgin* birth story was the perfect solution.

Alas, adding a virgin birth to the *curriculum vitae* of a fleshly Jesus now vitiated the genealogy that traced Jesus' ancestry through Joseph back to David! It was necessary to amend the genealogy so that we now may learn that "Jacob begat Joseph the husband of Mary, of whom was born Jesus, who is called Christ."

How do we know the genealogy was altered? The oldest manuscript of the Syriac versions of the Gospel of Matthew — the so-called *Sinaitic Palimpsest* or *Codex Sinaiticus Syriacus* — attests to the pre-virgin-birth state of the genealogy.[9] It simply states that "Jacob begat Joseph; Joseph, to whom was betrothed a young woman, Mary, begat Jesus who is called Messiah" [*my translation*].

The Matthaean genealogy and nativity tale have been so basic a part of our 'common sense' since our childhoods that it is almost impossible to step outside our imbedded framework for thought — our paradigm — to question why these components of Matthew's gospel are present in the first place, whereas they are absent from Mark and John. Rarely does any one of us get beyond wondering why Matthew's genealogy and nativity account differ so completely from those of Luke.

As was the case of what we might call proto-Matthew (the form of the newly expanded form of Mark's narrative that still lacked a genealogy and an account of the birth of Jesus), it seems quite clear that proto-Luke also had neither genealogy nor tale of a miraculous child. What evidence might we cite to support this idea?

Marcion of Sinope [*ca.* 84–*ca.* 160 CE] was one of the first 'heretics' of whom we have abundant information in the form of detailed refutations by early Church Fathers such as Tertullian, Irenaeus, and Epiphanius. Although all his writings were destroyed after the triumph of Nicene Christianity, it is known from the writings of his critics that he was the first Christian to create a canon of scripture, and his 'Bible' can be reconstructed in some detail. This is not as difficult as it might seem, as his Bible was *very* small. It had only one gospel — the *Evangelicon*, a form of the Gospel of Luke — and the *Apostolicon* comprised of ten of

9 Agnes Smith Lewis, *The Four Gospels in Syriac, Transcribed from the Sinaitic Palimpsest* [Cambridge University Press, 1894].

the so-called Pauline Epistles: Galatians, I & II Corinthians, Romans, I & II Thessalonians, Laodiceans (Ephesians), Colossians, Philemon, and Philippians. (Perhaps significantly, Marcion did not attribute his gospel to Luke by name, for which oversight he was criticized by Tertullian in his *Adversus Marcionem* 4.2.)

It was a scandal that Marcion did not include most of the first four chapters of Luke in his edition of the gospel. That means there was no Jesuine genealogy and no miraculous births of the Summer and Winter Solstice babies John the Baptist and Jesus of Nazareth. Also, it must be noted, there were four fewer mentions of 'Nazareth' — leaving none at all spelled with a *-th* or *-t* ending [10] — and there was no preface addressed to "most excellent Theophilus."[11]

In addition to the fact that Nazareth is not mentioned in any of the canonical epistles or Apocalypse, it is startling to find that the place is unknown also in Tischendorf's Greek text of *The Infancy Gospel of Thomas*, although it does turn up in "The Infancy Gospel of Thomas C: An Alternative Beginning" translated by Bart Ehrman from a fifteenth-century manuscript edited by Armand Delatte.[12] Nazareth is also not to be found in other 'infancy gospels,' including *The Proto-Gospel of James*, the Latin *Gospel of Pseudo-Matthew*, and

10 It is surely of significance that of the five times that Luke mentions the name of the alleged home-town of Jesus, the first four occur in the chapters that Marcion was accused of excising but which *he* claimed were interpolations. In all the MSS surveyed by Reuben Swanson in his *New Testament Greek Manuscripts: Luke* [Sheffield: Sheffield Academic Press, 1995], the first four occurrences are spelling variants of *Nazaret/th*. The fifth and last occurrence of the name — in Luke 4:16 — it is spelled *Nazara* in the best witnesses. It would appear that the earliest toponym was spelled *Nazara* or a variant thereof. Then, when the birth narrative was added (and in later harmonizing manuscripts) the name had somehow evolved into *Nazaret/th*. **It appears more than ever likely that the town was created for the sake of the birth legends. They, in turn, were created to counter the Docetists.**

11 "Forasmuch as many have taken in hand to set forth in order a declaration of those things which are most surely believed among us, 2 Even as they delivered them to us, which from the beginning were eye-witnesses, and ministers of the word; 3 It seemed good to me also, having had perfect understanding of all things from the very first, to write unto thee in order, most excellent Theophilus, 4 That thou mightest know the certainty of those things, wherein thou hast been instructed."

12 Bart D. Ehrman and Zlatko Pleše, *The Apocryphal Gospels, Texts and Translations* [Oxford: Oxford University Press, 2011].

The Latin Infancy Gospels (Arundel Form). It is, however, found three times in the Bohairic Coptic text of *History of Joseph the Carpenter*, which Pleše [*loc. cit.* 158] tells us was "most likely composed in Byzantine Egypt in the late sixth or early seventh century."

Nazareth is not to be found elsewhere in the entire corpus of apocryphal documents published by Ehrman and Pleše, although Ehrman uses the expression "Jesus of Nazareth" in this translation from the Greek text of *The Letter of Tiberius to Pilate* [*loc. cit.* 532–33]. This, however, is a KJV-type mistranslation of *Iēsou ton* [*sic*] *Nazōraiou* — 'of Jesus the Nazorean.' This means that Nazareth is not mentioned *even once* in *The Gospel of the Nazareans, The Gospel of the Ebionites, The Gospel according to the Hebrews, The Gospel according to the Egyptians, A gospel Harmony: The Diatessaron?, The Gospel according to Thomas,* the *Agrapha, The Gospel of Peter, The Gospel of Judas, Jesus' Correspondence with Abgar, The Gospel of Nicodemus (Acts of Pilate A & B), The Report of Pontius Pilate, The Handing Over of Pilate, The Letter of Pilate to Claudius* [sic!], *The Letter of Pilate to Herod, The Letter of Herod to Pilate, The Vengeance of the Savior, The Death of Pilate Who Condemned Jesus, The Narrative of Joseph of Arimathea, The Gospel according to Mary, The Greater Questions of Mary,* and ten ancient papyri published by Ehrman and Pleše!

It was, as I have noted, a scandal that Marcion's gospel lacked the birth narrative, and it was claimed that Marcion had deleted that and many other things from his text to accord with his heretical, Docetic, ideas. Marcion, we may suppose, must have responded that his short version was the original, true version, and that the proto-Orthodox versions had been swollen by interpolations. What were those interpolations? It seems likely to me that the interpolations were basically all the passages intended to refute a Docetic theory of Jesus. I see no reason to believe the Orthodox apologists' claims rather than Marcion's — especially for the text-critical reasons below.

According to the text of Marcion's *Evangelicon*[13] (available at www.marcionite-scripture.info) as reconstructed from Tertullian's

13 This reconstruction is based upon reconstructions by James Hamlyn Hill (1891), August Han (1823), and Theodor Zahn (1888). (Marcionite Research Library, www.marcionite-scripture.info © Melissa Cutter 2010).

Adversus Marcionem [*iv*.7] and Epiphanius's *Panarion* [42], Marcion's gospel began with what is now chapter 3, verse 1 of present-day Luke and followed it immediately by what now is verse 31 of chapter 4:

> "In the fifteenth year of Tiberius Caesar, Pontius Pilate being governor of Judea, Jesus descended [out of heaven[14]] into Capernaum, a city in Galilee, and was teaching in the synagogue on the Sabbath days; and they were astonished at his doctrine, for his word was in authority."

Instead of trudging out of the wilderness into Galilee and stirring up a lynch-mob at *Nazareth* (as in the canonical gospel of Luke) in a synagogue unknown to archaeology, in Marcion's version of Luke Jesus plops down from heaven — right into a synagogue in *Capernaum*! Only later does he go to the lynch-mob synagogue in Nazareth.

Now we know that Luke took his story from an early form of Mark. It is significant to note that in Mark — where the only mention of Nazareth is in the disputed passage Mark 1:9, the first place that Jesus visits after leaving the wilderness is *Capernaum*, not Nazareth

14 In Book IV, Chapter vii of his *Adversus Marcionem*, Tertullian dilates derisively concerning the "descent" of Marcion's Christ:

> In the fifteenth year of the reign of Tiberius (for such is Marcion's proposition) he 'came down to the Galilean city of Capernaum,' of course meaning from the heaven of the Creator, to which he had previously descended from his own heaven to the Creator's? ... I want also to know the remainder of his course down, assuming that he came down. For we must not be too nice in inquiring whether it is supposed that he was seen in any place. ... when it happens that a descent has been effected, it is apparent, and comes under the notice of the eyes. ... [We would like to know] further, at what time of the day or night, the descent was made; who again saw the descent, who reported it, who seriously avouched the fact, which certainty was not easy to be believed, even after the asseveration. It is, in short, too bad that Romulus should have had in Proculus an avoucher of his ascent to heaven, when the Christ of (this) god could not find any one to announce his descent from heaven... straight to the synagogue.

Is it not too bad as well, that Bart Ehrman and an army of historicists who have preceded him have been unable to dig up a Proculus to avouch the birth, death, or ascension of Jesus of Nazareth — after centuries of digging?

— *just as in Marcion's version of Luke*. In canonical Luke, by contrast, after Jesus's wilderness adventure and aerial tour of Jerusalem, Jesus comes into Galilee: Luke 4:16 "And he came to Nazareth, where he had been brought up: and, as his custom was, he went into the synagogue on the Sabbath day and stood up for to read."

Now it is an indisputable fact that *anyone* brought up in *any* town — not just Nazareth and with absolutely no exceptions known to history — has a body. Or *had* one during his or her residency there. Docetists beware! Jesus was brought up in Nazareth — why else would we call him Jesus of Nazareth? *Ergo*, he must have had a body. Q.E.D.

The question suddenly arises at this point in our inquiry: *Is it the case that Nazareth was invented precisely to thwart the Docetists?* Is it just an accident that Nazareth[15] fulfills the same anti-Docetic function in Matthew's otherwise totally contradictory nativity insertion?

Despite being an acknowledged expert in the art of detecting theopolitical bias in New Testament texts, Ehrman surprisingly is

15 Nazareth is unknown to the Old Testament, the two Talmuds (which name 63 places in Galilee, roughly one town for every 4.25 mile-square piece of land), to Josephus (who fortified a town less than two miles from present-day Nazareth and names 45 places in Galilee, roughly one town for every 5.00 mile-square piece of land), and to all other ancient sources. Moreover, archaeology reveals that Nazareth was not inhabited at the time Jesus of Nazareth should have been living there. (See René Salm's *The Myth of Nazareth: The Invented Town of Jesus*, American Atheist Press, Cranford, NJ, 2008) Ehrman rejects the archaeological evidence and argues further that Nazareth was just too small and insignificant to be noticed, even though (1) it was supposedly well enough known and notorious to give rise to the saying "Can anything good come out of Nazareth?" [John 1:46; *OCS* 57; *DJE?* 189]; (2) it is called a *polis* by Luke; and (3) it is claimed to have had a synagogue!

The Gospel of Mark already had described 'the Jesus' as a *Nazōrenos* or a *Nazōraios*, an epithet that I think was derived from the Hebrew word *netser* ('branch') — a word that appears in the messianic text Isaiah 11:1. ("And there shall come forth a rod out of the stem of Jesse, and a *Branch* shall grow out of his roots.") When it became necessary to invent a home town for a Jesus made of flesh and bones, it would have been natural that someone bearing the epithet *the Nazorean* must have come from a place called *Nazara* or even *Nazareth*. (The great variability in the MSS in the spelling of both the epithet and the city names makes it hard to know what specific etymology to pursue.) Also, I would argue, 'Jesus of Nazareth' is an epithet like 'Jimmy the Greek' — with the important distinction that the latter name describes a geographic and demographic reality, while the former does not.

unable to detect the polemical functions of Nazareth and the birth narratives:

> Jesus is said to have come from Nazareth in multiple sources (Mark, Q, John, L, M). And nowhere in any of these stories is there any hint that the author or his community has advanced its own interests in indicating Nazareth as Jesus's hometown. In fact, just the opposite: the early Christians had to explain *away* the fact that Jesus came from Nazareth, as seen, for example, in John 1:45-46 and in the birth narratives of Matthew and Luke, which independently of one another try to show that even though Jesus came from Nazareth, he really was born in Bethlehem... because the Old Testament prophet Micah said the savior would come from Bethlehem, not Nazareth (Micah 5:2) [*DJE?* 189].

How can it be that an expert in detecting *Tendenz* in literary texts could have failed to see the obvious anti-Docetic purpose of these texts? Perhaps this is because Ehrman is not a geologist trained to differentiate strata of deposition — in this case, redactional strata that have accumulated and been compressed under the weight of later textual sediments laid down at different locations over the course of changing theopolitical environments.

In his analysis of corruptions of the biblical texts, it would seem that Ehrman has not realized the possibility — indeed, probability — that several rounds of interpolation may be evidenced in any surviving witness. Has he considered the possibility that the orthodox scenario is fundamentally false and that he might be dealing with documents conflating (1) alterations of a very early stratum depicting Christ (not Jesus) as pure spirit; (2) alterations to reify Christ into Jesus a man; (3a) alterations to show that he was still a god, or (3b) to show how Jesus a man had become Christ a god?

It seems clear to me (1) that Nazareth (or Nazara) the *polis* was invented to prove the physicality of Jesus against the Docetists. The name was created by back formation[16] from *Nazoraios* or *Nazarenos* or one of the half-dozen variant spellings attested in the MSS. (2) Independently, some one else who was reading the Old Testament

16 *See* discussion of Matt. 2:23 below.

in search of oracles in order to determine where the Jewish messiah would be born fancied that Micah 5:2[17] was referring to a *place*, Bethlehem, not the *clan* Bethlehem. (Aviram Oshri,[18] an Israeli archaeologist has shown that Bethlehem in Judah was not inhabited at the turn of the era, and Jodi Magness[19] seems to have accepted this fact in her video course produced for the Teaching Company.) (3) Then we might suppose that there developed a north-south struggle between the claims of Nazareth and the claims of Bethlehem, ending with the various compromises found in Matthew and Luke. (4) As new theopolitical enemies arose, ever-changing types of redaction would take place.

While Bethlehem as a city is well attested in the Old Testament, it was a *clan*, not a city that was referred to in the Micah verse. Nevertheless, this messianic verse was mined to produce a place for the Messiah to be born. Unfortunately, archaeology has shown that neither of the places now called Nazareth or Bethlehem was inhabited when Jesus should have been living in them.

Before going further, I wish to return to Ehrman's claim that "Jesus is said to have come from Nazareth in multiple sources (Mark, Q, John, L, and M)." Lay readers can have no idea how controversial Ehrman's claim of multiple independent attestations of Nazareth is, and New Testament scholars can see immediately that this is a book of apologetics, not a scholarly contribution to knowledge. Ehrman goes from a highly questionable argument on pages 75-82 of *DJE?* that Mark, Q, M, L, and John are independent, multiple attestations of a

---

17 "But you, Bethlehem in Ephratah, small as you are to be among Judah's clans, out of you shall come forth a governor for Israel . . ." [NEB]
"And thou, Bethleem, house of Ephratha, art few in number to be reckoned among the thousands of Judah; yet out of thee shall one come forth to me to be a ruler of Israel." [LXX]

The Bethlehem *clan* is mentioned in Esra 2:21:

The children of Bethlehem, an hundred and twenty-three" [KJV]

"The children of Bethlaem (*huioi Bethlaem*) a hundred twenty-three" [LXX]

18 Aviram Oshri, "Where Was Jesus Born?" *Archaeology*, Vol. 58, No. 6, November-December, 2005.

19 Jodi Magness, "Holy Land Revealed," The Great Courses, The Teaching Company.

historical Jesus, to an even more questionable claim that they are multiple attestations of *Jesus coming from a place called Nazareth*. Ehrman has thrown all scholarly caution to the winds when he makes so reckless a claim without addressing even a single possible objection to such a claim. Perhaps Ehrman underestimates the sophistication of his readers.

First of all, he begs the question that these sources are multiple attestations of an *historical fact*, rather than attestations of a literary or theological 'fact.'

MARK

Secondly, Ehrman was well aware that I particularly have argued that the mention of Nazareth in Mark 1:9 was not original to 'Mark' and that the original author of that gospel had never heard of the place. Shouldn't Ehrman have noted here, at least in a footnote, that his claim of Markan attestation was controversial and shouldn't he have addressed my objections fully?

Q

Thirdly, he makes the shocking claim that the sayings source 'Q' attests to an historical fact of Jesus coming from a place called Nazareth. Where did he get *that* idea? It is so controversial, he should have devoted at least several pages to defense of that unsubstantiated claim. Consulting the Greek concordance of John S. Kloppenborg's *Q Parallels: Synopsis, Critical Notes, & Concordance*[20] fails to find any mention not only of Nazareth, but also of the titles 'Nazarenos' or 'Nazoraios.' Going further, consulting the scripture index of John S. Kloppenborg's *The Formation of Q*[21] fails to find any mention of the two verses in Matthew that mention Nazareth (Matt. 2:23; 21:11) or any of the five verses in Luke (1:26; 2:4; 2:39; 2:51; 4:16). This is not surprising, as five of the above seven references derive from the

20 Sonoma: Polebridge Press, 1988.

21 Philadelphia: Fortress Press, 1987.

birth narratives, and even Ehrman accepts the fact that those tales are not historical but "made up," as he might well have put it.[22]

It is only when one consults *The Critical Edition of Q*, by James M. Robinson, Paul Hoffmann, and John S. Kloppenborg[23] that one finds an entry—not for Nazareth or Nazarenos or Nazoraios—but for *Nazará*, with a reference for Q 4:16, ~~31~~. Turning to pages 42 and 43 that present the eight synoptic columns pertaining to this verse, the first thing we see atop the columns for Matt. 4:13 and Luke 4:15, 31 is the footnote siglum ^{0}/ signaling a note that asks the feeble question, "Is (at least) *Nazará* in Q?"

It seems safe to say, therefore, that the compilers of Q knew nothing of a place called Nazareth, even if they were familiar with Aesop's fables. Moreover, they seem to have known nothing of the appellations *Nazarenos* or Nazoraios! This leaves us to consider the claim that the *Sondergüter* 'M' and 'L' attest to Jesus coming from Nazareth.

MATTHEW

As already noted, there are only two places in Matthew where the Greek text indicates Jesus came from Nazareth. If they are not verses derived from Q or Mark—and indeed they aren't—then they must be part of what Ehrman refers to as 'M,' Matthew's *Sondergut* (material unique to Matthew). Ehrman begs the question not only that 'Matthew' derives this from written sources and hasn't made it up on his own to embellish his version of the story, but also the question as to whether this previous source can be considered to have been a *historical record* rather than a *literary* or purely *theological* one.

The first of these two verses (Matt 2:23) would seem to hold an important clue to the origin of the word 'Nazareth' and to its original function. It seems to me that *the word originated right here in this verse*. The verse reads:

22 See Bart D. Ehrman, *Forged: Writing in the Name of God— Why the Bible's Authors Are Not Who We Think They Are* [New York: HarperOne, 20011: 239–40].

23 Minneapolis: Fortress Press, 2000.

> Matt 2:23 And he came and dwelt in a city called Nazareth: that it might be fulfilled which was spoken by the prophets, He shall be called a Nazarene.

Quite clearly, Matthew thought the epithet 'Nazarene' meant 'coming from a place called Nazareth,' just as 'Jimmy the Greek' means 'someone coming from Greece' or 'Parisian' means 'someone coming from Paris.' But why would it be *necessary* to create the toponym *Nazareth* at all? As already noted, Ehrman admits the birth narratives and genealogies are fictions—but yet they still can be used as evidence that Jesus was born and existed! He also admits that some New Testament texts have been shaped to thwart the Docetists. In my opinion, then, the birth narratives were created to provide a physical body for Jesus. 'Nazareth' (or more likely, *Nazara*) in turn, was created to provide a hometown for him—a requirement for every flesh-and-blood person in history. It appears, therefore, that in this verse we have the origin—the moment of creation—of Nazareth. It is not a real place, it is an apologetic invention.[24]

The other Matthaean reference (Matt 21:11) in turn gives us a clue as to how 'Nazareth' found its way into Mark 1:9. Matthew has '*Iēsous ho apo Nazareth tēs Galeilaias,*' and Mark has '*Iēsous apo Nazaret tēs Galilaias.*' These are the only two places in the entire New Testament where this peculiar expression is to be found, and it seems likely that Mark was interpolated to bring it into closer harmony with Matthew.

LUKE

Ehrman claims that 'L'—the material unique to 'Luke'—is an independent attestation of the origin of Jesus from a place called Nazareth. It is true that none of the five references to a derivative Jesus-Nazareth association are to be found in Mark or Q, and so they must pertain to L. But

24 This is not to say that this verse does not fulfill another function long understood, *viz.*, creating a link to the Jewish scriptures. It seems likely that the very attempt to Judaize primitive Christianity was for the purpose of reifying and refuting a Docetic deity who previously had existed only in mythic time and space.

this assumes, of course, that I am wrong in my claim that the mention of Nazareth in Mark 1:9 is not original but rather a later interpolation. For if that verse is authentic as Ehrman claims, then he cannot consider Luke an independent witness to Nazareth, since it is known that Luke plagiarized most of the Greek text of Mark. That is to say, when Luke was copying Mark in order to write his expanded and improved version of the story, if 'Nazareth' had been present in Mark 1:9, Luke would certainly have gotten the city name from Mark and could not be the independent witness claimed by Ehrman.

The first four mentions of a Nazareth-Jesus connection in Luke all are part of the birth and childhood legends peculiar to Luke, and Ehrman admits they are not historically true. Nevertheless, it is well to remind ourselves why that is the case. Consider first the verse Luke 1:26:

> 1:26 And in the sixth month the angel Gabriel was sent from God unto a city of Galilee, named Nazareth. 27 To a virgin espoused to a man whose name was Joseph, of the house of David; and the virgin's name was Mary.

Could Ehrman believe that an angel's itinerary could be used as evidence of an historical event? Of course he couldn't! He does, however, seem to think that the story of Gabriel's trip to Nazareth *can* be used as evidence for the reality of Nazareth. Even if there is no such thing as the angel Gabriel, he might ask, why would an author make up a story about him going to Nazareth if no such place existed? Would Dorothy go to Emerald City in Oz if no such place existed?

Can anything good come out of Nazareth as witnessed by Luke? Only if one is willing to make it up.

JOHN

This brings us to consider if John 1:45, 46[25] can be considered an independent attestation of the 'fact' that Jesus came from a place called

25 John 1:45 Philip findeth Nathanael, and saith unto him, We have found him, of whom Moses in the law, and the prophets, did write, Jesus of Nazareth, the son of Joseph. 46 And Nathanael said unto him, Can there any good thing come out of Nazareth?

Nazareth. It has long been a strong minority opinion that one of the authors of 'John' knew of at least one of the Synoptic Gospels. The discovery that 'Aenon,' the place where John was baptizing, was the product of a dyslexic reading of a *Codex Bezae*-like manuscript of Luke does, however, seem to clinch it.[26] That means that 'John' is not an independent attestation of Nazareth, but rather it is an elaboration of information gleaned from Luke and perhaps other Synoptic Gospels. Although John may originally have been a Docetic or proto-Gnostic type of composition, in its present form it is strongly anti-Docetic and thus was in need of a residence for a god who had to be given a body of flesh and blood. Consequently, in the Gospel according to John we find not an independent attestation of Jesus coming from Nazareth, but rather a polemic application of the toponym 'Nazareth' employed by someone who had (mis)read a manuscript of the Gospel according to Luke.

While it is clear that John cannot be used as a witness of the fact that Jesus came from a city (*polis*) called Nazareth, this gospel's question "Can anything good come out of Nazareth?" is worthy of examination. It must be admitted that the origin of this verse is enigmatic. However, it is nevertheless a powerful refutation of Ehrman's unsubstantiated claim that the Nazareth of Jesus was "a one-dog town," so small that it left no remains for archaeologists of the twentieth century to find. If it was *that* small, how could it have given rise to an ostensibly well-known folk aphorism? It seems likely that we are dealing with an adaptation of something like "Can anything good come out of Possumtrot?" Like the made-up name 'Possumtrot,' the fictive name 'Nazareth' may have been substituted for some other made-up name. In any case, when biblical archaeologists tire in their search for the Nazareth of Jesus, they might find searching for the Possumtrot of Bubba a bit easier.

After claiming the absence of theopolitical impulses in the creation of the birth legends, and asserting multiple attestations of Nazareth as the hometown of Jesus, Ehrman goes on to assert that the Nazareth traditions would actually have been an embarrassment:

26 See footnote 26 on page 226 for details.

Bart Ehrman and the Body of Jesus of Nazareth

> Moreover, John reflects a more general embarrassment about Nazareth ("Can anything good come out of Nazareth?"). Nazareth was a little one-horse town (not even that, it was more like a one-dog town) that no one had ever heard of, so far as we can tell, before Christianity. The savior of the world came from *there*? Not from Bethlehem? Or Jerusalem? Or Rome? How likely is that? And so we have a multiply attested tradition that passes the criterion of dissimilarity. Conclusion: Jesus probably came from Nazareth. [*DJE?* 189]

Apart from wondering how Ehrman can know so much about the size and quadruped population of a place "that no one had ever heard of," *we have already questioned just how it could be that a one-dog "town" could simultaneously be so obscure that no one had ever heard of it and yet be famous enough to give rise to a saying that appears to be part of the common folk wisdom of ancient Palestine!*

One wishes further that Ehrman would have presented at least *some* evidence to show how the one-dog town could be equivalent to both the city that now bears the name, where no synagogue was ever built atop the hill above it as well as the biblical *polis* that was itself atop a hill that had a cliff and possessed a synagogue of which not a trace remains today.

So much for multiple attestation and the criterion of dissimilarity! Surely the facts of archaeology and logic must trump them both.

Critical examination of our texts, I have asserted, lends support to the notion that Marcion's gospel was an early form of Luke that did not yet have the anti-Docetic additions of genealogies and miraculous births. Why would I think so?

First of all, let us remind ourselves that in both Mark — the narrative framework for Luke's gospel — and Marcion, Jesus's first adventure after being tempted in the wilderness takes place in a synagogue in *Capernaum*. In canonical Luke, however, Jesus first makes an appearance in a synagogue in *Nazareth*. To compensate for skipping over the Capernaum adventure that appeared first-up in his *Vorlage*, Luke inserts a sort of flash-back of Jesus's activities in Capernaum — *something for which there is no room in Luke's chronology* since the Nazareth pericope is clearly *the first act of* Jesus's preaching career!

> Luke 4:23 And he [Jesus] said unto them, Ye will surely say unto me this proverb, Physician, heal thyself: whatsoever we have heard done in Capernaum, do also here in thy country. 24 And he said, Verily I say unto you, No prophet is without honor except in his own country.

"Whatsoever we have heard done in Capernaum"? How — *unless they had read Marcion's or Mark's gospels* — would they have known that Jesus had done anything before his debut at Nazareth? Do we not see here a seam in the textile fabric showing where a patch has been inserted?

Secondly, we must examine the implications of the fact that at the beginning of Marcion's gospel, "Jesus descended [*out of heaven, according to Tertullian's understanding*] into Capernaum, a city in Galilee, and was teaching in the synagogue on the Sabbath days." What were the consequences of this fact for the text of canonical Luke?

We might suppose that a heavenly descent of a person right into a synagogue would be a hard act to match. That, however, would be the case only if we had not read Luke's account of how Jesus descends into the synagogue at Capernaum.

It will be recalled that in canonical Luke Jesus's first adventure in Galilee is his encounter with a lynch-mob in a never-located synagogue in Nazareth. (It is his *second* adventure that requires him to descend (*katēlthen*) from Nazareth to Capernaum.)

> Luke 4:28 And all they in the synagogue, when they heard these things, were filled with wrath, 29 And rose up, and thrust him out of the city, and led him unto the brow of the hill whereon their city was built, that they might cast him down head long. 30 But he passing through the midst of them went his way, 31 And came down to Capernaum, a city of Galilee, and taught them on the Sabbath days.

Luke doesn't tell us how Jesus passed through the midst of the lynch-mob, but early Roman Catholic and Greek Orthodox traditions have it that Jesus *jumped into the air* to evade the mob. So, since escaping the mob and arriving in Capernaum are events recorded in the same Lukan sentence, we must suppose (*unless, of course, this is a seam indicating the precise point where someone has tampered with our text*!) that Jesus did indeed (1) launch into the air from the top edge of Nazareth Hill, (2) shoot like an artillery shell for 25 miles, and (3) land without cratering the Capernaum synagogue. (*Nota bene*: Occasional claims to the contrary notwithstanding, no first-century synagogue remains have ever been found at K'far Naḥum, the major site identified by Franciscan 'archaeologists' and tour guides as being the remains of ancient Capernaum — which, like Nazareth, was unknown to the world at the turn of the era. I have shown elsewhere[27] that claims that Josephus mentioned Capernaum are incorrect.)

Bart Ehrman's Discoveries

In 1993, Bart Ehrman published a devastating text-critical assault upon the canonical New Testament, *The Orthodox Corruption of Scripture: The Effect of Early Christological Controversies on the Text of the New Testament.* In that magisterial achievement of critical scholarship, he demonstrated beyond cavil how a bewildering variety of Orthodox potential and actual proof texts had been created as weapons with which to fight the battle between the proto-Orthodox and the Docetists, Separationists, Gnostics, and other early practitioners of Christianity. Unfortunately, almost all of his studies involved cases where manuscripts still survived in which could be found both orthodox and heterodox readings. He did not attempt, as I have done here, to apply his *Tendenz*-critical method backward beyond the point where all manuscripts with variant readings had either been destroyed by triumphal Orthodoxy or had ceased to be copied and transmitted for other reasons. Even so, as we shall see, he presented ample evidence to support my theory of Docetic priority and the invention of Jesus *of Nazareth* in the development of proto-Orthodox polemic.

27 "Capernaum — a Literary Invention," *Journal of Higher Criticism*, Vol. 12, No. 2 [Fall 2006:1–27].

Frank R. Zindler

After reading his book shortly after its publication — I had been watching his ideological and scholarly development for some time — I predicted (correctly) that he ultimately would become an Atheist, but I incorrectly expected him eventually to become a Mythicist. How, with all the discoveries he had made, could he continue to think there was anything historical in the New Testament beyond what one might encounter in a historical novel? How, after all the details of the life of Jesus of Nazareth had been stripped away as fictions created for myriad purposes, could he suppose that the grin of the Cheshire Cat that hovered over the text of the Gospels was actually the face not only of *Jesus*, but Jesus *of Nazareth* in particular? Nevertheless, Ehrman's early work still serves as a highly reliable database from which Mythicists can draw much valuable information and insight.

In his analysis of the disputed passage Luke 22:43–44, where Jesus is praying on the Mount of Olives and "his sweat became like drops of blood falling to the ground"[*OCS* 187*ff*], Ehrman — whether intentionally or not, I cannot decide — presents convincing arguments that lead me to conclude that *Ur-Lukas* (proto-Luke) was written as a Docetic reworking of the physicalist text of Mark and then in turn was subjected to physicalist interpolation by proto-Orthodox scribes. The conclusion of Ehrman's analysis [193–94] is worth quoting:

> The conclusion should now be clear. We do not need to *hypothesize* the usefulness of these verses for an anti-docetic polemic; we *know* that the verses were put to precisely this use during the period of our concern. Second-century heresiologists used Jesus' "bloody sweat" to attack Christians who denied his real humanity. Given the other problems that the verses have posed, there can be little remaining doubt concerning their status. The story of Jesus praying in yet greater agony, being strengthened by an angel from heaven, and sweating great drops as if of blood, did not originate with the author of the Gospel of Luke. It was inserted into the Third Gospel some time in the early second century (prior to Justin) as part of the anti-docetic polemic of the orthodox Christian church.

If the Gospel of Luke originated as a quasi-Docetist or fully Docetist reworking of the Gospel of Mark and ended as a collection of physicalist proof texts, what are we to think of the Gospel of Mark that underwent physicalist revision? I have argued elsewhere that the entire Prologue of Mark — including verse 1:9 where Mark's only mention of Nazareth is to be found — is an anti-Docetist interpolation. Was *Ur-Markus* (proto-Mark) itself a Docetist or quasi-Docetist document? This requires thorough investigation.

As important as the analysis of the Gospel of Luke may be, however, Ehrman's findings concerning the Johannine literature provide an even stronger basis for the Mythicist theory that Jesus began not as a man who became a god but rather was a god who ultimately — after long years of theopolitical strife — came to be believed had become a man. While a full discussion of the original nature of the Gospel of John is too complex to enter into here (I shall discuss its probable Docetic origins elsewhere), it is worthwhile for the Mythicist theory to examine what Ehrman has to say concerning so-called "secessionists" who are the target of the epistle 1 John 2:18–19. The NEB renders the relevant passage as follows:

> My children, this is the last hour! You were told that Antichrist was to come, and now many antichrists have appeared; which proves to us that this is indeed the last hour. They went out from our company, but never really belonged to us; if they had, they would have stayed with us. They went out, so that it might be clear that not all in our company truly belong to it.

Ehrman sums up his critique of this epistle by confirming my own opinion expressed near the beginning of this essay that "the epistle of 1 John counters a docetic Christology that is comparable to the one later espoused by the opponents of Ignatius. In this view Jesus only appeared to be human and to suffer and die, for he was not really made of flesh" [133].

Just who, in fact, were these "secessionists"? Ehrman explains that "the charge [*that the opponents of 1 John were antichrists*] has led some interpreters to assume that the opponents were non-Christian Jews who failed to acknowledge the messiahship of Jesus." Ehrman, however disagrees. "But because these opponents formerly belonged to the Johannine community [2:19], it seems more likely that they were in fact Christians who had developed their Christological views to an extreme that for the author amounted to a denial of the community's basic confession that the Christ, or the Son of God, is actually the man Jesus [*cf.* John 20:30–31]."

It is very significant that Ehrman confirms my opinion that there was a full-fledged Docetist group in existence as early as the composition of 1 John (90 CE, according to Archbishop Ussher). However, once again we must ask just how reasonable is it to suppose that *merely sixty years* after the alleged founder of their faith had suffered a brutal death by crucifixion — a physical nightmare that surely would have given rise immediately to oral traditions that were both lurid and vivid in their physically detailed descriptions — *he had come to be considered in fact to have been a phantom*? How plausible is that?

While it is not quite impossible to construct a scenario that could 'explain' such a development, it seems to me that all such attempts to account for such an implausible chain of events would be about as credible as the apologist's attempt to harmonize the account of Judas' death in Matthew 27:3–5 with the account in Acts 1:16–19 — Judas hanged himself and, after he had swollen up due to decomposition, the rope broke, he fell head-long onto the potter's field and his bowels gushed out.

It seems more likely that the interpreters who assume that the opponents were non-Christian Jews that failed to acknowledge the messiahship of Jesus are closer to the correct explanation. Once *Chreistos* or *Chrēstos* ('useful one,' 'goodness,' 'kindly,' 'worthy,' 'true,' or even 'prophet') had evolved into *Christos* ('anointed one,' 'messiah') [*see* "Bart Ehrman and the Crucified Messiah"], the Savior worshiped by the earliest Christians could now be identified with the messiah expected by the Jews, and attempts would be made to convince the Jews that the Christians' Savior — crucified in the heavenly realm at the vernal equinox where the intersection of the celestial equator and the ecliptic forms a chi-cross (as I shall argue elsewhere) — was indeed the Messiah awaited by the Jews.

Bart Ehrman and the Body of Jesus of Nazareth

Certainly, if Ehrman is correct in his assertion [*DJE?* 163] that the idea of a crucified messiah would have been extremely offensive to most first-century Jews, missionaries to the Jews would have been rebuffed more often than heard. Could being rebuffed by messianic Jews have been converted by the author of 1 John into the report that "They went out from our company, but never really belonged to us; if they had, they would have stayed with us" [NEB]? Could this be an ancient equivalent to the assertion "They didn't fire me; I quit"? I confess that this is uncertain and I might have to change my mind after deeper study of this text.

THE SUMMING UP

It seems abundantly clear that Docetism was one of the earliest forms of Christianity. Indeed, Docetism may be *the* earliest form of Christianity of which we have knowledge. Orthodoxy may be but a reified form of a mystery cult centered upon a savior who came to earth from the sky and somehow took human form and then substance.

The present Christian scriptures bear numerous scars and swellings that are the result of a long and bitter fight with Docetists. The birth legends of Matthew and Luke created Nazareth as a residence for a Jesus who had a physical body. According to these inventive authors, Jesus *inhabited* Nazareth like a man of flesh and blood. He didn't *haunt* the place as would a specter such as the Christ worshipped by the Docetists.

And so, *it seems highly likely that* Jesus of Nazareth *was the invention of proto-Orthodox propagandists in their long, drawn-out struggle against their Docetist progenitors.* We seem to be witness to a reversal of the classical myth of Kronos. Instead of Kronos eating his children, one of his children has served him up as a Eucharistic meal — and eaten *him*!

It is astoundingly difficult to do, but we must strive not to make the same mistake that Ehrman and historicists in general have always made, *viz.*, treating all references to *Christ* as though they were equivalent to references to *Jesus*. Still less has it been permissible to equate them to references to *Jesus of Nazareth*, a character practically never mentioned in the canonical new Testament and throughout the apocrypha, the Apostolic Fathers, and the Ante-Nicene Fathers. We know that 'Separationists' and others carefully distinguished Christ from Jesus and we too must always try to distinguish Christ from Jesus. We must always try to ascertain if any given source does this as well. We cannot presume that Jesus the man is anterior to Christ the god. Indeed, I argue that the opposite is the case.

*****

In studying the Christian scriptures we must always keep in mind not only the platitude that the victors write the history books, we must never forget that the victors also have determined which other books will be left on the shelves for us to read.

CHAPTER EIGHTEEN

The Epistle to the Hebrews and Jesus Outside the Gospels

A critique of pages 116–117 of *Did Jesus Exist?*

Earl Doherty

This chapter considers the nature of Christ and Jesus in the Epistle to the Hebrews

- God speaking through a Son in a new reading of scripture
- Hebrews' Son a heavenly entity like the Logos
- Hebrews 101: a sacrifice in a heavenly sanctuary
- an event of revelation at the start of the sect
- no words of Jesus on earth to be found
- another motif of "likeness" to humans
- "In the days of his flesh": not Gethsemane
- Christ "out of Judah"
- Hebrews' sacrifice in heaven
- taking on a "body" in the scriptural world
- Telling us that Jesus was never on earth
    - *First smoking gun: Hebrews 8:4 — a denial that Jesus had been on earth*
    - *Platonic parallels between heaven and earth*
    - *Christ could not be a priest in the same sphere as the earthly priests*
    - *no sense to a present sense*

- The Coming One
  - *Second smoking gun: 10:37 – "the coming one" has not yet been to earth*
  - *9:278 – a "second coming" or a sequence of events?*
- Jesus "suffered outside the gate"
  - *Jesus "passing through the heavens"*
- The inauthenticity of the epistle's postscript

* * * * *

Reading an historical Jesus into scripture

Those who have become familiar with my writings over the years will know that I have a soft spot for the epistle to the Hebrews. In many ways it is the most revealing of the New Testament documents.

- It gives us a Son who is entirely known from scripture.
- It presents a heavenly event that could only have been imagined out of a Platonic application of scripture: a sacrifice by the Son, performed in a spiritual sanctuary, in which he offers his own "blood" to God — a blood which can hardly be regarded as being human, hauled up from Calvary.

Indeed, anomalies like this have increasingly forced modern scholars to take refuge in interpreting Christ's sacrifice in the heavenly sanctuary as intended by the author to be merely a metaphor for the earthly Calvary event — an interpretation for which there is no justification in the epistle. Most significantly, Hebrews contains two verses which make it clear that *its Jesus had never been on earth*, two smoking guns that would do any Mythicist gunslinger proud.

Ehrman, true to form, simply seizes on any and all words and phrases in the epistle which he thinks could have an earthly or human application and declares them as such. He admits that this epistle, too, shows no knowledge of the Gospels — which he ought to have extended to no knowledge of the Gospel *story*, whether written or oral — but nevertheless "it contains numerous references to the life of the historical Jesus."

Ehrman itemizes some twenty of them [*DJE?* 116–117], beginning with:

- Jesus appeared in 'these last days' (1:2).
- God spoke through him (that is, in his proclamation; 1:2).

God speaking through a Son

First of all, the opening verses do not say, in any fashion, that "Jesus appeared." What has happened "in these last days" is that God, who formerly had spoken through the prophets, has now spoken to us "in a Son." Ehrman maintains that this 'speaking' was through Jesus' proclamation on earth. But we look in vain throughout the whole of Hebrews for a single word of proclamation by a Jesus on earth. Everything spoken by the Son is from scripture. *What the writer is referring to is a new reading of scripture in which the voice of the Son is now being perceived*, just as we have seen in epistles like 1 Clement.

The writer is presenting a new speaking by God through a Son, and he goes on to define that Son. If the latter were perceived as a teacher on earth, proclaiming on behalf of God, one would expect the writer's definition to include some reference to an incarnation and teaching ministry. Not a hint. Instead we get only the cosmic Son familiar from other hymnic passages (such as Colossians 1:15–20):

> . . . (a Son) whom he has made heir to the whole universe, and through whom he created all orders of existence: the Son who is the effulgence of God's splendour and the stamp of God's very being, and sustains the universe by his word of power. [Hebrews 1:2-3, NEB]

So far no sign of Ehrman's "life of the historical Jesus." Immediately thereafter, he lists:

> He 'made a purification for sins' (that is, he died a bloody death; 1:3).

Considering that no identification of the Son has been made with an earthly Jesus or his life, this comes up rather suddenly, and is followed immediately in the verse by his taking a seat at the right hand of God. (The throne room looks to be right next door to the heavenly sanctuary where the purification took place.) One gets no sense of a life and events that have covered earth and heaven.

Hebrews' heavenly sacrifice

By his parenthetical "that is, he died a bloody death," Ehrman shows himself to be woefully ignorant of the whole soteriology of this epistle. The "purification for sins" does not apply to any death event, but rather to Christ's (post-death) sacrifice—the *offering* of his own blood in the heavenly sanctuary. *That*, for this writer, is the "sacrifice," not the death, which remains obscurely in the background, unlocated. It is that act in the heavenly sanctuary which makes the "purification for sins."

This sacrificial offering of his blood on the heavenly altar is in Platonic parallel with, and a permanent replacement for, the traditional sacrifices of the high priests on earth, who have offered the blood of animals to God — first at Sinai, then in the Temple throughout Jewish history — on the Day of Atonement. (All this is Hebrews 101, which almost every scholar of this epistle recognizes, even if they try to compromise it by inserting an historical Jesus into the background.)

So after defining the Son in exclusively heavenly (and very Logos-like) terms, the author has followed this with a reference to a heavenly event: Christ offering his blood in the heavenly sanctuary. Once again, we look in vain for any reference to "the life of the historical Jesus."

Christ superior to the angels

Nor is that to be found in the remainder of chapter one, which the author devotes to proving that the Son is superior to the angels. (Such superiority is necessary since, while the angels delivered the Old Covenant, the Son through a superior sacrifice has delivered the New Covenant which supplants it.) This is demonstrated by means of 'proof-texts' from scripture, standard stuff such as "Thou art my

Son, today I have begotten thee," something God never said to any angel. (No mention of a voice from God out of heaven saying this very thing at Jesus' baptism by the Jordan.) No claim of superiority is made by virtue of his life on earth, or of his resurrection from the tomb. No "life of the historical Jesus" here.

Incidentally, when in 2:5–9, Christ is said to have been "made a little lower [*lit., lesser*] than the angels," applying Psalm 8:4–6 to him, the author is continuing his theme of comparing Christ to the angels. The verb means 'to make inferior,' not to place in a lower location. Thus it is not describing an incarnation to an earth which is lower than the angels' realm. This temporary 'inferiority' results from his assumption of corruptibility to undergo death, which could take place in the demons' realm below the moon (though this, too, is lower than the angels' location).

A time of revelation

As he did in regard to the Prologue of 1 John, Ehrman offers the event of revelation at the formation of the sect, described at the beginning of chapter 2, as a reference to the historical Jesus' own preaching. But the 'hearing' and 'confirming' are of the *message* of salvation, one provided by God. (The NEB gives us a particularly gratuitous translation which inserts Gospel Jesus implications that are not in the Greek.) In fact, the verse paraphrased by Ehrman (committing the same sin as the NEB),

> God bore witness to him [Jesus] and/or his followers through signs, wonders, various miracles, and gifts of the spirit (2:4)

raises the question of why it would be said that *God* supported Jesus' message by miracles, rather than Jesus himself. After all, according to the Gospels, this was the very purpose of Jesus' miracles. Rather, God is the one supplying the miracles here because it is God who is delivering the message at the time of the community's formation. This is a thought reinforced later in 9:10, in which the writer locates the inauguration of the New Covenant in the present "time of reformation," the time of understanding (*i.e.,* by revelation based on scripture), not the historical time of Jesus' sacrifice.

No words of Jesus on earth

This reading of the revelation event is confirmed by a later passage in the epistle, something which scholars have consistently overlooked or ignored. The account in chapter 2 has said: ". . . how shall we escape, if we ignore so great a salvation which was first spoken through the Lord?" If the latter refers to a preaching historical Jesus, why does 12:25 say: ". . .how much less will we (escape) if we turn away from the one who speaks from heaven?" This is in a context of quoting God from scripture. Shortly thereafter, 13:7 says: "Remember your leaders, who spoke the word of God to you." And back in 5:12, the basics of the faith have been referred to as "the oracles of God."

Throughout the epistle, any thought of the word of Jesus spoken on earth is utterly absent. Not even in 9:20 does the writer give us the Eucharistic words of Jesus at the Last Supper (see Mark 14:24) to illustrate the establishment of the New Covenant, despite the natural parallel — and this writer is fixated on parallels — this would have made with the similar words he quotes from Moses at the establishment of the Old. (They are similar, of course, because the Gospel scene has been determined by the Exodus passage.) Such a parallel with Moses would never have been passed up, regardless of the ineffectual excuses offered by various modern commentators.

Yet again, Ehrman's "references to the life of the historical Jesus" have evaporated into the wind.

The same void occurs in another key passage (2:11–18). To illustrate the paradigmatic link between Jesus and his devotees on earth, the writer presents him as acknowledging that the latter are his "brothers." (Which, of course, does not make them siblings — see Galatians 1:19.) But does he do this by appealing to any of several Gospel sayings which make such a point (as in Mark 3:35, "Whoever does the will of God is my brother")? No. Once more, *the voice of Jesus is from scripture*, in three passages from Isaiah and the Psalms (*e.g.*, "I will declare your name to my brothers" [Ps. 22:22]).

Another "likeness" motif

In this same passage, as part of that parallel counterpart relationship which makes Jesus' redemptive acts a guarantee of salvation, the writer says:

> Since the children have partaken of blood and flesh, so he in like manner [*paraplēsiōs*] shared the same things . . .

No matter what else this epistle lacks in regard to a human Jesus, this verse is seized upon by historicists as absolute proof of earthly incarnation. But we've seen it all before. As with other expressions of the "likeness" motif, the word "*paraplēsiōs*" means "similar to" not "identical with." And for what purpose does Jesus share in this similarity? So that through his death he could destroy the devil (v. 14), so that he might become a merciful and faithful high priest before God (v. 17). In other words, for his salvific role in the heavenly world — which required only the spiritual equivalent of blood and flesh. There is no mention of taking on literal human flesh and blood in order to a live an earthly life, to preach a ministry in Galilee, to perform miracles and heal the sick, to do anything else that could be associated with an historical man.

As for his being "tempted" (Ehrman refers to 2:18 and 4:15), nothing there suggests anything other than the temptation to refuse to obey God's will and fail to fulfill his mission of suffering and death. Such 'tempting' was limited entirely to activities in the spiritual world.

"In the days of his flesh
[en tais hēmerais tēs sarkos autou]"

There are two peculiarities about this phrase in 5:7, inevitably claimed to refer to Christ's incarnation on earth.

First is the language itself. What bizarre motivation would have led such a wide range of writers across a whole faith movement to consistently describe Jesus' life on earth in such awkward terms (and in combination with referring to his arrival on earth by using revelation verbs)? Why would they consistently have avoided more natural phrases, like "lived a life" or "when he was on earth" or "when he became a man among us"? (The NEB illustrates my point by translating the phrase: "In the days of his earthly life.") Not a single epistle writer uses such natural language. Not ever.

The answer does not need spelling out.

The second 'peculiarity' — though it is hardly peculiar within Hebrews or the rest of the epistles — is the description of what Jesus did "in the days of his flesh." Once again, the context is the narrow one of Jesus' obedience to God in fulfilling his redemptive role. Once again, such details are taken from scripture. "Offering up prayers and supplications" is drawn from Psalm 116:1 (LXX wording), while "with loud cries and tears" is an enlargement on Psalm 22:24 (LXX wording), "when I cried to him, he heard me."

This 'event' is sometimes interpreted as a reference to the Gethsemane scene, but scholars have noted an important incompatibility. There, Jesus prayed that he might be spared the cup of suffering, a prayer that was not answered, whereas in Hebrews he is asking to be delivered from death, *i.e.*, be resurrected from it. And so he was. The Gethsemane scene would have contradicted the writer's point, which is to present a Son whose prayers are answered by the Father. Besides, Gethsemane is virtually certain to be a literary invention of Mark, and this writer shows no knowledge of written Gospels. With monotonous regularity, Hebrews continues to deny Ehrman any "life of the historical Jesus."

A tribe and priesthood for a heavenly Son

- He was descended from the tribe of Judah [*lit., has arisen out of Judah*] (7:14).

This one is a complex point (see my *Jesus: Neither God Nor Man*: 228–231).[1] It entails an analysis of the figure of Melchizedek who appears throughout the middle section of the epistle. While this figure is based on the king and high priest of Salem (probably Jerusalem)

1 Earl Doherty. *Jesus: Neither God Nor Man. The Case For a Mythical Jesus* [Ottawa, Canada: Age of Reason Publications, 2009]

in Genesis 14:18–20, the writer also employs him as a heavenly personage akin to an angel (as one of the Dead Sea Scrolls does). In fact, he melds the two. First, historically speaking, Melchizedek was in a line leading to David and could thus be associated with the tribe of Judah. This provided Christ, in being linked with Melchizedek, with a High Priesthood of a different tribe than the Levites of the old priesthood of Aaron — a necessity, as he sees it, to accompany the new covenant and "change of law" (7:12), since the Levites were associated with the old law and covenant.

But because Melchizedek was also looked upon as a *heavenly* priest (see also 2 Enoch), this could give the heavenly Son a priesthood *in heaven*, and this the writer bases on Psalm 110:4: "You are a priest forever in the succession of Melchizedek." (We can see here, as well as in Christ's heavenly sacrifice, the extent to which a Christian exegete could 'tease' out of scripture a revelation of just about any scenario in the spiritual universe he desired.)

Immediately following 7:14, the writer notes:

> What we have said is even more clear if another priest like Melchizedek arises, *not according to a law about physical requirement*, but to the power of an indestructible life...

Not only does the writer dismiss physical descent as the basis on which Christ belongs to Judah and enjoys a legitimate priesthood, he derives that legitimacy from scripture. For "the power of an indestructible life" is in no way a reference to his resurrection on earth, but to the above-quoted Psalm 110:4, that Christ is "a priest forever," a promise made by God.

Clearly the writer knows of no life on earth, let alone a descent from David (whom he never refers to), for if Jesus as the new High Priest needed to be of a different tribe, no arcane link to Melchizedek should have been required. An appeal could simply have been made to the historical tradition that Jesus of Nazareth was descended from David and was automatically of the tribe of Judah. Thus, the "it is clear" of 7:14 is a reference to the information provided by scripture, not by "the life of the historical Jesus."

Earl Doherty

The sacrifice in heaven

Ehrman entirely skirts the heart of the epistle, chapters 8–9, which describes the sacrifice performed by Christ in the heavenly sanctuary, offering his blood to God on its altar for the propitiation of sins. Perhaps that was because the language conveying the parallel images of earthly sanctuary and heavenly sanctuary, earthly sacrifices by the high priests using the blood of animals and the heavenly sacrifice by Christ himself using his own blood, are so graphic and obvious, so Platonically spelled out, that it would be virtually impossible to interpret any of it as describing events of "the life of the historical Jesus."

The best that scholars (such as Harold Attridge) can do is label it all a metaphor, despite the gap between metaphor and the thing supposedly being represented. This author is not subtle about his parallels, even when they don't work (as in 13:11–14: see below). In the entire picture of the sacrifice in heaven, no parallel or comparison is even remotely implied to a death on a cross.

Besides, the writer is so preoccupied with comparing Jesus' sacrifice with the sacrifices of the high priests on earth, he has no room for any attention to be paid, by himself or his readers, to a presumed Calvary event. In fact, such an earthly event would have fatally compromised his elaborate Platonic parallels. (The "cross" is referred to in passing in 12:2, but not as part of the "sacrifice" which has made a purification for sin. Nor is that cross presented as located on earth.)

On the other hand, it is surprising that Ehrman neglected to bring up this passage (9:24/26) which is consistently given an earthly understanding by scholarship:

> For Christ did not enter a man-made sanctuary that is only a copy of the true one, but into heaven itself...
>
> ... but now, once, at the completion of the ages, he has been manifested/appeared [our old friend, the revelation verb *phaneroō*] to put away sin by his sacrifice.

The latter verse (26b) is invariably interpreted as a reference to his incarnation and earthly death on Calvary. But taking the thought in conjunction not only with verse 24, but the epistle's entire presentation of the sacrifice, the "appearing" must refer to Christ's entry into the heavenly sanctuary and the offering of his blood on the altar; this, as always, is what constitutes the "sacrifice" referred to at the end of the above quote. Otherwise, as I say in *Jesus: Neither God Nor Man* [243], the verse would be forced into saying: "Christ appeared on earth in order to offer his blood in the heavenly sanctuary."

Everything in this passage, as it has throughout the account of Christ's sacrifice, refers to activities taking place in heaven. As for the time reference "at the completion of the ages," the passage is sufficiently ambiguous in the Greek to allow that the 'putting away sin' is what has been accomplished, through the revelation of Christ and his role, at the completion of the ages, meaning in the writer's own time. Alternatively, perhaps the writer envisions that the sacrifice in heaven has actually taken place in the present period.

Christ takes on a body in scripture

- He taught about God: 'You have not desired or taken pleasure in sacrifices and offerings and burnt offerings and sin offerings' [10:8].
- He said, 'I have come to do your will' [10:9].

Ehrman is being particularly atomistic here if he thinks to label such things the voice of the historical Jesus. These are parts of a quote from Psalm 40:6–8 (LXX), with an introductory line:

> That is why, at his coming into the world, he says,
>
> Sacrifice and offering thou didst not desire,
>
> But thou hast prepared a body for me.
>
> Whole-offerings and sin-offerings thou didst not delight in.
>
> *Then I said: 'Here I am: as it is written of me in the scroll, I have come, O God, to do thy will.'* [10:5–7, NEB]

In no way is this presented as words of Jesus on earth. It is yet another example (and an excellent one) of the voice of the Son *being heard in scripture.* Note the present tense of the introductory line: "he says," used here and elsewhere, including in other documents like 1 Clement, to present the words of Jesus in scripture. While scholars are generally divided on how to interpret this, Paul Ellingworth nicely regards the "he says" as "a timeless present referring to the permanent record of scripture" [*NIGT Commentary: Hebrews*: 499–500]. I would call it a *mythical present*, reflecting the higher world of myth, onto which scripture provides a window.

The "at his coming into the world" must also entail a present sense, ruling out an historical reference to the incarnation. 'World' is kosmos *which* can encompass the entire universe, including heavenly spheres. These are perceived words of Christ as he enters the world where he will undergo sacrifice (a lower level of the heavens), where a body has been prepared for him to do this, and where he will obey the will of God.

The source of the Christ event is scripture

Right here, we can see one scriptural source which has led this community to envision a sacrifice for the Son in the supernatural dimension, as revealed in the new reading of the sacred writings: the voice of the Son himself spelling out the sacrifice that will supplant the earthly ones that God no longer wants. It has even revealed that he took on a "body" in order to do so.

When in the following verses the writer discusses certain parts of this Psalm quote (which Ehrman lists), there is no elucidation that such scriptural 'prophecy' was fulfilled on earth, on Calvary, or that the "body" was a human one. And further elucidation about the meaning of the sacrifice is in the form of more quotes from scripture. There is no sign of "the life of the historical Jesus" here either.

The Epistle to the Hebrews and Jesus

Smoking Guns at the NT Corral

Telling us that Jesus was never on earth

In addition to a smoking gun, I have called Hebrews 8:4 a "time bomb." The first half of the verse can be translated in either of two ways:

> In a present sense: "If he were on earth [*i.e., now*], he would not be a priest..." [NIV]
>
> In a past sense: "Now if he had been on earth [*i.e., in the past*], he would not even have been a priest..." [NEB]

Which 'time' does the writer mean?

Some state the general grammatical rule as the following: In a contrafactual (a condition contrary to fact) situation, the same tense of the indicative is used in both parts of the statement; the imperfect tense denotes present time, while the aorist or pluperfect tense denotes past time. In the Greek of Hebrews 8:4, the imperfect tense [*ēn*] of 'to be' is used in both parts.

Present or Past?

According to the rule, this would place the thought in the present time, such as the NIV translation above. But general rules generally enjoy exceptions, or are seen as not always so clear cut. Paul Ellingworth, appealing to *A Greek Grammar of the New Testament* by Blass and Debrunner, says [Hebrews: 405]:

> The second difficulty concerns the meaning of the two occurrences of ē n . The imperfect in unreal [contrafactual] conditions **is temporally ambiguous** (BD §360 [3]), so that NEB 'Now if he had been on earth, he would not even have been a priest' (so Attridge) **is grammatically possible**. However, it goes against the context, in at least apparently excluding Christ's present ministry, and **it could also be misunderstood as meaning that Jesus had never 'been on earth.'** Most versions accordingly render: 'If he were on earth, he would not be a priest at all' (REB, NJB; similarly RSV, TEV, NIV...). [*emphasis added*]

Past or present? But since the statement is meant as a contrafactual one (the "if" clause states something that is or was not the case), the choice is critical. To preserve an historical Jesus in the mind of this writer, we must understand a present sense for 8:4. The problem is, a present understanding makes little if any sense, and a past understanding is required by the context. If it is the past, this '*time* bomb' blows up in the historicist face.

The time of the context

The verses preceding 8:4 address the subject of the sacrifices performed by the respective high priests, those on earth at Sinai and in the Temple, and the one performed by Jesus the new High Priest in the heavenly sanctuary. In 7:27, a contrast is made: *the high priests on earth* offer sacrifices daily, as well as special ones once a year on the Day of Atonement, for the sins of the people*; but Jesus* was required to perform his sacrifice only once for all time, obtaining an eternal redemption. This is a contrast, then, that has application only in the past, for Jesus no longer performs any sacrifice in the present, nor is there any question that he would or could do so.

The parallel between the two is developed further in 8:3:

> Now, every high priest is appointed to offer gifts and sacrifices; hence (it is/was) necessary that this one [*Jesus*] too have (or have had) something to offer.

In the latter half, in regard to 'being necessary', the tense is again ambiguous (this time because a verb is lacking in the Greek), though again the NEB notes that it could mean either "must have something to offer" or "must have had something to offer." But the latter is the only choice possible, for Jesus' sacrifice has already happened; it need not and cannot happen again. *So a present sense is inapplicable, even in theory.*

Once Jesus and his sacrifice has been introduced here, the time frame must shift to the past, to a comparison between the high priests on earth and the High Priest in heaven *in the past*, because that is the only time when the comparison can be applicable. *There is not even a theoretical comparison to be made for the present.* The idea would be ludicrous, and the writer would have had no reason to offer it.

Each in their own sphere

What does this do to the succeeding verse 4?

> If he were/had been on earth, he would not be/have been a priest, there being ones [*i.e., earthly* priests] offering the gifts according to the Law . . .

The thought here is rather trivial, but the writer has expanded on verse 3 by stating that each type of high priest, in regard to their respective sacrifices, operated in his own territory: Christ in the heavenly sanctuary and the regular high priests in the sanctuary on earth. The two could not overlap.

Verse 5 goes on to emphatically state this Platonic separation of respective territories, with Christ having operated in heaven and the high priests on earth "in a sanctuary which is only a copy and shadow of the heavenly." *This emphasis not only rules out that the writer is constructing a metaphor for an earthly Calvary, but ought to rule out the very existence of such an earthly event.* Quite certainly, a graphic, historical crucifixion everyone would have remembered—one that had started the movement—would surely have compelled him to include it in his picture of the 'sacrifice' Christ made (the way most commentators on Hebrews regularly try to introduce it).

But then his Platonic comparison would be foiled throughout. (It would have been foiled even if there had been an earthly crucifixion and the writer chose to ignore it.) For then the blood was not spiritual but human; the sacrifice, being on earth, did not take place in a sanctuary not made by man (8:2), it was not "perfect, spiritual, and eternal" [9:14, NEB]; the blood of his offering was not heavenly, and could not cleanse heavenly things [9:23]. And if it was performed in the same territory as the sacrifices of the earthly priests, this would produce an outright incompatibility with the statement of 8:4.

Earl Doherty

A present sense makes no sense

That statement, to repeat, says that *the sacrifice of Jesus the High Priest could not take place on earth — he could not perform his function as 'priest' in regard to sacrifice — because there are already priests on earth performing the function of offering sacrificial gifts.* (Such a restriction ought to have been dubious in the context of an historical Jesus.) But this makes no sense in a present understanding. Did not that very situation exist in the past when he *was* on earth? How could the author make such a denial for the present time when it was actually the case in the past — if a Calvary sacrifice had taken place?

On any basis or for whatever reason, Christ could not be a priest on earth in the present. It simply doesn't need stating, whether for the reason given in verse 4 or any other. First of all, the 'sacrifice' would *have* to include the Calvary crucifixion if Christ were filling his role as priest *on earth*. But this would lead us to a nonsensical idea. Christ could not be crucified on earth in the present *because he has already been crucified in the past* (whether on earth or in heaven) and this was *once for all*, ruling out any further crucifixion in the present or future.

The writer would simply have had no reason, and certainly not a rational one, for making the 8:4 statement with a present understanding. It would have been both irrelevant and a *nonsequitur* in the context of his argument; essentially, it would be gibberish. Consequently, it must be understood as applying to the past. And in that case, the contrafactual nature of "if he had been on earth" makes it a *denial* that he had been on earth.

One presumes that the sound and smoke from this 'smoking gun' has been so obscuring that it has prevented the entire history of New Testament scholarship from reading the verse in any logical fashion. Ellingworth, despite a half-hearted suggestion, is, like everyone else, at a loss to explain it satisfactorily — and cannot hear its implications as a bell tolling for the historical Jesus.

[This has been a condensation of a 9-page argument in *Jesus: Neither God Nor Man*: 231–9.]

The Coming One

In 10:36–37, the readers are being urged to hold fast in the face of the persecution which has recently assailed them, and by way of encouragement the writer quotes Habakkuk 2:3 in the Septuagint version, prefaced by a phrase from Isaiah:

> You need to persevere, so that when you have done the will of God you will receive what he has promised. For "in just a little while" [Isaiah 26:20 LXX] "The coming one [*ho erchomenos*] will come, and will not delay."

Habakkuk was referring to God by "*ho erchomenos*," but in later times this became a prophetic reference to the messiah, and the phrase was adopted as a title to refer to him. If anything, this is a more immediately obvious passage than 8:4 to tell us that Christ had not been to earth. If "the Coming One" refers to Christ, the Savior figure of this community, and he is someone prophesied in scripture, then if he is still to come it follows that he has not come previously.

One advent or two?

The Jewish scriptures may traditionally have been seen as prophesying the coming of a messiah at the point of the world's transformation, the apocalyptic End-time, but early Christians are supposed to have reinterpreted that to refer to Christ's incarnation, and in that context we can assume that the writer of Hebrews would have shared in this reinterpretation.

Consequently, if an historical Jesus existed in the writer's past, the Habakkuk prophecy should have been applied to that first advent. This is how his readers would have understood it. *He could not have passed over that first coming in silence and directed the prophecy at the future Parousia without qualification or explanation.*

If "the Coming One" had already come, he would have had to specify 'return' or 'again.' (To read the word "*erchomenos*" as able to entail a thought of 'return' when so determined by the context would here be to beg the question, since, unlike the Gospels, no such context is supplied.)

Moreover, by ignoring the life of Christ on earth, he would have been tacitly dismissing any benefit or encouragement to be found in what Jesus had said or done in that life as a means of giving hope to his persecuted readers. Clearly, as the writer has expressed things, the scriptural promise of Christ's arrival on earth has not yet been fulfilled. It is instructive to imagine a modern analogous situation:

> In 1900, witnessing the rise of German militarism under the Kaiser, the Englishman Mr. Smith makes a prediction that "we will one day be at war with Germany."
>
> In 1930, witnessing the rise of Hitler and Nazism, Mr. Jones says, "soon Mr. Smith's prediction is going to come true and we will be at war with Germany."
>
> Mr. Brown objects, "But Mr. Smith's prediction has already come true. We were at war with Germany only a few years ago."
>
> "Are you sure?" asks Mr. Jones. "I guess I must have missed it."

And so have quite a few other writers of the New Testament, who in a similar way seem infected with memory loss.

> *Paul*, at the end of 1 Corinthians entreats the Lord to "come," *Marana tha.*

> *The writer of Revelation,* in his closing words, echoes the same prophetic words from Habakkuk that were quoted in Hebrews: "He who testifies to these things says: 'Yes, I am coming soon'."

A Second Coming?

Shortly before 10:37, a line at the end of chapter 9 is claimed to be the one 'clear' reference to a second coming by Christ to be found in the epistles, and I'm surprised Ehrman did not appeal to it in his list of references to "the historical Jesus." Of course, such clarity is exaggerated. Here are verses Heb. 9:27 and 28:

> Inasmuch as it is destined for men to die once, and after that comes the judgment, so also Christ, having been offered once to bear the sins of many, *ek deuterou* will appear to those awaiting him, not to bear sin but (to bring) salvation.

The "*ek deuterou*" is usually translated "a second time." But the phrase, like its sister "*to deuteron*," can also mean "second in sequence," without any thought of repetition of the first item but simply that of "next" or "second in time." (See Jude 5 and 1 Cor. 12:28.)

Moreover, such a meaning fits the context better. In verse 27, we have not a *repetition* but a *sequence*: men dying and afterwards the judgment. The "so also Christ" in verse 28 indicates that the writer is presenting a parallel to verse 27, one which specifies not a repetition of the 'coming to bear the sins of many' but a 'next' action after that one, namely to bring salvation at the Parousia. Since the "offered once to bear the sins of many" refers to the heavenly sacrifice, there need be no "second time" coming to earth.

Besides, the writer's sacrifice was a singular action, entering the heavenly sanctuary and offering his blood. The Parousia will also be a single occasion of "appearing," thus much more suited to be called a "second time"—should we wish after all to give the language any sense of repetition—to the "appearing" for his heavenly sacrifice than to a coming into an incarnated life on earth.

Suffering Outside the Gate

Finally, to complete our survey of Hebrews, this late passage may not quite qualify as a smoking gun, though when properly understood it again points to a heavenly setting. Considering that it is regularly appealed to as a strong indicator of historicism (Ehrman includes it in his list of "references to the life of an historical Jesus"), revealing it to be anything but such a thing can only support the compelling case which the epistle to the Hebrews makes in presenting an entirely spiritual Son and a sacrifice exclusively in heaven. (This passage was dealt with only briefly in *Jesus: Neither God Nor Man* [68–69]. For a more detailed examination, which I have summarized here, see Web-site Supplementary Article No. 14, "The Cosmic Christ of the Epistle to the Hebrews," Part Three.)

In 13:11–13, the author has the perfect opening to tell us, not only something about Jesus' sufferings, but where on earth they took place (he supplies neither):

> Those animals whose blood is brought as a sin offering by the high priest into the sanctuary, have their bodies burnt *outside the camp*, and therefore Jesus also suffered *outside the gate*, to consecrate the people by his own blood. Let us then go to him *outside the camp*, bearing the stigma that he bore. [NEB]

Like Hebrews 8:4 earlier, this passage has begged for a more careful analysis which it has never received. The first thing to note is that the writer is once again attempting ("and therefore Jesus also...") to make a parallel between Jesus' actions and those of the high priests on earth. The latter are spoken of as taking place "outside the camp" because the author, as much as possible throughout the epistle, has been making his parallels with the biblical accounts in which the first tent of sacrifice was set up outside the Israelite camp in Sinai.

A bad comparison

But this comparison is problematic. It is not really a parallel at all. The burning of the animals' bodies takes place after the sacrifice of their blood, and is a discarding of their bodies; nor does it cause the animal suffering. Jesus' suffering and death—with no burning involved—took place before the sacrifice and was an essential prelude to it; and his body was hardly discarded since he was resurrected. This inappropriate comparison is a signal that the writer's overriding object was to create as many parallels as he could with scripture, even if they didn't work very well.

Contrary to claims that the passage is governed by history, this shows the opposite: the author's process, and what he allots to Jesus, is governed by his focus on creating parallels with scripture.

But what of the change from verse 11 to verse 12, the change from "outside the camp" to "outside the gate"? Is that governed by history? Is it a reference to the gate of Jerusalem, as some claim?

Outside what gate?

Not necessarily. In any context, Jesus did not suffer outside any camp, and so a change needed to be made. If it were a reference to Jerusalem, why did the writer switch back to "outside the camp" in the next verse, urging his readers to join Jesus there? In fact, he is presenting his community as being 'outside the pale,' alienated from society and suffering persecution. Why not, then, have them join Jesus outside the gate of Jerusalem, a very apt symbolic image, where they could share in his own sufferings, his own "stigma"?

Furthermore, scholars have asked why, if Jesus suffered outside Jerusalem, did the author not make a comparison with Melchizedek, who in 7:1 is presented as king and priest coming out of Salem to greet Abraham and accept a tithe. Would that not have invited a parallel between the two priests (whom the author has paralleled in other ways), officiating outside the gate of Jerusalem?

I suggest that the 'gate' is the *gate of heaven*. Jesus had to suffer outside that gate, since suffering and death could not take place within the pure spheres of heaven (where the heavenly sanctuary was located). And since the readers could hardly be enjoined to join Jesus outside the gate of heaven, the writer had to revert to the initial "outside the camp." The latter may not have been the best solution, but it entailed the all-important image of being "outside" for both Jesus and the community: the community as "outside" the normal precincts of society. And thus it fitted his purposes.

Passing through the heavens

In this connection, I suggest we look at an earlier passage. In 4:14, as a concluding exhortation to hold fast to faith, the author adds this justification:

> Since we have a great High Priest *who has passed through the heavens*, Jesus the Son of God, let us hold to our confession.

If this is taken as a reference to Jesus' ascension after his time on earth (as is usually the case), it would serve little or no purpose. The ascension, as conceived by orthodoxy, had no role in salvation, and why it would be a reason for holding fast to faith would be obscure. Besides, in detailing Jesus' itinerary, *why mention the spheres of heaven but not earth itself?*

The answer is likely that the act of salvation directly involved this passing through the heavens. This would fit the concept of the descent and ascent of the Son, first descending to the lowest sphere to undergo death, then ascending to the heavenly sanctuary to offer his blood in a new atonement sacrifice to God.

I have made the point before that historicist scholars like Ehrman regularly indulge in and require a superficial reading (or rather, 'reading into') of the epistolary texts — with blinders attached — to make their case, whereas a less preconceived examination reveals a depth and dimension too readily overlooked, one pointing directly to Mythicism. The epistle to the Hebrews is perhaps the best example of this very deficient methodology.

A Pauline Postscript

A few words are needed about the ending of the epistle to the Hebrews. Uncertainty about the authenticity of the final verses (their number varies) has been common in scholarship, and particularly of 13:22–25. These constitute a 'farewell greeting' which, with its reference to Timothy, places us in the world of Paul. There are scholars, such as Harold Attridge, who maintain authenticity, but there are too many problems with this. In *Jesus: Neither God Nor Man*, Appendix 4, I discuss them at length, but here I will mention two. (That Appendix also discusses the question of dating, which almost certainly must be judged as pre-Jewish War.)

In ancient times, Hebrews came to be attributed to Paul, but this enjoys no support today, not least because the soteriology of the epistle is utterly unlike anything Paul has given us. But if the 'postscript' was written by the author of the epistle, this would mean that he moved in Pauline circles, leading us to expect his treatise to reflect at least some of Paul's thought. On the other hand, the postscript is obviously designed to give the impression that the epistle is by Paul.

That impression also creates a clear contradiction with the epistle itself. The implied Paul of the postscript is ostensibly writing to a community that he is not a part of. His remarks about Timothy point up the fact that he is a wandering apostle, accompanied on his travels by a companion. Yet the epistle itself presents the writer as a member of the community he is addressing (as in 10:24–25). (The same incompatibility is suggested in 13:17, which would make that verse a part of the addition as well.)

If Hebrews is truly an independent expression recognizable nowhere else, a unique interpretation of the Savior Christ on the first century scene, we are justified in postulating a Christianity which developed without a single founder or point of origin. It began in diversity, and only later coalesced around a Jesus on earth who seems, all things considered, to be a product of the imagination.

CHAPTER NINETEEN

Bart Ehrman And The Cheshire Cat Of Nazareth

Frank R. Zindler

Dubitando enim ad inquisitionem venimus;
inquirendo veritatem percipimus.
— Peter Abelard

When all that is left of a Cheshire cat is its grin, how can we be sure it is in fact the grin of a cat? To be sure, if we have watched a grinning cat disappear progressively until all we see is its grin, we can have some confidence that the aerial grin we perceive to remain is in fact that of a cat. As the grin further dissolves into the fog and mist of a perplexing day, however, it becomes harder and harder to determine if the motes that float before our eyes are still the remnants of the grin or just the random rubbish of polluted air. At some point, however, we will have to admit that the cat is gone — completely gone.

This all seems obvious enough and uncontroversial. But what if someone else were to walk by as you were standing at the wayside peering into the low branches of a tree and fixing your gaze on the fading remnants of the grin?

"What are you staring at?" the stranger might inquire.

"The grin of a Cheshire cat — a cat that used to live in Cheshire in England," you reply.

"Really?" he might ask. "Where exactly is it?"

You might point to a branch where the faint pattern of glowing dust still hovered in the air. "Right there," you'd explain. "A moment ago, the whole cat was on that branch, but he's faded away to just the grin you see up there now."

"What?!" the passerby might challenge you. "That's no cat! That's just a will-o'-the-wisp!"

"Well," you affirm, "*I* know it's a cat that grew up in Cheshire even though it's gone now and not even a trace remains."

Who would believe you? Who *ought* to believe you?

Just as with Alice wandering around in Wonderland, a walk through the field of New Testament studies comes again and again to faint, ethereal traces that one is told are remnants of the scowl, or grin, or grimace, or smirk, or leer, or glare, or smiley-face, or amorous glance, or winsome wink of another character of Western literature: Jesus of Nazareth.

Unlike the case of Alice and the Cheshire cat, no one now alive was around two thousand years ago to witness Jesus of Nazareth in his physical entirety before he started to fade into the blurry image of the past we now possess. Moreover, it certainly doesn't help when we learn that many of the earliest Christians didn't believe that Jesus ever *had* a physical entirety!

There is a further problem. Unlike Alice witnessing the fading of the Cheshire cat *from the beginning* and so being able not only to attest to the identity of the pattern glowing amidst the darkling leaves but even to confirm the *physical reality* of a feline philosopher of known provenience, no one today can even attest with certainty to the identity of the *character* they think they see in the Rorschach records of the past. Still less can they vouchsafe the reality of his physical existence. No two persons see the same Jesus, let alone the Jesus that Bart Ehrman describes in *Did Jesus Exist?* [1]

One thing now seems certain to all scholars who are theologically free to follow the trail of evidence whithersoever it might lead: the

1 Bart D. Ehrman, *Did Jesus Exist? The Historical Argument for Jesus of Nazareth* [New York: HarperOne, 2012].

original character — whose jigsaw-puzzle image has fragmented and been scattered to the point where only a few pieces of the face remain in the puzzle-box of history — could not possibly have been any of the Jesuses of the canonical New Testament.

From the time of the Enlightenment it has been understood that whoever Jesus of Nazareth might have been in real life, he could not have been the miracle-worker of Matthew, Mark, Luke, and John. That is to say, he could not have performed actual miracles that violated the laws of science. The Rationalists, however, held on to the stories as being history of a sort, but history that misunderstood what was really going on. Jesus wasn't *really* dead in the tomb; he had merely swooned. Jesus wasn't *really* walking on the water; the stones just below the surface weren't visible in the fog. And so on.

The Rationalists rescued the various gospel Jesuses from deconstructive demise for a time. But then in 1900 L. Frank Baum's wonderful *The Wonderful Wizard of Oz* was published, and the adventitious nature of Rationalist salvage efforts could eventually come to be seen as no more credible than arguments trying to prove that Emerald City isn't green because it is made of emeralds; rather, it is green due to paint pigments that exhibit high reflectance at wavelengths around 555 nanometers.

And so began the inexorable disintegration and disappearance of the Cheshire Jesus of Nazareth — a god long believed to have been a man but now known to have been no more real a man than was the Cheshire cat a real cat. After we briefly retrace the dissolution of 'The Historical Jesus' a bit later, we shall see that insoluble epistemological problems now rule out any possibility that Bart Ehrman — still less believing Christian apologists — can save the Savior long piously believed to have come from a place called Nazareth in the Galilee.

Problems Facing Historicists

The greatest problem faced by modern questers of the Historical Jesus — the problem of lack of physical evidence — actually existed already close to the time their quarry is imagined to have lived. Practically from the beginning of the literary record still at our disposal, there were Christians — 'heretics,' according to the victorious Orthodox

Party — who denied that Jesus or Christ (not necessarily equivalent characters) had had any physical reality at all. This problem was made extremely embarrassing by the apparent fact that no physical remains at all existed that could attest to the historicity of any Jesus at all, let alone to the physicality of a Jesus of an unknown place called Nazareth.

It is not surprising, therefore, to discover that a growth industry developed for manufacture and sale of holy relics — physical objects that could in some way be made to attest to the reality of Jesus, his Twelve Disciples, his parents, his step-siblings, his miracles, as well as the very geographical stage itself on which the drama of the ages was thereby certified to have been acted out.

Several foreskins of Jesus were produced for sacred edification of the faithful. Splinters of the True Cross, bones of the Apostles, and a mind-boggling array of artifacts soon filled the reliquaries of the churches of the Mediterranean world. All the relics were used to prove the unprovable — to bear false witness in support of a man whose existence had never been witnessed by mortal man or woman. What was necessary even in ancient times has become even more necessary in modern times. Forgeries such as the Shroud of Turin, the James Ossuary, and the bones of Saint Peter at the Vatican[2] continue to be needed props if modern Christians are to maintain contact with the historical Jesus.

Although there were no unbroken traditions of habitation and place-names to tie present-day sites such as Nazareth, Capernaum, Bethany, Bethphage, *etc.*, to the New Testament venues of Jesus' supposed ministry, by the time of Constantine's mother Helena tour guides seem to have been doing a handsome business leading the faithful to the place where Baby Jesus was born, where Gabriel spoke to Mary, where Jesus was crucified, buried, and did everything else men do except... Well, Jesus apparently did *those* things too, but there probably would have been no tourism potential in memorializing the places where the Savior of the World did *that* sort of thing.

2 The bones now venerated in the basement of the Vatican are actually the bones of two men, an old woman, chickens, pigs, and a mouse, as I have shown in my essay "Of Bones and Boners: Saint Peter at the Vatican," *Through Atheist Eyes. Volume One: Religions & Scriptures* [Cranford, NJ: American Atheist Press, 2011: 99–122].

Bart Ehrman and the Cheshire Cat of Nazareth

Before the tour guides could show credulous Christians the holy places of the gospels, of course, names of places to venerate had to be created by the reverend evangelists themselves. One of the places, Aenon,[3] was an unintentional invention resulting from dyslexia on the part of one of the authors of the Gospel of John trying to parse the sentences of a *Codex Bezae*-like manuscript of the Gospel of Luke. Nazareth apparently was created to provide Jesus with a hometown in order to thwart the claims of the Docetists — early Christians who believed that Christ and/or Jesus only *appeared* to have a body and undergo suffering. Others, like Capernaum,[4] Bethany, Bethphage,[5] Bethabara, *etc.*, were created for symbolic purposes. Most of the holy places of the gospels were unknown to ancient geographers and other writers.

As shocking as these claims may seem, there is an even greater problem with which Historicists must contend. In my *The Jesus the Jews Never Knew*[6] I have shown that there is no evidence in all of Jewish literature surviving from antiquity to show that the ancient Jews had ever heard of Jesus of Nazareth, due to the simple fact that they had never heard of Nazareth!

In recent times, René Salm[7] demonstrated that the city now called Nazareth was not inhabited between the end of the Bronze Age or beginning of the Iron Age and Late Roman times, and that the sites venerated by Roman Catholic Christians were the remains of an ancient necropolis — a cemetery, not the kitchen of the Virgin Mary

3 Details of how this came about can be found in my essay "Where Jesus Never Walked" [*ibid.*: 49–50].

4 An account of the outrageous 'archaeological research' that has been done at the present-day site of Telḥum as well as proof that Josephus did not in fact know of a town called Capernaum can be found in *ibid.* [38–44] and in my technical paper "Capernaum — A Literary Invention," *Journal of Higher Criticism*, Volume 12, No. 2, Fall 2006: 1–27.

5 Could there be a more appropriate place to curse a fig tree than Bethphage — 'House of Figs' in Hebrew?

6 Frank R. Zindler, *The Jesus the Jews Never Knew: Sepher Toldoth Yeshu and the Quest of the Historical Jesus in Jewish Sources*, Cranford, NJ, American Atheist Press, 2003. It appears that Ehrman did not read the copy of this book that I gave to him.

7 René Salm, *The Myth Of Nazareth: The Invented Town Of Jesus*,[Cranford, NJ: American Atheist Press, 2008].

or of anyone at all. The Historicist cause was not helped at all by the Israeli archaeologist Aviram Oshri,[8] who showed that Bethlehem in Judea also was not inhabited at the required time, even though a Bethlehem in Galilee was a going concern at the time in which the gospel stories are set.

Since no ancient writers had noticed the birthing and ministry of the Son of Man, a.k.a., the Son of God, it early on became necessary to forge witnesses by interpolating the texts of writers such as Josephus. Entire compositions such as "The Correspondence of Paul and Seneca" were needed to show that the Stoics had borrowed from Paul and not the other way around as it so strongly appears.

Perhaps most embarrassing of all, the historical Jesus never wrote anything — at least not during his lifetime. By the time of Eusebius [*ca.* 263–339 CE], however, Jesus had gotten around to dictating a letter in response to a letter sent to him by King Abgar of Edessa. The King, it became known, had written a letter to Jesus (now found in the *Doctrina Addaei* — 'the Doctrine of Thaddaeus')[9] asking him to come and heal his ills and find asylum from "the Jews." Jesus' letter basically was a dust-off, explaining that he was too busy at the moment ("I ascend again to my Father who sent me") but that he would have one of his secretaries attend to it.

It has become obvious at this point that there is nothing outside the canonical New Testament and the New Testament Apocrypha that can serve as a database from which to construct an image even of Jesus of Anyplaceatall. Is that sufficient to create even the image of a disembodied grin? Let us see what Historicists have to work with in the New Testament.

In the Pauline Epistles, there is no biographical material at all apart from creedal claims that the savior of the world was "born of woman" "according to the flesh" — passages that quite likely were put there to confute the Docetists.[10] There is nothing in the other

8 Aviram Oshri, "Where Was Jesus Born?" *Archaeology*, Vol. 58, No. 6, November-December, 2005: 42–45.

9 Eusebius, *Historia Ecclesiastica*, I, xiii, *ca.* 325 CE.

10 See my chapter "Bart Ehrman and the Body of Jesus of Nazareth."

epistles or the Apocalypse[11] from which one might infer the agenda of a coffee break, let alone important biographical details. That leaves only the Book of Acts and the Four Gospels in their disenchanted, demystified, skeletal forms. Is *that* enough to satisfy the ontological needs of Historicists?

Enter The Jesus Seminar, a group of biblical scholars led by Robert W. Funk and John Dominic Crossan. Convened in 1985, the group met several times a year to evaluate the more than 1,500 sayings that have been attributed to the historical Jesus. The makeup of The Jesus Seminar slowly changed over time, and even I was able to take part in the debates for a number of years. Then, in 1993, the scholarly equivalent of detonating a nuclear warhead at a fireworks display occurred: publication of *The Five Gospels: The Search for the Authentic Words of Jesus.*[12] Even though the scholars had included the noncanonical *Gospel of Thomas* in their database, a majority of them could only defend *about twenty percent* of the alleged Sayings of Jesus as likely to be authentic. (Of course, I argued that *none* of them were authentic, but being a mere geologist and neurophysiologist I repeatedly was voted down.) To this day, Fundamentalist Christians are trying to see if 'The Jesus Seminar' can be identified with 'the number of the name of the beast' of the Apocalypse — 666.

The Five Gospels were followed in 1998 by *The Acts of Jesus: The Search for the Authentic Deeds of Jesus.*[13] The findings this time were fairly predictable. Jesus did not rise bodily from the dead, the empty tomb is a fiction, Jesus did not walk on water, *etc.* Just as predictably, a majority felt that Jesus had been born in Nazareth, not Bethlehem, at the time of Herod the Great. His mother's name was Mary, his father's name might not have been Joseph, and so on.

11 Although an astral account of the nativity of Christ or Jesus is to be found in the twelfth chapter of Revelation, it is so symbolic and allegorical that nothing resembling biography can be gleaned therein. It is, however, the sort of nativity narrative one might expect for a divine figure.

12 Robert W. Funk, Roy W. Hoover, and The Jesus Seminar, *The Five Gospels: The search for the Authentic Words of Jesus* [New York: Macmillan Pub. Co., 1993].

13 Robert W. Funk and the Jesus Seminar, *The Acts of Jesus: The Search for the Authentic Deeds of Jesus*, [San Francisco, HarperSanFrancisco, 1998].

Frank R. Zindler

While The Jesus Seminar was not able to carry out what I had expected would be a complete dismantling and deconstruction of the gospel Jesuses, it was the beginning of the end of the historical Jesus. One of the more important scholars who had taken part in the deliberations was Dennis Ronald MacDonald. He had discovered copious evidence that there had been a considerable amount of imitation of Homer's *Odyssey* in the Gospel of Mark and other early Christian literature such as *The Acts of Andrew*. This means that at the same time that The Jesus Seminar was showing that the great majority of the sayings attributed to Jesus were not authentic, MacDonald[14] was showing that a substantial amount of the Jesus storyline was not authentic either.

While MacDonald was busy identifying Homeric imitations in the Second Gospel (Augustus Caesar's was the first), I was focusing on the so-called Q-Document, the hypothetical sayings gospel from which most of the sayings of Jesus had been derived in the construction of the gospels of Matthew and Luke.

Whereas Ehrman argues that Q is an independent witness of Jesus, I would argue that although it came to include material about John the Baptist and rudimentary narrative, it began merely as a list of wise sayings or proverbs. Perhaps it was used in some ancient school or other and then became attributed to Jesus fairly early in the manufacturing of gospels. How can I say this?

My answer will probably seem even more shocking than my claim. If Q was a true listing of the wise sayings of Jesus, then Ehrman could probably argue that Jesus had been well educated in Greek literature — including Aesop's Fables! In fact, Jesus had had such a good Hellenisic education that he even quoted Aesop in one of his sayings that is reported in Q and adapted as Matthew 11:17 and Luke 7:32.

> Luke 7:32: "They are like unto children sitting in the marketplace, and calling one to another, and saying, *We have piped unto you, and ye have not danced*; we have mourned to you, and ye have not wept.

---

14 Dennis Ronald MacDonald, *Christianizing Homer: The Odyssey, Plato, and The Acts of Andrew* [New York, Oxford University Press, 1994]; Dennis R. MacDonald, *The Homeric Epics and the Gospel of Mark* [New Haven, Yale University Press, 2000].

Bart Ehrman and the Cheshire Cat of Nazareth

> Mat 11:17And saying, *We have piped unto you, and ye have not danced*; we have mourned unto you, and ye have not lamented.

This passage incorporates a phrase from the Fables of Aesop, the fable of the "Fisherman Piping to the Fish" (Babrius 9 = Perry 11).[15], [16] In the fable, the fisherman plays his flute to attract fish, but it doesn't work. So, he throws his net into the water and brings up many 'dancing' fish: "When I piped you would not dance, but now you do so merrily."

As suggestive as the Aesop evidence might be to indicate that the Q sayings collection originally had nothing to do with Jesus of Nazareth — Q material then being unavailable for Ehrman's use — evidence from the Nag Hammadi 'Library' shows how originally non-Christian sayings actually came to be attributed to Jesus. James M. Robinson, the editor of the Nag Hammadi materials published in English, tells us that

> The Nag Hammadi library even presents one instance of the Christianizing process taking place almost before one's eyes. The non-Christian philosophic treatise Eugnostos the Blessed is cut up somewhat arbitrarily into separate speeches, which are then put on Jesus' tongue, in answer to questions (which sometimes do not quite fit the answers) that the disciples address to him during a resurrection appearance. The result is a separate tractate entitled The Sophia of Jesus Christ. Both forms of the text occur side by side in Codex III.[17]

With so much of the 'Historical Jesus' now having been pared away we may imagine his total dissolution. For nearly two centuries, one scholar after another has claimed that this or that feature of the

15 Ben Edwin Perry, *Aesopica: A Series of Texts Relating to Aesop or Ascribed to Him or Closely Connected with the Literary Tradition That Bears His Name, Vol. One: Greek and Latin Texts* [Urbana, Univ. Illinois Press, 1952: 326].

16 I was surprised to discover that John S. Kloppenborg, the famous Q authority, was unaware of this Aesop borrowing. Neither his *Q Parallels* [Sonoma, Polebridge Press, 1988] nor *The Critical Edition of Q* with James M. Robinson and Paul Hoffmann [Minneapolis, Fortress Press, 2000] notes the Aesopic origin of Q 7:32b.

17 James M. Robinson, *The Nag Hammadi Library*, 3rd rev. ed. [San Francisco: Harper, 1988: 8–9].

'Life of Christ' was borrowed from some Pagan source, adapted from the Hebrew scriptures or Septuagint, modeled after Homer, other divinities, *etc.* A large part of 'Jesus' can be seen to be 'The New Moses' or 'New Elijah,' and it is easy to see how all the 'Old Testament' so-called predictions of Jesus were actually the seeds that sprouted and turned into the various Jesuses of the various gospels.

Certainly, it is not possible to prove such a thesis in an essay such as this. Nevertheless, a fair number of scholars are busily at work adducing evidence to show that practically every detail of the Jesus biography is either borrowed and adapted from non-Christian sources, modeled after them, or was the creative fallout from ancient theopolitical equivalents of nuclear wars of attrition. What if these scholars succeed?[18]

What will Historicists such as Bart Ehrman do if it can be clearly demonstrated that eighty or ninety percent of the 'biography' of Jesus is bogus in the sense that it was created *ad hoc* to create a terrestrial itinerary for a heavenly being sojourning on our sublunary sphere? Some years ago I sent a questionnaire polling fellow members of The Jesus Project in which one question read something like "If it could be clearly demonstrated that the entirety of the gospel Jesus biography was inauthentic, would you still believe in the Historical Jesus? If 90%? If 80%? ...

To my astonishment, more than one of those hard-headed, secular scholars indicated that they would continue to believe in the Historical Jesus even if his entire biography were proven to be a fiction!

18 Thomas L. Brodie seems to have come very close to doing exactly this. In his *The Birthing of the New Testament: The Intertextual Development of the New Testament Writings* [Sheffield, England: Sheffield Phoenix Press, 2004] he demonstrates massive dependence of the New Testament upon the Septuagint version of Deuteronomy, Ben Sirach, and the Elija-Elisha narratives of Kings. Having 'come out of the closet' as a Mythicist, he summarizes this information in his personal, autobiographical *Beyond the Quest for the Historical Jesus: Memoir of a Discovery* [Sheffield, England: Sheffield Phoenix Press, 2012]. The "Epilogue" of the book is a brief critique of Ehrman's *Did Jesus Exist?*, and Brodie ends the entire book with the comment, "Ehrman's book is to be welcomed. Despite its ill-founded version of history, it helps bring the issue of Jesus' historical existence and other important issues about the nature of belief and religion to the centre of discussion." Brodie is the Director of the Dominican Biblical Centre at Limerick, Ireland, and remains a faithful Roman Catholic as this book goes to press.

Bart Ehrman and the Cheshire Cat of Nazareth

What Historicists Must Try To Do

Having no authority more credible than the fabled witness of the disembodied grin of a Cheshire cat, Historicists must look to see if there are any dots or spots or splotches in the blurred and broken image of the past that they can connect in such a way that it can produce a convincing and unambiguous picture of even a *character* they might call Jesus of Nazareth. Then, the picture must be sharp enough to convince not just themselves but skeptics as well that the character was an actual man — *not just a description of a character in a work of fiction.* And most importantly: they must take care to insure that the picture at which they gaze is not their own image in a mirror.

Throughout the ages, millions of men and women have been able to convince themselves and others not only of the identity of a pattern (actually, *patterns*) of traces that they identify as the spoor of Jesus of Nazareth, but also of his physical reality in Palestine around the turn of the era. Bart Ehrman is but one of millions of Alices who have affirmed an antecedent physical reality behind the grins they have strained to see. He must find his virtual quarry not amongst the leaves of trees, of course, but rather amidst the leaves of codices and papyrus rolls. The James Ossuary and the Shroud of Turin can no longer be called as witness to the 'physical entirety' of Jesus of Nazareth.

The image Historicists in desperation try to see is made more difficult to descry by the fact that the miracles ascribed to Jesus of Nazareth — what for Christian critics are the most illuminating features of the image — must be masked or eclipsed in the image at the outset. As a secular scholar who must always submit himself to the rule of reason, Ehrman knows that if he accepts the stories of Jesus of Nazareth raising the dead, healing the sick at a distance, walking on the water, *etc*., he must then admit not only the possibility but the probability that all the miracles attributed to Asclepius, Dionysus, Isis, Buddha, Allah, and thousands of other divinities who have been worshipped and talked about since the Stone Age are just as credible. He probably also knows that he must not fall into the old Rationalist error of trying to find 'rational' explanations for the 'miracles' lodged in narrative frameworks that to all appearances are fairy-tale fictions.

Frank R. Zindler

Once all the wonders and marvels have been removed from the canonical gospels, what remains for Historicists to use to demonstrate the historicity of a Jesus of Anywhereatall? What must they do?

Let us remember, as bearer of the Historicist banner, Ehrman has to stake everything on the gospels and other documents of the canonical New Testament because there are no eyewitnesses or contemporary writers who could vouch for the existence of Jesus *or any of his twelve disciples/apostles.*[19] Moreover, despite the thousands of fake relics ranging from body parts of Jesus and John the Baptist to splinters of the True Cross, no genuine physical materials are reliably traceable to Jesus of Anywhereatall. And then there is a further problem — a somewhat amusing one.

No one in early times ever described his physical appearance — even though according to 1 Corinthians 15:6 Jesus appeared to five hundred people at the same time. How did everyone know it was Jesus of Nazareth they were gawking at? How did they recognize him? Perhaps he announced himself in the words of Bart Ehrman[20] — "I am Jesus from a one-dog town called Nazareth"? Surely, if all five hundred had seen Jesus when he had been alive, someone would have left a record of what he looked like. But then, even if none of the 'witnesses' had ever known Jesus when he was alive, wouldn't some of them have left a record of what his virtual image had looked like? But then again, Saint Paul himself — apparently on face-to-virtual-image speaking terms with Jesus — is curiously silent concerning the visual details of his visions. Only rather late in the story did Christians begin to imagine just exactly what Jesus looked like. Is it unreasonable to ask Historicists if he was tall or short? Slim or

---

19 The absence of historical evidence of the Twelve is even more significant than the lack of evidence for Jesus. After all, what exactly would have been reported of Jesus if he didn't do any of the miracles? The apostles, however, had as their main function attracting the attention of the Roman world. My essay "The Twelve: Further Fictions From the New Testament" [*Through Atheist Eyes*, Vol. I: 81–98] examines this problem in some detail. I don't know if Ehrman simply did not read this essay in his obviously hasty preparation for *Did Jesus Exist?* or if he was unable to answer my argument and so avoided mentioning it.

20 "Nazareth was a little one-horse town (not even that; it was more like a one-dog town) that no one had ever heard of, so far as we can tell, before Christianity." *Did Jesus Exist?:* 189.

stocky? Black-haired or blonde as in portraits painted by German Lutherans? Was his hair long and curly, or short and kinky?

The gospels are the Historicists' last hope. For, in spite of the existence of many Jewish, Greek, and Roman authors living and writing at the turn of the era and having reason to take notice of Jesus, none of them mentioned either Jesus or Nazareth. Even more inexplicable: if the Twelve Disciples/Apostles had done anything at all to evangelize the world, *they* would have been noticed even if their master had spent most of his life in the cave in which he is imagined to have been born.

Surely, if Jesus of Nazareth had been real, Philo of Alexandria [20 BCE–50 CE] would have known about him and his disciples. Philo was a major developer of the Logos theory of Platonism, Stoicism, and Christianity. He had intimate ties to the goings on in Jerusalem, as his nephew Marcus Julius Alexander was the husband of the Herodian Princess Berenice who is mentioned in the twenty-fifth chapter of Acts. His other nephew Tiberius Julius Alexander became procurator of Judea [*ca.* 46–48] under Claudius. *Unless what Jesus and the Apostles were doing had no religious significance, Philo should have noticed them.* Historicists must try to find an answer to this problem that is more compelling than the answers one might get from a Josh McDowell or a Lee Strobel.

Justus of Tiberias [*second half of first century*], the great rival of Josephus living just fifteen miles from Nazareth as the angel flies, could not have been ignorant of Jesuine traditions in Galilee had there been any. Moreover, the evangelists Matthew, Mark, and Luke should have mentioned the controversial new city of Tiberias[21] had

21 When Herod Antipas founded Tiberias as a Roman city sometime around 20 CE, he violated Jewish ritual law by building it on the top of graves. At the time Jesus should have been traveling in the area, there would have been great and noisy tumult concerning the propriety of Jews living in the new city. Curiously, there is no record of anyone asking Jesus for his opinion about the city, which is mentioned only in the Gospel of John. In John 6:1 the *Sea* of Tiberias is mentioned simply as another name for the Sea of Galilee. In John 6:23, the city of Tiberias is mentioned simply as a departure point for boats needed in the narrative. The Sea of Tiberias is mentioned once more in the anti-Docetic appendix added later to the Gospel, in the first verse of chapter 21. Nowhere is there any hint that the authors of this gospel had any real knowledge of

they ever been in the Galilee themselves and if Jesus had ever done anything there as claimed by the evangelist John.

Although the works of Justus of Tiberias were not preserved, Photius, Patriarch of Constantinople [*ca.* 810-893] published a great volume of book reviews called the *Bibliotheca* in which he commented on one of the writings of Justus, *The Chronicles of the Kings of the Jews*. Obviously disappointed by the work, he sadly recorded that "of the advent of Christ, of the things that befell him one way or another, or of the miracles that he performed, [Justus] makes absolutely no mention"[Codex 33, my translation].[22]

Historicists must try to make up for the fact that no biographical material at all is found in the Pauline Epistles except for the disputed *Brother of the Lord*[23] of Galatians 1:19. Even if Ehrman is correct about "Brother of the Lord" meaning "Brother of Jesus,"[24] however, we must wonder why that would be significant. After all, in the Gnostic traditions Jesus had a *twin* brother named Thomas! If James be accepted on flimsy evidence to be a brother of Jesus, what reason might we give for rejecting Thomas as his twin brother? Of course,

---

the city and the religious controversy engulfing it at the time Jesus should have been in the neighborhood.

22 *Photius of Constantinople. Myriobiblon Sive Bibliotheca.* In Vol. 103, cols. 65–66 of *Patrologia Graeca.* Edited by J.-P. Migne [Paris, 1857–1886].

23 I have argued [*The Jesus the Jews Never Knew*: 75–88] that 'Brother of the Lord' being understood as signifying 'Brother of Jesus' is an anachronism dating from a later period when 'Lord' had become an epithet or title of Jesus alone not just of Christ or Christ-Jesus. In the Septuagint — the 'Old Testament' for most early Christians it would appear — the word *Kyrios* ('Lord') was used as a pronounceable substitute for the unpronounceable *shem* — the power-name *Yahweh.* In the Hebrew Bible, the name is written as a so-called Tetragrammaton — the four unpronounceable letters YHWH usually being written in Paleohebrew script. When the Hebrew text had to be read aloud, under pain of death [Leviticus 24:16] YHWH must never be pronounced correctly (*i.e., Yahway* or *Yahweh*). Instead, the Hebrew word *Adonai* ('my Lords') was spoken in its place.

When YHWH had to be *transcribed* into Greek, however, the magical, secret name of God could not be spelled out with all its vowels showing. So the substitute word 'Adonai' was *translated* into Greek as *Kyrios.* I have argued that 'Brother of the Lord' probably referred to a brotherhood of monk-like ascetics in special service to Kyrios-Yahweh. How this brotherhood became associated with early Christianity is unclear.

24 Bart D. Ehrman, *Did Jesus Exist?*:120 *et al.*

some Historicists might accept *both* James and Thomas, provided that Thomas be a fraternal twin, not an identical twin. It seems, however, that all Historicists are faced with a dilemma. They must decide if the Catholics are correct — that Jesus had no full siblings at all — or that a Gnostic-*cum*-Protestant position must be defended: Jesus had brothers and sisters and a twin!

Although Historicists need solid evidence to prove their Jesus, we must not fail to keep in mind that they are limited to the canonical New Testament as a source of information concerning Jesus of Nazareth. To make matters worse, most of the data contained in the canonical New Testament are not of any use at all.

So, to return to the Epistles: No Jesuine biography can be found in the non-Pauline epistles — including the one supposed by some to have been written by James the disputed brother of Jesus. Although "The General Epistle of James" is often supposed to have been written by a certain James the physical brother of Jesus, its author curiously does not even hint at any such privileged position. He does not begin his letter with anything at all resembling "James, a servant of God relaying to the twelve tribes the directives of his big brother Jesus the Messiah."

Instead, the letter begins "James, a servant of God and of the Lord Jesus Christ to the twelve tribes which are scattered abroad, greeting." Then follows what can only be described as an essay in Stoic philosophy.[25] (We may note that this is the infamous "Epistle of

25 A masterful analysis of the Stoic dimensions of the Epistle of James is to be found in *Logos and Law in the Letter of James: The Law of Nature, the Law of Moses, and the Law of Freedom*, by Matt A. Jackson-McCabe [Supplements To Novum Testamentum 100, Atlanta: Society of Biblical Literature, 2001]. Although the author accepts the historicity of 'James the Brother of Jesus' and the priority of Jewish Christianity, he nevertheless demonstrates the pseudonymity of the letter. He concludes his analysis on page 253 with the observation that

> James's interaction with Pauline ideas provides a secure basis for locating it [the letter] within early Christianity. More specifically, the Letter of James was produced in some circle of Christians for whom the Torah remained the central expression of love of God, and thus a critical criterion for inheriting the promised kingdom that would be given to the "twelve tribes" at the Parousia of the messiah, Jesus. Its precise date and provenance, however, remain elusive. Clearly it was not written prior to Paul's activity; and if it

straw" against which Martin Luther railed.)

An interesting feature of this letter is *the complete absence of any reference to Jesus as a man or as the Messiah of the Jews.* We have merely the formulaic "Lord Jesus Christ." Whatever the title 'Christ' may have meant to this author, it seems impossible to read any messianic reference into it. To be sure, there is an apocalyptic purpose to this piece, but it looks very much like an adaptation of Stoic eschatology to Christian use.

The database available to Historicists is shrunken further if, as we must, we eliminate the pseudopauline Epistle to the Hebrews. The first chapter does not even mention Jesus by name, but rather speaks of "The Son who is the effulgence of God's splendour and the stamp of God's very being, and sustains the universe by his word of power." [Heb 1:3, NEB]. In this verse it is rather difficult to make out the image of a fellow who just a few decades earlier had been living in "a one-dog-town" that no one had ever heard of.[26]

Can this "Son" be Jesus of Nazareth? Can this Son have been the physical Christ (Messiah) of the Jews? *That* Christ has to be anointed

---

> does assume some collection of Paul's letters, this would likely place it well after Paul's death, and thus after the death of James the brother of Jesus *ca.* 62 CE. In fact, while the letter's emphasis on the Torah seems consistent with our evidence for Jesus's brother, its enlisting, to this end, of the Stoic view of law seems more consistent with later developments in the Christian debates about the Torah. All things considered, it seems most plausible to view James as a pseudonymous work, written in the late first or early second century, perhaps in Syria or Palestine. In any case, the Letter of James provides important, if all too rare evidence for a form of the Christian movement where soteriology centered not on rebirth through "the Gospel," but on observance of the Torah.

If Jackson-McCabe is correct, this eliminates the Epistle of James from the database available for reconstructing the Historical Jesus. Interestingly, by placing the Jewish Christian author after the collecting of Paul's letters, he provides us with another example of Jewish Christianity being later than what has come to be viewed as proto-Orthodox Christianity.
A variety of views on the nature and significance of this epistle can be found in the symposium volume *Matthew, James, and Didache: Three Related Documents in Their Jewish and Christian Settings*, edited by Huub van de Sandt and Jürgen K. Zangenberg, Symposium Series No. 45 [Atlanta: Society of Biblical Literature, 2008].

26 Bart D. Ehrman, *Did Jesus Exist?*: 189.

with *real* oil. But we learn in verse 9 that this Son — assumed by Historicists to be equivalent to Christ who in turn is equivalent to Jesus — has been anointed (*echrisen*) in heaven, not on earth. Moreover, the anointment is not with olive oil and essences; rather, the 'oil' is "the oil of gladness" (*elaion agalliaseōs*). Can this Son be the carpenter's son?

As noted previously, no biographical data can be extracted from the astrotheological nativity brainstorm of the twelfth chapter of the Apocalypse or Revelation of John. That leaves the Gospels and Acts, and I will argue that this limitation will prove lethal to the Historicist cause. In trying to prove the quondam existence of any kind of gospel Jesus, it will be seen, Historicists come face to face with the greatest problem of all: a problem in epistemology and philosophy of science.

The Epistemological Jesus

The Historicists' problem in epistemology is straight-forward. It is even *theoretically* impossible for Ehrman — or anyone — to prove the existence of Jesus of Nazareth on the basis of the evidence available to us this late in history without falling into a scientifically meaningless argument.

Before we go any further, I must explain what I mean by "scientifically meaningless argument." Let us consider by way of illustration two propositions: (1) 'The moon is made of green cheese'; (2) 'Undetectable gremlins inhabit the rings of Saturn.' Although a non-scientist would be likely to say that both propositions are false, a scientist would claim that only one of these claims is false — the green-cheese proposition. The Saturnian gremlin claim, a scientist would explain, is neither true nor false; it is scientifically meaningless. 'True' and 'false' can apply only to meaningful sentences.

Well, then, how does one tell if a proposition is meaningless or meaningful? *To be meaningful a claim must in principle be falsifiable.* That is, one must be able at least to imagine a test that could be performed that conceivably could show the proposition to be false.

The green-cheese proposition can easily be tested today. But even before our astronauts went to the moon and discovered that moon dust is no good in salad dressing, it was easy to imagine what one could do to see if the moon were, in fact, cheese. But the gremlin sentence, by contrast, cannot be tested even in the imagination. Were we to send a rocket to Saturn that was carrying the finest gremlinometers that the creation scientists at NASA were able to build, *ex definitio* they would not be able to detect undetectable gremlins. Undetectable gremlins are forever undetectable and thus unverifiable. The gremlin proposition is thus meaningless and is neither true nor false.

Thus, the sentence 'Jesus of Nazareth once lived in Nazareth' is a meaningful sentence. It can be tested and it has proven to be false. The sentence 'The Jesus of the gospels once lived somewhere or other,' however, is meaningless. There is no conceivable way to falsify it. Even if every square inch of Israel/Palestine were excavated and no genuine Jesuine artifacts were discovered, one could always be told "You didn't search thoroughly enough," or "All traces disappeared long ago," or "He was too obscure to leave an identifying trace." The Jesus of Somewhereorother, thus, is just another undetectable gremlin.

Returning to Bart Ehrman and his book *Did Jesus Exist?,* we must look to see if his theses not only are correct or incorrect, but also we must see if any of them are *neither* true nor false — scientifically meaningless.

Let us consider the problem of Nazareth. René Salm and I have argued that Nazareth was not inhabited at the turn of the era. Ehrman rejects our evidence, siding with Franciscan archaeological apologists (who have destroyed most of the archeological stratigraphy at the venerated sites they control and made further truly scientific excavations impossible) and some recent archaeologists who have made claims of habitation at Nazareth at the turn of the era but never have shown their data for critics to evaluate. (It would, after all, be devastating to Christian tourism in Israel if it became certain that the present city called Nazareth was not the "one-dog-town" of Jesus that Ehrman claims it to have been.[27]

Just to be safe, however, Ehrman claims that it doesn't really matter if Nazareth of today isn't the Nazareth of Jesus or if Jesus

27 Bart D. Ehrman, *Did Jesus Exist?*: 189.

didn't actually come from there. He would still be Jesus, merely Jesus of Someplaceelse!

> "One supposedly legendary feature of the Gospels relates closely to what I have just argued and is in fact one of the more common claims found in the writings of the mythicists. It is that the alleged hometown of Jesus, Nazareth, in fact did not exist but is itself a myth (using the term as the mythicists do). The logic of this argument, which is sometimes advanced with considerable vehemence and force, appears to be that if Christians made up Jesus's hometown, they probably made him up as well. I could dispose of this argument fairly easily by pointing out that it is irrelevant. If Jesus existed, as the evidence suggests, but Nazareth did not, as this assertion claims, then he merely came from somewhere else."[28]

It is not clear in the above passage whether Ehrman has simply misunderstood the argument that I and other Mythicists have advanced or if he misunderstands the logic of science. The former possibility seems likely from the fact that even though on the page cited he discusses my article "Where Jesus Never Walked,"[29] he incorrectly summarizes the Mythicist argument by the statement "The logic of this argument... appears to be that if Christians made up Jesus's hometown, they probably made him up as well." Whether such a claim would in fact be "irrelevant" could be debated, but it is not the argument I would make and it is not the usual argument I have found other scholars to use.

Rather, the argument I have made is simply the fundamentally *scientifically relevant* argument that if Nazareth did not exist when Jesus and the Holy Family should have been living there, then of logical necessity *Jesus of Nazareth* could not have existed. By extension, that would mean of course that the Jesus of Matthew and Luke also

28 *Ibid,*: 191. It must not be thought that Ehrman is being facetious or alone in his judgment here. Some years ago I polled my fellow members of The Jesus Project, asking them the question: "If it could be shown conclusively that present-day Nazareth was not inhabited at the time of Jesus, would you continue to believe in his historical reality?" A large fraction answered "yes" to the question.

29 *Through Atheist Eyes, Volume One* [Cranford, NJ: American Atheist Press, 2011: 27–56].

could not have existed.[30] Why is this argument not only relevant, but relevant in a way that is *sine qua non*? Let us see.

The difference between Jesus *of Nazareth* and practically all the other gods and goddesses whose existence has ever been claimed is this. By being a character *who was defined* as being *physically* associated with a specific town at a specific place at a specific time, his existence could in principle be tested. Claims of his existence would thus be meaningful in the scientific sense. Exhaustive archaeological surveying of the site claimed to be Nazareth could in principle determine the existence claim to be false if the site showed no evidence of habitation at the requisite periods. On the other hand, it could only add a tiny bit of weight to the truth side of the claim if the archaeological evidence of habitation at the turn of the era were positive.

Claims of the existence of a Jesus of Someplace-Else, however, like claims of the existence of Zeus, or Thor, or Yahweh would be scientifically meaningless *since in principle they could not be tested or falsified.*[31] They are scientifically meaningless. It is unfortunate that so

30 Were it the case that Mark 1:9 ("...Jesus came from Nazareth in Galilee...") was *not* an interpolation (contrary to my opinion), then the Jesus of Mark also could not have existed!

31 Because they are not defined with respect to specific times, places, and physical properties, one is perpetually on a wild-goose chase trying to find them. No matter where we might look, we are told that we simply didn't look in the right place or at the right time. All such gods are the equivalents of undetectable gremlins. In the case of Jesus of Nazareth, however, an exhaustive search is possible in principle, and René Salm has done an exhaustive analysis of the Roman Catholic "venerated sites" owned and operated by the Franciscans and has found no compelling evidence of habitation at the turn of the era. Desperate claims are now being made that the right spots haven't been examined, and other parts of the Nazareth hill are being claimed to show proof of habitation at the proper time. Alas, by admitting that the venerated sites are not the correct locations for the holy homes of the Jesus family, it must now be admitted that the Roman Catholic Church was wrong in its profitable claim to the property deeds for Mary's home and Joseph's workshop. Perhaps an Evangelical Protestant-run theme park such as The Nazareth Village Farm Project will be able to stake a more durable claim.

It is worth noting, moreover, that the Gospel of Luke makes the claim that the Nazareth of Jesus had a synagogue at the top of the hill at the edge of a cliff. [Luke 4:28–30] These details absolutely rule out present-day Nazareth as the town of Jesus. Are there *any* hills in Galilee with first-century synagogue remains atop them bordering a cliff? I don't think so, but tour guides carrying out archaeological research might be able to find one. Or create one.

many biblical scholars have not had adequate training in the philosophy and logic of science. If Ehrman had read more of the first, second, and fourth volumes of my recent *Through Atheist Eyes: Scenes From a World That Won't Reason*, he could have avoided blunders such as the Jesus of Someplace-Else.

Nevertheless, Ehrman is still able to assert he could identify *some* Jesus, even if not Jesus of Nazareth. But just exactly which Jesus would that be?

The Face of Ehrman's Jesus

The image that Ehrman thinks he sees and describes in great and enhanced detail in the last part of his book *Did Jesus Exist?* most certainly is not the Yeshu of Jewish writings of late antiquity that can be interpreted to mean that Jesus was born a bastard at the time of Alexander Jannaeus [*r.* 103–76 BCE]. According to one version of the *Sepher Toldoth Yeshu*,[32] the scurrilous antigospel some have claimed was cited by the Greek philosopher Celsus around the year 177 CE, "In the year 671 of the fourth millenary (of the world), in the days of Jannaeus the king, a great misfortune happened to the enemies of Israel. There was a certain idle and worthless debauchee named Joseph Pandera, of the fallen tribe of Judah..." According to this version of the *Toldoth*, Miriam gave birth to Yeshu/Jesus at the time of Alexander Jannaeus — around a hundred years 'Before Christ'!

Of course, Historicists routinely dismiss this source as fanciful anti-Christian Jewish polemics — as though the canonical sources are measurably less fanciful. Nevertheless, Gibbon somewhere speaks of "the anachronism of the Jews, who place the birth of Christ near a century sooner." It is amusing to note that according to the Jewish calendar, which was not standardized until the fourth century CE,[33] the Julian year 1 CE corresponds to Hebrew year 3762, so that

32 Two thoroughly annotated versions of this antigospel have been reprinted as appendices A and B of my book *The Jesus the Jews Never Knew: Sepher Toldoth Yeshu and the Quest of the Historical Jesus in Jewish Sources* [Cranford, NJ: American Atheist Press, 2003].

33 Frank Parise, (editor), *The Book of Calendars* [New York: Facts On File, Inc., 1982: 12–43].

the year 3671 of the *Toldoth* would place the birth of Yeshu around the year 90 BCE.

Obviously, Ehrman's picture of Jesus of not-Nazareth does not look at all like the old photographs of Yeshu ben Pandera. Still less — here's no surprise — the Ehrman image exhibits no similarities at all to that of the early Jewish Christians discussed by Shlomo Pines in his famous paper "The Jewish Christians of the Early Centuries of Christianity According to a New Source."[34] According to Pines, those early Christians placed the ministry of their Jesus approximately *five hundred years* before the Council of Nicaea, which was held in the year 325 CE! Doing the easy subtraction, we find that Jesus lived around 175 BCE. Even *I* can agree with Ehrman that *that* Jesus could not have existed. After all, archaeological evidence[35] shows that Nazareth was not inhabited in 175 BCE.

Ehrman's Jesus also does not match up with that of the unknown author of "The Letter of Pilate to Claudius"[36] who thought that Jesus was done in during the reign of Claudius instead of Tiberius as everyone 'knows.' More importantly, he disagrees with Irenaeus, the Church Father [120–202] who also thought that Jesus lived into his late 40s, and thus into the reign of Claudius [*r.* 41–54]!

It is regrettable that Ehrman did not read the copy I sent to him of my *The Jesus the Jews Never Knew: Sepher Toldoth Yeshu and the*

34 Shlomo Pines, "The Jewish Christians of the Early Centuries of Christianity According to a New Source," *Proceedings of the Israel Academy of Sciences and Humanities* 2 [1966: 237–310].

35 See the extended arguments and evidence of René Salm in his *The Myth Of Nazareth, The Invented Town Of Jesus* [Cranford, NJ: American Atheist Press, 2008].

36 Not having taken the time to read my explanation of the tradition of Jesus living into his forties or even fifties [*The Jesus the Jews Never Knew*: 127–29], Ehrman writes in his introduction to "The Letter of Pilate to Claudius" [*The Apocryphal Gospels: Texts and Translations* (with Zlatko Pleše, Oxford University Press, 2011: 511], "It is not clear what to make of the anachronistic reference to Claudius as the emperor at the time of Jesus' death (rather than Tiberius; Claudius would not assume the throne for another decade). The author of this letter, living so long after the fact, may simply not have known the facts of Roman imperial history." Actually there appear to have been *many* attempts *post hoc* to locate Jesus in the frame of human history. *This is hard to understand only if he had actually lived.*

Quest of the Historical Jesus in Jewish Sources.[37] In that book I discuss the twenty-second chapter of *Against Heresies* by Irenaeus of Lyons [120–202 CE] who argued against the '*heretics*' who taught that Jesus was in his thirties when he died! Arguing from the text of John 8:56–57,[38] he explained "now such language is fittingly applied to one who has already passed the age of forty, without having as yet reached his fiftieth year, yet is not far from this latter period."

As if this all does not create enough confusion concerning the position Jesus of Nazareth may have occupied in Roman chronology, there is another oddity of history that seems somehow to relate to 'the Historical Jesus' and should have been investigated by Ehrman. This is the peculiar fact that Iberia for a long time used a calendrical system for which the commencement year corresponded to 38 BCE. According to an article in the on-line edition of *The Catholic Encyclopedia*,[39]

> Spain, with Portugal and Southern France, observed an era of its own long after the rest of Christendom had adopted that of Dionysius [Exiguus]. This era of Spain or of the Cæsars, commenced with 1 January, 38 B.C., and remained in force in the Kingdom of Castile and Leon till A.D. 1383, when a royal edict commanded the substitution of the Christian Era. In Portugal the change was not made till 1422. No satisfactory explanation has been found of the date from which this era started.

Wouldn't it be reasonable to conclude that the Iberians and their neighbors on the north began their era on a date they took to be the year of Jesus' birth? Remember, these were *very* Christian nations. Why would they so long resist the general 'Christian Era' of the rest

37 *The Jesus the Jews Never Knew*: 127–129.

38 John 8:56. "Your father Abraham was overjoyed to see my day; he saw it and was glad. 57. The Jews protested, 'You are not yet fifty years old. How can you have seen Abraham?'" This is followed by the apparently Docetic verses 58-59: "Jesus said, 'In very truth I tell you, before Abraham was born, I am.' They picked up stones to throw at him, but Jesus was not to be seen; and he left the temple."

39 The Catholic Encyclopedia (http://www.newadvent.org/cathen/03738a.htm), article "Chronology, General," section "Beginning of the year."

of Europe unless they had reason to believe they had better information than did Dionysius Exiguus when he set the starting point for his Christian Era at what so long has been reckoned as the year AD 1? It certainly looks as though an important part of Christendom believed that Jesus had been born 38 years 'Before Christ'![40]

Despite these problems in natal chronology, Ehrman seems quite certain that the dots and spots and splotches he has connected into the image of a man are traces of an actual man who was born and lived at the time the Gospel of Matthew says he lived, before the death of Herod the Great in 4 BCE. Or, maybe, at the time the Gospel of Luke says — during the Augustan census of Quirinius in 6 CE. Or, at any rate, *some* time around the turn of the era. Yes, he lived somewhere some time around the turn of the era.

But there is a far more interesting and historically important Jesus whom Ehrman has not called to sit to have his portrait sketched: the Jesus of the Docetists and Gnostics. Although he gives no reasons for his manifest preference, Ehrman doesn't think the true Jesus of Christian origins was the Jesus of the Docetists or Gnostics — traces of whose Jesus or Christ (sorting out the two is a difficult and daunting task) form a large chunk of the picture we might be able to reconstruct of any Jesus. Removal of the Docetic and Gnostic evidence from the data-set with which we might seek to test the historicity of the Jesus of some place and some time around the turn of the era makes that testing more difficult — and probably less meaningful. (By ruling out evidence that could disconfirm his hypothesis of historicity, Ehrman comes dangerously close to making his thesis scientifically meaningless by making it less open to testing and falsification.)

How comes it then that an expert in the apocryphal literature would ignore his own scholarship when trying to reconstruct his Jesus of Not-Nazareth? I am guessing that Ehrman ignored the Jesus of the Docetists and Gnostics because he realized their writings would be of no use whatever in reconstructing a *historical* Jesus or Christ.

40 The Egyptologist Margaret Morris (personal communication) has informed me that 38 BCE corresponds to the year in which worship of Octavian (Augustus Caesar) began in the Iberian Peninsula.

Given his powerful Historicist bias and the relative narrowness of his education, it probably never occurred to him to weigh the significance of those documents as evidence *against* historicity. Had he read my essay "What does it mean to be scientific?"[41] he would have realized the need to think like a scientist in order better to understand the relevance of his own research.

Ehrman has shown in his magisterial *The Orthodox Corruption of Scripture*[42] that a large number of passages in the New Testament were altered to refute the Docetists and Gnostics. How shall we evaluate this? If my thesis that both the genealogies and birth narratives in the New Testament were made up to thwart the Docetists and Gnostics, the veracity of a large amount of textual evidence is involved and so these passages now become unavailable for constructing an image of Jesus. We cannot know *a priori* who was correct — the proto-Orthodox or the Docetists and Gnostics.[43]

Ehrman is also the author of a *New York Times* best seller titled simply *Forged,* with the more expansive subtitle *Writing in the Name of God — Why the Bible's Authors Are Not Who We Think They Are.* Although I am not certain he would agree with me that the genealogies and birth legends were invented to confute the Docetists and Gnostics, nevertheless he agrees that that material is not suitable for use in any residue of data points to be used in connecting the dots of the Jesus picture:

> With regard to the stories of Jesus's birth, one does not need to wait for the later Gospels, mentioned above, to begin seeing the

41 Frank R. Zindler, "What does it mean to be scientific?" *Through AtheistEyes: Scenes From a World That Won't Reason, Volume Two: Science & Pseudoscience* [Cranford, NJ: American Atheist press, 2011: 110–126.]

42 Bart D. Ehrman, *The Orthodox Corruption Of Scripture: The Effect of Early Christological Controversies on the Text of the New Testament* [New York: Oxford University Press, 1993].

43 We are debating the historicity of Jesus of Nazareth merely because the Orthodox won the war. If any one of the non-Jewish 'heresies' had won out, the notion that Jesus of Nazareth had ever been born would then be the heresy. We have no reason to believe the Orthodox more than we believe the Docetists or Gnostics. There is danger in believing any of them. *Caveat creditor*!

> fabricated accounts; they are already there in the familiar versions of Matthew and Luke. There never was a census under Caesar Augustus that compelled Joseph and Mary to go to Bethlehem just before Jesus was born; there never was a star that mysteriously guided wise men from the East to Jesus; Herod the Great never did slaughter all the baby boys in Bethlehem; Jesus and his family never did spend several years in Egypt. These may sound like bold and provocative statements, but scholars have known the reasons and evidence behind them for many years. ...
>
> It is almost impossible to say whether the people who made up and passed along these stories were comparable to forgers, who knew full well that they were engaged in a kind of deception, or whether they, instead, were like those who falsely attributed anonymous books to known authors without knowing they were wrong. ... They may not have meant to deceive others (or they may have!), but they certainly did deceive others. In fact, they deceived others spectacularly well. For many, many centuries it was simply assumed that the narratives about Jesus and the apostles — narratives both within and outside the New Testament — described events that actually happened.[44]

It is unlikely that Ehrman realized what he had admitted here when later he composed *Did Jesus Exist? The Historical Evidence for Jesus of Nazareth.* We must emphasize the subtitle of that book here. *For it is precisely in the birth narratives that we find all but two references to Nazareth*[45] *in the entire canonical New Testament!* When we

44 Bart D. Ehrman, *Forged: Writing in the Name of God — Why the Bible's Authors Are Not Who We Think They Are* [New York: HarperOne, 2011: 140–41].

45 The first passage is Mark 1:9, that says that "Jesus came from Nazareth in Galilee and was baptized in the Jordan by John." For important technical reasons presented in my chapter "Bart Ehrman and Mark's *Jesus apo Nazareth*," I have argued that this passage is an interpolation, but Ehrman considers it authentic. The other passage is in Acts 10:38, where the Lucan author has made up a speech in which Peter says "You know about Jesus of Nazareth how God anointed him with the Holy Spirit and with power." (Readers may be warned that in reading the KJV books of Mark and Acts many more occurrences of the word 'Nazareth' are to be found, but they are mistranslations from the Greek text which uses titles that should be rendered *Nazarene* or *Nazorean*. Interestingly, Ehrman has also made such a mistake at least once. In his translation of "The Letter of Tiberius to Pilate" (*The Apocryphal Gospels: Texts and Translations,* Bart D. Ehrman and Zlatko Pleše [Oxford U. Press, 2011: 532–33]) he mentions "Jesus of Nazareth." This, however, is a KJV-type mistranslation of *Iēsou ton* [*sic*] *Nazōraiou* — 'of Jesus the Nazorean.'

eliminate the birth legends from our database we no longer have any compelling support for the existence of Jesus' purported hometown, and without Nazareth, Jesus becomes inevitably the Jesus of Someplace-Else — who, as we shall see, is a meaningless and identity-less character. It is hard to estimate how much of the Jesus of (Not)-Nazareth database is left now for Ehrman to use in reconstructing the face. Fifty percent? Forty percent? Even less?

It cannot be stressed too strongly: the more data Ehrman has to exclude from his database, the less likely it is that he can produce a meaningful hypothesis concerning a historical Jesus. By excluding all data that might argue against or falsify his thesis, his thesis is in danger of becoming worse than wrong; it risks becoming meaningless.

The Jesus of Nowhereatall?

The more Jesus becomes an ordinary component of the anonymous population inferred to have existed in first-century Palestine, the fewer falsifiable statements concerning him become possible. If Ehrman had understood this simple principle of science, he would not have written that

> It is also true, as the mythicists have been quick to point out, that no Greek or Roman author from the first century mentions Jesus. It would be very convenient for us if they did, but alas, they do not. At the same time, the fact is again a bit irrelevant since these same sources do not mention many millions of people who actually did live. Jesus stands here with the vast majority of living, breathing, human beings of earlier ages.[46]

The fallacious nature of this comparison is obvious to anyone educated in the sciences. By placing Jesus in the class of beings who could not be mentioned by ancient writers because nothing was known about them — not even how many of them there were, when they existed, where they existed — he is putting Jesus into the category of beings about whom nothing specific can be said. From our point in time, nothing can meaningfully be said *specifically* about any particular

46 *Did Jesus Exist?*: 43.

one of those millions of people we infer to have lived at the time in question. We can only make meaningful claims about the entire population and then, if we are lucky, we may make general, probabilistic claims about hypothetical individual members of the population.

It might be possible to say, for example, that a person selected at random from that population was 36% likely to be a woman over the age of 28, 92% likely to speak Aramaic, and so on. But we could not make any specific claim about a person who is completely and totally unidentified and unidentifiable. The nameless millions of whom Ehrman writes are an *inference*, not an *observation*. If Jesus is one of those unnamed millions, we can know nothing of him and can make no specific claims about him.

Carl Sagan's aphorism "Exceptional claims require exceptional evidence" was never more apt than in the case of the Historical Jesus — even without his miracles. What test could we do to learn if any claim regarding *any* one of the unknown millions of the past is true or false if he evaded the notice of all the writers of the time and left no physical remains that could yield clues to his identity? Could the Jesus of Nowherespecific be detected if we had a time machine? How would we recognize him if none of the gospels' identifying features were left for which to search and we couldn't know for sure that we had parked the Tardis at the right place and time?

We have come now to a point where the Historical Jesus is not yet completely gone, even though Ehrman himself has helped to cause the disappearance of his arms and legs and most of his torso. Nevertheless, soon all that will be left will not be the face of the Historical Jesus; it will be the grin of a cat that can't be traced to Cheshire. Historicists soon will have no more than the third derivative of a possibility in which to believe.

Like Alice in Wonderland, the reader of this essay has just witnessed the progressive dismantling and dissolution of a fascinating creation of the human mind. Like the Cheshire cat, Jesus of Nazareth was never a real, living organism. Like the Cheshire cat, who could not be beheaded because he had already lost his body, Jesus of Nazareth could not be 'beheaded' by the loss of his Nazareth identity. New

Bart Ehrman and the Cheshire Cat of Nazareth

Testament critics including Bart Ehrman had already hacked away most of his body by the time that empty excavations at Nazareth had erased 'the testimony of the empty tomb' at Jerusalem. All that now remains is the fictive face on the Shroud of Turin — the laser display-like death mask of the Cheshire cat of Nazareth. Sometime soon, everyone including Bart Ehrman will have to admit that the cat is gone — completely gone.

CHAPTER TWENTY

Ehrman's Concluding Case Against Mythicism

A Critique of Pages 332–339 of *Did Jesus Exist?*

Earl Doherty

This chapter examines Bart Ehrman's concluding charges of a Humanist/Atheist agenda:

- Are humanists and Atheists engaged in a religious exercise?
- Humanist and Atheist activism against religion: The Humanist self-definition
- Going against received wisdom
- The Jesus 'problem' for historicists: Replacing all the fantasy Jesuses with the 'real' one
- Is the Mythicist agenda anti-religion and anti-Christian?
- Ehrman's and traditional agendas
- An historical evaluation of religious tradition

* * * * *

Earl Doherty

Ehrman's reaction to humanism

Similar to his situation in having had little knowledge of Jesus Mythicism before he undertook to write a book in opposition to it, Bart Ehrman seems to have had little contact with or understanding of Humanism before being an honored guest recently at the national meeting of the American Humanist Association, where he received the Religious Liberty Award. He learned that they "celebrate what is good about being human." But another aspect of Humanism also struck him:

> But a negative implication runs beneath the surface of the self-description and is very much on the surface in the sessions of the meeting and in almost every conversation happening there. This is a celebration of being human *without God. Humanist* is understood to stand over against *theist.* This is a gathering of nonbelievers who believe in the power of humanity to make society and individual lives happy, fulfilling, successful, and meaningful. And the group is made up almost exclusively of agnostics and atheists.... [*DJE?* 332]

Evidently, Ehrman does not realize that the Humanist movement arose in great part as a *response* to religion, as a rejection of its traditional all-encompassing and rigid dictations of what life constituted, how it should be lived, how we should think, and how we should view and treat the world. Having come to realize that this tradition was flawed and even harmful — an ongoing impediment to rationality, science, and human rights — many people came together to try to counter these undesirable effects and offer an alternative.

Adopting a stance against religion in all its negative aspects was essentially one *raison d'être*. Those who were convinced that religion's foundation in a belief in God(s) and a supernatural dimension to reality was fundamentally erroneous felt a desire to correct that error in humanity's thinking — not through force, indoctrination, or legislation to impose one view of reality on everyone, such as religion has traditionally tried to do and is inherently 'set up' to do — but through reasoned persuasion and education.

Ehrman's Concluding Case Against Mythicism

> But what struck me most about the meeting was precisely how religious it was. Every year I attend meetings of the Society of Biblical Literature, conferences on early Christian studies, and the like. I have never, in my recollection, been to a meeting that was so full of talk about personal religion as the American Humanist Association, a group dedicated to life without religion. [*DJE?* 333]

Here Ehrman shows how the religious mind (even an ex-religious mind) can only evaluate other or opposing views in religious terms. It seeks to apply the concepts of religion to the non-religious. Thus, focusing on how one should live one's life in the Humanist way becomes a "religious" activity and fixation. "Life without religion" can only be achieved through "religion."

But this is a misuse of language and concepts. We can say "he works at his job religiously" because we have broadened the meaning of 'religiously' to apply to anything that is undertaken with dedication and faithful attention. This does not make working at that job a religion in the standard sense, because it does not involve belief in a god or the supernatural. Humanism may be promoted by some circles of non-believers quite 'religiously' but that does not make Humanism a religion. That is simply an attempt by members of actual religions to cast their own net over their opponents. "You criticize us for the qualities we value? You practice the same ones!" But what those respective qualities are used in the service of is quite different.

Humanist and Atheist activism

> I suppose there was so much talk about religious belief because it is almost impossible in our society to talk about meaning and fulfillment without reference to religion, and humanists feel a need to set themselves over against that dominant discourse. [*DJE?* 333]

Here, again, Ehrman seems to be saying that the very concepts of meaning and fulfillment only enjoy legitimacy, or ultimate reality, within the context of religion, or something given an essentially 'religious' interpretation (such as in the woolly and misleading terminology of being 'spiritual' so popular in our generation). That is indeed, and has always been, the "dominant" form of discourse in these matters, and it is precisely the *rejection* of that stance, one based ultimately on theism and supernaturalism, which leads Humanists and Atheists into actively setting themselves against it.

Modern medicine of the last couple centuries set itself resolutely (one might say *religiously*) against the longstanding medical practice of bleeding a patient to release harmful humors causing illness. Is modern medicine a religion? It recognized the harm created by older convictions and practices. Should they have been reluctant to set themselves "over against that dominant discourse," or be criticized for it? Should a religious belief based on no evidence whatever — the belief that two cells coming together within moments of conception are infused by a god with an immortal soul — be allowed to impede the potential cure of human illnesses through stem-cell research? Should the primitivism of two and three thousand-year-old cultures and their writings be allowed to dictate to the modern mind and society on everything from the origin of the world to what constitutes 'sin' to one's fate in an afterlife?

Ehrman, observing that Humanist meetings devote much talk to how to deal with family reaction when leaving the faith, or how to oppose the teaching of creationism in science classrooms and so on, laments that Humanists situate their Humanism in relation to something else, that they often define themselves in terms of what they are not, namely "agnostic" or "atheist" in relation to theism. Again, that is essentially their *raison d'être*, and even their positive stances and adopted lifestyles are necessarily "set over against" the traditional ones based on belief in a god and what that belief requires. Given the society in which we live, and its long history, this is inevitable and perfectly acceptable.

When astronomers of Copernicus and Galileo's day proclaimed a sun-centered world, this was a positive declaration of their view of the universe, based on scientific evaluation of the evidence. But it could hardly be promoted, let alone adopted, without setting itself against the traditional view of a Ptolemaic earth-centered one, a view fiercely adhered to by religious interests based on the bible's own presentation and on which its inerrancy was seen as dependent.

Modern Humanism and Atheism are in a similar situation, although they may not be facing the stake for their opposition. (That could change, though, if evangelical Dominionists gain the power they seek. Pat Robertson, in the first flush of the Moral Majority's influence in the 1980s, advocated passing federal laws against "defaming the Lord" — which no doubt would have included Jesus Mythicism — although he did not specify the penalty for such a crime.)

Thus, Humanism's self-definition should not come as a surprise to Ehrman, much less be something he ought to find fault with:

> "Humanism is a progressive philosophy of life that, without theism and other supernatural beliefs, affirms our ability and responsibility to lead ethical lives of personal fulfillment that aspire to the greater good of humanity." [*DJE?* 333]

Considering that religious belief has produced so much that has operated against that greater good, 'taking on religion' is a natural and necessary aspect of being a Humanist and Atheist in most societies around the world (even if a considerable number of Humanists have advocated against doing so) — with a few notable exceptions, one of which is unfortunately not the United States of America.

Going against received wisdom

Now, all of this has served as an introduction to the point Ehrman wants to make in his Conclusion. First, there is this claim:

> In my view mythicists are, somewhat ironically, doing a disservice to the humanists for whom they are writing. By staking out a position that is accepted by almost no one else, they open themselves up to mockery and to charges of intellectual dishonesty. [*DJE?* 334]

Well, this type of admonition could have been made against almost any individual or group who ever put forward a theory which bucked the going wisdom. Copernicus threw traditional astronomy into disrepute. Darwin was mocked by the religious establishment. Wegener was disowned by the discipline of geology and ridiculed by his colleagues for his theory of continental drift. If innovators and researchers not shackled by received tradition backed away through fear of such reactions we'd still be living in the Stone Age. Yes, we have had our share of new theories deserving rejection (alien visitors to earth as the source of human life is probably one such). But that rejection has usually been backed up by reasoned argument and counter-demonstration. And such rebuttal has had to stand up to scrutiny. Ridicule by itself or appealing to "the way we've always thought" doesn't do the trick.

The Jesus Problem

Before going on to explain why Jesus is a problem for Atheists and Humanists, Ehrman switches gears and examines why Jesus constitutes a problem for religionists. The problem is that he is "*too* historical," by which Ehrman means he is too adaptable. Christians at all times, and especially in the modern age, have been able to turn him into anything they wanted in order to suit different agendas, whether of televangelists, free-enterprise capitalists, racial supremacists, advocates of the welfare state, or any of a host of other self-interests. Of course, Ehrman sees the historical Jesus as none of these things, and he takes the opportunity to summarize the apocalyptic preacher he believes Jesus to have been. Then:

> The problem then with Jesus is that he cannot be removed from his time and transplanted into our own without simply creating him anew. When we create him anew we no longer have the Jesus of history but the Jesus of our own imagination, a monstrous invention created to serve our own purposes. But Jesus is not so easily moved and changed. He is powerfully resistant. He remains always in his own time. As Jesus fads come and go, as new Jesuses come to be invented and then pass away, as newer Jesuses come to take the place of the old, the real, historical Jesus continues to exist, back there in the past.... [*DJE?* 336]

Ehrman has summarized modern Jesus scholarship quite well here and, given the perennial failure of repeated quests to find the *real* historical Jesus, more and more of our modern New Testament scholars have begun admitting as much.

But what do many of them turn around and do? Just like Ehrman, they claim that they have finally identified the true, real, genuine historical Jesus to properly replace all those "monstrous inventions" of the past. No fad *my* theory. No problems with *my* evidence and argument to finally uncover the Jesus of history buried under all that early Christian superstructure and misguided preceding scholarship. If they live long enough (give it maybe a couple of decades), they get to see their own claims follow onto the scrap heap.

Like the difference between the Atheist and the Christian monotheist who rejects the existence of Allah, or Zeus, or any of a thousand other gods humanity has subscribed to, one could say: "But Dr. Ehrman, you're already a Jesus mythicist; I just believe in one less mythical Jesus than you do!"

The Mythicist Agenda

So now we've arrived at the crunch. Regardless of all the arguments pro and con, never mind the credentials business, forget all the misfirings of past historical Jesus quests, Mythicism can be rejected as unreliable and discredited simply because...MYTHICISTS HAVE AN AGENDA!

Of course, Ehrman is hardly the first to make that accusation. It has been an invaluable staple in most dismissals of the Mythicist case, going back to its earliest refuters, such as Maurice Goguel [1928] and Shirley Jackson Case [1912]. Mythicists are not to be trusted because they are motivated by their own anti-religion and anti-Christian biases.

Even given that alleged disposition, Ehrman wonders why such Humanists and Atheists do not focus instead on demonstrating that Jesus was not the person that Christian faith makes him out to be. After all, isn't whether Jesus existed essentially irrelevant to whether a god exists? Why not show, as Ehrman has done (though not with the same motivation), that he was simply a mistaken, misguided apocalypticist, neither right nor divine? Why go so far as to buck historical reality and go for the historical Jesus' own jugular? Ehrman supplies the answer:

Earl Doherty

> Mythicists are avidly antireligious. To debunk religion, then, one needs to undermine specifically the Christian form of religion. And what easier way is there to undermine Christianity than to claim that the figure at the heart of Christian worship and devotion never even existed but was invented, made up, created? [*DJE?* 337]

But what has Ehrman himself been doing? Is Christianity any more debunked by demonstrating that Jesus did not exist than by demonstrating that he was nothing like the character the Christian faith worships, a failed, somewhat crazy preacher of doom who got himself executed, never to be seen again? Either one would leave it in a "total shambles." (Personally, if I were a believer I would prefer Mythicism, because that would at least leave me in a position to fall back on Paul's heavenly Christ as an object of faith and salvation, a divinity unaffected by later delusions created by the Gospel writers that he had actually come to earth and been sacrificed there.)

The pot compared to the kettle

Could I not equally accuse Ehrman, in his promotion of a Jesus who was a failed apocalyptic preacher, of having an agenda, since his conclusion would be just as devastating to the Christian faith? After all, he has admitted to being at least agnostic on the existence of a god. Perhaps he is one of those "virulent, militant agnostics/atheists," but is being a bit more subtle about it. I am sure Ehrman's response would be to assure us that he is not, that he has good scholarly integrity and is honestly evaluating the evidence as he sees it. After all, he has studied the question of who Jesus was for years. I, for one, would be willing to allow him that honesty, without accusing him of something nefarious. Why is he not willing to do the same for committed Mythicists?

And just what are his *own* motivations? Why is he anxious to educate the world in the reality of who Jesus was, as opposed to what he is convinced Jesus was not? He would probably reply, "In the interests of historical truth."

An admirable motive. And why is the knowledge of that historical truth preferable to the naïve institutional beliefs of an indoctrinated

Christianity, a religion he himself has set aside as erroneous and unacceptable, just as Humanists and Atheists have? I won't guess at his exact words, but hopefully his answer would be along the lines that, in principle, a society should not govern itself, should not shape its laws, should not fashion its rights, should not educate its children, should not compromise its science, should not limit its technology, should not encourage superstitions of the supernatural, of angels and demons, of blissful afterlives and hellfire damnation, according to a belief system which can be judged to be based on a fiction.

In other words, Ehrman is surely as motivated by the same concerns about historical reality and its consequences as Humanists and Atheists are. Each of us has a perception of the truth and a desire to propagate it, perhaps the fundamental impulse of the human intellect. Why is Ehrman on the one hand an honorable and respected scholar, while Mythicists on the other hand are a bunch of ignorant agenda-driven charlatans? He may disagree with Mythicist arguments and conclusions, but the proper procedure is to approach those arguments and conclusions like a true scholar, with an open-minded eye, evaluate them honestly without prejudice or preconception, and measure them against his own. At the same time, he should do his best not to misunderstand, much less misrepresent, the Mythicist case. I think we can safely say that he has done none of these things.

The universality of agendas

> [T]he mythicists who are so intent on showing that the historical Jesus never existed are not being driven by a historical concern. Their agenda is religious, and they are complicit in a religious ideology. They are not doing history; they are doing theology. [*DJE?* 337–8]

Here again, Mythicism must be seen as a religion, which serves to cast aspersions on its claim to be first and foremost 'doing history.' Yet Mythicist books are full of that very thing: an often minute analysis of the texts, including in the original languages, a reasoned interpretation of those texts aided by the study of a much wider literature, an examination of ancient history, archaeology, religion, philosophy and mythology, and their relation to Christian origins and beliefs.

Earl Doherty

Precious little — other than knee-jerk dismissal and the tired old appeal to authority — has been offered by historicist scholars to discredit such historical exercises, much less to set more reliable alternatives in their place. (Remember Maurice Goguel, who was not going to "bother" addressing actual mythicist arguments in a book dedicated to demolishing them, relying on the same old timeworn 'proofs' of the existence of Jesus?) **And that a discipline, which has been traditionally dedicated to unabashedly "doing theology" in its study of Jesus and the New Testament, would accuse Humanists of doing the same thing, as though it were some sort of compromising activity on our part, is nothing short of comical**.

Religious or not, we all have agendas. The term itself has taken on a derogatory connotation these days, in many contexts. But understood neutrally, it is not a dirty word. Ehrman has his agenda. It can hardly be denied that New Testament scholarship has had its own agenda, though one with variations, particularly as the twentieth and twenty-first centuries have progressed. One of those agendas was and remains in many circles confessional, though increasingly another agenda has been to uncover the historical reality of Jesus the man.

Yet more often than not, those scholars who subscribe to the latter (such as Spong, Crossan, the late Robert Funk and the Jesus Seminar) have seen it as opening up some kind of avenue to 'spiritual' insight and progress; somehow, the 'real' Jesus, even if not the heavenly Son of God, is presented as serving the interests of theism, or at least of something a little more respectable and enlightened than — *hummph!* — mere science and earthbound reality and understanding of humans as humans. (But perhaps Ehrman's view signals a new phase: Jesus as misguided doomsayer, warts and all, though one wonders at the fierceness with which the existence of such a figure is defended against those who would call it into question.)

An historical evaluation of religious tradition

Atheism and Mythicism are not permitted to join the privileged club of debunkers. Never mind that 'believing in Jesus' — without whom Paul's Christ cult would never have survived — has led to untold misery and stagnation for an inordinately long time. The long litany of religious sectarian strife and international wars, of inquisition and pogrom, of conquest of 'inferior' cultures in the name of Jesus, of opposition to scientific and social enlightenment and the promotion of human rights, of impediment to investing in this the only world we are sure of having, is disheartening to say the least. Belief in a personal savior has never advanced human progress one iota. The fear created over the centuries, fear of devils and witches, fear of the infidel and non-believers, fear of the pleasures of the human body and intellect, and above all fear of 'God,' of sin, of eternal punishment, has wrecked millions of psyches and stunted millions of lives.

And don't let anyone tell you that faith in Jesus meek and mild, blood sacrificed for our transgressions, has relieved any of that. If anything, this bizarre primitive doctrine has accentuated fear and guilt. If the Christian god sent his own 'Son' to earth to undergo such suffering on our behalf, how much more do we owe that god and Jesus our allegiance, our every thought, word, and action in the service of conforming to their wishes and worship! For every Christian testimonial to how Jesus has changed his or her life, one can supply an Atheist testimonial to the intoxicating liberation from unjustified fear, guilt, and oppression — an opening up of life's potential once religion was abandoned.

Ehrman, commendably, goes so far as to admit sympathy for many of the concerns which Atheists and even Mythicists express. He acknowledges:

> They look at our educational systems and see fervent Christians working hard to promote ignorance over knowledge, for example, in the insistence that evolution is merely a theory and that creationism should be taught in the schools. They look at our society and see what incredible damage religion has done to human lives: from the sponsorship of slavery to the refusal to grant women reproductive rights to the denial of the possibility of gay love and marriage. They look at the political scene and see what awful political power the religious right yields [*sic*]: from imposing certain sets of religious beliefs on our society or in our schools to electing only those

> political figures who support certain religious agendas, no matter how hateful they may be toward other (poor, or non-American) human beings and how ignorant they may be about the world at large. [*DJE?* 338]

Much harm has been done, he admits, in the name of Christ, but he offers a 'counter-balance' which has become an almost pathetic cliché:

> I also see that a tremendous amount of good has been done in his name, and continues to be done, by well meaning and hard-working Christian men and women who do untold good in the world on both massive and individual scales. [*DJE?* 339]

(We've hobbled western civilization for centuries, but at least some of us have aided third-world children — while preaching Jesus — and brought hot meals to shut-ins.)

The fallacy here, of course, is that it doesn't take the influence of Christ, much less all its divisive and superstitious baggage, to do good in the world. Otherwise, Atheists — whose numbers are increasing — would be criminals and anti-social misfits, and clogging the jails. Cultures devoted to rival supernatural beings would be in social chaos, too. And non-theist organizations would not be concerned with ethics, social welfare, and human rights, as virtually all of them are.

Conclusion

If at the heart of Atheist concerns lies the realization that without any historical Jesus at all, western religion would not have taken the course it did, nor continue to have the negative results it has produced, it is only natural that Humanist scholars would have a disposition to focus on this issue. Ehrman notes, as though he has discovered a hand in the cookie jar, that it is only Atheists and Humanists who seem to be open to the idea that no historical Jesus ever lived. But this is hardly tantamount to being guilty of deliberately fabricating their theory for nefarious ends, of promoting their own wishful thinking based on no scholarly or legitimate evidence whatever.

Ehrman's Concluding Case Against Mythicism

Mythicism has too long a history, it has produced too much responsible literature to be dismissed with a simple stroke of the pen. (I have no hesitation in including my own *The Jesus Puzzle* and *Jesus: Neither God Nor Man* in that catalogue.) It has been in the hands of too many able scholars, even if some have been for the most part self-educated, though many have possessed 'proper' credentials such as the nineteenth-century Dutch Radical school and a few contemporary scholars. It has been too persistent and too tenacious not to be taken seriously. Through today's Internet, it has won over a broad constituency, comprising intelligent people who can recognize traditional bias, fallacy, special pleading — as against good argument and often simple common sense — when they see it.

Ehrman's case for an historical Jesus has been exposed as the weak effort and flawed exercise it truly is, by more than just myself (in a 34-part series on *Vridar.wordpress.com*). Capping that effort off with the ultimate, disreputable tactic of personally attacking the messengers and their integrity makes *Did Jesus Exist?* a dismal failure and an embarrassment. Ultimately, Mythicism will stand or fall on its own scholarly arguments, irrespective of any supposed agenda. Contrary to its longstanding mantra-like claims, traditional scholarship has done little to actually address those arguments, let alone refute them. Bart Ehrman has made the effort and been found wanting.

ENVOI

CHAPTER TWENTY-ONE

Bart Ehrman and the Emperor's New Clothes

Hans Unchristian Andersen,
a.k.a. Frank R. Zindler

Because in fact there is no obvious evidence for the historicity of Jesus of Nazareth that can be compared to the evidence, say, for Tiberius Caesar, when Bart Ehrman set to writing his book Did Jesus Exist? The Historical Argument for Jesus of Nazareth [HarperOne, 2012] *he was forced to resort to alleging the existence of evidence embedded in arguments so subtle and indirect and so far removed from straight-forward types of evidence that they become untestable. When stripped down to their logical structures, however, these arguments become the rhetorical equivalent of the Emperor's New Clothes. Ehrman is seeking evidence for the existence of Jesus of Nazareth. Mythicists are seeking evidence for the existence of Ehrman's evidence.*

Frank R. Zindler

Once upon a time there lived a vain Emperor whose only concern in life was to dress up in elegant clothes and regalia. He changed outfits almost every hour and always was eager to show them off to the people.

Word of the Emperor's refined habits spread across his kingdom and abroad. Two scoundrels, hearing of the Emperor's vanity, decided to take advantage of it to make a profit. They introduced themselves at the gates of the palace with an incredible scheme.

"We are expert clothificators," one of the scoundrels told the entry guard. I hold a doctorate in sartoriology, and my colleague here is a doctor of haberdasheristics. We are professors from Harvard University in America. The fame of your Emperor has spread even to the other side of the ocean and we realized that we could be of service to him. In fact, we can help him in a way that no one in his kingdom is able."

"In what way can you help His Majesty?" asked the guard.

"After many years of research," replied the sartoriologer — adding a comment about Harvard being a research University — "we have developed a wonderful method to weave a cloth so light and fine that it looks invisible."

"Wow!" replied the guard. "Is it *really* invisible?"

"Well," chimed in the haberdasheristicist, "in a technical sense, it isn't. Highly competent, intelligent, and appropriately educated people can see it — especially those holding doctorates in clothification. But people who are incompetent and stupid — or those holding doctorates in inappropriate areas of study — are utterly deficient in the refined sense required to perceive it."

The captain of the guards heard the impostors' strange story and sent for the court chamberlain. The chamberlain notified the prime minister, who ran to the Emperor and disclosed the astounding news. The Emperor's curiosity got the better of him and he decided to give the two visiting professors an audience.

"Besides being invisible, your Majesty, this cloth will be woven in colors and patterns created especially for you. Your Majesty's wisdom is evidenced by the fact that you have chosen to put your faith in expert clothificators instead of the amateurs who heretofore have been managing the royal wardrobe."

The Emperor gave the two experts a bag of gold coins in exchange for their promise to begin working on the wonderful textile immediately.

"Just tell us what you need to get started and we'll give it to you." The two impostors asked for a loom, silk, gold thread, and then pretended to start to work. The Emperor thought he had spent his money wisely. In addition to getting a fabulous new outfit, he would discover which of his subjects were ignorant and incompetent. A few days later, he called the wise old prime minister, who was considered by everybody to be a man with good, common sense.

"Go and see how the work is proceeding," the Emperor commanded him, "and come back to let me know what progress is being made."

The prime minister was welcomed by the two scalawags.

"We're almost finished, but we need a lot more gold thread. Here, Excellency! Admire the colors; feel the softness! The old man bent over the loom and tried to see the fabric that was not there. Cold sweat began to freeze on his forehead.

"I can't see anything," he thought. "If I see nothing, that means I'm stupid or incompetent! "If I admit that, I'll be fired from office."

"What a marvelous fabric," he exclaimed. "I'll certainly tell the Emperor." The two ne'er-do-wells rubbed their hands with glee. They were almost there! More gold thread and some platinum for buttons were requested to finish the work.

Finally, the Emperor was told that the two doctors of clothification had come to take all the measurements needed to sew his new garments.

"Come in," the Emperor commanded. At the same time that they were bowing before the Emperor, the two scoundrels pretended to be holding a large bolt of fabric.

"Here it is your Majesty: the result of our labor," the schemers announced. "We have worked night and day, but at last the most beautiful fabric in the whole world is ready for you. Look at these colors and feel how fine it is!"

Of course, the Emperor did not see any colors and could not feel any cloth between his fingers. He panicked and felt like he would faint. But then he realized that no one else could know that he did not see the fabric, and he felt better. Nobody could know that he was stupid and incompetent. Of course, the Emperor could not know that everyone else was thinking and doing the very same thing as he was.

The farce continued as the two scoundrels had planned. Once they had taken the measurements, they began cutting the air with scissors while sewing with their needles in and out of the invisible cloth.

"Your Majesty, you will have to take off your clothes to try on your new ones." The professors draped the new clothes on him and held up a large mirror. The Emperor was embarrassed, but since no one else seemed to be embarrassed he felt relieved and reassured.

"Yes, this is a beautiful outfit and it looks very good on me," the Emperor said — trying to look comfortable but not knowing if he was wearing a suit, a robe, a ceremonial gown, or a military uniform. (It never entered his mind that his new outfit might consist of less than a jock strap.) "You have done a very fine job."

"Your Majesty," the prime minister said, "the people have found out about this extraordinary cloth and they are anxious to see you in your new outfit." (The prime minister also wasn't sure what kind of garment it was that he wasn't seeing.)

The Emperor was reluctant to show himself naked before his subjects, but he quickly relinquished his fears. After all, nobody would see him that way except the ignorant and the incompetent.

"Okay," he said. "I shall grant the people this boon." He summoned his carriage and the ceremonial parade was formed. A group of dignitaries walked at the very front of the procession and anxiously scrutinized the faces of the people in the street. Everyone had gathered in the main square, pushing and shoving to get a better look at the clothing. Applause welcomed the royal procession. Everybody strained to learn how stupid or incompetent their neighbors were. As the Emperor passed, a murmur rose from the crowd.

Everyone exclaimed, loud enough for the others to hear, "Look at the Emperor's new clothes. How beautiful! What a magnificent train!"

"And the colors!" some exclaimed. "The colors of that fantastic fabric! I have never seen anything like it in all my life!" They all tried to conceal their disappointment at not being able to see the clothes. Since none of them were willing to admit their own stupidity and incompetence, they all performed exactly as the two scoundrels had predicted.

A child, however, a little boy who had no important job to retain and could only see what his eyes could actually detect, approached the carriage. "The Emperor has no clothes on him," he exclaimed loudly.

"Foolish child!" his father scolded him. "Don't talk so stupidly!" He grabbed the boy and started to take him away.

Before he could escape with his son, however, the sartoriologer shouted at the child. "What do you mean, he has no clothes on?"

"What evidence do you have for so ridiculous a claim?" demanded the haberdasheristicist."

"If he had no clothes on," sneered the sartoriologer, pointing at the slope-shouldered Emperor, "would he hold his shoulders like that? Can't you see that if he didn't have the weight of gold cloth pulling them down, he would be carrying his shoulders much higher up?"

The haberdasheristicist, pointing to the Emperor who could scarcely move due to embarrassment and fear, advanced another powerful argument to prove the existence of the exquisite apparel. "If he didn't have any clothing on," he asked, flailing his own arms around, "wouldn't he be able to move his arms about with greater ease?"

Affecting the tone of an oh-so-wise authority and with disdain so acrid his breath nearly corroded the gold plating off the royal crown, the sartoriologer wagged his finger around as though it were circling about the imperial body and inquired rhetorically, "Wouldn't the air circulate around him with less turbulence if in fact he had no clothes on?" The scoundrel congratulated himself on the ingeniousness of the argument he had just concocted.

"Indeed it would, Professor," the haberdashersticist agreed, delighted by the mental agility of his partner in crime. Glaring down, then, at the boy he lectured him in a voice as condescending as a waterfall.

"Tell me," he sniffed and pointed toward the Emperor's fingertips. Bending over and pretending to scrutinize the blue-from-the-cold hands of the Emperor — it was a rather chilly day for one to be parading around wearing such rarified textiles — he demanded, "Tell me, then — if you are so smart and qualified to pass judgment in matters outside your area of expertise — why would the Emperor's fingernails show such tiny marks of abrasion along their margins unless in fact he had been scratching them on the surface of these gorgeous buttons on this beautiful coat?"

"But I can't SEE any clothes on him," replied the child in bewilderment.

"And just who are YOU," the sartoriologer hissed, "to make such a silly claim when *real* experts such as I and my colleague — both of us Harvard professors who were educated and trained for years in the hyperfine arts of sartoriology and haberdasheristics in the most prestigious clothification centers in the world — can see with perfect clarity that these clothes exist?"

"But he's naked as a jay-bird," whimpered the intimidated child.

"You better give this boy a good thrashing," the clothificators in unison ordered the father of the boy. "Teach him to have more respect for the knowledge and wisdom of his elders and not pretend to have knowledge in fields outside his area of expertise," the sartoriologer commanded as he turned away from the boy and strode off toward the Emperor. The Emperor was standing half-frozen and rigid on the deck of his carriage in the midst of the crowd of subjects.

"Your Majesty," he fawned as he relieved the page of his responsibility to hold up the train of the imaginary cloak, "let *me* assist you."

Bart Ehrman and the Emperor's New Clothes

The Emperor by now had figured out that he wouldn't be so cold if in fact he actually was wearing clothing. He dared not, however, to admit his error. He decided to continue the imperial procession to further the illusion that anyone who couldn't see his clothes was either stupid or incompetent.

When he got back to the palace, however, he took a long soak in a hot bath. He never wore those fine regalia again — perhaps because he was never able to find them.